The Times
HISTORY
OF
THE WAR
VOL. VI.

PRINTING HOUSE SQUARE.

324

PRINTED AND PUBLISHED BY "THE TIMES,"
PRINTING HOUSE SQUARE, LONDON.

1916.

CONTENTS OF VOL. VI.

WAR ATLAS, STATISTICS, LIST OF PLACE NAMES.

CHAPTER XCVI.

THE

FRENCH OFFENSIVE-DEFENSIVE, NOVEMBER, 1914, TO APRIL, 1915.

SCOPE OF THE CHAPTER—REASONS FOR THE RETICENCE OF THE FRENCH AS TO THEIR OPERATIONS—FRENCH REVIEW OF THE POSITION ON FEBRUARY 1, 1915—STRATEGICAL PROBLEM OF GENERAL JOFFRE ON NOVEMBER 11, 1914—FIGHTING FROM LA BASSEE TO BELFORT BETWEEN NOVEMBER 11, 1914, AND FEBRUARY 1, 1915—ACTIONS ROUND ARRAS, BATTLE OF SOISSONS, BOMBARDMENT OF REIMS CATHEDRAL, ENGAGEMENTS IN CHAMPAGNE, THE ARGONNE, AND ON THE HEIGHTS OF THE MEUSE, AND IN THE VOSGES—EVENTS FROM FEBRUARY 1, 1915, TO MARCH 31—ACTIONS AT LES EPARGES AND VAUQUOIS—BATTLE OF PERTHES—THE FRENCH TAKE THE RIDGE OF NOTRE DAME DE LORETTE.

IN Vol. I. (Chapters XXIII., XXVI. and XXVII.) we dealt with the first offensive of the French in Alsace, their offensive in Lorraine and the Ardennes, the series of battles on the Meuse and Sambre and the glorious retreat of the Allies to the banks of the Marne ; while in Vol. II. (Chapters XXXII., XXXIV., XLV. and XLVI.) the Battles of the Marne and Aisne, the condition of Paris under the rule of General Galliéni during those terrible days when the fortunes of the Parisians, of France, and the civilized world hung in the balance, together with the extension accompanied by the Battles of Roye-Péronne and Arras of the western wings of the opposing armies from Compiègne to the North Sea at Nieuport Bains, were described and their strategical significance discussed. The Battle of Flanders, comprising the numerous struggles known as the Battle of the Yser, the first Battle of Ypres, and the Battle of Armentières-La Bassée, was the culmination of that extension. In Vol. III. (Chapters

XLVIII., LIV., LXII., LXIII.) and in Vol. IV. (Chapter LXV.) the desperate and successful resistance opposed by the Belgian Army, which had escaped from Antwerp, and by General d'Urbal's and Sir John French's armies to the last attempt of the Kaiser to turn or pierce the left wing of the Allies in the western theatre of war was narrated, and in Vol. III. (Chapter LXI.) and in Vol. IV. (Chapter LXX.) some particulars were given of the autumn and winter campaign in Central and Eastern France.

The present chapter is designed to provide a sketch of the main operations conducted by the French from the end of the battle of Flanders to the moves preliminary to the Battle of Artois, which began on May 9, 1915.

Between those dates, north of La Bassée, had occurred the bloody Battle of Neuve Chapelle, the combats of St. Eloi and Hill 60 and the Second Battle of Ypres, at which the Canadians first met the Germans and the Germans first began the use of poisonous gas. The fighting of the British, French and Belgian

1

THE FRENCH COMMANDER-IN-CHIEF AT THE FRONT.
General Joffre and members of his Staff have luncheon by the roadside.

troops north of La Bassée from November 11 to May 9, the Battle of the Aubers Ridge (May 9–10) and that of Festubert (May 15–18), both of which were contemporaneous with the beginning of the Battle of Artois and were intended to divert German reinforcements from it, have also been depicted.

It will be seen that a continuous narrative has been furnished of the doings of the Allied and German forces north of La Bassée to the date when Sir John French, after his gains at Festubert, was consolidating his position at the edge of the Aubers Ridge. Along the line, approximately fifty miles long, of the Allies from the sea to the western environs of La Bassée no decisive victory had been gained by either side. On the remainder of the Allied front, which measured, as the crow flies, about six times, and, if the windings of the trenches is taken into consideration, perhaps eight times that length, some 2,500,000 French troops were either engaged or were held in readiness to be thrown into the various battles or combats constantly going on along the far-flung line.

We must, therefore, never forget that severe as were the struggles in which we and the Belgians had been concerned, our gallant Ally had been and was still engaged in a long series of fights, none of them possibly of the first magnitude, but all of importance for maintaining the dam which kept back the German hordes from the centre of France.

During the momentous months in which the new British Armies were in training the strain endured by the French troops was tremendous. Week after week, by day and night, they were subject to continued assaults. against which they had to deliver repeated counter-attacks, frequently involving hand-to-hand struggles with the bayonet and bombs, to which an almost unending cannonade was the terrible accompaniment. The victories of the Battles of the Marne and of Flanders had saved France, but they had not broken up the gigantic machine constructed by Moltke and Roon, and remodelled and enlarged under the supervision of the Kaiser by the pupils of those formidable theorists and practitioners in the art of war. Joffre by every means in his power had to conceal his plans from the most vigilant and cunning Staff in the world, from men who, however deficient they might be in some of the higher qualities that distinguish great from mediocre captains, examined by themselves or their subordinates every scrap of information with the patience and care of scientists. The result was that the French *communiqués* and the official and semi-official reports, the best material available in 1915 for a narrative of the exploits of the French Army, were bald in comparison even with Sir John French's dispatches. As for the German accounts of the engagements, they cannot be trusted. The German authorities had to explain to the German and Austro-Hungarian peoples and to neutrals why it was that Paris remained untaken, why the French, Belgian and "contemptible" British Army had not been destroyed. To distort the facts was a necessity, and "necessity knows no law."

Before entering into the details of the fighting it will be as well to regard the situation on February 1, 1915. "The German offensive," said a French semi-official report, "is broken. The German defensive will be broken in its

turn."* How few of the Allied soldiers who were marching southward at the end of August, 1914, ever imagined that such words would be soberly penned by a Frenchman five months later !

The changes brought about in the composition of the French Army during the interval had been mainly these. Elderly generals and officers had, for the most part, been eliminated. Their places—and the places of others of proved incompetence—had been taken by younger or abler men. "Ability proved on the field of battle," it is observed, "is now immediately recognized and utilized. . . . The Army is led by young, well-trained, and daring chiefs, and the lower commissioned ranks have acquired the art of war by experience." As for the strength of the French Army, it was at this time, including all ranks, over 2,500,000—in round numbers the population of Paris. Imagine the capital of France entirely peopled by soldiers and one has then some idea of the huge force which with the British and the Belgians on February 1, 1915, barred the road

* The quotations are from a series of articles issued by Reuter's Agency and published by Messrs. Constable in book form.

THE SMOKE OF BATTLE.
A big French gun pouring shells into the enemy's position.

FRENCH GUN IN ACTION.

Inset : A German gun destroyed by French
artillery.

to the Kaiser. No less than 1,250,000 men
were at the depôts ready to replace losses.
"The quality of the troops," continues the
report, "has improved perceptibly since the
beginning of the war. . . . In August it neither
liked nor had the habit of using the spade.
To-day those who see our trenches are
astounded." During the preceding six months
the French infantry had acquired an ascendancy
over the Germans. From the outset its cavalry
had possessed the superiority. It "showed
itself perfectly adapted to the necessities of
fighting on foot." The artillerymen had unquestionably handled the "75" gun with a
skill that had won the admiration of the
Germans themselves. That precious weapon,
which had contributed so largely to the French
successes, had perfectly stood unprecedented
wear and tear.

The heavy artillery "in process of reorganization when the war broke out" had been one of

the weak spots in the French Army. By
February 1 this branch had been transformed
beyond recognition. The 155 cm. was an
accurate gun, firing a shell comparable in many
ways with our own 60-pounder ; the 105 cm, a
new and powerful heavy field gun. In addition
to these weapons, still larger guns and huge
howitzers had taken the field. The number of
machine guns had been very largely increased,
and, with regard to all the minor devices for
life-taking which the trench warfare at short
distance had brought into use, the position was
very favourable.

Enormous quantities of ammunition had
been accumulated. The blue and red uniform
had been or was being replaced by a uniform
of an inconspicuous colour. The transport
services had worked with a smoothness and
celerity beyond all expectation, and the
commissariat department, which had so signally
broken down in 1870, had kept the troops
regularly supplied with wholesome food. "The
Germans," confidently concluded this report,
"can no longer oppose us with forces superior
to ours. They will, therefore, not be able to
do in the future what they could not do in
the past, when they were one-third more
numerous than ourselves. Consequently our
final victory must follow by the imperious
necessity of the concordant force of facts and
figures."

THE SOUND OF THE FRENCH GUNS.
Soldiers stopping their ears during a bombardment.
Inset: A French 75 destroyed by a German shell.

Events alone could prove whether these calculations were correct, but that the hopes of the French of ultimate triumph were very reasonable the occurrences south of La Bassée between November 11, 1914, and February 1, 1915, establish.

The prodigious expenditure of ammunition during the first three months of the war had depleted the French arsenals, and for the greater part of the period under review Joffre could only, in his own word, " nibble " at the German line. Luckily for the Allies, the need the Kaiser was under to restore the prestige of Germany and Austria-Hungary, badly shaken by the victories of the Grand Duke Nicholas over Hindenburg and the Austro-Hungarians in the Eastern theatre of war, prevented the Germans taking advantage of the unfavourable situation. Otherwise it is conceivable that something similar to what happened the next year in Galicia, when Mackensen drove back Dmitrieff and Ivanoff, might have occurred in France.

We shall divide the vast battle or elongated siege into several sections: from La Bassée southwards to Compiègne, from Compiègne eastwards to Berry-au-Bac on the Aisne, from Berry-au-Bac south-eastwards to Reims, from Reims eastwards across the Argonne to Verdun, from Verdun south-eastwards round St. Mihiel to Pont-à-Mousson, on the Moselle, thence again south-eastwards, to the crest of the Vosges. The fighting in the Vosges and the Gap of Belfort will be the last or seventh action.

Despite their defeats at the Marne and in Flanders, the Germans were still on an extremely strong line for taking the offensive. Dixmude was theirs, so was the eastern edge of the ridge of the Mont-des-Cats—the key to the position north of the Lys. The heights at La Bassée and those from Notre Dame de Lorette, north-west of Lens, to the region of Arras, other heights from the south of Arras, east of Albert to the Somme, and both banks of the upper course of that river were held by them. De Castelnau had not advanced any considerable distance up the gap between the Somme and the Oise. From Compiègne along the Aisne to Berry-au-Bac the French since the Battle of the Aisne had made little progress on the north bank. The environs of Berry-au-Bac,

THE ASSAULT ON BEAUSÉJOUR REDOUBT IN CHAMPAGNE.
The final charge—the French infantry capture the redoubt.

where the road from Reims to Laon crosses the river, the whole line of the Aisne eastward almost up to the latitude of Verdun, and, south of the Aisne, most of that portion of Champagne which lies north of the Reims–St. Ménéhould–Verdun railway were retained by the enemy.

In this area behind the German lines ran from Bazancourt, a station on the Reims-Rethel railroad, a railway which crossed the Upper Aisne and the Argonne and terminated a little to the north of Varennes, so celebrated in the history of the unfortunate Louis XVI.

A glance at the map reveals that here no great natural obstacle barred the advance of the Germans southward to the Marne above Châlons-sur-Marne. The trenches of the army of Langle de Cary, connected with those of Sarrail defending Verdun and its environs, alone bridged this important gap.

The Southern Argonne and Verdun itself were, indeed, in little danger. General Sarrail had not wasted his time, and the glades and wooded hills of the Argonne, and the neighbourhood of Verdun, through which went the railway from Metz to Paris, had been so entrenched and fortified that they were probably by now impregnable. But between Verdun and Toul the Germans under Von Strantz had at the end of September broken the fortified line and obtained a crossing over the Meuse at St. Mihiel. If he could debouch in force from St. Mihiel, Von Strantz would either threaten Sarrail from the south or advance on Châlons-sur-Marne and the rear of Langle de Cary, or descend against the communications of the army of Lorraine defending the formerly unfortified but now strongly entrenched interval between Toul and Epinal.

At St. Mihiel, it is true, Joffre's main difficulties ended. From Pont-à-Mousson on the Moselle the French line extended east of St. Dié, along the western slopes of the Vosges to the Schlucht. From that pass it followed the eastern crest of the wooded mountains near Steinbach, Aspach and Upper Burnhaupt to the gap of Belfort. The fortresses of Toul, Epinal and Belfort, the entrenchments of the Grand Couronné of Nancy, and the forts between Epinal and Belfort were now well behind the southern part of the Allied right wing, the direction of which, since the departure of de Castelnau to the Somme-Oise region, had been given to General Dubail, one of the most competent and enterprising of the French commanders.

Born at Belfort in 1851, Dubail was sixty-three years old. He had been through the War of 1870-71. Appointed captain after the conclusion of peace, he had lectured on geography, strategy and tactics at the *Ecole Spéciale Militaire*, and had entered the *Ecole de Guerre* in 1876. Later, like Joffre, he had served in the East and in Algiers, where for ten years he was Chief of the Staff. On returning to France he had commanded the Alpine brigade at Grenoble and there familiarized himself with the problems of mountain warfare. Twice he had been *Chef du Cabinet* of the Minister of War. He had then filled the post of Commandant of the Military School of St. Cyr, the Sandhurst of France. At the expiration of his term of office he was placed at the head of the 14th Division, whose headquarters were his native town, Belfort. He had thus become thoroughly acquainted with the country in which he was now manœuvring. Finally, first as Chief of the Staff of the French Army, then successively Commander of the 9th Corps and member of the Superior Council of War, he had completed his education for one of the most responsible tasks set by Joffre to any of his lieutenants. When Pau's offensive in Alsace was abandoned, the command of the 1st Army and the defence of Alsace and the line of the Meurthe and Mortagne had been entrusted to Dubail, and he and de Castelnau on his left by their vigorous defensive–offensive measures had enabled Joffre to concentrate the bulk of his forces between Verdun and Paris and win the Battle of the Marne. Ultimately Dubail was given the direction of all the armies from Compiègne to Belfort, as Foch had been given that of the armies disposed between Compiègne and the sea.

With his right wing so placed and manœuvred by a man of Dubail's experience and ability, with Verdun defended by the indefatigable and initiative-loving Sarrail, Joffre could devote most of his attention to the many dangerous points on the line from Verdun to the North Sea. Large as his effectives were, the length and the shape of his front, the left wing of which was fighting with its back to the sea, rendered it liable to be pierced. Except for the flooded district between Nieuport and Dixmude, there was nowhere an obstacle which could be fairly described as almost impassable, and a frost might at any moment neutralize the effect of the inundations on the Yser. The Allied troops were disposed along or in the vicinity of two

GENERAL DUBAIL.

The north-western section of the Franco-German front—that from La Bassée to Compiègne—may be divided into three parts: from La Bassée to Arras, from Arras to the Somme, and from the Somme to the junction of the Oise and Aisne at Compiègne. In the first of these the immediate objective of the French was to drive the Germans from the hills and ridges on the edge of the plain of the Scheldt, recover Lens, and, with the assistance of the British Army attacking from the north, cut off the La Bassée salient and retake Lille.

The enemy had established himself on the chalky and ravined plateau west of the Lens-Arras railway, between the Lys and the Scarpe, which is a tributary of the Scheldt flowing through Arras. The northern edge of the plateau is dominated by the ridge of Notre Dame de Lorette, running west and east. South of the ridge are the townlets of Ablain St. Nazaire and Souchez, still farther south that of Carency, then the Bois de Berthonval, and the hill called Mont St. Eloi, north of the Scarpe. The high road from Béthune to Arras crosses the ridge of Notre Dame de Lorette and descends to Arras through Souchez and La Targette. From Carency to La Targette the Germans had constructed the entrenchments known as the "White Works," continued eastwards to the townlet of Neuville St. Vaast and then southward to "The Labyrinth," a veritable fortress of the new type, created to bar any direct advance up the Arras-Lens road. Between "The Labyrinth" and Arras the enemy were in or round the villages of Ecurie and Roclincourt, and south of Roclincourt, close to Arras, those of St. Laurent and Blangy. This region was destined during 1915 to be the field of some of the bloodiest fighting in the war.

The Notre Dame de Lorette-Labyrinth plateau could be turned from the north, if the French could penetrate between it and the La Bassée ridges. Accordingly General de Maud'huy, who was subsequently sent to serve under Dubail and was replaced by General d'Urbal—the local commander of the French in the Battle of Flanders—not only attacked the plateau from the south, west and north, but also endeavoured to approach Lens through Vermelles, Le Rutoire, and Loos. On December 1-2 three companies of infantry and two squadrons of dismounted Spahis carried the Château of Vermelles, and on the 7th Vermelles and Le Rutoire were taken. Later in the month further progress towards Loos was made.

sides of the triangular figure Verdun-Compiègne-Nieuport, nearly all the third side of which, that of Verdun-Nieuport and parts of the remaining two sides Verdun-Compiègne and Compiègne-Nieuport were in the possession of the enemy. An enormous artillery, an enormous store of munitions, a vast expenditure of life, and of labour and money on entrenchments were needed to render the new and temporary frontier of France secure.

Meanwhile the German positions on the plateau were being vigorously attacked. On December 7 some trenches south of Carency were captured, and the next day there was fighting close to " The Labyrinth." The weather was very bad and impeded the movements of Germans and French alike ; the mud often choked the barrels of the rifles and the fighting relapsed into that of primitive ages. The troops in the flooded trenches suffered terribly from the cold and the wet. On December 17–20 trenches of the Germans defending the ridge of Notre Dame de Lorette were carried, while from Arras the French attacked the enemy in St. Laurent and Blangy. On January 15 the Germans counter-attacked, and recovered some of the trenches near Notre Dame de Lorette and at Carency, and on the 16th they bombarded and assaulted the French in Blangy. The German " 77," " 105," " 150," and " 210 " guns and *minenwerfer* wrecked the foundry and malthouse of the village and destroyed the barricade in the main street, killing a lieutenant working a mitrailleuse. Soon after noon the fire of the German artillery was directed on the French reserves and at 2.30 p.m. the village was assaulted. The French in it were killed, wounded or taken prisoners. An hour or so later, however, the reserves at this point counter-attacked and the Germans were driven back to their former position. By February 1, 1915, in the section La Bassée-Arras, the balance of advantage lay with the French.

From Arras to the Somme there had also in the same period (November 11 to February 1)

been numerous combats. North of the Somme, between Albert on the Ancre and Combles to its east, there were, in the second fortnight of December, severe actions at Ovillers-la-Boisselle, Mametz, Carnoy and Maricourt. A German counter-attack on December 21 near Carnoy failed. On January 17-18 there was renewed fighting at La Boisselle. There again the French, on the whole, had had the upper hand.

General de Castelnau, too, in the plain between the Somme and the Oise, since his victory at Quesnoy-en-Santerre at the end of October, had not been idle. On him and General Maunoury devolved the most important duty of protecting the hinge, as it were, of the Allied left wing. On November 29 he had advanced a little in the region between the Somme and Chaulnes. During December there were various encounters south of Chaulnes and north of Roye, and also in the region of Lihons, a mile or so to the north-west of Chaulnes. Columns of the Germans counter-attacking on December 19 were, literally, scythed down by the French artillery and machine guns. Every day the possibility of the Germans recovering Amiens or marching on the Seine below Paris down the western bank of the Oise, became more remote.

In the second section of the front—that from Compiègne to Berry-au-Bac—affairs had not been so satisfactory for the French. The army of Maunoury had, indeed, secured the Forêt de l'Aigle in the northern angle formed by the Oise and Aisne. On November 13 he took Tracy-le-Val at its eastern edge, and his Algerian troops, on the 19th, brilliantly repulsed the German

BY MOTOR-RAIL TO THE FIRING-LINE.
Motor-car used on a railway to convey troops and provisions to the trenches.

counter-attack. Twelve days or so later (December 1) the enemy near Berry-au-Bac also failed to carry French trenches. From December 6 to 16 there was an artillery duel along the whole front. The French seem to have scored more than their enemy, and a German attack at Tracy-le-Val on the night of the 7th-8th met with no success. On the 21st, too, some German trenches in the region of Nampcel-Puisaleine were carried and retained. But in the first fortnight of January the centre of the army of Maunoury in the region of Soissons suffered a serious reverse. This engagement,

GENERAL MAUNOURY.

called by the Germans "The Battle of Soissons," deserves to be treated in some little detail.*

Since September Maunoury and Franchet d'Esperey had been vainly striving to dislodge Kluck from his formidable position, which has been already described in Vol. II., Chapter XXXIV., on the north bank of the Aisne, west of Berry-au-Bac. Generally speaking, the French remained at the foot of the heights occupied by Kluck with the river behind them.

* A brief account of this battle has been already given with Vol. IV., Ch. LXX. with a map (page 229) of the Soissons district.

Bridges through, above and below Soissons were in their possession, and on January 8, 1915, Maunoury, of his own initiative or by the orders of Joffre, made another determined effort to reach the plateau. From a barn, on a spot to the south of the river, affording a magnificent view, Maunoury himself, through numerous telephones, directed the attack. Owing to the torrential rain, he could, however, have seen with his own eyes very little of what went on.

A long line of closely set poplars on the horizon indicated the distant goal of the French. In the valley below a couple of chimney-stacks and some houses beyond Soissons in the loop of the flooded river marked the village of St. Paul. Between St. Paul and the poplars rises, to the right of the village of Cuffies, on the Soissons-La Fère road, the spur called "Hill 132." Nearer and to the right of "Hill 132," but divided from it by the village of Crouy on the Soissons-Laon road, is "Hill 151." The villages of Cuffies and Crouy are half way up the slope. The French were in Cuffies and Crouy and on a line from Crouy round "Hill 151" eastward through Bucy and Missy, higher up the Aisne than Soissons. At Missy was a wooden bridge, and between Missy and Soissons another at Venizel, opposite Bucy.

The attack was commenced by a heavy bombardment of the two hills and by sappers cutting the barbed-wire entanglements which had not been destroyed by the shrapnel or common shell. At 8.45 a.m. the infantry assaulted "Hill 132" at no less than ten different points. The rain falling in sheets, though it impeded the arrival of the supporting guns, probably assisted the foot soldiers. In a few minutes all three lines of trenches were captured, and guns were dragged up to the summit of "Hill 132" and of "Hill 151." The German artillery at once cannonaded the lost positions, and at 10.25 a.m., at 1 p.m., and 3 p.m., counter-attacks were delivered against "Hill 132." The last was beaten back by a bayonet charge of Chasseurs, a hundred of whom, carried away by their eagerness, were, however, surrounded and killed to a man.

The next day (January 9) at 5 a.m. the German attack on "Hill 132" was renewed, and a part of the third-line trench was recovered. Three and a half hours later the French artillery dispersed a German battalion being sent up to support the assailants. The bombardment continued, the French, dripping to the skin, constantly repairing trenches and entanglements.

During the night another counter-attack was repulsed, and on the 10th the French attempted to push eastwards. The Germans advanced to meet them, but, assisted by a body of Moroccans, the French flung them off, and at 5 p.m. had occupied two more lines of trenches and part of a wood to the north-east. They had lost in wounded alone 548. Throughout the 11th the struggle continued and the French progressed still farther eastward.

Meantime the river, swelled by the never-ceasing rain, went on rising, and during the night of the 11th-12th all the bridges of Villeneuve and Soissons, with the exception of one, were carried away, and those at Venizel and Missy followed suit. On a small scale the position of Maunoury's force resembled that of Napoleon's at Aspern, when it found itself with the flooded Danube and broken bridges behind it. Kluck, like the Archduke Charles

ABLAIN ST. NAZAIRE.
The surrender of a party of Germans to the French.

in 1809, violently attacked. Two Corps, it is believed, were hurled at the weak French troops, magnified by the Germans in their reports into the " 14th Infantry Division, the 55th Reserve Division, a mixed brigade of Chasseurs, a regiment of Territorial Infantry and " (unidentified) " Turcos, Zouaves and Moroccans." Before 10 a.m. on the 12th the Germans, as at Mons in solid masses, were thrown by Kluck at the French right above Crouy; at 11 a.m. a huge body was launched at the trenches on "Hill 132." Gradually Maunoury's men, inflicting terrible losses on their foes, were pushed back towards the river. Two pieces, rendered useless, were left behind.

To cover the retreat across the river, on the

13th a counter-attack at " Hill 132 " was delivered, and the Moroccans, covered with mud, endeavoured, towards Crouy, again to scale the heights. But the only bridge now remaining was that at Venizel, and Kluck was doing his utmost to fling the French from Crouy to Missy into the river. His artillery shelled Soissons. The Venizel bridge, the road to which was almost under water, might at any moment be destroyed. Maunoury, therefore, wisely decided to withdraw most of his men to the south of the river. They effected their retreat during the night of the 14th, but St. Paul, in the loop, was retained. An attack on it (January 14) was beaten off, and on the 15th the French artillery from the left bank dispersed a body of Germans mustering opposite it. The batteries on " Hill 151," handled with extraordinary skill, were saved, but at other points guns had to be left behind. Some 40,000 Germans had defeated but, under the most favourable circumstances, had been unable to destroy perhaps 12,000 French troops. The Germans are credibly reported to have lost 10,000 killed and wounded, the French 5,000.

This battle was absurdly compared by the Germans with the Battle of Gravelotte. In one of the German narratives occurred the statement that Kluck had " anew justified brilliantly his genius as a military chief. He appears more and more," wrote the journalist, " to be the Hindenburg of the West."

We here insert an account of *The Times*

THE WAR BY AIR.
A French airman about to start off.   The bombs are attached to the side of the machine.
Inset : A captive balloon being hauled down after reconnoitring.

CHARGE!

French troops leaving their trench to storm a German position.

correspondent's visit of inquiry on January 28 to Soissons and his meeting with General Maunoury. It will be seen how little the French General was affected by his defeat :

In Italy the German lie factories declare that as the result of the check sustained this month by the French on the Aisne the German troops are in possession of Soissons on the left bank of the river. I lunched to-day in Soissons as the guest of General Maunoury, the brilliant victor in the battle of the Ourcq, which contributed so greatly to the retreat of the German Army on the Marne.

General Maunoury, in bidding my two colleagues and myself welcome, said : " I am very happy to receive the representatives of our great Ally. It affords me particular pleasure to do so in Soissons. You will be able to see for yourself that, although we have undoubtedly suffered a check upon the opposite bank of the Aisne, that check is without strategic importance. We hold the Aisne as strongly as we did before. Our trenches on the other side give us two bridge-heads, and we are able to advance across the river with the same ease as before."

General Maunoury is a fine type of the modest, hard-working, and unselfish French soldier, who has made the Army of our Allies the splendid instrument it is to-day, and is turning it to best account. At the luncheon table were gathered three or four officers of his Staff, all of them men of the same unassuming nature. While the French Army is the most democratic in the world (the son of my concièrge is a sub-lieutenant), the officers of the active army remain nevertheless a class apart. They are drawn from families who have behind them a long record of military history. They are men of no wealth, and, although as representatives of the Army they are held in the highest esteem by the whole nation, their miserable pay is not compensated by the caste distinction which the officer enjoys in Germany and in a lesser degree in Great Britain. The work they do is in peace time the least recognized of any service for the State, and in war time they remain anonymous. The old class of soldier *à panache*, the general whose sword was for ever flashing in the sun, whose proclamations were epic poems, has vanished. His place has been taken by men such as I met to-day, hard-working, hard-thinking, and hard-fighting citizens, whose whole soul is given without personal thought to the service of France and her Army. Our conversation during luncheon showed that with all the national sense of the practical it is the ideal which the French Army has before its eyes in the conduct of this war.

With philosophical skill General Maunoury exposed the terrible retrogression in the German national character since 1870, which he remembers well. He dwelt upon the Bernhardi theory of war as practised by the German armies, the deportation of non-combatants, the placing of women and children as a protecting screen in front of their troops, as affording clear proof that the German morals had become swamped by materialism. Frank as are French officers in their condemnation of their enemy's morality, manners, and methods, they are none the less quick-to render tribute to their bravery.

The advance of the Germans in massed formation, described by our soldiers in letter after letter from the Flanders front as resembling the football crowd pouring into the gates of the Crystal Palace, was also seen in the Battle of Soissons. Flanders taught the Germans the value of extended formation more quickly than any drill instructor, and the return to this callously costly form of advance along the Aisne was due to the presence among the attacking troops of many young and untrained soldiers. " It is not surprising," said one of the officers at table, " that the Germans should deem it wise to send these young fellows forward with the courage which comes from contagion and the feeling of support given by massed formation. What is surprising is that these young chaps should obey."

In the old days the withdrawal of the French to the south bank of the Aisne in the region of Soissons might have caused a simultaneous evacuation of all their positions to the north of that river. But the new mechanism of war had changed both strategy and tactics. Troops could be protected by artillery sometimes posted twenty miles away from them ; the railway and motor traction enabled reserves of man-and-gun power to be shifted on a telephonic call from point to point with unexampled rapidity ; machine guns, repeating rifles, bombs and grenades, barbed-wire entanglements and properly constructed trenches permitted positions formerly regarded as untenable or perilous to be held with impunity. To fight with one's back to a river had been once considered the height of imprudence. The punishment inflicted by Napoleon on the Russians at Friedland, by Blücher on Macdonald at the Katsbach, had been imbedded in the memories of several generations of soldiers. Yet since the beginning of the second fortnight of September Generals Maunoury and Franchet d'Esperey, and, for a time, Sir John French, had kept large bodies of troops and a considerable number of guns on the north bank of the Aisne, on the outer rim of one of the most formidable positions in Europe. Apart from the reverse at Soissons, no serious mishap had occurred.

Farther east, near Craonne, an attempt by the Germans on December 1 to dislodge the French had failed; on January 23 they had bombarded Berry-au-Bac, but by February 1 they had not succeeded, except round Soissons, in clearing their enemy from the north bank of the Aisne between Compiègne and the last-mentioned crossing. Nor from Berry-au-Bac to the eastern environs of Reims had the Germans been more successful. Franchet d'Esperey and Foch had, in September, brought the enemy's counter-offensive from the valley of the Suippe westwards to a standstill, and the irritation of the Germans had been shown here as at Ypres by spasmodic renewals of their senseless practice of destroying architectural masterpieces. The Cathedral of Reims, which bears the same relation to so-called Gothic that the Parthenon bears to Greek architecture and sculpture, was, like the Cloth Hall at Ypres and the Cathedrals at Arras and Soissons, being gradually reduced to a heap of broken stones.

TELEGRAPHIC COMMUNICATION.

Listening post in an advanced trench: The white outlines in the background indicate the German trenches. Centre picture: Field optical telegraph. Top picture: Telegraphists putting their instruments in order.

of aircraft the summit of Reims Cathedral was being used by French artillery observers exhibits the childish side of the German character. That French generals for tiny technical advantages would expose to demolition a shrine associated so intimately with the history of their race, its art and religion, was inconceivable, though not to the minds of the men who perhaps believed that King Albert and the Belgians, King George V. and the British would sell their honour with the same alacrity as Ferdinand of Coburg. The nature of German *Kultur* was never more strikingly exemplified than

FRENCH TROOPS

On their way to reconstruct trenches from which they had previously driven the Germans.
Top picture: A dispatch rider cycling through a trench.   Bottom picture: A machine-gun in action.

The work of unknown medieval sculptors, which has not unfavourably been compared by competent critics with the masterpieces produced at Athens in the fifth century B.C., was being deliberately smashed by the new Goths, Vandals and Huns, probably at the bidding of the monarch who had caused Berlin to be disfigured with marble images of his ancestors almost as inartistic as the wooden idol of Hindenburg erected there in 1915. The excuse that in the age

in this absurd falsehood and in the action which it endeavoured to justify. The shelling of Reims Cathedral was a fitting epilogue to the scenes of drunkenness and debauchery which had accompanied the entry and departure of the German Army from the city to which Joan of Arc had conducted her exiled king.

The extent of the damage done to the Cathedral at so early a date as September 25, 1914, may be gathered from a report of the well-known New York architect, Mr. Whitney Warren :

Next day I was again at the cathedral from 7.30 in the morning until 4.30 in the afternoon, visiting it in detail and endeavouring to realize the damage done. On September 4, when the Germans first entered Reims, there was a bombardment of the cathedral by their guns and four shells fell upon it—one on the north transept— but little damage was done. The Germans themselves declared that this was either a mistake or caused by the jealousy of some corps which had not been given precedence in entering the city. The bombardment recommenced on September 14 and 15, after the Germans had evacuated the city, but the cathedral was not touched.

On the 17th two bombs struck it, one on the apse and the other on the north transept. The cathedral was again hit on the next day, the shell falling on the southern flying buttresses and on the roof, killing a gendarme and several wounded Germans. The building was fairly riddled with shell during the entire day on September 19, and about 4 o'clock the scaffolding surrounding the north tower caught fire. The fire lasted for about an hour, and during that time two further bombs struck the roof, setting it also on fire. The curé declares that one of these bombs was incendiary ; otherwise it is difficult to explain the extraordinary quickness with which the flames spread through the roof timbers.

The fire from the scaffolding descended until it reached the north door of the main façade, which caught rapidly, burned through, and communicated the fire to the straw covering the floor of the cathedral. This straw had been ordered by the German commander for 3,000 wounded which he intended to place in the cathedral, but the evacuation of the city by the enemy prevented the project from being carried out. When the French arrived the flag of the Red Cross was hoisted on the north tower, and the German wounded placed in the cathedral in the hope that it might be saved.

The straw, as I have said, caught ablaze from the fire originating in the scaffold, burning through the doors and destroying the fine wooden tambours or vestibules surrounding these doors in the interior, and also calcinating the extraordinary stone sculptures decorating the entire interior of this western wall. These sculptures are peculiar to Reims, being in high full relief and cut out of the stone itself instead of being applied. Their loss is irreparable.

All the wonderful glass in the nave is absolutely gone ; that of the apse still exists, though greatly damaged.

The fire on the outside calcinated the greater part of the façade, the north tower, and the entire clerestory, with the flying buttresses and the turret crowning each of them. This stone is irretrievably damaged and flakes off when touched. Consequently all decorative motifs, wherever the flame touched them, are lost. The treasury was saved at the commencement of the fire, and the tapestries for which Reims is renowned were fortunately removed before the bombardment. Half the stalls have been destroyed : the organ is intact, and several crucifixes and pictures in the apse are untouched.

If anything remains of the monument it is owing to its strong construction. The walls and vaults are of a robustness which can resist even modern engines of destruction, for even on September 24, when the bombardment was resumed, three shells landed on the cathedral, but the vaults resisted and were not even perforated.

It was in northern Champagne—in the section between Reims and Verdun—that perhaps most activity was shown during the months of November, December and January. This was one of the weakest spots in the five hundred mile long line of French front. Until the enemy were driven north of the Aisne (east of Berry-au-Bac) and completely expelled from the Forest of the Argonne, he might again resume the offensive, and by an advance to the Marne try to cut off the French right wing from its centre. To Generals Langle de Cary and Sarrail was deputed the task of preparing the way for an offensive which would finally dissipate that danger. Opposed to Langle de Cary, whose four corps in the middle of January, 1915, were strongly reinforced, was General Von Einem with an army of approximately the same size. The immediate objective of Langle de Cary was the Bazancourt-Grand Pré railway running behind the German front, crossing the Forest of the Argonne and terminating at Apremont, four miles or so north of Varennes. This line was connected through Rethel on the Aisne, Bazancourt, and, farther east, through Attigny on the Aisne, and Vouziers, with the Mezières-Montmèdy - Thionville - Metz railway. The country through which the Bazancourt-Grand Pré railroad could be approached was of a rolling nature ; the valleys were shallow, the villages small and poverty-stricken, the farms unimportant. Here and there clumps and plantations of fir trees planted in the chalky soil seemed to punctuate the austerity of the bleak landscape. It was in this forbidding country, against a system of entrenchments similar to that which the Germans had so rapidly constructed between Arras and Lens, that Langle de Cary cautiously advanced. Simultaneously Sarrail's troops worked northward up the Argonne. On December 10 Langle de Cary progressed towards Perthes. Twelve days later he was again advancing, this time not only against Perthes, but against the farm of Beauséjour, west of it on the road from Suippes, through Perthes and Ville-sur-Tourbe to Varennes. Up to December 25 the French pushed forwards and repulsed several counter-attacks, capturing many blockhouses, some machine guns, and a gun under a cupola. This advance was assisted by the

REIMS CATHEDRAL.
A portion of the front of the famous Cathedral before it was destroyed by the Germans.
(From a drawing by Joseph Pennell.)

pressure exercised by the forces round Reims, which to the north of Pranay between December 19–20, and again on December 30, attacked Von Einem's right flank. On January 15 the French Staff was only, however, able to announce that since November 15 it had advanced a kilomètre in the region of Prunay and two kilomètres in that of Perthes, where seventeen counter-attacks of the Germans had been repulsed and the village taken on the 9th.

THE BOMBARDMENT OF REIMS.

A portion of the wrecked Cathedral viewed from
a side street.

Two days later the French were on the outskirts
of Perthes and north of the farm of Beauséjour.

Equally stubborn had been the resistance of
the Germans in the Forest of the Argonne.

The ground in the Argonne is exceedingly
difficult, cut up by watercourses, alternate
ridges, and valleys which are covered with woods
with a thick undergrowth between the trees.
There is a sort of hog's back running through
the centre of it from north to south between
the Aire and the Aisne. Two main roads pass
through it, the one from St. Ménéhould to
Clermont, the other from Vienne-le-Château to
Varennes. Parallel to this last, and north of
it, there is a rough road through the forest
which, starting just above Vienne, goes to Mont
Blainville, traversing that portion of the
forest known as the Bois de la Grurie. Still
farther to the north there is a second rough
road, which goes from Binarville to Apremont.
In the southern portion of the forest the river
Blesme runs towards the north as far as Le Four
de Paris, then turns sharply to the west and
joins the Aisne below Vienne. Along its banks
there is a road coming up from the south and
joining the Vienne-Varennes one by the Four
de Paris. Just outside the main country of the
Argonne, on the east, there is also a good road
which goes up from Clermont through Varennes

and St. Juvin and Grand Pré, and there is on
the west another from Vilry-le-Fos through
St. Ménéhould, Vienne and then to the
north.

When the Germans were driven back from
the Marne their columns retired on both sides
of the Argonne, the available ways through
it being quite unsuited for the movement of
troops. They finally took a defensive position
about the line of the road running from Vienne-
le-Château to Varennes so as to hold the entries
to the district. Their pursuers, when they
arrived, moved up by the road in the centre of
the forest. The Germans, to hold off any possible
attack on the inner flanks of their troops at
Vienne-le-Château or Varennes, in their turn
advanced into the woods. The French could
not debouch from it on the western side, but
they took up a position facing the German
trenches which ran from Vienne-le-Château to
Melzicourt. Gradually the French extended up
the western border, turning the Germans out of
their trenches on the right bank of the Aisne
and occupying a few redoubts at Melzicourt up
to the point where a stream runs into the Aisne
to the north of Servon.

On the centre and east side the French were
stopped by strong forces of the 16th Army
Corps, which had entered the forest between
Varennes and Mont Blainville and held the
ground as far as Apremont. On November 24
the French were around Four de Paris;
on December 6 they were nearing Varennes
from the south-east. Very soon they were
over the Vienne-la-Ville-Varennes road and
round Four de Paris, Saint-Hubert, Fontaine-
Madame and Pavillion de Bagatelle. All these
positions are in the wood of La Grurie, and they
only reached the border at Barricade. Engagements ensued in which the Germans, at first,
were successful, but subsequently they were
pushed back by the French, whose forces,
back to back, faced the western and eastern
entries into the Argonne. One example will
suffice to give some idea of the nature of
the fighting here. The Germans on December 7 pushed out three saps from the first-
line trenches towards the French trenches
until the right and centre reached within a
distance of about 20 yards from the French, the
left sap getting as close as eight yards, but on
December 17 the French had mined the ground
over which this sap passed and blew it up.
The next day, the 19th, the Germans repaired
the damage done and the centre and right saps

reached to within about seven yards of their opponents. From here they drove two mining galleries beneath the French trenches, and on the 20th they blew them up. Meanwhile assaulting columns had been formed and advanced, covered by sappers provided with bombs, axes, and scissors for cutting the wire entanglements. On the 21st the French regained two-thirds of the lost ground. On January 5, after exploding eight mines, Sarrail's troops, aided by a contingent of Italian Volunteers under Constantin Garibaldi, attacked the German trenches north of Courtechausse. For a time they carried everything before them, but the Italians advanced too far, Garibaldi was killed, and at the end of the day the line here was much the same as it had been in the morning. Round Fontaine-Madame a violent engagement was also raging, which continued from the 8th to the 10th, but produced no important results. Similar incidents to these were of constant occurrence, but none of them had any real influence on the main struggle. It need hardly be said that the official bulletins in Germany claimed a series of victories in the Argonne, but then it must be remembered that, when the Austrians were driven back in the Bukovina, it was dryly announced that they were drawing nearer to the passes over the Carpathians, from which, as a matter of fact, they

had advanced but a short time before, only to be driven back by the Russians. Similar treatment was afforded to the defeats of the Turks in the Caucasus ; German official news stated that as a consequence of the bad weather operations in the Caucasus were suspended on both sides. The German public appeared to have an unrivalled capacity for swallowing official falsehoods.

From the eastern edge of the forest of Argonne south of Varennes, in the region of Vauquois, the line of Sarrail's trenches curved north and eastwards across the Meuse round the entrenched camp of Verdun, the perimeter of which was being constantly enlarged. In December the French were approaching Varennes from the east and south through Boureilles and Vauquois, were pushing down the valley of the Meuse in the direction of Dun, on the Verdun-Mézières railway, and up and over the heights separating Verdun and the Meuse from Metz and the Moselle. The town of Verdun, thanks to Sarrail's dispositions, had scarcely felt the pinch of war. Writing from it on December 2 a British war correspondent* observes : "The point of the German lines now nearest to the town is the twin hills known as the Jumelles d'Orne, and that is 10 miles from the town and four from the nearest fort—

* Mr. W. H. Perris.

REIMS CATHEDRAL ON FIRE.

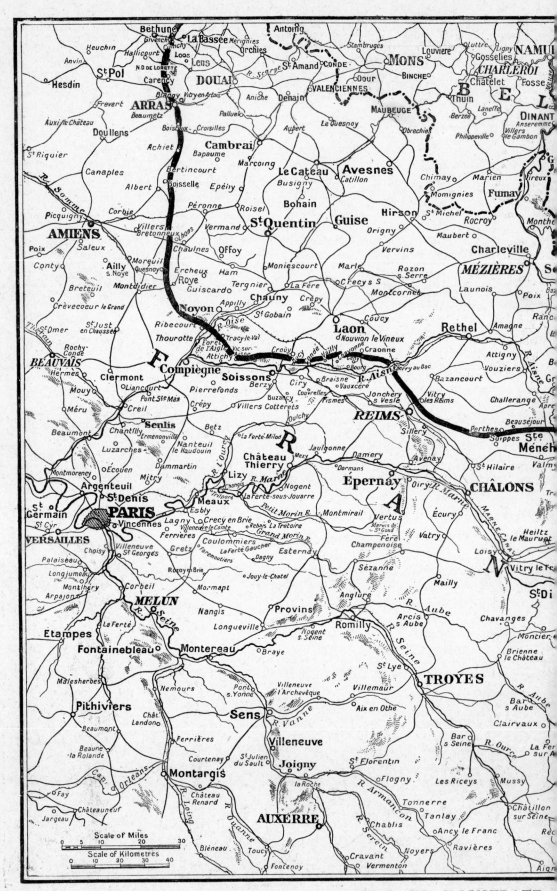

MAP TO ILLUSTRATE
The Line shows approximate

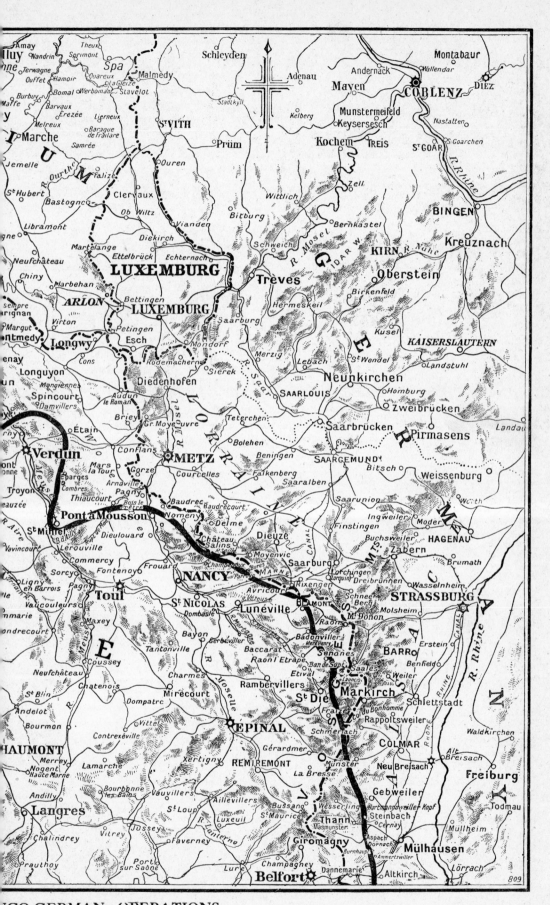

NCO-GERMAN OPERATIONS.
ront on November 11, 1914.

21

A BURNING VILLAGE NEAR REIMS.

generally speaking, the German batteries are about 20 miles from Verdun." The Verdun-Etain-Conflans-Metz railway was by then at several points under the fire of the French artillery, and the line of trenches went from Vauquois north-east through the Bois de Montfaucon, from Flabas to Azanne, south to Ornes, out away east towards Etain, and thence south-west through wooded, hilly country to Eparges, and from Eparges by Amorville to St. Mihiel, the sole crossing of the Meuse south of Verdun possessed by the Germans. The net effect of the fighting up to the beginning of December had been, in the words of Mr. George Adam, who was permitted to visit Verdun at this epoch, " to place the French at the top of the hills, from which their view stretches away into Germany. At the end of six months of siege," he added, "the Germans have not succeeded in throwing a single shell into Verdun."

As we have seen, the fortified lines from Verdun to Toul had been pierced at St. Mihiel. Happily, the forts to the right and left of the gap had held out long enough for Sarrail with two cavalry corps to head the columns of Germans crossing the Meuse and to confine them in the salient Les Eparges–St. Mihiel–Bois le Prêtre. The Bois le Prêtre is just north

and west of Pont-à-Mousson on the Moselle. But the Germans had secured a considerable portion of the heights of the Meuse between St. Mihiel and Les Eparges, and they had uninterrupted access to Metz and the railway from Metz to Thiaucourt.

The efforts of Sarrail and Dubail were directed against the western and southern faces of the salient, and its apex. On November 13 at both ends of the southern face there was fighting; and on the 17th there was an advance from Verdun against the western face. The next day the Germans blew up the barracks of Chauvoncourt, close to St. Mihiel itself. But on December 8 the French penetrated into the Bois le Prêtre, and took a mitrailleuse and several prisoners, who alleged that their officers had forbidden them to fire lest they should provoke the French.

West of the Bois le Prêtre the Germans on the southern face of the salient were being slowly pushed back from the forest of Apremont and the wood of Ailly to its left, and the communications of the defenders of the space between Les Eparges and the Bois le Prêtre were jeopardised by the French artillery. On January 18, and again on January 22, the station at Arnaville on the Thiaucourt–Metz railway was successfully bombarded. By the

17th all of the Bois le Prêtre was in French hands with the exception of the portion known as the Quart-en-Réserve. That day the Quart-en-Réserve was attacked and several trenches, some officers, and a company of infantry captured. On the 18th there was a further French success, but during the next few days the Germans counter-attacked and recovered a third of the lost trenches. On the 27th the German bridges across the Meuse at St. Mihiel were smashed by the French guns. St. Mihiel, the capture of which, in September, 1914, had raised the hopes of the enemy, and the salient, of which it was the apex, were proving a death-trap for the Germans.

Descending from Pont-à-Mousson the French line went east of Nancy protected by the Grand Couronné entrenchments and of Lunéville, The recoil of De Castelnau and Dubail, consequent on the crushing defeat of the French who had entered Lorraine in August, 1914, had ended with the battle of the Marne. By the close of November the French Staff were able to announce that Nancy was out of reach of the German artillery, that the French had progressed both north of Lunéville and also farther south to the north-east and

east of Saint-Dié, which had been recaptured. On December 2 Dubail's troops moved from Pont-à-Mousson, east of the Moselle in the direction of Metz and captured the hill of Xon and the village of Lesmésnils beyond it. Another detachment on December 24 was close to Cirey, east of Lunéville and within a few miles of Mt. Donon, the culminating summit of the Vosges on the north. North-west of Cirey the French were clearing the enemy from the Forest of Parroy, and east of the line Lunéville–St. Dié they advanced north and south of Senones and in the Ban-de-Sapt, where on November 29 they beat off three counter-attacks. The advance to the passes in the Vosges, seized by Pau in August, 1914, had again begun.

The operations in the Vosges during the winter months, like those in the Argonne, were favourable to the French, whose nimbler wits and greater individuality gave them the advantage. The Chasseurs Alpins of the French 15th Corps, often mounted on skis, performed feats as heroic as those of Ronarc'h's marines at Dixmude in October and November. Deep snow now encumbered the passes, and filled the ravines and glens up which General Pau's

BACCARAT.
Funeral of a French soldier.

A DUEL BETWEEN A FRENCH ARMOURED CAR AND A BODY OF GERMAN INFANTRY.

forces had swarmed to recover the lost province. Dubail's progress was necessarily slower than Pau's, but it obliged the German leaders to keep large forces in Alsace and to squander lives and waste their resources at a point where they could gain no decisive victory. Some incidents of the fighting may be referred to.

On November 9 the French had repulsed a German attack directed against their position on the heights near St. Marie-aux-Mines. On December 2 they moved once more south of the valley of the Thur on Mülhausen and captured Aspach-le-Haut and Aspach-le-Bas, south-east of Thann. The next day they advanced on Altkirch, between Belfort and Mülhausen. In the Northern Vosges they seized the Tête-de-Faux, near the Pass of Bonhomme. During the rest of December the struggle for the valley of the Thur continued, chiefly round Steinbach, stormed on December 30, and Cernay. On January 7 the French captured Burnhaupt-le-Haut, between Thann and Altkirch. The next day, however, it was recovered by the Germans. Snow storms then suspended the major operations for some time, but the French secured the summit of the Hartmannsweiler, a peak north of Cernay, but the detachment on it was killed or captured on January 21.

Our survey of the events which happened on the battle-front from La Bassée to Belfort in the period beginning with the discomfiture of the Prussian Guards in the Zonnebeke-Gheluvelt woods east of Ypres and ending on February 1 has been necessarily brief. The reader must imagine for himself the innumerable heroic and hideous scenes enacted, the daring exploits of the airmen—their duels thousands of feet above the surface of the ground, their expeditions to reconnoitre, to observe the effects of the fire of artillery, to bomb aeroplane sheds and railway stations—the thousands of guns of all calibres daily vomiting projectiles, some of which crushed in cupolas and casemates constructed by the most scientific engineers of recent years, others of which destroyed acres of barbed-wire entanglements and buried or slew officers and men hiding in deep dug-outs. By day and night the 450 miles or so of trenches which ran from the waterlogged plain of the Lys over the chalky plateau of Notre Dame de Lorette to Arras, from Arras across the hills, over the Somme and its plain to the Forest of the Eagle and the wooded heights to the north of the Aisne, thence to the outskirts of the battered city of Reims, from Reims over the bare downs of Champagne, through the glades and hillocks of the Argonne round Verdun to the tree-clad heights of the Meuse, by St. Mihiel to the Moselle, and from the Moselle and the Meurthe to the summits of the Vosges were, it must be remembered, alive with vigilant foot soldiers sniping at, bombing or bayonetting one another. In sunlight, fog, mist, haze, under torrential rain, or amid snow storms the struggle between the wills of the French and German nations-in-arms went on.

As in 1792, the representatives and agents of the houses of Hohenzollern and Hapsburg were again trying to subdue the spirit of the French. Then the tools of the Teutonic despots had been a few thousand mercenaries; now they had enlisted in their cause the armed millions of the German race. In 1792 the Hohenzollerns and Hapsburgs had fallen on a disunited France, whose capital was seething with revolution. They had fondly fancied that 122 years later the circumstances in France would be substantially the same; that when war broke out Republicans and Monarchists, Clericals and anti-Clericals, Socialists and anti-Socialists would fly at each other's throats.

Never were despots more dramatically disillusioned. The murder of Jaurès had been the prelude to no civil war, but to the most extraordinary consolidation of a people known to history. Not even under Carnot and Bonaparte had the French exhibited more prowess and military ability than they had under Joffre. When Namur fell it had seemed to many that nothing would be able to withstand the avalanche-like descent of the German army on the centre of Western civilization. By February 1, 1915, the danger of Europe relapsing into a barbarism, which being scientific was more appalling than the barbarism of primeval times, had vanished. The following extract from the French official report referred to above was the literal truth:

It may first of all be affirmed that the fundamental plan of the German General Staff has completely failed. This plan has been superabundantly set forth by German military writers, and also in the Reichstag by the Ministers of War. It aimed at crushing France by an overwhelming attack, and at reducing her to a condition of helplessness in less than a month. Germany has not succeeded in this. Our Army is, as we have seen, not only intact, but strengthened, full of trust in its leaders and profoundly imbued with the certainty of final success. Germany has not attained, then, the essential object which she publicly set before herself. But the defeat which she has sustained does not apply only to her fundamental plan. It extends also to the various operations in which she has essayed to secure partial

AFTER THE ASSAULT.
A view of the German first-line trenches.

advantages over us, in default of the decisive advantage which she had failed to win.

In the three days which followed the declaration of war the German General Staff massed great forces in front of Nancy. With what purpose ? A sudden attack which from its very beginning should break our lines. This attack did not take place, because the reinforcements of our frontier force at the end of 1913 and the defensive organization established on the Grand Couronné discouraged the enemy from an enterprise which, though possible a year sooner, had become full of risk. Being unable to strike at Nancy, the German command directed all its resources to the outflanking manœuvre which, by enveloping our left, would permit of the investment of Paris. Our left was not enveloped. Paris was not invested. And the German Army was obliged in the second week of September to save its own threatened communications by a precipitate retreat.

With a desperate effort the General Staff of the enemy attempted to offset the effect of this retreat by piercing our centre in Champagne. There, as elsewhere, he failed and had to withdraw in great haste. In the month of October, with more extended lines, he endeavoured to repeat his enveloping manœuvre and to turn our left ; but right up to the North Sea we built an impassable barrier against him. He accumulated his forces in Belgium to outflank us by the coast and reach our maritime bases. His attack was broken. With desperation he sought to cut our forces to the south of Ypres : we maintained all our positions.

To sum up, the German General Staff has placed upon its record since the beginning of the campaign—apart from the failure of its general plan, which aimed at the crushing of France in a few weeks—seven defeats of high significance, namely, the defeat of the sudden attack on Nancy, the defeat of the rapid march on Paris, the defeat of the envelopment of our left in August, the defeat of the same envelopment in Novem-

ber, the defeat of the attempt to break through our centre in September, the defeat of the coast attack on Dunkirk and Calais, and the defeat of the attack on Ypres.

The German Army, powerful and courageous as it may be, has therefore succeeded in gaining the advantage upon no single point, and its forced halt after six months of war condemns it to a retreat, the pace of which may or may not be accelerated by the Russian successes, but the necessity for which is now in any case a foregone conclusion.

Such was the proud but sober language in which the French described their own achievements. We proceed to narrate the main events from February 1 to the preliminaries of the Battle of Artois.

The birthday of the Emperor William II., January 27, and the next day had been celebrated by an ineffective German offensive at several points, La Bassée, La Creute, Perthes, Bagatelle in the Argonne, and also in the Woevre. The loss of the enemy was calculated by the French Staff at 20,000. It was a good omen for the Allied operations from Belfort to La Bassée. We propose now to work back through the seven sections of the battle-front from the frontiers of Switzerland to Artois.

In the Vosges, owing to the depth of the snow, which was frequently as deep as a man's height,

Dubail was content with maintaining an aggressive attitude, but for a time he made no serious efforts to enlarge his conquests in Alsace. There was a slight advance, indeed, during February in the regions of Amertzwiller and Altkirch at the southern, and in those of Senones and the Ban-de-Sapt at the northern end of the mountain chain, while French airmen bombed important points behind the German lines, notably, on February 5, the aeroplane sheds at Habsheim. Counter-attacks of the enemy at different points were repulsed, but in the region of the Col du Bonhomme the Germans obtained a temporary footing on a summit between Lusse and Wissembach, from which they were expelled on the 19th. Up the valley of the Fecht, down which runs the Münster-Colmar railway, the enemy advanced

on the 20th with the object of recovering the crest of the mountains. They were roughly handled, and on the 22nd the pursuing French gained a foothold in the village of Stosswihr. On March 2 the French gained a success at Sultzeren, north-west of Münster. Their grip on the Hartmannsweilerkopf was not abandoned, and on March 5 they captured a work, some trenches and two mitrailleuses. The preparations for obtaining a complete mastery of the valley of the Fecht leading to the Mülhausen-Colmar Strassburg railway continued. The barracks of Colmar were bombed by an airman on the 17th. The snow was melting and the operations could be more freely resumed. Seven days later (March 24) the second-line trenches of the Germans on the Hartmannsweilerkopf were carried and the French

THE RESULT OF THE FRENCH GUN-FIRE ON THE GERMAN
FIRST-LINE TRENCHES IN CHAMPAGNE.

A shell fired by the French artillery exploding in a German trench. In the foreground of the bottom picture are French infantrymen taking cover and awaiting the signal to charge.

AN ARTILLERY DUEL AS A PRELUDE TO AN INFANTRY ATTACK.

Chasseurs were once more close to the summit, which was secured on the 27th after severe fighting, no fewer than 700 German bodies being counted and 40 officers and 353 men, all unwounded, being captured.

Proceeding northwards to the region between the Meurthe-Moselle and the German borders : there was fighting round Badonviller at the end of February. The Germans claimed a great success for February 27, but their information given later with regard to it gives little to support their first claims, and it is probable that here there were only some partial engagements during February and March in which very little useful work was done by either side. The same remark applies to the combats in the forest of Parroy.

It will be recollected that the signal station on the hill of Xon, in the north-eastern environs of Pont-à-Mousson, had been captured by the French, who from its summit could observe the country to the gates of Metz. The hill Xon directly commanded the approaches to Pont-à-Mousson and the bridges over the Moselle there. During February there was a desperate but ineffective effort on the part of the Germans to recover this spot, which menaced their hold on the base line of the St. Mihiel salient.

Against the southern side from Pont-à-Mousson to St. Mihiel numerous attacks during February and March were made by Dubail. The possession of the Bois le Prêtre, the forest of Apremont, and the wood of Ailly were stubbornly disputed by the enemy. But it was the western side which became the theatre of the bloodiest engagements at this epoch. At Les Eparges, during the months of February and March, there were outbursts of violent fighting almost deserving the name of battles.

The first commenced on February 17 and lasted till the 22nd ; and the second took place from March 18 to the 21st. Les Eparges is situated on the heights east of the Meuse, on a height of over 1,100 feet, and the ground is difficult for the movements of troops. The Germans had occupied it on September 21, 1914, and their line went back from there to the wood known as the Forêt de la Montagne. The actual village of Eparges had remained in French hands, as well as the valleys and hills more to the north at Mont Girmont, and the hill known as the Côte des Hures, and on February 9 a surprise attack gave them St. Rémy. The German lines were strong and they held the ground to the north of Eparges—several lines of trenches

flanked by a redoubt at the east and west extremities. The line they held commanded from its left flank the road from Eparges to St. Rémy, thus cutting the communication between these two places and the line of hills from Hattonchatel to the Côte des Hures. This line of hills formed the northern defences of the position behind St. Mihiel. By February 17 the French had sapped towards the enemy's trenches and had constructed mines under the German line which, when blown up, formed a series of craters, in which the French troops assembled before making a further forward movement. A vigorous artillery fire was then directed against the German lines, especially against the western redoubt, and so great was its effect that the French troops were able to rush the first two lines of the trenches without much loss. During the night the redoubt was severely bombarded by heavy guns, and on the 18th the Germans began a counter-attack and at first drove out the French, but later in the day they in their turn made a fresh attack and recaptured the redoubt.

The same day another attack by the Germans was stopped. They then poured such a heavy artillery fire on the work that the French were compelled to evacuate it. But the French once more advanced to the attack. By the morning of the 19th they again held the redoubt, and on that day the same drama was performed. The French retired under artillery fire and then their guns drove out the Germans. Four times did the Bavarians, who were fighting here, assault the French, and each time they were driven back. But still the situation of the French was a precarious one. The shelter made by the craters was inadequate for the purposes of protection, and it was considered desirable on the 21st to take the work which supported the east end of the German entrenchments. This work followed the line of a pine wood, and the regiment told off to take it carried the work and even succeeded in penetrating into the wood. Here severe fighting took place, until at length both sides had dug themselves in. The French attack, delivered against the space between the two works protecting the flanks, was unsuccessful, but a fresh counter-attack by the Germans was also without result. During the night the French prepared their defences on the conquered position under a fire of bombs, and on the morning of the 22nd a strong counter-attack towards the work on the east of the lines forced back the French. Then the latter again assumed the offensive and managed to make some progress.

The second period of fighting took place between March 18 and 21. The object of the French assaults was to take the eastern redoubt, and three battalions were told off for the purpose. They managed to carry a part

of the first line of German trenches, capturing about one hundred yards on the right flank and three hundred and fifty on the left. A little later, on March 27, a Chasseur battalion was unable to close up nearer the eastern redoubt. The result of the fighting, which appears to have been very severe, was that the French gained a little ground, but the Germans state that no progress was made.

The French objective at Les Eparges was to clear the enemy from the heights of the Meuse. West of Verdun one aim of Sarrail was to dislodge the Germans from the banks of the Aire, to cross it and attack Varennes and Apremont (in the Argonne), where the Apremont-Grand Pré-Bazancourt railway terminated.

In the middle of February there was some fighting directed against the German position of Boureuilles-Vauquois, where, according to the French, some progress was made; but according to the Germans the French attack was completely defeated. On February 28 fresh operations were begun. At Hill 263, east of Boureuilles, the French captured about 300 yards of trenches, probably in front of the village of Vauquois, which is situated on this hill, and got a firm footing on the edge of the

GERMAN PRISONERS OF WAR.
Waiting to be marched off. Inset: Types of German prisoners.

plateau. The hill in question is about 300 feet above the valley of the Aire. It was a strong position, as there were numerous caves in it which were safe from artillery fire, and the woods behind it were cover for reserves. On March 2 the French claim to have held the captured ground despite two counter-attacks, and to have made some prisoners. If the Germans are to be believed, on each occasion these attacks were driven off with heavy loss. On the 3rd and 4th further progress was made by the French. As to this the Germans were silent. On March 5 fresh German attacks were made, which were defeated with heavy loss, the French taking a considerable number of prisoners. Later on in that day our Ally made still further progress on the west side of the village, the only part where the Germans still held out. The German reply to these statements of the French was that they had driven off all counter-attacks. It will be observed that the specific statements of the French were met only with general denials by the Germans. That the fighting here was very severe is proved by the French accounts published in the " Journal Officiel " of March 15, wherein it is stated that four assaults were made and were thrown back by the Germans. It would seem that on March 2 and 3 the French made progress. During the day of the 3rd the French appear to have occupied themselves in consolidating their position, and the fighting was renewed during the night of March 3–4, the Germans having received reinforcements. Their counter-attack was repulsed and so was a further attempt made during daylight on March 5.

Across the Aire, from Varennes to Vienne-le-Ville on the Aisne, the forest of Argonne, continued to be hotly contested. At 8 o'clock in the morning of February 10, after a heavy preparatory artillery fire, the enemy blew up 15 yards of the fort of Marie-Thérèse, in the wood of La Grurie, by mines, besides throwing on the two faces of the salient very large bombs, the explosion of which produced damage to the parapet. Immediately after, three German battalions advanced to the attack. The first line carried bombs, which they threw into the French trenches. It seems probable that the artillery and the big bomb explosions had somewhat cowed the French, and there was very little active resistance to the German advance. The centre of the German attack succeeded in pushing the French out of their

AFTER FIGHTING IN CHAMPAGNE.
German prisoners being interrogated by a French Intelligence Officer.

front trenches, and the men falling back carried with them the garrison of the supporting trenches immediately behind, but it was only over a short space that this occurred. To right and left the troops held their ground. The French made a counter-attack, but it was brought to a standstill by the German machine guns, and only a small portion of the left of the captured trenches could be regained, but the Germans were unable to carry the second line of the trench. In the afternoon a fresh counter-attack succeeded in regaining 160 yards on the right of the lost front-line trench, but no progress was made in the centre. The fighting continued during the night without any great results, but our Allies recaptured a bomb-thrower and a gun which had been lost in the morning. The enemy dug themselves in about 400 mètres from the French first line, where they entrenched themselves. It will thus be seen that the Germans had made a slight gain, though nothing of any importance.

It was west of the Argonne, between the Aisne and the Suippe, that the most important of the battles in the early part of 1915 was fought by the Allies. We have pointed out that Von Einem's forces, deployed as they were from the borders of the Argonne west and south of the Aisne to Berry-au-Bac, constituted a serious menace to Joffre's whole position from Belfort to La Bassée. Should the German and Austro-Hungarian operations in the Eastern

AFTER A SUCCESS IN THE BOIS D'AILLY, NEAR ST. MIHIEL.

French infantry returning to their cantonment, preceded by a band and with their colours flying.

theatre of war be successful, the enemy's army
in France and Belgium would be reinforced
and the German offensive, closed by the battle
of Flanders, probably be renewed. Until the
German Crown Prince's and Von Einem's
troops were expelled from the Argonne and
the Champagne-Pouilleuse respectively, the
new German offensive might be directed to
cutting off Joffre's right wing from his centre,
or to an advance westward against Reims,
and, behind Reims, the rear of Maunoury's
army. The sooner, then, Von Einem was
driven to the north bank of the Aisne, the
better it would be for the Allied cause.

There was also an imperative reason, uncon-
nected with the situation in France, why Joffre
should take the offensive. Just as we now
know that one of the motives for the Dardanelles Expedition was the urgent request of
the Russians, so it was afterwards explained
that the French offensive in Champagne during
February had for its ulterior motive " to fix on
this point of the front the largest possible German
force, to oblige it to use up ammunition, and to
prevent any troops being transported to Russia."

Accordingly, in February, Langle de Cary
was ordered by Joffre to attack Von Einem in
the region of Perthes. During December the
French had conquered about one and a half
miles of ground on the line Perthes-Le Mesnil-
Massiges and made an important capture in
winning the Hill 200 on the road to Souain,
about a mile and a quarter west of Perthes.
This dominated the ground in front and
was a favourable point of observation against
the German trenches. From January 25
to February 4 had been a period of counter-
attacks by the enemy, which were driven
back by the French, who advanced their line
still farther to the north to a small wood
about 500 yards to the north-west of Perthes
and to another nearly a mile to the north-
east of Le Mesnil. In front of Massiges there
was no change in the position, so that early in
February the line here ran from the north of
Souain, north of Perthes, back to Beauséjour.
But on February 16 Langle de Cary captured
nearly two miles of trenches to the north of
Beauséjour, and a number of counter-attacks
made by the Germans were beaten back, our
Allies taking a considerable number of prisoners.
The fighting was extremely local in character,
with here partial successes and there partial
repulses, but on the whole the French got the
better of the day.

On the 17th the French gained still more
ground, capturing many more of the
German front line of trenches. They were
subjected to a number of counter-attacks
all of which were beaten off and some
hundreds of prisoners taken. Amongst these
were included officers and men of the 6th
and 8th German Army Corps, and the 8th,
10th and 12th Reserve Army Corps. On the
night of the 17th–18th, and on the morning of
the 18th, two very severe attacks were made
by the Germans to reconquer the positions they
had lost. They reached quite close up to the
line held by the French, but were eventually
driven off by the bayonet. On the next night
(18th–19th) five more counter-attacks were
made by the enemy, but they were all defeated.
The German explanation was that " at a few
important points the French succeeded in
penetrating our advanced trenches." On the
20th the fighting still went on, and the French,
besides holding their ground, made some further
progress to the north of Perthes, though according to the Germans the latter enjoyed, in comparison with the last few days, comparative
tranquillity. On the 21st the Germans still
claimed the same relative cessation in the
fighting, but, according to the French, German
counter-attacks were driven off with great loss,
the enemy pursued, and the whole of the
trenches to the east and north of the wood
above Perthes were captured and held. Some
progress was also made to the north of Le
Mesnil.

There is the same discrepancy in the accounts
of the fighting on February 22, the French
claiming to have captured a line of trenches
and two woods besides beating back a couple of
severe counter-attacks. On the 23rd a further
advance was made to the north of Le Mesnil,
and the German attacks were as usual beaten
back. According to the Germans, the whole
of the fighting of the 23rd and 24th ended in
their favour, a categorical statement being
made that the French had completely failed in
their object. The same monotony of falsehood
is to be found in the German narratives of the
fighting right up to March 12. The result of the
battle, as a whole, was that, although no great
successes were obtained by the French, they
distinctly pushed the enemy back and gained
positions one to two miles in front of the line
they had originally held and over four and a
half miles in length. But they had done more :
they had secured a line which dominated the

ground in front, and formed, therefore, a favourable jumping-off point for future successes. The German losses had been heavy ; the Guards, who had been brought to this part of the line, being very severely handled. Four to five and a half Army Corps had been engaged by the enemy, of whom two thousand were taken prisoners and ten thousand killed ; and in addition a considerable amount of material had been captured.

Generally speaking, the operations must be regarded as successful from the Allied point of view. The French had held a considerable German force and they had attracted to this region further numbers. Thus, on February 16, the Kaiser's troops in the Champagne numbered 119 battalions, 31 squadrons, 64 field batteries, and 20 heavy batteries. By March 10 these had been strengthened by 14 battalions of Infantry of the line and six of the Guard, one regiment of Field Artillery and two heavy batteries. Notwithstanding this increase of strength, the enemy had been unable to win back the lost ground, and he had not only been compelled to hold troops in the Champagne, but to add to them, and so great had been the need of reinforcing the German armies at this point of the long line of battle that they had even been compelled to draw from the troops facing the British Army six battalions and eight batteries, two of the Guard. Even the German bulletins were obliged to recognize that their losses had been very heavy, from which it may be deduced that their numbers engaged were very numerous. In one of their bulletins they admitted that the German Army had lost more troops in the Champagne than in the fighting round the Mazurian Lakes in the Eastern theatre. There they had 14 Army Corps and three Cavalry Divisions, yet they had the effrontery to assert that they had only in Champagne two feeble Divisions fighting against the French from Souain to Massiges, a distance of 10 miles, a statement which is plainly absurd.

Though the Battle of Perthes, as it may be called, did not produce the retreat of Von Einem to the Aisne, by hindering or preventing the transport of German troops to the Russian front it was probably a material cause of the Russian victories between February 25 and March 3 on the Nareff, and certainly, by diverting German troops from Flanders, it facilitated the gaining by the British of the Battle of Neuve

KEEPING FIT BEHIND THE FIGHTING LINE.
French cavalrymen exercising their horses. Inset : Awaiting orders to advance.

THE EFFECT OF A GERMAN BOMBARDMENT.
An old parishioner visits her ruined church in an Alsatian village.

Chapelle. Before leaving the Battle of Perthes we shall describe the combat for the Sabot Wood, a subsidiary action in the region to the left of the battle-field.

From Perthes to Souain there ran a road more or less along the crest of the hills which stretched out to Souain. To the north of this were the German trenches; on the south, sheltered by the ground, the first French position. To hold the French position it was necessary to capture the crest line which went east and west through the Sabot Wood. It had been strongly fortified by the Germans; furnished with frequent bomb-proof covers bristling with machine guns and with every possible means of defence. It was held by Bavarian Landwehr.

The French trenches at this time were at a distance of from thirty to two hundred yards from the Germans, the nearest being at the point of the Sabot, the farthest towards Perthes. The German position was ordered to be captured on March 7, when two French battalions prepared to storm it. The assault was naturally preceded by a severe artillery fire, and then one battalion advanced from the west against the toe of the Sabot, while the other made a more or less direct attack on its right. The left attack

had but a short space to go, and at the first rush reached the extremity of the wood, but here a tremendous fire from many machine guns brought it to a standstill. The southern attack, notwithstanding that it had farther to go, was more successful. The rush of the French infantry, gaining momentum as it went along, broke with an irresistible vigour on the Germans, drove them back from their first line, and captured the second. Moving still onward, they reached the northern border of the wood, but here a trench, made by the Germans perpendicular to their foremost lines, took the French in flank and they were obliged to retire to the second German line, where they proceeded to instal themselves without interruption from the enemy. During the night no less than four attempts to regain the lost ground were made by the Germans, but all without success. At the first dawn of day a fresh attempt was made and some of the French yielded to the shock, but the Colonel commanding the regiment at once advanced to meet the Germans with the bayonet, which dislodged the enemy from the toe of the Sabot and thrust them back farther to the east. Thus in two days' fighting a considerable gain had been made. From the 9th to the 12th

GERMAN BOMBARDMENT OF A
The German gunners having found the range of the church, shells rained

numerous small encounters enabled the French to strengthen their position and to extend it more towards the heel of the Sabot. Large working parties also excavated communication trenches which led from the rear to the French position, thus facilitating the approach of reinforcements and the removal of the wounded.

On the 14th a further attempt was made to capture a German trench which connected together the heads of three communications. The first attempt was unsuccessful; a second was deferred till the 15th. At 4.30 two French companies were sent forward to the assault, and in a moment the rival troops were engaged with the bayonet. The result at first was a success, but the way was stopped by a blockhouse armed with machine guns, and these drove back the French troops. Yet another attack was made, but it took two hours of heroic efforts before the blockhouse could be penetrated. Even then the enemy did not give up, and two smart counter-attacks were made shortly after daybreak. These were beaten off with bombs and then the Germans gave up the contest. They evacuated the wood, leaving it in the hands of the French and merely hanging on to a small trench at its north-eastern extremity.

We have noted that if Von Einem—reinforced—were to take the offensive, one course open to him would be to advance westward between the Aisne and the Marne towards the Oise. During the Battle of Perthes there was an indication that he was, perhaps, contemplating a step of the kind. During the night of

The Postern.

THE FORT OF

PEACEFUL VILLAGE IN FRANCE.
upon the village, causing fires which rapidly spread from house to house.

March 1-2 the whole of the French front from Bétheny through Reims to Prunay was violently bombarded. At 2.15 a.m. the Germans launched an attack near Cernay, and three-quarters of an hour later, under cover of a clump of firs, another between the farm of Alger and Prunay. These attacks were, however, feints, and at dawn the main German effort was made against the farm of Alger, north of the fort of La Pompelle. Preceded by a flight of aerial torpedoes, two columns of Germans rushed forward, but, caught by the fire of the French mitrailleuses and by a hail of shrapnel, this charge, like the fight during the night, was a complete failure.

In the meantime, on the Aisne from Berry-au-Bac to Compiègne, there had been a succession of artillery duels but no action of any importance. The Cadmean victory of Soissons had been followed by a cessation of the German offensive. Maunoury's guns kept Kluck from crossing the river and bombarded the roads leading to the latter's front, the stations and railroads utilized by him, and his gun or mitrailleuse emplacements. Kluck's artillery was almost equally active, but its targets were not of a merely tactical character. Thus, on March 1, two hundred shells were thrown into Soissons, the continued existence of which, like the existence of Reims, Arras and Ypres, annoyed the representatives of Teutonic *Kultur.* One piece of misfortune to the Allies must be recorded. On March 12 General de Maunoury and General de Villaret, one of his corps

MANONVILLER.
The Ditch. showing the destruction of the iron fence on the scarp and counterscarp.

THE HEAVY FIGHTING IN THE MAIN STREET OF VAUQUOIS DURING THE FRENCH ATTACK, MARCH 1, 1915.
The French obtained possession of the village and drove the Germans from their positions.

commanders, were badly wounded while inspecting from the first-line trenches the German position, at this place thirty or forty yards away. Maunoury's left eye was injured. The brave and able victor of the battle of the Ourcq—the action which more than all others decided the battle of the Marne—had to go into hospital. In August he paid a visit to his estate at Loir-et-Cher, where the veteran had been spending in retirement the latter days of his life engaged in agricultural pursuits. Like Cincinnatus, with whom he was compared by his fellow-countrymen, he had rejoined the army and proved that it is a mistake to suppose that an old soldier is necessarily timid and incompetent. "A little place," he said with a smile to an inquirer, "will soon be found for me." That place was to be the Governorship of Paris, vacated by General Galliéni—his coadjutor at the battle of the Marne—when Galliéni succeeded M. Millerand as Secretary for War in the Briand Cabinet. The news of the wounds inflicted on Maunoury and Villaret may well have encouraged the Germans.

On March 14, and again on the 22nd, they bombarded the Cathedral of Soissons. The French reply took the form of airmen dropping on March 22 explosives on the barracks of La Fère and the stations of Anizy, Chauny, Tergnier, and Coucy-le-Château. The French airmen at this period were particularly active. One of them dropped bombs on the barracks and station of Freiburg, in Baden. On March 27 a squadron of ten airmen attacked the airship sheds of Frescaty and the railway station at Metz, and also the barracks, east of Strassburg. The enterprise of the German airmen was also shown on several occasions. For example, on March 30, one of them dropped bombs on the apse of Reims Cathedral.

Turning to the area between the Oise and Arras, in February and March there was, unless judged by the standards of most previous wars, little to mention. On January 28—the day following that of the anniversary of the Kaiser's birth—the Germans had made a vain and costly attack in the region of Bellacourt. On February 1 there was an engagement north of Hamel. The night of the 6th-7th the Germans exploded three mines on the face of the group of houses in La Boisselle, north-east of Albert, held by the French. As the smoke and dust cleared away it was perceived that three companies of the enemy had left their trenches and were clambering among the ruined

buildings. The French infantry and artillery kept the Germans, however, to the craters formed by the explosions. At 3 p.m. the enemy was then assaulted by a company and, losing 150 dead and many wounded, the Germans were dislodged. During the next few days there was more mining, followed by explosions, on both sides, but the balance of advantage lay with the French. Throughout January and February the artillery duels went on, the barrages of fire frequently preventing German or French attacks maturing. On March 1, at Bécourt, near Albert, a German force mustering to assault the French trenches was stopped before recourse had been had to bayonet or bomb. At Carnoy, in the same district, the Germans on March 15 exploded a mine, and the usual crater-fighting ensued for several days. The reader who has followed our narrative of the struggle for Hill 60 will realize for himself what that meant. As was truly pointed out by the French military authorities on March 1, although in the then present stage of the War it was rare for important masses to grapple with one another, there were daily operations of detail, " destructions by mines or gun-fire, surprises, offensive reconnaissances," and the more active of the adversaries by constantly threatening his opponent obtained a moral ascendency.

While everything from Reims to Arras tended to remain in a state of equilibrium, it was different north of Arras. Just as in Champagne, in the Argonne, on the Heights of the Meuse, and the southern face of the St. Mihiel salient, and in parts of French Lorraine and in Alsace, the fighting between Arras and La Bassée was fierce and sanguinary. The prize at stake was Lens, and, if Lens fell, La Bassée, probably, Lille and perhaps the whole plain between the Scarpe-Scheldt and the Lys. To achieve these objects, to recover the whole of Artois, to cut the communications of the enemy in Flanders and to menace those of the enemy south of the Scheldt and Sambre two initial steps had to be taken—the seizure of the Notre Dame de Lorette-Ablain-Carency-La Targette-Neuville St. Vaast-Vimy plateau, and the piercing of the German line between the heights of Notre Dame de Lorette and those of La Bassée.

Here, as elsewhere, the Germans were not content with a passive defensive. In the morning of February 1 they attacked the hinge between Sir John French's and Maud-

'huy's army near La Bassée, but were beaten with heavy loss. On the 4th it was the turn of the French to advance, not on this side, but in the region of Arras. The road from Arras to Lens was barred by the fortress, already referred to, called by the French " The Labyrinth." A little to the west and east respectively of the road before it traversed " the Labyrinth " and nearer Arras were the villages of Ecurie and Roclincourt. Having blown up with five mines enemy's trenches north of Ecurie, three small columns—two of Zouaves and one of African Light Infantry— were directed into the mine-craters, which were occupied, fortified and connected by a communication trench with the French position in the rear. On the night of the 6th-7th the French mines blew up a German trench on the outskirts of Carency. The next day, February 8, a mill on the Béthune-La Bassée road was captured by the French, and the Germans massing for a counter-attack dispersed with shrapnel. Near Roclincourt, east of Ecurie and south of " The Labyrinth," a German trench on February 17 was blown up and a counter-attack repulsed with heavy loss. On the other hand, at the beginning of March the Germans won a trench of the French near Notre Dame de Lorette, and apparently captured a considerable number of prisoners. The next day, March 4, the French counter-attacked and recovered part of the lost ground and in their turn made

150 Germans prisoners. On the 6th the French claim to have gained further ground and to have inflicted a severe check on the Germans. The next day a further attack by the enemy was also driven back. On the 8th the Germans claimed another success, but the French reports of the 10th state that notwithstanding the severe fighting the position was unchanged. The 16th was another critical day in the long and bloody struggle for the plateau. The French stormed three lines of trenches, captured a hundred prisoners, and destroyed two machine guns. In the region Ecurie-Roclincourt other trenches were blown up that day. In spite of counter-attacks, the French pushed on for the crest of the ridge of Notre Dame de Lorette, gaining on the 19th the communication trenches descending towards Ablain, but they lost some of these on the 20th. By the 23rd most of the ridge was virtually in their possession. The next day they captured and destroyed a German trench, south of Ablain, near Carency. Two German assaults on the Notre Dame de Lorette ridge were defeated on the 25th. On the 27th, perhaps out of revenge, the Germans again bombarded Arras.

At this point we break off the narrative. The British during March had regained Neuve Chapelle, the French the ridge of Notre Dame de Lorette. The opening moves of an Allied offensive against the Germans in the triangle Lille-La Bassée-Arras had been made.

MANONVILLER.
A destroyed gun emplacement.

CHAPTER XCVII.

SCIENCE AND THE HEALTH OF ARMIES.

War and Disease—Vindication of Science in Recent Military Experience—Bacteriology in the Field—Tetanus—The Use of Serum—Gangrene—"Getting Back to Lister"—Antiseptic Methods—Sir Almroth Wright's Teaching—Vaccination—The Conquest of Typhoid Fever—Inoculation—"Typhoid Carriers"—The Water Supply Problem—Cholera and Anti-Cholera Vaccines—Typhus Fever in Serbia—Plague and Health Problems in Egypt—The Achievements of Science—German Gas and Counter-Measures.

PRACTICALLY all the great wars of past ages were carried on in conditions of dirt and misery and privation which to-day are scarcely to be found in the whole world. The association of famine and sword and of disease and war was no fortuitous one : these scourges were in fact indissolubly associated, and war without plague and epidemic was unknown.

It is easy in the light of modern scientific knowledge to realize how this state of matters arose. In those days men lived, in homely phrase, very near the soil. The margin of safety so far as disease was concerned was always a narrow one. There was no effective sanitation ; and modern ideas in regard to sewage disposal and public health simply did not exist. Almost all the diseases which we now speak of as epidemic were then endemic, that is to say, they remained permanently fixed in a locality and attacked all members of the community.

War broke down instantly what slender protection the people had built up against disease, and so engulfed whole populations in the terrible disasters which are known by such names as " black death " and " great plague." War, too, swept away the ordinary necessities of life, and thus brought in its train diseases like scurvy, which often decimated armies as

no hostile weapons could. The fighting man was exposed to a thousand risks, and usually in the end fell victim to one of them. Danger from the enemy was the least of all the menaces which threatened him.

This state of matters existed without any alleviation right down to the period when scientific thought began to predominate in Europe. That period may be placed about the middle of last century, for in the beginning science was occupied for the most part with her own warfare against superstition and ignorance. The battle had been won, however, when the discovery of micro-organisms finally vindicated the scientific claims and swept away for ever the idea that pestilence was a special manifestation of Divine wrath. It was realized, as it were, all of a sudden, that pestilence could be prevented just as pests could be prevented—by killing it, and, further, that so far as war was concerned the horrors of disease could be eliminated.

It is unnecessary to trace the growth of these ideas in the great wars of this generation—the Russo-Japanese War, the Boer War and the Balkan Wars. These wars were from the scientific point of view, experiments. The Boer War was an unsuccessful experiment out of which success was snatched by a study of many errors and mistakes ; the Russo-Japanese

SIR ALMROTH WRIGHT.

War was a triumphant vindication of science. The Japanese attained the ideal; that is to say, their losses from disease were trifling as compared with their losses from the bullets of the enemy.

Britain and France and Germany therefore went into this war with a full knowledge of the scientific needs of the situation. Scientists, as differentiated from medical men, were attached to the armies of all the belligerents, and these scientific forces included bacteriologists and public health officers.

From the point of view of the scientist war is a test on the grand scale. Unlike the medical man, he does not chiefly deal with the individual. His business is with the mass. His mission is prevention. From his point of view the hospitals and the ambulances, in so far as they minister to cases of disease and infection, are proofs of failure; they show that prevention did not achieve the perfection hoped for from it. He visits the hospitals therefore in order to study failure, so that from failure he may win success.

Science, as will be shown, anticipated many events in this war and failed to anticipate many others. Science anticipated the probability of an outbreak of typhoid fever on the grand scale; but she did not foresee that the soil of

France, the soil of an ancient land, intensively cultivated through many generations, would play a part of almost crucial importance in connexion with the health of armies. With the soil of France, therefore, the scientific history of the war properly begins.

For a considerable period it has been known that there are certain bacteria inhabiting soil, or commonly found in soil, which, when introduced into the human body, give rise to most deadly diseases. These bacteria are probably put into the soil in the first instance in manure, for they are found in greatest abundance in well-manured or intensively cultivated soils—the soils of old agricultural countries like France. One of the best known and also one of the deadliest of these germs is the tetanus bacillus (bacillus of lockjaw). This bacillus is normally present in manure, and in times of peace claims a certain number of victims each year. The usual history in these cases is that some small wound was suffered in connexion with work in the garden; very often the wound was made by a rusty nail which had been lying near or in a manure heap. The trivial character of the wound causes it to be neglected, until some days later the early signs of lockjaw show them-

PROFESSOR METCHNIKOFF.

THE FLY PEST.

**Bonfires to destroy flies.—Inset : The Fly-net,
which was used in the Dardanelles, covered the
head and shoulders and afforded complete protection
against the fly pest.**

selves. Horses are subject to the disease, and
infection is usually conveyed to them through
some small crack in a hoof.

Before bacteriological knowledge was available many erroneous ideas prevailed as to the
cause and character of the disease. And even
to-day the superstition that a cut between
thumb and first finger will give rise to lockjaw
is widely believed. Bacteriologists showed,
however, that the site of the wound does not
matter. What does matter is the character of
the wound and the character of the ground upon
which the wound was sustained.

The bacillus of lockjaw has certain individual
peculiarities which determine its powers of evil.
Of these the chief is the fact that it cannot
flourish in air ; only when the atmospheric air
has been completely excluded from the wound
in which it lodges can this deadly germ survive.
For this reason it is known as an anaerobic
organism.

Bullet wounds, however, and wounds made
by small pieces of shell are exactly the type of
wounds into which air is not likely to penetrate ;
they are small, deep wounds and they tend to
heal quickly upon the surface, so that the air
is shut off and the bacteria are left in the kind
of surroundings most favourable to their growth.

At the beginning of the Great War, that is
to say in the autumn days, when the British
Army was fighting its way back through
Flanders and Artois to Paris, the terrible
danger which lay in the soil of France became

clear. The soldiers, during the Great Retreat, were subject to many hardships and privations. They had to fight all day in order that they might be free to retreat under cover of night,

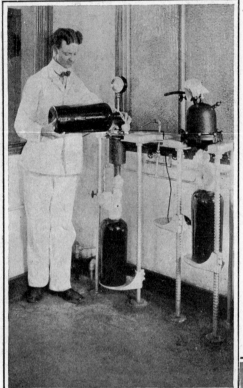

and they snatched what sleep they could get as opportunity offered. They slept by the wayside, in the fields, in stables. Their clothing, which they had no chance to change, became saturated with mud and dirt, a veritable breeding-ground of bacteria, especially the bacteria of the soil. When a bullet hit one of these men it carried with it into his body shreds of the dirty uniform he wore, and so inoculated him successfully with bacilli. Nor was there any time or opportunity to have small wounds treated in an adequate manner. The evacuation of the seriously wounded was far too great a problem for the small body of men engaged in solving it.

For these reasons the doctors in charge of Army hospitals soon found themselves confronted with cases of lockjaw of a severe and deadly type, and had to acknowledge with apprehension that this disease seemed likely to prove one of the horrors of the Great War. For lockjaw is an affliction terrible alike in its manifestations and in its mortality.

Nor at this period was any cure to be obtained. Shortly after the great discovery that a serum could be prepared against the disease diphtheria,

PREPARATION OF SERUMS.   [*By courtesy of Parke Davis & Co.*
Withdrawing blood from immunised horse. Inset: Filtering the serum.

LORD MOULTON.

efforts were made to prepare an anti-tetanus serum. But unhappily the good results which had been obtained in the case of diphtheria were not obtained with tetanus. Diphtheria yielded at once to the serum ; tetanus did not yield, and the cases indeed showed no improvement. It was therefore concluded by many that anti-tetanus serum was a failure and scarcely worth using—though it continued to be used, or rather tried, in a number of cases.

The serum is prepared in a manner which illustrates how close and careful scientific reasoning has become. A horse is used, and the animal is given a very mild dose of the disease, from which it soon recovers. A more potent dose is then administered, and again a still more potent dose, until the animal is capable of standing deadly doses without showing any sign of illness. In other words, the blood of the horse has been able to prepare antidotes to the poison and the animal has acquired what is known as "immunity" to the disease—somewhat as a smoker acquires immunity to the ill-effects of tobacco or an opium-eater to the ill-effects of opium, but to an incomparably greater degree.

When this stage has been reached, some of the blood of the horse is drawn off and made up in bottles for injection into patients suffering

from the disease. Before being made up the blood is standardized by means of guinea-pigs, so that exact doses may be administered.

The serum, however, failed in most instances to save the lives of the men affected with tetanus. More and yet more cases arose, and the situation, early in September, 1914, was exceedingly alarming.

Help however was at hand, and once more it was science which came to the rescue. It had been suggested on many occasions that if anti-tetanus serum could be administered immediately after the wound was sustained, the results would probably be better. It now occurred to doctors to put this idea to the test. Orders were given to the hospitals that cases with wounds of the type likely to be infected with tetanus should receive at once a dose of serum, and that careful records of the results should be kept.

This policy was not at first an easy one to carry out upon an extensive scale, for the simple reason that supplies of serum were limited. But that fault was quickly remedied. Inoculation at a very early date became general, most of the badly wounded men receiving their antitetanic serum at the field hospitals.

The result was remarkable and justified to the fullest possible extent the procedure adopted. Within an exceedingly short period— corresponding roughly to the period of the Battles of the Aisne and Ypres—tetanus had

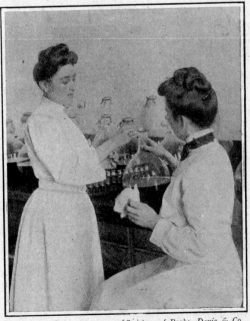

[*Courtesy of Parke, Davis & Co.*

CULTURES OF BACTERIA PLANTED
IN BOUILLON.

ceased to be a serious problem. A little later the disease actually ceased to occur. The victims of wounds which, judging from the experiences of the early days, would most probably have proved to be infected with the lockjaw microbe, suffered no ill, and passed safely through the danger period. This was nothing less than a great scientific achievement which in times of peace would have attracted universal attention ; it passed almost unnoticed, except amongst doctors and nurses who had good reason to be thankful that so dreadful a scourge had been met and defeated. The practice of injecting serum became, of course, universal, so that every wounded man received his injec-

TO PREVENT EPIDEMICS.
A French soldier disinfecting a captured German trench in the Champagne.

tion simply as a matter of course. What the state of matters would have been had this discovery not been made and this work not carried out, it is difficult to say ; this much is certain, a heavy tetanus mortality would have been encountered, and the horrors of the war added to in a manner calculated to terrify even the bravest.

But the lockjaw bacillus was not the only one found in the soil of France. In addition, there were found to be present a group of organisms which gave rise to severe suppurations, and often the so-called " gas gangrene." It is unquestionable, however, that much misapprehension existed in the public mind con-

cerning the nature of the various form of gangrene met with. Gangrene is a word which inspires so great dread that the mere mention of it was enough to excite morbid interest and curiosity. It was not generally recognised that some of the cases of gangrene were not infections at all, but were the result of tight bandages applied to stop bleeding and kept too long a time in position. In other cases, gangrene supervened as the natural result of a wound which cut off the blood supply of a limb. The true " gas gangrene " was of a different type. It owed its origin to infection, and it was, in fact, a severe violent infection which frequently proved fatal in a very short period. Dr. Delorme, the Inspector-General of the French Army Medical Corps, described it in his book on " War Surgery " as " acute, violent, excessive, constringent." " Nearly all the patients," he said, " ascribe it to the construction of the apparatus, or of the dressings, but if these are taken off it is found that swelling may not, as yet. exist." This gangrene was naturally regarded as a terrible complication of wounds, and every effort was made to cope with it. Unfortunately the early attempts of surgeons were not crowned with great success. Surgeons in these early days had not fully realised the immense difference between the methods of peace and the necessities of war. They had not yet come to see clearly that the technique of the operating theatre in a great hospital and the technique of the field were two totally different matters.

Moreover, a gigantic problem faced them. Most of them had to deal not with a few, but with hundreds of infected wounds—wounds, moreover, infected with germs of such virulence that unless measures were prompt and thorough a fatal result might be looked for in a large percentage of the cases. Prompt and thorough measures were often exceedingly difficult to carry out, because in these early days hospital accommodation was scanty, and medical com forts and appliances were difficult to obtain.

From the soldiers' point of view the Retreat from Mons was a great military achievement ; from the point of view of the statesman it was a calamity, until the Battle of the Marne brought salvation ; from the point of view of the surgeon it was a tragedy—he found himself suddenly face to face with the greatest emergency of his life, and the means to deal with the emergency were wanting. But there remains yet another point of view, that of the scientist.

THE DARDANELLES.
A dressing station, an operation in progress.

47

TO PREVENT THE SPREADING OF DISEASE.
Disinfecting the clothes of German wounded.

In his eyes the Retreat from Mons, the battles of the Marne, Aisne, Ypres, and the Yser were events the result of which was one of the greatest epidemics—if we include the Eastern front, probably the very greatest epidemic—which the world has seen. The fact that the victims were wounded men in no way altered this view. Men seldom die of a clean wound if it be not immediately fatal ; it is the poison in the wound, and not the wound itself, which is lethal. The man of science, the bacteriologist, saw all Europe living under the scourge of blood poisoning on the grand scale ; every fresh wound created a fresh victim, because almost every wound was infected. Every wound served to multiply the evidence of infection, and to prove more and more conclusively that this was not only a matter for cure, but also, like other infections, a matter for prevention.

But at the beginning the scientist had to give place to the surgeon. It was a moment for the best possible treatment in the circumstances and the best possible treatment was afforded—in the circumstances. Surgeons very soon found out that their methods of asepsis—scrupulous cleanliness—were useless where everything was already as dirty as it could be, so almost with one accord they abandoned the aseptic method and began to clean up these terrible wounds with the same chemicals which Lord Lister had used a generation earlier when he discovered his antiseptic treatment.

This " movement " was called, appropriately enough, " getting back to Lister." It very quickly became universal. The old solutions of strong carbolic acid, of mercury, of iodine, were to be found in every hospital. Surgeons at the Front swabbed iodine into the wounds they had to treat. It was considered that the one essential was to disinfect as quickly as possible and as strongly as possible.

This was exactly Lister's teaching. Lister's work was built up on the fact that a wound did not suppurate unless germs had gained entry to it ; the germs entered from the patient's skin or from the hands or instruments of the surgeon. Operations were deadly because this fact was not recognized. Lister began to operate therefore in conditions of " antisepsis." He used sprays of carbolic acid to kill the germs and his results were so immensely superior to those of all his surgical colleagues that very soon his procedure was adopted by everyone.

But it was a natural assumption that operations would be still more effective were there no germs to kill. Carbolic acid did not affect the bacteria only ; it acted also upon the tissues of the patient's body. So modern surgery began to aim at absolute cleanliness rather than at efforts to destroy dirt already present. The new doctrine was not "kill the germs," but "exclude them." This was called the aseptic method.

The aseptic method was as vast an improvement upon the antiseptic method as the antiseptic method had been upon the early days of dirt and ignorance. By means of scrupulous cleanliness germs were banned altogether, and it was no longer necessary to use the irritating fluids which in Lister's early days had so often caused trouble alike to doctor and patient. Operations became much less dangerous and much more successful in the broadest sense of the term. Surgeons declared that their technique was now perfect. The few wounds which were dirty at the time of treatment were still dealt with by means of antiseptics, but these were for the most part mild conditions when compared with the wounds which Flanders and France were soon to show to an astonished world.

"Back to Lister" was therefore a reversal of the order of evolution; it was, speaking in the strictest and most formal language of science, a retrograde step, though clearly justified by circumstances; and, in the circumstances, science condoned it and even applauded it. But this applause could not be expected to continue when the circumstances had changed and when opportunities offered for research and investigation. And, in fact, so soon as the military situation improved and medical work on a great scale became organized at centres like Boulogne and Havre, the scientists began to devote themselves to the problem of infected wounds—by far the greatest medical problem of the war.

The scientists viewed the problem from a new angle. They were concerned (1) to prevent infection at all, if this should be found possible, and (2) to destroy it in such a manner that only the infecting germs and not the tissues of the patient should suffer. In the eyes of the scientist the pioneer methods of Lister lacked precision; they resembled the shot-gun, which discharges many pellets in the hope that some will hit—and in this instance with the added fear that not only the invading germs will be hit but also the body tissues of the patient. Scientists hankered after the exactness of the well-sighted rifle. They wanted to hit the germs only and to spare the patient;

THE DISINFECTION OF CLOTHES.
A chamber at a hospital in Petrograd. Clothing of patients placed into a cylinder.

in other words, they wanted to evolve a remedy or a remedial treatment which should be specific for the infection and should destroy the infection with absolute certainty.

The first scientific efforts were dominated to some extent by war experience, and a number of antiseptics were produced and tried. Many of them were found to be little better than the agents already in use, though there were notable exceptions to this rule. Meanwhile a second, very robust school of scientists had begun to preach a new doctrine, and to state openly that their investigations had led to the conclusion that the "back to Lister" movement was being overdone, that harm was frequently wrought by the too free use of antiseptics, and that a halt must be called in this indiscriminate application of strong chemicals to open wounds.

This new school owed its origin to Sir Almroth Wright, and commanded an attentive hearing the moment it made its opinions known. It spoke at an opportune moment, for many observers were beginning to distrust the antiseptic treatment as applied and to wish for a more exact and scientific method.

Sir Almroth Wright, at the Royal Society of Medicine, stated the case unequivocally. He said that he had never seen a wound rendered aseptic by chemicals inserted into it with the object of killing the bacteria infecting it. Some of the bacteria might be killed, but all of them were not, and there were grave objections to the process in any case.

These objections he dealt with in great detail, revealing the fact that a vast amount of most careful scientific work had already been accomplished in his laboratory at Boulogne. This work had gone to show that, other things being equal, the most efficient preventive a man possesses against infection, that is against germs, is to be found in his own blood. Nature, as soon as a wound is sustained, floods the wound with a fluid known as lymph. This lymph is highly bactericidal and if left to work is able to kill the invading germs. The lymph, however, is a very unstable product. If it is dammed up it quickly becomes changed; it "decomposes"; and soon the fluid that was possessed of the power of killing bacteria becomes in fact an excellent food for them so that they grow and flourish in it.

Recognition of this vital and fundamental truth made it apparent at once that all circumstances which tended to dam up the flow of

AN INSTITUTE FOR INFECTIOUS DISEASES.
The Royal Robert Koch Institute, Berlin. In the Plague Department. Inset: The Serum Department.

lymph—that is, to prevent its free drainage from the wound, tended to increase rather than to diminish the infection. Dressings applied to the wound and left in position after they had became soiled and dried dammed up the lymph and produced this evil effect—as was well seen in the early days when the conditions of the military situation made the frequent changings of dressings an impossibility. So also did coagulation of the lymph fluid itself, for if the lymph coagulated it formed an obstruction to the free flow, and so acted just as a dirty dressing acted.

But one of the effects of strong antiseptics was to make the lymph exuding from the wound coagulate. So that one of the effects of strong antiseptics was to dam up the very flow which it was so important to encourage and stimulate. Reasoning a little further, strong antiseptics in the last issue did more harm than good because they interfered with Nature's own antiseptic methods and mechanism, and gave little or nothing in exchange for what they took away.

Sir Almroth invited his audience to consider the character of a wound made by shrapnel— perhaps the commonest cause of wounds. The wound was not clean cut, it was jagged, a tearing of the tissues. It was full of "pockets," some shallow, others very deep. Often it was contaminated by pieces of clothing and other foreign matter which had been carried into it in the first instance. This wound Nature soon flooded out with her lymph. Her object was to wash out the impurities and to kill the germs, and so to allow of rapid healing. The question was, in what manner Nature might be assisted.

It was not assisting Nature to fill that wound with a strong and irritating solution. The solution might penetrate a certain distance and would no doubt kill some bacteria ; but it did not penetrate to the deep pockets. It missed these, and meanwhile it coagulated the lymph and so formed obstructions over the openings of the pockets. In the pockets the germs were able to multiply at their leisure, the decomposed lymph forming an excellent pabulum for their nourishment. Within a very short time the number of germs which had been destroyed was fully replaced, and far exceeded, and the latter state of the wound tended to be worse than the first.

Needless to say this attack upon established ideas produced an immediate effect. Sir

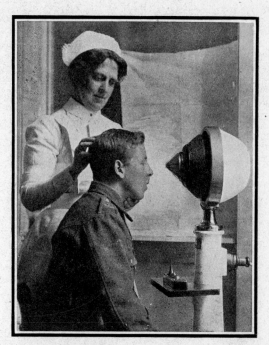

A POWERFUL ELECTRIC MAGNET
At the Western Ophthalmic Hospital, Marylebone Road, London, where an electric magnet was used for extracting fragments of shells and bullets from the eyes of wounded soldiers, the magnet attracts the fragments to the front of the eye and a smaller magnet was then used to extract them.

Almroth Wright had practically impugned the basal idea of the "back to Lister school." He had dealt a heavy blow at the antiseptic treatment of wounds ; he had refused to accept the idea that the process of evolution must be reversed in this special case. He stood, therefore, as a pioneer in the true sense. He demanded a new conception of infection, and a new treatment founded on this new conception.

But he did much more than this. As will be seen in a moment, it followed from these researches that if Nature can be assisted along strictly scientific lines when disease has become established, so also can she be assisted along scientific lines in her continuous effort to prevent the beginning of disease. In other words, it is not possible to say that the natural germ-killing power of the body can be augmented during an invasion of germs without inferring that it can be strengthened before such an invasion takes place.

Sir Almroth's second line of reasoning was directed to the elucidation of this latter problem—the problem of prevention as opposed to the problem of cure. And here he found himself upon the sure ground of science, for science, as has already been said, is interested

WOUNDED HELPING THE WOUNDED.

A pathetic episode between Le Cateau and Landrecies during the retreat from Mons, September, 1914.

to prevent disease as well as to deal with it, and views the hospital ward, thronged with sick and infected men, as a phenomenon, demanding a change of method or an improvement in technique. Sir Almroth saw the problem of prevention of infection in wounds as he had at an earlier date seen the problem of the prevention of typhoid fever—that merciless scourge of armies in the field. He saw it whole, and he saw it clearly.

The wounded man falls a victim to bacteria which have become lodged in his wound because he cannot mobilize in his blood sufficient germ poison to kill the invaders. His blood, so far, is not accustomed to the new poison, and so has not developed any antidote to it. After a time, however, in favourable circumstances, an antidote will be produced and the poison killed off. The aim of the scientist must be, therefore, to prepare the blood beforehand to meet the danger to which it is likely to be exposed.

This conception of preparation is at the root of the vaccine therapy which now bulks so large in medicine. It has been found that it is not the actual presence of the germ which causes disease, but the poison which the germ produces during the course of its life—the poison which it "excretes." This poison circulates in the blood and sets up disease processes, often in remote organs. But the blood is armed with methods of destroying the poisons, and also the bacteria which produce them. Long ago the great French scientist, Professor Metchnikoff, showed how the white cells of the blood are in reality warrior cells capable of attacking bacteria and destroying them. This is one phase of the subject. The body itself is able, as has been shown, to secrete into the blood antitoxins, or antidotes, of great subtlety, which are exactly calculated to meet and annul the poison—are, indeed, specially prepared for the special type of poison present. Thus, by a double action, bacteria and their poisonous products are removed and normal health regained. This process takes place during acute fevers, like pneumonia.

Occasionally, however, the germ which makes the attack is so virulent, or in so great numbers, that the normal reaction of the body is not shown, and then the patient dies of the infection. Or the patient himself may be in a weak state of body, as from exhaustion, or cold, or strain, or shock, and be capable of only a feeble resistance to the invaders. He may,

GERMAN RED CROSS WORK.
A splint used by the German Red Cross for treating wounded with a shattered hand.

for example, be a soldier who has fought hard through long days and nights, taken part in forced marches while heavily loaded, had insufficient sleep, food, rest, or water, been subjected to terrible anxiety or weather conditions of exceptional severity. In these circumstances how shall his wearied and enfeebled body bear up against the added shock of a wound, with the loss of blood and of nervous energy, and the wracking pain? His wound is soil very favourable for the growth of any hostile germ, and he lacks the strength to

TO RECOVER THE USE OF STIFF JOINTS.
German soldiers working a pedal of a sewing-machine and turning a cart wheel fixed to the wall.

SIR WILLIAM LEISHMAN.

produce an immunity as quickly as may be necessary.

How to prepare this man's blood for the danger it may be exposed to ? It has been found that the response of the blood is related, in ordinary circumstances, to the quality of the poison. But the poison itself depends on the number of germs and on their character and virulence. The blood, therefore, seems to be guided in its output by the special characters of the microbic enemies it has to contend against.

If now a few of the germs which commonly infect wounds, the cocci as they are called, are taken and grown in a test-tube and then killed by heat, we shall possess in that test-tube a quantity of the poison which, had the germs been present in a wound, would have been circulating in the victim's blood. If now we take that poison and measure out a minute dose of it (and it is to be noted that the germs have been killed, only the poison, not the actual germ is used), and inject that dose

into the body of a healthy man we shall occasion in his blood a reaction to the poison. His blood will at once prepare an antidote on the assumption that an invasion of germs has occurred. But as the poison was introduced in very minute dose, so it will easily be neutralized. The blood of the man will now possess a certain power against this particular infection.

If we repeat our injections, giving each time a little more poison, we shall presently produce a high degree of immunity in the blood of the man. His blood will indeed be in a state of preparedness against invasion by this particular poison—that is, by this particular germ. If he is wounded and his blood is infected by this germ unpleasant results are not likely to follow because the germ will not be able to hurt him. He will be, in short, vaccinated against wound infection.

It was this idea which Sir Almroth suggested as the preventive measure against the war epidemic of infection. Needless to say it was hailed with great interest. It was not seriously assailed, because it was founded upon scientific reasoning of a very close and cogent order, and, moreover, because another application of the same reasoning had already produced, as will be shown later, the great triumph of anti-typhoid inoculation.

But a reply of another kind was made by another school of workers. Ever since the great German chemist and bacteriologist, Prof. Ehrlich, had shown that chemical bodies could be found which had a special action upon special germs and little or no action upon the tissues of the body containing these germs, investigators had been busy studying the chemistry of antiseptics. Ehrlich had shown

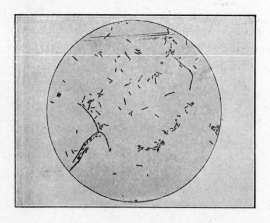

BACILLUS TYPHOSUS.

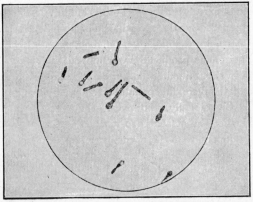

Courtesy of Parke, Davis & Co.

BACILLUS TETANI.

AFTER A BATTLE IN THE ARGONNE.
French troops removing their dead and wounded from the trenches.

ANTI-TYPHOID VACCINATION IN THE FRENCH ARMY.
Filling phials with vaccine.

that the micro-organism of the disease syphilis —the so-called *spirochaete pallida*—was killed immediately if a compound of arsenic and an aniline body, "Salvarsan" or "606," was injected into the patient's blood. Salvarsan did not injure the patient : its action was "specific" for the *spirochaete*. The research workers who devoted themselves to the treatment of infected wounds upon chemical lines aimed at finding a substance which should prove destructive of the germs of infection and yet be innocuous to the tissues of the body. They aimed, in fact, at producing a sighted rifle to replace the blunderbus of indiscriminate antiseptic treatment.

Some success attended this effort. In the *British Medical Journal* of July 24 there appeared an account of an antiseptic, which had been used by Professor Lorrain Smith, of Edinburgh, and three members of his department. This substance was hypochlorite of sodium, and the research work in connexion with it was assisted by the National Health Insurance Medical Research Committee. Curiously enough, antiseptics belonging to the same chemical group were used almost simultaneously in the Organic Chemistry Department, Leeds University, by Dr. H. D. Dakin. Dr. Dakin worked in collaboration with the distinguished American surgeon, Dr.

Alexis Carrel. Later Dr. Carrel and Dr. Dakin used the preparations in a field hospital at Compiègne, behind the French firing line, with, they stated, very satisfactory results. With the cooperation of the French War Office and the Rockefeller Institute, a large hospital and laboratories were established at Compiègne. Professor Landouzy read a paper on the antiseptic before the French Academy of Sciences on August 4, 1915, and said that hypochloride of lime was the most powerful antiseptic known to science, but that up till that time this substance had been of no practical utility on account of the difficulty of preserving it, and because of its alkalinity, which was injurious to human tissues. These difficulties had been surmounted by various means, and might now be said to have passed away. The new preparation had been applied to the most frightful wounds, with the result that within eight days their aspect had been modified in a way quite unknown under the old antiseptic processes. Cases of gangrene had been radically prevented at the very outset. Indeed, if the antiseptic was applied in time it was not too much to say that the infection of wounds might henceforward be considered impossible.

The antiseptic, during the first few months of its trial, gave certainly very good results.

But the claim that it was the ideal antiseptic which would destroy the septic agents in wounds without damaging the tissues was not allowed by all observers, and meantime interest continued to be focussed upon Sir Almroth Wright and upon his researches.

Sir Almroth had laid it down that every wound should be kept as wide open as possible during the period when septic matter remained in the wound, and he had also suggested that means should be employed to induce a freer flow of lymph from the wound. Such means were "wicks" placed in the wound, and also the application of the solutions having the effect of stimulating lymph flow. Later, at the Royal Society of Medicine, October 8–14, he elaborated the idea. The application of a strong solution of salt to a wound would, he said, cause the sweeping away of all obstructions from the wound. The result would be a wound absolutely clean. This clean wound would, however, still be very easily re-infected as it would be open. The next step, therefore, was to bring forward the army of white blood corpuscles—the army whose duty it is to attack invading germs. In order to do this the solution of salt must be diluted very considerably, from 5 per cent. to .85 per cent., or so-called "normal saline solution." This normal saline solution acts by drawing to the surface the white blood cells, so that in a little while a fine grey film—composed of the white "warrior

cells," appears on the surface of the wound. This is another great advance. But it is a fact that these warrior cells do not long survive exposure on the surface of the wound. Soon they break up and die and then again the wound is likely to become infected.

What then is the next step? Sir Almroth suggested what is known as "secondary suture of the wound." The wound was clean. It was protected by leucocytes. Danger no longer lay within, but threatened from without. The time had come to shut the door in the face of danger.

Meanwhile vaccination ought to have prepared the blood for resistance. Sir Almroth held that every wounded man should be inoculated as soon as he reached the first-aid post. A second opportunity would present itself if there was any sign of a spread of infection along the skin near the wound. In the case of the wound which was sewn up after being cleaned vaccination seemed to be a method of completing the work and destroying the bacilli that might remain in the wound.

Sir Almroth made the following suggestions regarding the treatment of wounds to be applied to work in the actual field of operations :

(1) An injection of vaccine at the first-aid post—*i.e.*, of vaccine prepared from micro-organisms commonly infecting wounds. "There would," he said, "follow upon the inoculation

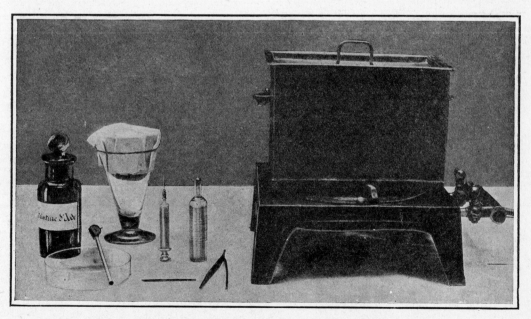

ANTI-TYPHOID VACCINATION IN THE FRENCH ARMY.
The apparatus employed includes a cistern for sterilising instruments in boiling water, bottle of tincture of iodine (with brush), injection-syringe, phial of vaccine, and forceps.

BRITISH SAILORS IN SERBIA
Being inoculated against typhoid.

a rapid immunising response, which would, one is entitled to anticipate, in a bullet wound perforating only tissues, extinguish the infection, and would in other wounds do the same in those regions where the physiological conditions were not too unfavourable."

(2) At the field ambulance simple operations should be performed for the excision of projectiles and foreign bodies and securing thorough drainage of the wounds. Also here all wounds, except those promising to get well of themselves, should be treated with strong solutions of salt ("hypertonic salt solution") "wicks" made of bandage soaked in salt and sodium citrate should be put into the wounds in order to encourage a flow of lymph from them.

(3) At the Casualty Clearing Station, the next step in the journey from the front, X-rays and other equipment became available, and so more extensive operations could be carried out and fuller drainage of the wound secured. It was important to realise that travelling was, for the sick soldier, mostly a time of retro-

gression, and so every effort must be made to prevent the wound becoming "lymph bound," and so a seat of infection.

(4) At the base hospitals the full procedure should be carried out.

The importance of those researches and suggestions must be evident to everyone. They stimulated the minds of medical men in regard to the whole treatment of wounds, even though at the end of sixteen months of war they were still so new as to be tentative. It was felt even by opponents of Sir Almroth Wright's views that the vast problem of infection had been placed upon a new footing, and that a new conception of surgical treatment had been afforded. Sir Almroth's own words may be quoted (*Lancet*, November 13, 1915).

" It has come home to everybody that every wound is infected, and that the infection is the really serious element in wounds. Coming on the top of this, practically everybody has become aware that the antiseptic system has— so far as the treatment of the wound infection is concerned—completely broken down. So finally it comes to this that the progress of knowledge has filched away from the ordinary medical officer everything, other than the knife, which he was relying upon for the treatment of bacterial infections of wounds." Clearly the ideal antiseptic remains to be discovered.

If the treatment of infected wounds was the big scientific problem of the war, because the wounds were actually there to be treated, the prevention of the old-time scourges of fighting men was also a huge difficulty, because no man could doubt that unless measures were taken in advance the old foes would soon show themselves, and the old story of death and wretchedness be repeated. But here, happily, science was well prepared. The lessons of the past had been learned ; doubts and suspicions scarcely existed ; there was no battle against doubt or misgiving to be fought. It was known and accepted as a fact that by means of vaccination these diseases could be met, and could be held at bay.

The history of this remarkable movement is like a romance. With it the names of Wright and Leishman will ever be associated, as its success was due largely to their painstaking efforts. The story may be said to have begun when the specific germ of typhoid fever was discovered. The bacillus is a minute body with small hair-like projections, the so-called cilia by which it is able to move itself about. It was known that after the entrance of typhoid bacilli into the human body, the tissues ultimately developed an antibody or antidote, which destroyed the invaders. Advantage was taken of this fact by Widal, who invented a subtle bacteriological test for the disease. The essence of this test consisted in taking a few drops of the blood of the suspected victim, and adding them to a solution containing living typhoid germs. If the patient had had the disease his blood would for some time contain some antibody and so the germs would be altered and be clumped into masses. If on the contrary the patient was not affected, his blood would not possess this power of "agglutination." The "Widal test" proved a very helpful adjunct to the physicians' powers of observation, and came into general use. It contained the germ of the future vaccine treatment as will presently be seen.

The idea of vaccination was of course no new one. Ever since Jenner made his great discovery, the conception of cure "by a hair of the tail of the dog that bit you" had been prevalent. Koch, too, the discoverer of the Tubercle Bacillus, had introduced a substance "tuberculin," which was, in fact, a vaccine, and had claimed for it diagnostic and immunising powers.

The step to the production of a vaccine against typhoid fever was thus a short one. All that seemed to be necessary was to secure some of the poison or toxin excreted by the bacilli and inject this in gradually increasing doses into the patient's body.

Theory is one thing, however, and practice another. The Boer War afforded a great opportunity to those who hoped to render the soldier immune against typhoid. Coming as it did shortly after the Spanish-American War, in which the death rate from typhoid fever was terrible, the Boer War may be regarded as the first testing ground of the new medicine. The test was a severe one, because the conditions were severe and the climate difficult. The results were, on the whole, good, though they are not usually spoken of as satisfactory. In the first place, the correct dosage was not clearly known, and in the second the technique of the process had not been fully worked out.

The result was that a tendency arose to belittle inoculation as a useless method. Stories

TO DESTROY GERMS.
British troops in France placing uniforms and blankets in an oven.

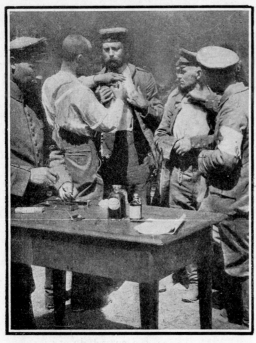

GERMAN TROOPS
Being vaccinated as a precaution against cholera.

men were killed by the injections, and that injected men fared no better—sometimes worse—in respect of the disease than did uninjected men. The arguments, which are familiar, concerning "preserving a pure blood pure," were heard in many quarters.

This was not an encouraging atmosphere for patient and earnest research work. Nevertheless, workers were found to carry on the investigation, and to reap success where only partial success appeared to be. Technique was perfected; results were watched; deductions were made, and as a result of a vast bulk of evidence it was proved to the satisfaction of exacting minds that in this anti-typhoid inoculation science possessed in fact a most potent weapon against the onset of the disease. This result was due in large measure to the splendid work of Sir Wm. Leishman in India.

When the war broke out the army authorities decided to give immunising injections in all cases in which the soldier himself consented. The matter was discussed in public, and notably in the columns of *The Times*, and pleas on behalf of vaccination were entered by such distinguished authorities as Sir W. Osler, Sir Almroth

were told by ignorant people which suggested that evil effects followed the inoculation, and that good effects did not exist. It was proclaimed by the enemies of the treatment that

RUSSIAN SANITARY TRAIN.
Sterilising Clothes.

TYPHUS IN SERBIA.
British nurses who attended to the stricken Serbians, wearing special costumes. Inset: Nurses on the way to Serbia being inoculated against typhoid.

Wright and Sir Lauder Brunton. Sir W. Osler wrote :

" The work of the French Army doctors and of British Army surgeons, particularly in India, has shown conclusively the remarkable reduction in the incidence of typhoid when vaccination is thoroughly carried out. The experience of the American Army is of special value, as the disease is so much more prevalent in the United States. The number of cases in the home army has fallen from 3.53 per thousand men to 0.03 in six years, and the death rate from 0.28 in 1909 to zero in 1913."

Sir Wm. Osler then called attention to the work of the Vaccine Department of the Army Medical College, the Lister Institute, and other laboratories.

The work of the Army Medical College was indeed, of supreme value at this hour. As has already been stated, Sir Wm. Leishman had placed the whole world in his debt by his splendid services upon anti-typhoid vaccination. He may be said to have worked this problem out with the patience, the courage, and the honesty of purpose which alone can triumph over great obstacles. Very large numbers of men owe their lives to his efforts.

Sir Almroth Wright declared that " the absolute necessity of making provision against this disease by inoculation is now a commonplace of military hygiene." In the same letter (September 5, 1914) Sir Almroth referred to the use of vaccines in wound treatment, stating that his department at St. Mary's Hospital had supplied gratuitously to our Army and Navy, and also to the French military hospitals, a total of 180,000 doses of " anti-sepsis " vaccine. In addition this department had, by working long hours in response to a War Office request, furnished, as a contribution, for the use of the

DR. STRONG,
Medical Director of the American Sanitary Red
Cross Commission.

Army, nearly 280,000 doses of anti-typhoid vaccine."

These letters, and the publicity given to them, undoubtedly influenced the public mind to a great extent, and as a result the vast majority of recruits accepted vaccination with alacrity. They received their small doses of the virus, and the number who suffered any serious inconvenience in consequence was found to be exceedingly small, so carefully had the procedure and technique been studied and worked out. Our army went to France and to the East as a vaccinated force, with its blood prepared against the typhoid danger, to which it was so likely to be subjected.

But the case of the scientist was not determined nor his vigilance bounded by this one great method of prevention. Experience had taught that disease does not arise spontaneously, but is in fact propagated from man to man. Therefore, in order to produce typhoid fever in one man, typhoid bacilli must be present in another man, and must be conveyed from infected to uninfected. This is so self-evident that it seems too simple to require emphasis. Experience, however, has often proved that it is just the neglect of these simple truths which lead to disaster.

It was known of typhoid fever that men might suffer from it and retain a very considerable amount of health and strength, or they might pass through an attack and recover from it and yet remain infected with the bacilli for long periods. These latter patients were known as " typhoid carriers," and in civil life very many epidemics had been traced to the presence in a community of even one of these carriers. Thus, a whole water supply might be poisoned through the instrumentality of a typhoid carrier.

It was obvious that in addition to preparing the soldiers against disease efforts must be made to secure them from unnecessary infection, and therefore plans were laid to carry out a careful scheme of prevention on what may be described as sanitation lines.

Typhoid bacilli are " water borne," but they can be carried also in food and by other means. It was clearly essential that those men handling the food of the troops should be guaranteed free from infection. A " typhoid carrier " in the commissariat would have partaken of the nature of a calamity.

So all the men in the food services were examined with a view to determining their suitability for the work to which they were about to be sent. Suspicious cases were, of course, rejected at once. Other cases were dealt with as occasion arose, and thanks to unremitting care it was secured that no carrier was in a position to bring disease to his fellows.

In addition to these precautions the question of water supply had to be considered. It was, of course, obvious that in a country which had been fought over, and which had been the scene of fierce conflict, the water supply was exceedingly likely to be contaminated. There was, moreover, no assurance that contamination with typhoid or other water-borne bacilli might not have taken place or might not take place. It was therefore necessary to supervise with the utmost care the drinking and washing water supplied to the troops. This problem was no easy one, for while sterilisation by boiling is, of course, quite sufficient and efficient on a small scale, when one comes to deal with millions of men it is cumbersome. Therefore various other expedients were tried, including the addition of certain disinfectant substances to the water. At the end of sixteen months of war the problem had been met and solved, but scientific workers were even then busily engaged in suggesting and testing new and improved methods so that the maximum of efficiency and safety might be secured with the minimum of labour and trouble. Labour and trouble, and more especially a troublesome technique, are the great enemies of all-round success, because the more they are multiplied the greater becomes the possibility of error or carelessness on the part of some subordinate worker; and this is emphatically a chain which must have no weak links.

Safety was therefore secured in three definite directions and by three separate proceedings.

(1) The men were protected by vaccination; (2) "carriers" and other human sources of infection were eliminated; (3) the means of propagation, water and food, were brought under the strictest possible supervision.

These three factors undoubtedly achieved one of the greatest triumphs which this or any other war has demonstrated. Thanks to them, and to the men who so boldly conceived them, and so vigorously and unselfishly carried them out, typhoid fever simply did not count in the British Army in France and Flanders. When the size of that Army is taken into consideration, indeed, the number of cases encountered was almost ludicrously small. When, as it seemed, all the circumstances favouring the onset of a great epidemic were present together, no epidemic occurred. Pessimists prophesied again and again that terrible trouble was almost sure to breed upon those dead-strewn fields, but their forebodings were falsified; the autumn wore on into the winter, and the winter again gave place to summer, and still the anticipated outbreak of typhoid fever did not come. Typhoid fever had been beaten—defeated before the battle as it were. Our Army went

TYPHUS IN SERBIA.
Patients outside the American Hospital.

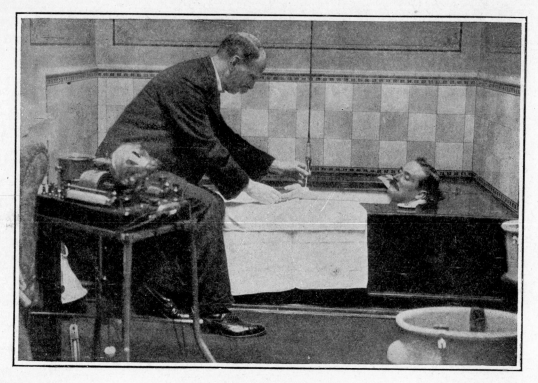

"TAKING THE WATERS."
A wounded soldier taking an electric bath.

scathless, and hundreds, nay thousands, of supremely useful lives were saved to the service of the country.

This great triumph passed almost unnoticed, as the triumph over tetanus had done, for in time of war it is mistakes which loom up large upon the public horizon. Yet it will stand for all time as a vindication of the scientific mind and of the scientific method.

But science had not finished her work with this enemy after a year of war. There remained certain difficulties, particularly in the detection of "carriers," which required further patient research. One of these difficulties was the direct outcome of vaccination. A vaccinated man, if by any chance he did develop the disease—and these instances were exceedingly few—could not, of course, be expected to give for diagnostic purposes so clear a reaction to the Widal blood test — seeing that his blood had been rendered immune in advance. By far the best way to make sure of infection by the typhoid germs in his case was by finding the germ and conclusively demonstrating its identity. But unhappily in these cases many other types of germs were usually present and it was difficult to separate out and to find the typhoid germs—often exceedingly difficult.

The matter received careful attention, and at length a chemical was discovered which had the effect of destroying practically all the types of germs from the intestinal contents except the typhoid and allied germs. This chemical, named "Brilliant Green," belonged to the aniline dye series which has been so prolific in potent drugs during the past decade. As applied by Dr. Browning, Director of the Bland-Sutton Institute of Pathology at the Middlesex Hospital, the results were highly successful. When it was added to any solution containing the typhoid germs, these were permitted to flourish, so that discovery of them became relatively a much easier matter. Other methods directed towards the same end were evolved, and some of them have also proved useful.

The only outbreak of typhoid fever on the western front occurred in connexion with the Belgian Army after the battle of the Yser, and at a time when the whole of the medical equipment had been lost during the retreat from Antwerp. The outbreak was quietly stamped out by a vigorous application of the scientific method—i.e., by vaccination and segregation of infected soldiers. It served to show how quickly any relaxation of a vigilance (in this case vigilance was rendered impossible temporarily by the exigencies of the military situation) was followed by an outbreak of the disease; and secondly, how quickly the disease could be mastered when the weapons of the laboratory were brought to bear against it.

It is not possible to leave this part of the subject without a reference to the allied condition "paratyphoid." This disease was met with in Gallipoli, and occasioned there a great deal of trouble and anxiety. It is not true typhoid, nor is it due to the true typhoid bacillus, and hence the fact of its presence was no kind of proof that vaccination had failed. On the contrary, it merely served to show how precise and exact the typhoid vaccination was for while the patient was securely protected against the one type of germ he was not protected against the other type. Inoculation with several strains of germs allied to the typhoid germ is, happily, within the powers of scientific technique, and therefore the problem of paratyphoid is essentially similar to the problem of typhoid. Commenting upon this, the *British Medical Journal* of November 13, 1915, stated that paratyphoid inoculation had been carried out upon a large scale in Serbia. The process " consists in preventive inoculation

with cultures of Paratyphoid A and B bacilli which have been killed by carbolic acid. In view of the special conditions existing in that country (Serbia) inoculation against paratyphoid has been combined with inoculation against typhoid fever, and cholera as well. Professor Castellani therefore employs what he calls a ' tetra vaccine,' or preferably a quadruple vaccine, to protect against these four infections. His paper shows that it has been administered to over 170,000 persons among the military and civil population of Serbia without the occurrence of any untoward results. Naturally we have no means as yet of judging the success attained by the use of this quadruple vaccine up to the present time. But if it is at all comparable to the success which has attended the employment of anti-typhoid inoculation in our own armies, Professor Castellani and his medical colleagues will have effectively conferred a most valuable benefit upon the inhabitants of that much-vexed country, and prospectively a comparable benefit upon the armies of the Allies which are going to its assistance."

The great success of the work upon typhoid naturally led to a careful consideration of the

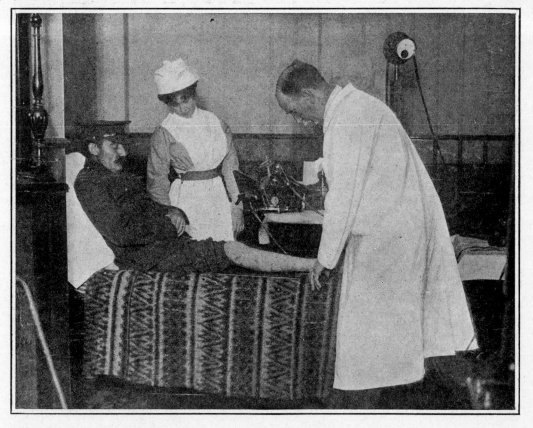

TAKING AN X-RAY OF A SHRAPNEL WOUND.

AN X-RAY AMBULANCE IN FRANCE,
Showing the special apparatus.

danger of cholera, and early in 1915 an effort was made to bring a strain of the cholera germ to this country from Russia so that inoculations might be prepared. The Medical Research Committee of the National Insurance Act enabled Dr. Freeman, of St. Mary's Hospital, to go to Galicia to secure a strain of the bacilli, and this he did. In Paris, too, at the Pasteur Institute, due preparations were made against the danger of an epidemic, and very large numbers of anti-cholera vaccines were held in readiness. These "weapons in test tubes" were despatched to the danger areas, and were used there with excellent effect, so that outbreaks which in other days might have proved disastrous were countered and quelled.

The cholera vaccine is prepared upon the lines already described. It depends for its utility, of course, upon the presence of a specific germ, just as the typhoid vaccine does. Its great worth was proved conclusively in the Greek Army during the recent war, when a catastrophe was prevented by its use.

Cholera is, of course, the scourge *par excellence* of armies in the field; should it gain the upper hand, terrible suffering and loss are certain. That science should have been able to hold this terror also at bay is, indeed, a matter for deep thankfulness, and proves once more how far-reaching, how momentous and how triumphant has been her share in this world struggle. Disease, the enemy of armies, has played but a minor part; its ancient decisive character has been filched away from it. Between the soldier and the epidemic that would devour him there has stood a figure new in the history of wars, a fighter whose weapons are his eyes and his ears and his faculty of close reasoning and stern self-discipline. The man of science has often been impugned as "cold blooded" and as lacking the good and warm impulses of his brother the doctor. It may be so. But this at least shall also be said, in the early days of the Great War he saved more lives by his "laboratory methods" than all the engines of war were able to destroy.

The war against dysentery, which proved so troublesome in certain theatres of action, cannot well be dealt with at this time. In spite of the fact that dysentery is an old disease, as the age of disease is reckoned, science had not yet—at the end of fourteen months of war—compassed its prevention as it had compassed that of typhoid fever. The " carrier " problem had indeed been attacked, and a serum had been produced which was of great value when bacilli were the cause of disease. This serum was used with excellent effect in many cases, as also was the drug " emetine," which has a special power over another of the causative organisms, the *Entamœba histolytica* (for there are two distinct types of this disease, each having a separate causative organism).

The terrible outbreak of typhus fever in Serbia during the early months of 1915 naturally directed scientific attention to this, in England, well-nigh extinct disease. Typhus fever, which used to be known as " gaol fever," from its prevalence in prisons, was at one period a scourge dreaded as much in this country as was smallpox. What vaccination accomplished in the case of the latter affliction cleanliness and hygiene accomplished in the case of the former. Typhus fever, essentially a dirt disease, disappeared with the dirt in which it bred and flourished, and its exit was hailed, and rightly hailed, as a triumph won by the public health official.

But the conditions of armies are not those of great cities in times of peace. Serbia had been invaded; twice over she had repelled the invader. Her national life was disturbed, her systems of government and control were unhinged. The normal protection against disease—never, it is to be feared, very adequate in Eastern countries—was broken down. Typhus reappeared, and reappeared in a form of great virulence, so that the whole country was plunged into calamity, and terrible scenes of suffering and death were witnessed.

When the great need became known in this

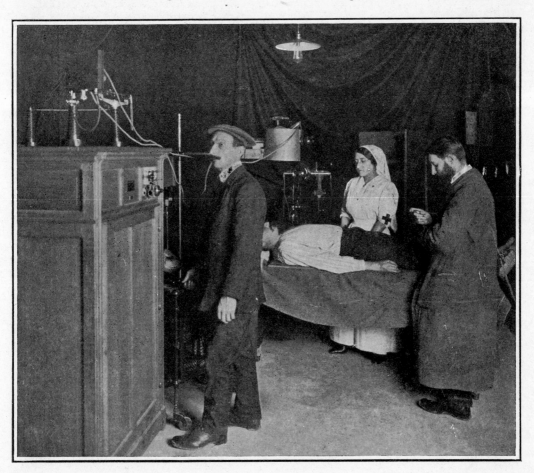

MICHELIN HOSPITAL.
Taking an X-ray photograph.

country heroic bands of doctors and nurses at once offered their services, and with these there went to the stricken land a large number of bacteriologists and men of science in the strict sense.

In the eyes of the man of science typhus fever is a disease belonging to the class known as "insect-borne," just as typhoid fever belongs to the class "water-borne." Another great member of the insect-borne class is, of course, malarial fever, and still another member is plague. Malarial fever is carried by a mosquito, plague by the rat flea; typhus fever is conveyed in the body of the louse.

This knowledge, gained by much patient labour, was, of course, the bed-rock upon which all measures of amelioration were built up. The question in Serbia was, first and fore-most, how to get rid of the lice. Lice are not, of course, themselves infected with typhus fever in the first instance, and a man may harbour many of these loathsome pests and never contract the disease. But if the lice settle upon the body of a patient who has typhus fever and pass from him to the body of another man the fever will be transmitted. It is easy to understand how in the conditions prevailing in Serbia at this period practically no soldier was free from the chance of infection, and so the infection spread with fell rapidity throughout the country. The problem was therefore a problem of prevention—a problem of cleansing. It was discovered that the lice tended to gather upon the inner garments, and that if these were removed and burned the insects were killed with great ease. Vast

A REMARKABLE CAMERA-PICTURE RECORDING A SHELL EXPLODING
IN A TRENCH.

CANNED POISON-GAS OPENED BY RIFLE SHOTS.
Tins containing poison-gas deposited by Germans at night outside the French wire entanglements.
By daytime the cans were hit by enemy rifle fire, so as to release the asphyxiating fumes.

measures designed to segregate the contacts, to destroy their clothing and to sweep away the infected lice were instituted. Other measures to prevent lice from reaching the body, and to keep them away, were devised and all manner of applications tending to secure this end were in use. *Eau de Cologne* was found to be very effective in this respect, as were a number of other substances having a pronounced perfume. Little by little these measures won the fierce battle, and the country was rescued from its evil plight—or, at least, that plight was ameliorated. And these measures were carried on with energy and determination, so that treatment may be said to have moved hand in hand with prevention

WITH THE FRENCH IN THE WOEVRE.

French Infantry, wearing respirators and goggles, awaiting a German poison-gas attack.

When treatment ended, with the subsidence of the epidemic in its acute form, this was in reality a victory for prevention. Prevention held the field which it had won.

Typhus was not confined to Serbia during this period, though it was only in that country that its full horror was realized. Wherever lice are to be found and infection is able to penetrate, there may the disease be expected to show itself.

For this reason strict measures were enforced in connexion with the armies operating in France and Flanders—which armies suffered, as all armies do, from the attacks of vermin—what have been described as "the minor horrors of war." On the British front elaborate and careful precautions were enforced in order to keep the pest down as far as possible. These consisted of frequent bathings as often as opportunity allowed, also of frequent fumigation of clothing, and especially of underclothing. Elaborate arrangements were in force for securing that infected or suspected cases were removed at once to a place of segregation, and all "contacts" kept under observation. Clothing, too, of a dangerous character was at once destroyed, and every effort exerted to see to it that the troops were shielded as far as might be from every possible source of danger. The ideal—no vermin in the trenches—cannot be attained so long as thousands of men of all kinds are congregated together, but there can be no reasonable doubt that those measures had the effect of preventing outbreaks of disease which, had no such measures been taken, would have occurred. Here again the Army owed a deep debt of gratitude to its scientific advisers.

While these great works were in progress another piece of scientific war work of a totally different character was being carried out in Egypt, under the auspices of the Royal Army Medical Corps, and with the help of the Medical Research Committee of the National Insurance Scheme. This research was undertaken with a view to determining the nature and mode of propagating what was in fact one of the most ancient and most troublesome of the plagues of Egypt.

This plague, known as "Bilharziosis," from the name of the discoverer of the worm which is the cause of it (Bilharz) was a source of great economic loss to Egypt, and was spoken of by Lord Kitchener in his annual report on Egypt

INTERIOR OF RUSSIAN SANITARY TRAIN.

for 1913. He said, "It is high time that serious steps should be taken to prevent the continuity of infection which has been going on so long in this country."

The research was entrusted to Lieutenant-Colonel Leiper, Helminthologist to the London School of Tropical Medicine. Colonel Leiper, in his report which was submitted to the Royal Society of Medicine, and afterwards published in *The Journal of the Royal Army Medical Corps* (July–August, 1915), described the evil effects of this disease. "During the Boer War," he said, "625 men were infected with bilharziosis in South Africa. In 1911, 359 of these were still on the list, exclusive of those meanwhile permanently pensioned. The cost to the State for 'conditional' pensions for these 359 men was about £6,400 per annum. The 'permanent pensions' already allotted amounted to an additional sum annually of £4,400."

The bilharziosis of the Nile delta is much more widespread than that of South Africa and more severe. It was therefore needful, since troops were being concentrated in Egypt, that preventive measures should be taken against the disease. But unhappily, though the parasitic nature of the disease was known, nothing definite concerning the life-history of the worm parasite had been discovered. In other words, it was known that a certain small worm caused the condition by entering the body of the victim. But how that worm lived outside of the body before entry was a mystery. And unless this mystery could be solved it was manifestly impossible to kill the worm and so prevent the disease. Many ideas had been formed on the subject, but these had not been proved.

The great antiquity of the disease is proved by the fact that evidence of its occurrence has been found in early Egyptian records, and in the bodies of mummies now in the Cairo Museum. The disease was prevalent among the French troops during the Napoleonic invasion of Egypt.

The worm belongs to the order known as "trematode." It had already been shown that some of the worms of this type complete their life-cycle in the bodies of molluscs—*e.g.*, the snail. This, therefore, was a reasonable basis for investigation, and, moreover, some earlier researches made by Lieut.-Colonel Leiper in China had led him to regard this hypothesis as a reasonable one. This idea had also been present to the minds of other workers. The investigation was therefore organized under several heads, of which the following are examples.

To collect and specifically determine all the fresh-water molluscs in the selected endemic

VICTIMS OF THEIR OWN GAS.
German prisoners who were captured by the French. They were about to pump gas into the trenches of the Allies, but a French 75 shell fell on to the cylinder with the result that they themselves were gassed. Inset: Two of the prisoners suffering from the effects of poison-gas.

"FLAMMENWERFER" (FLAME-PROJECTOR) IN ACTION.
German method of spraying liquid fire in the British trenches in Northern France.

area—*i.e.*, within half a day's journey from the laboratory in Cairo.

To dissect large numbers of all species found for trematode larvæ.

To ascertain which, if any, species of mollusc showed chemiotactic attraction for bilharzia.

To ascertain experimentally whether infection took place through the skin, or by the mouth, or in both ways.

This was necessarily a very great work. But so carefully was the investigation organized that within a relatively short space of time a large collection of these fresh-water shell-fish had been made. The shell-fish were recovered from the field drains—" agricultural drains "—both near villages and away from them. It soon became clear that large numbers of snails " found at spots daily frequented, such as the praying ground, at the embankment crossing, in front of the cafés, and at the bend of the Canal daily used for washing " were infected with bilharzia. The same species of snail was common at other parts of the Canal, but was not infected in these situations

The next step was to discover whether animals could be infected experimentally. It was noted that in the regions affected by the disease rats and mice were very scarce. A professional rat-catcher who was employed failed entirely to secure any of these animals. A possible inference from this was that rats and mice are susceptible to the disease, and so do not live near infected areas. On June 13, 1915, a positive result was obtained when a rat was experimentally infected. In addition to tame white rats and various types of mice, " the Egyptian desert rat, obtained from the neighbourhood of the Pyramids, was found to be susceptible to experimental infection, while guinea-pigs were peculiarly so. Mangaby monkeys were also capable of being infected."

It was thus shown that a snail inhabiting the Canal and ditches was the intermediate host of this worm. But it remained to be discovered in what manner the worm passed from the snail to man, or again from man to the snail. This was determined by experiment— permitting animals to drink infected water, and also to wade in infected water. Those which drank the infected water were infected much more severely than those which merely waded,

BRITISH TROOPS IN FRANCE.
An inspection of respirators.

but both classes were infected. In the experimentally infected water were large numbers of the so-called bilharzia " cercaria "—free swimming forms with tails and suckers. It was concluded that the chances of infection are much greater in bathing than in drinking, " because under the former circumstances a much larger quantity of water comes into contact with the body."

The question of naturally infected water next demanded attention. One of the difficulties was that it was known that the general water supply of Cairo, the same for natives as Europeans, was of a very high quality supplied from filters. How, it was argued, could this water affect anyone with a disease like bilharziosis ? The matter engaged the attention of the research workers, who found that " in addition to the series of pipes supplying Cairo with filtered water, it appears that there is a second system, carrying to the numerous gardens of Cairo unfiltered water drawn direct from the Nile in the neighbourhood of the Kasr Nil bridge, a spot where in recent years numbers of European troops have, while bathing, become infected shortly after their arrival in Egypt. It is well known that the children even of better-class Egyptians are allowed to run about in the privacy of their own courtyards in a state of semi-nudity during the summer months, and are thus continually exposed to the risk of infection from the hose used in the garden or stable. The lower classes probably derive their infection from the same source, although under different circumstances. To them water is a dear commodity in Cairo. There is no free supply. In the poorer quarters one frequently sees water being hawked about in large skins, and there is the standing inducement to the middleman to increase his margin of profit by arranging to draw his stock, possibly surreptitiously, through a friendly gardener from the unfiltered supply, for which the water companies make a lower charge."

It was shown also that the eggs of the worm pass from its human host into water : there they enter the body of the snail—and only of the particular snail concerned—and undergo a process of evolution, and *six weeks later* the mollusc has become a disseminating agent of the disease. It retains its power of dissemination during considerable periods. The following conclusions have therefore been formulated :

(1) Transient collections of water are quite safe after recent contamination.

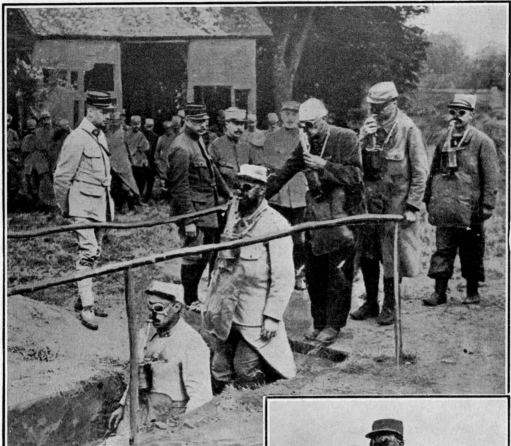

FRENCH ARMY SCHOOL OF ASPHYXIATING GASES.

Training troops to accustom them to the German poison-gas attacks : Soldiers wearing the protective masks descending an underground chamber filled with poison-gas. Inset : A French soldier's anti-asphyxiating-gas equipment.

(2) All permanent collections of water, such as the Nile canals, marshes, and birkets are potentially dangerous, depending upon the presence of the essential intermediary host— the snail.

(3) The removal of infected persons from a given area would have no effect, at least for some months, in reducing the liability to infection, as the intermediate hosts discharge infective agents for a prolonged period.

(4) Infected troops cannot reinfect themselves or spread the disease directly to others. They could only convey the disease to those parts of the world where a local mollusc could efficiently act as carrier.

(5) Infection usually takes place both by the mouth and through the skin. Recently contaminated moist earth or water is not infective.

(6) Infection in towns is acquired from unfiltered water, which is still supplied, even in Cairo, in addition to filtered water, and is delivered by a separate system of pipes.

(7) Eradication can be effected without the cooperation of infected individuals by destroying the molluscan intermediaries.

This last conclusion contained the germ of the protective measures which the research was designed to suggest. Egypt is fortunately

NOVEL FORM OF AMBULANCE USED BY THE RUSSIAN RED CROSS SERVICE.

Russian troops removing their wounded by means of a kind of sledge made of ski-sticks lashed together, with layers of straw on top. The ski-sledges were drawn by stout leathern thongs fastened to the belts of the bearers.

situated in that her irrigation work is in the hands of the Government. Every year during the dry season the small pools and canals are emptied, and the molluscs which live in them die. But many small pools are left, and it is in these that the disease is kept alive. Lieut.-Colonel Leiper suggested that action on the part of the irrigation authorities was necessary to have these pools filled up or treated chemically. The molluscs would then be killed off, and the worm, robbed of its necessary intermediate host, would gradually become extinct. The difficulty in Cairo was the unfiltered water supply, which, it seemed, was essential to the gardens. Happily it had been found that the free swimming form of the bilharzia does not live for a longer period than 36 hours. If it were possible to store Cairo's daily requirement of unfiltered water for two days or a day and a half, there was no doubt that it would become practically free from danger so far as bilharziosis was concerned. One-third of the 30,000 children born annually in Cairo became infected with the bilharzia.

The immense importance of this work must be obvious to everyone. At the meeting of the Royal Society of Medicine, at which Lieut.-Colonel Leiper recounted the story of his work, Lord Cromer stated that " the whole people of Egypt owed him an undying debt of gratitude." There could be little doubt that the result of these very careful experiments would be both far-reaching and in the highest degree valuable.

These, then, were the most notable scientific achievements of the first year of war. But scientists were at work in very many other fields, and great advances in knowledge were recorded. The use of X-rays, for example, became much more accurate and well understood than had been the case before the war. Many workers dealt with this subject, and especially with the difficult matter of the localization of bullets and pieces of shrapnel, and various methods were evolved and improvements on older methods suggested. Amongst methods which commended themselves to a large number of workers was the stereoscopic method—by which a bullet can

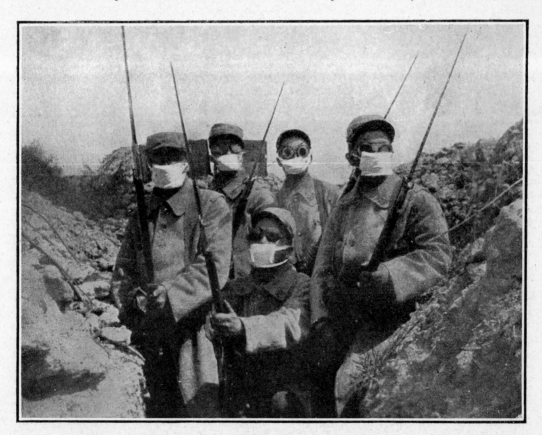

" WARE GAS."

When the Germans released a wave of asphyxiating gas—French troops wearing their masks awaiting an infantry attack at the entrance of their trenches.

be seen in perspective, like a view in a stereoscopic picture. This method naturally afforded a useful idea of the exact whereabouts of a foreign body and of its relations to the surrounding structures. The installation of X-ray apparatus became a matter of necessity in every well-organized military hospital. A great deal of work, too, was performed in connexion w.th the investigation of disease conditions arising from causes peculiar to the conditions of trench warfare. This work included a careful inquiry into the nature of frostbite, so-called "trench-foot," and some valuable suggestions for its amelioration. The "frost-bite" was found to be dependent not only upon cold, not even chiefly upon cold, but upon the association of cold with wet, and hence various means. including the use of oiled-silk foot and leg wear, by which wet could be excluded, were suggested. The results of these researches were submitted to the military authorities.

The problem of supplying artificial limbs also engaged attention, and several remarkable new pieces of apparatus were shown at the Queen Mary's Hospital, Roehampton. These artificial limbs were of so ingenious a character that their wearers seemed often to be " as good as whole men." Further work upon this subject was proceeding.

It would be impossible to close a chapter of this kind without a brief reference to the work of the Medical Research Committee of the National Insurance Scheme, presided over by Lord Moulton. This committee, early in the war, offered its help to the War Office, and soon made its potentiality for good felt in connexion with the majority of the great scientific efforts being carried out. The committee granted assistance to Sir Almroth Wright and many other workers in the field of wound infections ; it played a part in the work of bringing the strain of cholera bacilli to England from Galicia ; it afforded to Lieut.-Colonel Leiper all necessary field and other expenses incidental to his research. These, however, were but a few of its activities, for it also aided and encouraged researches in many other fields. The study of gunshot and shell wounds and various injuries occasioned by bullets, of nervous disorders, heart conditions, and the like was included in this wide purview. These most valuable researches proved of great assistance both to doctors and patients, and conferred a boon upon humanity. This splendid organiza-

tion thus placed the whole profession of medicine under a debt of gratitude.

Surveying, as a whole, this vast field of scientific labour, one sees that a great war was waged against the minute, unseen forces of disease during all the days and nights in which the war of nations continued. Science fights without noise or dust of battle ; she has no heralds, no trumpeters. Her victories do not bulk large in the eyes of men. But her victories are, nevertheless, splendid with the splendour of patience and care and selflessness which from defeat have won triumph, and from death life. There are tens of thousands to-day among our bravest and best who owe their lives in full measure to this silent warfare—with its precision and its hard logic. And the sum of the suffering which has been saved to humanity who shall reckon ? The enemies of science have often pointed to her as a figure of cruelty rejoicing in the infliction of pain and deaf to the appeals of sympathy. Let them now regard the work which she has accomplished, and let them ask themselves which, after all, is the nobler pity, the pity which is vocal or the pity which, in silence, achieves.

This recital of the work which science has accomplished has so far gone to show only the good which was wrought. There is, unhappily, another side to the picture, for our enemies devoted much of their brilliant scientific genius to the production of means of death rather than means of life. The most notorious of these efforts was, of course, the use of poison gas in Flanders and on the Russian Front.*

The use of this gas must be attributed directly to the laboratory, because the gas employed, chlorine, is essentially a laboratory product. Chlorine is an element, one of the so-called halogen group. It is found freely in combination in nature as sodium chloride, or common salt. It remained for the chemists to split up this substance and other chlorine-containing matters, and so to produce the element in its pure state.

Chlorine is a heavy gas, with a yellow-green colour, and having a pungent effect on the mucous membranes of the mouth and nose. Owing to its heavy character, it tends to lie upon the ground, and not to disperse, and so it

---

* The first great German gas attack in April, 1915, has been described in Vol. V., Chapter LXXXII.

WOUNDED BELGIANS IN ENGLAND.
A scene at an English country house.

fills up all holes in the ground, like trenches, and remains there, making life in these areas impossible. Moreover, it is "irrespirable"— that is to say, when it enters the mouth and air passages spasm, and then a serious inflammation, is set up, leading to bronchitis and terribly distressing breathlessness.

A careful consideration of these facts shows

WITH THE RUSSIAN RED CROSS.
Bringing in a Russian soldier suffering from the effects of poisonous gas.

that the use of chlorine was very deliberately calculated beforehand with the utmost ingenuity. It was seen that, given a still day, with a light wind blowing towards the enemy trenches, and given a sufficient supply of the gas released from cylinders at high pressure, the cloud would pass almost across to the enemy trenches, would cling to the ground and would then fill up the trenches, and render it impossible to remain in them. The victims would be unable to breathe, and in their agony would lose control of themselves, and rush anywhere for safety. Moreover, the gas would be carried back over line after line until a process of demoralization should have been accomplished.

To a great extent these ideas were justified. The gas did in fact sweep away the men in the front trenches at Ypres. But it did not demoralize their comrades—in this respect the enemy had miscalculated, and had failed to comprehend the heroic qualities of the British and Canadian troops. These men held on, though suffering great agony, and by their

supreme valour saved the day. Their sufferings were too terrible to describe. Deaths from suffocation, from injuries to the lungs, from remote poisoning were all too common. The pain was often continued over many days and even weeks.

But science which had made this abomination was able to meet and counter it. Thanks to the fact that no time was lost by the authorities in dealing with the matter, the use of respirators was quickly ensured. Science saw that the only way to deal with chlorine was to combine it again with some other chemical substance, and so, by " chaining it up," render it innocuous. Happily there are substances which will immediately combine with free chlorine gas to form harmless compounds like common salt. Several of these substances were used in solution upon respirators, so that the deadly gas was unable to penetrate to the mouth of the soldier, and became destroyed, as it were, upon his lips. He was able to face the deadly cloud with equanimity, and to await calmly and sternly the onset of the foe who should follow his hateful weapon.

CHAPTER XCVIII.

THE DARDANELLES CAMPAIGN (III): TWO MONTHS' LAND FIGHTING IN GALLIPOLI.

SECOND DAY OF THE BATTLE OF THE LANDING—ANZACS HOLD THEIR GROUND—HOW COLONEL DOUGHTY-WYLIE FELL AT HILL 141—THE THIRD DAY'S ADVANCE—SCENES AT ANZAC—RESULTS ON THE FOURTH DAY—EXPLOITS OF BRITISH SUBMARINES—FIRST BATTLE OF KRITHIA—SECOND BATTLE OF KRITHIA—CHARGE OF THE NEW ZEALANDERS—THE GOLIATH TORPEDOED—GREAT ATTACK ON ANZAC ON MAY 18—BATTLESHIPS SUNK BY GERMAN SUBMARINES—THIRD BATTLE OF KRITHIA—HEROISM OF THE MANCHESTER TERRITORIALS—BRILLIANT EXPLOIT BY THE FRENCH CORPS—BATTLE OF THE GULLY RAVINE—ENVER PASHA AND THE ANZACS.

IN Chapter XCIV. the problem of the land attack upon the Gallipoli Peninsula was examined in considerable detail, and the configuration of the coast and the various landing beaches, as well as the more prominent points of the interior, were fully explained.* The stirring episodes of the first day (April 25) of the great Battle of the Landing were described, and the whole narrative was carried through the night to the early morning of April 26. The present section of the story deals first with the next three days' fighting, on April 26, 27, and 28, which may properly be held to form part of the Battle of the Landing.

By the afternoon of April 26 the Australian and New Zealand Corps had firmly established itself in its isolated position at "Anzac," and though fighting in the Anzac sphere never ceased afterwards, its share in the opening battle may be considered to have terminated on the evening of that day. The forces which had landed on the southern beaches of the peninsula fought hard all through

April 26, and made a general advance without much opposition on April 27. The great general advance from the south was made on April 28, and constituted the final phase of the Battle of the Landing. By the afternoon of that day some of the troops were within three-quarters of a mile of Krithia, but further progress was impossible, and all hopes of obtaining a footing on Achi Baba upon that occasion were abandoned. With that admission the Battle of the Landing closed, and the troops dug themselves in as best they could.

Then followed the first three battles of Krithia, and what may for convenience be designated as the First and Second Battles of Anzac. The two days' fighting at Anzac on April 25 and 26, when the troops were first put ashore, are reckoned as part of the Battle of the Landing. The First Battle of Krithia lasted for parts of two days, and consisted of a Turkish attack on the night of May 1, followed by a British counter-attack on May 2. The Turks were heavily repulsed, and also suffered great losses in the counter-attack, but the British gained no ground. The Second Battle of Krithia began on May 6,

---

* For topographical details Chapter XCII. should also be consulted.

THEIR FIRST FOOTHOLD ON LAND.
British troops in their newly made trench.

and lasted three days. It was mainly an attempt to occupy the Krithia ridge, the ultimate object being the capture of Achi Baba. The British front was advanced over 500 yards, but the main purpose was not achieved, and the battle must be counted extremely indecisive. The First Battle of Anzac was simultaneously fought on May 6, 7, and 8, and continued during May 9 and 10. The Anzacs were attacked by the Turks, and adopted defensive tactics, but beat off the attack and maintained their ground. The Second Battle of Anzac was on May 18, when the Turks delivered an attack in great force. Their assault completely failed, and they were slaughtered in large numbers. The British forces before Krithia won a little ground during the following fortnight, and on June 4 the Third Battle of Krithia was fought. It was another British attempt to reach Krithia and Achi Baba, but the line was advanced by less than 500 yards. There was persistent fighting during the remainder of June, marked by heavy losses on both sides. On June 21 the French Expeditionary Corps captured a work known as the Haricot Redoubt, and brilliantly stormed the enemy's positions above the stream called the Kereves Dere. On June 28 the British left attacked, carrying several lines of trenches, and during the next two nights strong Turkish counter-attacks

were driven back. This action of June 28 became known as the Battle of the Gully Ravine. The Anzacs had much vigorous fighting at the end of June and the beginning of July. On July 12 the Fourth Battle of Krithia was fought, but it only resulted in a gain of between 200 and 400 yards. Desultory encounters followed until the landing of fresh British forces at Suvla Bay on August 7, which coincided with a general advance by the Anzacs upon the ridges towards Sari Bair.

These various conflicts will now be described in greater detail, though necessarily not with the minuteness which was possible in dealing with the clear-cut and unprecedented episodes associated with the first day of the Battle of the Landing. That was a day without parallel in British history. Thereafter the fighting grew more confused, and also more normal, until at length it lapsed into a variation of the trench warfare which became so familiar in France and Flanders. From the time the first landings were effected on April 25 the British troops were always more or less under fire. Every day brought its encounters, and hostilities were practically continuous. Certain larger actions, such as the battles just noted, stand out in great prominence, and lend themselves to consecutive narrative. The story of May, June, and July on the Gallipoli Peninsula can, however, only be handled in a selective manner. Even Sir Ian Hamilton, when he came to write his second long dispatch, dated August 26, felt the impossibility of recording in full the incessant attacks and counter-attacks of this crowded period. "Several of these daily encounters," he said, "would have been the subject of a separate dispatch in the campaigns of my youth and middle age, but, with due regard to proportion, they cannot even be so much as mentioned here." He contented himself, therefore, with giving one example each of the later activities during this period of the French, British, and Australian and New Zealand Forces respectively.

The general position on the morning of April 26, the Second Day of the Battle of the Landing, may be briefly recalled. There were two separate spheres of action, one at Anzac and the other based on the beaches at the extreme end of the peninsula. These two broad divisions of the land attack at the Dardanelles never effected a union, and each requires to be dealt with separately. The Anzacs had shortened their line on the evening of April 25, and were holding a semi-circular area at the top of the cliffs next morning. There was a small isolated force at De Tott's Battery, above Beach S. At Beach V the troops which had landed from the River Clyde were gathered under the shelter of the old fort near the shore, awaiting the order to attack the village of Sedd-ul-Bahr and Hill 141. The forces landed at Beaches W and X had effected a junction, and held a small corner of the peninsula in front of Cape Tekke. The 1st King's Own Scottish Borderers and the Plymouth (Marine) Battalion of the Royal Naval Division were being withdrawn from Beach Y. Sir Ian Hamilton made an error about Beach Y in his first dispatch, which was repeated in Chapter XCIV. He said that the attack on Beach Y was commanded by Lieutenant-Colonel Koe, who afterwards died of wounds. Long afterwards it was officially announced that this was a slip, and that the attack on Beach Y was commanded by Lieutenant-Colonel G. E. Matthews, C.B., of the Royal Marine Light Infantry, who was responsible for all that took place there. The battalion of Marines fought throughout with the utmost gallantry and resolution, and fully shared with the Borderers the brunt of heavy odds.

In describing the second day of the Battle of the Landing the separate Anzac zone may

SEDD-UL-BAHR.
The graves of Lt.-Col. Doughty-Wylie and Capt. G. N. Walford, R.A.
Both Officers were awarded the V.C. on April 26, 1915.

BRITISH BLUEJACKETS LANDED AT THE DARDANELLES.
In the background are warships of the Allied Fleet.

be taken first. Dawn disclosed the Anzacs in possession of a square mile of ground. Sir Ian Hamilton wrote that "despite their losses and in spite of their fatigue, the morning of the 26th found them still in good heart and as full of fight as ever." They had got up machine guns, and even on the first day had wrought deadly execution on the Turks advancing in close formation. The landing of men, guns, and stores had continued during the night, although movement on the narrow beach was much hampered owing to the returning stream of wounded. The units and formations were still intermingled, and it was not until three or four days afterwards that the force was partially sorted out and reorganized. The great change from the first day was that the front had been straightened out and defined, and the period of indiscriminate fighting was over.

In the early morning hours it became clear at Anzac that the enemy had received further reinforcements. The watchers on the warships could see the Turks creeping in large numbers over the northern shoulder of Sari Bair. The enemy were obviously adepts at taking cover, and they steadily drew nearer, sniping the Anzacs as they came. By 9.30 a.m. the conflict was once more in full progress. The Turks had brought up more guns in the night, and were "plastering" the Anzacs with shrapnel. They had the range of the beach, which was swept with shrapnel also. They even fired shrapnel at the warships lying off the coast, not always entirely without result. As the Turkish snipers gathered round the Anzac position, some of them actually ensconced themselves on the cliffs towards Suvla Bay, and began a fusillade against Rear-Admiral Thursby's squadron. Their object was to pick off officers and men, and many of their bullets fell on the decks. The war had seen many strange developments, but nothing stranger than this pitting of rifles against battleships. Nor was this all. The Turks had again brought warships into the Narrows, and one of these was firing over the peninsula. H.M.S. Triumph dropped a few shells around her, and apparently she then retired to a safer position, though her fire continued intermittently throughout the day.

The Anzacs were not idle. They were hauling field guns up the steep slopes of the coast, and reinforcements were still trickling ashore. Admiral Thursby's seven battleships had moved closer in, and were maintaining a terrific bombardment. The amount of actual execution wrought against the scattered Turks was doubtful, but the din was terrific, and the moral effect probably considerable. The mighty Queen Elizabeth had been summoned to give her aid, and an eye-witness declared that wherever her shells struck the ridges were transformed into "smoking volcanoes." Her 15-inch shrapnel shells each contained twenty thousand bullets, and it was a pity she had no more concentrated target. As it was, she conveyed on the whole a sense of comparative impotence. The 15-inch shells were not much more effective against hordes of snipers concealed over a wide tract of country than were the bullets of the Turkish riflemen against the battleships. Yet the ships helped the troops more than might have been expected. They covered the landing, and they cowed the Turks.

and delivered a dashing counter-attack, before which the Turks broke and fled, though with manifest reluctance. On that day, as on many others, the Turk showed himself a gallant and not unworthy foe. There were local conflicts later in the day, and the Turkish shrapnel was never long silent ; but at Anzac on April 26 the principal fighting occurred between 9.30 a.m. and noon. On the day's results the Anzacs gained some ground, and they were never shaken in the least. They deepened their trenches, and the reserves, which they were by this time accumulating, began to prepare dug-outs and shelter-trenches on the coastal slopes. The resemblance to the warfare of Flanders and Northern France was unconsciously developing. All experts had foreseen that the great war would produce many changes in tactics.

Lafayette.

Elliott & Fry.

MAJOR-GEN. SIR A. J. GODLEY
Who commanded a portion of the Anzac front.

MAJOR-GEN. W. P. BRAITHWAITE, C.B.,
Chief of Staff.

Sometimes their shells found a Turkish unit, and when they did death was scattered broadcast. Above all, they gave the gallant Anzacs a sense of backing which was sorely needed ; and the naval gunners must have felt that their bombardment was not wholly in vain when Admiral Thursby received from the shore the following signal : " Thanks for your assistance. Your guns are inflicting awful losses on the enemy."

Towards noon the Turks gathered for an attack, and instantly the combat reached its height. The artillery and rifle fire on both sides deepened into an almost continuous roar, and the Anzacs from their shallow trenches poured in a concentrated hail of bullets upon the advancing foe. The Turks wavered and hesitated. The Anzacs rose from their trenches

None had realized the extent to which the spade would come into its own again. All over Europe the progress of ordnance was compelling men to burrow once more into the earth. And just as this change was not fully foreseen, so when the attack upon Gallipoli was planned no one seems to have recalled that at Plevna, nearly forty years earlier, the Turks had proved themselves masters of spade warfare. It was eminently suited to their temperament.

Next in the story of the second day of the Battle of the Landing come the beaches of death at the southern end of the peninsula. Beach V claims foremost place. By dawn two officers of the General Staff, Lieutenant-Colonel Doughty-Wylie and Lieutenant-Colonel Williams, had gathered together the survivors of the Dublin* and Munster Fusiliers, and a couple of companies of the Hampshire Regiment, under the shelter of the old fort on the beach. The gaping sides of the transport River Clyde had long since yielded up the balance of her human freight, and during the night the lighters and other craft between the ship and the shore had been firmly lashed in position. The task before Colonels Doughty-Wylie and Williams was formidable. They had to restore organization to the shattered units who had spent the night on the open beach. They had then to clear the village of Sedd-ul-Bahr, still packed with Turkish snipers, and afterwards to direct an attack on Hill 141, the swelling height covered with trenches and entanglements which dominated the whole position.

Early in the morning General Hunter-Weston, the gallant commander of the 29th Division, arranged with Rear-Admiral Wemyss for a searching bombardment of all the enemy positions beyond Beach V. The warships poured their shells upon the old fort, the village, the Castle beyond, and the trenches on the hill. Covered by this bombardment, and led by Colonel Doughty-Wylie and Captain Walford, Brigade Major R.A., the troops, who had completely rallied, quickly cleared the old fort. They then entered the village, between 9 and 10 a.m., and were assailed by a hot fire from concealed riflemen and machine guns. Des-

---

* In Chapter XCIV. it was correctly stated that the landing in open boats at Beach V was made by three companies of the 1st Royal Dublin Fusiliers, but thereafter, on p. 469, Vol. IV., they were more than once referred to as "the Munsters." The Munsters were on the River Clyde, and not in the open boats. How well the Dublins fought at Gallipoli was shown in a speech made to the battalion by Major-General Sir Aylmer Hunter-Weston, K.C.B., D.S.O., commanding the 29th Division, on their relief from the firing line, after fifteen days' continuous fighting, in the Gallipoli Peninsula :

"Well done, Blue Caps ! I now take the first opportunity of thanking you for the good work you have done. You have achieved the impossible ; you have done a thing which will live in history. When I first visited this place with other people we all thought a landing would never be made, but you did it, and therefore the impossibilities were overcome, and it was done by men of real and true British fighting blood. You captured the fort and village on the right that simply swarmed with Turks with machine guns ; also the hill on the left, where the pom-poms were ; also the amphitheatre in front, which was dug line for line with trenches, and from whence there came a terrific rifle and machine gun fire.

"You are, indeed, deserving of the highest praise. I am proud to be in command of such a distinguished regiment, and I only hope when you return to the firing line after this rest (which you have well earned) that you will make even a greater name for yourselves. Well done, the Dubs ! Your deeds will live in history for time immortal. Farewell."

perate hand-to-hand fighting followed, and many fell on both sides. A naval officer who entered the village next day saw Turks and Britons still lying dead side by side in the streets, one poor soldier with his little red book of prayers near his hand. Every house had to be emptied in turn, and it was not until noon that the northern edge of the village was reached. Captain Walford had already fallen, and in recognition of his gallantry the Victoria Cross was posthumously conferred upon him. When the village was won, the Castle and the hill had still to be carried. There was a pause while the troops were formed up afresh by Colonel Doughty-Wylie, and while H.M.S. Albion provided a final bombardment. She ceased firing at 1.24 p.m., and the storming party of Dublins, Munsters, and Hampshires advanced undauntedly into the open. They were led again by Colonel Doughty-Wylie, whose tall, commanding figure inspired general confidence. His coolness in these last moments won an admiration that can never fade. Carrying only a light cane, he showed the way up the green slopes with intrepid and unfaltering courage through a storm of fire. Though he fell at last, being instantly killed, the spirit he had kindled carried the rank and file to victory. Other brave officers died on those fatal slopes, none braver than Major Grimshaw of the Dublins. But the attack surged on. The last trenches were passed, the Castle at the summit was gained, and before 2 p.m. the whole position was in the hands of the British, and the 29th Division had gained fresh laurels.

Men who saw most of the Battle of the Landing afterwards declared that in a series of conflicts in which heroism abounded the boldest exploit of all was the storming of Hill 141 by the Irishmen and the Hampshires. They were the remnants of a force which had faced death time and again, and they had then been struggling for thirty-six hours against terrific odds. Nothing stopped them long on that second day. They swept the amphitheatre and the old barracks bare. They did their task thoroughly, and never ceased fighting until it was completed. Amid all the incidents of those deathless hours, one other must receive special record. In the last assault on the Castle a party of the Dublins was checked by a murderous fire from a concealed machine gun. A young officer, Lieutenant Bastable, rushed forward and emptied his revolver into the embrasure, killing or wounding the men

H.M.S. "ALBION" AT THE DARDANELLES.

Shells from the Turkish batteries falling round the warship when she stranded near Anzac. The enemy gunners did not open fire until they observed the hawser of H.M.S. "Canopus" showing above the water. Bottom picture: H.M.S. "Albion" replying to the fire from the Turkish batteries.

"THE SOUL OF ANZAC."
Lieut.-General Sir W. R. Birdwood, K.C.S.I.,
D.S.O., Commander of the Australian and New
Zealand Army Corps, outside his dug-out. On
May 14, 1915, General Birdwood was slightly
wounded.

around the gun and silencing its fire. Miracu-
lously he escaped unhurt, but soon afterwards
he received a rifle bullet through his cheek.

No man who fell in the Battle of the Landing
was more deeply regretted than Colonel
Doughty-Wylie. Before the war he had gained
distinction as a Consular Officer in Asia Minor.
He it was who, accompanied by his brave wife,
had gone to Adana in 1909 and sought to check
the massacres of Armenians in that city.
Although then wounded, a shot having broken
his right arm, he and Mrs. Doughty-Wylie
remained at Adana protecting and succouring
the unfortunate Armenians under circum-

stances of great danger. His devoted wife,
twice widowed by war, had established and
personally directed plague hospitals in India,
and worked among the wounded in South
Africa. In the Levant Service both had won
great esteem. Colonel Doughty-Wylie received
the Victoria Cross posthumously, and the
height he died to win was ever afterwards
known to his comrades and to all Britons as
"Doughty-Wylie's Hill."

The forces landed at Beaches W and X, who
had effected a junction across the landward
slopes of Cape Tekke on the afternoon of the
first day, passed out of sight altogether in the
early published records of the war. Sir Ian
Hamilton waxed eloquent about the exploits
at "Lancashire Landing"; special correspondents employed their most thrilling phrases;
artists drew vigorous pictures of the penetra-
tion of the wire entanglements on the beach.
But having got the Lancashire Fusiliers and
the Worcesters on the high ground beyond,
having told how they were unable to reach
Beach V on the first day owing to the heavy
rifle fire from the ruins of Fort No. 1, Sir Ian
Hamilton and the unofficial recorders alike
left them behind a veil. Their story was never
continued either in the official dispatches or in
the other leading narratives of the time. What
really happened was that they had a good deal
of miscellaneous fighting on the 26th, found
their way through the remaining wire entanglements, cleared the nest of snipers in
Fort No. 1, and ultimately joined hands with
the Beach V forces above the "amphitheatre"
after Sedd-ul-Bahr and Doughty-Wylie's Hill
were carried. During the remainder of the
afternoon consolidation of the whole position
was rapidly continued. By nightfall the
French Expeditionary Corps was being landed
with comparative ease at Beach V, and sufficient troops moved across towards De Tott's
Battery, near Beach S, to relieve the South
Wales Borderers established there from their
isolation.

The general results of the second day of the
Battle of the Landing may be briefly summed
up. The Anzacs had steadily maintained
and slightly enlarged their position. All the
remaining defences directly commanding the
southern beaches had been carried. Contact
had been established all the way across the
peninsula from Beach S to Beach X. More
troops, including the French, were being landed
without immediate exposure to rifle fire. At

nightfall on the first day the British were still holding on "by teeth and eyelids." At nightfall on the second day they had a continuous line across the southern end of the peninsula, and knew that their foothold was won.

The third day of the Battle of the Landing, April 27, was comparatively uneventful, though marked by substantial progress. The Turks had been heavily hammered, and had realized that their opposition, though desperate, had been in vain. The British were well ashore, and were evidently going to stay. The enemy had suffered great losses, and needed reinforcements. The landing at Anzac had served one good purpose. It distracted the Turks, who seemed to fear it most. They had flung against Anzac reinforcements which had a much better chance of success on the Krithia line. Throughout April 27 their opposition in front of Krithia was desultory and spasmodic, and during the chief movements of the day they offered no opposition at all.

Sir Ian Hamilton considered the situation on the morning of April 27. He saw that the main beaches were now at his disposal, but they were becoming congested. Troops and stores and weapons were still pouring ashore. He needed more elbow-room, but he also needed water, for the problem of thirst was becoming serious. Accordingly, he ordered a general advance. It was fixed for midday, and was accomplished without difficulty. The line he desired to occupy was drawn from Hill 236, near De Tott's Battery, across to the mouth of a small stream two miles north of Cape Tekke. The stream emerged upon Beach Y2, described in Chapter XCIV. The new line, which was three miles long, was reached and consolidated in the course of the afternoon. It was held on the left and centre by the three brigades (less two battalions) of the 29th Division, under General Hunter-Weston. Then came four French battalions, and finally the South Wales Borderers on the extreme right. Long before nightfall the British left was at the mouth of the "nullah" known as Gully Ravine, which was afterwards to give the name to an important action.

The Anzacs had a busy though never a menacing day on April 27. During the night of April 26 the enemy had brought up many more field guns. With these he rained shrapnel on the trenches, the beaches, and on the boats plying to and fro between the transports and the shore.

All attempts to establish guns in positions whence they could enfilade the beaches were promptly checked by the warships, which also dealt effectually with a renewed bombardment from Turkish warships in the Narrows. There were no organized infantry attacks on Anzac on this day, the enemy relying chiefly upon their guns and upon snipers. A special correspondent, describing the scene on April 27 at Anzac, wrote :

The stretch of foreshore and cliffs occupied by the Australian and New Zealand troops has been named the Folkestone Leas, and the ground certainly does bear a striking resemblance to what Folkestone must have looked like before the town was built on the cliffs. On going ashore through an avalanche of bursting shrapnel you land on a beach about 30 yards wide between the water and the cliffs, which then rise very steeply for several hundred feet. There are regiments waiting to move to the trenches, fatigue parties unloading boats and lighters, others making great pyramids of tinned meat and biscuits, others fetching water, of which a supply has been found on shore. There are trains of mules endeavouring to drag field guns into position, Indians in charge of mountain guns, dressing stations where the wounded are hastily tended before being piled into barges and sent to the ships. Other fatigue parties are laying telegraph and telephone wires, and still others carrying supplies up the cliffs.

You run across your beach parties from the battleships,

GENERAL ELLISON,
Quartermaster-General, outside his quarters.

[Elliott & Fry.

MAJOR-GENERAL SIR W. T. BRIDGES,

Late Commander of the Australian Division, who,
on May 15, 1915, received a severe wound which
proved fatal a few days later.

and see young midshipmen who have been working
incessantly for days now building themselves bomb-
proof shelters and complaining that their last one was
considered such a perfect model of its kind that some
superior officer no sooner saw it than he appropriated
it for his own use. Thousands of hardy New Zealanders
and Australians are concentrated on this narrow shore,
each engaged in some occupation, for no sooner does a
man get out of the front trenches than he is required for
fatigue work, and very few have had more than a few
hours' sleep for days past.

The whole scene on the beach irresistibly reminds you
of a gigantic shipwreck. It looks as if the whole Army
with its stores had been washed ashore after a great gale
or had saved themselves on rafts. All this work is
carried on under an incessant shrapnel fire which sweeps
the trenches and hills. The shells are frequently
bursting 10 or 12 at the same moment, making a deafening noise and plastering the foreshore with bullets. The
only safe place is close under the cliff, but every one is
rapidly becoming accustomed to the shriek of the shells
and the splash of the bullets in the water, and the work
goes on just as if there was not a gun within miles.

These Anzacs are extraordinarily cool under fire, often
exposing themselves rather than taking the trouble to
keep in under the shelter of the cliff. One of the
strangest sights of all was to see numbers of them
bathing in the sea with the shrapnel bursting all around
them.

This colony suddenly planted on the shores of Gallipoli
is now assuming a definite form. The whole face of the
cliffs is being cut away into roads, dug-outs, and bomb-
proof shelters. Thus a kind of improvised town is rising
up as the troops slowly dig themselves in and make

themselves comfortable. As you climb up the newly-
made paths to the front trenches you realize some of the
difficulties the Australians and New Zealanders had to
face when they first advanced from the beach on April 25.
We are now holding a semi-circular position. The
trenches are well made and provide ample cover, but
if you show your head above the parapet for a second
you are certain to get a bullet in or close to it.

This incessant sniping is one of the great puzzles of the
men in the trenches, and presents the great problem
to be dealt with at the present time. Apparently even
when an advanced post is thrown out to hold some
commanding point the enemy's sharpshooters remain
behind and continue to pick off any unwary man who,
either through carelessness or indifference, exposes
himself. Volunteers go out at night and hunt about for
these snipers, but up to the present they have not been
able to keep them under.

The cheerfulness of the men in the trenches is most
marked. They feel they have overcome the initial
difficulties and have paved the way for success. These
Anzac divisions now occupy a position and have entrenched it so thoroughly that all the Turks in Thrace
and Gallipoli will never turn them out of it.

The Anzacs were, however, becoming exhausted, and reinforcements were sent up to
them next day.

On the night of April 27 Sir Ian Hamilton
once more examined the situation at the
southern end of the peninsula. He had got
his three-mile line, but it was, as he himself
acknowledged, "somewhat thinly held." His
troops had suffered heavy losses, and some
units had sadly diminished in size. The lull
of April 27 was not likely to continue. The
Turks would assuredly bring up further reinforcements as quickly as possible. To the
anxious Commander-in-Chief it seemed imperative to push on as rapidly as possible. The
village of Krithia and the heights of Achi Baba
lay before him. His sorely tried men needed
rest, but he could not afford to wait. He
therefore ordered a great general advance for
next morning upon Krithia and Achi Baba.

April 28 was the last day of the Battle of
the Landing. The great attack was delivered,
and though a whole mile of ground was gained
upon most of the front, it failed in its principal
object.

The line advanced at 8 a.m. The 29th
Division were under orders to advance on
Krithia, their left brigade, the 87th, leading.
The French were to extend their left in conformity with the British movements, but
apparently they were not to advance beyond
the river Kereves Dere, which lay athwart
their path in a deep bed a mile ahead. Krithia
was the main objective, and from the village
it was hoped that the western slopes of Achi
Baba would be reached. The 87th Brigade
included the Drake Battalion of the Royal

Naval Division, which had been used to replace the King's Own Scottish Borderers and the South Wales Borderers. The Brigade advanced rapidly for a couple of miles, and then the 1st Border Regiment found a strong enemy work on their left flank. The battalion halted and prepared to attack, but before they could advance the Turks delivered a fierce counter-attack. The enemy were beaten off, but had attained their purpose, for the British advance was held up at this point. The Queen Elizabeth came to the assistance of the men of the Border Regiment, and her shells prevented the Turks from continuing their success, but the Border Regiment got no farther. The men eventually entrenched for the night where they stood. The 1st Royal Inniskilling Fusiliers, on the right of the Border Regiment, fared rather better. They reached a point about three-quarters of a mile from Krithia, but the check elsewhere prevented them from continuing their advance, and eventually they fell back into line. The 88th Brigade, farther to the right, had pushed forward very steadily until 11.30 a.m., when they were brought to a stand-still by heavy opposition. Their ammunition

THREE OF THE PERSONAL STAFF OF GENERAL SIR IAN HAMILTON.
Lieutenant McGregor, Colonel Pollen (Military Secretary), and Colonel Maitland, A.D.C.

TURKISH PRISONERS.
British Staff officers questioning Turkish officers on the battlefield. Centre picture: Turks delighted with their new occupation. Bottom picture: Wounded Turks being brought into the British lines.

was also failing. The situation was growing anxious. Both the leading brigades of the 29th Division were stationary.

The 86th Brigade, under Lieutenant-Colonel Casson, had been held in reserve. It was ordered to pass through the 88th Brigade, and to endeavour to reach Krithia. The new bolt was launched at 1 p.m., but it fell short. Small advance parties got ahead, and even reached within a few hundred yards of the village. The bulk of the brigade was unable to advance beyond the line held by the 88th. The French had met with an almost similar fate. They had arrived on the western verge of the Kereves Valley, but found the enemy strongly posted. Their left, in contact with the 88th Brigade, got well in advance of their right, as was intended, and at one time they were within a mile of Krithia. But our Allies found further progress impossible. The Turkish resistance increased, and later in the day they were even forced to give ground.

By 2 p.m. it was seen that the full objects of the day would probably not be won. All the

THE ENEMY'S AMMUNITION.

Examining arms and ammunition left behind by the Turks. Centre picture : An interval for lunch. Bottom picture : Men at work making bombs. Old jam tins and other similar receptacles were used, also fragments of Turkish shell and enemy barbed wire were cut up and used as filling.

available troops, with the single exception of the Drake Battalion of the Royal Naval Division, were then in the firing line. Sir Ian Hamilton in his dispatch wrote :

The men were exhausted, and the few guns landed at the time were unable to afford them adequate artillery support. The small amount of transport available did not suffice to maintain the supply of munitions, and cartridges were running short despite all efforts to push them up from the landing-places.

At least it was hoped to hold the ground gained, but even this limited purpose was jeopardized when an hour later masses of Turks advanced with the bayonet against the British centre and right, and against the French. There was a partial retirement, and for a time it seemed as though the line would be pierced at the point of contact between the British and French. The right flank of the 88th Brigade was uncovered, and the 4th Worcesters suffered heavily in consequence. The French were also forced back, as has been mentioned, and their casualty list was high, especially among their gallant officers. At six o'clock

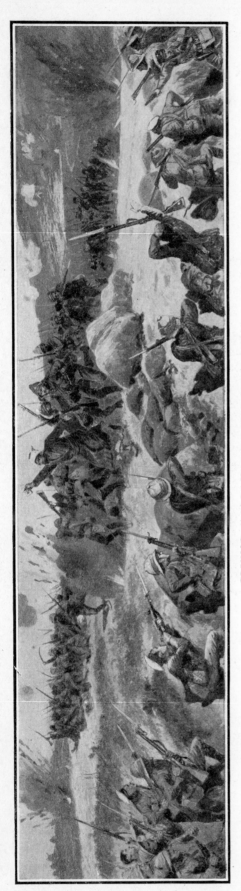

CRYING "ALLAH! ALLAH! DIN! DIN!"
Turkish Imams heading a bayonet charge in the first battle near Krithia shortly after the landing of British troops.

the whole line was ordered to entrench and endeavour to hold on where it stood. This was successfully done, and with the invaders brought to a complete standstill the Battle of the Landing came to a close.

If on the last day Sir Ian Hamilton's purpose was not fulfilled, yet it must also be said that the day was not lost. The attacking forces had gained a mile of front, and never afterwards during the months of fighting which followed was so much ground placed to the credit of the Allies in a single day in the southern sphere. Sir Ian Hamilton, summing up the results of the last day's fighting, wrote:

Had it been possible to push in reinforcements in men, artillery, and munitions during the day, Krithia should have fallen, and much subsequent fighting for its capture would have been avoided.

Two days later this would have been feasible, but I had to reckon with the certainty that the enemy would, in that same time, have received proportionately greater support. I was faced by the usual choice of evils, and although the result was not what I had hoped, I have no reason to believe that hesitation and delay would better have answered my purpose.

It was afterwards said, with obvious truth, that the men, artillery, and munitions needed before Krithia were engaged in the Anzac adventure. Had Sir Ian Hamilton been able to fling the dashing Anzac Corps in a completely fresh condition against the Turks in the south, instead of the exhausted 29th Division, he might perchance have slept in Krithia on the night of April 28, and seen Achi Baba crowned by his troops at sunrise on the following morning. But the suggestion does not cover the whole of the possibilities of the situation. If the Anzac attack weakened Sir Ian Hamilton in the south, it also weakened the Turks in that area. They were terribly perturbed about Anzac, and a large proportion of their reserves were sent thither. Had the British operations been solely directed against Krithia and Achi Baba, the Turks would have been able to face the attack on these positions in far greater strength than was actually the case. Nevertheless, on a balance of probabilities it would perhaps have been better if Anzac had been left severely alone.

The Battle of the Landing succeeded in its initial object, because the landing was effected. It failed in its later objects, which were to effect a junction between the Anzac and the Southern Contingents, to take Krithia and Achi Baba, and to advance upon Maidos and the Narrows. The primary cause of the failure was that the Allies delivered their attack in

A NEW ZEALAND OFFICER HURLING JAM-TIN BOMBS.

An incident during the recapture of a trench by the Inniskillings, near Achi Baba. A New Zealand officer attached himself to the Royal Inniskilling Fusiliers during an attack on a trench which had been rushed by the Turks the preceding night. As the Irishmen crept up a small communication-trench from a nullah, the New Zealander armed himself with half-a-dozen jam-tin bombs and, with an orderly to assist him, created a diversion by hurling them into the midst of the Turks. One of the bombs had to be re-lit and the shortened fuse caused it to explode prematurely—wounding him severely. The Fusiliers, meanwhile, had dashed on to the main trench held by the Turks, whom they destroyed or captured.

insufficient force. The secondary cause was that the forces available were unduly dispersed. Behind these lay a third cause, that of lack of accurate topographical knowledge of a peninsula which had been for centuries an object of deep interest to ardent soldiers, and especially to British soldiers. To these causes may be added the complete and most unwise elimination of the element of surprise, due to

the original decision to rely on naval strength alone.

The total losses in the Battle of the Landing were not stated separately, but were probably over 10,000 of all ranks, exclusive of the French losses, which were proportionately heavy.

One reason why Sir Ian Hamilton found himself exceptionally short of reserves on April

28 was that he had been obliged to send assistance to General Birdwood at Anzac. Four battalions of the Royal Naval Division were dispatched as reinforcements. The Chatham and Portsmouth Marine Battalions, together with the Brigade Headquarters, under the command of Brigadier-General C. N. Trotman, C.B., R.M.L.I., landed near Gaba Tepe at 5 p.m. on April 28. They were attached to the Australian Division commanded by Major-General Sir W. T. Bridges, K.C.B., and at once proceeded up the slopes to relieve certain Australian units. The Anzacs had not then succeeded in dealing fully with the mixing of units which inevitably occurred on the first landing. The Turkish lines had approached them within a stone's throw at various points, and the enemy were maintaining a continuous and intense fire against the Anzac trenches by day and night. A company of the Motor Maxim Section of the Royal Naval Division landed next morning, and was placed in reserve. Another Marine Battalion, and the Nelson Battalion of the Royal Naval Division, also disembarked on April 29, under the command of Brigadier-General David Mercer, C.B., R.M.L.I. The Australians thereby relieved were able to obtain a little of the rest they so greatly needed, and to reorganize their scattered and depleted units. The newcomers soon found that the Turkish artillery had got their range accurately, and the constant bursts of shrapnel caused many casualties. On several occasions at this period the Turks conducted minor attacks, and on April 30 they captured a section of a front-line trench held by the Chatham Battalion ; but the Chathams regained it during the following night. After three days and four nights of arduous strain the British battalions were relieved by a reorganized Australian Brigade under Brigadier-General Walker, D.S.O.

One of the objects of the Allies at this juncture was to prevent reinforcements and supplies from reaching the Turks in Gallipoli. The enemy's land communications were difficult. The nearest railway was far away in Thrace, and the single available road which entered the peninsula was liable to be shelled at the Bulair lines. It was common knowledge that men and stores were being chiefly sent to Gallipoli by marine transport through the Sea of Marmora. Admiral de Robeck therefore decided to attempt to harry the Turkish sea communications by means of submarines. The experiment was conspicuously successful from the outset, although at the very beginning one submarine was lost. AE.2, a submarine of the Royal Australian Navy, commanded by Lieutenant-Commander Henry Hugh Gordon Dacre Stoker, R.N., was sunk on April 30 while endeavouring to enter the Sea of Marmora. Lieutenant-Commander Stoker, Lieutenant Geoffrey Arthur Gordon Haggard, R.N., Lieutenant John Pitt Cary, R.N., and seventeen men were made prisoners, and twelve men were lost. Submarine E14, commanded by Lieutenant - Commander Edward Courtney Boyle, R.N., had better fortune. She passed the mine-field in the Narrows on April 27, sinking on the way a Turkish gunboat of the Berk-i-Satvet class. She remained in hostile waters until May 18, when she successfully traversed the Dardanelles once more. She sank a transport on April 29 ; a gunboat on May 3 ; a very large transport full of troops on May 10 ; and compelled a small steamer to run aground on May 13. For these services Lieutenant-Commander Boyle, who had ranged the whole Sea of Marmora right up to the entrance to the Bosphorus, received the Victoria Cross. The other officers of E14, Lieutenant E. G. Stanley, R.N., and Acting-Lieutenant R. W. Lawrence, R.N.R., received the Distinguished Service Cross, while the Distinguished Service Medal was granted to every member of the crew. Submarine E11, commanded by Lieutenant-Commander Martin E. Nasmith, R.N., performed an even more brilliant exploit in the Sea of Marmora later in the month. She sank a vessel containing a large amount of howitzer ammunition, several gun mountings, and a 6-inch gun. She then chased a supply ship with a great cargo of stores, and most daringly torpedoed her alongside the pier at Rodosto. Afterwards she chased and ran ashore a smaller store ship. Emboldened by these successes, she actually entered the Golden Horn and torpedoed a transport lying off the arsenal. Finally, while on the return journey, she turned back to torpedo a transport. Lieutenant-Commander Nasmith received the Victoria Cross for his " most conspicuous bravery," his subordinates, Lieutenant Guy D'Oyly Hughes, R.N., and Acting-Lieutenant Robert Brown, R.N., were awarded the Distinguished Service Medal, and every member of the crew was decorated. These incursions inaugurated a period of British submarine activity in the Sea of

BRITISH TROOPS MAKING A ROAD ON BEACH X.

Marmora which was long continued. The greatest consternation was caused in Constantinople, the sea communications of the Turks were incessantly interrupted, and the list of Turkish losses between Constantinople and Gallipoli grew very long indeed.

It may be noted that on April 27 British airmen reported a Turkish transport of about 8,000 tons near the Narrows, off Maidos. The Queen Elizabeth was notified, and fired three shells, the third of which struck and sank the vessel. It was not known whether she contained troops. The Fleet occasionally fired at the forts in The Narrows in the days which immediately followed the Battle of the Landing. H.M.S. Triumph bombarded Maidos across the peninsula on April 29, and at night the town was reported in flames.

For two days after the Battle of the Landing terminated on April 28 the troops on the Krithia line had a comparatively quiet although an extremely busy time. They had partly lost their normal formations during the abrupt check in the last phase of the battle. Some of the units of the 86th and 88th Brigades had become mixed, and there were flaws in the line, especially at the points of contact between brigades. All through April 29 the work of straightening and strengthening the line continued, and though there was some exchange of both rifle and artillery fire, the enemy offered little hindrance. On April 30 much the same work proceeded. The Allies finished landing their artillery, and the French, who were growing in numbers, increased their share of the line. Two more battalions of the Royal

INDIAN TROOPS AT THE DARDANELLES.
Bringing up forage for their mules.

A DAYBREAK EXPLOIT AFTER
Two companies of the Royal Inniskilling Fusiliers making a flank attack on the

Naval Division were disembarked, and were formed into a temporary reserve in conjunction with three battalions of the 88th Brigade, withdrawn from the trenches. On May 1 the 29th Indian Infantry Brigade arrived, and was placed in reserve, thus enabling the 88th Brigade to regain its three battalions.

The First Battle of Krithia began at 10 p.m. on the night of May 1, and was by no means expected by the British. After half an hour's artillery preparation, the Turks advanced in three solid lines just before the moon rose. The enemy had made very careful preparations under German supervision. The men in their front rank had been deprived of ammunition, in order to compel them to rely upon the bayonet. Sir Ian Hamilton said :—" The officers were served out with coloured Bengal lights to fire from their pistols, red indicating to the Turkish guns that they were to lengthen their range ; white that our front trenches had been stormed ; green that our main position had been carried." If the green lights were ever used, it must have been in error or in hope ; and very little justification was gained for the use of the white lights. The orders to the Turkish rank and file were to crawl on their hands and knees until the word was given to charge. They had been exhorted to fling the British into the sea in an address which read thus :

Attack the enemy with the bayonet and utterly destroy him !

We shall not retire one step ; for, if we do, our religion, our country, and our nation will perish !

Soldiers ! The world is looking at you ! Your only hope of salvation is to bring this battle to a successful issue or gloriously to give up your life in the attempt !

These inciting apprehensions about the possible fate of the Turkish race and religion bore the not very Ottoman-like signature, " Von Zowenstern." The first impact of the Turkish charge struck near the centre of the British line, on the right of the 86th Brigade. It was " an unlucky spot," observed Sir Ian Hamilton, for " all the officers thereabouts had already been killed or wounded." The rank and file were taken unawares by the silence of the Turkish advance, and the enemy got into their trenches with the bayonet and made " an ugly gap." The emergency was instantly met. The 5th Royal Scots, the fine Territorial battalion which formed part of the adjoining 88th Brigade, faced to their left flank and charged the intruders impetuously with the bayonet. The Essex Regiment, belonging to the same brigade, was detached by the brigadier for a similar purpose, and the gap was closed. The attack against the rest of the British line was not pressed home with the same vigour, and General Hunter-Weston did not have to bring his reserves into action. But the French left, which adjoined the right of the 88th Brigade, was in difficulties very soon afterwards. The French left consisted of a force of Senegalese, behind whom were stationed two British Field Artillery Brigades and a Howitzer Brigade. The Turks smote the Senegalese with persistent vigour, and after the conflict had swayed to and fro with great violence for some time, the Africans began to lose ground.

A TURKISH NIGHT ATTACK.
Turks near Achi Baba.   The Inniskillings secured a "bag" of 152 prisoners.

The moonlight revealed what was happening, and a company of the 4th Worcesters, belonging to the much-tried 88th Brigade, hurried to the aid of the Senegalese. The Turks did not desist, and another company of the Worcesters came up, after which the enemy's attack gradually ceased. At 2 a.m. a battalion of the Royal Naval Division was sent from the reserve to strengthen the extreme French right, and the first phase of the action terminated.

Three hours later, at 5 a.m., the Allies began a counter-attack. The whole line advanced. The British left had gained 500 yards by 7.30 a.m., and the centre had also gained ground and punished the enemy heavily. The British right and the French left also progressed, but the remainder of the French line was checked, doubtless because the Kereves Dere was very strongly held. Thus the counter-attack, which had looked very promising at the outset, began to languish. The British centre and left came under a heavy cross-fire from machine guns, and it was found impossible to maintain the ground won. The whole force, therefore, withdrew to its original line of trenches.

Nevertheless, the First Battle of Krithia left the honours in the hands of the Allies. They had beaten back the Turkish attack, and had killed "great numbers" of Turks. Sir Ian Hamilton afterwards declared that "had it not been for those inventions of the devil— machine guns and barbed wire—which suit the Turkish character and tactics to perfection, we should not have stopped short of the crest of Achi Baba." Unfortunately, modern in-struments of warfare must be taken into account, even if handled by Turks, and the crest of Achi Baba was still two miles away. The Allies took 350 prisoners in the course of the action.

The Turks buried their dead under a Red Crescent flag during May 2, and at night they attacked the French portion of the line, being once more repulsed with heavy loss. They came forward once more against the French on the night of May 3, the reason why they chose the French section of the line presumably being that the approaches were easier. During the three night attacks the French casualties mounted up to such an extent that on May 4 they relinquished a portion of their line to the 2nd Naval Brigade. Welcome reinforcements arrived for the British on May 5, when the Lancashire Fusilier Brigade (5th, 6th, 7th, and 8th Lancashire Fusiliers) of the East Lancashire Territorial Division were disembarked from Egypt and placed in reserve behind the British left. Preparations for a fresh British advance had been steadily continued, and the receipt of reinforcements made it possible to give battle again.

The losses of the land forces up to and including May 5 (not counting those of the French) were :

177 officers and 1,990 other ranks killed.
412 officers and 7,807 other ranks wounded.
13 officers and 3,580 other ranks missing.

The Second Battle of Krithia was decided on by Sir Ian Hamilton on May 5, and was fought on May 6, 7 and 8. It deserves careful attention,

WITH FIXED BAYONETS AND COLOURS FLYING: TU
British troops beating back the en

SURGING FORWARD UNDER THEIR CRESCENT BANNERS.
from machine guns and rifles.

because it was in many respects the most significant land battle fought during the Dardanelles operations. Its lessons ought to have been considered conclusive, for it demonstrated clearly the growing strength of the Turkish line before Krithia and of the defences of Achi Baba. Sir Ian Hamilton afterwards wrote that his immediate object was to seize some of the half-mile of debatable ground which lay between the opposing forces, because he needed more room on the peninsula. He gained a depth varying from 600 to 400 yards ; but the real object of the three days' battle was manifestly to seize Krithia and Achi Baba, and this object was completely frustrated by the Turks. The Second Battle of Krithia plainly proved that there was not the slightest hope of carrying the Gallipoli Peninsula, or any important portion of it, with the culminating rush of a manœuvre battle. It therefore led to the definite adoption of the alternative of siege warfare. It ought to have led to the careful reconsideration in London and Paris of the whole position at the Dardanelles. The battle was one more of those occasions for re-examination of the project, so frequently offered to the Allies, but so invariably ignored until the late autumn. Siege warfare in the Dardanelles might imply operations as protracted as the

siege of Troy. The whole peninsula was being converted into a vast fortress, upon a scale that Vauban and Brialmont had never dreamed of. Its configuration offered possibilities of line after line of almost impregnable defences. When the Japanese burst one point of the inner ring of forts at Port Arthur they knew that the fortress had fallen. At Gallipoli the capture of one line of defences could only mean the revelation of a fresh and almost endless series of lines behind. It was at this stage that the true object of the attack upon the Dardanelles—to provide means for the passage of the Fleet—was apparently lost sight of both on the spot and at home. The obstinate attempts to carry a series of Turkish defences became an object in themselves. Britons wished to show that they were never beaten, a laudable desire, but not of vital importance in a world-wide war. Even when men began very properly to ask what the Fleet could do if it gained access to the Sea of Marmora, few connected the question with the continuance of the stubborn and unavailing efforts to overthrow the well-entrenched Turks in Gallipoli. These efforts were blindly continued, and many ingenious but evasive reasons were offered in apologetic excuse.

The Allied forces had been gradually reorganized after the First Battle of Krithia.

"SPLINTER VILLA."
A quaint name given to a dug-out by Australians.

A FRENCH SOLDIER GOING TO HELP A WOUNDED COMRADE.

Inset : Carrying a wounded Frenchman from the trenches.

Sir Ian Hamilton had at last been able to create a General Reserve. He had brought down the 2nd Australian Infantry Brigade and the New Zealand Brigade from Anzac, and had formed them, with a Naval Brigade consisting of the Plymouth and Drake Battalions, into a Composite Division, held in reserve. The 29th Division had been reconstituted into four brigades, consisting of the 88th and 87th Brigades, the Lancashire Fusilier Brigade (Territorials) and the 29th Indian Infantry Brigade. The French Corps had been reinforced by the 2nd Naval Brigade. On the first morning of the battle the 29th Division held the British line, the other portion of the front being held by the French Corps and the 2nd Naval Brigade. Communication between the two sections was maintained by the Plymouth and Drake Battalions. The broad purpose assigned to the 29th Division was to seize the ground about Krithia, while the French were to carry the ridge above the hollow through which ran the Kereves Dere. The French attack was very important, because unless it succeeded the left of the Allied front would have been advanced too far, and would have been in danger of being enfiladed.

The gallant 29th Division, wearied but undaunted, marched into battle at 11 a.m., supported by the fire of warships in the Gulf of Saros. The French 75 guns near the village of Sedd-ul-Bahr simultaneously opened fire upon the Turkish positions beyond the Kereves Dere, sending salvoes of four shells at a time. At 11.30 a.m. the French Corps advanced to the attack, the Senegalese troops leading. Some of the British warships endeavoured to help them by directing their fire into and beyond the Kereves Valley. The British advance on the left was steady but slow, for every yard was stubbornly contested by the Turkish sharp-shooters. A few isolated Turkish trenches were carried, but the main positions of the enemy were not reached at all. In two hours the line had advanced between two and three hundred yards, and three hours later it was still in the same position. The fight had raged backwards and forwards, but the front had not materially altered. The 88th Brigade was held up by a furious fire, apparently from concealed machine-guns, trained on a clump of fir-trees which the Brigade sought to carry. Time after time companies tried to storm the clump, but were repulsed. The Lancashire Fusiliers Brigade had also suffered much from machine guns. After the battle had continued on the British front for five hours the men were ordered to entrench where they stood. For that day, at any rate, their attack had practically failed. The French Corps had fared little better. They had topped the crest overlooking the river valley, to find themselves under a fire so galling that they could go no farther. Again and

again the Senegalese advanced, only to give way before the tremendous fusillade which greeted them. They had further discovered a concealed redoubt on their left which greatly impeded their movements. They were not even able to entrench until after dark. They had to face a bayonet attack during the night, but on the rest of the line the night was quiet.

The second day of the battle opened with a fierce bombardment from the warships directed against the ground around Krithia, before the British left. A watcher on a distant hill-top wrote that "the shell smothered every yard of the ground, and it seemed impossible for anyone to live within this zone, as the shrub and ravines were yellow with bursting lyddite." A quarter of an hour later, at about 10 a.m., the Lancashire Fusiliers Brigade moved out into the open to renew the attack. They had to cross the partially cultivated area near Krithia, but there was much dead ground, in which machine guns had been cleverly hidden. A terrific blast of fire greeted their appearance,

AN AUSTRALIAN FIRING A TRENCH MORTAR.

A MACHINE GUN IN THE TRENCHES.

and it was at once clear that the naval guns had neither destroyed nor demoralized the Turks. The brigade was unable to cross the open ground. Nevertheless, the advance progressed on their right, for the 88th Brigade pushed forward, and the 5th Royal Scots rushed the obnoxious fir clump. Its secret was immediately revealed, for it was full of Turkish snipers on platforms hidden away among the trees. The snipers were soon disposed of. The 1st Royal Inniskilling Fusiliers, of the 87th Brigade, moved up on the left of the 88th Brigade, and for a time it really seemed that further progress was possible. At 1.20 p.m., however, the Turks recaptured the firs in a counter-attack. The battle still hung in the balance. The plucky Inniskillings took three Turkish trenches, which were made good by the 1st King's Own Scottish Borderers. But the Lancashire Fusiliers were absolutely held in check by the cross-fire from machine guns, and at 3 p.m. they reported that they were "stuck." The French, on the right wing, had been quiet during the morning, but soon after 3 p.m. they gained some ground.

Sir Ian Hamilton decided to make one more supreme effort. He ordered a general attack for 4.45 p.m., at which hour the Turks brought fresh guns into action against the French on the right. The whole line advanced at the time named, and there was no sign either of fatigue or reluctance. The British made progress, except on their extreme left. The fir clump was carried once more with the bayonet. The French met an incessant shrapnel fire from the new Turkish guns, which was so disconcerting that their line wavered and melted away. General d'Amade threw forward his reserves, who quickly saved the situation. The British again advanced at 6.10 p.m., and far back at Sedd-ul-Bahr the khaki lines could be seen slowly moving onward. But they, too, were smothered by Turkish shrapnel, and at nightfall the combat slackened. The great effort had only met with a limited success.

It was resolved to make one more try next day. The tired troops again dug themselves in, and were not seriously molested in the darkness. The Lancashire Fusiliers Brigade was withdrawn into the reserve, and was

BRITISH TROOPS RETURNING FROM THE TRENCHES.

replaced by the New Zealand Brigade. Everything was made ready for a final attack after breakfast. Sir Ian Hamilton's reason for resolving to continue the battle was that he knew fresh Turkish reinforcements were coming up, and it was desirable to lose no time if he sought to snatch a victory.

On the third day, May 8, the action began afresh more fiercely than ever. for all ranks realized that success must be attained that day, if at all. Soon after 10 a.m. the warships resumed their bombardment, with equally little result, for when the New Zealand Brigade began to march on Krithia it instantly encountered a furious outburst of rifle and machine gun fire. The resolute New Zealanders pressed on, supported by the British artillery and by the machine guns of the 88th Brigade. Their centre got well beyond the fir clump, and was then checked, but by 1.30 p.m. the New Zealanders were 200 yards nearer Krithia than any unit had got before. Small parties of the 87th Brigade were meanwhile working through a ravine on the left, in the hope of getting in among the enemy's machine guns. An on-

looker who saw the whole New Zealand advance wrote :

It looked as if some annual manœuvres were taking place. Successive lines of khaki figures were pressing forward, across the green fields and through the farms and orchards, towards the firing line. The enemy's shrapnel burst over them, but inflicted small damage, owing to the open formations adopted. When each successive line reached the fire zone it doubled across the open ground, resting in the vacated trenches, and then passing on to the next. The whole of the plain seemed alive with these khaki-clad infantry. It was, indeed, a perfect example of the classical British attack, carried out over a broad front so as to concentrate the maximum number of men in the firing line for the final assault on the enemy's position with a minimum of loss.

But the Turks held back the attack, and the French over towards Kereves Dere sent word that they could move no further unless the British line advanced. There was a long lull, and many thought that the day was over. Sir Ian Hamilton was, however, concerting measures for the greatest moment of the battle. At 4 p.m. he ordered the whole line to fix bayonets, slope arms, and march on Krithia at 5.30 p.m. A quarter of an hour earlier the whole of the warships and every battery ashore opened " a most stupendous bombardment," and " the noise was appalling." The thunder of the guns died away, and long lines of glittering bayonets were seen moving outwards. They passed into the smoke-wreathed zone of the bombardment, and disappeared from view. The French vanished into the battle-smoke with drums beating and bugles sounding the charge. The whole scene was blotted out by the smoke, and when darkness fell the results were still only vaguely known. They can be told in a sentence. More ground was gained, but the Turkish line remained unbroken. Such was the end of the Second Battle of Krithia, and with it ended all hope of taking Krithia and Achi Baba by direct assault.

The full story of the closing episodes only became known next morning. The first lines of New Zealanders had passed the enemy's machine guns without discovering them, and their supports had suffered heavily in consequence. The brigade, which was commanded by Brigadier-General F. E. Johnston, had nevertheless got within a few yards of the Turkish trenches, and its first line had dug itself in. The 2nd Australian Infantry Brigade, under Brigadier-General the Hon. J. W. McCay, had shown equal valour, and though badly mauled, had won nearly 400 yards of ground. The 87th Brigade, under Major-General W. R.

Marshall, on the extreme left, had tried to advance over the open area between the ravine and the sea, but was checked by machine guns, which worked sad havoc among the South Wales Borderers. After sundown the men of the brigade begged to be led again against the enemy, and actually won another 200 yards. The French had been battered by the fire of the heaviest Turkish artillery, and though the 2nd Division attacked with ardour, the Senegalese broke. The attacking column was most gallantly rallied by General d'Amade and General Simonin in person. It recovered momentum, and stormed and held the redoubt at the end of the Kereves Dere hollow which had proved so troublesome. The 1st Division had very hard fighting in the Kereves valley, and a battalion of Zouaves was temporarily repulsed, but Lieut.-Colonel Nieger, of the 1st Regiment de Marche d'Afrique, gripped the position in the nick of time, and in the end the Division found itself master of "two complete lines of Turkish redoubts and trenches."

By general consent, the honours of the day on the British section of the front rested with the Anzacs, who suffered severely. They were warmly praised by Sir Ian Hamilton for their "determined valour," and for the "admirable tenacity" with which they clung to the ground they gained. The eye-witness already quoted, in describing the final attack wrote :

The New Zealanders and the Australians advanced at the same moment, over open ground which provided little or no cover. They were met by a tornado of bullets, and were enfiladed by machine guns from the right. The artillery in vain endeavoured to keep down this fire.

The manner in which these Dominion troops went forward will never be forgotten by those who witnessed it. The lines of infantry were enveloped in dust from the patter of countless bullets in the sandy soil and from the hail of shrapnel poured on them, for now the enemy's artillery concentrated furiously on the whole line. The lines advanced steadily, as if on parade, sometimes doubling, sometimes walking. They melted away under this dreadful fusillade, only to be renewed again, as reserves and supports moved forward to replace those who had fallen.

Although some ground was won, the broad result of the Second Battle of Krithia must be frankly said to have been failure. Sir Ian Hamilton admitted that it compelled him to realize that the operations had reached "the limit of what could be attained by mingling initiative with surprise." He observed :

Advances must more and more tend to take the shape of concentrated attacks on small sections of the enemy's line after full artillery preparation. Siege warfare was soon bound to supersede manœuvre battles in the open. Consolidation and fortification of our front, improvement of approaches, selection of machine-gun emplacements, and scientific grouping of our artillery under a centralized control must ere long form the tactical basis of our plans.

It is time to turn once more to Anzac, which had been strongly attacked on each day of the Second Battle of Krithia. The task of the Anzacs at Gaba Tepe was defined as being, first, "to keep open a door leading to the vitals of the Turkish position" ; and second, "to hold up as large a body of the enemy as possible," in order to lessen the strain at the end of the

BRITISH BATTERY IN ACTION ON A SAND-RIDGE.

AN ARMOURED CAR OF THE NAVAL DIVISION "GRAPNELLING" WIRE ENTANGLEMENTS.
A British car in Gallipoli uprooting and tearing down barbed-wire defences in front of a Turkish trench.

peninsula. The Anzacs were then holding a semi-circular position at the top of the cliff, with a diameter of about 1,100 yards. They were constantly under shell fire, and it was recorded that as many as 1,400 shells had fallen in this tiny area within an hour. All round the semi-circle the Turkish trenches were close at hand.

The Homeric conflicts on this little patch of ground above the cliffs were so incessant and so similar in character that probably even those who took part in them lost all count. They were never adequately recorded. One typical example of dozens of such encounters may be mentioned. On the night of May 2 the Anzacs, whose sturdy conception of acting on the defensive was to attack on every possible occasion, made a thrust at the Turks through a deep narrow ravine, which had been called "Monash Gully." They succeeded, and dug themselves in, but the Turks responded with a withering machine gun and shrapnel fire, and the position grew critical. The Anzacs were being hard hit, and the Chatham and Portsmouth Battalions of the Royal Marine Brigade were sent up the gully to their aid. It took the whole of the following day and the next night to consolidate the position, and in that one episode, so small that it found no mention in any dispatch, the Marines alone lost 500 officers and men killed and wounded. The First Battle of Anzac was so overshadowed by the Second Battle of Krithia that it received no allusion in the dispatch of Sir Ian Hamilton. It began on May 6, and practically lasted five days. For the first three days the Turks repeatedly attacked, and made desperate attempts to overwhelm the depleted Anzac forces. On the fourth day the 15th and 16th Battalions of the 4th Australian Infantry Brigade sallied forth with the bayonet and took three lines of Turkish trenches. On the fifth day, at dawn, the Turks retook the trenches but could make no impression on the main Australian position.

More reinforcements began to reach the British at Cape Helles. The 42nd Division was landed towards the end of the Second Battle of Krithia, and on May 11 the heroic 29th Division was withdrawn from the line for the first time for eighteen days and nights. The whole front before Krithia was divided into four sections, and regular siege warfare began.

On the night of May 12 H.M.S. Goliath, a

battleship of 12,950 tons, completed in 1902, was torpedoed off Morto Bay, in the entrance to the Straits, while she was protecting the French flank. Over 500 officers and men were lost, including the captain, and 20 officers and 160 men were saved. The occurrence was as startling as it was entirely unexpected. The Mouavenet-Milieh, 620 tons, a Turkish destroyer of German construction, built in 1909 at one of the Schichau yards, had slipped down the Straits under cover of darkness. She managed to torpedo the Goliath and to get back safely.

try to capture the position by escalade from the beach after dark. Their scouts had made a reconnaissance up the precipitous cliff on the night of May 10, when they were discovered by the enemy and fired upon. Major-General H. B. Cox, commanding the 29th Indian Infantry Brigade, then submitted an elaborate plan, which included a bombardment from the sea and shore, and an infantry demonstration, under cover of which the Gurkhas were to repeat their escalade in greater strength. The plan succeeded perfectly. At 6.30 p.m. on

"STRIPPED TO THE WAIST."
Anzacs working their guns on Gallipoli Peninsula.

The Goliath had been on the east coast of Africa before she went to the Dardanelles, and had bombarded Dar-es-Salaam.

The same night the British left was advanced nearly 500 yards by a successful stratagem. On a bluff north-east of Beach Y, which had been abandoned in the Battle of the Landing, the Turks had established a strong redoubt armed with machine guns, which constantly harried the British line. The Munsters and the Dublins unsuccessfully tried to take the bluff on May 8 and 9. Lieut.-Colonel the Hon. C. G. Bruce, of the 6th Gurkhas, himself an expert mountaineer, suggested that his men, who could climb like cats, should be allowed to

May 12 the cruisers Dublin and Talbot began to pour in shells, while the 29th Divisional Artillery bombarded from the British lines. The Manchester Brigade of the 42nd Division co-operated with rifle fire, and in the midst of the din a double company of the Gurkhas scaled the cliff and "carried the work with a rush." Another double company followed by the same route, and next morning the gain was consolidated and joined to the British front. The knoll was ever afterwards known as "Gurkha Bluff." The losses in this attack were 21 killed and 92 wounded. The early months at the Dardanelles teemed with such exploits, though perhaps few were so dramatic.

The French completed the disembarcation of a second Division during the second week in May, and on May 14 General Gouraud took over the command of the whole French Corps from General d'Amade. General Gouraud was 47 years of age, the youngest officer of his rank in the rejuvenated French Army, and he had been so successful in his command of the Argonne section of the front in France that his countrymen had dubbed him " the Lion of the Argonne." Sir Ian Hamilton sent the following letter of farewell to General d'Amade :

12th May, 1915.

MON GENERAL,—With deep personal sadness I learn that your country has urgent need of your great experience elsewhere.

From the very first you and your brave troops have done all, and more than all, that mortal man could do to further the cause we have at heart.

By day and by night, for many days and nights in succession, you and your gallant troops have ceaselessly struggled against the enemy's fresh reinforcements and have won from him ground at the bayonet point.

The military records of France are most glorious, but you, mon Général, and your Soldiers, have added fresh brilliancy if I may say so. even to those dazzling records

The losses have been cruel. Such losses are almost unprecedented, but it may be some consolation to think that only by so fierce a trial could thus have been fully disclosed the flame of patriotism which burns in the hearts of yourself and of your men.

With sincere regrets at your coming departure, but with the full assurance that, in your new sphere of activity, you will continue to render the same valuable service you have already given to France

I remain,

Mon Général,

Your sincere friend,

IAN HAMILTON,

General.

During the remainder of May, and for the first day or two of June, there was more fighting on the Anzac front than on any other part of the position. The Turks never liked Anzac, and were always fearful that the Anzacs might launch an attack against the heart of their stronghold overlooking the Narrows. At the outer edge of the Anzac curve was a spot known as Quinn's Post. It was so named after Major Quinn, of the 15th Australian Infantry, who met his death close to this very point during an Anzac counter-attack on May 29. At Quinn's Post the Anzac fire trenches were " mere ledges on the brink of a sheer precipice falling 200 feet into the valley below." The enemy's trenches were a few feet away, and the post was never securely held until some weeks later a body of New Zealand miners made elaborate underground shelters. Quinn's Post was soon renowned for its unending series of sorties, attacks and counter-attacks. For instance, on May 9 the Anzacs carried the enemy's trenches before Quinn's Post by bayonet attack at night. On May 10 the enemy counter-attacked at dawn and won the trenches back, but they were so severely dealt with by the Anzac guns that, according to records afterwards captured, two Turkish regiments alone lost on that day 600 killed and 2,000 wounded. There were no safe corners at Anzac, and even the generals in high command had to disregard the usual wise precautions and take the same risks as the men. On May 14 Lieut.-General Sir W. R. Birdwood was slightly wounded, but did not relinquish his command. Next day Major-General Sir W. T. Bridges, commanding the Australian Division, was so severely wounded that he died in a few days. Sir Ian Hamilton wrote of him that he was " sincere and single-minded in his devotion to Australia and to duty."

During May 18 reports of unusual activity among the enemy came to Anzac from many sources. The warships could see troops massing at various points near the coast. The airmen saw other bodies of troops landing near the Narrows and moving across from the direction of the Pasha Dagh. The Turkish bombardment grew in intensity throughout the day.

IN THE TRENCHES.

Using the Periscope.

TURKISH PRISONERS

Being led through a deep gully. Inset: Giving a
drink to a wounded Turk.

Shells rained upon Anzac from 12-inch and
9-inch guns, big howitzers, and field guns.
The portents were not misleading. General
Liman von Sanders himself proposed to clear
away the Anzac thorn by throwing it into the
sea. He had planned a great attack, and was
about to fling massed columns, numbering
30,000 in all, against the Anzac zone. Word
passed down to the trenches for the defenders
to be alert and ready

At midnight the storm burst, and machine
gun and rifle fire of unprecedented volume and
force was concentrated on the Anzacs. They
lay snug in their trenches, and were very little
injured. At 4 a.m. the Second Battle of Anzac
began, and a dense Turkish column advanced
to the assault. It was beaten back, chiefly by
rifle fire. Other columns followed, and various
sectors of the Anzac line were assaulted in turn.
At 5 a.m. the Turkish attack had so far
developed that it had become general, and the
heavy artillery was once more participating.
For the next five hours the enemy strained
every nerve to press their onslaught home.
They never had a chance of succeeding. No
Turkish foot ever touched a single Anzac
trench that day. The close Turkish formations were mown down. The Turks died in
heaps. The battle became a butchery, for the
Anzac field guns and howitzers were doing their
share of execution. The attack of General
Liman von Sanders was sheer folly, and the
punishment of his unhappy instruments was
terrible. When the fight ended he had lost at
least a fourth of his attacking force, for it was

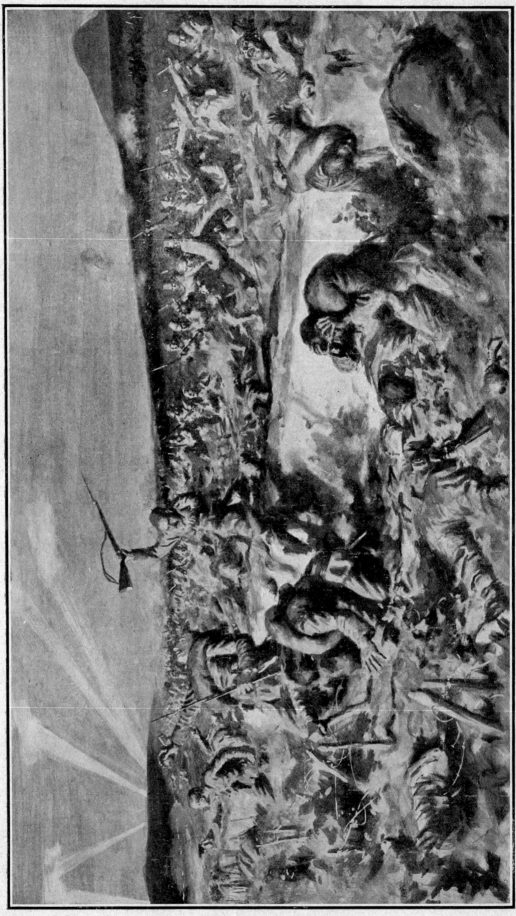

TURKISH NIGHT ATTACK NEAR ACHI BABA.

estimated that the Turkish losses on that one morning alone numbered over 7,000. The estimate was moderate, and was perhaps too low. Over 3,000 Turks lay dead within actual view of the Anzac trenches. In one corner, 100 yards by 80 yards, 400 corpses were counted. A large proportion of the losses were afterwards found to have been caused by artillery fire. The Anzac losses numbered about 100 killed and 500 wounded, including nine officers wounded. There were few more remarkable examples in any theatre of the war of the disproportionate advantage which modern weapons sometimes confer upon the defence in prepared positions.

A visitor who went round the Anzac front lines after the battle wrote :

The ground presents an extraordinary sight when viewed through the trench periscopes. Two hundred yards away, and even closer in places, are the Turkish trenches, and between them and our lines the dead lie in hundreds. There are groups of twenty or thirty massed together, as if for mutual protection, some lying on their faces, some killed in the act of firing ; others hung up in the barbed wire. In one place a small group actually reached our parapet, and now lie dead on it shot at point-blank range or bayonetted. Hundreds of others lie just outside their own trenches, where they were caught by rifles and shrapnel when trying to regain them. Hundreds of wounded must have perished between the lines.

There were some curious negotiations during the days following the Second Battle of Anzac. At 5 p.m. on May 20 the Turks displayed white flags and Red Crescents, and various Turkish officers came out into the open. They were met by Major-General H. B. Walker, commanding the Australian Division, and asked for an armistice to bury their dead and collect their wounded. General Walker pointed out that he was not empowered to treat, and in any case the principal Turkish officer had no credentials. It was noticed that the Turks were massing afresh, and General Birdwood ordered all trenches to be manned as a precaution. The Turkish object seemed to be to effect a fresh concentration without being harassed by artillery fire. Towards sunset masses of Turks advanced behind lines of unarmed men holding up their hands. Intense firing broke out, and was continued until 1.20 a.m., when the enemy attacked Quinn's Post in strength. They were beaten back, and these strange proceedings, which had a strong flavour of German inspiration, came to an end. When Sir Ian Hamilton heard what had happened, he sent Major-General W. P. Braithwaite, C.B., on May 22 to assist General Birdwood in further negotiations. General Braithwaite was

the Chief of the General Staff at the Dardanelles, and Sir Ian Hamilton described him as the best Chief-of-Staff he had ever known in war. A formal armistice was then arranged with the Turks, and lasted from 7.30 a.m. to 4.30 p.m. on May 24. Considerations of health made such a truce desirable. The Turkish burying parties were supplied with cotton wool soaked in solution to deaden the stench. They worked expeditiously, and the armistice was scrupulously observed by both sides. But thereafter, until June 5, there was more exciting fighting of the episodical kind around Quinn's Post than even that most unrestful corner had ever known. A whole chapter could be filled with descriptions of the stirring events of those ten days on that one section of the Anzac front alone.

A new menace against the Allied Fleet at the Dardanelles developed during the month of May. Weeks earlier large German submarines had been seen going south through the Bay of Biscay, and afterwards near Gibraltar and off the north coast of Africa. Neither the Admiralty nor Admiral de Robeck were for a moment under any illusions about the meaning of these movements. Admiral von Tirpitz was about to take a hand in the Ægean, and his move was difficult to counter. The Army needed support from the naval guns. On the other hand, even old battleships could not be kept stationary near the peninsula to be picked off like sitting partridges. The first result of the news was that the Queen Elizabeth was hurried back to the North Sea, despite the anxious though unwarranted representations of the War Office. The other battleships were gradually removed, and certain effective refuges from submarines were prepared for those which remained. Great risks had to be taken, however. Until the new shallow-draught monitors, then being built in England, could be sent out, some at least of the battleships had to lie at times off the Dardanelles coast in very exposed positions.

According to Mr. Ellis Ashmead-Bartlett, whose accounts of the first months at Gallipoli must always be of inestimable value to historians, the earliest sign of the presence of enemy submarines off the Dardanelles was detected on May 22. As a consequence, H.M.S. Albion went ashore in a fog off Anzac at 4 a.m. next morning. H.M.S. Canopus came to her rescue, but it took six hours to get the stranded battleship off the sandbank on which she had

REAR-ADMIRAL STUART NICHOLSON, M.V.O.,
Leaving the Naval Observation Station and making his way to Cape Helles.
Inset: Rear-Admiral Nicholson.
(*Photo by Elliott & Fry.*)

grounded. During all that time both battle-ships were under a strong fire from Turkish field guns, but fortunately the Turks were not able to bring heavy guns to bear. On the morning of May 25, at 8 a.m., a submarine was seen and fired upon by H.M.S. Swiftsure, but the shots took no effect. The submarine made off towards Anzac, chased by British destroyers. At 10.30 a.m. she unsuccessfully fired a torpedo at the battleship Vengeance, near Gaba Tepe. At lunch-time H.M.S. Triumph (Captain Maurice Fitzmaurice, R.N.), a battleship of 11,800 tons displacement, originally built for the Chilian Government, was torpedoed and sunk south of Gaba Tepe. She had her torpedo-nets out, but both the two torpedoes fired at her pierced the netting and took effect. Eight minutes after being struck she turned turtle, and she finally plunged beneath the waves half-an-hour after-wards. The captain and nearly all the crew were saved by destroyers.

All the available destroyers and patrols set out in search of the two submarines, for another had been seen off Rabbit Island. H.M.S. Swiftsure was sent to the protected waters of Mudros Harbour, and the Admiral's flag was transferred to H.M.S. Majestic (Captain H. F. G. Talbot, R.N.), the oldest battleship on the station, displacement 14,900 tons, built in 1895. On the night of May 26 the Majestic was anchored off Cape Helles, opposite Beach W, and inside a line of transports. At 6.40 a.m. next morning a submarine found and torpedoed her. At once she listed heavily, and in a very few moments she was lying on her side. The officers and crew took to the water, and all the vessels near hastily sent launches and small boats. Very few lives were lost. The Majestic sank quickly in shallow water, and as her bows were resting on a sandbank a small piece of her ram remained exposed to view. Mr. Ashmead-

Bartlett, who was among those rescued, stated: —" As she turned over and sank, a sailor ran the whole length of her keel and finally sat astride the ram, where he was subsequently taken off without even getting a wetting." Thousands of troops on shore saw the disaster. Captain Talbot was picked up by a launch, but afterwards plunged in again and rescued two of his men from drowning. Although these losses caused considerable apprehension, for a long time afterwards the German submarines were much harried and met with little further success·

The British losses in killed, wounded, and missing at the Dardanelles up to May 31 numbered in all 38,636, including 1,722 officers. Thus in this one theatre alone there had been more casualties in less than six weeks than were recorded during the whole of the South African War, when the casualties in conflict numbered 38,156, spread over a period of three years.

The Third Battle of Krithia was fought on June 4, and was finished in one day. Both British and French had been sapping and mining during the latter half of May, preparatory to a further attempt to rush the Turkish trenches. There had been more than one small advance, and the Turks had delivered many attacks without definite result. Sir Ian Hamilton deemed that the time had come for a further concerted and general effort. In the Third Battle of Krithia large losses were inflicted on the Turks, and there was a gain of from 200 to

400 yards over three miles of front ; but much of the ground won in the early stages of the battle could not be retained, because the Turks drove in the French left in a powerful counter-attack, and the British line was in consequence enfiladed. The British and French losses were also heavy. One sentence in Sir Ian Hamilton's dispatch told its own story. " The Collingwood battalion of the Royal Naval Division," he wrote, " which had gone forward in support, (was) practically destroyed."

The line of battle was formed, from right to left, by the French Corps, the Royal Naval Division, the 42nd (East Lancashire) Division, and the 29th Division. The British had 24,000 men massed on a front of 4,000 yards, and General Hunter-Weston, now commanding the 8th Army Corps, had 7,000 men as a corps reserve. The enemy's position had by this time been developed into rows and rows of trenches stretching right across the peninsula. Achi Baba was honeycombed with works and galleries, and crowned by a strong redoubt. " The barrier," wrote a special correspondent the day before the battle, " constitutes one of the strongest defensive positions any army has held or captured during the present war." The facts might have been even more strongly defined. The battle began with an intense land and sea bombardment at 8 a.m., which continued for 2½ hours, stopped for half an hour, and then resumed for twenty minutes,

A BATTERY OF FRENCH 75's ON A SAND RIDGE.
(Exclusive to "The Times.")

THE LAST MOMENTS OF H.M.S. MAJESTIC,
Torpedoed off Gallipoli, May 27, 1915.

SURVIVORS OF H.M.S. TRIUMPH

Arrive on board H.M.S. Lord Nelson. The Triumph was torpedoed by a submarine at the Dardanelles on May 26, 1915. Inset: The Captain's clerk of H.M.S. Triumph who swam with the ship's ledger until he was picked up by a destroyer.

after which a brief feint attack was made. At 11.30 the Allies recommenced their bombardment, which continued until noon, when the signal was given for a general advance. Accompanied by parties of bomb-throwers, the whole line dashed forward with bayonets fixed. The assault met with swift success. The French 1st Division, on the extreme right, took the trenches before them, and the French 2nd Division stormed and captured the strong "Haricot" redoubt at the head of the Kereves Dere hollow, which previously they had three times sought in vain to seize. The weak spot was at the point of contact between the French and British forces, on the extreme left of the French front. There the Turks, who were well served by communication trenches, developed rapid counter-attacks and effected a marked check. Their discovery of a flaw in the line eventually changed the aspect of the whole battle.

The Royal Naval Division, next in the line, fought with the utmost gallantry, and never did better than it did that day. In fifteen minutes the naval men had charged the Turkish trenches and obtained possession of the whole position immediately before them. The Anson battalion stormed a Turkish redoubt which formed a salient in the enemy's line, and the Howe and Hood battalions were consolidating captured Turkish lines by 12.25 p m. The

Manchester Brigade of the 42nd Division did even better, and wrought deeds which made their city thrill with pride, while they made the name of the Territorial Force immortal. The Manchester Brigade carried the first line of trenches before them within five minutes. By 12.30 they had advanced a third of a mile, overwhelmed the second Turkish line, and were calmly establishing themselves in their new position. Lancashire, Ireland, Australia, and New Zealand share the tragic glories of Gallipoli. The 29th Division, on the

THE CHARGE OF THE ROYAL NAVAL DIVISION.

left, was soon desperately engaged. The 88th Brigade had a fierce bayonet struggle with the Turks, but with the Worcesters in the van, the entire brigade swarmed into the Turkish first line and could not be dislodged. On the extreme left was the Indian Brigade, which was much baffled by barbed wire entanglements which the British artillery fire had failed to destroy. The 14th Sikhs lost three-fourths of their effectives while checked by these obstacles, and a company of the 6th Gurkhas, which had gone along the cliffs, was temporarily isolated. Eventually the Indian Brigade had to withdraw to its original line, where it was reinforced.

But the shining success of noontide did not endure. The Turks had poured in a terrific counter-attack against the French in the Haricot redoubt, which they regained with the aid of their well-served guns. The French fell back, and thereby exposed the Royal Naval Division to enfilading fire. The Ansons had to relinquish their redoubt with heavy loss, and the Howe and Hood battalions were in turn enfiladed and forced back across open ground under a terrible rifle and machine-gun fire. It was while rendering succour to these harassed battalions that the Collingwoods met with such a disastrous fate. It may be noted that in the early phase of the action the Naval Division had been supported by its armoured motor-

cars, armed with maxims. By 1.30 p.m. the Naval Division had lost all its new trenches, and was back on its old line, and the enemy were enfilading the Manchesters in their turn. The fire was maddening, and the Manchesters were cruelly reduced in numbers. They lost their brigadier and many other officers, but Lancashire grit was not to be intimidated. For five hours the Manchester men stuck to their position in the hope that the Turks who were enfilading them would be driven back. They faced round their right flank to confront the foes who had got such an advantageous position. Reinforcements were sent to them. The Royal Naval Division was told to co-operate with the French in a fresh attack, timed for 3 p.m. Twice General Gouraud postponed the advance, and at 6.30 the gallant French commander was obliged to report that he was unable to move. The Manchesters had to be brought back to the first line of captured trenches, and such was the spirit of the men that when first told to withdraw they refused to move. The Royal Fusiliers had meanwhile made a local advance, but they were also directed to withdraw, in order to maintain an even front. The French 1st Division was twice counter-attacked during the succeeding night, but with this exception the conflict had ended before nightfall. Most of the reserves had been brought into the firing line, and it was not considered desirable to renew the attack next day. The British took 400 prisoners, including 11 officers, and most of these captures were effected by the 42nd Division, which was commanded by Major-General W. Douglas. The prisoners included five Germans who formed part of a machine-gun crew furnished by the Goeben. The Third Battle of Krithia could not be counted a success. Much of its original gains were lost, and its chief result was to reveal the increasing strength of the enemy's resistance.

The French had a brilliant action to themselves on June 21, when they fought from dawn to dark with the object of seizing the Turkish works overlooking the hollow of the Kereves Dere. By noon the 2nd Division had stormed two lines of trenches, and captured again the coveted Haricot redoubt. On the right the 1st Division struggled for hours to take lines of Turkish trenches, which passed into the alternate possession of Frenchmen and Turks time after time. General Gouraud made a last inspiring call to the 1st Division at 2.45 p.m. He said that if the trenches were not taken before dark the gains of the 2nd Division would be lost. The youngsters who had been brought out from France to reinforce the 1st Division responded nobly. Their general had his wish, and by 6.30 the whole of the positions above the Kereves Dere were in French possession. A battalion of the Foreign Legion and a battalion of Zouaves made the brilliant final charge which ensured complete success. During the day the French battleship Saint Louis bombarded the Turkish artillery on the Asiatic side of the Straits from a point near Kum Kale. No more notable, compact, or valuable action was fought by the French during the whole of the operations on the peninsula. The French losses during the day were 2,500, and the enemy's casualties were estimated at 7,000. General Gouraud was badly wounded by a shell on June 30, and the command of the French Corps passed to General Bailloud. The injuries to General Gouraud proved very serious, and on his passage back to France it was found necessary to amputate his right arm. His right thigh and left leg were broken. Vice-Admiral Nicol, the youngest vice-admiral in the French Navy, had been appointed some days earlier to command the French Fleet at the Dardanelles, Rear-Admiral Guépratte remaining as second in command.

The heartening French success had marked the end of the phase of general attacks all along the line, for which sectional attacks were thenceforth substituted. On June 28 the British left repeated in an even more striking manner the French victory on the right. The Turks had always been very strong, and extremely pertinacious, on the coast of the Gulf of Saros, opposite the British left. They were helped by a deep cleft, known as the Gully Ravine, which ran inwards towards Krithia from a point near Beach Y; and the action of June 28 was recorded as the Battle of the Gully Ravine. The plan of the attack was prepared by General Hunter-Weston, and the battle was fought by the 29th Division, the 156th Brigade of the Lowland Division, and the

Elliott & Fry.

MAJOR-GENERAL W. R. MARSHALL
Who commanded the 87th Brigade.

Indian Brigade. The 29th Division had lost a very large proportion of its original effectives, and some battalions had not a single officer left of those who landed on April 25; but large drafts had been sent out, and the Division was up to strength. The attack delivered was in the form of an arc; five trenches had to be carried near the sea, but only two farther inland. There was the usual artillery preparation, and H.M.S. Talbot (carefully guarded by destroyers and trawlers) steamed round Cape Tekke and enfiladed the nearest Turkish trenches with her fire. The enemy seemed short of ammunition, and throughout the day their field guns fired less than 300 rounds. The 10th Battery, R.F.A., did effective work in smashing wire entanglements, and the French had lent some trench mortars which proved useful. The bombardment, which began at 9 a.m., lasted nearly two hours. Just before 11 the 1st Battalion of the

Border Regiment rushed a small work called by the British "Boomerang Fort," on the right of the ravine. Ten minutes later the 87th Brigade (the King's Own Scottish Borderers, Royal Inniskilling Fusiliers, and South Wales Borderers), commanded by Major-General W. R. Marshall, stormed three lines of Turkish trenches between the ravine and the sea. Many Turks were found to have been buried in the trenches by the bombardment, but about 100 surrendered. On the right of the ravine the 4th and 7th Royal Scots of the Lowland Division took two lines of trenches, but the remainder of the 156th Brigade were checked by the Turkish fire. At 11.30 the 86th Brigade, led by the 2nd Royal Fusiliers, passed through the three trenches held by the 87th Brigade and took the remaining two trenches on the coast. The Indian Brigade had meanwhile moved along the cliffs and seized a spur running from the west of the furthest captured Turkish trench to the sea. This was the limit of the British objective. The trenches on the right of the attack, nearer Krithia, were not taken. The enemy made several counter-attacks on the two following nights, but without avail. The British losses in this spirited action were 1,750, and they were considered small. The distinguishing feature of the engagement was the splendid culminating charge of the 86th Brigade. The gains were definite and considerable; "a whole mile along the coast, five lines of Turkish trenches, about 200 prisoners, three mountain guns, and an immense quantity of small arms ammunition and many rifles." No action since the first landing did more to cheer the British forces. It seemed to promise further progress. The Turks had been turned out of strong positions, and had been utterly unable to retake them.

Mr. Ashmead-Bartlett, who visited the Gully Ravine next day, wrote:

All the way up that portion of the gully, only 24 hours before in the enemy's possession, there is a litter of *débris* of the camp and of the great fight. Scattered bodies half protruding from the ground, hastily-dug graves, hundreds of rifles and bayonets, some broken, but the majority intact, thousands upon thousands of rounds of ammunition—we made a very big haul indeed in this last engagement—entrenching tools, loaves of bread, soldiers' packs, Turkish letters, a Mullah's prayer stool (a souvenir eagerly sought after), great coats and kits, blankets and old sacks, cooking utensils, and firewood, left just where the enemy abandoned them when our gallant infantry broke through at the bayonet's point. Great fires are burning at intervals. They are avoided by all, and give forth a horrid, a sickly stench. On these the Turkish dead, who have been hastily collected, are being burnt, for it is all important

to get the dead out of the way as quickly as possible in this hot climate.

The last prominent episode at Gallipoli during June was a determined attack upon Anzac, personally directed by Enver Pasha. He had come down from Constantinople, and ordered the Army to drive the Australians and New Zealanders into the sea. On the night of June 29 a heavy musketry and artillery fire developed at midnight, principally against that portion of the Anzac front commanded by Major-General Sir A. J. Godley. At 1.30 a.m. a heavy column advanced to attack, and was quickly broken by the rifles and machine guns of the 7th and 8th Light Horse. Another attack an hour later against the left and left centre melted away with equal rapidity, and Enver returned to the capital, presumably discomfited.

There was further heavy fighting during July, which will be dealt with later; but the essential fact of the situation at the Dardanelles at the end of June was that the difficulties were increasing daily. Sir Ian Hamilton thus summed up a portion of them:

The efforts and expedients whereby a great army has had its wants supplied upon a wilderness have, I believe, been breaking world records.

The country is broken, mountainous, arid, and void of supplies; the water found in the areas occupied by our forces is quite inadequate for their needs; the only practicable beaches are small, cramped breaks in impracticable lines of cliffs; with the wind in certain quarters no sort of landing is possible: the wastage, by bombardment and wreckage, of lighters and small craft has led to crisis after crisis in our carrying capacity, whilst over every single beach plays fitfully throughout each day a devastating shell fire at medium ranges.

Upon such a situation appeared quite suddenly the enemy submarines. On May 22 all transports had to be dispatched to Mudros for safety. Thenceforth men, stores, guns, horses, etc., etc., had to be brought from Mudros—a distance of 40 miles—in fleet sweepers and other small and shallow craft less vulnerable to submarine attack. Every danger and every difficulty was doubled.

A far more vital factor was the formidable and growing strength of the Turkish positions. It was true that sectional attacks, such as that at the Gully Ravine, had proved successful; but there were 50 miles of ravines on the Gallipoli Peninsula, and the Turks seemed ready to contest each one of them. The end of June was clearly another period at which careful re-examination of the whole problem should have been made in London. The problem did receive some consideration, but the only result was the acceptance of plans for a fresh landing north of Anzac and the dispatch of large fresh forces, who went straight to disaster on the rolling and arid uplands above Suvla Bay.

CHAPTER XCIX.

THE SPIRIT OF ANZAC.

AUSTRALIA'S PREPAREDNESS FOR WAR—THE NAVY—WAR LEGISLATION—DOMINION LEADERS—GENESIS OF THE ANZACS—THE EXPEDITION TO GALLIPOLI—HISTORY OF THE CAMPAIGN—AUSTRALASIAN EPISODES AND ACHIEVEMENTS—DEEDS OF VALOUR—THE SITUATION AT HOME—RELATIONS WITH THE BRITISH GOVERNMENT—MUNITIONS AND OTHER WAR WORK—NEW ZEALAND—AUSTRALIAN FINANCE—THE TRAGEDY OF GALLIPOLI—MR. FISHER AS HIGH COMMISSIONER IN LONDON.

AUSTRALIA and New Zealand from the beginning played their part in the war with vigour and wholeheartedness. Their enthusiasms rivalled those of the Mother Country, and their direct and practical methods gave promise of valuable developments in the governance of Empire. The Imperial structure had been prepared for war so far as war had been foreseen. But an abundance of thinly developed Imperial Defence schemes, and of advice from the Imperial General Staff on early steps to be taken to protect local interests, was not real military preparedness. Of the Dominions generally, it must be said that their military strength was unorganized, although it was a potential military strength fully half that of the Mother Country. A few months before the war an effort had been made in New Zealand and Australia to prepare more definite plans, and the leading military officers, on the advice of the Imperial General Staff, had suggested that certain sections of the Dominions' armies should be organized on the basis of expeditionary forces, ready at a few days' notice to move to any part of the Empire. In Australia certain Scottish militia battalions were to be allowed to wear kilts, instead of the distinctive Australian Garibaldi uniform, in recognition of their pledge to go where the Empire required their services. The reception of this scheme was distinctly unfavourable,

because neither Australia nor New Zealand had concluded the organization of its home-defence civilian armies.

No such risks had been run with preparations on sea. The Australian Navy, purposely kept at greater strength than that of Germany in the Pacific, was ready to take its station in the Admiralty's prearranged plans. The ships were maintained at an efficiency very nearly bordering on complete mobilization, and their part in the event of war had been mapped out in detail. The organization was used for protecting the trade routes, for snapping up Germany's possessions in the Pacific and for destroying her commerce. These objects were so efficiently pursued that the German Navy was unable to interfere with a single British ship in the South Pacific. Our commerce proceeded as in times of peace, except for variations in routes ; and the strong German squadron could do no more damage than a " thorough " but easily remedied disturbance of the Pacific Cable Board's station on Fanning Island. When this scourge was removed, H.M.A.S. Australia, a battle-cruiser paid for and maintained by direct Australian taxation, took her place among her sister ships in Admiral Beatty's battle-cruiser fleet, leading the second squadron ; and the light cruisers, torpedo craft and submarines filled their respective rôles. The Australia reached northern waters too late for the engagement of January 24, but she had an

OFF TO THE FRONT.

Sir George Reid, the High Commissioner for Australia, inspecting an Australian Contingent at Romsey.

unequalled steaming record to her credit, and she soon earned a reputation for cleanliness and readiness. The Grand Fleet dubbed her the " wallaby ship," because her mixed Australian and British crew received " wallaby " rates of pay. Their physique was unequalled in the Fleet, and their keenness for battle was intense.

There were soon regrets in Australasia that a better perspective of the war had not been obtained in these early months. The difficulties of judgment can readily be seen from the uncertainties which characterized the situation everywhere. No Australian leader had felt quite certain that many thousands of the country's young men would leave their new homes and friends and risk all for a cause that seemed assured of quick victory. On the eve of the appeal for the first twenty thousand men, several of the political leaders felt some anxiety as to whether reinforcements could be promised in addition. It was not at once recognized that war had precipitated a spirit of supreme self-effacement. During those months the public showed eagerness to spend all, and there was far more restlessness at the lack of demand for sacrifices than there was contentment with the part, vigorous though it was, that Australasia was playing. Throughout cities and country, private opportunities

for sharing the trials of the Allies were eagerly sought. Goods of high value and extraordinary assortment were given to the Defence Department. It became almost a mark of lack of sympathy to ride in a motor-car which was not doing some war work, or on a horse which had not been offered to the troops. Estates were handed over to the Government for use as camping grounds, large gifts of flour and meat were made for the armies. By November, 1915, the sums contributed to the War Funds in Australia amounted to more than three millions and a half sterling. Of this, nearly one million was subscribed for Belgian relief, a cause that secured a great outpouring of sympathy in Australia. More than that sum was raised for the benefit of Australian wounded. In one day £700,000 was raised for the " Australia Day " Fund. South Australia alone contributed £250,000, or ten shillings per head of population. The demonstrations of private generosity were no less conspicuous in New Zealand. The sinking in the English Channel by a German submarine of a ship specially chartered to carry chosen gifts from the people of New Zealand to those of Belgium did more than many official cables to make the Dominions realize the conditions prevailing in Europe. All the people asked was that their whole resources should be mobilized and thrown into the scale. They asked that the cost should be shared, that it should be a national effort, and that all should be spent rather than defeat risked. True, there was a certain feeling, encouraged by official delays in London, that Australasian strength could not weigh in the scales. Only a small section of Australasia really believed that their country itself was in danger from the Germans. The appeal for military action could not be a direct appeal for defence of Australian homes. Everything done was done, as in other parts of the Empire, from broad and honourable motives of pursuing the common cause of the Empire.

Towards the Germans in Australasia restrained but obstinate feeling was displayed. Throughout the latter half of the last century Germany provided Australasia with more immigrants than any other foreign country. They were for the most part Prussians, Bavarians, and Saxons, who went into farming districts where the pioneering had already been done. They formed their colonies, and German was the language spoken in several thickly settled districts in South Australia, and in a few localities in the Geelong district of Victoria and the Riverina district of New South Wales. Some

efforts were made by Berlin to organize pro-German opinion before the war, and an energetic Consul-General, Herr Kiliani, toured the German settlements with a retinue of naval officers. Though many Germans made conditions unpleasant for themselves and compelled the creation of large concentration camps, in which they were interned, and though it could not be said that the sympathies of the older German colonists were wholly alienated from their Fatherland, a remarkable cordiality towards the land of their adoption was the outstanding characteristic of the problem which their presence raised. Their Church Synods passed resolutions supporting the cause of Australia, and they sent their sons with the expeditionary forces. Many German

THE NEW ZEALAND FLAG
Flying over the New Zealand Hospital, Cairo.

assemblies which had found fondness for Germany as they remembered it stronger than their loyalty for the country which had given them their homes hurried to renounce their old faith when the Lusitania was sunk. The number of German names in the Australian casualty lists must have struck every observer. These men for the most part would not admit that they were fighting for Great Britain; they were at war for Australia, which they were bound to defend. The distinctive characteristics of Australia and its people, the newness and freshness of life there, had thus captured the Australian-Germans of the second generation.

The strongest demonstration against aliens came after the loss of the Lusitania, when wild riots occurred, and the Governments closed all German clubs and halls and interned large numbers of men. Germans were compelled to

THE NEW ZEALAND FLAG IN EGYPT.
Lady Maxwell (wife of General Sir John Maxwell, commander of His Majesty's forces in Egypt) unfurling the flag at the New Zealand Hospital, Cairo.

WAR HORSES FOR THE FRONT.
Australians returning to camp after breaking-in remounts.

resign from public positions. No one whose patriotism and support of the war was not intense could remain in any official situation. In South Australia the Attorney-General, Mr Homberg, although his sympathies were beyond question, resigned from office in face of public feeling. The public resented the treatment given to the interned men, many of whom had been earning scanty livings as bandsmen and had been interned at their own request, in conformity with international law. The imprisoned Germans showed their inherent capacity for orderliness by making the internment camps models of well-lit, well-built, and well-managed institutions. Australians had to confess that these were better camps than their own military encampments. The New Zealand Germans were interned on an island in shark-infested Wellington Harbour, where they could do what they liked without troubling anybody. The Imperial Government used the comparative harmlessness of German concentration camps in Australasia to good advantage, and large numbers of Germans arrested for internment in Ceylon and other dependencies were taken charge of by the Australasian authorities. The New Zealand public demanded a wholesale rounding up of the alien enemies in the Dominion, and included a section of the naturalized Germans. But the policy of both Dominions was to follow Imperial advice in all

matters affecting international law, a rough and ready line of demarcation faithfully followed by all the Dominions.

The measures of Federal and State Parliaments to adapt life to war conditions became of lasting interest to the rest of the Empire because of their courageousness. In the attitude towards the enemy nothing was left to chance. No attacks were made on things German simply because they were German. But the Attorney-General of the Federal Ministry, Mr. William Morris Hughes, who introduced the principal Acts, and who was throughout the principal spokesman of the irreconcilable anti-German community, gave his countrymen a satisfying feeling that nothing remained undone through lack of detestation of the enemy. His rights under the Patents Acts disappeared. The rush for naturalization was abruptly stopped. The German hold on Australian industries was gradually relaxed. Acts controlling alien enemies gave drastic powers to the authorities. Under the Trading with the Enemy Act prosecutions showed marked determination to root out the evil, regardless of the standing of the persons concerned. The military authorities were encouraged to make searches of establishments where business with Germans had previously been done. In one such place a collection of rifles was found, but no attempt at organized rebellion was discovered, nor indeed

FROM AUSTRALIA'S SMALLEST STATE.
Soldiers from Victoria on a route march.

would it have had the slightest support of any large body of Australian Germans. Apart from such measures and the long and hard fight for release of the metal industry from German control, the attention of the Governments was fully occupied in raising the armies and in regulating the new industrial situation. In all States and in New Zealand drastic methods were taken to prevent exploitation of the public's new circumstances. Legislation instituting boards to fix prices was hurried through. Thus in New South Wales, where the State Government commandeered wheat and founded State bakeries, the price of flour remained considerably lower than the world price. The Government acquired more than 300,000 bushels of wheat from its farmers at a set price of 5s. a bushel, when the world price was over 8s. These boards met with varying success, and their utility changed with the seasons. They could not prevent an increase of nearly 30 per cent. in the cost of living, but it was noticeable that the increase was lowest in those States in which their work was continuous. As trade became more settled the tribunals relaxed their activities, until, after a year of war, only a few fixed maximum prices remained.

For many months the State legislatures seemed unable to settle down to any legislation not directly bearing on the war, and they gave the bulk of their time to reforms in the industrial legislation and to directing the employment of men who had lost their occupations owing to restriction of employment. It must be remembered that, unlike the United Kingdom and Canada, Australia received little share of the munition and war material manufacture which maintained industrial activity at a high standard elsewhere. Yet there was no part of the Empire where relations between employers and their men remained on such excellent terms. The unions never attempted to bring pressure upon employers by threats of strikes. The severe limitation of profits on war contracts, followed by the decision of the Federal Ministry to commandeer all profits on war material manufactures above the average percentage for the three years preceding the war, satisfied the workers that their industries were not being exploited for the gain of the masters.

The policy enunciated at first from seemingly authoritative sources, that of " keeping Australia going with as little hindrance to sound industry and local development as possible," never had more than a temporary popularity. Australia worked as if war was at its own doors, and an invader was being dealt with. Women on all sides engaged on a mass of ill-directed war work which at any rate eased their minds. There was a great national demand to have an individual part in the war, and where the

Governments failed to provide outlet for energies private organisations stepped in. Rifle clubs were thronged with new members, new clubs sprang up in all parts of the country. Volunteers for home service pressed their claims upon the Defence Department, and when refused official recognition formed large organizations of their own. In New South Wales, where the movement was led by the ex-Minister of Education, the Hon. Campbell Carmichael, M.L.A., who later formed a battalion of 1,000 sharpshooters from his reservists and enlisted for service with them as a private, 20,000 ablebodied men were enrolled in a fortnight. The idea behind these organizations, which

organized criticism from the Opposition benches. Both Dominions went through the pangs of general elections, and five Australian States had State elections close upon the heels of the Federal elections. These did not excite the outbursts of feeling which formerly characterized Australasian political contests. It was common for rival meetings on opposite street corners to end about the same time, and the notes of the National Anthem would arise from the opposing camps. In the Parliaments, the Governments had only to say that their measures were war measures to ensure quick acceptance. In New Zealand, where the elections gave the Massey Government an unworkable majority, both

AUSTRALIAN NAVY'S FIRST IMPORTANT ENGAGEMENT.
The last of the raiding German cruiser "Emden," which was destroyed by the H.M.A.S. "Sydney" in one hour and forty minutes after the firing of the first shot off Cocos Keeling Island, November 9th, 1914.

flourished particularly in the south island of New Zealand, was that men who could not then be accepted for foreign service, or whose position was such that they would be amongst the last to be called up, should secure what training could be given in the city parks.

In the political sphere there was a wise tempering of opposition with action. The old class jealousies largely died down, hushed by the seriousness of the common crisis; but in all the Australian Parliaments, and for eight months in the New Zealand Parliament, there remained

parties joined forces to ensure efficiency and ease in war administration.

The Dominion had in Mr. W. F. Massey, Sir Joseph Ward and Mr. Allen typical Australasian leaders, who had risen from working boys to be men of substance. An Ulsterman who had gone through the heartaches of colonial farming, Mr. Massey showed himself a plain-thinking and practical man, and he was typical of that unquestioning New Zealand loyalty which no disaster could ever shake. Sir Joseph Ward, more adroit, perhaps, in Parliament and on the platform, brought into service a wide experience of Imperial adminis- tration, and personal knowledge of those leaders in London who had never thought it worth while to travel within the Empire. Mr. Allen was a cautious administrator, economical, and a zealous student of London models. No coali- tion was achieved or even seriously considered in Australia. Powerful newspapers, nervous about the prospects of radical legislation passed as war measures becoming permanent, de- manded a fusion, but neither side in the Federal Parliament believed that its leaders could work with strength alongside the men they had fought in some of the bitterest and most advanced political contests in the history of the Empire. Mr. Andrew Fisher, who took rank during the war as one of the strongest men in the Empire, thoroughly disbelieved in coalitions. He remained until October, 1915, the supreme head in Australia, settling the most troublous questions in all departments, and controlling Parliament without difficulty. Like Mr. Massey and his own lieutenant, Mr. Hughes, Mr. Fisher was a native of the United Kingdom. He was a product of the coal mines of Ayrshire, and hard experiences in boyhood had evolved that policy of caring for lives more than for property, which for five years had been the outstanding note in the Australian Parliament. Mr. Fisher secured the Opposition's representation on a war com- mittee of twelve, six from each side, who shared the secrets of the Prime Ministry and the Defence Department and assisted in recruiting. But though the Opposition appointed the ex- Prime Minister, Mr. Joseph Cook, who, like Mr. Fisher, had begun life in a British coal mine- Senator E. D. Millen, an aggressive and re- sourceful ex-Minister of Defence, and Sir William Hill-Irvine, the ex-Attorney General, a North Irishman who had been the first to sound the note popularly called " pessimism " and who brought a well-equipped and powerful intellect into the counsels, the Cabinet retained respon- sibility and control of all measures. The war committee was never accepted as an authorita- tive body in the community, and it achieved little. Better success attended the treatment of the demands of the Government that refer- endums should be taken to enlarge the Federal Constitution at the expense of the States. This was in reality a search for the key of the Labour programme, which entailed the estab- lishing of national industries on a large scale, beginning with iron and shipping, and the regulation of prices, wages and profits. The

Government certainly found itself hampered by the sovereign rights of the States, and in such matters as the acquiring of the meat output at the request of the Imperial Government there were serious conflicts between Federal and State authorities. The sacrifice by which all parties agreed that the Federal Parliament should have full powers during the war and for one year afterwards was one that only those who had lived through the transition stage in which Australia passed from a collection of autono- mous and jealous States into a continental nation could appreciate. It showed how Aus- tralia recognised that in party politics the clock had stopped. It was another exemplification of that policy of " setting our teeth and seeing it through," expressed by Mr. Hughes after the early casualty lists. The nation was in no mood to fight in factions. Its anxiety for its men in Gallipoli, and its desire to use more of its strength, had become acute. It suffered from an itch of impotence, feeling helpless and un- happy through not being fully organized and led to supreme efforts. It was generally said that those men only were happy who had donned the Australian uniform and taken rifles to the firing lin . The spirit of Anzac had per- colated through the two nations, and changed their fibre. The thoughts of Australia and New Zealand were following the fortunes of their sons on those dreary and inhospitable cliffs where the destiny of Turkey was being so strangely linked with theirs. They were busy, too, with visions of a new Australianism and a new Imperialism, and for the first time in their history were be- coming conscious of their place in the troubled orbit of conflicting nations.

The Australian and New Zealand Army Corps had achieved an historical feat, and its com- position and work require examining. Its renown as one of the finest fighting forces any Empire has produced led to its being called a *corps d'élite*, but it was characteristic rather than specially representative of Australasia. It was merely the first assembling of early volunteers after the declaration of war. The men came into the camps from all parts of the Dominions, many journeying hundreds of miles on horse- back or on foot to enlist. Both Dominions had been roughly mapped by the military leaders into territorial areas, from each of which a quota of recruits was to be accepted. It was thus arranged that the men from one district should fight side by side—that the man from

NEW ZEALANDERS IN CAMP NEAR CAIRO.

the Snowy should find himself beside a comrade from his own locality in the Light Horse, and men from the West Australian minefields should be together in the engineers. Except that restriction of employment through drought increased the quotas from Victoria, it was found that similar enthusiasm prevailed in all parts, and recruits came forward from States and Provinces in about equal percentages of population. They were drafted into training camps in each State, and took naturally to that open-air life which for six months before their supreme trial toughened their muscles and hardened their spirits. It was all new work, both in Australia and New Zealand. But the Kitchener compulsory training schemes—the outcome of Lord Kitchener's visit to Australasia in 1910—though insufficiently advanced to provide many trained men for the expeditionary armies, had set up administrative machinery which proved invaluable. Working upon raw material of the finest quality, this machinery was able to produce within two months a fully equipped division in Australia and half a division in New Zealand, both ready to the last button, and locally provided with every necessity except heavy howitzers. Australia indeed had set about its military administration so earnestly that in addition to equipping its own forces it was able to assist other Dominions. It had for four years had the

advantage of the strongly developed war administration of Senator George Foster Pearce, an Australian-born carpenter whose name is indissolubly linked with the creation of the Australian Army and Navy. It helped South Africa with ammunition, and was in the early days applied to by that country for artillery. It raised a heavy siege brigade for European service, and sent a flying corps to General Nixon's expeditionary force in Mesopotamia. As they watched their little army grow, Australians regretted that they had not taken still greater heed of warnings given their statesmen, on the subject of German aggression, at the 1911 Imperial Conference. But they could justly claim that on land as on sea they were more ready than any other self-governing Dominion. They were in the peculiar position of having a higher military annual cost per head than even Germany, and yet finding themselves without trained men to send out of the country. They had to improvize, to expand, and to create. A few years more of preparation would have made their early war measures very different indeed. Australia and New Zealand could then have launched, within a month, armies of fully 150,000 men, fit to march against any troops in the world.

Such was the genesis of the Anzacs. Here, among their own people, they were equipped. Much they owed to Major-General William

Throsby Bridges, who began his work for the first Australian Division with the first sound of war, and ended by giving his life for it on the sands in Gallipoli. Before he could lead the Division, General Bridges had to organize it. His energy and force infused the factories which produced uniforms from mere wool, rifles from mere steel, boots from new hides, and hats from the furs of rabbits. Much the Division owed, too, to the workers in the factories, who joyfully laboured day and night that the Dominion's forces should have the best of everything ; to the railway employés and the tentmakers, the sock-knitters, and those who had horses and motor-cars to give. In both Dominions it required such generous and indefatigable efforts as came from all classes to secure the results achieved. Both communities, led by their small staffs of military experts and by politicians who did not falter at any expense, laid aside other work in order that this should be well done. There were scenes of great rejoicing when, two months after the declaration of war, the men marched through the cities, as magnificent an array of manhood as the Empire had seen. Thirty-three thousand men were ready to sail by the end of November ; fifteen thousand men were training in camp, getting ready to fill the places of those who, jaunty now in confidence of their strength, might fall.

It will never be claimed, however, that the Australasian Army Corps was made in the

MAORI WARRIORS AT BAYONET EXERCISE.
Inset: Maori Chiefs in Egypt.

training fields of Australasia. There, on their own land, in the sunshine they had not yet learnt to prize, the men from the factories, the warehouses, and city offices, the long, "lanky" Queenslanders from the Warrego, the farmers' sons from the Parramatta, and the wiry country-men from the Hunter, the Murrumbidgee pastor-alists, and the kangaroo shooters from the Murray Plains—there, with broad-backed miners from Bendigo and Kalgoorlie, and stocky South Australians, they were given their first martial training, their company drill and musketry courses. But it was in Egypt that they were made into soldiers. It was the desert that made them. On the long marches on the sands and in the long watches round the Pyramids and

HELIOGRAPH SIGNALLING.
New South Wales Signallers at their camp in the Desert at Heliopolis, Cairo.

Heliopolis camps, they passed through the ordeal of labour which is the essential prepara-tion for every achievement. It was there that the first 30,000 men from Australia and the first 10,000 from New Zealand were moulded into an army corps. Lieutenant-General Birdwood, chosen by Lord Kitchener as their commander, met them. The new discipline of foreign service settled down upon them, the *esprit de corps* of their force became a thing to be reckoned with. The men grew to hate the desert. They were in it for three months. They became jaded, mentally and physically, under the iron soldiers' régime. As draft after draft came forward from Australasia, and the army grew into three divisions, and all gaps in the ranks were filled by the regular inflow, the process was always the same. Egypt preceded the firing line, and

rigid training under an Imperial officer—at first under Lieutenant-General Birdwood, then under Major-General Spens—was imposed on all except those reinforcement drafts urgently wanted after heavy losses. It was so loyally and cheerfully gone through that General Bridges declared that the Australians had won their first victory on the sands of Egypt. Their commonsense and desire to become an efficient unit in the Imperial armies triumphed over the self-dependence learnt on their own free and limitless spaces, and many men wrote home to say that, though they loathed the sands of Egypt, they owed to them their strength as fighting men.

It was with great joy and eagerness that the men embarked for Gallipoli. They were at last to fight. Training had taken more time than they had bargained for. They had begun to fear those disintegrating forces which, in the midst of the strange, monotonous soldier's life in a country that was ever remote from their ideas of home, had shown themselves in such incidents as the mild riots in the Whasa district of Cairo. They had confidence in their leaders and them-selves, and though they knew that casualties would be high in their early fighting, they had no doubt about the result. General Birdwood had made the First Australian Division the first division of his corps, and his second division he had formed out of the two brigades of infantry and the mounted infantry sent by New Zealand, together with the Fourth Australian Infantry Brigade and the First Australian Light Horse Brigade, part of which were divisional mounted troops. Commanding the first division was General Bridges, who proved in fighting as in organizing to be "a leader possessing in rare strength the greatest qualities of a soldier," as General Hamilton said after his death. General Bridges had on his staff the most bril-liant young Australian professional soldiers produced by fifteen years of Federal army work, and it should be mentioned that in his Chief of Staff, Colonel C. B. Whyte, *p.s.c.*, who received one of the many decorations bestowed on Aus-tralian officers, he possessed an inspiring young Australian leader who became a great force in Anzac. In command of the mixed Australian and New Zealand Division was Major-General Sir A. Godley, of the Irish Guards, who for some years had been tutoring New Zealand in its uni-versal service scheme. General Godley had Imperial officers in the principal positions on his staff, and his division more nearly approximated

TRENCH DIGGING IN THE DESERT SANDS.
Party of the New Zealand Contingent in Egypt.

to a British division than did either of the Australian divisions—a difference to be expected from the absence in New Zealand of that distinctive nationalism which had developed in Australia. The complete success of the landing spoke much for the two divisional and the six brigade staffs. It was difficult to realize what an enormous amount of work and strain had to be borne in preparation for such a feat, in which no detail could be left to chance if disaster was to be avoided. The loss suffered by the force when General Bridges fell to a Turkish sniper could be weighed in lives. A cold man with an ideal of meticulous accuracy, he had nevertheless endeared himself to his troops, and they were not satisfied until they had taken a revenge upon the Turks, in the actions of May 18–19, described in Chapter XCVIII., so severe that the enemy was compelled to seek an armistice to bury his dead. General Bridges was posthumously knighted, and his body was taken from its grave in Egypt to Australia, where it was interred on the Federal capital site at Canberra, in the wild bush near the Royal Australian Military College he had created.

After General Bridges's death, Brigadier-General Walker, an Indian Army soldier brought by General Birdwood on his staff, took over the First Division. The Federal Government sent from Melbourne the apostle of compulsory service, Colonel J. G. Legge to take over the First Division, and promoted him brigadier-general. But he had been only

a few days on the peninsula when it became necessary to give the division a rest from the trenches, in which they had been for nearly five months. He was given the onerous task of organizing and commanding the Second Australian Division, which he formed out of large drafts from Australia then completing their training in Egypt. With this he returned to Gallipoli in September, thus enabling the First Division to rest and refit. It was a disappointment to Australia that General Legge, who with Colonel Whyte was the military hope of the Australian democracy, did not find scope in the nation's first military operations until the story of Anzac was so far advanced, but in General Walker the division had a hard-hitting, downright soldier, who shared with his men the Anzac spirit of enduring comradeship.

In previous chapters the narrative of the earlier episodes at Anzac has been given. There are, however, considerations and incidents which should be set forth here. They help us to weigh the Imperial importance of the Australasian effort in the war, and explain the spirit which promised much after the war. What was expected from the Australasian Army Corps during the first days in Gallipoli was not made clear. Certainly the prevalent opinion was that the task was simple, that the naval fire would have a shattering effect on the Turks, and that the peninsula would soon be straddled. Although General Bridges and Colonel Howse, V.C., a New South Wales country doctor, who did heroic work as director of medical services on General Bridges's staff, arranged as far as was in their power for evacuation of 5,000 wounded, others were not so long-sighted. There were very few hospital ships prepared for casualties from the landing.

With each force, the British at Helles and the Australasian at Sari Bair, artillery horses and full ambulance transport were sent, indicating the existence of hopes and expectations which were doomed to disappointment. On the other hand, though calculations were made upon an over-estimation of the power of the naval artillery to cover the advancing army, it was fully expected by the Australasian staffs that the landing would be sternly opposed and would lead to very heavy losses. As a matter of fact, great feat though it was, the Australasian landing was assisted by an extraordinary mishap. The Navy in the darkness, steaming without lights and in unknown waters, had landed General Birdwood's pioneer force one mile north of the position chosen. They hit upon a spot so rugged and barren that the Turks, thinking that no force could be landed there and that no commander would be foolish enough to attempt it, had prepared few defences. On the wide point of Gaba Tepe, on the other hand, where clear undulating plains open an easy way across the peninsula, the Turks had erected barbed wire entanglements in the sea and made a landing almost impossible. Had the Australasians been put ashore here, as proposed, they would have won an exposed foothold, but they might have been utterly broken in the first assault upon the Turk. " Our orders were to land, to get into contact with the enemy, and to push in," wrote a senior Australian officer. " We had thought of all contingencies, and had decided our policy in the event of mistiming in landing or of overwhelming opposition. That policy was to send in boatload after boatload, until in the end as much of our programme as was possible was achieved, or we ourselves were wrecked in this honourable but hazardous task."

The Australasians' qualities as fighters proved equal to every change in the situation in Gallipoli. At first, when a thin line, stretched along the edges of the cliffs and gullies, was precariously holding back great bodies of Turks, it was indeed a question whether the corps should not be re-embarked. Twice the transports lying off the coast were ordered to send in their small boats, lest withdrawal

should be forced upon the Australasians. The army corps commanders were doubtful on the first evening about the advantages or possibility of holding on, and the decision was referred to General Hamilton on his staff ship off Helles. For some days the Turks had all the best of things. Their snipers enfiladed the gullies, their artillery poured shrapnel from each side upon the beaches and trenches. Only the slight protection afforded by the cliff itself made the future Anzac possible. The strain upon physical endurance was intense. Great difficulties were experienced in getting water and ammunition across the roadless gullies, through the thick scrub, up the precipitous sides to the few defenders. There seemed to be none of the elements of victory and all the elements of disaster. Months after, when the survivors looked back on those awful days, they agreed that it was sheer physical strength that had enabled the corps to hold on. The men had the will and physique to endure. In the extremes of tiredness, they were slightly less tired than the Turks. From the first day a wonderful spirit was displayed. The wounded staggered back from the dressing stations to the trenches. Men died with the same simple, unquestioning heroism with which they had fought. The mortally wounded did not complain. Those being carried down from the hills roused themselves, as they passed the reserves, to breathe a word of encouragement or defiance. It was a fiery spirit, and it carried forward these forty thousand men, trained to the last ounce in physical strength, with irresistible momentum.

Anzac became theirs. But its problems never became simple. No one could see how it could be used, so broken and precipitous was the country into which it led. No one could see, for a time, how it could be held. It was merely a foothold on cliffs, on a deep gully and on the gully-sides beyond ; the posts along the side were slenderly held, and to be swept off at one would mean that the others were untenable. At the gully head was a position commanding the whole of Anzac, known as " Dead Man's Ridge," which the Australasians lost large numbers in several efforts to capture, and from which only the resourcefulness and skill of the Australasian snipers—old " rifle club " men for the most part—kept the Turks. The weather was beautifully calm and mild, but no one could tell when the exposed anchorage would become tossed by winds for days on end, and neither stores nor reinforce-

PARADE OF TERRITORIAL AND COLONIAL TROOPS.
The march past before General Sir Ian Hamilton at Mena Camp, near Cairo.

ments could be landed. For protection on the flanks, the navy's guns had to be relied upon ; and the appearance of enemy submarines compelled the disappearance of the fleet until such time as specially adapted monitors and old cruisers arrived to take up the work. It was a situation calling for not only endurance and courage, but engineering skill and resource in organization. The use of hand grenades had not been foreseen ; bombs had to be improvised, and bomb-throwers instructed. The way these civilian soldiers—farmers' sons fresh from their ploughshares, solicitors and clerks brought from their libraries and desks—made of Anzac an almost impregnable fortress was one of the finest feats of the war. Remarkable defences were improvised at such places as Quinn's and Courtney's Posts. Tunnelling, barricading, and sap making proceeded uninterruptedly for five months.

Resource and initiative were developed in unsuspected quarters. A New Zealand solicitor, Colonel Malone, proved himself a military engineer of great ability. Having transformed Quinn's Post from a vital point of danger to a foothold for offence, he died there.

The Post was the key to Anzac, and the encounters upon it would alone make an epic. It was held on the night after the landing by the remnants of several companies driven back to the edge of the gully, and the Turks were never nearer victory than when they faced these lonely and worn-out infantrymen. Major Quinn, a Queensland officer, after whom the Post was named, was killed whilst organizing an attack from it, and later a Light Horse company went to its doom from it as part of the costly operations of early August. It should be recorded that artillery officers, among whom were the first graduates of the Royal Military College, got their guns into the very trenches throughout Anzac, and suffered always from the handicap that their emplacements were necessarily few and well known to the Turks, whereas the Turks had square miles in which to choose their positions. A young private invented a periscope rifle, which, until the enemy copied it, gave the whole corps a marked ascendancy over Turkish trench fire. In many extraordinary ways the Dominion men's self-reliance and initiative displayed themselves. Perhaps the most notable of all was the resourcefulness of

NEW ZEALANDERS IN EGYPT.
Field Artillery returning to camp from the desert.

AUSTRALIANS IN EGYPT.
A scene on the Quayside. Inset: The Camp
Donkey.

AUSTRALIANS IN EGYPT.
A scene on the Quayside. Inset: The Camp
Donkey.

the snipers. By sheer obstinacy and skill the
Australasian riflemen overcame the Turks,
until it became perfectly safe to walk in gullies
which the Turks commanded, and even to show
oneself over the Australasians' lines. The
Turks contrived wickerwork boxes which,
placed slantingly in their sandbags, seemed to
defy detection. But they soon learnt that they
could not fire without attracting a deadly return.
Nor could they throw one bomb upon the
Australasians without getting two or three
back. The Australasians became ascendant.
The Turks were obviously afraid of them.
Their prisoners told how for some weeks no
men would go into the trenches opposite Quinn's
Post unless given special promotion, so frightful
was the Australian rain of bombs. It was said
that Enver Bey, during a visit to his countrymen's lines, stopped this procedure, and ordered
a charge which ended in complete disaster.

To those who went through it, more striking
even than the facing of death in Gallipoli was
the capacity of the soldiers to endure. They
were faced with hardships comparable with
those of the Crimea. They were never, at

any point, out of range of Turk guns. Their
dug-outs afforded them more moral than physical shelter. They were in reality safer in the
trenches than on fatigue duty on the beaches
or in the gullies. The weather until late
October was indeed a glorious calm, the sky
scarcely clouded, the blue waters of the Ægean
scarcely ruffled. Sometimes, for a few minutes
only, when bathers were in the sea, and North
Sea trawlers were steaming leisurely about with
stores, one could imagine, at Helles, at Anzac, or
at Suvla, that in this wild and inhospitable
country all was at peace—that war could not
take place for such barren shores, and that the
dread reality would prove a dream. But the
guns were seldom silent. The rain of shells
and the whistle of bullets were everlasting. The
work in the trenches was continuous. Our
hold was never firm. It always required all
the efforts of all the men we could land and
feed in Gallipoli. The food could never be what
it was in France. There was nowhere to forage,
except the little Greek island villages on Imbros,
which was inaccessible except to a very few.
Bully beef, onions, biscuits, tea, and water were
the staple, almost the only, articles of diet.
There were three great days in Gallipoli—the
first when the troops first got news through the
issue at General Headquarters of a daily broad-
sheet, *Peninsular Press*; the second, when
they got meat ; the third, when they got bread.
But bread as known in Gallipoli was different
from what these men had consumed at home.
Once the Army Service Corps got fresh eggs to
the Suvla trenches, and it performed other
feats. But the monotony of the food meant

a great deal. The men could get no change, and they suffered. They could get no relief from work. They were never without great hopes and determination, or without full confidence that the Turks could and would be beaten. But there was throughout the Peninsula a mental and physical strain which was often manifest.

Few armies have borne so much over such a length of time, few have risen better to perilous tasks at the call of their commanders. When after the great Turkish assault on Anzac lines on May 18-19—an assault in which the enemy changed completely in one hour the Australasians' feelings towards the Turks, by an exhibition of unsurpassable bravery—the Turkish dead brought flies to the scene, the agony of dysentery was added to those of the prolonged and obstinate fighting. The dysentery could never be overtaken. It smote down nearly everyone in Anzac. The place was septic, and men in ill-health had small chance of picking up again. Though not a particularly virulent form of the disease, it had mortal effect in many hundreds of cases, owing somewhat to the difficulties encountered in hospital transport. When the flies disappeared with the first signs of winter, the illness abated. But by that time dysentery almost more than Turkish bullets and shell had sadly reduced the armies in each zone. As an army of offence, the Australasian Army Corps had lost its original vigour after the great assaults of early August, when the first Australian Brigade won the Lone Pine position on the right of Anzac, the sixth and eighth Light Horse Brigades were flung in a great and hopeless charge against " Baby Seven Hundred," and the Fourth Australian Infantry Brigade and two New Zealand brigades suffered terribly in the brilliant work against the Sari Bair Ridge to the left of the New Zealand outposts. But nothing cheered the men more than to be told that a Turkish attack was expected, or an Anzac attack was being planned. They would manage to struggle round, at all costs, while there was real fighting in sight. Heroic endurance was the order of the day. Men scarcely able to stand remained by their guns, because they knew they could not well be spared. The cases of those whose sickness fully justified removal, but who kept resolutely to the trenches, were to be numbered in thousands.

The most moving part in the Gallipoli story will ever be the splendid feelings it called forth in the breasts of young Australasians. To them it was no ordinary adventure in warfare. These single-minded, loyal youths had different conceptions of God. But every conception fitted into the sublime conception that this work for their race and country was God's

AUSTRALIAN OFFICERS IN EGYPT.
A lunch in the desert.

THE SCENE AFTER THE HISTORIC LANDING AT SUVLA BAY—
Enemy snipers driven from their lurking-

work. Upon the tissue of their natures, the warm affections, the cleanliness and the liberty among which they had been brought up, this fighting call in Gallipoli precipitated something that seemed to them the highest thing possible. They did not stop to give it a name, or they would have been able to distinguish it, by its accompaniment of home-longings and fierce connection of this enterprise with Australian people and Australian soil, as Australianism. What they knew was that they wished to go to Anzac, that they were prepared to die there, that the Australian army had become for them a sacred institution. Their hearts were touched by the death of comrades, their eyes took fire at the sight of the distinctive Australian uniform. Gallipoli proved, if it did not in itself go far to produce, a warmth and generosity in the Australian character. The difficulty experienced by the commanders was not to get men to this shell-torn place of hardship, but to keep them from it. Half the members of the Light Horse Brigades and all the drivers of artillery and ambulances had been left behind in Cairo or Alexandria, to attend to the horses. But it was impossible to keep them there. They decided amongst themselves who could be spared. Everyone wished to go, those chosen were thought lucky. They boarded transports at Alexandria, stowed away until the ships were at sea, and then reported themselves to the officers commanding. One artillery brigade lost 39 of its men in this manner. General Hamilton could never find it in his heart to send back men who came with tears in

their eyes and asked for nothing better than to be given privates' work in Anzac. There were cases in which sergeants gladly forfeited stripes and pay for the chance. Men could not bear to go back to their homes and say they had not done their share in Anzac.

And of their discipline, which was attacked because it was sometimes unorthodox, what better can be said than what was told in the undying story of the Southland? The Southland was torpedoed by a German submarine in the Ægean Sea, when conveying the 21st Australian Infantry Battalion and part of the 23rd, 1,500 strong, from Alexandria to Mudros They were Victorian country boys, recruited for the most part from the farms and stations of the Wimmera and the Goulburn Valley. Panic ensued among the ill-assorted crew of this converted German liner. Three of the four holds filled with water, the hatches of the hold first damaged were blown out and in the water there the Australians could see the dead bodies floating of their comrades killed by the explosion. No one thought that the ship could keep for long above water. But the soldiers stood at their stations They waited for their turn. One went to the piano, and played favourite airs. Others, when volunteers were asked for, jumped into the water to right overturned boats. When at last all the men were off the stricken vessel, standing on half-submerged rafts, clinging to the edges of boats, swimming alongside improvised supports, volunteers were called for to stoke the ship into port, all the men within hearing offered for the hazardous task. Six officers and seventeen men

A BUSH FIRE ROUTING OUT BOTH BRITISH AND TURKS.
places and hunted out by the Anzacs.

climbed the rope ladders again, and with her bows under water and her stern low down, the ship was brought into Mudros and beached. It was a triumphant vindication of the discipline of Dominion troops. "The discipline was perfect," wrote Captain C. E. W. Bean, official reporter at Anzac. "The men turned out immediately. There had been boat drill on the voyage and the men ran straight to their proper places and lined up." They sat down on the decks, under orders, and removed their boots. "There were officers shouting, 'Steady, boys; that's the only thing, steady!' The men's stations were partly in the half darkness of the 'tween decks and partly in the sunlight on the upper deck. . . . Occasionally a man would turn his head and look down to see how the water was making. 'Bad luck, that two and a half months in the desert should end in this,' said one. 'Are we downhearted?' called another. 'No!' they all shouted. 'Are we afraid to die?' called someone else. 'No!' they shouted again." A letter home, which was published in *The Times*, paid a generous tribute to the raw young soldiers :—

I received orders to go to Anzac to join the batteries. We had an infantry regiment which should go down to history for a deed only equalled by the Marines on board the Birkenhead. After two days' sailing, at 10.14 a.m., I heard a sentry shout, "My God, a torpedo," and we watched this line of death getting nearer and nearer until crash ! and the old ship reeled with the shock. Then the order "Ship sinking," and "Abandon ship"; without a cry or any sign of fear, without any more hurry than a brisk march and singing "Australia will be there." I cannot say how magnificent, how fine they were. They went to their stations and lowered the boats in an orderly, careful way; taking the places they had been told off to, the injured going in first. . . . The

only losses out of 1,600 of the soldiers is one officer and 36 men, of whom 12 were killed by the explosion, two from boats crushing them, and the rest were drowned from overturned boats. The moment when the torpedo came towards us was the most awful experience I can ever remember. To wait and keep calm in the face of what seemed certain death. Never can men have faced death with greater courage, more nobility, and with a braver front than did the Australian troops on board the Southland. The song they sang was "Australia will be there," and by God ! they were. They were heroes ; we knew they were brave in a charge, but now we know they are heroes. Long live in honour and glory the men of the 21st and 23rd Australian Infantry.

The narrative of military operations contained in our earlier chapters on the Dardanelles campaign will be continued later, but several episodes may be related here. The first capture of a Turkish trench and its retention deserve special notice because this brilliant exploit fired the whole of Anzac, after fifteen weeks of monotonous trench fighting, for the great aggressive operations of August and September. The work was known as Northern Turkish Despair Trench, or Tasman Post, and it was stormed under severe fire on July 31 by a composite company of the 11th Battalion (West Australia) of General E. G. Sinclair-MacLagan's Third Brigade, under Captain R. L. Leane. After two days a heavy counter-attack was launched by a battalion of Turks, who regained a section of the work, but were again driven out. The episode cost Anzac 300 casualties, but showed what could be done. Near the close of the series of attacks which this success began was another charge, the simple truth of which was worth accomplishing, even at the cost. It was the charge of the First and Third Light Horse Brigades, differing from the charge of the Light Brigade at Balaclava only in that it was made by horsemen who had volunteered to fight on foot, and that it succeeded in one object—that of holding large bodies of Turks who would otherwise have been used against the new British landing at Suvla Bay. The Eighth and Tenth Regiments of the Third Brigade went out from Walker's Ridge. It was a charge into death from the first moment, and before the men of the second line leapt from their trenches they shook hands, knowing that they could not survive. They were met by a fusillade that became a continuous roaring tempest of machine gun and rifle fire, and out of the 300 men in the first line only one returned. The Second Regiment of the First Brigade was sent out from Quinn's Post, charging into so impossible a fire that the first line had to be left to its fate, and the second, third, and fourth lines held in the trenches. The First Regiment of the First Brigade charged up the slopes of Dead Man's Ridge and found a similar fate. It was all over within ten minutes—in the case of the charge from Quinn's Post within a few seconds. "The Turkish machine guns drew a line across that place which none could pass," wrote Captain C. E. W. Bean, official observer with the Australian Division, "and the one man who

went out and returned unwounded put his escape down to the fact that he noticed the point on our sandbags on which the machine-gun bullets were hitting, and jumped clear over the stream of lead. The guns were sweeping low, and a man who was hit once by them was often hit again half-a-dozen times as he fell through the stream which caught him. The whole of the first line was either killed or wounded within a few seconds of their leap from our trenches." But though the charges shattered four regiments of as good fighting men as the Empire possessed, they created an imperishable impression. "As for the boys," wrote Captain Bean, "the single-minded, loyal Australian country lads who left their trenches in the grey light of that morning with all their simple treasures on their backs, to bivouac in the scrub that evening, the shades of evening found them lying in the scrub with God's wide sky above them. The green arbutus and the holly of the peninsula, not unlike their native bush, will some day claim again this neck in those wild ranges for its own. But the place will always be sacred as the scene of this very brave deed—this charge of the Australian Light Horse into certain death at the call of their comrades' need during a crisis in the greatest battle that has ever been fought on Turkish soil." They helped the Fourth Australian Brigade and the New

NEW ZEALAND TROOPS IN EGYPT.
At work near the Pyramids.

DUG-OUTS AT GABA TEPE.

On top of the famous hill which was successfully carried by the Australians and New Zealanders.

Zealanders in their night march among the hills to the north, and they made the Suvla Bay landing at least a bit safer for the raw youths, much like themselves, from Lancashire, Essex, and Ireland.

To understand the Australian soldier it was necessary to appreciate his open-handed liberality. He was built on generous lines in every way. His physique was the wonder of the Mediterranean. Some squadrons of Light Horse averaged six feet in height. The regular life and hard work in the deserts filled out the city men and gave uniformity to the magnificent infantry. No doubt also a consciousness of stalwart manhood brought to them a dignity and confidence of bearing which, as they swung themselves down the steep sides of Anzac or worked, stripped to the skin, beside the guns in their emplacements, brought emotion to the observer at the sight of so much fine life. But generosity in mind and spirit was as characteristic as generosity in physique. The Australasian's views, his sympathies and his sacrifices were alike liberal. He went to death, as at Walker's Ridge and Lone Pine and on the shoulders of Chunuk Bair, with the same generosity with which he spent his money. "He shed his blood in

Anzac," said Colonel Nash, M.P., who left a large Sydney practice to minister to his countrymen on their first battlefield, "as prodigally as he spent his substance in Cairo." The Australasians were often misunderstood, but never by those alongside whom they fought. Paymasters were overwhelmed with requests from soldiers in the field to make over their pay to comrades in hospital. "They may have a chance to spend the money, it is no good to us here." British regiments recorded how when, as sometimes happened, they ran short of tobacco, the Australasian force alongside subscribed and bought enough for all. The Australasians' generosity to each other in action was equally marked. There were terrible times after a charge, when wounded had to be left alone in the dead country between trenches to languish and die. Many Australasians lost their lives in vain endeavours to venture out for comrades after dark. Others spent day and night in digging saps to bodies, in the hope that they would recover them before suspicious Turks, noticing the hasty spade work, put artillery on to the spot.

Amongst the heaviest sufferers at Anzac were the ambulances and stretcher bearers, who ventured into all parts of the field and followed

ON THE GALLIPOLI PENINSULA: THE AUSTRA
The great landing of troops and supplies; on the

EW ZEALANDERS AT GABA TEPE, APRIL 25, 1915.

s Dressing Station, protected by sandbags.

the infantry in their charges.   The Fourth Field Ambulance, an Adelaide force, lost more than half its men.   The bearing of the Australian wounded was beyond all praise.   It seemed almost as if they were proof against pain, so uncomplaining and cheerful they remained.   Will and spirit triumphed over body.   It was a point of honour with the wounded to make no sound. It seemed a point of honour, too, to make no call for medical men, to fight on until strength departed, and even then to ask that others should be treated first.   Such things are expected.   But with a shaken force, battering against a victorious and numerically overpowering enemy under distracting conditions of hardship, the factors making for demoralization are sometimes irresistible.   Where the Australian soldier was not liberal was in his hatred of the Turk.   Until May 18 the hatred was of heart and soul.   But on that memorable day, when wave upon wave of Turks broke against the Australasian lines until 7,000 of the enemy lay dead and wounded, the feeling in Anzac was convulsed.   There were always strange threats and oaths, bitter feelings and desires, when a sniper sighted a Turk or machine guns began to play upon rest camps or reserves down on the plains.   But for " Achmed," as the Australasians called the Turk, there grew up a strong respect.   There was respect for such glowing bravery as the Turks showed in charging, and more specifically in chancing death for their wounded comrades.   Except where there were German officers, who were confined in Gallipoli to a small number of commissioned and non-commissioned men in charge of artillery and machine guns, the Turks fought fairly.   They respected the Red Cross, they sought to minimize suffering, they even braved danger for the sake of Australasian wounded.   One striking instance was given on Anzac's left.   In the dusk a Turk was seen crawling forth from his trench, wriggling across the ground, and disappearing into a hole not far from the Australian lines.   The operation was three times repeated.   The Australian fire was withheld, despite fear of mining, because it was suspected that a wounded Turk was being succoured.   But when in the dead of night a small Australian party made its way to the indentation, they found not a Turk but an Australian, with a Turkish blanket covering him, a Turkish fly-net over his face, Turkish food beside him, and Turkish bandages upon his wound.   General Birdwood, early in the

history of Anzac, sent a company down to Gaba Tepe by sea, more for reconnoitring than for a serious landing, but with some hopes that the place would be found undefended and the emplacements of the mysterious guns in the olive groves discovered and destroyed.   The party found occupation of the little peninsula impossible.   They were met by withering fire, they found the beaches defended by stout, sunken barbed wire.   They had to take again to their boats.   And the Turks stopped their fire while the Australians were lifting their wounded from beach to boats, and did not re-open until the wounded had been removed into comparative safety.

It is necessary to say a word in praise of the Australian officer.   He was born of the occasion. Australia was able to call upon very few professional officers to take up the work.   New Zealand was in an even worse position. Although military science had been more seriously studied in Australia than in any other Dominion, it seemed when war broke out that the Commonwealth was in no way capable of officering even the first expeditionary force of twenty thousand men.   For the headquarters staff General Bridges had several well-trained young Australian officers who had passed through the Imperial schools under the system of exchange and study sedulously encouraged by Senator Pearce during his creative periods of administration at the Defence Department. Such men as Colonels Whyte, Brand, Blamey, and Cass justified expectation of brilliance. In addition General Bridges was fortunate in having serving in Australia at the time of the war several expert officers lent by the War Office for special organizing purposes, and these, of whom Colonels Glassfurd, Marsh, and Mackworth were specially trained in infantry control, army service work and signalling, merited much of Anzac.   The appointments of brigadiers was Australia's chief difficulty. The Government had available various brigadiers under the compulsory training scheme. They were civilians, had had little or no field work, and had not impressed General Hamilton during his visit to the Commonwealth.   Of the eleven Brigadier-Generals appointed to the four Light Horse and seven Infantry Brigades, nine reached the front with their commands. Brigadier-General Linton, a typical Australian self-made civilian turned soldier, was lost when the Sutherland was torpedoed, being thrown into the water from an overturned boat and

ON BOARD A GERMAN PRIZE.
The Australians take possession of the S.S. "Lutzow" near Sedd-ul-Bahr.

refusing assistance till all the men had been got into shelter. Colonel Spencer Browne, a Brisbane journalist, found when he got to Egypt with the Fourth Light Horse that other brigades had been so reduced that his men were needed as drafts. The Second and Third Light Horse had found it hard to leave their horses behind them in Egypt and go to war as

ANZACS IN GALLIPOLI—WATCHING A BATTLE.

infantry, especially as with true Australian sympathy for horses they had become greatly attached to their mounts, and they had had no training for war without them. But the Fourth Light Horse was called upon to surrender not only its character as mounted troops, but also its formation. It was soon seen that the early appointments of brigadiers had been happy. This is not to say that permanent and skilled soldiers, who had given all their lives to the study of war, would not have been even more successful, or that lives were not lost through the later appointment of men too old for the rigours of Gallipoli. But it certainly showed that the type of Australian civilian appointed to the senior commands—successful business men who had put in their holidays for many years at training camps, solicitors, engineers, and journalists—quickly became resourceful, determined and clever soldiers. If anything, they were too contemptuous of personal danger. General J. W. M'Cay, of the Second Brigade, was first from the rest trench in the great charge made by his brigade in May at Krithia. Exclaiming, "Now is the

time for me to do the heroics," he walked along the top of the trench, in face of heavy fire, rallying his men and giving that inspiration which carried them on to the enemy's lines. General M'Cay was later wounded in the leg, and he was not the only Australian General who in defiance of the medical corps returned to Anzac before fit for work again. As a result his leg broke at the old wound, and he missed command of the First Division. A solicitor with a large practice in Melbourne, General M'Cay had been State and Federal politician and Minister, Minister of Defence, Chief Censor and representative banker before his soldiering took him to Gallipoli. On return to Australia he became Inspector-General of the Forces. Another lawyer-brigadier, General M'Laurin, was killed with his brigade-major, Major Irvine, a trusted and valuable Imperial officer, on the day after the landing. Like many other officers, including General Bridges himself, they exposed themselves freely to Turkish snipers in order to increase the men's sense of confidence when for the first time under heavy fire. Officers of both divisions suffered very heavily during the early days, but though it robbed the army corps of many trained men who could never be replaced, it was a sacrifice no less conscious and no less noble in that it was premeditated recklessness, designed to inspirit men under fire for the first time. The two professional soldiers given brigades were Colonel Chauvel, an Australian cavalry officer who at the outbreak of war was succeeding General Legge as Australian representative on the Imperial General Staff, and Lieut.-Colonel Sinclair-MacLagan, of the Yorkshire Regiment, to whose work at the Australian Royal Military College at Duntroon the training of the cadet-officers was largely due. Lieut.-Colonel Sinclair-MacLagan, who became temporary Brigadier-General after the landing, was generally adjudged the most successful of the Anzac brigadiers. A disciplinarian with tact, a skilled soldier, and above all a clever tactician, he was given the most responsible work on April 25. It was his Third Brigade which General Hamilton sent to Mudros in March to practise landing on an exposed beach from small boats. The Brigade was first ashore. It drove back the Turks from the cliff trenches. It got far inland towards Maidos, and it suffered heavily. A composite brigade from the four least populated States, it had that element of wiry and resourceful Queenslanders and tough West Australian miners generally considered the best composition in Australian forces. General Sinclair-MacLagan was compelled to take a great

ANZACS AT THE DARDANELLES.
Australians at the entrance of a dug-out on the Gallipoli Peninsula. Inset: Using a periscope and a periscope-rifle in the trenches.

THE BATTLE BY THE LONE PINE, ON 400 PLATEAU, NEAR ANZAC.

The First Australian Brigade attacking the hidden Turks through scout-holes cut in the enemy's roofed trench.

decision on the day of landing, inclining his men towards the left and thus happily striking the undulation later famed as Shrapnel Gully. In General Godley's Division, General Russell and General Monash, the former a New Zealand city man and the latter a Melbourne civil engineer, were given the bulk of the work. General Monash, in command of the Fourth Australian Brigade, led the ill-fated attempt to capture Baby Seven Hundred, in which his brigade lost heavily. He later led his brigade, brought up after severe wastage to a strength above 4,000, in support of the New Zealanders in the great advance from Anzac's left, in which the shoulder of Chunuk Bair was reached, and the force was terribly reduced. It will never be decided whether the utmost was made of the gallant New Zealand and Australian brigades on this occasion, when the Second Division lost to an extent which was tragical. But to say that the general officers were worthy of their men in Anzac is to say no more than is their due.

It was, in fact, no easy matter to lead such a force. Where intelligence in the ranks is high only brave and skilled officers will command respect. The younger officers were frankly amateurs. The majority had had no military training. They had learnt their first drills as privates at the Australasian camps, and had gone through hurried training at officers' training schools in Australasia and Egypt. They started only with keenness, energy and ability, but they understood their men, and their sympathy won a confidence which in the Imperial Army is won by military skill and courage. They were for the most part athletic young adventurous Australians, of a similar type to the men in the ranks. Except at the very beginning of the war, everybody had to enlist as a private in the ordinary way ; an age limit of twenty-three was fixed, and commissions were awarded in open competition. It was a democratic army, and it should be said that the young men weighed carefully the responsibilities of officers' work before they sought commissions. Large numbers of educated men remained in the ranks. The extra pay for commissioned rank, 21s. a day for lieutenants and corresponding increases for each promotion, did not appeal. The Australasians rather scouted the idea of payment for their fighting. Their pay was high, 6s. a day for privates, including 1s. deferred until discharge ; their non-com-

missioned officers received more in some classes than British lieutenants. But to Australasians their pay was a means to an end, and they spent it so freely that orders were given limiting the amount drawable to 2s. a day, balances to be drawn only when really required. In the ranks was to be found an extraordinary mingling of rich and poor, of educated and raw human material. One tent of eight men in the Fourth Light Horse Brigade owned pastoral property and stock worth £500,000. Of nine members of the Perth City Club who enlisted in the Third Light Horse Brigade only three secured commissions, and the remaining six agreed that they would remain steadfastly together in the ranks. Every member of their regiment, the only Light Horse regiment

[*Elliott & Fry.*

BRIGADIER-GENERAL SINCLAIR-MACLAGAN, D.S.O.

raised in West Australia, brought his own horse into camp when he enlisted. Throughout every battalion and every squadron, and particularly in the artillery brigades, were men of wealth and substance ; youths whose fathers were amongst the most distinguished and wealthiest men in Australasia maintained throughout their service the humble rôle of privates, and met the private's varying fate. General Birdwood found in the ranks of the Light Horse two sons of the Australian branch of his family ; General Hughes's and General Linton's sons enlisted in their father's brigades as privates ; Mr. John Wren, who had racecourse interests throughout Australasia and owned a newspaper, served as a corporal.

The plain story of Gallipoli will be enough to stir the pride and rouse the emulation of the British race for generations. But some of the distinctive acts in Anzac were so remarkable as

CORPL. P. H. G. BENNETT.
Wellington Battalion, awarded
the D.C.M.

CORPL. C. R. BASSETT.
New Zealand Divisional Signal
Company, awarded the V.C.

SERGT. TINSLEY.
Auckland Battalion, awarded
the D.C.M.

to compel mention. General Walker, after the Lone Pine attack, found it necessary to mention more than 150 men, each of whom had performed what would in normal conditions be acts justifying decoration. The first Anzac V.C. was a typical Victoria Cross deed. Corporal Jacka, a young Bendigo miner, was the

LANCE-CORPORAL JACKA.
Victorian Battalion, Australian Expeditionary
Force, the first Australian to be awarded the
Victoria Cross.

sole survivor in a trench in which seven Turks secured a footing. Instead of retreating down the communication trench he sprang into a sniping post, and by covering their line of advance kept the Turks where they were. Jacka must have expected death from behind from other Turks who would be following their comrades, but he held his position until an officer approached with men. " It is not safe to come round there, sir," he called to his officer. Asked for suggestions, Jacka replied that the only thing to be done was to send a party along the trench to rush the Turks. He agreed to lead the party, but the first man round the trench was shot, and this form of attack was seen to be impossible. " Send a larger bombing party," called Jacka. But when after an interval the party was ready and arrived, they found seven dead Turks, with Jacka sitting on the body of the last, smoking a cigarette. He had leapt across the trench, got behind the Turks, shot five and bayonetted the other two. It should be said that all the nearest men volunteered to form the first attacking party, several remarking, " It's got to be done. Let's do it now." This admirably stated the Australasians' point of view of danger. None courted death. To regard the Australian or New Zealander as reckless is to misunderstand. It seemed reckless that they should bathe in the sea while the guns from the olive grove were casting shrapnel over the waters. It seemed reckless that the officers should expose themselves as they did in order to observe positions and get the best results for their men. It seemed reckless that they should go out singly and in twos and threes to search for hidden snipers. But they did nothing without a purpose, and if they risked death for a bathe, it was because they felt so much better fighting men after their customary swim. The Australasians had, indeed, every possible reason for wishing to live. The warm affections of well-established homes were awaiting them, good careers in a free and peaceful country stretched ahead, life to these young men seemed very sweet indeed. They measured the sacrifice by the stake, and knew that the great aim of maintaining the happiness of their nation justified the giving of themselves. The early August operations at Lone Pine, and in the ridges along the north, when for one brief moment the Australasians saw the waters of the Narrows and the Straits beneath them, produced a crop of nine Victoria Crosses. There were few finer incidents in the war than the work for which Captain Shout, who succumbed to his injuries, was decorated. With a very small party he charged down trenches strongly occupied by the enemy, killing with his own hand eight Turks, and assisting in the rout of the

remainder. From this captured trench he led a similar charge against another section, capturing it, and maintained until his wounds became unbearable a heavy bomb fight with the enemy under severe fire. Nor could anything be more picturesque than the way in which Lieutenant Throssell and Corporals Dunstan and Burton, although badly wounded, built up a barricade under fire and thus saved a critical position. Yet every Victoria Cross man declared, when his wounds were dressed, that every man in the battalions had done work as good.

The story of Australasian efforts would be incomplete without reference to the work of the Australian Army Medical Corps. The medical resources of Australia and New Zealand were fully mobilized, and in addition to providing a large section of the treatment for the Mediterranean Expeditionary Force wounded and sick, more than a hundred doctors were sent at the War Office's request to France. The doctors of Australasia seemed unanimous in their desire

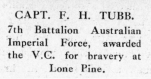

CAPT. F. H. TUBB.
7th Battalion Australian Imperial Force, awarded the V.C. for bravery at Lone Pine.

LIEUT. JOHN SYMONS.
7th Battalion Australian Imperial Force, awarded the V.C. for bravery at Lone Pine.

PRIVATE J. HAMILTON.
1st Battalion Australian Imperial Force, awarded the V.C. for bravery in the Gallipoli Peninsula.

DINNER TIME.
A Quarter-Master of the Canterbury Rifles.

to go with their sons and their sons' friends into battle, and the applications for positions came in such numbers that the Defence Department was able to choose the best. Several leading consultants and surgeons went to Egypt at their own expense, when they found that room could not be made for them ; one took with him his assistant, two nurses, and full equipment. In Sir Alexander McCormack, Drs. Syme, Stawell, and Maudsley, and many others, Australia had the services of its most distinguished medical men. The work in the Mediterranean was not only distressing, continuous, and extremely fatiguing, it also required a self-effacement and submission to discipline which to less patriotic men would have been a severe trial. The sands of Egypt and the islands of the Ægean were against quick healing. The medical corps was continually fighting its septic surroundings, and the system grew up of sending as many cases as possible direct in hospital ships from Gallipoli to England. The Australian Army Medical Corps suffered severely in Gallipoli, but it established traditions. In one man alone, Dr. Mathieson, of Melbourne, Australian Universities lost a life which had been judged infinitely precious. It was felt that in public interests a different system from that followed in the army should prevail, and brilliant men with proved capacity for research work should not be allowed to risk

their lives. But the Australian Army Medical Corps was proud to bear its heavy sorrows without complaint. The men at the front lived under fire, they had their little hospitals on the beaches. The ordinary system of stationary hospitals behind the firing line could not apply to warfare on the peninsula, where the ground held was so slender. There were many incidents showing the heroism and self-sacrifice of medical workers in Gallipoli, but nothing more appealing than the refusal of a hospital unit at Suvla Bay to hoist the Red Cross flag, lest the Turks should think we were sheltering under it the army corps headquarters close by As a whole it may be said that the Dominion medical corps, which in the Mediterranean included Australian, New Zealand, and Canadian units, brought something new into army medical work. The Dominion men were extraordinarily quick in their methods. They did much that might have been left to orderlies, and waited on no man. Australia organized no less than ten fully equipped and staffed general hospitals, and added seven auxiliaries to its two hospitals in Cairo. Where convenient, Australian wounded and sick were sent to Australian hospitals, but as a general rule British and Australian lay side by side in the nearest hospital able to deal with them. The Governments agreed to pay each other a daily allowance for each of their soldiers treated in a hospital established by another, but as the war progressed these charges appeared by common consent to be cast aside. Both New Zealand and Australia sent many more doctors and nurses than were required for the treatment of their own sick and wounded, excessively large in numbers though these were. They sent also numerous hospital ships, chartering the best liners in their waters, and sparing no expense. There was a striking rally of Australasian men and women to the Red Cross, and the keen anxiety of the nation to know that their wounded were getting the best that could be provided was shown by the display of public indignation when convalescent men were instructed to travel by ordinary train between Melbourne and Sydney.

It is now necessary to take up in detail the narrative of the war activities of the six million people from whom the Anzacs, in regular drafts, had come. There were regrets and recriminations when it was thought that another ten thousand men landed in Gallipoli on the first day, or another two divisions added to the five British divisions landed at Suvla Bay in August, would have made the difference between success and failure. It could not be said that in the Dominions the men did not exist, or that the training would have been impossible. Governments and people, however, never had the information upon which drastic and complete action could be based. Lord Kitchener's cable in June that he could arm and use "every available man" was the first direct intimation that all was not well. Several of the offers of brigades and reinforcements were accepted so tardily that there were doubts as to whether they were really needed. The utmost news that the Government received from Downing Street for many weeks about the Dardanelles was that there was reason for "satisfaction." Mr. Fisher was led in the House of Representatives to make public complaint that he had to rely

for valuable Imperial information upon what the Press reported by cable of answers given by Under-Secretaries to questions in the Imperial Parliament. He was compelled to "express the opinion that the British Government does not yet realize to the full the real position of the distant Dominions in matters that very nearly affect us." There was, of course, good reason for secrecy. To send confidential information to Australia was to take a risk, under some circumstances, which did not make for Imperial efficiency. No risk with regard to the arrangements for the Gallipoli landing, for instance, could well have been justified. But the Dominion Governments were throughout more jealous of official secrets than was London, and one of the episodes which puzzled the Australians was the noising about of great secrets in London, and their discussion in the House of Lords, before they were entrusted to

INTELLIGENCE OFFICERS.
Outside their dug-out at Gaba Tepe.

their Governments. There could be no complaint about the complete confidence reposed in Dominion Prime Ministers when they visited London, but the lack of clear Imperial leadership distinctly delayed emergency efforts in Australia. No adequate attempt was made to use the Dominion Press, which was allowed to flounder along in the dark, with two articles in its creed—faith in Great Britain, and downright certainty of victory.

After early vain offers to turn Australian factories into munition workshops, and to accelerate recruiting if the Imperial Government would provide rifles, the Fisher Government

AN AUSTRALIAN DESPATCH RIDER IN GALLIPOLI.

settled down into steady efforts to produce what Australia could within its own strength and in a high state of efficiency turn out. The policy was persistent, thorough work, instead of an emergency effort that could and would have produced 250,000 able-bodied men within fifteen months of war. A severe medical test was imposed on volunteers, and the average number of rejections was as high as 46 per cent. What was done was done without regard for vested interest and with thorough regard to the men's fitness as soldiers. Equipment was of the best. All militia officers were called to work at the training camps, which became great semi-permanent institutions. There was quick response to every suggestion from London. At a mere hint the whole of the

frozen meat trade was taken over for Imperial soldiers. Horse-buyers were sent into the remotest parts to make sure that the best available should be secured for the forces. Though surprised when Lord Kitchener answered a plaintive appeal for further directions with a cable, "Send a motor transport column," the Government searched every city for motor wagons, bought the best they could find, and set the State railway workshops to work to build repairing shops on wheels. As soon as fear of surprise attacks on the coast was over, a large section of permanent Australian Garrison Artillery men were formed into a siege brigade, under Colonel Coxon. These men created a most favourable impression in England, where their stature was generally commented upon amongst artillery officers. A bridging train was raised under naval officers, and put through thorough training in Government House Grounds, Melbourne. The tasks set the Australian and New Zealand Governments were performed with characteristic directness and completeness. What was lacking was a mobilization of all resources on a final scale, a thorough education of the public in the necessity of supreme efforts if they were to gain the one outstanding desire of the nation.

The question of equipment became paramount in the Government's considerations of what could be done, both in New Zealand and Australia. In New Zealand the one requisite of which an ample supply was soon assured was khaki cloth. The Otago and Canterbury mills were soon busy producing the typical New Zealand khaki, which had a shade of green, and they adapted their looms to serve Australian needs. The whole cloth output of the Australian mills was taken over by the Government, the Federal Clothing Factory, a national enterprise established by Senator Pearce four years previously to make uniforms for the citizen soldiery and the Post Office, was trebled in size and put on double shifts, and large private clothing factories became practically national concerns. The Government fixed conditions of work, exercised a general control, and took the whole of the output. This was in keeping with the practical policy of rigid regulation of private war efforts, and resulted in a system similar to the new munitions scheme in Great Britain being instituted in the Commonwealth long before the Ministry of Munitions was thought of. A Federal saddlery factory had been established for army and postal

HEROES OF GABA TEPE.

Tending wounded on the heights after they had been stormed by the Australians and New Zealanders.

ON BOARD H.M.S. "CANOPUS" AT THE DARDANELLES.
Australians calling for their mails.

requirements in peace time. This was at once extended, and again private output was regulated. Export of hides except to Great Britain was prohibited. Care was taken to select the local boot factories which produced the best possible service boots. The same policy was pursued in connexion with underwear, hats, and general accoutrements required by the troops. No better equipment was sent into the firing line than that of the Australasian soldiers. "The most perfectly equipped soldiers I have seen," wrote *The Times* Special Correspondent in Egypt. "Everything is of good quality, and stands wear well." The Australian tunic, a pure woollen flannel garment, became distinctive. The Australasian overcoats were eagerly sought after. An officer of the Lancashire Territorials told in his diary how eagerly the troops at Suvla Bay wrapped themselves in them when lucky enough to come upon the piles collected from the Australian dead.

There was never lack of clothing at Anzac. Other troops suffered through being sent on an autumn expedition in tropical uniforms, but though the Australasians ruthlessly cast aside everything but abbreviated "shorts" during the hot months, they got back into their native wool when the nights became cold again.

Conscription had been discussed at the first mention of war. A large section of practical

opinion held that the nation had a right to its best, and that the fate of generations was too serious a matter to take the slightest risk with. It was not, however, until late in June, 1915, that the utmost efforts were put into recruiting. The Australian force had then grown to 90,000, the New Zealand to 23,000. By July 13 Australia had reached 100,000. Recruiting campaigns were instituted by the State Parliaments, and that in Victoria brought in 19,000 men in three weeks. The Governments adopted the uncompromising attitude of mobilizing the last man and the last shilling. "The struggle is titanic, and will have to be fought to the death," said Mr. Hughes. "We must win; but we can only do this by bringing into the scale every ounce of energy we possess and every resource at our command." The New Zealand Government compiled a compulsory register of all men between the ages of 17 and 60 years, with full particulars of status, occupation, physical condition, military experience and number of dependents. Men of military age were asked if they intended to serve, and "if not, why not." The Australian Government compiled in September, 1915, a record on the same lines, in addition to full particulars of the wealth of the community. Every person was compelled to state his wealth, and the Government became possessed of information on which complete mobilization of gold could be based. By November the number of men enlisted for active service, including those preparing in the training camps, was nearly 170,000. When the full extent of the losses at the Dardanelles was at length estimated, it was decided to raise another full army corps of 50,000. The reinforcements necessary for the armies in the field were then 9,000 a month, and the new corps promised to bring Australia's total by June, 1916, up to 300,000. There was never doubt that the men could be raised. Nor was there any real split on the question of forced service if necessary. Several trades-union organizations protested against compulsion before the first boatloads of wounded returned from Gallipoli, but the real issue was whether it was necessary. A Universal Service League was formed in August, with branches in all the States, its leaders including men of such different political views as Mr. J. C. Watson, ex-Labour Prime Minister and principal leader of the unions, Mr. Wade, ex-Premier, and Professor Edgeworth David. The general sentiments of the Dominion were well expressed by the *Sydney Bulletin,* an outstanding Socialist journal :

There is no party that questions the justifiableness of this war ; it is not being waged for territory ; and even if we won it in an unthinkably short time there would still be no financial profit in it. It is one of those Imperial death-struggles which occur but once in centuries ; the sort of war that Carthage waged—and lost. It is peculiarly our war. . . . The first anomaly that ought to go is voluntary service. The business of wailing for recruits by means of posters, politicians' speeches, white feathers, and so forth is as degrading as those other appeals by which our hospitals are periodically rescued from insolvency. Speaking broadly, the system gets the wrong men—the best—leaving the bad patriots and the cowards behind. There is everything against voluntary service as a means of raising a national army and nothing but a few deceptive old catchwords in its favour. It is especially fatal in a war where every fit man is wanted, inasmuch as it can never rope in all the nation's fit men.

In New Zealand Mr. Massey guaranteed that he would stick at nothing, and Mr. Allen declared on November 4 "There is much evidence that the public mind is veering towards compulsory service. The evidence in the South Island is overwhelming, and the matter is receiving very serious consideration." In both Dominions the Derby Scheme methods were used to the full in the months preceding

AFTER THE BATTLE OF GABA TEPE.
Turkish prisoners guarded by Anzac Troops.

Christmas, 1915. There were never two opinions as to the conditions on which peace could be accepted. Such statements as the following, by the New South Wales Labour Premier, Mr. W. A. Holman, came from all the leaders :

I am one of those who hope that, when victory is achieved, there will be no weakness on the part of the Allied Governments; that, acting in the interests of civilization, they will avail themselves of so unprecedented an opportunity to declare that the public law of Europe is no longer a law without sanction and without punishment, but that those who break the public law of Europe are to be treated like criminals who break any other law. I hope we shall have the pleasure of seeing some of the members of the Great General Staff of the German Empire and some members of the German Ministry placed upon their trial for wilful murder and brought to account for the various acts committed at their instigation. If I live to see that day I shall feel that I have belonged to a nation and a race that deserves well of humanity and has

nothing. In Australia the war and drought acted as co-ordinated scourges, which imposed a discipline on the country such as many generations will remember. The drought followed seven bountiful years, and was easily met in the financial world by a conservative banking policy, and by drawing upon the great reserves which squatters, traders, and working class savings banks had piled up. Its effect was, however, most unfortunate, for it meant that Australia had to import wheat at high prices instead of sending forth a great surplus to command the war returns ruling in Europe. The meat trade, which during 1912 and 1913 developed with Great Britain and the United States, was less badly hit, but the export was obtained very largely by reckless marketing of

AT THE DARDANELLES.
An Australian gun in position on Bolton's Ridge.

justified its existence in the long and melancholy history of mankind. It is to the resolute hearts, the clear heads, the strong arms, and the determined spirit of our race that we must look now to guide us through this crisis and bring us triumphantly out.

New Zealand prosperity increased during the first year of war. A series of bountiful years culminated in one of remarkable productivity, and high prices ruled. For the staple exports, wool, wheat and frozen meat, the Dominion secured the full benefit of war prices. This made the task of financing the war comparatively easy. Mr. James Allen, who was Finance Minister as well as Minister of Defence until the Coalition, when Sir Joseph Ward relieved him of the former office, had to place no serious new imposts on the people. There were complaints in the north island of drought, but compared with the sufferings in Australia the damage was

valuable stock. Stockowners depleted their breeding stocks and sold their ewes to such an extent that even the pastoralists' newspapers suggested preventive legislation, saying with true Australian opportunism that " it is always risky to leave it to the individual to act in the interests of society." In New South Wales the sheepbreeders estimated that the drought cost them one-third of their flocks, while in Western Queensland and South Australia the calamity was even worse. While drought thus reduced trade in the main requirements of armies, the war for a while killed the wool and coal export. At a word from the Imperial authorities, wool export was prohibited. It had been going in large quantities to the United States, the usual markets of Belgium, Northern France, Germany and Austria having been suspended ; and upon it a considerable number of American factories were dependent. The stoppage had a double effect, as intended. It brought pressure upon the United States, and prevented supplies from going to the enemy. When at length a trust was formed in New York guaranteeing that the German alliance would get none of the product, export was again allowed, and abnormal prices were obtained. The uncomplaining way in which Australia submitted to the dislocation of its wool trade, which as the main export of the continent amounts to nearly £40,000,000 a year, was another of the many instances of the patience and sacrifice of Australian loyalty. The butter export, which had reached an average of four millions sterling annually, was reduced to little more than half that figure for the drought year and that following. Fine rains during autumn and spring in 1915 assured all States of a return to prosperity, and as the Governments had in every way encouraged the increase of acreage under crops the harvests became such that serious problems of transport developed. The official estimates for New South Wales and Victoria, which had in their best previous years produced thirty-five and thirty-three million bushels respectively, were that each would harvest sixty million bushels in the summer of 1915–1916. The Federal estimate was an

exportable crop of 150,000,000 bushels for all States. Railway departments set to work to improvise trucks for this rich result, and even carriages were reduced to wheat waggons. The women went into the fields, and the school boys of the cities were sent in organised bands to assist, but the main work of this great harvest had to be done by the farmers and those farmers' sons who subdued their fighting spirit until they had seen " the old people " through the good year. The release of the metals by the establishment of a metal exchange freed from foreign influences promised also to bring money to the country, and Australasia looked forward into 1916 with confidence that it could pay its share of the war expenditure and subsist. In general, the effects of the war upon trade were that the large import and export trade which Germany had secured was paralysed and that the United States and Japan, whose commercial travellers swarmed over Australasia, secured a greater share of this available connection than did the slower moving exporters of Great Britain.

In its public finance Australia did not face the task of getting on with less borrowed money than in normal years. New Zealand borrowed least of all Dominions, Australia most. Mr. Fisher, as Federal Treasurer, used all the Commonwealth Government's authority to

GALLIPOLI.
Graves of the New Zealand Mounted Brigade.
(*Exclusive to " The Times."*)

AUSTRALIAN WOUNDED IN THE DARDANELLES.
Red Cross men at work on board a war vessel at Lemnos.

curb loan expenditure by the States. But the State Premiers, who in the majority of cases were the Treasurers also, found their requests to London for money for public works were consistently well received by the Imperial Treasury, and they accepted the easy policy of borrowing in preference to that of stopping public works on hand, or even curtailing them, and interfering with the livelihood of the several scores of thousands of men employed. During the year ended July, 1915, the six States borrowed £25,990,000—more than a million more than in the previous year of profound peace, and eight millions more than in 1912–13. The point of view expressed by the State Treasuries was that Great Britain was quite willing to lend the money, and that there was so much money in London that there was a danger that the Imperial Treasury might forget it had lent any to the States. This view was encouraged by the attitude of the British Treasury when requests were made by State Premiers, against the wishes of the Federal Prime Minister, that an agreement entered into in December, 1914, should be broken on their side. This agreement provided that the British Treasury should lend to the Commonwealth

Treasury eighteen million pounds, which it must use for war expenditure, but which would enable it to finance the States to a similar extent ; and that the States would agree not to borrow elsewhere during the next twelve months except for renewals or by merely normal sales of Treasury bonds. London accepted the Premiers' assurances that more money was needed, and in seven months allowed the States nearly twelve millions more.

Being well into the field before the States with a strong case for war taxation, the Commonwealth Government led the way with stiff income taxes, a new inheritance tax, an increased land tax, and new import duties. Mr. Fisher, who a few years ago had surprised Australia by budgeting for an expenditure of eighteen million pounds, found himself in 1914–1915 faced with an outlay of £38,000,000, of which £14,792,000 was war expenditure, and when he left office in October, 1915, to take up the High Commissionership in London, he forecasted that the expenditure for 1915–1916 would be £74,045,000, of which £45,749,450 would be upon the expeditionary forces and the Fleet. He proposed that taxes should raise more than enough for the swollen " normal " expenditure, now increased by war pensions and interest on war loans to £24,466,025. His income tax was to begin at 3d. in the £ on incomes of £157 a year, rising by steep gradations to 53d. in the £ on those over £7,750. The heavy taxation was accepted throughout Australia with scarcely a protest.

A first war loan of £20,000,000 was successfully floated in Australia in September, and Mr. Fisher announced that another of £25,000,000 would be raised soon after. Of the first loan, which was issued at 4½ per cent., with immunity from taxation—a concession that for investors with the highest scale incomes brought the interest up to £6 4s. per cent.—£13,000,000 was immediately subscribed.

Although the part played by Australia and New Zealand in the supply of munitions was small, it could not be said that the failure was due to lack of local desire or effort. Both Dominions had been taught to rely upon Great Britain—and to some extent, in the case of cartridge cases, upon Germany—for their own needs in artillery and ammunition, and they had not even experts available for sudden adaptation of their industries. As far back as September, 1914, Senator Pearce offered all Australia's shell-making facilities to the Imperial Government. The war pressure in London naturally delayed receipt of full information, but on December 31 the High Commissioner was instructed to obtain quotations for a complete manufacturing plant. When the outcry for shells came in May, 1915, the people of both Dominions reproached themselves for not having done more. They eagerly repeated their offers. The controllers of all private enterprises concerned—mining, smelting and engineering companies—as well as the State Governments, placed their works at the disposal of the Minister of Defence. But though these works contained the essential lathes in abundance, and though the new steelworks of the Broken Hill Proprietary Company at Newcastle soon produced a steel fit for shellcases, it was late in the year before work could be begun. The time passed in securing formulæ from the Imperial authorities, and general disappointment was caused by the impression that London regarded Australian workshops as a negligible factor not worth troubling about. In New Zealand munitionmaking followed a similar course. It was felt to be unfortunate that the strong resources in metals and metal working in Australasia should

not have been mobilised early in the war, and the objection that shells made in Australia had to be transported half way round the world before they got to the filling factories of Great Britain was answered by the consideration that such cargo could take the place of ballast. The Commonwealth Government sent officers to London early in 1915 to become specially trained in shell-making, but these proved so valuable in British factories that their services were requisitioned, and it was not till several of the larger workshops in the Dominion had been converted, after long and intricate negotiations, into shell factories that they were allowed to return. In October tenders for the manufacture of shell-cases were accepted from the New South Wales, Queensland, Victorian and South

AT THE AUSTRALIAN HOSPITAL.
The Sultan of Egypt and General Sir John Maxwell visit the wounded from the Dardanelles.

Australian Governments, nine Victorian firms, two South Australian firms and the War Munitions Company of West Australia, first deliveries to be between November 1 and January 1.

The tragedy of Gallipoli was long in unfolding itself to the Australasian people. Inherent in them was a confidence in Great Britain capable of withstanding many rude shocks. The homesickness of the pioneers and settlers had passed down to Australasians of the second and third generations, and the Mother Country was regarded with strong veneration and affection. Those disposed to criticise the methods of the Englishman had faith in his powers, and the ability of the Empire to win the war was never questioned. In the early stages of the Gallipoli campaign anxiety was limited to a few political leaders, and even they believed till many months after the Battle of the Landing that the Imperial armies would get through. News was scant, and unreliable. Official reports told little, official press representatives were never allowed to touch on the strategical situation, and the lurid tales from Athens filled the place of legitimate news. In the Dominions it was believed that on the first days the Australasians had straddled the peninsula, that Maidos had been taken, that the fall of the Turkish army was a matter of days. The letters home from the wounded brought first particulars of actions that absorbed the public mind, and their exaggerated optimism supported the popular theory of infallibility. Casualty lists were long and numerous ; family after family was smitten, until it could be said that those who had not a relative in the lists had at least a friend ; the total of casualties rose with alarming rapidity to the full number of the first expeditionary force. But nothing could shake the patient confidence in the race.

The main product of the Dardanelles adventure in Australia, apart from the new national spirit it aroused, was a renewed determination to see the war through. The Dominions felt drawn even closer to Great Britain in common suffering and disappointment, and they stiffened their backs. There were many who expressed their disappointment candidly, but there were none who cast blame. What Australasia looked for as a result of the lessons of the Dardanelles was avoidance of mistakes in future. Misfortune on the battlefield could not daunt the Dominions ; the only thing that could weaken their Imperial affection was weakness or indecision in the supreme control of the war.

The effect upon the political leaders was more definite. The Australian Cabinet had in January, 1915, sought a meeting of Dominion leaders in London, in order that the full resources of the Empire should be mobilised. This suggestion was put forward by Mr. Fisher to Mr. Lewis Harcourt, then Secretary of State for the Colonies, but it had a poor reception in London. Mr. Massey, after accepting the London view that an Imperial Conference in war time was unworkable, supported the Australian Prime Minister, but Sir Robert Borden and General Botha were understood to be against it. The rejection of this project made the Dominion leaders feel even more in the dark than before, and they reached out

anxiously for such scraps of official information and guidance as came over the cables. Mr. Fisher's Imperialism was never to be questioned, and his admiration of London institutions and ability was always frank. But he stated in the House of Representatives that he was disappointed with the means of communication between the Dominions and London in war time, and that he could not regard a promise made by Mr. Harcourt, that the Dominions would be consulted before peace was accepted, as a satisfactory recognition of the Dominions' rights. What was feared was that Dominion opinion might count for little in peace, except as regards any suggestion that the German colonies should be returned ; whereas what really mattered was effective organisation of Dominion resources, and their co-ordination in Imperial plans. At length the leaders could stand it no longer. Mr. Harcourt, in rejecting the plan for a round table conference, had informed the Prime Ministers that he would be glad to see them and any responsible Ministers from the Dominions in London, and to lay before them all the information available to the British Cabinet. This invitation was repeated by Mr. Bonar Law when he assumed control of the Colonial Office. By the end of October, when the mistakes of the Dardanelles were more or less bare, Mr. Fisher, Mr. Hughes, Mr. Massey and Sir Joseph Ward decided to visit London. Mr. Fisher, whose recent experiences had convinced him of the importance and necessity of official work for Australia in London, decided to follow Sir George Reid as High Commissioner, and to take over the position in January, 1916. Mr. Hughes, who succeeded Mr. Fisher as Prime Minister, decided to make a brief visit to London about the same time, and Mr. Massey and Sir Joseph Ward were asked by their Ministers to take a similar journey as soon as could be arranged. The visits were looked forward to in the Dominions with intense interest. It was felt that they would mark a new, and perhaps a startling, departure in Imperial governance, and that from them would arise an enduring and invincible cohesion in the elements of Empire. Something, too, was expected from the visits paid to London by large numbers of Australasian soldiers. By November 11,000 sick and wounded Australians and 5,000 New Zealanders were in Great Britain, and the broadening effect of travel had been added to the discipline of Anzac. Everywhere an undeniable demand was arising for more vigorous co-operation of the Empire as a whole.

CHAPTER C.

RAILWAYS AND THE WAR.

IMPORTANCE OF RAILWAYS IN WAR—THE SOUTH AFRICAN WAR—GERMAN STRATEGIC LINES—
THE INVASION OF BELGIUM—THE FRENCH RAILWAY SYSTEM—RUSSIAN AND ITALIAN SYSTEMS
—THE BALKANS—BRITISH RAILWAY EXECUTIVE COMMITTEE—THE EXPEDITIONARY FORCE SENT
TO FRANCE—THE RAILWAY TRANSPORT OFFICER—AMBULANCE TRAINS—MAKING MUNITIONS.

O**N the outbreak of the Great War it was not easy for the average person to grasp the essential fact that the railways over which in normal times he travelled for purposes of business or pleasure were not only an indispensable part of the war machine, but perhaps the most powerful weapon in the armoury of the nations. There were wars before railways were built, and mankind will probably retain force as the final international court of appeal when railways shall have been superseded by other methods of land transport. The European War was, however, more than any conflict between the armed forces of mankind which preceded it, a war of railways.

There had, of course, been many interesting examples of the successful use of railways by armies in the field, and it was a subject which had received for a generation or more the very closest attention of the Military Staffs of the great nations on the Continent of Europe. The first examples of the use of railways on a large scale for military purposes were furnished by the wars of 1859 and 1866 in Europe, and the War of Secession in America. On the lessons then taught Germany framed a military railway policy which, in the war of 1870, had much to do with the rapid success won by the German armies. In France the teachings of earlier wars had been insufficiently regarded, and the rapidity of mobilization of the German forces, due to the efficient use of the railways, found

the French military authorities inadequately prepared. Moreover, what had been done in Germany itself enabled the Germans to make a more efficient use than would otherwise have been the case of the French railways of which possession was gained at an early stage of hostilities.

The fall of Toul and Metz gave uninterrupted railway communication between Germany and Paris as far as Nanteuil, 52 miles distant from the capital. The bridge over the Marne had been blown up by the French in their retreat, and this break in the line hampered the German advance, but when Soissons capitulated in October, 1870, the German armies held the line from the valley of the Marne to Reims, Soissons and Crespy. The Orleans Railway, and then the Western line to Rouen and Havre were also secured, although in the case of the Orleans Railway the retreating French army succeeded in destroying the railway bridge over the Loire.

In comparison, however, with the feats in railway transport which were accomplished in the war of 1914, the use made of the railways in the war of 1870 appeared to have been almost trivial, at least in the occupied territory. Owing to the general hostility of the civilian population and the more active tactics of bands of *Francs Tireurs*, the German provision, troop and hospital trains were only permitted to travel over the French railways by daylight, and it is stated that such trains occupied five

VOLUNTEER TRAINING CORPS AT WORK
Shovelling ballast out of railway trucks at Banbury.
Inset : Unloading cars.

British as a nation have lacked the gift of creating iron-bound systems and have, therefore, had to start *de novo* on the outbreak of every war in connexion with the work of supply and transport, the national characteristic of improvization had not infrequently stood us in good stead. The old British Army was not to be judged by Continental standards ; it had to fight its battles in many parts of the world and always under different conditions. It is certain that no organization planned in days of peace could possibly have served the needs of British campaigns in the Soudan, India, and in South Africa.

When the South African War broke out the whole of the British military railway organization consisted of two railway companies of Royal Engineers, amounting to 300 men of all ranks ; an organized railway staff and a scheme of operations were non-existent. The story told in *The Times History of the War in South Africa* is a fascinating narrative of the way in which the transport problem was solved under circumstances which were new in warfare. The work done by the staff under

days on the journey from railhead in France to the interior of Germany. No proper system of guarding occupied railway routes from raiders was put in force, and not until the South African War was an example given of the use of efficient methods of protecting long railway communications in areas subject to enemy raids.

The experience of that war in connexion with the use made of the railways was unique. At that time Great Britain possessed no military railway organization such as had been created on the Continent, and perhaps until England appeared likely to be involved in a great Continental war there was no real need to set up an organization in imitation of the German system. In this instance the policy of drift could be defended. If, however, the

the direction of Captain and Brevet-Major E. P. C. Girouard, afterwards Sir Percy Girouard, was one of the best examples of successful improvization for a special occasion which the annals of warfare contain. From the outset the Continental system, under which the Director of Railways was to be in absolute control of the railways, subject only to the Commander-in-Chief, was adopted. That principle was borrowed from Germany; the rest of the plan was British. The railway conditions were quite different from those on the Continent of Europe. The many thousands of miles of railway which had been constructed from the coast into the interior were nearly all narrow gauge single line, often constructed, owing to the nature of the country traversed, on heavy radients and curves of short radius, so that the carrying capacity was far below that of the standard railways of Europe.

The strategical concentration for the march on Bloemfontein under Lord Roberts was under the circumstances a great feat in troop transport. The railway was called upon to collect the men, horses, transport, guns, and stores and supplies from many points, and to concentrate them on the short section of line between the Orange and Modder rivers. The troops had to be detrained at various stations, where no accommodation existed, on a single line railway, while the concentration had to be done in a certain time and be carried out with the greatest secrecy. With supreme confidence in the system which he had devised, the Director

THE BRITISH IN FRANCE.

Loading pontoons on a train in Northern France. Inset : British and French troops guarding a railway.

SIR SAM FAY,
Great Central Ry.

MR. J. A. F. ASPINALL,
L. & Y. Ry.

MR. GUY CALTHROP,
L. & N.W. Ry.

THE RAILWAY

THE RT. HON. WALTER RUNCIMAN.
President.

of Railways undertook the whole responsibility for the task, and in fifteen days a total of 152 trains passed northward and 30,000 troops with horses, guns, etc., were detrained.

It was only gradually that the 5,000 odd miles of railway in operation in South Africa at the beginning of the war passed under British control, and at the commencement of hostilities the Boers, from the strategical standpoint, were in a very favourable position. Like Germany and Austria in the European War, they were acting on interior lines and could move troops from one frontier to another with great rapidity. The chief defect of the Boer railway system, in which respect it resembled the railway systems of Germany and Austria, was that only one of its lines connected with neutral territory and was available for the importation of supplies. The Boer railway management had, however, taken advantage of the fact that the loosely-knit network of South African railways was worked as a single economic system to retain for their own use a favourable balance of rolling stock on the eve of the war, the loss of which was severely felt as additional railway mileage came under British control. So cleverly indeed did the Boer Railway Department handle the question of rolling stock, that it was not until a comparatively late date that what had not been destroyed in the Boer retreat was recovered.

MR. C. H. DENT,
G.N. Ry.

MR. F. H. DENT,
S.E. & C. Ry.

SIR GUY GRANET,
Midland Ry.

SIR A. KAYE BUTTERWORTH,   MR. DONALD A. MATHESON,   SIR. WILLIAM FORBES,
N.E. Ry.   Caledonian Ry.   L.B. & S.C. Ry.

EXECUTIVE COMMITTEE.

Only the rapidity of Lord Roberts's advance, which was rendered possible by the excellent use made of the railway facilities, prevented the Boers from destroying all the engines and rolling stock which they were unable to retain. They did, of course, on some of the routes destroy the railway itself with a considerable degree of thoroughness—stations, telegraphs, water supply, permanent way, and bridges being wrecked wholesale, and thus threw a great strain on those charged with the repair of the line. Fortunately, however, Elandsfontein Junction, the key of the railway system in South Africa, was recovered in an undamaged condition.

In the later stages of the war, when the whole of the South African railway system was in possession of the British Forces, the railways were subject to the persistent attacks of Boer raiders, which on one occasion stopped all traffic for over a fortnight. It became necessary to adopt effective measures to protect the long lines of railway on which the supplies of the British Army depended, and the steps taken by the establishment of the blockhouse system

not only secured the communications but had the effect of converting the railways into fortified barriers, which played an essential

SIR HERBERT A. WALKER.
Chairman.

part in the policy of separating, enclosing, and hunting down the Boer Commandos.

Originally, the railways had been protected

Elliott &   *Fry.*

MR. GILBERT S. SZLUMPER,   MR. A. WATSON,   MR. FRANK POTTER,
Secretary to the Committee.   L. & Y. Ry.   Great Western Ry.

FIRING A BRIDGE IN BELGIUM, SEPTEMBER, 1914.
An heroic act by an eighteen-year-old Belgian Corporal. J. de Mante ran along the plank by the side
of the bridge, lighted torch in hand, which he plunged into the barrels of paraffin already prepared.
They blazed up instantly. Bullets whizzed round him, but he climbed upon the bridge and completed
his task by rubbing his torch on the paraffin-soaked boards, after which he left the bridge a roaring furnace.

by small parties of mounted men, but in addition to the large drafts which such a system made on the fighting forces it was ineffective against raiders in any force, and the idea of establishing definite fortifications was evolved. The type of blockhouse ultimately adopted took the form of two cylinders of corrugated iron without woodwork, the spaces between the cylinders being packed with shingle, and the construction roofed and loop-holed. It was possible to build these blockhouses at a very low cost, and the defence which was thus provided, in conjunction with armoured trains provided with quick-firing guns, as well as Maxims and searchlights, made the railways safe from raiders. On some sections of railway blockhouses were erected at such short intervals as 200 yards and, in addition, the lines were fenced with barbed wire. It was a system designed to meet the needs of a special case, and the conversion of long lines of railway into permanent fortifications for the successful prosecution of a war was a feat which was only made possible by local conditions.

Brief reference should also be made to the work carried out in the shops of the various South African railway companies, an example which was so largely followed in the European War. The resources of the manufacturing departments of the railways were diverted for increasing the output of munitions. The control works at Pretoria successfully undertook the production of gun ammunition, and the repair of ordnance, while the wagon shops provided the necessary number of ambulance trains. The South African campaign as a whole was a revelation even to the great military nations of the uses to which railways could be put for the purposes of war.

In the American War of Secession excellent use had been made of the rail transport facilities available, but in view of what was achieved by railways in the European War of 1914, attention was directed in the American Press to the lack of strategic railways in the United States in the light of modern experience. It was pointed out that owing to the great distances over which troops would have to be transported in the event of the United States being threatened on either of its exposed seaboards, the lack of strategic railways would prevent that rapid mobilization which war had shown was one of the first essentials of a successful campaign. Attention was particularly directed to the need of providing improved terminal facilities at those ports and harbours at which an enemy might seek to make a landing in order to avoid the congestion which took place in the dispatch of troops to Cuba in the Spanish-American War. A demand was made for a transportation survey and the preparation of plans so that a comprehensive programme might be worked out with a view to providing against the danger of invasion.

The disadvantages which arise from the want of adequate transport facilities were very vividly illustrated in the Russo-Japanese War. In that case the only method of transporting troops to the scene of warfare was by means of the Trans-Siberian Railway, which at that time was mainly a single line track, and it was partly

BRIGADIER-GENERAL TWISS,
Director General of Railway Transport.

for want of adequate transport that Russia concluded a peace when she had only put a comparatively small number of her available men into the field.

In the Great War the railways exercised a constant influence on the course of the fighting. The campaigns in Belgium, France, Russia, in Northern Italy, and the great thrust into the Balkans, by which the enemy sought to gain possession of the through railway route to Constantinople, furnished many illustrations of the tendency in modern warfare to wage battles for the possession of transport facilities, and to utilize to the fullest extent the mobility which railways confer. Germany made free use of her railway system to transfer large forces from one battle front to the other and to hold up each in turn during the early stages of the war; the excellent employment made of French railways enabled our Ally to be at least partially prepared to deal with the invader, and it was largely by means of her railways that Russia mobilized in a period of time which surprised the enemy and occupied territory in East Prussia at a moment when Germany was concentrating on the march to Paris. The fine use which was made of the railways by the combatant armies was often overlooked for the simple reason that they were common features of every-day life.

In Great Britain there was, of course, with

ON THE UGANDA RAILWAY IN BRITISH EAST AFRICA.

British troops preparing to resist an attack by the enemy on an armoured train.

one possible exception, no such thing as a strategic railway. The main lines of communication and practically every branch railway were constructed to serve ordinary commercial needs. The building of strategic railways had always been the business of the State, and in Great Britain there were no State railways, although the Government in virtue of the powers vested in it took possession of the railway system when war was declared.

The position on the Continent was very different. The policy of building railways by which military forces could be rapidly placed on artificially created frontiers had been pursued for many years. In this respect Germany had taken the lead, and had constructed a large mileage of railway lines for which there was military but certainly no commercial justification. It was a simple task indeed for any railway expert to destroy the whole edifice of German sophistry regarding the responsibility for the war by a reference to the policy pursued by Germany in strategic railway construction. It was plain that the invasion of France through Belgium was an essential part of the plan of invasion. There could be no other reason for the remarkable network of lines which had been constructed on the frontiers of Belgium, and which when the time came were employed for the invasion of that unhappy country. The only excuse that the Germans could offer for their railway policy was that the best defensive consists in preparedness for an offensive. The work of constructing these railways was simplified by the fact that the German railway system was owned and worked by the Government.

In a war which in its character was so often a struggle for lines of communication, every mile of the railway was an asset. The following table, compiled for the *Great Eastern Railway Magazine*, from which some of the maps in this chapter have been reproduced, may, therefore, be regarded as possessing historical interest, as it represents the railway conditions as they existed at the outbreak of war :

[Swaine.

LIEUT.-COL. H. O. MANCE, D.S.O.,
Assistant Director of Railway Transport.

The table reveals the disadvantage at which Russia was placed in relation to Germany, and why the latter country was confident of holding up the slow-moving Russian armies while France was being beaten to her knees. That, with a railway system so inferior to that of the enemy, Russia was able to mobilize her forces for the invasion of East Prussia at so early a stage in the conflict was one of the marvels of a war which was full of surprises.

Germany, with that genius for organization which proved to be one of her great assets in the long struggle, had, during the forty years of peace which followed the war with France in 1870, created a railway system which, however well it may have served the needs of the

—	Miles of Railway.	Area Sq. Miles per Railway Mile.	Population per Railway Mile.
Great Britain ... about	23,450	5½	1,930
Belgium ... ,,	5,000	4	2,400
France ... ... ,,	30,000	8	1,650
Russia ... ... ,,	39,000	234	3,500
Germany ... ,,	38,000	6	1,700
Austria-Hungary ,,	27,000	10	2,000
Italy ... ... ,,	10,800	10¼	3,211

Mr. H. W. THORNTON,
General Manager, G.E. Ry.

GENERAL BOTHA'S CAMPAIGN IN SOUTH-WEST AFRICA.

A railway engine "pontooned" across the Orange River, March 14, 1915.

travelling and commercial community, had, as indicated above, been largely built with a view to military needs. It is obvious to anyone who studies the accompanying maps that the possession of railways which covered the frontiers of France, Belgium, and Poland, which provided duplicate routes between East and West, which linked all the railway centres by direct lines with the frontiers, was a great military asset. The trunk lines were all important, but it was some of the smaller railways on the frontier that held the main interest for the military chiefs. These were, indeed, of supreme importance to Germany. The line between Emden and Munster afforded connexion across the marshy country of Ems ; its branch lines were also of military value. In the triangle formed by Cologne, Aix la Chapelle, Emmerich, Limburg and the Rhine, Germany had multiplied strategic lines to the point of apparent confusion. These, in addition to controlling the frontiers, served Essen and other industrial towns.

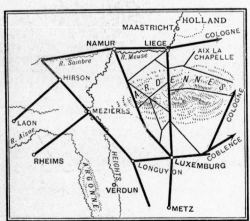

A glance at a map shows how important, apart from its influence on the Belgian campaign, was the seizure of Luxemburg. It gave a straight road from Verviers to Metz, with connexions on the Rhine. Into this line and the territory behind it between Cologne and Saarburg many branch lines and connexions had been constructed. So military in purpose were some of the railways on which Germany relied for the rapid invasion of Belgium that they had never been used for ordinary traffic before the war. One of these secret lines was that connecting Malmedy and Stavelot. Yet its existence was almost essential to the success of German military plans. The line linking Malmedy with Weymertz was another important strategic route. Major Stuart Stephens had reminded us that without the aid of these short lines the troops entrained at Coblenz, Cologne, Bonn and Gladbach could not be secretly projected on the Belgian frontier. As a blind to the real intentions in constructing these particular railway links, Germany had provided an alternative route between Aix and St. Vitti, but this was not built as a military railway, and had, before Germany was ready for war, to be superseded by a high-level line. As a corollary to the little Stavelot–Malmedy line four million pounds were expended in building this high level line between Weymertz and Malmedy. It was designed to be finished in June, 1914, and as is now known war broke out at the beginning of August in that year. Such was the gigantic "bluff" put up by Germany in regard to the reasons for building these two lines—the Stavelot–Malmedy and the Weymertz–Malmedy—that a considerable portion of the capital was provided by Belgium, and that country actually at its own cost linked these lines, designed to facilitate the rapid invasion of its territory, with the Belgian railway system. The annexation of Luxemburg was, of course, a very simple affair. The railways were already in German hands, and it was an easy task to transport an army into the capital of the Duchy and announce its annexation for the purposes of the war.

There were other points in the German railway policy before the war to which attention should be directed to show the determination to be ready for war, although it was known, in the phrase used by Sir James Yoxall, that in the months preceding the outbreak of hostilities "grass grew hay-high between the rails of the few French strategic railways." The same writer furnished some striking information as to what the Germans had been doing in constructing railways through the volcanic province of the Eifel, just inside the German frontier. Ten years ago the railway was a simple single line, but by the time war was declared it had been straightened, doubled, and throughout its steeper gradients flattened ; in certain sections it had been tripled and quadrupled, and sidings, absurdly large for the trading or social needs of the population, were laid out near any railway station which was in flat open country and itself

situated on level ground with plenty of space in the vicinity of the station. At Gerolstein, a village with 1,200 inhabitants, sidings suitable for the traffic of a large town had been laid out.

A marked feature of German railways was that there were very few heavy gradients, and that on many of the main lines there was not a single tunnel. That routes had been selected for the railways which presented so few natural obstacles was a great advantage as long as the railways remained in German possession, but in the event of invasion, which a military Power such as Germany probably never contemplated when laying out the railway system, it would clearly be very difficult for German armies in retreat to damage the railways to an extent which would prevent their use by an invading army for anything more than a short period.

It may be pointed out that even during peace time German railways were administered by military methods. On the mobilization of the army they were immediately taken over by the military authorities, under the guidance of the Railways Section of the Great General Staff. The German railway administration was of a somewhat complicated character, but the Imperial Government had always possessed arbitrary powers in connexion with railway construction, and it had been no unusual circumstance for military lines to be constructed through territory in opposition to the will of

GERMANS OVERCOMING DIFFICULTIES CAUSED BY BROKEN BRIDGES.

Transporting engines and rolling stock by pontoon across a river in Russia.

the inhabitants. To such a degree of completeness had the German railway organization been brought that rules had been framed before the war governing the administration of railways in foreign countries which were occupied by the German army.

No doubt many fine feats in transport were achieved by German railways during the war, but some of the stories concerning the rapid movement of troops from east to west or the converse which were published in the Press were obvious exaggerations. There is a limit

in transportation of which every practical railway man is fully aware, and some of the performances with which rumour credited the German railway organization were of an impossible character. One fine achievement, however, stands to the credit of Von Hindenburg who, in spite of the handicap of air reconnaissance, succeeded by the transfer of a large force from the Cracow and Czenstochau districts in effecting a surprise upon the Russian forces in the neighbourhood of Kalisch. In a period of four days Von Hindenburg transported a force of nearly 400,000 men over a distance of 200 miles. The fact that it took four days to move this army over a comparatively short distance, although in itself a good performance, gave an index to the time which would be occupied in transferring any large body of troops from the eastern to the western front, a journey which in peace times occupied about twenty hours by express train and which, even when the necessary rolling stock had been assembled at the point of departure, a long and wearisome business in itself, would under military traffic conditions take many times as long. Even when credit is given for all the

GUARDING RAILWAYS AT THE FRONT.
German Landsturm in Belgium. Inset: A German armoured train.

TRANSPORTING A BRITISH TWELVE-INCH GUN.

advantage which followed the fact that Germany was fighting on interior lines, a majority of the stories which gained currency at various times during the war may be relegated to the same category as that of the transport of a Russian army through England.

The French railway system, although it was not constructed for strategic purposes, was admirably adapted for the rapid transport of troops and material of war. The lines along the eastern frontier from Boulogne, through Amiens, Tergnier, Laon, Reims and Verdun commanded the German frontier and that through Cambrai and Mons to Brussels enabled troops to be transported to the Belgian frontier. These, however, were commercial railways, not strategic in the ordinary meaning of the word, nor was the frontier, as was the case with Germany, a maze of railways whose only functions were that of army transport. Under normal peace conditions the French railways were under the control of the Minister of Public Works, but as was the case in Great Britain, they were automatically taken over by the Government on the outbreak of war.

It will be interesting to show in some detail how the French railways were managed during the war. The whole of the railways were operated under the condition even in times of peace that if the Government required to transport troops and supplies to any point on any railway system the Company must immediately place all its facilities at the service of the State. As this obligation had existed for a period of forty years a permanent military organization was in existence whose duties were to prepare the railways for service in time

of war. According to an account of the system in force which appeared in the *Journal des Transports*, each of the large railways had attached to it a Committee of two, known as the Commission de Réseau, composed of a technical member, usually the general manager of the railway, and a military member, who was a high officer of the general staff nominated by the Minister of War. The duties of this Committee were to investigate in all its bearings in the light of strategic requirements the manner in which the railway could be utilized for the purposes of war. In addition to the Commissions de Réseau a Military Railways Committee had been created in the year 1898. This Committee, which was presided over by the Chief of the General Staff, consisted of six military officers of high rank, three representatives of the Ministry of Public Works, and the members of the Commissions of the different railways. The functions of this Committee were mainly advisory, but it sat in judgment on all questions relating to military transport, and assented or dissented from measures proposed by the Commissions de Réseau.

Special regulations affecting railway employees came into force on the declaration of war. These provided that when a railwayman was called to the colours he was mobilized as a railwayman, and the working of this system was successfully tested during the railway strike of 1910, the railway men being then called out under martial law. On the first day of mobilization the railways were required to place at the disposal of the military authorities the whole of their transport facilities either over the whole of the systems or on certain specified

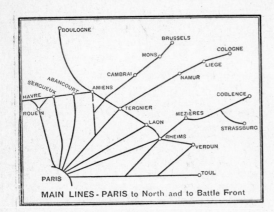

MAIN LINES - PARIS to North and to Battle Front

routes. The railway system of France was on mobilization divided into two zones which, although administered by different authorities, were both under military control. The army zone was placed under the control of the Commander-in-Chief of the armies in the field, to whose staff was attached an officer whose status was that of Manager of the army railways. This zone was subdivided into the sections of line which were within and without the actual sphere of military operations. Within the zone of actual field operations the service was conducted by military units, while the sections of line outside that area were manned by the employees of the company who were mobilized under a territorial system for that purpose. The other railway zone, known as the interior zone, was under the direction of the Minister of War, who gave authority to the Commission de Réseau of each railway to carry out executive functions, each of the two members of the Committee retaining individual responsibility, the military member being entrusted with military measures, and the technical member being charged with the provision of rolling stock and other technical requirements.

While precedence was given to the transport of troops and materials of war, provision was also made for the carriage of food-stuffs and general commercial merchandise. Within the army zone ordinary traffic was entirely suspended except on the order of the Commander-in-Chief. In the interior zone ordinary passenger and goods traffic was carried according to the conditions prescribed by the Minister of War, who had the power after mobilization and concentration were completed to authorize the partial or complete resumption of ordinary passenger and freight traffic.

The French Army at the outset of the war was undoubtedly under the handicap of having a much smaller mileage of strategic railways

than Germany. The deficiency was to a certain extent remedied during the progress of the war. The French had a valuable asset in a fine corps of railway engineers, and in connection with the repair of railways damaged during the march on Paris and the subsequent advance the services of British railwaymen were requisitioned both for this repair work and for the building of new lines.

An account of the fine work done on the French railways during the early days of the war was furnished by the French authorities, and the report indicated with what remarkable precision the transport system worked. Its first great task was the transport of the "troupes de couverture," the army sent to the frontier to meet the first shock of the enemy, a proceeding which enabled the mobilization of the main armies to be carried out undisturbed.

This was the work of the first department of the three heads into which the French transport service was divided. The second department was charged with the regular supply of men, horses, provisions, ammunition and material to the armies in the field. The third department was responsible for the transport of troops from one part of the theatre of war to another where their presence would contribute to the success of an operation. The transport of the "troupes de couverture" commenced on the evening of July 31, 1914, and was completed on August 3 at noon without any delay either in the departure or arrival of trains, and before any of the ordinary services had been suspended. Nearly 600 trains were required on the Eastern system alone, and the merit of this fine feat in transportation was enhanced by the fact that the transport of troops in connection with the general mobilization commenced on August 2 and was, therefore, partially concurrent with the movement of the first armies to the frontier. The transports needed for the concentration of the armies generally commenced on August 5, the most urgent period ending on August 12. During these eight days no fewer than 2,500 trains were dispatched, of which only 20 were subjected to slight delays, and during a period of fourteen days nearly 4,500 trains were dispatched, and in addition 250 trains loaded with siege supplies for the fortresses. These excellent results of French railway organization were rendered the more noteworthy from the fact that the original destination of four army corps was changed after mobilization had commenced.

ITALIAN SOLDIERS LEAVING FOR THE FRONT.
The last few moments before departure.

In the transport of troops from one part of the theatre of operations to another some remarkable performances were accomplished by French railways. During the French offensive in Lorraine and Belgium in August, 1914, at which time the transport in France of the British Expeditionary Force had also to be undertaken, during the retreat beyond the Marne, and the subsequent advance, and again at the time of the extension of the left of the armies operating in France to the North Sea, over 70 divisions were moved by railway from one point to another, the journeys varying in length from 60 to 360 miles, and necessitating the employ-

WRECKED BY BELGIAN ENGINEERS.
German soldiers repairing a train that was overturned on the line to obstruct the advance in Belgium
of the German Army.

ment of over 6,000 trains. The report which made these facts public rightly attributed a large measure of the success attained by the Allied armies to the manner in which the railway transport problem was solved, and in particular assigned to the railway arm the main credit for the erecting of the impassable barrier against which the enemy made his vain attacks in Flanders.

With regard to the ordinary transport service of the Army which was directed from the control stations on the railways, as described in Chapter LXXII. dealing with the feeding of the Army, this worked with perfect regularity from the beginning of the war. During the retreat on Paris the control stations had to provide for all sorts of unforeseen needs, such as the removal of military and other stores, of the inhabitants from abandoned towns, and the withdrawal of French and Belgian railway rolling stock. In doing these things ample proof was given of the skill with which the organization had been worked out. Magnificent service was rendered by the French railways from the first day of war.

In regard to railway facilities for the movement of troops, Russia was throughout the war at a great disadvantage as compared with Germany. She was, when war was declared, engaged in the building of certain strategic lines to the German frontier, and it was suggested that one of the reasons for the selection of 1914 as the year when the war cloud should burst was the need for making war on Russia before her strategical railway system had been completed. The figures in the table on page 169 show the disparity of the Russian railway system in comparison with that of the enemy.

The Russian system had its focus at Moscow, and the German frontier was by no means well served. There was a line from Moscow to Warsaw and Brest, a railway from Petrograd to Warsaw, a railway from Wilna into East Prussia, and the Kursk, Krew-Lemburg and Odessa-Lemburg lines. In Poland the chief railways were those between Thorn, Kalisch, Grancia to Warsaw, and Grancia, Ivangorod to Warsaw, with various branch lines. In comparison with conditions on the German side of the frontier there was a lamentable absence of rail transport for the armies of the Tsar. It was, as previously stated, the superior railway facilities on the German side of the Poland border which enabled Von Hindenburg to effect his first great concentration for the attack on Kalisch. When Poland and Russia were at last invaded by the Austro-German armies a good deal of the advantage of gaining possession of certain railways was lost owing to the difference in gauge between the German and Russian systems, which prevented through traffic from Germany, and, as the Russians removed the rolling stock when the time came for them to retreat, the possession of these lines was made a still more barren asset for the German Army.

It is true that the German railways had provided convertible axles on some of the rolling stock to enable them to employ German trains on the Russian 5 ft. gauge, while a corps of engineers was set to work to build new lines of standard gauge, for which purpose some of the Belgian railways were taken up and the material transported to Russia. The break of gauge was, however, a serious disadvantage to the Russian and German armies in turn when invading the other's territory.

In the early stages of the war, when the French Army was being beaten back on Paris, it was the heroic efforts of the Russian railway men which saved the military situation. With a greater rapidity than could possibly have been expected, and at a moment when Germany, deeming any immediate Russian offensive impossible, was seeking to deal a smashing blow in the west, a Russian army appeared on the banks of the Niemen and the Vistula and invaded East Prussia. In spite of the counter-blow which, owing to superior railway facilities, Germany was able to make, new forces were poured without cessation along the Russian railways, and enabled the Army of the Tsar to apply a pressure which was one of the decisive factors in arresting the blow aimed at the heart of France. When all the circumstances are

taken into account, this was one of the greatest railway achievements of the war.

The employment of the railways as an adjunct to military strategy by Italy, although of the first importance, was restricted by the mountainous character of the frontier where the Italian and Austrian forces first made contact. The accompanying map shows the principal railways on the northern frontier of Italy. Free use was made of the direct Milan–Udine and the Milan–Codogno–Padua–Udine route, and the railways from Verona to Franzenfeste, and that from the latter place to Villach. The possession of the latter line through the mountains was, indeed, essential to a successful offensive, as these northern lines were in direct rail communication with Austrian and German railways, and it was through them that if Italy lost the offensive an enemy might descend in force on the Italian northern plains with little hope of help coming from France.

The railway links with the French armies were the single line along the sea coast to Nice and the railway from Turin through the Mont Cenis Tunnel. It was plain to the

A GERMAN LIGHT RAILWAY.
Transporting supplies on light trucks.

RUSSIA: CONVEYING A GERMAN ENGINE ON THE RUSSIAN RAILWAYS.
The gauge is too broad for German trains to run on.

military authorities that for any active co-operation between the Italian and the French armies it would be necessary to rely on sea transport.

The need for securing possession of the frontier railways was therefore urgent. It is true that they could not, owing to the fact that for long distances the railways were single lines, separated from each other by difficult country, give to the military force in possession any great power of concentration, which is the function of railways in war, but once these lines were in Italian hands there was little chance of a successful Austrian offensive. To gain the mountain lines a rapid blow was necessary, as the railway

facilities possessed by Austria were much superior to those of Italy, and would under normal conditions have enabled an Austrian force to be concentrated on the frontier before Italy was ready to parry the blow. The military organization knew the disadvantage under which it stood in relation to transport in comparison with the enemy, and took steps to counter it by a determined stroke at the frontier railways. Since the year 1905 the majority of the Italian lines had been under State control, but little or no building of strategic lines was undertaken by the Government, although considerable sums were expended in improvement of and additions to rolling stock, and in converting some of the single railways into double line tracks. During the war the railways were operated under military control on methods which differed only in detail from those already described.

The campaign in the Balkans focussed attention on other railway systems of Europe. There were several important main lines of railways for the possession of which the struggle in the Balkans was forced by the Germanic Powers. It will be noted that ordinary methods of communication were few in number, the difficulties which faced railway construction being such as could only be overcome by wealthy countries. The natural obstacles which the armies in the field had to face were chiefly the mountains and rivers.

Between the VISTULA and the ODER

As was pointed out by a correspondent of the staff magazine of the Great Eastern Railway, which published a series of articles on the War, the mountain ranges in the Balkans were so closely connected that the construction of roads which could be used by large armies was practically impossible. From the Adriatic Coast to the River Vardar, from the River Vardar to the River Mesta, and from the River Mesta to the River Maritza, owing to the trend of the mountains north by south, communication from east to west was very difficult. The Transylvanian Alps and the Balkans formed an almost impenetrable barrier, and from the mountain ranges unnavigable winding rivers presented frequent obstacles to an army on the march. These natural conditions very much enhanced the military value of the railways, and explained why any destruction of railway bridges or of the permanent way hampered the pursuing forces more than would have been the case in less difficult country. The great high road along the valleys of the Morava and the Maritza connecting Central Europe and Asia through Constantinople was selected as the route that the railway from Vienna to Constantinople should follow. The important line from Laibach and Budapest entered Serbia at Belgrade by a bridge across the Save, and was thence carried down the valley to the heart of Serbia at Nish. The Nissava was traversed through a remarkable gorge by Pirot, Serbia's eastern gate, and the railway builders entered Bulgaria between the mountains of

Northern Frontier of ITALY

Zaribrod. The succeeding section to the Vakarel Pass was built over the plateau leading to Sofia, and was then constructed along the Maritza, through Mustapha Pasha, the Turkish junction. At this point the railway emerged from the mountain ranges which had been entered at Nish, the succeeding section of the line followed the River Ergene and making the passage of the famous lines of Tchataldja entered Constantinople.

It is not surprising that, hemmed in as they were on the sea, the Germanic Powers should seek to open up communication with Constantinople. It was realized at the outset of the Balkan campaign that an army which could cross the Danube and gain a footing on the high side of the river at Belgrade could obtain possession of the railway as far as Nish, if it

FRENCH MOVABLE HOWITZER FORTRESS.

DEPARTURE FROM LONDON OF THE TRENCH TRAIN: A SCENE AT VICTORIA STATION.

was in sufficient force to drive the Serbian Army into the mountains, and protect the bridges, three in number, between Belgrade and Nish. The possession of Nish, the natural centre of Serbia, was vital to the success of the plans of the invader, as it gave into his hands not merely the Oriental Railway as far as Nish, but the railways up the Timok to the Roumanian frontier, and the lines going south to Uskub, Monastir and Salonika.

Much interest attached to the Salonika–Nish section of the line, as it was by means of this railway that the Anglo-British forces landed at Salonika might hope to effect a junction with the Serbian Army. It was only a single line railway, partly in Serbian and partly in Greek territory, and, apart from the political question which arose out of Greek ownership of the Salonika section, the capacity of this line of railway for transporting troops and material became of vital importance to the cause of the Allies. Vulnerable points on the line were the four bridges which carried the line over the Vardar between Salonika and Bania. Between the latter place and Uskub there was fairly open country in which to operate, and the River Vardar afforded the railway some protection from Bulgarian raids. Uskub and Veles were, however, uncovered at other points between Kara Dagh and Veles, and this section of the railway could also be used for an attack on Sofia by way of Kostendil.

Turning to the Bulgarian railways, Adrianople assumed importance as the Bulgarian terminus on the through route. Another link in the system was the line from Dedeagatch, trains on which were shelled from the roadstead by the Allied Fleet operating in near Eastern waters. North of the Balkans was the line to Varna on the Black Sea, a port which received the attentions of Russian warships, with connections to Nicopoli and Rustchuk on the Danube. The line to the last-named place from Varna was built by an English company, and was the first of the Balkan railways.

The long cherished dream of making an attack on Egypt through the Suez Canal was intimately linked up with the provision of the necessary railway transport. The fine use which was made of the railways in the early part of the war doubtless led the German military party to the view that the transport difficulties of an attack on Egypt had been exaggerated, and that a great deal could be

accomplished by means of the lines which had already been constructed. Hindenburg was credited with the statement that the organization of the railway weapon had solved the problem of waging successful war over long distances. Distance, however, was not the real difficulty in the case of the projected grand attack on Egypt. The question to be answered was the extent to which the existing railways, aided by light railways, could be expanded to make possible the transport across the desert of a large and well-equipped force. The choice of Meissner Pasha, the German builder of the Hedjaz and Bagdad Railways, to supervize the railway preparations for this advance was an intimation of the extent to which the idea of making a successful attack on Egypt had taken root in German military circles.

IN THE AUSTRIAN LINES.
An Austrian General's car used for quick transit from the Base to the lines occupied by his army.

Before the European War indicated the exact character of the services which railways could give to an advancing army, it had been imagined that an almost prohibitive amount of railway construction must precede an Egyptian campaign from Turkey. It may be taken for granted that Meissner Pasha was not misled by the fact that the small forces used for the first invasion of Egypt succeeded in crossing the desert. That was a feat which had been accomplished before. No doubt if he could have had his way, and the necessary time had been available, Meissner would not only have undertaken the construction of light railways across the desert, but the doubling of a large mileage of the single track line from Hedjaz to Damascus, of the railway from Damascus to Aleppo, as well as of the Bagdad railway from Aleppo to the Bosphorus. These were ambitious plans and would have involved the driving of important tunnels through the

IN NORTHERN FRANCE.
French Soldiers cutting out chalk for roadmaking.

Taurus and Amanus ranges, if the tremendous handicap of breaking bulk in the transport of supplies was to be overcome. Whatever might be the case in the future, it seemed certain to those acquainted with local conditions that any force advancing on the Suez Canal from Turkey, while it might succeed in drawing its food supplies from Asia Minor, would have to be munitioned from Europe, a circumstance which opened up a new problem, that of dealing with the munition traffic on the single line from Constantinople to the frontier of Palestine. This was the situation from the railway standpoint which had to be faced by those responsible for attacking any force on the Suez Canal.

In England, despite the absence of strategic lines, the railways did excellent work, the railway interests of the nation being the one great business undertaking to give efficient and loyal war service without the prospect of a penny of extra profit for the proprietors. The scale of payment to the railways was based on the earnings in a normal period before the war, although it soon became common knowledge that with depleted staffs the railways were carrying far more traffic both in passengers and goods than in years of peace.

It was a ready criticism during the war that Great Britain—not by any means for the first time in her history—had been caught by the enemy in a state of unpreparedness for the struggle that was thrust upon her. Nobody ever really questioned the truth of the criticism or the ability of the nation to win through

in spite of the slow start. Even the bitterest critic, however, always modified his condemnation of our unreadiness for war by excepting from it the Navy, which from the first day of war assumed command of the seas. To the Navy should have been added the railways, which were placed on a war footing by the stroke of the pen which gave notice of Government control, and which immediately put into practice plans which had been devised, tested, and perfected during long years of peace.

It will not be without interest to give an account of the steps which enabled the railways in a day to become efficient instruments of military transport.

Immediately following the declaration of war the Government, exercising the powers it possessed under the Regulation of the Forces Act, took possession of the railway system of Great Britain—but not of Ireland. The control was exercised through an Executive Committee, which was composed of General Managers of the various railway companies. The President of the Board of Trade was the official Chairman, but to Sir H. A. Walker, the General Manager of the London and South Western Railway, was entrusted the Acting Chairmanship. The task of the executive was to operate the whole of the railways of the country as one undertaking, or, as it was expressed in the public announcement, "the railways, locomotives, rolling stock, and staff shall be used as one complete unit in the best interests of the State for the movement of troops, stores, and food supplies."

The Executive Committee was not as many believed a new body, it having existed in the form of a War Railway Council for some years past. It was this Council which had drawn up plans which were to be put into operation in the event of Great Britain being involved in a European war. Nor had the subject escaped attention in earlier years. As long ago as 1865 the Engineer and Railway Staff Corps came into being. This corps was formed with the object of directing the application of skilled labour and of railway transport to the purposes of national defence, and for preparing plans to meet the direct shock of war. Even when the Territorial force was created, the Engineer and Railway Staff Corps, although merged in the Royal Engineers of the Territorial Force, remained under the administration of the War Office. The corps, as originally constituted, was composed of a certain number of engineers, several of the great contractors, and the general managers of the principal railways, the contractors forming what was known as the "Labour Branch' of the Corps. It was intended that in the event of war the officers of this corps, acting under the direction of the military authorities, would superintend the working of the railways, and it was hoped that by making the best use of the organization and resources available no difficulty would be experienced in concentrating a considerable body of troops within a brief period upon any point of the coast which might be threatened

by a foe. The spirit which had been infused into these early plans to repel invasion was present in the British railway organization when the war cloud burst in 1914, and the cruder plans of the Victorian era had been worked out and perfected when King George, the grandson of the Great Queen, saw his Empire plunged into war.

In a lecture which the late Sir George Findlay delivered before the School of Military Engineering, this eminent railway manager put upon record the duties of railways in time of war. There would be general agreement with the statement that in Great Britain, where the whole of the railways had been constructed by private enterprise, the antecedent conditions differed so widely from those obtaining on the Continent that any such arrangements as had been devised in Germany, Austria, France or Italy would be inapplicable. Hence the decision to give the State the powers of control embodied in the provisions of the Act of 1888, and the drawing up of plans by which the Executive Committee, who were all Lieutenant-Colonels in the Railway Staff Corps, should operate the whole of the railways under the direction of the military authorities as a single system.

It would be more correct to write that the railways were during the war administered, not by the Government, but for the Government, the management of the railways and the Staff control being the same as in the days of peace. Orders for necessary facilities were issued by

IN NORTHERN FRANCE.
French Sappers constructing a railway.

BRITISH MOTOR TRANSPORT IN FRANCE:

the Transport Department of the War Office and the Railway Executive furnished the trains. The only thing which the public noted during the early days of the war was that the railways were placed under military guard—an essential precaution—and that the number of trains carrying troops increased. Otherwise—except for a rise in the percentage of trains which did not keep time—there was no public inconvenience. Behind the scenes, however, all grades of railwaymen, from the members of the Executive down to the humbler members of the uniform and clerical staffs, were passing through days and nights of stress. The outbreak of war was a bolt out of the blue ; the holiday traffic was at the flood and simultaneously with the extra call on the railway for transport facilities there was an appreciable reduction of staff owing to the return to the colours of the large number of railway reserves and the enlistment of the new armies. The number withdrawn from railway service by the call of the Army and Navy was even before Lord Derby's great recruiting effort over 100,000, and it became necessary, after a certain period, in order to ensure the efficient working of the railways, to forbid the enlistment of railwaymen.

It was a great national asset when war was declared that British railways were ready to put into practice the programme of working which had been evolved by the War Railway Council. Everything worked smoothly from the first day of war.

The elaborate arrangements which had been made in advance for troop transport were soon put to the test, for the decision to send an Expeditionary Force to the Continent was taken immediately and the work of transporting this force to the port of embarkation put in hand at once. Southampton, which had been similarly used in the South African War, was selected as the port for this purpose. That the work was well done by the railways the public knew later from the public statements of Lord Kitchener and Sir John French. The actual words used when the work of placing our first little army by the side of the French forces had been accomplished should be put on record, for the appreciation had been well earned.

Lord Kitchener wrote : " The railway companies, in the all-important matter of transport facilities, have more than justified the complete confidence reposed in them by the War Office, all grades of railway services having laboured

THE PETROL-DRIVEN LORRY.

with untiring energy and patience. And it is well to repeat that the conveyance of our troops across the Channel was accomplished, thanks to the cordial cooperation of the Admiralty, with perfect smoothness and without any untoward incident whatever."

Sir John French added his word of praise. He wrote from France under date September 9, 1914:

"The transport of the troops from England both by sea and rail was effected in the best possible order and without a check. Each unit arrived at its destination in this country well within the scheduled time."

A surprising fact not brought out in either of these testimonies was the secrecy which shrouded the whole of this important operation. Many hundreds, indeed thousands, of those engaged on the railways must have known of the work which was being done, and yet it was stated on good authority that in spite of the wide knowledge of the transport work in railway circles, and in a community which at that time at least was teeming with spies, the first knowledge which Germany had of the transference of the British forces overseas was when they found their army corps opposed by Sir John

French's army during the historic retreat from Mons.

The transport of the Expeditionary Force to the Continent was only the beginning of a period of enormous demands on the railways for facilities for the movement of troops, supplies, provisions, horses, mules and equipment of all descriptions.

Of this early work and of some of the subsequent services given to the military and naval authorities an excellent account was given in the special supplements issued by the *Railway News*. It was impossible, however, for the full story of the work of British railways in the war to be then put on record, if only for the reason that the period of greatest demand on the Railway Executive for transport facilities came somewhat late in the war. That an organization which had never contemplated having to move armies of the size which were ultimately raised should have come so successfully through the ordeal without inflicting greater inconvenience on the non-military portion of the community was a wonderful achievement for which, owing to the secrecy which veiled the military traffic, full credit was never given.

Figures could be quoted which would give an

index at least to the vast volume of traffic handled, but they would furnish nothing more than the dry bones of the narrative. It would be foolish, however, for the historian to attempt to rid himself altogether of the incubus of statistics. Thus in the first five months of war the London and South Western Railway provided nearly 15,000 special trains for the naval and military traffic. The strategical position of this Company's lines, the fact that the port of Southampton, owned and managed by the Company, was an important port of embarkation, and that so many military camps had been established on this system, accounted for this large volume of traffic. Other railways also provided many thousands of special trains during the same period. On the small Brighton Company's system 4,400 such trains were required, and even the Metropolitan Railway passed over its lines during the five months in question nearly 2,750 troop trains. That meant in the case of the London and South Western Railway the running of 100 special trains every twenty-four hours in addition to a vast volume of ordinary traffic. The fact that such a feat was possible, and moreover that every one of these trains reached its destination at or before schedule time, constituted an achievement of

which the Railway Executive had every reason to be proud. On the Great Western system during the first seven months of the war no fewer than 6,684 special military trains had to be provided, apart from the very great amount of military traffic carried in ordinary trains. The Great Eastern Railway during the same period was called upon to put into its time-table over 3,000 military and naval trains, representing a considerable daily average. The Company also converted its hotel at Harwich, which fortunately had been reopened shortly before the war, into a military hospital. In the case of the Great Northern Railway, while no actual figures were available, a great many troop trains passed over the system, and the Company, which carried an enormous traffic to and from the London docks, handled more wagons at the London end of the system than at any previous period in its history. In addition to what might be regarded as the normal increase in both troop and horse traffic, an increase which made the running of thousands of special trains necessary, the Lancashire and Yorkshire Railway had its accommodation severely taxed by the activity of the Yorkshire woollen trade and the partial renewal of the cotton trade in East Lancashire. Many other

A BRIDGE OVER THE MEUSE.
Destroyed by French Engineers.

WATER BY RAIL.
A special on the French railway carrying water to the troops in the trenches.

details and figure could be quoted, but these may serve as an index to a traffic intensity which had never before been approached on British railways. Yet it must be confessed that bulk figures of this sort, however instructive in a general way, would have no meaning unless the reader could analyse them and split them up into the component ceaseless activities which they represented. They implied that more traffic was being handled on British railways than at any previous period of their history, that reinforcements were being rushed to the front to aid the original gallant little army, that wounded were being brought back to hospitals in England, that a vast tonnage of food for the feeding of the army, more artillery, more munitions, more material of war of all descriptions for both the army and the navy were daily passing over the railways into the theatre of war.

Subsidiary causes also contributed to the pressure on the resources of the railways. It was not merely Government traffic which caused that congestion of the railways with which the Railway Executive wrestled with such success : there were other traffic demands, and these coming on top of naval and military requirements made necessary the provision of new sidings for marshalling and storage purposes. There was also much traffic ordinarily carried by sea which was thrust on the rail-

ways. This was a direct result first of the closing of certain ports to ordinary traffic, and, secondly, of the tremendous rise in freights. To take only one case : it was stated in the railway Press at the time that coal for London and the south of England which was usually water-borne was carried by the railways during the war in very great quantities, the tonnage conveyed by one of the larger railways to places in the metropolitan area exceeding the normal tonnage by one-third. This was quite a normal rate of increase. Was it to be wondered that there was congestion in various quarters, especially at junctions and exchange stations ? The surprise was that the handling of ordinary traffic was not at times entirely suspended, and it is but fair that the extra work thrown on the railways in dealing with the ordinary demands of the mercantile community while meeting without delay urgent Government commands should be recorded.

What has been already written refers to the broad general principles on which railways were employed in the war, the measures adopted in connexion with mobilization and concentration of the armies ; what ought to be regarded as the main line traffic of the military railways. In the actual fighting zone the work which had to be carried out was of a somewhat different and certainly of a more strenuous character. Just as on an ordinary railway in days of peace

BRITISH TROOPS IN THE BALKANS.
On the way to the fighting line.

the area of dense traffic is on the lines which converge towards great centres of population, so it was at the front to which the many millions of troops converged that the railway problem was most acute. Here, where the Railway Transport Officers had control of what might be termed the local traffic of the war, men of whose activities the public knew nothing grappled with a great task. The work was of a character to call for the services of men skilled in railway traffic management. The French authorities had the advantage that all the railwaymen were automatically enlisted for the period of the war, and were available wherever their services were required ; the British Army was fortunate in having attracted so large a number of railwaymen to the colours.

Transport in the case of the British forces was not a simple matter. An account of that part of the work connected with the provisioning of the Army was given in an earlier chapter. The story there told indicated the difficulties arising out of the need for dealing with transport in its three phases, rail transport in England, the sea carriage to the French port used as an overseas base, and the rail and mechanical transport to the front. The feeding of the Army was, however, only one department of the work of transport. The railways had also to provide for a constant stream of troops, horses, guns, stores and equipment of all kinds.

At the ends of the long line of rail communication the strain on the transport staff was relaxed ; the blow fell on the Railway Transport Officer, whose station was anywhere near the fighting line, with full force. In civilian life the officer was probably high railway official —men from the traffic department of all the

railways of the Empire had answered the call— in the war zone he was merely a more or less subordinate officer of the railway transport, responsible to his superiors for a link in the chain of communication which must never break, or he would be broken with it. There was no room in this service for inefficients.

The main work of such an officer, who was invariably understaffed, was to take hold at the particular point on the railway to which he had been ordered and perform miracles. He had to deal with a never-ending stream of men and guns, horses and mules, stores and materials, until he gained the impression that the populous places of the earth had been denuded to form the procession of men he passed on, and that the workshops of a nation were pouring their production along his particular piece of line. He had not only to regulate trains, but to manage men, to understand how to deal with horses and mules, and to be familiar with a bewildering variety of articles, for which insistent demands were reaching him by letter, telephone and wire. Even during the war in fixed positions the work was arduous and wearisome ; when active operations were in progress it was one long struggle to keep faith with his military superiors. Against difficulties such as those which enveloped transport during the retreat on Paris, at a time when the system had not been completely organized, it was a hard fight, but the men in charge withstood the strain. The rail transport system was always harassed, but never overwhelmed. A change of railhead, orders to transport large numbers of men by new routes, the need to provide travelling facilities for the civilian population of the invaded territory, a call to aid a division in retreat, or to rush forward reinforcements to a point where a stand might be made; this was the lot of the railway transport officer. He often worked for twenty-two hours out of the twenty-four. Many qualities and gifts were demanded of him. If he were an Englishman

ARMOURED TRAINS NEAR THE BATTLE-LINE.

An Austrian train in the Eastern Campaign. Top picture: A British train crossing a bridge in East Africa. Bottom picture: Giving final instructions to a driver in Northern France.

serving in France he was required to speak fluent French and to have the command of several kinds of English; he had to draw upon all the knowledge of railway work it was possible for man to acquire and to make, in addition, large drafts on the quality of instinct to get things done. When not actually engaged in superintendence of the traffic, he was required to write innumerable reports, and to answer perpetual inquiries as to why he had done this and left undone that. His office, more often than not a disused railway wagon, was a target

for a constant stream of remonstrances, entreaties and complaints, which he had no means of evading. He was there to be shot at and riddled by all kinds of people who wanted things he had not got, and by other persons who had got the things they did not want. He had to be all things to all men; to give to this man the soft answer that turned away wrath, and to that the decisive word that ended discussion. The fact that mattered was that the work went on smoothly or with difficulty as the case might be, and that the general high level of efficiency maintained had a profound effect on the fortunes of the campaign.

There was other railway work in the war zone apart from that of traffic regulation. This was rather a matter for the railway engineer. Broken lines had to be repaired, bridges reconstructed, telegraphic communication restored, light railways laid down beyond the limits of permanent track. It was a revelation to those unacquainted with railway work with what rapidity temporary lines could be put in place, and even little narrow gauge trench railways constructed in order to link the actual front with the complex system of main and branch line railways on which the armies were based, and by which they lived and moved.

The public in England knew little and understood less of these feverish activities. Even the services being rendered by the railways in Great Britain were never appraised at their real value.

The public whose imagination was aroused by the fable of the Russian legions passing over the British railways for an unknown destination paid little regard to the work which passed in daily review before their eyes. They saw something of it—no traveller by railway in England could help seeing it—but little thought

OFF TO THE FIRING-LINE.
British Territorials on a railway in France.

was given to the organization which at the period of intense pressure provided at the appointed place the necessary engine power and rolling stock, with so little disturbance of ordinary schedules, and with a watchful eye on the need which might have arisen at any moment for having trains in readiness to transport an army to any threatened point on the coast.

The picture drawn by a correspondent of *The Times* of a night scene at one of the great railway junctions gave a vivid impression of the work of the railways in troop transport:

"There are times," he wrote, "when the military element is so predominant that the station looks as if it were a strategic point of the first importance. There are soldiers and sailors camping out in booking halls, yarning round waiting-room fires, sitting in groups at refreshment room tables, resting tired limbs on trucks and trolleys interminably pacing the platform in twos and threes. Trains and soldiers, soldiers and trains, the heart of the boy that beats in the breasts of all of us leaps to greet them. A dozen trains roll in one after the other. Special coaches bring sailors from Devonport returning to the Grand Fleet from leave. Hands in pockets they swing along the platform as if it were falling away from them like the more familiar battle deck. A military relief train draws in with a strangely mixed company. Wounded soldiers homeward bound for a brief period of convalescence, eager Territorials on their way north to say good-bye before leaving for the front, keen young fellows in the new army returning to their billets for the final stage of their training. New contingents leap from the crowded corridors of other trains, some in kilts, others with the shamrock in their caps, flying men, Red Cross workers, cavalry men, booted and spurred, men of the line regiments with hands encased in sheepskin gloves and ears deep in woollen helmets, men with rifles and men with canes, men in khaki and men in blue, but never a red coat amongst them. So the great trains come and go, are shunted and remarshalled all night long in this gathering-ground of the forces on furlough. It is the halfway house between north and south, giving fresh steam to down trains splashed with rain and to up trains plastered in snow. There are two distinct service tides; that for the fleet is setting north; that for the army is setting south. Like ships that pass in the night, soldiers and sailors have just time enough to exchange signals before they are swallowed up behind the blackened windows and drawn blinds of trains which speed unseen through the night in war time."

Before the war had been long in progress steps were taken to provide facilities for both rest and refreshment for soldiers and sailors, who had frequently to wait long hours at railway stations for connecting trains, and in some cases it was possible for men in uniform to obtain a bed at the railway terminus.

The difficulty of the task was greatly increased by the constant depletion of the railway staffs as more and more men flocked to the fighting line, or were lent to the French railways, and the news that the Executive Committee sat night and day at the offices in London, so that all requirements of the Government could receive immediate attention, did not come as a surprise. The railway officials grappled with a complex problem in a business way, and the military authorities, wisely recognizing that while the demands were made by those trained in war their fulfilment was a commercial undertaking, left the purely transport part of the work where it properly belonged—in the hands of the railway experts.

The results were eloquent of sound method, and it was not surprising that when Mr. Lloyd George was looking round for men wherewith to fill important positions at the Ministry of Munitions his choice fell in many instances on highly placed railway officials. It was one of the first indications given of a desire on the part of the authorities to enlist directly in the service

WOUNDED FROM THE BATTLEFIELD.
An officer of the R.A.M.C. on the footboard of a fast-moving train going from carriage to carriage
to attend to urgent cases.

of the Government the business training and instinct which it was then realized could alone in a war of this character ensure a successful issue.

The provision of train transport was only, however, a portion of the work which was carried out by the railways. It was a fortunate circumstance for the nation that railway enterprise had been so closely associated with dock and harbour development. In the acquisition

and improvement of harbour facilities the railways had expended between £40,000,000 and £50,000,000 in the years preceding the war. As a result the Government not only acquired the control of the railways, but of the magnificent chain of railway docks, which are without rival in the whole world. The existence of facilities at Southampton for the largest ships which have yet been built, the services of men long trained to the work of loading and unloading between train and ship, and who from experience gained during the South African War were acquainted with military transport work was a great asset. Similar accommodation—if on a less lavish scale —had been provided by the Southern railways at Newhaven, Folkestone and Dover, all of which ports were available for the important cross-Channel services. On the East Coast there was Harwich, where the great quay at Parkeston —used in peace time by the Continental steamers of the Great Eastern Railway and other services—was handed over to the Admiralty. Further North the Government had the use of the twin ports of Grimsby and Immingham—both the outcome of the effort made by the Great Central Railway to extend its commercial boundaries. At Hull, Hartlepool—the scene of a bombardment by German warships—at Middlesboro' and on the Tyne were a series of fine docks owned by the North Eastern Company, the largest dock owning railway in the world. The general use made of these East Coast docks by the Admiralty must remain a closed chapter of naval history, but from the purely railway aspect it should be recorded that it was in the warehouses of the

new dock at Hull that the battalion of the Northumberland Fusiliers, raised and equipped by the North Eastern Railway from its own employees, were housed during their training. Good service was also rendered by the Bristol Channel railway ports, Newport, Cardiff, Barry, Swansea. It was into Newport that the first German steamship to be captured after the outbreak of war—the Belgia, of the Hamburg Amerika line—was brought, mainly through the exertions of the railway officials. It was typical also of the use made of other railway dock property that owing to the congestion of the regular passenger ports some of the principal steamship companies diverted their services to Newport, where an improvement scheme completed on the eve of the war made the port accessible to the largest liners. The large fleet of steamships owned by the railways was also available for Government work, and some were lost in the hazardous duties of transport service. Of the 200 odd ships built by the railways for cross-Channel traffic over 100 were, under arrangements with the Railway Executive Committee, at once taken over by the authorities and the rest usefully employed in maintaining

A HOSPITAL ON WHEELS.
Ward in an ambulance train, showing cots suspended in ship's berth fashion.

GUARDING RAILWAYS IN ENGLAND.
Royal Dublin Fusiliers lined up for inspection.
Inset: Guarding the line at Rochester.

communication with Ireland and the countries of our Allies.

One or two examples of the manner in which the port and dock facilities of the railways were employed during the war will be of interest. The possession of the dock at Fleetwood, which had always been closely associated with the fishing industry, enabled the Lancashire and Yorkshire Railway to provide a home port for many of the trawlers which had been accustomed to fish the North Sea and to take their catch into East Coast ports. The maintenance of the food supplies of the country was also materially assisted by the Lancashire and Yorkshire steamship services between Fleetwood and Belfast and between Liverpool and Drogheda. The London, Brighton and South Coast Company, in addition to the running of the special trains for troop transport referred to above, undertook the carriage of large quantities of food and supplies in connexion with the feeding of the Army. The Continental Department of the Company, in cooperation with its French partners, also maintained services to France, and except when mines were reported to be in close proximity to the sea route followed, kept these going daily in both directions. Newhaven was required for other purposes, but the passenger boats to Dieppe were run from Folkestone, and the cargo boats from either Folkestone or Southampton. The pressure

BRITISH TROOPS IN FRANCE.

Repairing a railway point.   Going back to the fighting line.

on the resources of these ports became so great, however, that while the war was in progress it was decided by the Brighton Company to develop yet another port on the South Coast.

The early services of the railway steamers were arranged partly with the object of bringing to this country Belgian refugees, goods which English firms had in warehouses in Belgium, while an increased service of cargo boats brought over food-stuffs from Holland. Through the gates of Harwich, Folkestone, and the Port of London Belgian refugees poured into England. The first party reached Liverpool Street station at the beginning of September. Those who witnessed their arrival in London saw these victims of a calamity, the extent of which they appeared too dazed to realize, standing in forlorn groups on the railway platform around the boxes and bundles containing the few personal belongings they had been able to gather together in their hasty flight from the German hordes which were then overrunning their country. Many of them were country people, speaking no language but Flemish, and for the most part they remained silent and listless, resigning themselves without comment into the hands of their new-found friends. Torn, at a moment's notice, from the cottages and the fields in which their simple life had been mainly passed, they seemed strangely out of place in the whirlpool of the great London terminus. British refugees from Germany were also brought back in railway steamers

from the Hook of Holland. Again and again, while there was a possibility of refugees desiring to take passage to England, the railway steamers braved the dangers of the North Sea passage, and on more than one occasion were chased and attacked by German submarines. The case of the steamship Colchester should be referred to in this connexion, Captain Lawrance, who was in command of that ship, exhibiting a fine courage which earned for him not only the praise of his immediate employers, but the thanks of the Board of Trade.

The South Eastern and Chatham Company's part in bringing refugees to Folkestone was also a fine piece of work. When Germany began to invade Belgium an arrangement was made by the Local Government Board that the Company should put on an additional service between Folkestone and Ostend, and as Germany gradually occupied the whole of Northern Belgium, a great demand was made for additional boats to carry the war refugees from Belgium. The Admiralty one day requested that every available boat should be sent to Ostend, and on one day alone the South Eastern Company's fleet landed over 6,000 war refugees at Folkestone. Reference should also be made to one or two incidents in which familiar cross-Channel steamers were concerned. The Invicta, known to multitudes of voyagers to the Continent in happier days, was instrumental in saving some of the survivors of His Majesty's ship Hermes, and the Queen—the first turbine boat to be put into the Dover-

Calais service, rescued over 2,000 panic-stricken refugees from the Amiral Gauteaume, when that ship was attacked in mid-channel by a hostile submarine. Other railway steamers were fitted up as hospital ships and rendered most useful service.

Nor does this record complete the story of the part which British railways played in the Great War. The leading railways had in operation—and this applied to the railways of the Allied nations as well as to those of Great Britain—many large and well-equipped establishments in which during years of peace locomotives were built and were repaired and railway carriages and wagons constructed. Following the example set by the South African railways during the Boer War, the whole of these establishments were placed at the disposal of the Government. One of the first demands made upon the manufacturing resources of the railways was for the construction of ambulance trains for the transport of the wounded both on Continental and home railways. In view of the urgency of the demand the usual plan adopted was to make up the ambulance train from vehicles taken from ordinary service, the carriages being altered to suit the required conditions. Most of the trains were completed in the course of a few days, the record for rapid construction being held by the London and North Western railway mechanics, who succeeded in providing a naval ambulance train within a period of thirty hours. All the larger companies undertook the provision of trains for the transport of wounded, the numbers being apportioned among the railway manufacturing establishments in proportion to the manufacturing capacity. Many of the public had an opportunity at a later date, when additional trains were ordered, of gaining through personal inspection an idea of the care lavished in the design and arrangement of these trains so that the wounded should receive every possible attention. A typical ambulance train—one of those constructed by the Great Western Railway—included a saloon with beds for orderlies and stores compartment, a restaurant car, five ward coaches, each with accommodation for eighteen patients, a pharmacy coach containing dispensary, operating room, and linen stores, a saloon with beds for eight patients, and accommodation for two nurses

REMOUNTS FOR BRITISH TROOPS IN FRANCE.

and two doctors. This train would carry ninety-eight patients, in addition to the doctors, nurses, and orderlies. The pharmacy coach was divided by partitions into the dispensary, operating room, office, and linen stores, and a sliding door giving admittance to the operating room was designed of such width as to admit a stretcher being taken in sideways. Special arrangements were devised to ensure that a plentiful supply of hot water was available for sterilizing and other purposes from a boiler in the coach, and the floor of the operating room was covered with zinc. The heating was by steam, and the lighting by oil-gas,

BRITISH FIELD-KITCHENS
On the way to Northern France.

which was also used for the warming and heating of food.

At a very early stage of the war the passage of these ambulance trains over British railways became a sad but familiar feature. A *Times* correspondent, dealing with the night traffic at Crewe, wrote : " While the merry-go-round is in full swing a train of a kind with which Crewe is becoming only too familiar creeps in out of the station smoke and the fog beyond. It is an ambulance train, one of four or five that are on their way this night from the South Coast to the Northern hospitals. The singing and the dancing cease as sound fighting men crowd behind the barriers and catch glimpses of wounded comrades, some propped up in bed with bandaged head or limbs, others

limping on crutches to the carriage doors. The long string of luxuriously furnished Red Cross coaches seems a haven of rest after the impression of incessant strife that one has caught from exploding fog signals, shrill whistling of giant engines and creaking carriages scrunching over points. The train of mercy passes out into the night, as it seems on silent wheels, leaving the station staff still battling with the novel demands of war."

On French, German, and Russian railways elaborate arrangements were in force for the care of the wounded, which in the case of the German Army must have thrown a prodigious strain upon the organization. What was done by France will serve as an index to the general arrangement on Continental railways for the transport of the wounded. The complexity of the problem which the French Railway Administration had to solve may be gathered from the statement that on an average there were 5,000 casualties during each terrible twenty-four hours of battle. Mr. Walter S. Hiatt, writing in the *Railway Age Gazette*, described how by slow degrees the wounded man was carried to the rear and placed in trains that were always waiting to whirl the wounded back to Paris, Orleans, Bordeaux, Lyons, to the sea coast at Toulon in the distant south, to Tours or to St. Nazaire at the mouth of the Loire. At the end of a year of war these trains of mercy had carried nearly a million men into the hospital country. One phase of this service was the evolution of a life-saving hospital car out of a rudely constructed cheap box car. At the beginning of the war, when the railways had rendered the first-rate service of launching the soldiers towards the frontiers, the problem of caring for the wounded was in a state of infancy. It was, however, soon recognized that the only hospital in which a seriously wounded man could be treated effectively was one in a building away from the heat, the noise, and the life of the camps, and that the only way to get the soldiers to these hospitals was by train. In the early days of the war it sometimes took a long period owing to scarcity of hospital trains to convey the wounded to the hospitals, but after three months of war 600 ambulance trains were in service on the French railways. At first the sleeping and dining cars were used as temporary moving hospitals, but, although they rendered excellent service, their weight made too great a demand for engine

A FIGHT AT A BROKEN BRIDGE IN CAMEROON
During the Anglo-French Expedition's Battle with the Germans at Nlohe, December 6, 1914.

power, and hence there was evolved the idea of converting the often despised box-car into a travelling hospital. Wherever the idea originated credit must be given to Commandant E. Loiseleur, in charge of the Fourth Bureau of the War Department, for putting the plan into operation. The 30 ft. car, when rebuilt, was divided into three parts—an operating room, a medical store, and a kitchen. The effect that the provision of these trains had in

saving the lives of wounded soldiers was quite remarkable. One report showed that of 350 men taken at one time to Brest, a long slow ride from the front, across Brittany, there were no deaths. Another report showed that, of 418 wounded taken to Rouen, 200 had been treated on the train. Another case was that of a train with 611 wounded, where the lives of five were saved by operations, and many others had their wounds dressed. The service was raised to such a level of efficiency that a soldier wounded on the Yser in the North could be delivered at a Paris hospital within thirty hours if in a condition to be moved at all. The services rendered by the railways both in Great Britain and on the Continent in providing for the transport of the wounded were a revelation of the scope and usefulness of railways in war, which at the time were only dimly understood. There were cases in which men were in hospital in London within 24 hours of being wounded in France.

The workshop staffs in which the ambulance trains had been built having filled this urgent need turned to the supply of other military requirements. There was a call for motor-lorries which was beyond the capacity of the motor manufacturing industry proper, and the railways undertook to deliver large numbers of these useful links for transport work between rail-head and the front. Many other branches of war work were also undertaken, including the supply of the regulation army wagons used by horse transport, gun limbers, and other auxiliaries of the artillery or transport arm. In some of the great railway works special steels for ordnance manufacture were produced, in others ordnance itself was manufactured ; in all of them work was undertaken for the Ministry of Munitions. Existing works

were not only fully manned to assist the successful prosecution of the war, but new factories were erected and equipped in response to the call for more and yet more munitions. The building of locomotives and all but absolutely essential repair work were suspended ; wagon and carriage construction except for the needs of the war was a dead industry. The manner in which equipment designed for an entirely different purpose was adapted to the execution of military contracts was a fine example of the resourcefulness of the railway engineer.

Not only in Great Britain but throughout Europe the same thing was being done. In France, in Austria, in Russia, in Italy railway activities, altogether apart from the transport problem, which was the primary duty of the railway arm, were mobilized to aid the successful prosecution of the war. The building of armoured trains for use on lines within the war zone was an important part of this task, and on many occasions excellent work was done by these mobile forts both in attack and defence. Special vehicles for armament traffic were constructed in every railway workshop in the belligerent countries. In England wagons to carry heavy guns up to 130 tons in weight were built for the Woolwich Arsenal railways, and armour-plate wagons for the

EAST AFRICA: TRAIN CROSSING A BRIDGE
Guarded by Sentry and Blockhouse on top of cutting at right.

THE CARPATHIANS.
Handing out bread from a Russian supply train.

Sheffield and Manchester districts, and many other types were to be seen passing over British railways. An English railway—the Great Eastern—recognizing the difficulty of feeding troops when travelling by train or when on the march, got out designs for a commissariat train to supply every four hours a hot meal for 2,000 men. The German railways, which furnished many examples of resourcefulness, provided trains to enable men coming back from the firing line for rest to enjoy the luxury of a bath. These trains consisted of a locomotive, tender, a wagon with water in a reservoir, three wagons for hot baths and several wagons to serve as cabins. The reservoir was capable of holding 2,300 gallons of water, and fifty men could bathe at the same time. Each train could give a bath daily to at least 3,000 soldiers. Some fine feats in restoring broken railway communication, following the repulse of the German Army from the gates of Paris, were done by the French railwaymen with the assistance of the railway works.

In all the combatant nations the new significance of railways in war was recognized, and steps were taken with varying, but in all instances a great measure of success to obtain from the railways the maximum assistance they could afford either for attack or defence. The mobility conferred on an army by the possession of either permanent or temporary railways on many occasions enabled assaults to be pressed home or a threatened position saved. The successful retreat of the hard-pressed Russian Army, the repulse of the fierce German thrust at Calais, owed much to the skilful use made of the railways by those in charge of the operations; the possession of the Belgian railway system, with its high percentage of mileage to the area of country traversed, was an incomparable asset to the invader.

Railway work in the Great War was so intimately connected with the incidents of the various campaigns that its history is the history of the war itself. If the illustrations which appear in this chapter were the only means by which the importance of the railway arm could be measured they would tell a wonderful story. By their aid alone the world-wide character of the Great War could be easily mirrored. They would call up a picture of the first great rush of troops to the frontiers of threatened territories, of the dispatch of the British Expeditionary Force, the arrival of the Empire soldiers from overseas, the ready response of the Princes of India to the call of the King-Emperor. There would be revealed glimpses of the Russian Army in Galicia going on from success to success as new and important positions were secured, the subsequent rolling back of the tide of Russian invasion, when, such was the devastation wrought by the invading armies, the peasants who owed allegiance to the Tsar were forced to seek temporary homes in railway wagons. From the desolation of Russia the mind could turn to the brighter picture of the Italian Army coming into the war when the Allies had reached a dark hour, and advancing with high hopes into the mountains which guard the Northern frontier. Another change of the kaleidoscope and the mind could see an image of the Austro-German rush on Serbia, of the Bulgarian Army leaving for the front, and other incidents of the campaign against heroic Serbia. A fresh turn of the wheel, and there would be a vision of Africa, where by means of the Windhoek-Keetmanshoep line, at a moment when the South African forces were rounding up the rebels, Germany might have hoped to strike swiftly at Cape Colony. There would also be shown the work of armoured trains and other incidents of the war in the back places of the Empire. Then he who would seek to reconstruct the story of the war would be once more in France; he would see the measures being taken to facilitate the French advance on the trenched-in, dispirited German Army on the Western front.

Next he would be with the British Army, its long line stretching from the front in France to the great camps in England. It was commonly said that except for occasional raids of enemy airships England did not feel the breath of war. Those who spoke thus overlooked the daily reminder given in London itself of how near the war was to the heart of the Empire. The scene at Victoria Station when the train with those returning from leave left on the first stage of the journey to the front formed a definite link with the great conflict being waged only a few miles away. To pass within the platform barriers and stand beside this " trench train " on the eve of its departure was to touch the fringes of the fighting area. That last word " Good-bye " was being said by men who on the morrow would be facing the enemy. The story told in Frith's famous picture of the scene at a great railway terminus was of trivial significance compared with the daily drama of the war train, where brave women smiled through their tears and looked the farewells they could not speak. Finally, the picture would tell of the journey by rail and sea, and rail again to the British front, where a million men awaited with calm confidence the victory which was destined to give safety to the Empire and to civilization the assurance that the menace of militarism had been definitely quelled.

BRITISH TROOPS IN FRANCE.
Returning to Camp on a Light Railway.

CHAPTER CI.

OPERATIONS ON THE WESTERN FRONT, APRIL TO SEPTEMBER, 1915

REASONS FOR THE COMPARATIVE INACTION OF ALLIES FROM MAY TO SEPTEMBER—FIGHTING IN THE AIR—THE BELGIANS—BRITISH OPERATIONS ROUND LA BASSÉE AND YPRES—EXTENSION OF BRITISH LINE—BATTLE OF ARTOIS—ACTIONS OF HÉBUTERNE AND QUENNEVIÈRES—GERMANS REPULSED AT BEAUSÉJOUR AND VILLE-SUR-TOURBE—GERMAN CROWN PRINCE'S OFFENSIVE IN THE ARGONNE—FRENCH STORM LES EPARGES CREST—FIGHTING IN THE WOOD OF AILLY—CAPTURE AND RECAPTURE OF THE "HEIGHT OF THE BAN DE SAPT"—FRENCH ADVANCE IN ALSACE—EVE OF THE SEPTEMBER OFFENSIVE.

IN Chapter XCVI. we described the operations on the Western front between La Bassée and the Swiss frontier down to March 31, 1915. The fighting from La Bassée to the sea at Nieuport-Bains, which included the Battle of Neuve Chapelle, the Second Battle of Ypres, and the Battles of the Aubers Ridge and Festubert, had been already narrated. The last two battles, which occurred in May, 1915, were closely connected with the Battle of Artois, the name which may be given to the French offensive in May and June south of La Bassée and north of Arras. The present chapter continues the story of the Franco-German campaign from March 31, and of the Anglo-Belgian campaign from May 25—the last day of the Battle of Festubert—up to September 25, when French and Joffre again struck heavily at the German lines in Artois and Champagne.

During the period under review vast changes occurred outside the Western theatre of war. By sinking the Lusitania (May 7), and by numerous interferences in the domestic politics

of the United States, the German Government further exasperated the American people. On May 12 General Botha captured Windhoek, and German South-West Africa was speedily conquered. On April 25 British and French forces were landed in the Gallipoli Peninsula. On May 23 Germany's ally, Italy, declared war on Austria-Hungary.

Nevertheless, the Germans and Austro-Hungarians and their leaders from April to September displayed the utmost energy. Taking advantage of the fact that the French and British in the West had not yet accumulated sufficient men and munitions to pierce the network of barbed-wire, trenches, redoubts, and underground fortresses which had been so skilfully constructed by the German engineers along Germany's new frontier, the Kaiser threw overwhelming forces against the Russians, who were suffering from a grievous lack of weapons and munitions. Przemysl, captured by the Russians on March 22, had to be abandoned by our Allies. On June 22 Lemberg was evacuated. In August the Germans

NEUVILLE ST. VAAST.
A strongly fortified German trench captured by the French, and remains of a German gun.

entered Warsaw and, one by one, the fortresses —Ivangorod, Kovno, Novo Georgievsk, Brest Litovski, Grodno—protecting Russia proper from invasion were lost, and on September 18 the Germans were in Vilna.

Thus the Allies did not succeed in seriously retarding the Austro-German re occupation of Galicia and invasion of Russia. Huge as were the forces and the store of munitions of the Allies in the West, they were not proportionately so great as those possessed by the Kaiser when in August, 1914, he had invaded Belgium and France. If William II., with all the advantages of a vast superiority in numbers, heavy artillery, and machine guns, had been unable to batter his way through the French defences, it is not to be wondered that the French and British in 1915 made slow progress against a baffled but not badly defeated enemy, who were numerically perhaps their equals and were magnificently equipped and supplied with new and hideous engines of destruction. It was evident that, except at a ghastly sacrifice of life, no advance which had not been prepared by a prodigious expenditure of shells could be made. The danger in face of an enemy— amply provided with shells and cartridges— of depleting the reserve stores of munitions was soon brought home to the French Staff by the battles in Galicia and Russian Poland. Each section of Joffre's four hundred mile front had to be kept supplied with a sufficiency

of ammunition to prevent the German commanders from blasting their way through it. The railroads and motor-traction permitted the German leaders rapidly to concentrate their reserves behind any point in their immense battle front, and a temporary absence at any point of ammunition on the part of the Allies might have led to an irretrievable disaster. The German gas-and-flame-aided offensives round Ypres and in the Argonne proved that the enemy was far from considering that his cause was hopeless in the West, and there was always the chance that the invasion of Russia would be suspended and that Mackensen with his phalanx and gigantic artillery would be transferred to Belgium or France.

With these preliminaries, we commence our account of the main events which occurred on the Allied front from April 1 to September 24, 1915. We shall, as in Chapter XCVI., treat them not in strictly chronological order, and we shall ask the reader to accompany us along the line of battle from the sea at Nieuport-Bains to the Vosges.

Before doing so we devote some lines to the war in the air. On April 1 a German aeroplane, whose occupant was dropping bombs on Reims, was brought down by a lucky shot. The next day British aviators bombed Hoboken and Zeebrugge, and French aviators wrecked the railway stations at Neuenburg and Mülheim.

On April 3 St. Dié was attacked by a Taube. Zeebrugge was again, on the 8th, bombed by British airmen. The French on April 11 launched explosives on the railway station and a foundry at Bruges. German airships were busy the next day. One caught fire at Aeltre, another did some damage to Nancy. On the 14th French aviators disquieted the German headquarters at Mézières-Charleville; others, soon afterwards, inflicted damage on the military railway station at Freiburg. A French airship on April 19 attacked the railway station at Strassburg. A few hours later some French aeroplanes set fire to stores of fodder at Mannheim. Mannheim and Mülheim were bombed on the 21st; Friedrichshafen, on the Lake of Constance, and Leopoldshöhe on the 28th, and the railway station at Valenciennes on the 30th. In May, on the 3rd, French airmen dropped bombs into the headquarters of the Duke of Würtemberg. A German aeronaut on May 11 attacked St. Denis and another (May 22) Paris itself. The French, on May 26, sent a squadron of aeroplanes to destroy factories at Ludwigshafen. June 7 was memorable for the exploit of Lieutenant Warneford, who destroyed a Zeppelin between Ghent and Brussels, while other British aviators bombed a hangar near the Belgian capital. A week later (June 15) civilians in Nancy were killed and wounded by German aeronauts. Carlsruhe that day was visited by Allied aircraft and the castle there damaged. This operation was undertaken by way of reprisal. Zeebrugge, Heyst, Knocke, and Friedrichshafen were all attacked in the last days of June. In Belgium, on July 2, the German airship sheds at Ghistelles, which had been destroyed and rebuilt, were again rendered useless. Near Altkirch a duel in the air between German and French aviators ended in the defeat of the Germans. On August 26 a British aviator dropped bombs on a German submarine off Ostend, while British, Belgian, and French aviators set fire to a large portion of the Forest of Houthoulst, which during the end of August was almost daily bombed. Concentrations of German troops there had been signalled. On August 31 the celebrated French aeronaut Pégoud was killed in a duel near Belfort, a serious loss to the Allies. He had exhibited extraordinary courage and skill in a class of fighting where the individual counted as much as he had done at sea in the days of Elizabeth.

While the Allied aircraft chased Taubes and Zeppelins, and interfered with the communications of the German armies, the 400-mile long battle continued to rage. On the extreme left of the Allied line the Belgians in the period under review maintained their position. The floods of the Yser were drying up, and the country from the sea to the south of Dixmude was becoming a morass. In this muddy region a number of minor actions took place. On April 4 a German detachment took Driegrachten and crossed the Yperlee Canal. They were driven back across the Canal on April 6. Three days later, the enemy, on rafts armed with machine guns, tried to reach St. Jacques-Cappelle, on the western side of the Yser, south of Dixmude. They were repulsed by the French marines. Reinforced, the Germans again, on April 14, attacked near Dixmude, but unavailingly. Eight days later an effort on

A FRENCH TRENCH.
Showing bombs and hand-grenades placed in readiness for an attack.

their part to take the Château de Vicoigne, in the loop of the Yser, north of Dixmude, met with no success. On April 26 they used south of Dixmude some of the poisonous gas which they were employing in the Second Battle of Ypres. They were, however, unable to break the Belgian line. Three bridges of boats, by which they tried to cross the Yser at Dixmude, were destroyed by the Belgian artillery on April 29. The day before, a monster Krupp gun in a concrete casemate near Dixmude threw shells into Dunkirk, killing some civilians. It was promptly put—at least temporarily—out of action by the Allied aeronauts and gunners. On May 9 Nieuport was violently bombarded by the enemy. In a blinding sandstorm he advanced up the sea shore, but was beaten back.

It was now the turn of the Belgians to take the offensive, and on May 11 they obtained a footing on the right bank of the Yser. The Germans, towards the end of May, again endeavoured to advance from Dixmude, and between Dixmude and the loop of the Yser. Their efforts led to nothing of importance. In June the monster gun or, if it had been smashed, another of the same calibre, once more bombarded Dunkirk. On July 10 there was a skirmish at the House of the Ferryman on the Yser Canal. Forty British men-of-war bombarded the Belgian coast from Ostend to Zeebrugge on August 25. The object of the bombardment partly was to destroy the submarine base at Zeebrugge. The bombardment was repeated in September, and was supported by the Belgian and French artillery on the Yser front. The aim of Joffre was, it seems, to induce the German commanders to believe that he was about to take the offensive in Belgium with the assistance of troops landed from England east of Nieuport. To draw the German reserves to Belgium and Alsace, while he pierced the enemy's line in Artois and Champagne, was apparently his plan.

The Belgian right wing joined on to the French troops defending the Yperlee Canal in the neighbourhood of Ypres. The attempts of the Duke of Würtemberg to obtain a footing on the western bank of the Yperlee were everywhere foiled.

From the expiration of the Battle of Festubert in the fourth week of May to the beginning

IN THE ARGONNE.
An outpost in the woods.

FIRED BY GERMAN SHELLS: ON THE WESTERN FRONT.

The farmhouse in the background was so pounded by the enemy's shell-fire that it was almost unrecognisable as a house. The flames of the burning lit up the countryside for miles around.

of the Battle of Loos on September 25 the British Army was comparatively inactive. The Germans, who had calculated that with their poisonous gas they would achieve results in Flanders similar to those to be secured by Mackensen's overwhelming artillery, remained, generally speaking, after their failure at the Second Battle of Ypres, on the defensive.

To the disappointment of many people in England still bemused by optimistic politicians and writers, Sir John French imitated the German example. The number of the trained officers and privates, who had performed such prodigies of valour and exhibited such skill in the fighting from Mons onwards, had sadly dwindled. Time was needed to complete the training of the Territorials and to convert into soldiers the brave civilians in the

LOOKING OUT FOR ENEMY AIRCRAFT.
A French searchlight station.

ranks of the New Armies. Our heavy artillery was still inferior in quantity, if not in quality, to the enemy's. The enormous mass of shells and grenades required in the trench warfare had not yet been provided. Our experiences at the Battles of Neuve Chapelle, the Aubers Ridge, and Festubert, the experience of our French Ally in the Battle of Artois, about to be described, had driven home the lesson that the Art of War had been revolutionized by high explosives, aircraft, machine guns, barbed wire, and motor traction. " Festina lente," the favourite maxim of the founder of the Roman Empire, was now that of the British leaders.

It must not be supposed, however, that the last week in May, the months of June, July, and August, and the first three weeks of September were for the British troops uneventful. Numerous incidents occurred which in our previous wars would have caused columns of the newspapers to be filled with glowing narratives. Some of these engagements may be briefly recorded.

The character of the fighting which followed the Battle of Festubert in the La Bassée region, is admirably delineated by an eye-witness :

Fighting had been in progress for nearly a week, and the British were gradually working their way from left to right (that is, from north to south) along the old German line. The general position was thought to be favourable, and the German infantry were showing signs of demoralization, but the right extremity of the British progress was still a dangerous and difficult place. Part of the old German breastwork had been captured by a charge across the open, after a most destructive British bombardment. The Canadian garrison were, of course, holding the old rear side, originally thinner than the front and now severely battered by our shells. For more than 200 yards on the left the whole breastwork was so much knocked about as to afford no cover at all.

The communication trench which had been run back to the old British lines had been made under heavy German shelling, and was little more than a track across the field. Not only was communication with the left and rear thus made dangerous by night and almost impossible by day, but on the right there were several hundred yards of the trench still in German hands, with a fort at the end in which were two machine guns and a trench mortar. Another German fort stood in a communication trench running straight out from the front of the breastwork. A counter-attack with hand grenades might begin at any minute from both these places, and if it were successful from the communication trench, the troops to the right would be cut off and attacked from both flanks.

Two companies of the Post Office Rifles went to take up this position on the night of May 22. Until the 27th the whole battalion was almost unbrokenly at work, either winning more of the trench to the right or putting the place into a state of defence and improving its communications with the rear. On their way up the first two companies found the road blocked by parties of stretcher-bearers taking away the wounded. The German trench mortar and light guns were already active, and no sooner was the relief completed than—in the fearful thunderstorm of that night—the expected counter-attack with bombs was begun. Perhaps it was only defensive in intention ; at any rate it was kept down by the courage and enthusiasm of the Post Office bombers, both in fighting and in bringing up boxes of bombs from the stores behind.

The next day was Whit Sunday. It was a quiet day as those days went, but the French and British gunners were busy : there was a little bombing, and there was much fatigue work on the defences. The strong effort to clear things up was planned for the following dawn.

At 2 a.m. Major Whitehead attacked with his company towards the right, and cleared 250 yards of the trench. When that length had been gained, all the bombers were either dead or wounded, and two of the three subalterns in the company had come by mortal wounds. It was necessary to stand fast and block the trench. Meanwhile the Canadians had taken the fort in front by an assault across the open, only to be shelled out of it. For more than seven hours the Germans bombarded with the greatest violence. By midday the platoons on the left had less than a third of their men unwounded.

As the front to defend was now, of course, longer, another platoon, with the machine-gun section and two troops of Strathcona's Horse, had reinforced under machine-gun fire across the gap on the left. They, too, had casualties, and in the evening, when the shelling was again heavy, the men were tired out. All day they had had neither food nor water. The trench was choked with dead and wounded, and in many places the parapet had been blown down by shells. Fortunately, a fresh company came up from support to press the bombing attack on the right, but it had little success.

The attack had to be pushed on at all costs, and next evening, at 6.30, in conjunction with an assault by the brigade on the right, it was carried on till the last bend before the little fort. The fort had to be left for yet another time. An infantry assault in the moonlight was made. When Major Whitehead jumped on the parapet the Germans had hoisted the white flag and thrown down their arms. One officer and 36 men (nearly half of them wounded) gave themselves up, along with one Canadian who was their prisoner. The booty included the trench mortar, a machine gun, and 400 rifles, a great store of equipment and comforts, and, curiously enough, a drum.

The whole section of trench captured by the battalion was under a quarter of a mile in length, and there had been a casualty for almost every yard of it. Five of the officers had lost their lives and four more were wounded. After the fighting came the heavy and disgusting work of clearing up the breastworks and rebuilding them. On the night of the 26th the riflemen were so much exhausted that the officers and N.C.O.'s did all the sentry duty in order at last to let them snatch some sleep. On the 27th the battalion marched away to another part of the front.

It will be recollected that the Canadian Division had, after the Second Battle of Ypres, taken part in the closing stages of the Battle of Festubert. On May 20 the intrepid Colonials had captured the orchard near La Quinque Rue which had defied the efforts of other troops during the last-named battle. The next day they had attacked a redoubt known as "Bexhill." It was captured on May 24. In these and subsequent actions the Canadian artillery greatly distinguished itself.

Monday, May 24, was also noteworthy for an attack delivered by the Germans against the Ypres salient. At 2 a.m. a violent bombardment with gas and other shells along the British front from a point north of Wieltje to near Hooge began. Simultaneously a vast quantity of poisonous gas was discharged from the cylinders in the German trenches. The

LOOKING OUT FOR ENEMY AIRCRAFT.
A French 75 being used as an anti-aircraft gun in France.

FRENCH SOLDIER'S LIFE-SAVING HELMET.

The "Adrian helmet," which was a means of preventing wounds and saving the lives of many French soldiers. 1. A helmet struck by a bullet which ricocheted without penetrating. 2. Helmet that saved its wearer's life : showing the crest torn by a shell-splinter and brim bent by the soldier's fall. 3. Helmet pierced by a bullet which was deflected : showing the holes of entry and exit. 4. French sniper's helmet that saved his life : exhibiting marks of bullet which struck it as he was lying down.

enemy then attacked from the neighbourhood of St. Julien, Zonnebeke and the Polygon Wood. They gained some trenches near Shelltrap Farm, with others on both sides of the Ypres-Roulers railway and south of the Bellewaarde Lake. Counter-attacks during the day, however, were at most points successful, and the Germans secured little by the renewal of their treacherous tactics. Captain Francis Grenfell, V.C., one of the most promising of the younger officers in the Army, was killed. In the vicinity of Hill 60 and near Bois Grenier there was also fighting in which the British had the upper hand.

For several days the struggle in the Festubert region went on, but led to no decisive results. On the evening of May 31 the British recaptured the stables of the Château of Hooge. About this time the British Premier, Mr. Asquith, visited the front. He was accompanied or followed by the Postmaster-General, Mr. Herbert Samuel, M.P., and by Mr. Ben Tillett and Mr. Will Crooks, M.P. The last two had

been enthusiastic recruiters for the New Armies. Mr. Tillett and Mr. Crooks published their impressions. "On leaving the Army," wrote Mr. Tillett, "I had a mixed feeling of humiliation and of gratitude to our men."

On June 2 the enemy made a violent attempt to pierce the British position round Hooge, but the troops of the 3rd Cavalry Division and the 1st Indian Cavalry Division beat him back, and the next day the British seized some out-buildings of the Château, or rather the ruins of it. The 2nd Army took over the French trenches as far as Boesinghe on the Yperlee Canal, and on June 15 the 1st Canadian Brigade carried the front-line German trenches north-east of Givenchy, pushing towards Rue d'Ouvert and Chapelle St. Roch, but, the flanks of the Canadians being exposed, they were withdrawn to their original position.

The next day, June 16, the 5th Corps attacked the Germans south of Hooge, cleared their first-line trenches, and reached the edge of the Bellewaarde Lake. The British subsequently retired a little, but a thousand yards of trenches had been gained. The Honourable Artillery Company and other Territorials behaved very gallantly in this engagement. At the same time the 2nd and 6th Corps delivered holding-attacks and the artillery of the 36th French Corps shelled Pilkem. On Tuesday, July 6, Lord Kitchener paid a visit to the army, and stayed till Thursday evening inspecting the troops. The day of his arrival, at 6.20 a.m., in misty weather, after a brief bombardment by British and French guns, the 11th Infantry Brigade captured a German salient between Boesinghe and Ypres. From the 10th to the 13th July the Germans endeavoured to recover the trenches which they had lost, but were repulsed. They bombarded the position with gas shells and carried some of the trenches, but were expelled by our troops with bombs and grenades. East of Ypres, about 10 a.m. on the 13th, they rushed one of our advanced posts on the Verlorenhoek road. It was at once retaken.

Six days later (July 19) a German redoubt near Hooge was successfully mined and destroyed and some trenches captured. Both sides were frequently exploding mines, but the days when fortresses could be breached by a few bags of gunpowder were over. The struggle round Hooge went on, and on July 30 the Germans introduced to the notice of our men a new weapon. It was the *Flammen-werfer*, a steel cylinder resembling a milk-can in shape and filled with inflammable liquid. To one side was fitted six feet of rubber hose with a long steel nozzle at the end. By padded metal arms the cylinder was attached to the back of the operator. Stamped on the top was the German Imperial crown.

The interior was divided into two chambers, the lower containing a compressed gas to furnish the pressure. A valve released the gas, which pushed the inflammable fluid into the rubber pipe. Two other valves held the fluid in check before it reached the device for igniting it at the nozzle. This device consisted of a small tube containing a spring, a detonator, some gun-cotton, and a wick soaked in paraffin. When the gas pressed the fluid against the spring, the wick ignited and a jet of flame projected from the nozzle for twenty yards or more. It was accompanied by volumes of black smoke, and could be made to last two minutes. For each ignition, however, a firing tube had to be fitted into the end of the steel nozzle.

This diabolic instrument had been employed against the French in October, 1914, and was then being used in the Argonne. With the assistance of the *Flammenwerfer* the Germans gained some trenches at Hooge on the Menin-Ypres road.

On August 9, at 4 a.m., the British and French artillery directed a terrific fire on the trenches secured by such unnatural means, and these, with 400 yards of German trench north of the Menin road, were recovered.

From the end of the action at Hooge to the Battle of Loos there was, in Sir John French's words, " relative quiet along the whole of the British line, except at those points where the normal conditions of existence comprised occasional shelling and constant mine and bomb warfare." The preparations for the great offensive at the end of September were being made. Detachments of the New Armies were constantly arriving, and the British line was gradually extended south of La Bassée towards the plateau of Notre Dame de Lorette. The New Armies filled the French with admiration. M. Pichon, ex-Minister for Foreign Affairs, who had been to the British front, published on August 25 an account of his visit :

It is certain that at first sight the rapid formation of a huge British Army might appear impossible and the difficulties almost insurmountable, but British tenacity has overcome them. It has been a huge task, involving enormous expenditure, a method and co-ordination of effort without pause or limit, and a will which would not bend before any obstacle. That is exactly what has happened. Kitchener's Army is in being and is now on our soil with all the requisite services provided and equipped in a manner which excites our admiration.

It was on the plateau of Notre Dame de Lorette, and south of it, that the bloodiest battle in the West during the spring and summer of 1915 was fought.

On April 28 General von Mackensen commenced his great offensive for the recovery of Galicia, and by the evening of May 2 it is probable that Joffre was informed of the gigantic forces in men and artillery opposed to the Russians defending the space between the Carpathians and the Upper Vistula. Although the Russians had an enormous tract of country into which to retreat, every indirect form of pressure consistent with the safety of the Allies in the West had to be exercised on the Germans to force them to recall troops to Belgium and France.

The question for the French Generalissimo to decide was at what point in the long line

TRENCHES LOST THROUGH GERMAN "LIQUID FIRE" RECAPTURED.

from the North Sea to Switzerland he should use his reserves of men and munitions. For various reasons he selected the region south of La Bassée and north of Arras. If, pivoting on Arras, he could drive the Germans from the heights between the Lys and the Scarpe into the plain of the Scheldt and, capturing Lens, advance towards the line Lille-Valenciennes, he would threaten the communications of the armies facing the French from Arras to the junction of the Oise and Aisne, and also be able with the British forces from the west of La Bassée to Armentières to dislodge the enemy from the ridges north of the La Bassée-Lille Canal, and remove once and for all the danger of a German thrust from La Bassée in the direction of Boulogne. Assuming success, Lille might then be invested.

The difficulties in the way of carrying out a plan of this kind were very great. South of the Béthune-La Bassée-Lille Canal the French, who had captured Vermelles and Le Rutoire in December, had indeed made some progress in the plain towards Loos and Lens. But the high ground round Loos, the ridges north of the stream of the Souchez, and most of the hilly ravined plateau, which from the ridge of Notre Dame de Lorette extends west and south of Lens to the banks of the Scarpe below Arras, were held by the Germans, and had been converted by them into one of the most formidable fortified positions in the world.

Lille, too, had been put into a state of defence by the German engineers. The forts, unfinished or dismantled at the outbreak of war, had been made, so far as German science could make them, impregnable. Electrified barbed wire entanglements encircled the city. Fifteen miles or so east of Lille an entrenched camp had been formed at Tournai on the Scheldt, and heavy guns placed on Mont St. Aubert, which, north of Tournai, commands the plain for several miles. Courtrai, on the Lys below Armentières, had also been strongly protected. Even if Joffre expelled the enemy from La Bassée and Lens, the fortified area in the triangle Courtrai-Lille-Tournai would present a redoubtable obstacle to a further advance. In the centre of the side Courtrai-Lille were the cities of Tourcoing and Roubaix, which, like Lille, Tournai, and Courtrai, would be defended not only by artillery but by innumerable machine-guns. If farms and villages held by machine gunners delayed, as they had done

at Neuve Chapelle, the advance of overwhelming numbers, it was to be presumed that cities bristling with mitrailleuses would be impenetrable.

The alternative plan of marching on the Scheldt above Tournai and descending on the communications of the German armies between the Scarpe and the Oise was perhaps more promising, but the Scarpe and the Scheldt would have to be crossed, and the forests of Vicoigne and Raismes, between the Scarpe and the Scheldt, and the high ground south of Valenciennes would provide the enemy with excellent defensive positions, while from the triangle Courtrai-Lille-Tournai he could attack the left flank of the French moving on the Scheldt.

The above considerations must be borne in mind or we shall not understand why Joffre, despite the straits to which the Russians were reduced in the summer of 1915, was content with comparatively small gains at the Battle of Artois.

Another reason for the French Generalissimo selecting the Arras-La Bassée region for his offensive was that a stroke at Lens was calculated to assist the Allies engaged since April 22 in the Second Battle of Ypres. On May 2 Sir John French had ordered Sir Herbert Plumer to retire to a new position nearer to the walls of Ypres, and there can be little doubt that, up to the opening of the Battle of Artois, the situation of the British and French round Ypres was distinctly dangerous. The battles of the Aubers Ridge, Festubert and Artois were in the nature of counter-strokes. That they were effective, events were to prove. Though, as mentioned, the Germans on May 24 attacked the British, they had broken off the battle for Ypres on May 13, four days after the Battle of Artois began, and they had suffered General Putz on May 15–17 to drive them from the west bank of the Yperlee Canal, which they had reached by the use of chlorine gas. The Battle of Artois may not have acted as a brake on the German war machine in the east, but it brought to a close the last great offensive of the enemy in the west during 1915.

We will now describe the earliest of the exhibitions on a large scale of the power of the French heavy artillery. In 1914 the Germans had shown the value of high explosive shells discharged from gigantic guns and howitzers transported by railroad or motor traction. At Neuve Chapelle, in Champagne, at Les Eparges, in

BRITISH GUN IN DIFFICULTIES.
Owing to the sudden rising of a river in Flanders, a temporary bridge collapsed and the gun overturned
into the water.

the Wood of Ailly and elsewhere the Allies had already taught the enemy that they had no monopoly of the machinery which tended more and more to transform war from a contest between soldiers into one between chemists and mechanics. The French leaders perceived that without a superabundance of heavy artillery the Allies would never be able to overcome their enemy. When the war broke out, that branch of the French Army was, according to a semi-official report, " in process of reorganization." Whatever the phrase may mean, we learn from the same semi-official report that Joffre sent to the Battle of Flanders no more than 60 heavy guns. It is unquestionable that the Germans in 1914, though their light artillery was inferior to that of the French, were, so far as heavy artillery was concerned, ahead of their enemies.

Since November 11, 1914, an immense change had come over the scene. Under the direction of Joffre, M. Millerand, the Minister of War, and M. Thomas, the Minister of Munitions, a large part of the civilian French population had been mobilized for the production of artillery, machine-guns, rifles and munitions. With feverish haste men worked day and night in arsenals, factories and shops to turn out the implements which would free France from the despised and hated " Boches." The labour of the men was supplemented by that of the women. The average French woman has always

taken kindly to business, and some of the chief commercial establishments in France have been under female control. After, and even before, the fall of Napoleon III. education in France was every year becoming more scientific and less literary. Universal military service had spread the knowledge of strategical and tactical problems. The result was that the Government could call upon a host of chemical and mechanical experts of the two sexes both able and willing to help it in its stupendous task.

The French, unlike the Germans, had not for a generation been considering every invention and discovery from the point of view of a soldier bent at all costs on conquest. In this crisis, however, they swiftly applied their knowledge and wits to the purposes of war. From Ancient Greece and Rome the catapult was borrowed to discharge, not spears and bolts, but bombs and grenades. Helmets and shields manufactured of a compound of steel, which for its hardness, lightness and toughness would have astonished mediæval knights, were provided for the trench warfare. Improved forms of aerial torpedoes were invented. New kinds of grenades and bombs to be thrown by hand ; baby mortars to launch projectiles a score of yards, monster howitzers and guns to hurl them almost as many miles, issued from the cannon foundries. If Great Britain and Russia had been proportionately as well equipped as was France in May, 1915, the

British repulse at the Battle of the Aubers Ridge and the victories of Mackensen in Galicia might never have occurred.

On May 8, while Sir Douglas Haig was putting the finishing touches to his preparations for storming the Aubers Ridge, General d'Urbal, who had replaced General de Maud'huy—the latter had been sent to serve under General Dubail in Alsace—as leader of the 10th Army, gave his final orders for the battle which, it was hoped, would end in the recovery of Lens. General d'Urbal, it will be remembered, had been Sir John French's coadjutor in the Battle of Flanders. There had been a recent re-distribution of commands. The local direction of the French troops north of the Lys had been assigned to General Putz, who, later in the year, was succeeded by General Hely d'Oissel. South of d'Urbal's army, that between the Somme and Oise had been transferred from General de Castelnau to General Petain. The former now directed the armies of the Allied centre from Compiègne eastward. General Dubail continued to superintend the operations of the right, General Foch those of the left wing.

Foch was with d'Urbal, and during the Battle of Artois both were joined by Joffre himself. To d'Urbal had been allocated seven corps. Some 1,100 guns of all calibres were concentrated for the task immediately to hand. Since January the French sappers had been undermining the enemy's defences. In the sector of Carency alone the underground works constructed by the French engineers measured in length one and a half miles, and the quantity of explosives in the mines weighed more than thirty tons.

Ample as were the preparations, large as the numbers of the men at d'Urbal's disposition, they were none too many. The position to be carried by assault had been converted by the Germans into a fortified area the like of which had never existed before the Great War. The

A BRITISH STAFF CAR ON THE WESTERN FRONT.
An episode during a bombardment : the car skimming past a cavity formed by a shell.

NORTH-WEST OF HULLUCH.
The Quarries occupied by the Germans.

engineering skill of an age which had witnessed the tunnelling of the Simplon and the piercing of the Isthmus of Panama had been applied to the ridges, hollows and ravines between Arras and Lens. Manufacturers of barbed wire and *chevaux-de-frise* had assisted the efforts of the engineers. In tunnels, caves and trenches, in cellars and loopholed buildings were ensconced thousands of Germans armed with every instrument of destruction which the perverted ingenuity of the Fatherland's chemists and mechanics could devise. An enormous collection of guns and howitzers in the background were ready to deluge with high-explosive shells and shrapnel the avenues of approach to the position and, if it were lost, to bombard it. Mackensen's task in Galicia was child's play to d'Urbal's in Artois.

Although there was fighting north of the plateau of Notre Dame de Lorette, the battle may be said to have been confined to an assault of the German line from the region of the Chapel on that plateau to the Labyrinth, which was the name given to the two square miles of trenches, tunnels and roofed-in pits across the Arras-Lens high road north of the villages of Ecurie and Roclincourt. The ridge of which the plateau is the eastern extremity is the southern boundary of the plain that stretches to the Béthune-La Bassée Canal. The ridge

is six miles long and, in places, wooded. The plateau at the eastern end is bare. From the north the slopes of the ridge are easily mounted, but on the southern side it is approached up steep spurs separated by ravines. West of the village of Ablain St. Nazaire is the Spur Mathis, then, going eastwards, the Great Spur, the Arabs' Spur, the Spur of the White Way and the Spur of Souchez, which dominates both the eastern edge of Ablain St. Nazaire and the Sugar Refinery between Ablain and Souchez.

About March 20 the French had worked their way up to the foot of the Great Spur, and by April 14 they were close to Ablain St. Nazaire. But the Germans retained most of the plateau of the Chapel of Notre Dame de Lorette, and the whole of the Spur of the White Way and the Spur of Souchez.

On May 9 the French line ran some 1,100 yards west of the Chapel to the summit of the Arabs' Spur, and thence by the Great Spur and the Spur Mathis descended into the valley west of Ablain.

No less than five lines of German trenches had been dug from the Arabs' Spur across the plateau to the Arras-Béthune road near Aix-Noulette. These trenches were very deep and covered with double and triple iron networks, and protected by sacks of earth or cement and by *chevaux-de-frise.* At every hundred yards or so they were crossed by barricades in which were fixed machine guns. Several small forts supported the defenders, and the one north-east of the Chapel contained dug-outs over 50 feet deep. The artillery and machine guns in Ablain raked the southern slopes of the ridge, those in Souchez the eastern face of the plateau. Guns hidden in the houses of the villages of Angres and Lievin, north-east of the plateau, shelled troops attacking the trenches from the plain to the north or advancing against them along the ridge. This part of the German line was defended by troops from Baden of excellent quality.

Nestling below the southern side of the plateau of Notre Dame de Lorette were the considerable villages of Ablain St. Nazaire and Souchez, both in possession of the enemy. Between them, closer to Souchez, was the Sugar Refinery—a collection of buildings 200 yards long on the banks of the rivulet Saint Nazaire. A little to the south of it were three ruined houses called the Mill Malon. The ground to the east of the Sugar Refinery was very marshy. The Sugar Refinery and the Mill Malon had been powerfully fortified by the Germans

To the south of Ablain St. Nazaire rose the wooded heights of Carency, with the townlet of that name situated in a hollow. It consisted of five groups of houses, one in the centre and the others facing north, west, south and east. Four lines of trenches defended Carency.

Each street and house in it was fortified and connected by underground passages. Four battalions—Saxons, Badeners, and Bavarians—and more than six companies of engineers garrisoned this important point. A great number of guns and mitrailleuses had been installed in the gardens and orchards and behind the church. It was only possible to attack Carency from the south or east. Trenches connected it with Ablain St. Nazaire and Souchez.

Souchez is on the Béthune-Arras high road. Between Souchez and Arras lies the hamlet of La Targette. The Germans had cut lines of trenches, known from their chalky parapets as the "White Works," from Carency to La Targette. The ruins of La Targette covered another underground German fortress. A short distance east of La Targette was the town of Neuville St. Vaast, also in German hands, situated between the Arras-Béthune and Arras-Lens roads. Neuville St. Vaast was a straggling village some one and a half miles long and seven hundred yards broad. It, too, had been turned into an underground fortress.

South of Neuville St. Vaast extended the Labyrinth on both sides of the Arras-Lens road. "Possibly," wrote a Special Correspondent of the *Morning Post*, "never has a similar stronghold been planned and constructed . . . . Inside it there is a complete and cunning maze, containing every species of death-dealing device known to science, including numbers of gas and inflammable liquid

ANOTHER VIEW OF THE QUARRIES.

engines. Underground tunnels, coupled with mines, compete with small fortresses containing guns for the better destruction of the daring invaders. In a maze one constantly turns corners to meet blank walls of hedge. In the ' Labyrinth ' such blank walls are death traps, and from their subterranean refuge bodies of the enemy are liable to appear to the rear of the advancing attackers. The ' Labyrinth ' is linked up by underground tunnels to Neuville St. Vaast, and probably to Thelus, near Vimy. Anyhow, it is an integral and consummately important part of this fortress land—an entire district which constitutes one concentrated fortress." About two miles east of the Labyrinth and Neuville St. Vaast was the edge of the heights bordering the plain between the Scarpe and the Béthune-La-Bassée-Lille Canal.

Such was the subterranean fortified area which the French were called upon to carry. Their aeronauts and other observers could give them but a faint idea of its nature. The Germans had made the fortresses of Brialmont seem as obsolete as those of Vauban. Could the French miners and gunners solve the problems set them by the murderous intelligences who had designed the Labyrinth ? On the answer to that question seemed almost to depend the issue of the Great War. If the engineer had got the better of the artilleryman and the miner, the Germans, with countless " Labyrinths," would hold up the Allied offensive, and the War might continue indefinitely.

On Sunday, May 9, as the last stars were fading in the grey of the morning, the assaulting French troops were inspecting their rifles, filling their water bottles, inserting cartridges into their belts and hand-grenades into their bags. The sappers had cut steps in the sides of the trenches to enable the men to climb out more quickly. At sunrise there was the sound of firing in the distance. A British aeroplane from the direction of La Bassée was crossing the German lines. It was hit, but the aeronaut managed to descend behind the French trenches. Three French aeroplanes immediately afterwards ascended, and the observers in them took a last look at the gashes and holes in the ground, the ruined chapel of Notre Dame de Lorette and the remains of the villages of Ablain St. Nazaire, Souchez, Carency, La Targette and Neuville St. Vaast, in, or under which were lurking the German infantry and the enemy's guns and mitrailleuses.

At six a.m. the signal was given for the bombardment to open. The sound produced by the discharge of the thousand and more French pieces resembled the rolling thunder of a tropical storm. The British engaged in mounting the Aubers Ridge were startled by the intensity of the distant cannonade. "I am quite well," wrote, four days later, a French artillery officer who was present at the battle, " although I am still stunned by the noise of the cannon."

The sound produced by the French howitzers, heavy artillery, *Soixante-quinze* guns and trench mortars, suggested the storm ; the effects of the bombardment were seismic. "I went," says the same officer, "and afterwards looked at one of the enemy's trenches. It was a terrible sight. Everything was upset ; there was blood everywhere, and, as the excavations are narrow, we had to walk over heaps of corpses, legs, arms, heads, rifles, cartridges, machine guns, all in a confused mass. That," he adds, " was the work of our artillery."

The heavens had rained projectiles, which blew in the sides of concreted trenches, formed huge craters, smashed to fragments the *chevaux-de-frise*, cut lanes through the barbed wire entanglements, and caused bags of earth and cement, baulks of timber, and iron nettings to collapse on the heads of the Germans. More than 20,000 shells rained upon the houses of Carency alone. The other villages and buildings in the area received similar attention. Over 300,000 shells were discharged that day. To complete the work of destruction, at 6.45 a.m. the seventeen mines in the sector of Carency were fired. The subterranean refuges of the enemy were uprooted. His counter-mines were buried or the wires for detonating them destroyed. Most of the German sappers were killed or buried alive, but one company of French engineers rescued seventy cowering in a gallery. On the plateau of Notre Dame de Lorette and at other points French mines were also exploded with analogous effects.

The assault did not immediately take place. For three hours the bombardment continued, the French in the trenches loudly applauding. At 10 a.m. the order was given to attack. Of the five lines of trenches on the plateau of Notre Dame de Lorette, three were carried by the French Chasseurs and supporting infantry, but with heavy losses. The little fort in the centre of the German line, however, held out ;

AT THE POINT OF THE BAYONET.
British Infantry attacking a German trench in France.

the men of Baden putting up a desperate resistance. From Angres, the German batteries played on the lost trenches, or rather on the depressions in the ground and craters. From Ablain St. Nazaire the enemy's mitrailleuses continued their ceaseless fire. On the plateau men struggled confusedly with bayonets and knives and hurled bombs and grenades at each other. Night fell, and, amidst the explosions of the shells, the cries of the wounded and the whistling of the bullets, the French dug themselves in.

Meanwhile, south of the plateau, across the valley, a no less bloody struggle was proceeding from Carency to the Labyrinth. At the same moment that the attack was delivered on the plateau the French attacked Carency. They carried the German trenches and, despite the orders given, endeavoured to storm the village. They were unable, however, to break in, and a fortified work to the east of the village, which the Germans retained, forced them to halt. Nevertheless they pushed

A BATTERY OF FRENCH GUNS ON THE WAY TO THEIR POSITIONS.

forwards towards Souchez and approached the road leading from Carency to that place. Many prisoners—over 500—had been captured, and thirty machine guns. It was no longer possible for the Germans to use their communication trenches between Carency and Souchez, and the only connexion of the Carency garrison with the rest of the line was by the trenches from Carency to Ablain St. Nazaire.

Carency was almost isolated. Not only had the French reached a point from which they could take it in reverse from the east side, but the bastioned trenches of the White Works which had joined it to La Targette had, with La Targette itself, been captured. At 10 a.m. two regiments had left their trenches in the Wood of Berthonval and, bayoneting the enemy in their path, speedily placed the White Works behind them. Ignoring the fire of the mitrailleuses which had not yet been put out of action, the mass of enthusiastic soldiers made for the Arras-Béthune Road between Souchez and La Targette. A Brigadier-General fell shot through the chest. A Colonel was seriously wounded ; and the loss in officers was very heavy. But the heroic band rushed up the slopes and reached the crest. By 11.30 they had covered over four thousand three hundred yards. A German Colonel was captured and the equivalent of a German brigade put out of action.

Meantime, across a meadow, other French troops had marched on La Targette, where the road from Mont St. Eloi crosses the Arras-

Béthune road and continues through Neuville St. Vaast to the Arras–Lens causeway. The strands of barbed wire, thick as a finger, had been destroyed by the artillery. To cross the trenches, light wooden bridges were carried by the men. But so eager were they that they threw them down and leapt the obstacles, which, as usual in the case of German trenches, were very narrow. In front of La Targette were two big works armed with artillery. So rapid, however, had been the French advance that the Germans, with the exception of a few machine-gunners, disappeared into their dugouts. Some of the French stormed the village, which was in their hands by 11.15. Three hundred and fifty prisoners, several "77" guns and numerous mitrailleuses had been captured. The sappers rapidly organized the defences of this important point, and batteries of French artillery galloped up, unlimbered, and opened on the German reserves.

Passing round and through La Targette, the French next attacked Neuville St. Vaast. The right wing was held up by the defenders of the Labyrinth, but the centre succeeded in both gaining a footing in a group of houses at the southern end of Neuville St. Vaast, and in approaching the cemetery of the village. Twice during the day amid the tombs a desperate hand-to-hand combat took place. Half of the village itself remained by nightfall in the possession of the French, who took many prisoners. The dirty, terrified Germans were directed to the rear by cavalrymen.

Such was the battle of May 9. The French had proved that defences which the Germans regarded as impregnable could be stormed. They had taken 3,000 prisoners, 10 field guns, and 50 mitrailleuses.

By Monday, accordingly, the French had wedged themselves into the centre of the German position. To keep the enemy's reserves employed, a feint attack was made north of the Notre Dame de Lorette plateau in the direction of Loos. The fighting on the plateau continued. Some progress was made on the left until it was brought to a standstill by the artillery hidden in Angres. The little fort by the side of the chapel was a thorn in the side of the French. A strong counter-attack from the Sugar Refinery between Ablain and Souchez was signalled, and the French offensive was here suspended. The artillery by a barrage of fire prevented the Germans from debouching, and the French infantry, heartened by this, descended from the plateau towards the Ablain ravine. From the note-book of Captain Sievert, who commanded a German battalion, and was subsequently killed, we learn the importance attached by the Crown Prince of Bavaria and his Staff to the Germans retaining the Loretto plateau and the line Ablain–Carency, also the insufficiency of the means at the disposal of Captain Sievert. His first company had been

reduced by May 10 to four non-commissioned officers and twenty-five men; his second company to one officer and eighty non-commissioned officers and men. The third and fourth companies were of about the same strength, and the battalion now mustered only three officers and 272 non-commissioned officers and privates. "I demand again," he wrote, and he underlined the words, "reinforcements. I must, at all costs, have a large number of the hand-grenades which I have already sent for."

Carency was undoubtedly in great danger. The Germans appear, indeed, from the French official narrative, to have recovered some of the communication trenches and tunnels connecting it with Souchez, but during the day some houses east of the village were stormed, and the enemy cleared out of a hollow south of the Carency-Souchez road. On the right, beyond the Arras-Béthune road, the cemetery of Neuville St. Vaast was carried, and the German reserves who had been motored up from Douai and Lens were repulsed with loss.

The 11th was another day of sanguinary combats. The French in the evening, after a terrific encounter, mastered the lower slopes of the Arabs' Spur. In the night the Germans counter-attacked from the Spur of the White Way. They were beaten back. The guns in Angres and the machine guns in Ablain

WITH THE FRENCH ARMY.
Filling a captive balloon with hydrogen gas from cylinders. The cylinders are attached to the supply tube of balloon.

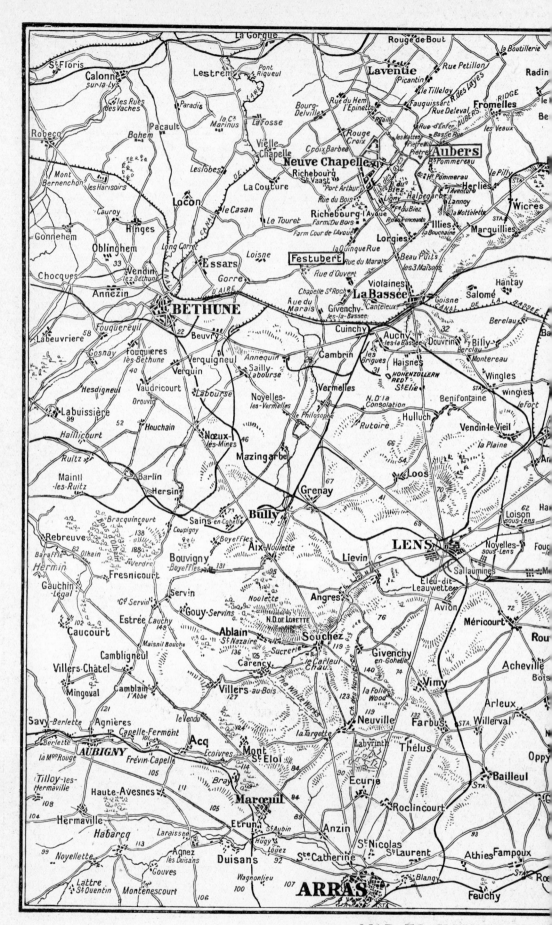

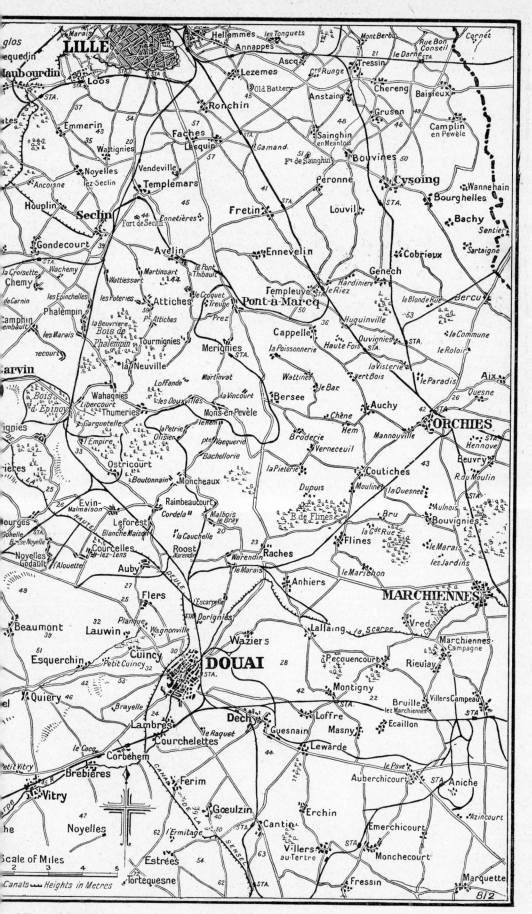

OF ARTOIS.

RUINS AT PERTHES-LES-HURLUS.
The French bombarded the village and at the point of the bayonet took the German trenches close by.

kept up a never-ceasing fire at the French positions. The conditions on the plateau were unusually disgusting. The bursting shells had disinterred the corpses of the hundreds of French and Germans whose lives had been sacrificed during the preceding months.

The days of the garrison of Carency were now numbered. On the 11th the French gained the wood east of the village, and the communication trenches with Souchez could no longer be used by the enemy. A woody hillock, fortified by the Germans, still kept the French from storming the east end of the village. Their approach from the west was checked by the infantry in a stone quarry nearly 300 feet deep. The Germans, however, in this sector were beginning to despair. Captain Sievert and his officers had refused to take part in a night attack because they had too few projectiles and grenades. "The enemy's artillery," he notes, " fires uninterruptedly and inflicts losses on us."

Away to the south the French were still attacking Neuville St. Vaast and the Labyrinth. They had at last established their hold on the cemetery of the village, but the Labyrinth had not been reduced.

The next day, Wednesday, May 12, saw the capture of the little fort and the Chapel of Notre Dame de Lorette, also that of Carency. General Joffre had arrived to observe the operations. In pitch darkness the French Chasseurs clambered into the *fortin*, and, after

a desperate hand-to-hand combat, it and the remains of the Chapel were at last gained. At daybreak, under the fire of the enemy's artillery, the French pushed towards the Spur of the White Way, which commanded the valley beneath from Ablain to Souchez.

Before the *fortin* and Chapel fell, Carency had been taken. The French infantry, well supported by the artillery, routed the three companies defending the wooded hillock to the east of the village. After violent fighting, the stone quarry to its west was cleared of the enemy. The French entered the western block of houses, whilst the eastern group was also assaulted. The enemy sold their lives dearly. Firing through windows and trap-doors, they retreated from house to house. At 5.30 p.m., what remained of the garrison surrendered. A motley collection of Bavarians, Saxons and Badeners crying " Kamerad, Kamerad " issued from the village. They numbered over a thousand. The officers, stiff as usual, clicked their heels together and saluted the French General.

" Who is in command ? " asked a French officer.

After some hesitation, a Colonel advanced and explained that he had only arrived that morning and that he was not the director of the defence. Whether the Brigadier-General in command had been killed or wounded, was uncertain.

The German officer, with all his faults,

respects ability, especially ability in the art of destroying human life. "Your fire," said one officer to his captors, "has been mathematically precise. Your infantry have charged so quickly that it was impossible to resist them."

From Carency the conquerors pushed on to Ablain St. Nazaire. The night was suddenly illuminated by an immense fire. Ablain, or at least part of it was in flames. The Germans, who were evacuating the village, retained some houses at the eastern end. Two thousand prisoners, guns, howitzers, minenwerfer, machine guns, rifles, ammunition, and other material of war, had in this region alone fallen into the hands of the French.

On Thursday, in drenching rain, d'Urbal tried to seize the Spur of the White Way, but the French were held up by machine-gun fire. That day M. Millerand despatched this letter by telegraph to General Joffre :

My dear General,—I do not wish to await the end of the operations begun on the 9th inst. by our troops in the Arras region before sending you and asking you to express to your soldiers my grateful congratulations for the results already obtained by our action, which demonstrate the excellence of the preparations made, the splendid way it was carried out, and the superiority we have gained over an opponent who recoils from no crime. It is a new and happy presage of his ruin. You and your armies have once more won the admiration and gratitude of the country, and I am happy to convey them to you.

A. Millerand.

On the 15th another French attack on the Spur of the White Way failed. Thenceforward up to the 21st the French on the plateau, under the fire of the German artillery in Angres and Lievin, were engaged on consolidating their position.

Below in the valley the Germans still clung to Ablain. They had apparently recovered the church and they were also occupying the cemetery. Neither in Ablain nor in Souchez, east of it, was their position enviable. On the 17th Captain Sievert made this note. "Covered in sweat, we arrive at Souchez. The sights are indescribable. It is one hideous mass of ruins. The street is littered with fragments of shells. The staff of the 11th Infantry Reserve Regiment is in a cellar. Souchez has been completely destroyed by the artillery." From Souchez he proceeded the same day to Ablain, which, it seems, was also a heap of broken building material. Only a quarter of the church tower was left. "When," he observes, "we were in the ravine of Souchez we did not believe that there could be any worse position. Here we perceive that it is possible. Not only are we exposed to frontal and flank fire, but the French are firing at our backs from the slopes of the plateau of Notre Dame de Lorette." Still, and it must be

AFTER A FRENCH OFFENSIVE.
French trench-diggers in steel helmets on the way to reconstruct the trenches.

CROSSING A HALF-SUBMERGED PONTOON BRIDGE.

An Exploit by the French Artillery : Saving a battery of " Seventy-Fives."

admitted to the credit of this member of a stubborn race, he did not despair. "We have become tolerably apathetic in this mouse-trap. I ordered the battalion to fight to the last man."

Notwithstanding this affirmation, it is clear from the Captain's entries on the 19th and 20th that his spirits were sinking. Food was running low. The road by which the portable kitchens reached Ablain was swept by the fire of the French artillery. The nerves of his men were shaken. Threats of bringing them before a court-martial failed to keep them at their posts when the shells fell. He demanded that he and his men should be relieved, but the German Higher Command has no mercy. There is something pathetic in the last lines which he wrote. "How much longer," they run, "shall we have to stay in this mouse-trap ? I am in a state of nervous collapse. The fire of the enemy has reached its greatest violence. Indescribable."

It was on May 21, in the afternoon, that the French from the north, south and west attacked the German trenches on the Spur of the White Way. Leaving its position on the Arabs' Spur, one body, in a few minutes, captured the lines of the enemy in front of them. From the north another seized the German central communication trench. Surrounded on every side, the enemy threw down their arms and threw up their hands. The assault directed from Ablain was equally successful. The houses west of the church were secured and the communications of the White Way with Souchez cut. Three hundred prisoners and a gun had been captured. At 2 a.m. on the 22nd the Germans, who retained a few houses in Ablain, counter-attacked, but were repulsed. In the course of the combats, from the 9th to the 22nd, the enemy had lost very heavily in dead and wounded. On the plateau and its slopes over 3,000 German corpses were counted.

The Germans had been dislodged from the plateau of Notre Dame de Lorette. The next step of d'Urbal was to expel them from Ablain. On May 28 an attack was launched against the doomed handful of brave men who, in obedience to orders, still occupied the trenches round the cemetery. It was a beautiful, clear day, and the houses in the village, through the broken walls of which one perceived the Loretto spurs or the blue sky, stood out as if in a painting. The French artillery threw a curtain of shells east of the cemetery so as to prevent the garrison from being reinforced. Cheering

FAMOUS FRENCH GENERALS.
General de Castelnau (left) and General Franchet d'Esperey (right).

loudly, the assaulting infantry with fixed bayonets made for the cemetery. The Germans offered no resistance, and soon afterwards 400 men, including seven officers, surrendered. During the night the business of clearing the enemy out of the group of houses to the south of the church was undertaken, and outside Ablain a *fortin* stormed. On the morning of the 29th the church and the rectory, defended by three companies, were attacked. Only twenty Germans escaped and were made prisoners. The French in this last combat had lost 200 killed and wounded. The majority had been struck by fragments of " Jack Johnsons " rained on Ablain by the German gunners, who may have believed, what was afterwards asserted, that Ablain had been evacuated. Five hundred German corpses in the ruins, about as many prisoners and 14 machine guns attested the French victory.

AFTER A BATTLE IN THE CHAMPAGNE.
French soldiers filling their water-bottles at a well at Perthes-les-Hurlus.

With Ablain in their possession, the French descended the valley, and on May 31 drove the enemy out of the three ruined houses, known as the Mill Malon. From these houses a communication trench ran to the Sugar Refinery already referred to. The French infantry, flinging grenades in front of them, rushed up it, chasing the flying foe before them. They entered the Refinery on the heels of the surviving fugitives. By nightfall they had killed or expelled every one of the garrison. Hastily the defence of the place was organized. Towards midnight the Germans counter-attacked, and gradually pushed the French back into the communication trench. A telephone message was at once sent to the artillery to isolate the enemy by a curtain of fire, and to the troops on the outskirts of Ablain to march on the Refinery along the bed of the rivulet. The men in the communication trench were rapidly re-formed and they counter-attacked. The Germans fled, and by the evening of June 1 the conquered position was connected with Ablain by communication trenches.

Throughout June, and indeed up to the great offensive on September 25, the fighting in the region of the Battle of Artois went on. The French from May 25 to 28 had made some little progress eastwards in the direction of Angres. In June and the succeeding months they nibbled at the German trenches traversing the plain to the Béthune–La Bassée Canal.

South of the plateau of Notre Dame de Lorette, which remained in their possession, they penetrated from the Sugar Refinery into the outskirts of Souchez. But it was in the section of Neuville St. Vaast that there was the hardest fighting. An officer wounded there on June 19 has graphically described what the conquest of the Labyrinth entailed :—

The war of the trenches is nothing compared with the struggle of the burrows that we had to carry on for three weeks. Picture to yourselves narrow galleries, feebly lit by flickering oil lamps, in which the foes are separated only by sandbags, which they keep pushing against each other. As soon as an opening shows a terrific hand-to-hand fight begins, in which grenades and the bayonet are the only arms possible. Sometimes the Germans take to knives and revolvers, and one day they even began throwing corrosive liquids, which burnt badly ; but, in spite of these cowardly tricks, our men always had the best of it, showing a marvellous spirit of initiative. They fought with clubbed rifles and fists when required, and their courage was never shaken, as the Germans soon saw.

The passages in which we were advancing were 18 ft. deep, and often 24 ft. or more. The water was sweating through in all directions, and the sickly smell was intolerable. Imagine, too, that for three weeks we were not able to get rid of the dead bodies, amongst which we had to live night and day ! One burrow, 120 ft. long, took us thirteen days of ceaseless fighting to conquer entirely. The Germans had placed barricades, trap-doors, and traps of all descriptions. When we stumbled we risked being impaled on bayonets treacherously hidden in holes lightly covered with earth. And a.i this went on in almost complete darkness. We had to use pocket electric lamps and advance with the utmost caution.

Besides the strategic advantages of the future occupation of the famous "Labyrinth" position, its capture has had another result. The Germans had come to consider "The Labyrinth" as an impregnable fortress, and their men were accustomed to this belief. Their disillusionment was proportionately great when they learned that we were masters of it. We were able to notice this ourselves when we announced the news to our prisoners, who at first refused to believe the news, and when they were confronted with the reality were completely demoralised. One of them gave expression to the prevailing impression when he said, "Nothing resists these French devils." *

With this quotation we end our account of the Battle of Artois. Joffre, Foch and d'Urbal, if they had not succeeded in breaking the German line, or indirectly reducing the pressure on the Russians, had forced the enemy to desist from his offensive round Ypres. They had, too, proved that, diabolically ingenious as the German engineers had shown themselves to be, it was possible, if there was an adequate gun-and-mine preparation, to storm at comparatively small cost the German entrenchments and burrow-fortresses. The losses of the Germans in the battle have been estimated at 60,000, perhaps they were considerably more. What the French losses were is problematical, † but it is said that the casualties of one division

---

* Published in the *Standard*.
† The Crown Prince of Bavaria fixed them at 60,000, a curious coincidence.

which killed 2,600 of the enemy and took 3,000 prisoners were only 250 killed and 1,250 wounded.

While the last stages of the Battle of Artois were proceeding, south of Arras, which, like Ypres, was being constantly bombarded by the Germans, General d'Urbal took the offensive between Serre and Hébuterne. Hébuterne is nearer Albert on the Ancre than Arras. The French had occupied Hébuterne, the Germans Serre. The villages were a mile and three-quarters apart, each situated on a slight rise. Halfway between, in front of the farm of Tout Vent ran two lines of German trenches. The fields of the farm were enclosed by a line

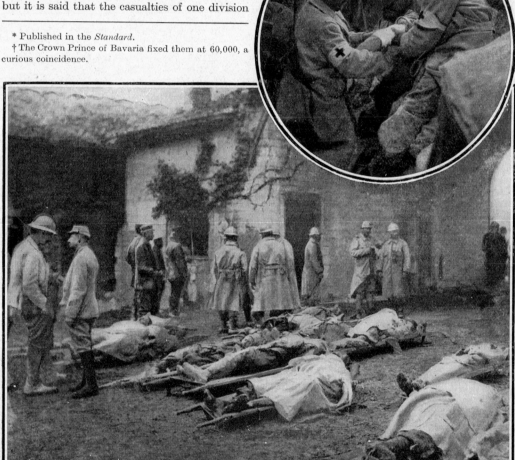

AFTER A FRENCH VICTORY IN CHAMPAGNE.
Wounded being removed to a farm in the rear of the battle-line.   Inset : First aid in a French trench.

of big trees. The 17th Baden Regiment was entrusted with the defence of the position. They were attacked on June 7 by Bretons, Vendéens and troops from Savoy and Dauphiné.

From 3 a.m. on the morning of June 7 the Germans, who had been forewarned by the intensity of the French artillery preparation, kept up an incessant fire at their enemy's trenches. The French guns replied with a continuous stream of projectiles. At 5 a.m. the assault was delivered. In ten minutes the men from the coast and mountains were east of their opponents' trenches and digging themselves in. The next day, under the fire of the German heavy artillery, the conquered area was extended to the north and also in

A BOMB-PROOF SHELTER.
Showing part of the ceiling made of steel plates.

depth. On June 9 there was severe fighting in the German communication trenches, and on the 10th a few hundred yards of trenches to the south were captured. The number of prisoners taken was 580, including ten officers. The 17th Baden Regiment had virtually ceased to exist, and two battalions of another German regiment suffered severely.

The day before the action at Hébuterne began, General de Castelnau, in the northern angle of the Oise and Aisne, had made a gap in the German line east of the Forêt de l'Aigle, which is a continuation of the Forest of Compiègne, and is divided from it by the Aisne. On the east it is bounded by a vast plateau through which rivulets flow down to that river. The country is highly cultivated. Spinneys mark the situation of the large farms which, like the farm of Tout Vent, are, or were, surrounded

by tall trees. The farms of Ecaffaut and Quennevières were within the French, those of Les Loges and Tout Vent were behind the German lines. Facing the farm of Quennevières the enemy's front formed a salient, at the point of which was a kind of small fort. Where the northern and southern ends of the salient touched the rest of the German position flanking works had been constructed.

Along the arc of the salient ran two lines of trenches; in places there was a third. The chord of the arc was defended by an indented trench. In a ravine which descends towards Tout Vent were several German guns. As the plateau sloped slightly towards the salient, the French had a considerable advantage. Normally the salient was garrisoned by four companies of the German 86th Regiment, recruited from the Hanseatic towns and Schleswig, but on June 5 the reserve companies posted in the Tout Vent ravine had been brought up, their place being taken by other troops. The titular commander of the 86th Regiment was the German Empress. Four battalions, Zouaves, sharpshooters, and Bretons, had been detailed by the French commander for the assault.

During June 5 the French artillery methodically pounded the little fort, the trenches and the accessory works. Throughout the night the guns went on firing, and to prevent the enemy repairing the damage done in the daytime the French infantry kept up an incessant musketry fire, while from time to time aerial torpedoes were discharged. Between 5 a.m. and 9 a.m. on the 6th the bombardment became fiercer. For three-quarters of an hour it ceased, and then, at short intervals, gusts of shells succeeded one another. A mine under the little fort was exploded. The Germans, in groups of four, six or ten, had taken refuge in their dug-outs, but the roofs of many of these had been blown in by the large shells, and the inmates were either dead or dying slowly of suffocation. At 10.15 the French gunners lengthened their fire, and the infantry, who had discarded their knapsacks, dashed forward. Each man had three days' rations, 250 cartridges, two grenades, and a sack. The sack was to be filled with earth so that the defence of the position to be captured might be rapidly organized.

The bayonets glittered in the sun as the line of cheering soldiers crossed the 200 yards which separated them from the enemy. The

THE FRENCH AT QUENNEVIÈRES.

Infantry storming a deep German trench.

German infantry and machine gunners fired wildly, and in a few minutes the first trench was taken. Two hundred and fifty prisoners, the sole survivors of a couple of German battalions, were made. From the ravine of Tout Vent the companies in reserve had rushed to the aid of their comrades. A hurricane of shells from the *Soixante-quinze* guns laid them low. Nearly 2,000 men had in under an hour been put *hors de combat*.

Encouraged by the execution wrought by the French artillery, the Zouaves, preceded by patrols, headed for the Tout Vent ravine. In a clover field they came on a work armed with three guns and protected by a wire network. The gunners had sought refuge in a dug-out. Guns and gunners were captured, but the attack on the ravine was not pushed home. The German local reserves had arrived, and French aviators signalled the approach of new reinforcements. It transpired that two battalions were being motored from Roye to the east of the Oise. Before they reached the battle-field the Germans counter-attacked, and were mown down by machine-guns and shrapnel. At the extremities of the salient the French sappers, with sacks of earth, were erecting barriers. By nightfall the position had been put in a state of defence.

It was time that it was. During the night the troops from Roye made eight fierce attacks, and on the morning of the 7th endeavoured to storm the barriers at the northern and southern ends of the salient. Recklessly they advanced up the communication trenches, but were kept at bay by a hail of grenades. Towards sunset the attack died down. Some 2,000 German corpses were lying in the area where the counter-attacks had taken place. The German losses in dead alone exceeded 3,000. This brilliant little victory had cost de Castelnau 250 killed and 1,500 wounded. Twenty machine-guns, numerous shields, telephones, field-glasses, and a quantity of ammunition were among the spoils.

As has been pointed out in Chapter XCVI., one of the weak points in the French line from the North Sea to Switzerland was the section from Rheims to the Forest of the Argonne, defended by the army of General Langle de Cary. Until the Germans had been driven back across the Aisne at every point the French centre and also the right wing from Verdun to Belfort were in jeopardy. We have previously described (see Chapter XCVI.) the efforts made by Langle de Cary to expel Von Einem from the Champagne Pouilleuse. The preliminary step was to deprive the enemy of the use of the railway which ran from Bazancourt across the Upper Aisne through the Forest of the Argonne to a few miles north of Varennes. Langle de Cary had met with considerable success, and in the course of his operations on February 27 had taken the little fort of Beauséjour, to the north-

A HEAVY FRENCH GUN
Bombarding the German trenches.

AFTER A BATTLE IN CHAMPAGNE.
Carrying water to the wounded at Perthes-les-
Hurlus. Inset : Carrying a wounded French soldier
from the firing-line.

east of Perthes.   On April 8 the Germans
attempted to recapture it.

A violent cannonade on the fort and the
communication trenches preceded the attack.
The French look-outs reported a concentration
of the enemy in his trenches.   The northern
salient of the fort, which jutted out like an
arrow towards the German position, was
assaulted from east and west by two companies
of volunteers belonging to all the regiments of
the German division in this region.   They
acted as a forlorn hope.   On the eastern side
the enemy met with little success.   Caught by
the fire of machine guns and the French
artillery, the assaulting infantry was soon
mown down.   The other attack was more
successful, and a footing was obtained in the
western trenches and the extreme point of the
salient.   The next day, however, the French
artillery rained projectiles on the intruders,
who, crowded elbow to elbow in the narrow
cuttings, lost heavily.   Those who escaped
the shells were bayoneted.   By nightfall the
fort was again entirely in the possession of the
French.

The assault on Beauséjour was not the only
German offensive between Rheims and the
Argonne during the spring and summer of 1915.
At Ville-sur-Tourbe, some seven miles east of
Beauséjour, where the undulating plains of

Champagne approached the wooded heights
of the Argonne, the Germans on May 15
delivered a serious attack.   Ville-sur-Tourbe
was garrisoned by the French Colonial Infantry,
who had taken Beauséjour on February 27.
Our Allies held a bridge-head on the north
bank of the stream of the Tourbe.   The village
had been reduced to a mass of ruins by the
German artillery.   Two hillocks, separated by
the high road from Saint-Ménéhould to Vou-
zieres, had been converted by the French
engineers into miniature forts.   A zigzag of
communication trenches connected them with
the village.   If the works on the western of the
two hillocks, which extended north-westwards,
could be carried, the French hold on the
eastern hillock and on Ville-sur-Tourbe would
be jeopardized.   It is an interesting fact,

THE ST. MIHIEL SALIENT.

showing the meticulous attention given by the German Higher Command to details, that a reproduction of the French work to be attacked had been made behind the German line, and the troops selected for the assault had been trained in mock attacks.

Three mines had been driven under the French trenches. On May 15, at 6.25 p.m., they were fired, producing the effect of an earthquake. Simultaneously the enemy's guns opened on the village, on the rest of the French trenches, and on the positions where it was presumed that guns were hidden. Immediately afterwards the Germans succeeded in capturing two lines of trenches on the northern face of the *fortin.* During the night a desperate struggle ensued. At daybreak the French, with grenades, counter-attacked, and their artillery threw a curtain of shells in front of the German trenches, so that the retreat of the enemy who had entered the fort was cut off. By 3 p.m. the attacking force had been killed, wounded or taken prisoners. It consisted of Westphalians, Hessians and Thuringians.

During June and July the Argonne was the theatre of a considerable offensive on the part of the Germans. The German Crown Prince, whom rumour had killed several times, was in command of the enemy at this point. He was strongly reinforced from the army in the St. Mihiel salient, and the aged Marshal von Haeseler, one of the most experienced soldiers in the German Army, was on the spot to advise. The French, it will be recollected, had worked across the Vienne–Varennes road into the Bois de la Grurie. Their enemy's front ran eastwards from the south of Binarville, which is five miles north of Vienne-le-Château, north of Bagatelle—a shooting lodge—and the woodland spring known as Fontaine Madame, and then descended across the Vienne–Varennes road and issued from the forest south of Boureuilles, which is in the same latitude as Vienne-le-Château.

On June 20 the German attack began. It was accompanied, as usual, by a tremendous bombardment, which, however, owing to the wooded, broken nature of the country, was less effective than elsewhere. It was at first directed against the western side of the French position. The Germans tried to work down to Vienne-le-Château, and the Württembergers and Prussian Landwehr gained some ground. According to the German official account, seven officers, 627 privates, 6 machine guns,

and fifty trench-mortars were captured. The French, from June 21 to 29, counter-attacked, and, according to the veracious German Staff, used liquid fire. This was an untruth designed to excuse further German breaches of International Law.*

The next move of the enemy was to endeavour to thrust his way down the centre of the forest. They attacked the French in the neighbourhood of Bagatelle, and on the 7th advanced between Fontaine Madame and the ride in the wood called the Haute Chevauchée, capturing a hillock called La Fille Morte. This was subsequently recovered by the French, who also drove the enemy back in the direction of Binarville.

A French corporal, René Destouches, who was captured and afterwards escaped, has recorded the interview which he had with the German Crown Prince. The Crown Prince, with whom was an elderly officer, perhaps von Haeseler, according to Destouches looked thin and tired. He paced up and down his tent with his hands in his pockets, and, if Destouches is to be believed, spoke excellent French with a nasal accent. He assured Destouches that life in a German prisoners' camp was not very terrible. After asking several questions, which were answered evasively, he threw away his half-smoked cigar, and with a sad smile remarked : " I am afraid you are rather stupid, Destouches, and don't keep your eyes open. I suppose," he added, " your chiefs never tell you how badly things are going with you." The answer of the French corporal was : " that every Frenchman saw for himself that the situation was excellent." A weary expression passed over the Crown Prince's face. He shook his head, and with his companion passed out of the tent.

Whatever we may think of Destouches's story, there is no reason to believe that the Crown Prince felt elated. Some time before the war he had expressed to an Englishman the hope that he would soon have a chance of fighting with—to use an expression, which, in his mouth, is not offensive—" the French swine." He had had his wish, but apart from the curios he had collected in French châteaux he had gained little out of the cataclysm which he had helped to produce.

---

* The German official narrative claims that 7,000 to 8,000 French were put out of action between June 20 and July 2 in the Argonne fighting.

We have narrated in Chapter XCVI. the various efforts of the French to dislodge the Germans from the St. Mihiel salient. They had attacked it on both sides and also near the apex. The advance to the crest of the Eparges hill, which dominates the plain of the Woevre, had been proceeding since February. It culminated on April 9 in a decisive French victory.

The German engineers had protected the summit by tiers of trenches one above the other, at points no less than five in number. Guns of all calibres and mitrailleuses were concealed on the flanks of the hill and its summit. On April 5, at 4 p.m., the French began their final move to reduce the fortress. Rain was pouring in torrents, and the ground was almost impassable. The troops were in places up to their thighs in mud. Wet to the skin, covered in sweat, they, however, pressed forward, and, after numerous mêlées, established themselves in a part of the German trenches. To the east their progress was stopped by flights of aerial torpedoes, each one of which, when it burst, destroyed whole ranks. At 4.30 a.m. on the 6th the Germans counter-attacked. Fresh troops had been sent up from Combres, and they drove back the worn-out French. At nightfall the latter, reinforced, returned to the attack. A trench at the eastern end of the plateau was captured. On the west progress was made towards the summit, but in the centre the Germans put up a fierce resistance. During the night, in a pitiless downpour of rain, the French with the bayonet drove the Germans back foot by foot. When day broke several hundred yards of trenches had been taken and many prisoners and officers, but the Germans did not immediately give way. Counter-attack succeeded counter-attack. The French artillery, with its shrapnel, assisted the infantry toiling up the slopes. A furious charge by the Germans at 5 a.m. on the morning of the 7th failed. More troops from Combres arrived on the scene. The masses were mown down by shrapnel. But at one point the French fell back.

Meanwhile the French General directing the operations was sending up fresh troops. At 9 a.m. on the 8th the advance was resumed. Two regiments of infantry and a battalion of Chasseurs were ordered to storm the summit. The magazines of the rifles were choked with mud, and the men had to rely on the bayonet. An hour later the summit and the western crest were in their hands. They pushed forward to the crest on the eastern side, reversing the parapets of the German trenches. By midnight, after fifteen hours of uninterrupted fighting, the whole of the summit, with the exception of a small triangle at the eastern extremity, had been gained. Sixteen hundred yards of trenches had been lost by the Germans and also the formidable bastion on the summit, which was the key of the position.

Both sides rested on the morning of the 9th, and another French regiment arrived soon after midday. It had taken fourteen hours to climb up the muddy, slippery paths. At 3 p.m. the French once more attacked, in a hurricane of wind and rain. The ground in front of them was honeycombed with deep holes, but, covered by the fire of their artillery, they approached the last refuges of the enemy. Suddenly the summit of the hill was shrouded in fog. The French guns ceased firing, the enemy counter-attacked, and the French fell back. Their officers called on them to make a new effort and they again advanced. At 10 p.m. they held the whole ridge and summit of Les Eparges. During the 10th there was no fighting, but on the night of April 11–12 the Germans made a final counter-attack, which failed.

Such was the capture of Les Eparges. We leave the French Staff to draw the moral:

To keep this position the Germans left nothing undone. We have seen the strength of their defensive works. We have noted the fact that at the end of March they brought to Les Eparges one of their best divisions. To this were joined five pioneer battalions with machine guns from the fortress of Metz and a large number of trench mortars of 21 and 24 cm. Their shelters were caverns dug at their leisure. They had constructed a narrow-gauge light railway. Their troops were provided with rooms for resting in, their officers had a club, and they could bring up reinforcements unobserved, while ours were exposed to the fire of their artillery and machine guns and even of their rifles. Under these circumstances supply difficulties, both in the matter of food and of munitions, may be imagined.

Here was every indication of a fixed determination to resist all our attacks. Indeed, we found on officers taken prisoners orders to hold out at all costs. The German General Staff was resolved to sacrifice everything in order to retain this dominating crest, and the German troops offered the maximum of resistance. Their conduct was magnificent.

In order to deprive the machine-gun detachment of any temptation to cease fire the men had been chained to their weapons. Nevertheless, we conquered in spite of all. The German resistance was singularly favoured by the conformation of the ground. The steep slopes and the waterlogged soil constituted the most formidable obstacle to our attacks. We lost unwounded men drowned in mud and many of our wounded could not be rescued in time from the morasses into which they fell. The German howitzers and trench mortars had an easy mark in our advancing men, so long as the enemy held the summit.

TAKING A SUMMIT IN THE VOSGES, JUNE 14, 1915.
French Chasseurs defending a trench with the aid of stones rolled down the hillside against the Germans.

THE ARMY OF THE GERMAN CROWN PRINCE.
Regiments marching past the Crown Prince in the Argonne.

Two months ago the Germans at Les Eparges had a full view of our lines. Now it is our turn to overlook their positions. Even the height of Combres, which they still hold, has been reduced to a kind of islet between our machine-gun fire from Les Eparges and St. Remy. We have achieved this result at a cost of half the losses which we inflicted on the enemy.

What does this mean if not that the victory of Les Eparges is one among other proofs of the growing superiority of our Army? We are attacking. The enemy is on the defensive. He holds the heights and we take them from him. He has the advantage of position. We are driving him from his trenches. Those who have survived these battles know that our triumph is certain and that it has already begun.

While the French were beginning their final assault of Les Eparges, they also attacked the southern side of the apex of the St. Mihiel salient, capturing the Wood of Ailly, on the edge of the Forest of Apremont.

This little action aptly illustrates the nature of the great struggle raging for months from La Bassée southwards to the region of Compiègne, from Compiègne eastwards along the banks of the Aisne to Berry au Bac, thence south-eastwards to the environs of Rheims, again eastwards across the Forest of Argonne to Verdun, from Verdun once more in a southerly direction round St. Mihiel to Pont-à-Mousson, from Pont-à-Mousson through the Gap of Nancy to the summits of the Vosges. A description of the conflict may enable the reader to understand with what effort, at what risk, and with what human suffering each step leading to the deliverance of France was taken.

The road to St. Mihiel ran west of the Wood of Ailly, now no longer a wood, but a wilderness of stumps, traversed by the irregular lines of trenches. Branching off this road was a path leading to Apremont. Where the St. Mihiel road and the Apremont path crossed the Germans had made an important work. From it a trench went northwards parallel with the St. Mihiel road, another eastward parallel with the route to Apremont. These two trenches were connected behind the work by two others, crossed by a communication trench running back from the work to the north-eastern border of the wood. The word "trench" gives an inadequate idea of the deeply sunken excavations, covered in at places, which the Germans had constructed.

The French process of preparing the attack was almost as scientific as a modern surgical operation. The "75" guns blew wide breaches in the barbed-wire entanglements, which were over 36 feet wide and 6 feet high; the larger "155" guns (about equivalent to our 6-inch guns) crushed down the skilfully hidden emplacements of the German mitrailleuses. The effect of the French bombardment may be gathered from the following extract from an unfinished letter of a Bavarian taken prisoner: "At 7 a.m.," he wrote, "the French commenced a terrible bombardment, principally with their heavy artillery and with shells as big as sugar loaves . . . When this storm of fire had lasted about an hour a mine exploded and blew up our trench many feet into the air, by which we lost 30 men. Huge stones cast up fell back on us, killing and burying many soldiers. The bombardment increased in intensity. The air was filled with shrapnel bullets and the fragments of high-explosive shells, and to add to this there came a terrible fire from the rifles of infantry and machine guns. I have taken part in many actions, but this battle of five days surpasses all I have ever seen. To add to our trials it rained without ceasing, the dull, leaden sky and the air charged with moisture condensed the smoke so that we could scarcely see through it."

The utmost care had been taken by the French commanders to ensure success. "The Colonel," says a soldier present, "had shown to each of us the tree he was to make for." The French infantry contained miners and mechanics. Light bridges had been prepared by the engineers to throw across the trenches.

At last, on April 5, the signal for the advance was given. In three waves the French, now relying on the bayonet and hand grenades alone, dashed forward. The infantry had been ordered to pass over and not to descend into the trenches, which were to be cleared by the supporting troops. Two companies attacked the St. Mihiel road trenches, two more those on the Apremont side. When it had passed through the wood, the battalion was to unite. The work at the salient of the wood had been destroyed by the artillery.

The trenches on the St. Mihiel road were carried by the first rush, and the rearmost German trench was reached, in which the French proceeded to establish themselves. The two companies storming the German entrenchments on the Apremont path at first were equally successful, but, taken in flank by the fire of concealed machine guns, were compelled to fall back. Their retirement entailed that of the companies on the St. Mihiel road front. But the fortified work and the first line, and some of the second line trenches north of it, were retained and lined with mitrailleuses. A counter-attack at 4 p.m. was repulsed chiefly by the French artillery. The fighting went on during the night, and at daybreak, April 6, the French were masters of the line. Fresh attacks were organized against the German position, and these resulted in hand-to-hand fighting

THE VILLAGE OF CLERMONT-EN-ARGONNE.
Recaptured by the French.

AN ARMOURED SHIELD,
Used in the French Army for protection
against enemy fire.

with bayonet and bomb. The Germans fought
bravely, but were unable to resist the more
vigorous efforts of their adversaries, and when
night fell the whole salient of the wood was in
the hands of our Allies, who had even pushed
some distance up the road to St. Mihiel. The
whole German garrison had been killed,
wounded or taken prisoners. It was only on
the 8th, after a rest of two days, that the
Germans ventured to counter-attack, and then
unsuccessfully. The French maintained and
consolidated their position.

The capture of the Wood of Ailly was one of
a number of similar engagements along the
southern side of the St. Mihiel salient. There
was fighting in the Forest of Apremont, in the
Wood of Montmare and in the Bois Le Prêtre,
which latter wood is just west of the Moselle,
and was christened by the Germans the " wood
of death," and the " wood of widows." Into.
the Bois Le Prêtre the Germans constantly
poured troops from Metz, but the French
gradually expelled them from it, and in May
reached the northern edge. From this position
they could threaten the communications from
Metz to Thiaucourt along the narrow valley of
the Rupt de Mad.

South of Pont-à-Mousson, on the Moselle,
through the gap of Nancy to the summits
of the Vosges, the French line in the spring,
summer and early autumn remained, broadly

speaking, unchanged. Round La Fontenelle, in the Ban-de-Sapt, the Germans took
the offensive in April and June. East of
La Fontenelle the French engineers had, on
Hill " 627," created a fortress similar to that of
the Germans on the summit of Les Éparges.
The enemy, unable to storm it, had recourse to
mines, but this was a slow process, as the sub-
soil consisted of a very hard rock. Nevertheless, with the tenacity of their race, the German
sappers bored galleries beneath the French
works. The French counter-mined, and from
April 6 to 13 there was a succession of underground combats. The enemy's sappers progressed, but were tempted into a communication gallery which had been mined, and they
were blown up. All through the night (April
13) the German officers could be heard shouting
to their men to renew the attack, but the latter
replied with " Nein, nein ! "

On June 22 another, and this time a successful, attack was made on the hill. The pleasure
this achievement gave to the Germans is
evidenced by an order of the General commanding the 30th Bavarian Division. " I have
confidence," he said, " that the height of the
Ban-de-Sapt "—the name given by the
Germans to Hill " 627 "—" will be transformed
with the least possible delay into an impregnable fortress and that the efforts of the French
to retake it will be bloodily repulsed." The
General was speedily undeceived. At 7 p.m.,
on July 8, after heavy bombardment, a French
column burst through the five lines of trenches
and carried the block-house on the summit,
which was protected by trunks of trees, corrugated iron and gun shields. Another column
attacked the enemy's trenches on the left and
surrounded the hill from the east. A third
column, by a vigorous demonstration, kept the
enemy employed on the French right flank.
Two battalions of the 5th Bavarian Ersatz
Brigade had been killed or taken prisoners.
The number of the prisoners was 881, including
21 officers. Among the officers were professors
and clerks and a theological student.

In Alsace the advance by the French was,
in April, impeded by snowstorms, but despite
the bad weather General Dubail pressed on.
For many reasons it was advisable to give the
enemy no rest in this region. In Alsace the
French were directly in touch with the German
civilian population. Defeats in Belgium and
France might be hidden from the subjects of the
Kaiser, and even transformed into victories by

a few strokes of the pen. But, if the Germans were routed on the eastern slopes of the Vosges in the plains of Alsace or on the banks of the Rhine, the news would travel throughout Germany. The crossing, too, of the Rhine itself between Bâle and Strassburg might be a stupendous operation. But before Germany could be brought to her knees the Allies would probably have to cross the river. Here they were within a few miles of it. At all other points they were divided from the natural boundary of Germany by rivers, hills, woods, entrenched positions and fortresses.

The step preliminary to gaining the plains of Alsace and the banks of the Rhine was the seizure of the valleys on the German side of the Vosges. During the spring and summer months particular attention was bestowed on the valleys of the Ill and Fecht. On April 26 the Hartmannsweilerkopf, which commanded the communications of the Ill and the Thur Valleys, was again the scene of very severe fighting. It was, however, further north, in the valley of the Fecht and the surrounding mountains, that the main effort of the French was made. Their object was to descend the valley and reach Münster, and the railway which served the mountain railways and roads leading to the crest of the Voges. In the course of the mountain campaign one episode peculiarly heroic occurred.

On June 14 a company of Chasseurs was isolated. Surrounded by Germans, they did not surrender, but constructed a square camp and prepared to defend themselves to the last man. In this place, attacked from below, from above, and on the flanks, they held out till June 17, when they were relieved. The ammunition running low, the soldiers resorted to the primitive device of rolling rocks on their enemies. The incident of the defence of this camp throws a flood of light on the transformation which had taken place in warfare. The Chasseurs were saved by curtains of shells discharged by the French artillery miles away.

IN THE WOODS IN ALSACE.
Loading a French heavy gun.   Inset: After firing.

REMAINS OF GERMAN TRENCHES IN A WOOD ON THE ST. MIHIEL SALIENT.

While the company of Chasseurs was thus engaged, the advance down the Fecht and the ascent of the mountains commanding the valley were proceeding. On June 15 and 16, the summit of the Braunkopf was stormed and the Anlass attacked. From the Braunkopf, the Chasseurs turned Metzeral by the north. The Germans set fire to the town, which blazed through the night of the 21st and 22nd. The capture of Metzeral forced the enemy to retire, and the whole of the valley of the Fecht as far as Sondernach was acquired by the French. In July and August, the Lingenkopf and the Schratzmännele were captured. From the summit of the Schratzmännele, which was cleared of the Germans on August 22, the French troops saw below them the valley of Münster, the plain of Alsace and the city of Colmar. Joffre was in a position to take, if he chose, the offensive in the plains of Alsace. The fact that he had unbolted most of the gates into the lost province proved of great importance. It forced the Germans to keep large bodies of troops away from the regions—the Champagne Pouilleuse and Artois — where the next blows were to be struck by the French generalissimo towards the end of September.

CHAPTER CII.

PRISONERS OF WAR.

Prisoners of War in History—Napoleonic Times—First International Agreement—Calculated Frightfulness—Shooting of Prisoners—German Hatred for the British—German Treatment of Irish and Mahomedans—Irish Brigade—The Commandant and the Camp—Treatment of Enemy Civilians—Submarine Reprisals—Exchange of Prisoners—Relative Treatment—Conflicting Reports, Discrepancies Explained—Inspections by United States Officials—Brutalities on Capture—The Journey to Captivity—Major Vandeleur's Report—Official German "Reply"—German Hospitals: The Brutal Doctor—Internment Camps—Wittenberg—Discipline—Camp Brutalities—Food—Treatment of Officers—Use of Prison Labour—Work Camps—Enemy Civilians in Germany—Murder of Henry Hadley—Ruhleben—German Prisoners in England—Neutral Reports—Prisoners in Russia—The Y.M.C.A. in Germany—Prisoners' Help Organizations.

THE lot of the captive, whether wounded or unwounded, has throughout history been painful and hard to bear. The level of treatment has usually been below the level of the morality of the period. War, that so often brings noble qualities to the surface, brings the evil ones into even greater prominence. The history of captivity has suffered especially in this way. From the earliest dawn down to a period of little over two hundred years ago capture on the field of battle meant selling into slavery, slavery in the mines, the hulks or the galleys. Even chivalry, which alleviated the lot of the knight and the noble, made no effort to uplift the condition of the ordinary man-at-arms.

During the Napoleonic Wars the position of the prisoners of war began to improve, but even then the French prisoners in England were fed on "weevily biscuit" and other food "which sowed the seed for a plentiful harvest of scurvy, dysentery, and typhus."

The terrible sufferings in the campaign which had its consummation at the battle of Solferino caused the Swiss Government to summon a conference at Geneva which resulted in the First General International Agreement in the year 1864. So little advanced was public opinion even at that date that the Agreement made no alteration in the treatment of unwounded prisoners of war.

Before the treatment of prisoners by the belligerents in any war can be seen in its true perspective many matters must be taken into account. The size of the problem to be dealt with is not the least important, although its importance diminishes as the months pass. The difficulty of making adequate arrangements is obviously greater in the early days of rush, when everything, or almost everything, must be sacrificed to the necessity of getting men and munitions to the war zone. As the months pass the character of this necessity changes. With time the facilities for dealing with prisoners increase at a greater ratio than their increasing numbers. As in all other problems, whether civil or military, experience provides the greatest assistance.

In the Russo-Japanese War the Japanese had to handle 67,701 prisoners. That struggle, on the other hand, provided Russia with no real experience of the difficulties surrounding the care of captives. Her total of Japanese captured only amounted to 646.

Though the Boer War put 32,000 prisoners into British care, the only nation possessing any real acquaintance with a problem comparable to that presented by the Great War was the German. In the débâcle of the Franco-Prussian War, when army corps and armies were compelled to surrender, about 400,000 Frenchmen passed under the Prussian yoke.

AFTER THE BATTLE OF LOOS.
German Prisoners from France at Southampton, on their way to the Internment Camp,
September 29, 1915.

After the present war had lasted five months the German Headquarters claimed to have captured 8,120 officers and 577,475 men, being composed of :

		Officers.	Men.
French	... ...	3,459	215,505
Russian	... ...	3,557	306,294
Belgian	... ...	612	36,852
British	... ...	492	18,824

By August, 1915, as the result of twelve months' war, the Austro-German claim had swollen to 2,000,000, of whom 300,000 were British, French, and Belgian, the remainder being Russians. Without accepting the German figures as correct, the number of Russian prisoners was enormous, the majority being captured in the great German "drive" in Galicia. It is, of course, obvious that a retreating army, the roads blocked not only with wagons and artillery, but by fugitives, civil and military, loses a large proportion of its wounded. To stop, even for the simplest cause, whether exhaustion, a sprain or sleep, means inevitable capture. Altogether apart, however, from the losses on a prolonged retreat, the fluid character of the war on the Eastern

front was favourable to the making of prisoners. The official figures of Austro-German prisoners in Russia in May, 1915, were 600,000, whilst by October they were reported to have reached 1,100,000.

The official figures for British prisoners in Germany stood, in December 1915, at 33,000, a large proportion of whom had been captured during the retreat from Mons. The number of naval and military prisoners interned in England in December, 1915, was 13,476.

Any estimate of the numbers of prisoners requires checking by so many factors—by no means the least important being the veracity of Governments—that any true conception is difficult, but it is probably well within the mark to say that on Christmas Day, 1915, not less than two and a half million people were eating the bread of captivity.

Included in the armoury of German warfare was the idea that calculated frightfulness might attain victories denied to arms. It was doubtless upon this ground that Brigade orders were issued from time to time instructing the troops that no prisoners were to be made, but that all soldiers, whether wounded or not, who fell into German hands were to be shot. It is probable, however, that this "frightfulness" was intended to apply only to troops in the field. Taking into account the calculating character of the Teuton, it is unlikely that the harsh treatment of prisoners after removal from the field—whether upon the journey or in the prison camp—can have been any part of a concerted plan. Though inhuman and uncivilized, it was not of the character either to break the moral of opposing troops, or to terrify the civilian population.

It is certain that the German was brutal towards his prisoners of whatever race. That his malignancy was specially directed towards the British soldier is equally proved. Those innumerable cases where the German refused to give the British wounded even those small considerations which he gave to the French showed that the German venom was specially directed against England.

Just as the British suffered from the hatred,

the Russian writhed under the contempt of the Germans. The Russian, speaking a language known to few not of his own race, of a civilization differing in degree, and almost in kind, from that of either his captors or his fellow prisoners, poor, ill-nourished, and from a land whose vast distances and inadequate intercommunication made the sending of relief almost impossible, suffered terribly from hunger, tubercle, typhus, cholera, and hard enforced labour.

The hatred for the British soldier carried with it two interesting phenomena. If hatred for the British people was stronger against any one of its component parts than it was against any other, it was directed more strongly against the Canadian, whilst at one time, and for some unaccountable reason, there seemed to be a possibility of preferential treatment being given to the Australian.

Direct and transparent political motive dictated German treatment of Mahomedan and Irish prisoners. French and British Mahomedans were segregated in a special camp at

GERMAN PRISONERS IN ENGLAND.
Marching through a peaceful country lane on their way to the Detention Camp at Frimley.

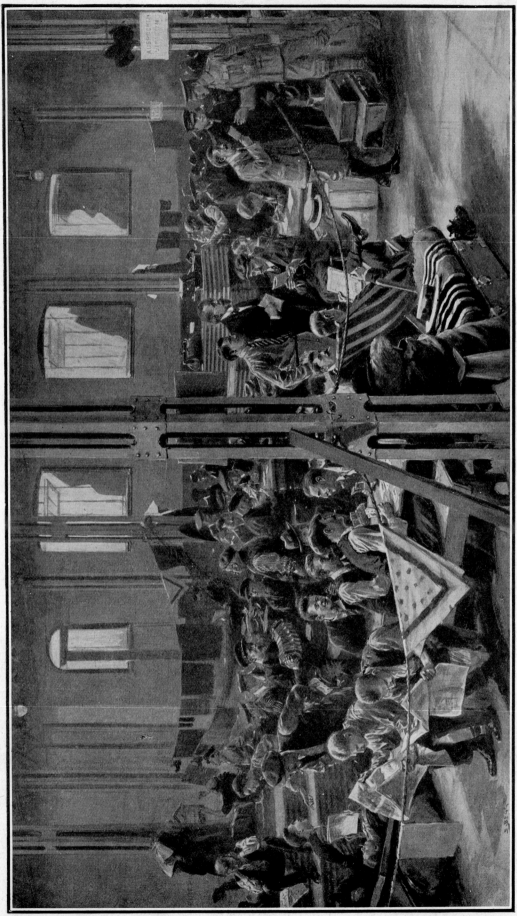

"ENEMIES" OF GREAT BRITAIN IN LONDON: GERMANS UNDER DETENTION IN THE ANNEXE OF OLYMPIA, AUGUST, 1914.

Zossen, where their religious susceptibilities were scrupulously regarded, and a special mosque was built for them.

The Irish, the majority of whom were assembled in a separate camp at Limburg, were supplied with special literature, had the number of their fatigue duties reduced, and, having been warned that failure to do as they were desired would be rewarded with correspondingly harsher treatment, were privileged with a visit from an ex British Consul-General, Sir Roger Casement, who made his way to Germany early in the war by way of Scandinavia, and was received with open arms by the German Government. Sir Roger, having described the historical woes of Ireland, called for volunteers to form an Irish Brigade. Despite oratorical exhortations, secret inquisitions and persuasions, the screw of hunger and the lure of freedom, the Irish, to their eternal honour, forgot what to many of them had been a life-long political quarrel, and remembered only their oath of allegiance to their King and the weal of their realm. Fewer than sixty out of two thousand succumbed to the temptation, and the ruse failed.

For both officers and men the discipline was " German." One returned prisoner said of the treatment that, " the fact is the prisoners were treated just as the German soldiers were treated." The " atmosphere " of a camp depended chiefly on the commandant. In general the German commandants appeared, to the American authorities, disposed neither to make life harder than seemed to them to be necessary nor to discriminate intentionally against the British.

Some commandants were popular and the prisoners, therefore, happy. Some were hated and feared, with the consequence that all was unpleasantness, bickering, and trouble. The camp at Schneidemühl was a good example of this. During the year 1914 there was nothing but complaints. Discipline could only be maintained by brutality. Men were held over barrels and beaten with sticks. In January, 1915, a new commandant was appointed. Immediately the thrashings ceased, guards who ill-treated prisoners were punished, and the general character of the camp showed a marked improvement.

Similar changes, usually for the better, but sometimes for the worse, were made in other camps. Of the camp at Torgau the American Ambassador said, " From being one of the worst it has become one of the best camps." The possible—and, as events showed, the actual—variation was greater in Germany than in Britain chiefly because the lowest in the former country was so markedly—and monstrously—lower than the worst in the United Kingdom. There appears to have been at least one camp in Germany as good as anything to be found in the countries of the Allies. It was a small officers' camp at Blankenburg i/Mark, and was described by Mr. J. B. Jackson, of the United States Embassy in Berlin, as " a four-storeyed house, well built, heated throughout and lighted by gas. It is surrounded by attractive, well-kept

MAJOR VANDELEUR,
of the Scottish Rifles.

grounds, in which a tennis court has just been made. The house itself is as comfortable as any of the places where I saw interned officers in England, although the neighbourhood is not so attractive as that of Dyffryn Aled or Donington Hall. There are several modestly-furnished mess and recreation rooms, and a terrace which is used for afternoon tea and in connexion with the canteen. The older officers occupy single rooms. . . . Officers below the rank of major occupy the larger rooms, which are apparently well ventilated, no more than ten persons being in any one room, nationalities not being separated. . . . On each floor there are baths and water-closets, and a general washroom for the use of the junior officers, all of which are in good condition. Officers are allowed to remain in the garden until 6 p.m., and in the open-air court of the building until dark. . . . Smoking is permitted generally. . . .

The commandant is interested in his work, and evidently does all he can to make conditions agreeable." The misfortune was that Blankenburg held only 110 officers, of whom but nine were British.

The correct procedure in the case of civilian alien enemies within the borders of an opposing belligerent had been, for many years, to expel them, or to grant them permission to remain with such restriction of movement as the exigencies of the military situation demanded. They were to be regarded as honourable though unfortunate.

Never since the days of the French Revolution had there been any internment of alien civilians upon a large scale. It can only be justified upon military grounds, such as general espionage, threatened revolt, or the presence of enemy civilians in such numbers as to be a probable impediment to military operations, or a possible specific danger to the existence of the State. In any case, whatever may be the grounds of their detention, or internment, the alien enemy civilian, even more than the enemy soldier, has the right to demand and receive the fullest privileges and consideration.

That in many places besides Ruhleben the action of the German authorities did not accord with this view was shown by Mr. Jackson's report in March, 1915, on the camps of Burg, near Magdeburg, and Magdeburg. "These camps had already been visited several weeks earlier by other members of the Embassy, and the interned officers stated that conditions had improved in the meanwhile. Even as they were, however, it seemed to me that the prisoners were treated more like ordinary offenders than they were like officer prisoners of war."

The Great European War saw nations, not soldiers, ranged in arms. Normally for a nation to allow, or to compel, alien civilians to return to their native country had little result other than that of relieving the nation of their maintenance. In the Great European War, fought with the uttermost of the reserves both of men and wealth, such repatriation, at least in the case of men of fighting age, strengthened, rather than burdened, the opposing belligerent. The German authorities, knowing that the German population in Britain far exceeded the British population in Germany, and considering that, owing to conscription and industrial organization, the German of

suitable health and age was a greater military and economic asset than the average individual Englishman, desired the mutual exchange of all enemy civilians. Wisely the British Government, though with some incomprehensible delay, laid an embargo on Germans of potential military value between the ages of 17 and 55 leaving the country.

In a somewhat similar manner the British Government, having to deal with alien enemy population great in numbers, largely trained in arms and the tenets of obedience, feeling intensely the national character of the struggle, the subjects of a State whose political and military ethics had induced it to regard wholesale espionage as not merely a legitimate but a natural and essential weapon, and driven by a Press and public horrified by conditions prevailing in German prison camps, proceeded to intern the more dangerous portion of the alien enemy population.

A new chapter in naval warfare was opened when, as we have seen in earlier chapters, the German Admiralty decided to use its submarine fleet as merchant raiders. The victims were to be both British and neutral ships trading with England, which might be found within an area proclaimed by the German Government as a "war zone." In the case of British ships no notice was to be given, and no difference of treatment made, whether the vessel was carrying contraband or innocent cargo. All vessels falling under the German ban were to be sunk forthwith. At this point it seemed probable that, though such procedure was contrary to International Law, the British Government would content itself with a vigorous protest. The German authorities then made another move in their underseas policy which was destined to have considerable influence on the treatment of prisoners of war. Though never very careful to ensure the safety of the crews upon the ships they sunk, the submarines usually gave them some stated period of time, whether wholly sufficient or not, in which to leave their vessel. The new move consisted in torpedoing these merchant ships without warning, no time being given for the crews or passengers to make their escape from the doomed vessels. In some cases the torpedoed ships sank in less than ten minutes. Their crews, when lucky enough to reach their boats, were left to find their way to land as best they might. The treatment proceeded from bad to worse, as in the case of the

CROSS-EXAMINING A GERMAN PRISONER.
A scene at the Battalion Quarters of the Coldstream Guards in France.

Grimsby trawler Acantha. This small vessel was torpedoed and sunk. While the boats were being lowered several shots were fired at the crew, and even after the men had taken to the boats the crew of the submarine continued to fire at them with rifles.

England was ablaze with resentment and indignation. The British Government, with slightly unnecessary pomposity, declared that, in future, the crews of submarines believed to have been guilty of such offences would not, in the event of capture, be regarded as honourable prisoners of war, but, whilst being well and humanely treated, would be separated from the other prisoners. This was done in the case of three German submarines.

AT THE CAMBERLEY COMPOUND.
German prisoners returning to camp after their day's work.

Reprisals are always the mothers of reprisals. In this case the child was quickly born. On April 13, 1915, Berlin declared her views on the British treatment. For every member of a submarine crew, whether officer or man, who received differential treatment, the German Government resolved to treat a British officer in a corresponding fashion. A number of officers of distinguished names or connexions were sent to gaol, some to Cologne, some to Burg, the majority to Magdeburg. Two slight errors on the part of the German Government provided the only amusing relief. Lieutenant C. F. ffrench, of the Royal Irish Regiment, was chosen because of the erroneous idea that he was Sir John French's relation, whilst Lieutenant Baron W. Allistone owed the attention to the assumption that his first name was derived, not from the font, but from the fountain of honour. The German Government affected to believe that their prisoners were treated as " ordinary prisoners."

The conditions under which these prisoners were actually confined in England is, perhaps, best shown by the following telegram sent on May 3, 1915, by the United States Ambassador in London to the United States Ambassador in Berlin. The telegram refers to twenty-nine officers and men interned at the Naval Detention Barracks, Chatham Dockyard. Their treatment was typical of that accorded to all those interned for these offences :

Lowry reports officers and men at Chatham in good health, and supplied with money. Officers receive 2s. 6d. per day from British Government. None in solitary confinement, but are kept in separate rooms at night. Size of room 8 feet by 12 feet. Men eat together in one mess, and officers together in another mess. Officers and men have same food. Dietary composed of bread, cocoa and tea, sugar, potatoes, suet pudding, pork and pea soup, cheese, beef, mutton and milk. Officers may have butter. Men supplied with margarine. All supplied with books and tobacco. Officers are allowed servants from among the crew. All have use of well-equipped gymnasium daily at stated periods. Permitted to write letters once a week, and to receive money, parcels, and letters. Both men and officers exercise in association, but at different times. Recreation quarters indoors as well as out of doors. Officers complained of being held in detention barracks rather than in officers' camps, but no complaint as to quantity or quality of food. No complaint as to treatment, or as to character of accommodation. Hygiene and sanitary requirements excellent. Rooms and all surroundings specklessly clean.

The German " reply " to the British treatment of submarine prisoners can with most authority be shown by the report of the American representative :

At Magdeburg 14 British officers have been placed in solitary confinement in the police prison, which we were informed has been put at the disposal of the military authorities during the war. . . . A number of prisoners, other than military, are quartered in the same building, but are in no way brought in contact with the British officers. The building has the advantage of having been built in 1913, and of being scrupulously clean. The bathing and other sanitary arrangements are of modern construction, and appear to be thoroughly clean.

Each of the officers is locked in a cell, which he is only allowed to leave between the hours of 8.30 and 9.30 in the morning and 3 and 4 in the afternoon, during which time all the officers are permitted to exercise together in a courtyard, roughly 35 metres in length, and about 20 metres wide at one end and 25 metres wide at the other. . .

During the period of exercise the officers are allowed to talk together, but during the rest of the day they have no opportunity of seeing or communicating with one another. The cells are approximately 12 feet long and 8 feet wide, but those in which the lieutenants are imprisoned are only about 5 feet wide. Each cell has a window, a bed, with which a sheet and one blanket are furnished ; the beds, however, are chained up to the wall during the day. There are also shelves where things may be kept, a chair and a table for writing, etc. The light is good and the cells are clean.

The meals, for which 1.60m. per day is paid, are the same as those furnished in the officers' camps; for breakfast two pieces of bread and butter, and a cup of coffee; for lunch, at 12.30 o'clock, a piece of meat and potatoes and bread; and for dinner, at 6.30 p.m., two pieces of bread, one of them with sausage, and a cup of coffee. The officers are allowed to have whatever food supplies, books, etc., they had received from home, and which were in their possession before they were placed under arrest, and the regulations about receiving parcels in prisoners' camps apply equally to the officers under arrest. Smoking is permitted at all times. . . .

On the whole, the officers looked as well, and appeared as cheerful as is possible under the circumstances There were no complaints as to the treatment received from the officers and non-commissioned officers under whose immediate jurisdiction they are placed.

The treatment of the "reprisal" prisoners at Burg was very similar to that described at Magdeburg. The treatment in Cologne was very much worse. The food was of a lower standard, smoking was prohibited, and the facilities and hours for exercise were fewer. By May 7, however, the general conditions were raised to those described as prevailing in Burg.

Early in June, 1915, the British Government decided to abandon its policy of differential treatment. Automatically Germany abandoned hers. So closed a rather pitiful chapter in the history of reprisals.

After much delay the various Governments agreed to the mutual exchange of physically incapacitated prisoners of war. The agreement between the British and German Governments was concluded in December, 1914. August, 1915, saw two further important arrangements, one for the repatriation of civilians unfit for military service—the decision as to "unfitness" resting entirely with the Government holding the prisoner—the other a tentative scheme under the auspices of the Swiss Federal Government for the internment of sick or convalescent prisoners in Switzerland. Only too slowly the broken men of the different belligerents reached their native shores.

If the condition of exchanged prisoners is any criterion of the treatment received, the humane treatment of prisoners in England and the brutality and inhuman character of the treatment of British prisoners in Germany is abundantly proved. The evidence of the Dutch neutral Press upon this point is conclusive. In the one case the returning prisoners looked well fed, were well clothed, and had few complaints, whilst in the other the men were wrecks, garbed in tattered, thin, and miscellaneous clothes, and showing every sign of bad feeding and ill-treatment.

GERMAN PRISONERS IN A BRITISH COMPOUND.
In the Concentration Camp at Frith Hill, Camberley. In the compound various games, including football, were played, and concerts were arranged by civilian prisoners.

AN EXCHANGE OF PRISONERS.

Germans who had been taken prisoners on the battlefield of Flanders marching through London to the
railway-station for transference back to Germany, in exchange for British troops
who were arriving back from the prison camps in Germany.

No charge is made, or material fact alleged,
in the course of this narrative unless the particular act complained of has been spoken to,
directly or inferentially, by more than one
person or circumstance, except in those
cases when the evidence upon similar incidents is so strong as to render it humanly
certain that the particular thing alleged really
happened. Great use has been made of the
official evidence supplied by officers of the
United States Diplomatic Service. The
accuracy and veracity of this evidence is
unquestionable, as was the utility of their
labours to humanity in general and the British
prisoner of war in Germany in particular.
Although unimpeachable, this evidence is not
conclusive except upon the things seen by these
officials. Cases of apparent discrepancy are
often explained by reference to dates. Similarly,
negative is never so strong as positive evidence.
Taking, by way of example, the charges against
the Iseghem Hospital, to be found on page 257,
the first case appears to have happened after

the visit of the American representative;
whilst in the second it appears probable that
the victim had been removed before that visit.

Whilst admitting, on the one hand, that
prisoners of war, like all classes of witnesses,
are prone to exaggeration, it must always be
remembered that as soldiers they are accustomed to discipline, which inclines them to
answer questions truthfully, and to hardship,
which inclines them to minimise harshness. But,
above all things, whilst accepting thankfully
and wholeheartedly the American official
accounts, it is well to recollect that the absence
of complaint in a hospital or camp may as
easily arise from fear of consequences as from
lack of grounds. Even had this fear of consequences had existence only in the minds of the
prisoners themselves it would have been sufficient, but evidence exists, and has been given,
of cases where, after the Ambassador's visit was
concluded, men who had made complaints to
him were punished with more or less severity.

When the American representative asked

the British prisoners at Merseburg whether they had any complaints, three men stepped forward.* In the case of one man his complaint was merely that the parcels were kept so long in the parcel room before delivery that the food in them became uneatable. On the following day he was sent to the cells, where he was kept for some days in solitary confinement. During this time his food consisted of four ounces of black bread and one pint of water per day. He was without an overcoat, and was obliged to sleep on the cold floor at night.

Although in several cases the American officials made "surprise visits," the great majority appear to have been announced beforehand. A great body of evidence shows that special preparations were made for these visits, and many features normally present in the camps were removed or hidden. Ship's Steward Higgins, of Grimsby, reported that he and his companions, seized in the North Sea on the charge of being mine layers, were lodged in an open field at Sennelager for fourteen days in September, 1914. From the 4th to the 7th they were without food. Rain descended on twelve out of the fourteen days. They were then lodged in a large tent full of holes. When

* "The others, myself included, were afraid."—Pte. R. Gainfort, Royal Irish Regiment.

word came that the United States representative was coming they were removed to new quarters, but after he had gone they were moved back.

In some cases the military authorities requested that no communication should be held with any or with particular prisoners. This applied not only to ordinary visitors but to the accredited representatives of the United States Embassy, and even to the Ambassador, Mr. Gerard, himself.

Dr. Ohnesorg, United States Naval Attaché, reported that in April, 1915, he went to Salzwedel, where "the General asked me, showing me a letter from the General Kommando supporting his request, that I would please refrain from conversing with any prisoner in an undertone or alone."

At another camp "the military authorities remarked that they had had considerable difficulty with" three detained British medical officers, "and requested the Counsellor of the Embassy not to speak with them."

In April, 1915, the American Ambassador himself had to report: "I went to Halle, where there is also an officers' camp, and was there kept waiting for half an hour and, at the expiration of this time, was told that I would be permitted to visit the camp, but under no

EXCHANGE OF PRISONERS.
These British soldiers arrived in England, from Germany, on December 7, 1915.

BRITISH MARINES IN HOLLAND.
A game of Rugby in the Internment Camp.

circumstances would be allowed to speak to any prisoner out of hearing of the officers accompanying me. As this was directly contrary to the arrangements which I made with the General Staff and the Kreigs-Ministerium . . . I refused to make any inspection."

That the United States reports are not conclusive was shown by a letter from the American Ambassador :* " In these camp matters, in order to obtain speedier and more effective action, I deal directly with the bureau of the War Ministry which has charge of prisoners of war." The officers' camp at Hanover-Münden " is not in good condition, and I do not send the report by this mail as I wish to secure a betterment of conditions rather than to furnish ground for controversy."

The volume of evidence relating to German brutality upon Allied soldiers at the moment of capture is both large and weighty, and is illustrated by the cases where British wounded, having been left in a trench, were found, on its subsequent recapture, with their throats cut.

Early in the war some of the German soldiers developed the habit of stripping both the dead and the wounded. A typical example of this is the case of Private Palin,† of the 2nd South Lancashire Regiment, whose spine was pierced by a bullet in the battle of Mons. His legs

became paralysed. The Germans stripped him of his clothes, and for two days and two nights he lay helpless on the field.

No indictment more precise or repulsive has ever been laid than that found in the diary‡ of a German officer of the 13th Regiment, 13th Division of the VIIth German Corps. The extract is dated December 19, 1914 : " The sight of the trenches and the fury—not to say the besti-

‡ Eye-witness (Official), April 16, 1915.

BRITISH MARINES IN HOLLAND:

ality—of our men in beating to death the wounded English affected me so much that for the rest of the day I was fit for nothing."

The journey to captivity was ever terrible, for the unwounded as well as the wounded. Perhaps the most remarkable document on this subject was a report by Major C. B. Vandeleur, who escaped from Crefeld in December, 1914.

Attached to the Cheshire Regiment, Major Vandeleur, of the 1st Cameronians (Scottish Rifles), was captured near La Bassée in October, 1914. Although otherwise well treated by his actual captors, he was compelled to march until, owing to a wound in his leg, he was unable to move further. Being taken to Douai, he was detained, under guard, in the square in front of the Hôtel de Ville, and "subjected to continual abuse and revilement.

"On the arrival of the other prisoners we were all confined in a large shed for the night. No food, except a little provided by the French Red Cross Society, was given, also no straw, and we spent a terrible night there, men being obliged to walk about all night to keep warm, as their greatcoats had been taken from them."

This habit of depriving prisoners of their overcoats, and in some cases of their tunics, was particularly cruel, as the vitality of the men, lowered by exposure, inadequate food and frequently by wounds, rendered them ill able to resist the fatigues of travelling and the rigours of the climate. It was also a direct breach of both Articles 4 and 7 of the Hague Regulations.

"On October 17, in the morning, the French Red Cross gave us what they could in food, and did their very best, in spite of opposition from the Germans. At about 2 p.m. we were all marched off to the railway station, being reviled at and cursed all the way by German officers as well as by German soldiers. One of our officers was spat on by a German officer.

"At the station we were driven into closed-in wagons from which horses had just been removed, fifty-two men being crowded into the one in which the other four officers and myself were. So tight were we packed that there was only room for some of us to sit down on the floor. This floor was covered fully three inches deep in fresh manure, and the stench of horse urine was almost asphyxiating.

"We were boxed up in this foul wagon, with practically no ventilation, for thirty hours, with no food, and no opportunity of attending to purposes of nature. All along the line we were cursed by officers and soldiers alike at the various stations, and at Mons Bergen I was pulled out in front of the wagon by the order of the officer in charge of the station, and, after cursing me in filthy language for some ten minutes, he ordered one of his soldiers to kick me back into the wagon, which he did, sending me sprawling into the filthy mess at the bottom of the wagon. I should like to mention

TAKING EXERCISE IN THE INTERNMENT CAMP.

A BRITISH MARINE
and his little Dutch friend.

that I am thoroughly conversant with German, and understood everything that was said."

Thoroughly to understand the gravity of Major Vandeleur's story it must be remembered that at this time he was not only a prisoner but a wounded prisoner. The condition of the wagons in which many of the prisoners were transported has been spoken to by so great a number of witnesses as to lift it beyond the realm of possible doubt. The ammonia rising from the floor caused agonies to the chests and eyes of many men, whilst wounds, untended except for the hasty bandaging of field dressing stations, suppurated and gangrened.

"Only at one station on the road was any attempt made on the part of German officers to interfere and stop their men cursing us. This officer appeared to be sorry for the sad plight in which we were. I should also like to mention that two men of the German Guard also appeared to be sympathetic and sorry for us ; but they were able to do little or nothing to protect us.

"Up to this time I had managed to retain my overcoat, but it was now forcibly taken from me by an officer.

"On reaching the German-Belgian frontier, the French prisoners were given some potato soup. The people in charge of it told us that none was for us, but that if any was left over after the French had been fed we should get

AT THE INTERNMENT CAMP IN HOLLAND.
British sailors making models. To prevent the men "running to seed" mentally and physically, Commodore Wilfred Henderson, in command of the interned Naval Brigade, assisted the men to adopt useful occupations, such as rug-making, knitting garments, carpentering, tailoring, boot-making, and net-making.

BELGIAN PRISONERS WAITING FOR THEIR MID-DAY SOUP RATION.

what remained." Major Vandeleur then adds that a little soup and a few slices of bread were divided amongst the twenty-five British prisoners confined in the same wagon with him. Major Vandeleur's is, unfortunately, far from having been a solitary case. The differentiation of treatment against the British was as marked a feature of many camps as upon the journey.

Although both food and drink were supplied to their guards, many British wounded were refused either for long periods, sometimes for 58 hours. In some cases even German Red Cross sisters would only supply refreshment to the guards upon the condition that they did not give it to the English. It is well to remember that this injunction was not always complied with.

Screaming crowds of men and women appeared at many of the stations, anxious to see and revile any English prisoner who might pass through. "Women, men and little children howled and in many cases spat" at the prisoners, "while the sentries," who had made them get out of the train, "stood by and laughed."*

Major Vandeleur's terrible report proceeds : "It is difficult to indicate or give a proper idea

* Report of Corporal W. Hall, 1st Life Guards, wounded and captured October, 1914. *The Times,* March 12, 1915.

of the indescribably wretched condition in which we were after being starved and confined in the manner stated for three days and three nights. As is well known, one of these wagons is considered to be able to accommodate six horses or forty men, and this only with the doors open so as to admit of ventilation. What with the filth of the interior, the number of people confined in it, and the absence of ventilation, it seemed to recall something of what one has read of the Black Hole of Calcutta.

"I found out that the wagon in front of us was full of English soldiers. This particular wagon had no ventilation slit of any sort or description, and men were crowded in this even worse than they were in the wagon in which I was. They banged away continually on the wooden sides of the van, and finally, as, I supposed, the Germans thought that they might be suffocated, a carpenter was got, who cut a small round hole in one of the sides."

Major Vandeleur's report, together with those of other exchanged or escaped prisoners, were of such a grave character as to produce in June, 1915, an official reply from the German Government. The reply is particularly interesting as being more an apologia than a defence or denial. Only three short quotations need be given :

"If the English pretend that they were attended to during the journey only after the French, the reason is to be found in the quite comprehensible bitterness of feeling among the German troops, who respected the French on the whole as honourable and decent opponents, whereas the English mercenaries had, in their eyes, adopted a cunning method of warfare from the very beginning, and, when taken prisoners, bore themselves in an insolent and provocative mien."

To the charges of brutalities committed after capture the German official retort is a simple *tu quoque* :

The question refers perhaps to individuals who have been found by German soldiers in the act of killing helpless German wounded and have met with their just reward.

The German reply to the allegations levelled by two exchanged Russian doctors contained a sinister remark. One of the doctors, it asserted, had complained "in a loud and unseemly

fashion" to a sergeant on duty, saying that officers were lodged in barrack rooms ordinarily inhabited by German soldiers. "After the unseemliness of his behaviour had been brought to the attention of this doctor no further opposition was made to the camp regulations."

The general character and equipment of German hospitals appears to have been good, and the medical and surgical treatment and nursing of the patients in them satisfactory. A very large number of them were the normal hospitals of the country, but even in those improvised for the purpose modern scientific appliances were, in the majority of cases, installed. The most prevalent complaint concerned the food, which was very similar to that provided in the camps and, however suitable for the healthy, was unappetising to the sick. The hospital bread was made from wheat and rye in equal proportions. Although distasteful at first, this bread was wholesome and sufficient.

In the hospital, however, as in the prison camp and upon the field, the human equation was of the greatest importance. Any departure from the normal dictates of humanity in the hot blood of battle is to be deprecated but understood ; brutality in the prison camp, brutality, that is, to a healthy, able-bodied man, assumes great importance only when frequent or generally prevalent. The hospital is the home of inevitable suffering, and inhumanity, even in isolated hospitals and in isolated cases, must be

AT THE CIVILIAN INTERNMENT CAMP, RUHLEBEN.
A game of chess. Inset : Eagerly awaiting parcels sent by friends in England.

AT WORK AND PLAY.

On the sports ground in the civilian internment camp, Ruhleben.

Inset : A civilian sets up in business as an engraver.

placed upon an entirely different footing. Unfortunately the brutal doctor and inhuman hospital treatment were neither unknown nor rare. Brutality does not appear to have been in any way usual, but it was not infrequent. The American representative visited the hospital of Iseghem some time before June 12, and the English prisoners " of their own accord," but apparently in the presence of the Commandant, " spoke in praise of the Surgeons and attendants."

Private George Foote, of the 3rd Royal Fusiliers, was wounded on May 21, and after more than three weeks arrived at Iseghem. His account, and some others, are here taken from an interesting series of articles contributed to the *Daily Mail* by Mr. F. A. McKenzie.

" This hospital was in the charge of a very clever, but very brutal doctor. My mate and I (my mate is in the ward here in this London hospital with me) were placed in beds opposite the operating room and saw far more of what was going on than we liked. The doctor did not believe in using chloroform. He used it as seldom as ever he could, particularly on Englishmen. He would do all kinds of operations without it. He would take a mallet and a chisel and get a bit of bone off a man's leg with the man in his full senses."

Private McPhail, a Canadian, was hit outside Ypres on April 24 ; after eight days he arrived

at the Iseghem hospital. He was blind in one eye. " They led me to an operating table and put me on it. Three attendants and a sister held me down. The sister asked a doctor a question, and he answered in English for me to hear : ' No, I will not give an anæsthetic. Englishmen do not need any chloroform.' He turned up my eyelid in the roughest fashion and cut my eye out. He used a pair of scissors, they told me afterwards, and cut too far down, destroying the nerve of the other eye. . . . Suddenly I lost consciousness, and I remembered no more all that day nor all the next

BRITISH PRISONERS OF WAR AT DÖBERITZ.

night." " Soon after this " McPhail was moved from Iseghem.

Other operations without chloroform are alleged to have been performed at a hospital in Hanover. At least one similar case occurred at a general hospital where, after being treated in a rough and brutal manner, a man was subjected to an operation to his face necessitating 16 stitches. No anæsthetic was given.

At Mülheim Ruhr dangerously wounded men were made to take baths in the open in bitter weather. Bandages were left on until they reeked. Helpless men were handled brutally, their bandages, when changed, torn from their wounds. " I will not soon forget Mülheim Ruhr."

Paper was sometimes used as a dressing for wounds. " I myself saw one of the German doctors go up to a party of Russian prisoners lying asleep by the roadway and press the burning end of his cigarette into their cheeks. He was insulted, I suppose, because the men had not been standing at attention when he passed. I saw another take a running kick at a Russian soldier in the tenderest part of his body."

After an operation a man of the Royal Horse Guards was in intense pain. The intensity of the pain, and semi-delirium, made him pull some of the wool dressing from under the bandages The dressing fell over the floor and so annoyed an orderly that he struck the patient and knocked him on to the floor. " There were also * two Englishmen, Philips (Royal

Scots) and Dickson (Lincolns), who, after lingering between life and death in the hospital, were literally kicked out of bed by a newly arrived German doctor, and sent out at the beginning of March with nothing on but thin cotton jackets, old pants, a shirt and wooden sabots. They could not stand alone, and were so emaciated that one scarcely believed it possible for a human being to exist with such a total absence of flesh. Dickson was half crazy through his sufferings and starvation. In endeavouring to aid each other up the step leading to the bunk Dickson fell, being unable to stand the few seconds his one foot was lifted to step over ; Philips, in trying to save him, fell also, and neither could rise without the assistance of bystanders.

"Some French surgeons, who had been sent to Langensalza to fight the growing typhus, pitied these two men, and ordered Dickson some milk each day. Of course he could not fetch it himself, so another Lifeguard (Geeves) went to the hospital for it. En route he encountered the medical officer, an enormously big man, who angrily asked him what he was doing there. When he showed the written order of the French doctor the M.O. tore it up and drove him back."

The internment camps and hospitals in Germany appear to have run the whole gamut from good to terrible. Of many hospitals and some camps no complaint of substance has been made. Of the officers' detention camp at Mainz it has been said that " a spirit of con-

---

* Report by Mr. John Burke, an American subject, in the New York World.

tentment pervaded the entire prison." Some, such as Erfurt, are reported to have been "good"; a few, such as Schloss Celle, a small civilian camp, excellent. Again, others, like Burg, were bad; whilst a few, like Torgau and Wittenberg, were terrible. On November 8, 1915, or fifteen months after the outbreak of war, the conditions at Wittenberg compelled the American Ambassador to forward two reports to London. The first report, prepared by Mr. Lithgow Osborne, said :

The matter of clothing was the chief source of trouble. Upon arriving in the camp I asked the commandant whether there were stores of clothing. He replied, "Yes." To my further enquiries I distinctly understood both the commandant and his assistant to say that every English soldier had been provided with an overcoat. When I investigated among the prisoners, who were drawn up in line, I was informed that practically no overcoats had been given out by the authorities. On the contrary ten overcoats which men had had sent out from England had been taken from their owners and given to other British prisoners who were going to work camps. When I brought this to the attention of the commandant, he stated that the property of the prisoners could be disposed of by the authorities as they saw fit. When I pointed out the fact that exceedingly few of the British had received overcoats he modified his former statement to the extent of saying that they would be supplied in the near future, in so far as possible, but that it was at present very difficult to get overcoats. I was later shown the overcoats, and then I received a third version of the story. I inquired whether these overcoats were to be given out upon application, and the commandant replied in the affirmative ; when I asked if these would be given to British prisoners who asked for them and needed them, he again answered affirmatively.

From many of the men I had heard complaints that one of the watchmen had a large and fierce dog which he took inside the barracks, and which had attacked and torn the clothes of the prisoners. I informed the commandant that I did not know how far this was in accordance with facts, but suggested that it was unnecessary to bring the dog inside the compound, particularly as I had never heard of it being done in other camps. He replied that he considered it necessary, and that this could not be changed, as the prisoners were in the habit of remaining up late at night, keeping their lights burning, playing cards, etc.

The evidence of brutalities of this character is overwhelming. A French priest reported that in the camp at Minden "the German soldiers kick the British prisoners in the stomach and break their guns over their back." It is only proper to add that in some cases, as at Münster, the German soldier was punished when his conduct was brought to the attention of his officers. This priest added that the British were almost starved, "and such have been their tortures that thirty of them asked to be shot."

The report on Wittenberg continued :

My whole impression of the camp authorities at Wittenberg was utterly unlike that which I have received in every other camp I have visited in Germany. Instead of regarding their charges as honourable prisoners of war, it appeared to me the men were regarded as criminals, for whom a régime of fear alone would suffice to keep in obedience. All evidence of kindly and human feeling between the authorities and the prisoners was lacking, and in no other camp have I found signs of fear on the part of the prisoners that what they might say to me would result in suffering for them afterwards.

BRITISH PRISONERS AT DÖBERITZ.
A mid-day meal at the prison camp.

ON THE WESTERN FRONT.

Prussian Guardsmen surrendering to the Middlesex Regiment on March 10, 1915.

So horrible was this report that the U.S. Ambassador requested that it should be regarded as confidential until he had inspected the camp personally. The subsequent visit by the Ambassador compelled him to report as follows :

I was anxious that Mr. Osborne's report should not be made public until I had had an opportunity of viewing actual conditions myself, and I regret to have to state that the impression which I gained upon careful examination of the camp, and after long conversations with the prisoners, was even more unfavourable than I had been led to expect.

Upon my arrival at the camp I was not received by the general who acts as commandant, but by a major, who, together with certain other officers, took me through the camp.

At the present time there are over 4 000 prisoners of war in the camp, 278 of whom are British. There is also a small number of British prisoners in the hospital at the camp, and there are 500 British soldiers employed in a number of working camps through the Province of Saxony. There are also 36 British civilians interned in the camp. Among these I found that 12 were without overcoats.

I next visited the three barracks where British military prisoners are interned, and where the men were lined up together, so that I had an opportunity of speaking to them collectively as well as individually. In the first barrack which I visited there were 68 men, none of whom had overcoats ; in the next barrack, 136 men, of whom 8 had overcoats ; and in the third barrack, 74 men, of whom 8 had overcoats. This makes a total of 16 overcoats among 278 men.

One of the chief complaints which I received was that overcoats had been taken away from British prisoners to be given to other British prisoners who were going out on working parties, and who were without overcoats. This was at first denied by the authorities. but finally the officer with me said that this course was perfectly proper. . . .

. . . It must be said that on the whole they were insufficiently clad.

The Ambassador then proceeds to point out another case of assault, upon a doctor, which does not seem to have been included in those mentioned in the previous report :

The men also told me that one of the British medical officers at the camp had been recently struck by a German non-commissioned officer, and upon investigation this fact proved to be true. . . .

Many of the prisoners complained that dogs were brought in by German soldiers on duty at night, and that in certain cases the prisoners had had their clothes torn by these dogs. . . .

Two prisoners informed me that conditions in the camp had unquestionably improved greatly in the last months, that last year, when an epidemic of spotted typhus existed in the camp, conditions had been indescribably bad. My impression of the camp as a whole was distinctly unfavourable. The entire atmosphere is depressing, due not so much to the conditions under which the men live, which are practically identical with those existing at other camps, as to the fact that nothing appears to have been done towards bringing about any organization among the prisoners themselves which would be of mutual benefit to them, and to the authorities. The attitude which is taken towards the British prisoners seems to be based upon suspicion, and they are not given positions of trust. It is true that they are now housed in barracks together, which is a great improvement, but they have no opportunities for playing games such as football, or for exercise

other than walking. A theatre, however, has now been started, and it is hoped that it will prove a success.

A report of this character which condemns the commandant, who, in this case, was a general and not an "under-officer," must by implication condemn also the German Government. Exaggeration cannot be alleged of the U.S. Ambassador when he wrote, more than a year previously, that the case of British prisoners of war in Germany "is a matter which requires the immediate attention of the British Government."

Of camp brutalities there was evidence without end. Of the more petty tyrannies but one example is given. In the camp at Sennelager were interned—but for a long period unhoused—a number of North Sea trawler men with one half of their hair, beards and moustaches shaved clean. This

RUSSIAN WOUNDED PRISONERS
DRAWING A CART.

must have been done either at the instance or with the concurrence of the commandant, as so notorious and remarkable a spectacle could not, for long, have been kept from his notice.

At Ohrdruf, at Soltau, at Sennelager and at other camps, prisoners for very small offences were tied to posts, sometimes in the snow, usually for a few hours only, but in some cases for many hours, with the result that in some cases when they were released they "just tumbled to the ground." At Zerbst this treatment was admitted by the Commandant to the American official visitor. In other cases men were punished with solitary confinement, and in others were held over barrels and beaten with sticks.

Considering the physical condition of many of

BRITISH PRISONERS AT WORK.
Digging trenches in Germany.
Inset : Preparing wood for supports for the trenches.

tinuous use of which was monotonous to the German, and the views concerning military ceremonial and discipline were so radically different in the land of the captor and the captive. In speaking of the camp at Döberitz the U.S. representative said :—" There were no general complaints, except with regard to the German character of the food—and those were the exact counterpart of complaints made to me by German prisoners in England."

That the food complaints of British prisoners in Germany did not arise from mere fastidiousness is shown by the general remark of the U.S. representative that " frequent protests were made to me concerning the food—not so much because of its quality as because of the insufficient quantity and the monotony of the diet."

The food provided for the non-commissioned ranks consisted for the most part of 300 grammes of black bread per day. This bread was served out every five days and was composed of rye and wheat flour. It was dark, unpalatable and exceedingly heavy and hard. A little weak coffee or tea was given each morning and evening, and at midday one dish of thick vegetable soup, sometimes with a little meat or fish in it. The " vegetables " were principally soya beans, turnips, potatoes, carrots and maize.

The evening ration was a thick soup, sometimes meal soup, with the occasional addition of a small piece of sausage or cheese.

the prisoners, and the poor, strange diet, the general health of the German camps was good, and deaths were relatively few. The Russian prisoner was the greatest sufferer, apparently, from all diseases. Tuberculosis, pneumonia and diabetes were prevalent, probably, in the main, due to exposure in the trenches. Both typhus, the child of dirt, alleged to have been introduced by the Russians, and dysentery claimed many victims and visited a large number of camps.

In Germany all the prisoners were vaccinated against small-pox and immunized against typhoid and cholera, whilst in England such precautions were offered for voluntary acceptance.

An exceedingly fruitful source of complaint lay in the fact that the views in relation to food, as, for instance, raw pickled herrings, which British soldiers detested, or white bread, the con-

At the work camps, such as Süder-Zollhaus, where men were employed in tilling the soil, or other labour, they were called at 5.30 a.m., and at 6 a.m. were given a ration of gruel. On this breakfast they were supposed to work till noon.

By Article 17 of the Hague Regulations all officer prisoners receive the same rate of pay as officers of corresponding rank in the country in which they are detained. When this is done the officer is expected to feed and clothe himself. On September 24, 1914, Sir Edward Grey declared the intention of the British Government to adhere to this Article subject to a similar adherence on the part of the German Government. Until the intentions of the German authorities could be ascertained only half these rates of pay were to be given, but free messing was to be supplied.

Germany did not adhere to the Hague Regulations, but allowed only 60 marks per month to lieutenants and 100 marks to officers of superior rank. The result was that in many cases junior officers had nothing left after paying obligatory mess charges.

As a consequence the British Government, whilst still declaring its willingness to adhere to the Hague Regulations, was obliged to abandon its previous scale. The new scale bore the same ratio to minimum British infantry rates for captains and lieutenants as the pay issued by the German Government to British officers prisoners of war in Germany bore to ordinary German minimum rates for captains and lieutenants. Even under the new conditions the British rate was approximately double the German, the British subaltern in Germany receiving sixty marks a month, or approximately 2s. 0d. per day, whilst the corresponding ranks amongst the German prisoners in England received 4s. 0d.

The refusal of the German authorities to adhere to the Hague Regulations is rendered the more curious and significant as they contain a clause requiring the amount which has been paid to officer prisoners to be refunded by their respective Governments, thus entailing no permanent cost to the Government of the country in which the officer is interned.

The labour of prisoners was considerably used in Germany, France and Russia, though little resorted to in Britain. By Article 6 of the Hague Regulations the labour of all prisoners of war, except officers, may be used according

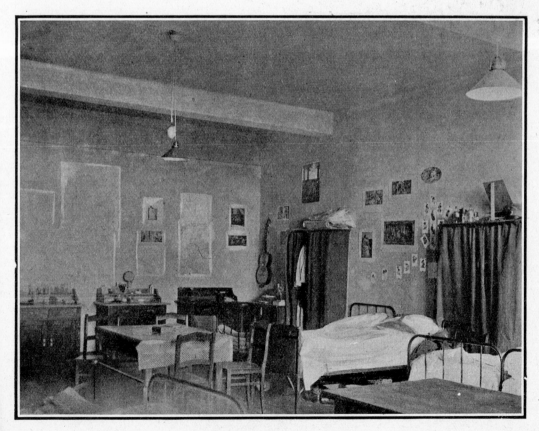

IN THE CAMP AT FRIEDBERG.
British officers' quarters. A room in which there is accommodation for six officers.

to their rank and capacity. The work, which must not be excessive, must "have no connexion with the operations of the war." The Germans used many prisoners for the purposes of grooming and exercising horses intended for subsequent military purposes, and even employed these prisoners to entrain horses for dispatch to the front. Whether or not this was a violation of the prohibition is rather a question for the international lawyer than the historian. The labour may be employed in the public service, for private persons, or on the prisoners' own account. Road making, levelling, clearing and draining the ground, and building huts for

A LETTER HOME.
A wounded British officer dictating to a German Red Cross nurse a message for home.

themselves are examples of labour for State purposes which found favour—least so in Britain—in all the countries of the Allies and the Central Empires. Prisoners were largely used on the land in the employment of private persons in Germany. In Germany prisoners of war were also used in mines and factories, and in other ways. Of course, in all countries maintaining prison camps, the barber and tailor quickly became recognized institutions for whom huts or rooms were usually provided.

As was to be expected, it was in Germany that the greatest use of this labour was made. In addition to, and quite separate from, the ordinary prison camp, the German Government established "Arbeitslager," or "working camps." To these camps were sent those who volunteered for work, and many others besides.

The camp at Süder-Zollhaus was a typical working camp, and contained, in May, 1915, about 2,000 prisoners of war, of whom 479 were British. In that month Dr. Ohnesorg, U.S. Attaché, reported :

The barracks are larger than the ordinary barracks seen in other prison camps. The men sleep on straw, which is placed directly on the floor of the building. There are no mattresses ; each man is supplied with a blanket. In the centre of the compartment is a double-decked arrangement for sleeping. One small stove heats this large compartment.

The latrines are of the trench system, housed over lime, and a substance similar to moss being used as a disinfectant. . . . The diet is about the same as that described in previous reports.

For working camps the official allowance for food was 10 per cent. in excess of that allowed in ordinary camps. There seems considerable doubt whether this was given in all cases. At Süder-Zollhaus the official dietary for Monday, April 26, 1915, was :

Morning.—Coffee, 10 grammes sugar, 300 grammes bread.

Midday.—Swedish turnips and potatoes and pork.

Evening.—Meal soup with vegetables.

For Tuesday, April 27, 1915 :

Morning.—Rice soup, with meal and turnips, 300 grammes bread.

Midday.—Fresh fish with potatoes.

Evening.—Meal soup with vegetables and potatoes.

The hospital arrangements were primitive, and the medical attention inadequate. The report says : "A small portion of a building is set aside for hospital purposes, containing, perhaps, forty bunks. The conveniences are very crude, the bunks being in double tiers, made out of plain pine boards, with mattresses of burlap stuffed with straw ; each patient is supplied with a blanket. There was no doctor living at the camp, a civilian from the city of Flensburg making periodical visits and being summoned by telephone whenever an emergency arises. The immediate care of the sick is intrusted to prisoners who have been roughly trained in this work."

The supply of blankets would seem to have been quite inadequate, and the medical attention in striking contrast to the regulations in force in England, where a resident medical officer formed part of the staff of each place of internment. Süder-Zollhaus was twelve miles from Flensburg.

As this camp is supposed to be a working camp, it seems to me that only prisoners who are physically fit to do the work should be quartered here. Cripples and men who are sick or are not physically fit for the work

DÒBERITZ: SOME OF THE BRITISH PRISONERS

IN THE CONCENTRATION CAMP AT MÜNSTER.
British prisoners taking compulsory exercise.

THE FRENCH VICTORY IN CHAMPAGNE: SOME OF THE

required of them should not be retained in a camp of this type. In the so-called hospital were probably thirty patients at the time of my visit. Of these six were British. One of them had been there for a month with an attack of dysentery. His condition was pitiable—nothing more than skin and bone, and very weak. Although he received medicinal treatment, there was no effort made to give him special diet, which he sadly needed. I obtained the promise of the commandant that he would be immediately transferred to the military hospital in Flensburg. The other cases were those with a dropsical condition of the extremities due to a weak heart. There had been, I was given to understand, several cases of this cardiac trouble which had developed previously in the camp. There was one British prisoner who was still suffering from the effects of frost-bite of toes. Men in such poor physical condition have no business being quartered in such an encampment. They are in need of special diet and careful nursing, and should either be transferred to some hospital or returned to the parent camp at Gustrow.

By the Hague Regulations, when the work is done for the State, payment must be made at rates proportional to those paid for similar work when executed by soldiers of the national army, or, if no such rates are in force, at rates proportional to the work executed. When the work is for other branches of the public service, or for private persons, the rates are to be fixed in agreement with the military authorities. In Britain military prisoners, and civilians if they volunteered, were, when used,

paid at the same rates as British soldiers doing similar work. The position in Germany is best indicated in the American Official Report on Süder-Zollhaus :

There is no stated scale of wages for those employed at work in the fields. I should say that the average labourer received about 30 pfennige per diem for his work. The British do not accept any payment for work done. They say that their Government pays them while they are prisoners of war and they think that if they accept anything from any German individual their pay from their Government will be forfeited. The work which these prisoners do is for private individuals, *i.e.*, the farmers of the surrounding neighbourhood.

Under the Hague Regulations the wages of prisoners must be used for the purpose of improving their position, and the balance paid to them on their release, " deductions on account of the cost of maintenance excepted."

The camp of Friedrichsfeld on the Lower Rhine, near Wesel, was typical of the majority of those holding prisoners of war. It was a mighty camp, and in May, 1915, it held 20,000 prisoners, of whom rather fewer than 300 were British. Probably the best description of the camp itself is that contained in the report of the American representative who inspected it :

The dwelling shacks are all alike, about 200 feet long by 50 feet wide, and not more than 15 feet in height. They are solidly built enough, but they are roughly put

TWENTY-THOUSAND UNWOUNDED GERMAN PRISONERS.

together and finished, and they look uncomfortably low. Each of them is designed to house 750 prisoners, and is divided in the middle by a wall without doors. Against either side of this wall there is a room for non-commissioned officers, and at either end of the building there is a room for a barber or tailor, etc. Bunks fill the remaining space in each shack. They are ranged across the floor in sets of twenty-five or more, with a low partition behind them on which there is a shelf and a place for hanging clothes. The bunks are small and close together, and are not separately detachable from the floor.

Perhaps because of their shape the shacks give the impression of being overcrowded and of being unfitted for very hot or very cold weather. By calculation they provide for more than five cubic metres of space per inmate. The air in them was good, but, on account of the width of the buildings, their windows do not give a great deal of light. . . .

The kitchens are housed in small shacks of their own and were simple and clean, easy of access and egress, and not very different from one another. In each of them there were three large cauldrons over separate fires, all necessary utensils, and their floors were of brick or concrete. The latrines are ranged along one edge of the camp, 100 yards distant from any other building. They are identical as to design and structure, and contain a long room with two inclined benches in it, and a urinating room. They can accommodate about forty men each, are cleaned and disinfected daily, and were free from pronounced odour. They will not become a source of annoyance in hot weather, but they are somewhat distant for night use, notwithstanding the fact that the dwelling shacks are never locked.

In many camps the shacks were locked at night, necessitating the calling of a sentry when men desired to leave them. Many of the camp brutalities arose from the annoyance of the guard on these occasions. The report continues :

The most striking thing about the Friedrichsfeld camp is the pace at which it is being improved by the interned. Surface drainage is being completely done away with, concrete ducts and water troughs are being built, gardens are being laid out and embellished, electric wires near woodwork are being encased in tubes, shacks are being bettered internally, etc. The prisoners have initiated little of this work, but they have almost complete charge of its execution. There is still room for further improvement, of course, but the camp is already in very fair shape, and its further improvement lies largely in the hands of the prisoners themselves. This applies especially to housing conditions, for beyond the standard of cleanliness fixed by their warders, prisoners can clean their dwelling shacks as much as they like.

The outbreak of war saw no general internment or even ill-treatment of British civilians in Germany. In isolated cases only was violence, and, in some instances, murder resorted to. Of such was the murder of Henry Hadley. The following report was officially furnished by the German Government on April 17, 1915 :

The British subject, teacher of languages Henry Hadley, behaved most suspiciously in every respect during his trip in the corridor train from Berlin leaving at 1.25 p.m. to Cologne on August 3, 1914, in company of his housekeeper, Mrs. Pratley.

In the first place, he gave the conductor to understand by shrugging his shoulders, when he was asked how far he was travelling when the train was leaving Berlin, that he could not speak German, while the conductor heard him speaking German several times. Further he talked with his companion several times in foreign languages. While in the dining car Hadley had acted in a conspicuous and impolite manner and also had an excited dispute with a waiter. Finally he made, according to the conductor's statement on oath, ironical remarks and gestures regarding passing officers.

The conductor drew the attention of First Lieutenant Nicolay, who was in the same train, to the stranger, whereupon First Lieutenant Nicolay watched Hadley from the corridor. As the train approached Gelsenkirchen, Hadley came to the conductor, who was standing with First Lieutenant Nicolay, and asked him whether this station was Cologne. First Lieutenant Nicolay asked Hadley where he intended to travel. Hadley replied, "Well, I think to Paris," which caused First Lieutenant Nicolay to remark that it was remarkable that he (Hadley) did not know where he desired to travel. Hadley, who was listening, overheard this, and began a conversation with the conductor. First Lieutenant Nicolay forbade the conductor to answer, and the conductor informed the stranger to this effect. Hadley told the conductor in German that the officer had no right to command him (the conductor), whereupon the conductor answered that under these circumstances the officer was his superior. First Lieutenant Nicolay now blocked Hadley's way by stretching out his arms, and told him in English that he was not to leave the train, letting him know at the same time that he was a Prussian officer. But as Hadley assumed an aggressive attitude, First Lieutenant Nicolay called

"Hands up" several time, in German and English. Hadley paid no attention, but raised his sticks so that First Lieutenant Nicolay was led to expect an actual attack, and he called again, "Hands up or I shall shoot." He thereupon fumbled with his hands under his waistcoat, saying that he was a British subject. As First Lieutenant Nicolay believed that the stranger intended to bring out a weapon and use it against him, he fired at him, in order to be first. Thereupon Hadley was taken to the door and on to the platform by the people who were present, resisting with all his might ; at the station First Lieutenant Nicolay handed over Hadley and his companion to two civil police officials. Hadley, who was brought into a hospital and placed under doctor's care, died on August 5, 1914, at 3.15 a.m., in consequence of the wound caused by the bullet.

Court-martial proceedings were instituted against Captain Nicolay, as he now is, for killing Hadley which proceedings were discontinued upon the completion of the investigation of the case.

This dastardly murder of an unarmed civilian occurred on August 3, the day before the declaration of war.

But outrage, though not unknown, was not general. British citizens, whilst bound to report themselves to the police, were not interfered with, though their movements were restricted. Following upon the increased stringency of the British Government in dealing with alien civilians, the German Press commenced a

FRENCH TENDING THEIR OWN WOUNDED AND ENEMY PRISONERS.
French wounded on their way to entrain for hospital, and, on the left, German wounded prisoners waiting to be conveyed to a base hospital.

AFTER THE FRENCH VICTORY IN CHAMPAGNE.

German officers who were discovered by the French hidden away in cellars and dug-outs. They were conveyed by motor-'bus to the French headquarters.

campaign calling for "reprisals" against the British subjects in Germany. An article, entitled "The Persecution of Germans," appeared in the *Frankfurter Zeitung*, which said :

The Government has caused thousands of Germans and Austrians, who have committed not the smallest offence, to be arrested, in order to bring them into the terrible concentration camps in which Germans, declared to be prisoners of war, are interned. The disgusting nature of these places scandalously defy all sanitary requirements. . . . One must assume that the condition of these camps is known to the Government. But the Government has made no changes, and if it now throws further thousands into them, the object no doubt is similar to that pursued by a former British Government in the internment of Boer women and children. It is desired to take vengeance upon Germany for defending herself with all her strength against England, and for winning victories, and although that may not have been the primary intention, the English have no doubt the miserable idea that it does England no harm if a few thousands perish in these camps They are only Germans.

The article then deals with the possibility of espionage, and denies that any real fear existed in England :

If the British Government does not stop persecuting shamelessly the Germans who are in its power, it becomes necessary to show this Government plainly that Germany is both able and willing to reply with reprisals of equal severity. The English subjects may then become conscious that they owe the deterioration in their position

to those same Ministers of his Majesty of Great Britain who, like mad gamblers, plunged England and Europe into this terrible war, and who are now not content to fight the war by military means between State and State, but extend hatred and destruction to spheres and to persons that, in the spirit of International Law, ought to remain protected from the violence of war.

Almost every paper contained "interviews" and accounts, true or apocryphal, of the conditions in the internment camps of England. The German Government yielded, and the first general internment of British civilians commenced in the first week of November, 1914.

The interning was done in a wholesale, systematic, thorough and German manner. Though small bodies were scattered in various gaols and camps throughout Germany, the majority of civilians were interned at Ruhleben, near Berlin. The camp, which was situated on a large trotting track, soon contained about 4,000 British subjects. The prisoners, who were of all ages, social classes, and conditions of health, were lodged in the yards, stables and grand-stand of the racecourse.

Of Ruhleben it is peculiarly difficult to write, as the conditions were in a constant flux, though with a steady tendency towards improvement.

Under the régime of Count Schwerin—described by one prisoner as a "kindly man"—and Count Taube, the "patience and devotion" of both of whom the American Ambassador praised in the warmest terms—the camp greatly improved.

In the earlier days the horse-boxes, some 10 ft. 6 in. wide, were made to house six people, whilst the lofts were also grossly overcrowded. For bedding a very limited supply of straw was provided. The straw was simply strewn on the damp concrete floors of the horse-boxes, and, trodden and damp, soon became unwholesome and verminous. A little later, sacks were provided into which the damp straw was placed and mattresses made. Apparently only one blanket was provided. No proper washing or sanitary arrangements existed. There were only two taps for each stable, which accommodated over 300 men. The latrines for the use of the prisoners were at a considerable distance from the stables. There were no baths except a shower bath, which was situated some way from the camp. All prisoners were roused at 6 a.m., and, after "dressing," had to go more than 500 yards to get their morning coffee. Everyone had to go to bed at 8 p.m., with "lights out" at 9 p.m.

The lofts and stables, which were dark and cold during the day, were cold, clammy and unventilated at night. Particularly when the age of many of the prisoners, the variety of the social classes, and the fact that a very large portion of the British population in Germany was there solely for reasons of health, Ruhleben, particularly in its early days, was a disgrace not only to the civilization, but to the humanity of Germany.

Largely in consequence of the efforts of the American Ambassador improvements were gradually introduced. New barracks, which improved the conditions and relieved the overcrowding, were gradually erected, recreation grounds provided, new and better latrines constructed, some hundred persons removed to sanatoriums, and a similar number released. The greatest improvement of all, however, was the formation of a prisoners' committee, into whose hands a large part of the internal camp management was placed. Life then became tolerable in Ruhleben.

Unfortunately, whilst their removal to a sanatorium did something to relieve the congestion in Ruhleben, it did little to benefit the patients. The sanatorium belonged to one Weiler, and those patients who were unable to pay for themselves were supported by the British Government. As late as November 16, 1915, the American Embassy reported on the main building of the sanatorium, Nussbaum Allee, "we found here, as in the house on Akazien-Allee, that there was no effort made to segregate communicable disease. In a previous visit the attention of the authorities was called to cases of tuberculosis and a suggestion made that they be removed from the immediate association with those not so afflicted. No effort to do this has yet been made, nor does there appear any likelihood of it being done."

The report adds : "This last visit has convinced us more than ever that the proprietor of this sanatorium cares more for pecuniary

UNDER ALGERIAN CAVALRY ESCORT.
Cavalry attached to the French Army bringing into a base town German prisoners from West Belgium.

GERMAN PRISONERS IN FRANCE.
Outside a farmhouse in the Champagne.
Inset : Sweeping the roads in the North of France.

gain than the humanitarian side of his
work."

Of the man Weiler it is unnecessary to say
more. The vital fact remains that these sick
civilian prisoners of war, the cost of whose
maintenance was not even borne by the
German Government, were kept interned in
this sanatorium under the surveillance of and by
the orders of that Government. It is well that
such an indictment is laid in the official docu
ments of a neutral Power, for the history of
captivity must, before this war, be traced far
back before a similarly authentic and repulsive
incident can be found. The history of civilization is the debtor of the American people.

In England the German prisoner was housed
either on ships or in the usual land camp. The
ships, about which a great outcry arose in
Germany, were principally looked upon as
winter camps, as it was easier to keep them
warm and comfortable than those ashore. The
principal defect lay in the limited accommodation which they provided for exercise. This

defect was felt more acutely in those ships in
which military prisoners were interned. In
fact, the ships had distinct advantages in the
case of civilians, particularly owing to the ease
with which the authorities were enabled to
separate the various classes. For a small extra
payment the wealthier prisoners could obtain
the use of a cabin.

The British Government having given the
U.S. Ambassador at Berlin permission to
appoint any person to inspect prison camps in
England, he thereupon gave the German Foreign
Office the choice of selecting any member of
his Embassy staff for that purpose. The

German Foreign Office selected Mr. J. B. Jackson, former American Minister to Cuba and Roumania. Mr. Jackson, having been a Secretary of the American Embassy at Berlin for a period of about eleven years, and having been responsible for the inspection of a large number of prison camps in Germany, was both well known to the German Government and well qualified for the task.

Mr. Jackson received a general passport, which empowered him to visit all prison camps in England without being previously announced. He was also permitted to converse freely with the prisoners without any other person being present.

In April, 1915, Mr. Jackson reported that he had been able to inspect nine ships and thirteen other places in which German prisoners of war were interned. Approximately there were 400 officers (including a few Austrians), 6,500 soldiers and naval sailors, and between 19,000 and 20,000 merchant sailors and civilians (German and Austrian) interned on February 1, 1915. Probably less than one-third of the total number of German subjects or persons of German birth in the United Kingdom were interned, and many of those interned had no wish to return to Germany. Besides seafaring persons there were a considerable number of boys under 17 and men over 55 who were interned, but in every case which came to his attention note had been taken of the fact by the local commandant and reported to the authorities, with a view to repatriation, except where men had no wish to be sent to Germany.

He heard of no cases where women were interned. Wherever he went he was granted every facility to see all that there was to be seen and to converse freely with the prisoners without any kind of control or supervision. On two occasions he lunched with the German officers, no British officer or soldier being present. The officers were under practically no supervision so long as they remained within the camps themselves, and there was no direct contact between them and the British officers and soldiers, except when they left the barbed wire enclosure.

The German fatigue and police work was done by the prisoners themselves.

An investigation of Frith Hill Camp, Frimley, near Aldershot, by an independent American showed that " the prisoners run their own little republic under their non-commissioned officers, who are responsible to the military authorities. They have their own

GERMAN OFFICERS.
Officers captured by the French from the Army of the Crown Prince.

FRENCH PRISONERS IN GERMANY
Lined up for inspection. Centre and bottom
pictures : Erecting barbed-wire enclosures in which
they are confined.

police, even their secret police." This organization of secret police has a characteristically
Teutonic flavour.

In continuation, Mr. Jackson reported that
opportunities were given for exercise, but that
it was not obligatory, although all prisoners
were compelled to spend certain hours every
day outside their sleeping quarters.

Up to the date of his report very little had
been done to provide occupation or employment for interned prisoners, military or civil.
Soldiers and sailors were allowed to wear civilian
clothes when they had no uniforms, and
civilians were provided with blankets, shoes
and clothing of all kinds by the British Government when they had no means to purchase
such articles. Soap was provided, but towels,
tooth paste, brushes, etc., usually had to be
provided by the prisoner himself, or through
the American Embassy in London on account
of the German Government. Books printed
before the outbreak of the war were permitted
in English and other languages, and English
newspapers after January, 1915. The regulations relating to the receipt of parcels, letters

COSSACKS CONVOYING GERMAN AND AUSTRIAN PRISONERS IN THE CARPATHIANS.

and money and for outgoing correspondence were similar to those in Germany.

An interesting sidelight on the food supplied in British prison camps was shown by the infinitesimal number of parcels received, whilst the number of parcels containing food and clothing which were sent to Germany mounted week by week, and ultimately achieved colossal proportions.

Mr. Jackson then adds that in certain cases the right to receive correspondence was suspended as punishment for breaches of discipline, such as the receipt or transmission of clandestine letters, or the attempt to send letters through bottles thrown from the prison ships.

The food supplied to prisoners * was practically the ration of the British soldier, and seemed to be generally satisfactory, both as regards quality and quantity, though there were a considerable number of individual complaints, mostly concerning the monotony of the diet—there was too much beef and too little pork ; white bread instead of brown · and not sufficient fresh vegetables.

The free use of tobacco was permitted everywhere, and in most of the camps visits were permitted. In general the hospital arrangements were primitive, but appeared to be sufficient, and the health of the camps had been good.

The officers without exception told Mr. Jackson that they had always been treated like officers and honourable men by the English soldiers, and many of the German soldiers told him of instances where they had been protected by the English from assaults by the mob on their way through France. From the civilians, however, there were many complaints, especially from those who had been taken from neutral ships or had been arrested in the Colonies, as to the manner of their arrest and their treatment before being brought to the detention camps.

Mr. Jackson's report made a noteworthy conclusion :

On the whole the present treatment seems to be as good as could be expected under the circumstances. The new camps are all better than the older ones, and everywhere there seemed to be an intention to improve on existing conditions. Lack of organization and preparation would account for most of the hardships which

prevailed at first. Absolutely nowhere did there seem to be any wish to make the conditions any harder or more disagreeable for the prisoners than was necessary, *and I saw no instance, and heard of none*, where any prisoners had been subjected either to intentional personal annoyance or undeserved discipline.

This report, which has been quoted at such length on account both of the interesting character of its contents and the unimpeachable character of its author, relates that all prisoners on board the ships were locked below decks at night, and that this caused some nervousness among them owing to the apprehension of danger from Zeppelins.

The International Red Cross Association in Geneva appointed Professor Eduard Naville and M. Victor van Berchem to visit and inspect the various prison camps in the United Kingdom. In February, 1915, they reported that

ON THE EASTERN FRONT.
An Austrian officer under cross-examination.

out of the 10,000 German officers and men who were prisoners in England, not one was dissatisfied with his food or treatment.

The prisoner had only to make representation that his clothes or boots were tattered or insufficient, and he received what he required. Unlike those in France and Germany, the prisoner in Britain was not in any way dependent for his clothing upon supplies provided from his own country.

In an interesting report * on the prison camp at Holyport, Mr. T. E. Steen, a Norwegian, says : " We passed through a number of large well-furnished rooms. In the largest we found some fifty prisoners, smoking, chatting, or reading. In the centre

---

* The rations which were issued free consisted of :—
Bread, 1 lb. 8 oz., or biscuits 1 lb. ; meat, fresh or frozen, 8 oz., or pressed, 4 oz. ; tea, ½ oz., or coffee, 1 oz. ; salt, ½ oz. ; sugar, 2 oz. ; condensed milk, 1–20 tin (1 lb.) ; fresh vegetables, 8 oz. ; pepper, 1-72 oz. ; 2 oz. cheese to be allowed as an alternative for 1 oz. butter or margarine ; 2 oz. of peas, beans, lentils, or rice.

* *The Times*, January 29, 1915.

ALLIED PRISONERS IN GERMANY.
Russian, Belgian, French and British flanked by an Algerian and a Senegalese.

was a large Christmas-tree, which gave a picturesque and gay note to the room. In the large dining-room I saw on the wall the German flag spread out with a freedom which went far to prove the broadminded spirit of the British."

Similar toleration was occasionally shown in Germany. In the camp at Hameln the prisoners made a flower-bed representing the Allied flags. In this camp "the great majority of the prisoners . . . spoke well of the warders and especially of the Commandant."

When leaving Holyport Mr. Steen asked the (German) colonel whether he had any complaint to make, and received a reply in the negative. The colonel added : "The English are very kind. I tell my people in Germany of their kindness in every letter I write . . . everywhere the English seem intent on providing their prisoners with comfortable and healthy accommodation. And as to the food, it is the same as that provided for the soldiers, and it is a well-known fact that no soldier is better fed than those of the King of England."

From the earliest days the British authorities endeavoured to enlist the cooperation of the prisoners in the conduct of the camp.

By June, 1915, the American Ambassador in Berlin was able to report that, except with regard to the confinement on board ships, which was still a sore point, "the German military authorities have now satisfied them-

selves that German prisoners in England are being treated as well as the conditions permit."

In May, 1915, the Budget Committee of the German Reichstag, ignoring the conditions prevalent in German prison camps, declared itself shocked at the "brutalities" to which German prisoners in Russia "were exposed."

Russia, with her vast distances, her scanty means of intercommunication, solved the difficulties surrounding the care of prisoners characteristically.

The great bulk of her unwounded prisoners were removed to Siberia and billeted on the population. During the winter months the prisoners were conveyed to their destination in well-warmed trains. On arriving, the prisoners were supplied with clothing suitable to the climate. The attitude of the Russian authorities towards their charges was well shown by the official Proclamation issued by the Governor of the province of Akmolinsk, in which many prisoners were detained. A portion of the proclamation was in the following terms :

The Russian people have too noble a soul for them to be cruel to those in misfortune. Peasants ! Receive not the prisoners sent to you as your enemies. Have consideration for others' sorrows. Our great ruler, His Imperial Majesty, has relieved them from enforced labour ; and they are permitted to enter into work by voluntary agreement. Peasants ! By instituting friendly relations with the prisoners, but not oppressing them, you will meet on their part a readiness to be friendly and helpful to you.

Perhaps the most interesting statement on Russian hospitals which appeared during the war was the letter from an exchanged invalided prisoner given on November 10, 1915, in the Vienna *Arbeiter Zeitung.* This prisoner, who had lost his leg by amputation, had experience of no fewer than eight hospitals in Stanislau, Schmerinka, Tscher, Kassy, Kiev, Moscow, Jaraslow and W——. The letter is here given, with both its praise and blame, and without comment of any kind. After stating that "conditions varied in each Russian military hospital," it says :

Practically the treatment of the wounded depends on those to whom they are handed over, or those who deliver them up. . . .

To speak truthfully, I must admit that on the whole in Russia *no difference* is made between prisoners and Russians, hospital trains are well arranged and the nursing is better than in hospital.

I should like here at once to correct the very general impression that Russian doctors are too ready to amputate, that they, as has been asserted, would rather amputate at once—that is, at least not right in all cases. For instance, I know a case, a North Bohemian, severely wounded in the lower part of the thigh, who repeatedly begged Russian doctors at five places to remove his leg ; they did not do it, and I can testify that before I parted with him he had once more been operated on and was then himself convinced that his leg could be saved. One of the worst evils is that wounded prisoners, as in my case, were dragged from one hospital to another. That may partly be caused by the immense distances

that have to be traversed to reach the interior of Russia. For example, we travelled three nights and two days from Kiev to Moscow. That is not only harmful for the recovery of the wounded, but it has also the result that prisoners can hardly ever hear from their belongings and especially that no money reaches them. By the time letters or money reach them the wounded have gone on to the second, or a third hospital. . . .

Food in the hospitals, unless one is especially fastidious is quite sufficient.

The hospital attendants consist mostly of good natured, if not very intelligent folk. It is at first unpleasant that the orderly uses no handkerchief and seldom a towel. He rises early, quickly washes, and not having a towel, dries himself on his far too wide and soiled blouse. There, too, he cleans his nose and immediately afterwards with the hands which he has used for this purpose, he distributes bread and sugar ! One only notices that at the beginning ; later on one gets used to it.

Once we were four weeks without clean body linen ; the consequence was—vermin.

The nursing sisters perform their duties conscientiously.

AUSTRIANS IN RUSSIA.
Prisoners arriving in Petrograd. Inset : Round a camp fire.

Their position towards doctors and patients is much more independent than with us.

The large number of medical men in every Russian hospital astonished me. Nowhere was a lack of doctors to be noticed. Certainly the majority were not genuine doctors, who had studied at a University, but army doctors (Feldscherer), in the interior generally students, but still intelligent people. In most cases well educated, and especially fairly experienced in the treatment of wounds. The doctor generally leaves the whole work to them—himself reading newspapers, and only appearing when called by the assistant to notice some case. But there are also hospitals where the assistant may not bind the wound until instructed by his doctor. But these hospitals are in the minority. Also the doctors, qualified and unqualified, are mostly humane towards the prisoners —at least as conscientious as towards their own country-men. On the other hand, the necessary furnishings are often lacking in the hospital. Of all the towns in whose hospital I was, Kiev and Moscow were the only ones possessing Röntgen apparatus, and so the medicos have to do without the right requisites. . . .

Many were the devices for whiling away the hours—all the time-worn schemes of prison history. In most of the camps games such as football were permitted, in a few tennis was allowed, the courts being laid largely by the labour, and usually at the expense, of the prisoners. Of the making of knicknacks there was no end, the Russian excelling all others in this. Then concerts and theatrical per-formances, even Shakespeare was essayed, the most delicately featured and complexioned of the prisoners being cast for the female parts. It was often asserted that if you kept your eyes away from the boots the illusion was complete. Probably the most ambitious attempt was a " Revue in Eight Episodes," entitled " Don't Laugh ! " given in Ruhleben in May, 1915, complete with Lyrics, Prologue, Episodes, and Beauty Chorus.

" The Ruhleben Song," in particular, was a great success :

Oh, we're roused up in the morning, when the day is
    gently dawning,
And we're put to bed before the night's begun.
And for weeks and weeks on end we have never seen a
    friend,
And we've lost the job our energy had won.
Yes, we've waited in the frost, for a parcel that got lost,
Or a letter that the postmen never bring.
And it isn't beer and skittles, doing work on scanty
    victuals,
Yet every man can still get up and sing :
                    Chorus.
    Line up, boys, and sing this chorus
    Shout this chorus all you can ;
    We want the people there,
    To hear in Leicester Square,
    That we're the boys that never get downhearted.
    Back, back, back again in England,
    Then we'll fill a flowing cup ;
    And tell 'em clear and loud of the Ruhleben crowd
    That always kept their pecker up.

February, 1915, saw the commencement of an interesting experiment in German prison camps.

ON THE EASTERN FRONT.
A group of Russians captured by the Germans.

RUSSIAN PRISONERS AT WORK.

Unloading potatoes. Bottom: Marching through
a Polish village.

The American branch of the Y.M.C.A. extended
its sphere of operations, Göttingen and Alten-
grabow being first attacked. A building was
erected at Göttingen with rooms for prayer,
for reading, for concerts and lectures,
equipped with a library of English, French
and Russian books, pianos, blackboard,
maps and pictures. The building was erected
by the men themselves. Never was labour
more willingly given. At the opening ceremony,
on April 15, one of the prisoners of war called
the new building " Our Home," and many a
head bent low when one of the Camerons,
with a high tenor voice, sang, " Be it ever so
humble, there is no place like home."

In any account of the life of prisoners in
the Great War mention must be made of the
work done by prisoners' help organizations.

In England this necessary work lay at first
in the hands of individuals, or separate organizations. In March, 1915, the War Office
sanctioned the appointment of a Prisoners of
War Help Committee with an executive council,
consisting of Sir Charles Lucas (chairman),
Mr. Rowland Berkeley (hon. treasurer), Lieut.-
Colonel C. J. Fox, Mr. W. J. Thomas, Mr. N. E.
Waterhouse, and Mr. B. W. Young (hon.
secretary). Increase in the facilities and
efficiency for dealing with prisoners, and the
prevention of overlapping and waste, were

amongst the principal duties of the Committee.
In order to make full use of local patriotism
and *esprit de corps*, the subsidiary organizations
were arranged on the regimental plan. The
interests of prisoners were placed in the care
of their regimental organizations, those of
native troops being in the care of the Indian
Soldiers' Fund. Although the regimental plan
possessed the inestimable advantage of using
intimate knowledge and sympathy for the
benefit of the prisoner, it was subject to one
grave disadvantage. Each regimental organization was primarily responsible for its own
finance.

Unfortunately the resources and the obligations of the different regiments varied. In
some cases regiments with a long list of wealthy
subscribers had had few men captured, whilst
in others, particularly so in the case of
many gallant Irish regiments, the losses had
been heavy, and the subscription lists were

meagre and inadequate. The Prisoners of War Help Committee dealt with the difficulty in three ways. Any money or offers of help received were handed over to the regimental organizations whose needs were most pressing. In addition to the regimental organizations there were others, such as the Royal Savoy Association, which were ready to deal with any prisoner, civil or military, whose needs were not otherwise provided for. Relief was given to an overburdened organization by apportioning some of its obligations to one of these unattached associations.

Finally the Committee controlled the " adoption " of prisoners by individual sympathizers. Anyone desiring to help a prisoner otherwise than by subscribing to an organization, could " adopt " a prisoner. This plan worked excellently in the hands of conscientious people, but was always open to the defect that the " parents " might tire or become irregular in

their attention to the prisoner's needs. This was a particularly grave offence, as weeks might pass before either the regimental organization or the Committee learnt what was happening. During this time the prisoner was helpless and his position deplorable.

By Article 16 of the Hague Regulations all letters, money orders, valuables, and postal parcels intended for prisoners of war were exempt from all postal charges or import or other duties. Whilst the British Post Office dealt with all packages not exceeding 11 lbs. in weight, the Committee, immediately on its formation, secured the services of the American Express Company. This company, as a neutral carrier having agencies throughout Germany, had special advantages. All parcels for Germany were sent via Rotterdam. On April 8 the number of packages handled was 23, whilst on November 15 this had risen to 870, weighing about $4\frac{1}{2}$ tons.

SERBS CAPTURED BY THE AUSTRIANS.

CHAPTER CIII.

THE KING'S NEW ARMIES AND THE DERBY RECRUITING SCHEME.

The Army at Outbreak of War—Army Reserve and Territorials—First Rush of War Recruits—The Government's Call for 100,000 Men—Formation of the New Armies —Appeal for Another 100,000 Men—Separation Allowances—Administrative Blunders and Misunderstandings—The Policy of Secrecy—More Appeals and Raising of Age Limit to Forty—Mr. Lloyd George and "Conscription"—The National Register and "Pink Forms"—National Service Movement Revived—The Government and Labour— Lord Derby as Director of Recruiting—The Derby Scheme—The Group System —Unmarried Men First—The Derby Canvass—The King's Letter to His People— Mr. Asquith's Pledges to Married Men—Armlets for the Attested—Four Groups Called Up in January, 1916—Results of the Derby Canvass—Cabinet Hesitations—The Cabinet Adopts the Principle of Compulsion—Opinion in the Country.

THE outbreak of war found the British Army consisting of two different parts, each self-contained. The first-line Army, which provided the so-called Expeditionary Force and the British garrison in India and elsewhere abroad, was composed of professional soldiers, who served for twelve years, part of the time (generally seven years) with the colours and the remainder in the reserve. The periods devoted to the colours and the reserve respectively varied according to the arm of the Service. The old Militia had been abolished and had been replaced by the Special Reserve, a force destined on mobilization to maintain the fighting strength of the Regular Army overseas. The second-line Army was composed of the Territorial Force, which had superseded the former Yeomanry and Volunteers, and which had a complete divisional organization analogous to that of the Regular Army.

The strengths of the Regular Army on January 1, 1914, were as follows:

On Home and Colonial Establishment ...	156,110
On Indian Establishment	78,476
Total ...	234,586

The age limits for enlistments were from 18 to 25 (in some cases 30), and the height standard varied from 5 feet 11 inches for the Household Cavalry to 5 feet 2 inches for the Royal Flying Corps.

The rates of pay on enlistment for the various branches of the Regular Army were the following. Lodging, uniform and kit were provided free, but as much as 5½d. a day might be deducted for messing and washing. A considerable increase was granted to men on attaining proficiency.

	Pay per week	
	s.	d.
Household Cavalry	12	3
Cavalry of the Line	8	2
Royal Horse Artillery (gunners)	9	4
Royal Horse Artillery (drivers)	8	9
Royal Field Artillery	8	5½
Royal Garrison Artillery	8	5½
Royal Engineers	8	2
Foot Guards	7	7
Infantry of the Line	7	0
Royal Flying Corps (2nd Class Mechanics)	14	0
Royal Flying Corps (1st Class Mechanics)	28	0
Army Service Corps	8	2
Royal Army Medical Corps	8	2

The Army Reserve, consisting of the trained Regular soldiers who had returned to civil life after service with the colours and remained

LORD DERBY INSPECTING THE DOCKERS BATTALION.

liable to be called up on general mobilization, numbered on January 1, 1914, 146,756 men.

It was composed (1) of reservists who had volunteered to come up, if called upon, to complete to war establishment units detailed for a minor expedition, and who received 7s. a week reserve pay ; (2) of reservists liable only to be called up for general mobilization, and who received 3s. 6d. a week reserve pay ; and (3) men who, after their twelve years' service, had re-enlisted for a further four years in the reserve on the same terms as (2). They were only to be called up after (1) and (2) had been embodied. Reservists were liable to be called out for twelve days' annual training or twenty drills.

The Special Reserve consisted of a fixed number of battalions, representing an allotment of one or more reserve battalions to every line battalion at home, in addition to twenty-seven extra reserve Battalions for fortress defence and lines of communication. The term of enlistment was six years, and all ranks were liable for foreign service in war. Recruits were trained by a " regular establishment " of officers posted to the depôt, the training consisting of an initial course of five to six months with an annual training of three to four weeks in every subsequent year of the man's service. The war function of the Special Reserve was to act as a feeder to its battalion in the field, and to assist in the work of coast defence. Belonging to it were three regiments of cavalry, the " North " and the

" South " Irish Horse and King Edward's Horse, which were not drafting reserves, but service units resembling yeomanry. A special reservist, while undergoing training, received Regular pay, together with certain bounties. The strength of the Special Reserve on January 1, 1914, was 63,089, some 17,000 below its establishment.

The Territorial Force, with a period of enlistment of four years, and a height standard of 5 feet 2 inches and age limit of 17 to 35 inclusive, was only liable for home service. When the war came, however, a large proportion of the Force volunteered for foreign service, and was employed in the first instance on garrison duties abroad, thereby releasing units of the Regular Army for the front. The raising and equipping of the Force was in the hands of County Associations. Every man was liable to attend camp for at least eight days in each year unless excused, and to make himself efficient under a penalty of £5. In 1913 66 per cent. of the Force attended camp for fifteen days, and 23 per cent. for less than fifteen days. While in camp a man received Regular pay and rations, and a further sum of 1s. per head per day was allowed for additional messing purposes. On January 1, 1914, the Territorial Force numbered 251,706, its establishment being 315,485.

It will thus be seen that, on paper at all events, the British Army at home at the outbreak of war numbered approximately 366,000 of the first line and 251,000 of the second. To these must be added the National

Reserve, consisting on January 1, 1914, of 217,680 men, of whom a large proportion were old soldiers and sailors fit either to take their place in the field or for garrison and administrative duty at home. Within a few weeks of August 4, 1914, about 80,000 of the National Reserve had joined the Regular Army.

With regard to officers, there were on the establishment of the Regular Army before the war about 10,600 officers, who had either been trained at the Royal Military Academy, Woolwich, or at the Royal Military College, Sandhurst, or were University candidates trained in the Officers Training Corps. In the case of the Special Reserve and the Territorial Force, officers were appointed either after service in the Officers Training Corps or direct from civil life. The Officers Training Corps was composed of senior division contingents belonging to the Universities, and junior division contingents belonging to the public schools. The total strength of the Officers Training Corps was approximately 25,000, of whom about 5,000 were undergraduates of military age available for immediate service. The Territorial Force contained about 9,500 officers.

The Expeditionary Force was originally intended to consist of six divisions of infantry, each of about 20,000 men, all ranks, and one cavalry division, about 10,000 all ranks. The

RECRUITING AT NORTHAMPTON.
Recruits receiving the King's shilling.

number actually landed in France in the first instance did not exceed 60,000 officers and men.

With the outbreak of war came a remarkable rush of recruits to the colours. No better evidence of England's unpreparedness for war can be imagined than the complete lack of any adequate provision for dealing with this rush. During the first week of the war pathetic scenes were to be witnessed at the recruiting stations.

RECRUITS OUTSIDE WHITEHALL RECRUITING OFFICE.

**LORD DERBY ARRIVING AT THE
WAR OFFICE.**

After hours of weary waiting, sometimes in
heavy rain, it was no uncommon thing for as
many as 700 men to be left standing outside
one station alone when the doors were closed.
Nothing could exceed the enthusiasm of the
would-be recruits, who were occasionally so
eager in their desire to join the Army as to
require the services of mounted police to pre-
serve order. On August 10 it was reported
that 1,100 men had been enrolled in London
alone in the previous twenty-four hours, and
that 500 or 600 had been left over. Large
numbers of reservists applied to extend or
renew their service. The City of London
Territorial units, with five or six exceptions,
had already been filled up to their full strength.
Veterans' corps throughout the country
accepted men between thirty-five and sixty.
Various irregular corps were being well supported.

It will be remembered that on August 6
Lord Kitchener had been appointed Secretary
of State for War, and that on the same day
Mr. Asquith asked the House of Commons
to sanction an increase of the Army by
500,000 men. Next day an advertisement
appeared in the Press which, for the first time,
although this did not appear on the face of

it, contained an appeal for the formation
of what was to become the first of the new
Armies. The advertisement ran as follows :

YOUR KING AND COUNTRY NEED YOU.
A CALL TO ARMS.
An addition of 100,000 men to his Majesty's Regular
Army is immediately necessary in the present grave
National Emergency.
Lord Kitchener is confident that this appeal will be
at once responded to by all those who have the safety
of our Empire at heart.
TERMS OF SERVICE.
General service for a period of 3 years or until the
war is concluded.
Age of enlistment between 19 and 30.

Old soldiers up to the age of 42 were also
acceptable.

On the same day, August 7, the Government
made clear its intention in a circular addressed
to the Lords-Lieutenant of counties and
chairmen of the Territorial Force County
Associations, which was published on August
10. The curious inability of the authorities
to come straight to the point which dogged
the steps of the voluntary system of recruiting
throughout the war was illustrated in this
circular by the fact that not until the last
paragraph did the War Office explain that

RECRUITING—OLD STYLE.
Before the war.

ROTHSCHILD'S BANK AS RECRUITING OFFICE.
Major Lionel de Rothschild, M.P. (X), and a number of recruits outside the bank in St. Swithins Lane, E.C.

this was "not an ordinary appeal from the Army for recruits, but the formation of a second Army." This explanation was very necessary, for, as a matter of fact, the appeal was an invitation to the county authorities to cooperate in the work of raising "the additional number of regular recruits required at once for the Army." Only gradually was it made clear that the desired "addition of 100,000 men to His Majesty's Regular Army" had nothing to do with the Territorial Force, which was not to be responsible for their clothing or equipment, nor with the existing cadres of the Army, but was an entirely new army altogether.

As for the Territorial Force itself, it was not to recruit over its establishment until the 100,000 men were forthcoming. Individuals were to be permitted to transfer into the new Armies, but the Force was not asked to volunteer *en masse* for foreign service. In a circular opening with a phrase which was later to become only too familiar—" there seems to be a certain amount of misunderstanding "— Lord Kitchener desired the County Associations to divide the Force into two categories, those able and willing to serve abroad and those precluded " on account of their affairs "

from volunteering. By August 26, 69 whole battalions had volunteered. The first Territorial regiment to be in the firing line was the Northumberland Yeomanry, which was in action with the 7th Division on October 12.

Considerable difference of opinion existed in military circles as to the wisdom of Lord Kitchener's method of creating "his" army. Many eminent officers, including Lord Roberts, considered that he would have been better advised if he had merely expanded the Territorial Force, the cadres of which would have provided a ready-made organization, and which, without any serious dislocation, would, while retaining its existing character, have been enabled continually to throw off fresh divisions for service abroad.

For whatever reason, the public was some time in realizing exactly what the official appeal meant. Thus another " misunderstanding " had to be disposed of by a War Office announcement, which ran as follows :

It has been freely stated in the Press during the last few days that " Lord Kitchener's new army of 100,000 men is to be trained for home defence." This is totally incorrect. Lord Kitchener's new army of 100,000 men is enlisted for general service at home and abroad, and when trained to the proper standard of efficiency will be employed wherever their (*sic*) services may be most required.

[Russell.

LORD DERBY,
Director-General of Recruiting.

[Elliott & Fry.

MR. ARTHUR HENDERSON,
Chairman Joint Labour Recruiting Committee.

A considerable, though not a very remarkable, increase of recruiting followed immediately on the Government's appeal. The country was in no sense awake. Long years of peaceful prosperity had produced a frame of mind not easily to be moved, even by the advertising campaign, as gigantic as it was humiliating, which was subsequently set on foot by the joint Parliamentary Recruiting Committee created, at the suggestion of the War Office, on August 31. More than a year, indeed, was to elapse before the mass of the people can be said to have become alive to its

responsibilities. Meanwhile there were many circumstances which tended to abate the early flush of enthusiasm. Apart from the general ignorance of what was happening, due to the misguided obscurantism which from the first characterised the Government's attitude towards the public, the difficulties and discouragements which faced those whose only wish was to serve their country could not fail to have an unfortunate result. Owing to the complete unpreparedness of the War Office for dealing with the flood of recruits—an unpreparedness which, in itself perfectly natural in

[Swaine.

MR. JOHN W. GULLAND,
Joint Chairman, Parliamentary Recruiting Committee.

[Elliott & Fry.

GENERAL SIR HENRY MACKINNON.

LORD SYDENHAM, G.C.M.G.
(Chairman).

MR. CYRIL JACKSON

view of the fact that it was now receiving as many recruits in a week as it had been accustomed to receive in a year, was infinitely accentuated by its incapacity to shake itself free from the trammels of red tape which in peace time checked initiative in every direction —the mere process of enrolment was compassed about by fatuous routine. In those days the practice of merely attesting men and allowing them to return to their civilian occupations until needed found no acceptance with the authorities. Hence the men, after they had succeeded in enlisting, were huddled together, often in the most insanitary conditions.

and, devoid of uniforms, rifles and equipment, were set to make the best they could of circumstances of which the only redeeming feature was their own inextinguishable zeal.

An officer of the new army, himself a member of one of the learned professions, has given a lively description * of the difficulties which had to be overcome. He believes, he says, that his battalion, which was formed about September, 1914, and belonged to the second new army, started with three officers, one a young

* *The New Army in the Making.* By an Officer. London : Kegan Paul.

SIR GEORGE YOUNGER,
M.P.

MR. G. J. TALBOT,
K.C.

SIR FRANCIS GORE,
K.C.B.

COMMISSIONERS OF CENTRAL APPEAL TRIBUNAL.

THE MAGIC PIPES: HIGHLAND PIPERS' RECRUITING MARCH IN LONDON.

Regular, and two straight from the Officers Training Corps. Upon them fell the duty, one wet night, of receiving about a thousand recruits, nearly all quite raw, who were deposited by train at the depôt:

> There were about 45 to 50 tents ready, but there were no blankets, practically no arrangements for cooking, and the new recruits had nothing but their civilian clothes and their enthusiasm. Think of it, you who have managed a big office or factory, you who have organized political campaigns or governed schools and colleges! A thousand miscellaneous, unknown men, from every class in society, from a hundred different trades, a hundred different towns and villages, of whom a mere handful had the least conception of military discipline, and all of whom were glowing with the rather hectic enthusiasm of patriotic self-sacrifice, and with the belief that they were at once to set about killing Germans. . . .
> In late autumn and winter it rained—cats and dogs—and round the tin huts which had taken the place of the original tents the trampled earth turned into loose mud a foot deep, with eccentric watercourses and oozy ponds which made the camp intolerable.

No praise can be too high for those who, in these miserable circumstances, stuck to their work with patriotic fervour. It is in conditions such as these that the spirit of the voluntary system finds its highest expression. In spite of the many unsatisfactory features—amounting in some cases to a pressure lacking little of compulsion but the name—which were to characterize the final efforts of the voluntary system, it must always be remembered that this spirit enabled the men who enlisted during the early period of the war to endure without grumbling hardships such as no army recruited under compulsory service would be called upon to bear. England would have lasting cause to be proud of these gallant fellows, even if they had never proved their merit in the field.

On August 12 Lord Kitchener announced that the response to his appeal " had enabled him to decide on and define the framework to be employed and to make all the necessary arrangements for the infantry training." (Curiously enough, this important decision, which was essential to the proper distribution of the troops, seemed to have been postponed until after, instead of preceding, their enlistment.) Six divisions were to be formed, each consisting of three brigades, the battalions of which, as was announced five days later, were to be additional battalions of the regiments of the line, with numbers following consecutively on the existing battalions of their regiments. These divisions were to be known as the Scottish, the Irish, the Northern, the Western, the Eastern and the Light Division. The Irish Division, consisting entirely of Irishmen, was to be stationed at the Curragh, the Western

Division on Salisbury Plain, the Eastern at Shorncliffe, the Scottish and Light Divisions at Aldershot. The station of the Northern Division was still " under consideration."

By August 25 Lord Kitchener was able to inform the House of Lords, on his first appearance as a Minister of the Crown, that the 100,000 recruits had been " already practically secured." He added a note of warning:

> I cannot at this stage say what will be the limits of the forces required, or what measures may eventually become necessary to supply and maintain them. The scale of the Field Army which we are now calling into being is large and may rise in the course of the next six or seven months to a total of 30 divisions continually maintained in the field. But if the war should be pro-

THE NATIONAL REGISTRATION.
Officials instructing the heads of families how to fill up the forms.

tracted, and if its fortunes should be varied or adverse, exertions and sacrifices beyond any which have been demanded will be required from the whole nation and Empire, and where they are required we are sure they will not be denied to the extreme needs of the State by Parliament or the people.

In commenting on Lord Kitchener's speech, *The Times* pointed out that, proud as we might be of the national spirit, the rest of the nation had no right to shelter itself behind the sacrifices of those who, at the call of duty, had left their businesses and homes to face, if need be, the issues of life and death. It urged that the age limit of thirty was too low, and that the Continental nations were calling up men many years older. It further drew attention to the vast numbers of young men who might serve

M. Marcel Samett, a French soldier from the trenches; Sir Peter Stewart Bam and Miss Katie Botha, C. W. Neimeyer, of the
APPEALING FOR RECRUITS IN

but who preferred to loaf at home "attending cricket matches and going to the cinema—in short, the great army of shirkers," and summed up by declaring:

It is a national scandal that the selfish should get off scot free while all the burden falls on the most public-spirited section of our available manhood; and if the voluntary system can do no better it will have to be changed.

The fact of the matter was that, although the men who were coming forward were the

IN TRAFALGAR SQUARE.
Answering the call.

pick of the nation, both in physical fitness and in *moral*, the maintenance of the supply of recruits, in view of the greatness of the emergency, could not fail to arouse serious misgivings. A strong feeling in favour of compulsory service began to manifest itself in those organs of the Press which were unaffected by party shibboleths. For the prevailing ignorance which led, for example, to the impression that, because the Government had asked for 100,000 men, only 100,000 were required, the Government alone was to blame. The columns of *The Times* at this period teemed with suggestions from correspondents for the enlightenment of the country. The majority of these were carried out in the course of the next fifteen months, but at the moment they were curtly dismissed by the Government whenever questions relating to them were asked in the House. Mr. Asquith, asked on August 26 whether the Government intended to introduce a measure for compulsory service, replied that the answer was in the negative, and referred the inquirers to Lord Kitchener's speech.

On August 28 the first 100,000 men had apparently been obtained, for the following appeal for another contingent of the same size was issued:

YOUR KING AND YOUR COUNTRY NEED YOU.
ANOTHER 100,000 MEN WANTED.

Lord Kitchener is much gratified with the response already made to the appeal for additional men for His Majesty's Regular Army.

niece of General Botha; Mlle. Marie Somers, a Belgian Red Cross Nurse from Antwerp; Sergeant
First Canadian Contingent.

TRAFALGAR SQUARE, LONDON.

In the grave National emergency that now confronts
the Empire, he asks with renewed confidence that
another 100,000 men will now come forward.

TERMS OF SERVICE.
(*Extension of Age Limit.*)

Age of Enlistment, 19 to 35 ; Ex-Soldiers up to 45
and certain selected ex-Non-Commissioned Officers up
to 50. Height, 5 ft. 3 in. and upwards. Chest, 34 inches
at least. Must be medically fit.

General service for the war.

Men enlisting for the duration of the war will be
discharged with all convenient speed at the conclusion
of the war.

PAY AT ARMY RATES

and Married Men or Widowers with Children will be
accepted and will draw Separation Allowance under
Army conditions.

It will be noticed that the age limit was
now raised to thirty-five. Attention may also
be drawn to the appeal to married men.

On the same day Mr. Asquith, moved at
last by the mass of evidence supplied by the
Press as to the ignorance and indifference of
the country, informed the Lord Mayor of
London, the Lord Provost of Edinburgh, and
the Lord Mayors of Dublin and Cardiff that
" the time has now come for combined effort
to stimulate and organize public opinion and
public effort in the greatest conflict in which
our people has ever been engaged." He proposed, as a first step, that meetings should be
held throughout the United Kingdom " at
which the justice of our cause should be made
plain, and the duty of every man to do his part
should be enforced."

The campaign was inaugurated by an
invigorating meeting on September 4 at the
Guildhall, when Mr. Asquith made a stirring
speech, and was followed by Mr. Bonar Law,
Mr. Balfour and Mr. Winston Churchill.

Whether as the result of the campaign thus
set on foot, which rapidly spread throughout
the country, or, as is more probable, of the
publication of a list of nearly 5,000 casualties
and the return of wounded from the front,
the second 100,000 was enlisted far more

IN TRAFALGAR SQUARE.
Swearing-in a Recruit.

VETERANS AS RECRUITING SERGEANTS.
A Crimean hero addressing a meeting at the village pump in a village in Somerset.
Inset: A Chelsea pensioner shaking hands with a new recruit in London.

in London revealed groups of men who had been waiting their turn for six or eight hours.

The attitude of the trade unionist leaders at this juncture was illustrated by a manifesto issued on September 3 by the Parliamentary Committee of the Trade Union Congress. After expressing gratitude for the manner in which the Labour Party in the House of Commons had responded to the appeal made to all political parties "to give their co-operation in securing the enlistment of men to defend the interests of their country," the manifesto declared the conviction of the Committee

That in the event of the voluntary system of military service failing the country in its time of need, the demand for a national system of compulsory military service will not only be made with redoubled vigour but may prove to be so persistent and strong as to become irresistible. The prospect of having to face conscription, with its permanent and heavy burden upon the financial resources of the country, and its equally burdensome effect upon nearly the whole of its industries, should in itself stimulate the manhood of the country to come forward in its defence, and thereby demonstrate to the world that a free people can rise to the supreme heights of a great sacrifice without the whip of conscription. . . .

The mere contemplation of the overbearing and brutal methods to which people have to submit under a Government controlled by a military autocracy—living as it

rapidly than the first. The following figures for the London area were published:

August 26	...	1,725	August 31	...	1,620
„ 27	...	1,650	September 1	...	4,600
„ 28	...	1,780	„ 2	...	4,100
„ 29	...	1,800	„ 3	...	3,600
„ 30	...	1,928	„ 4	...	4,028

The physical difficulty of enlisting still remained. A visit to several recruiting stations

were, continuously under the threat and shadow of war —should be sufficient to arouse the enthusiasm of the nation in resisting any attempt to impose similar conditions upon countries at present free from military despotism.

Only a cynic or a neutral could find fault with this characteristic expression of the Englishman's love of freedom. The remainder of the manifesto was equally characteristic, for it drew the attention of the Government to the necessity of its taking, in return for the performance of the citizen's duty, "a liberal and even generous view of its responsibilities towards those citizens who come forward to assist in the defence of their country." The basis of this appeal for generous treatment of recruits, "not so much for themselves as for those who are dependent upon them," rested doubtless on the Englishman's natural love of home and family, which he shrinks from leaving unless he is assured that "they will be looked after when he is gone." And it is certain that many hesitated to come forward from uncertainty as to what might happen to those dependent on them. The necessity, under the voluntary

BRIGADIER-GENERAL OWEN THOMAS (On right) with Mr. Lloyd George. General Thomas, who raised many Welsh battalions, was charged with the duty of raising a Welsh Army under Lord Derby's scheme.

system, of rendering the duty of serving the State less unpalatable, as it were, to those who undertake what, under compulsory service, is regarded as a privilege is none the less extravagant because it is inevitable.*

Meanwhile, in spite of the inability of many employers to realize that the best way of promoting their own interests was to contribute men to win the war—an obstacle to recruiting so great that it called forth from Lord Kitchener a special appeal—and in spite of defects in organization which even the Under-Secretary of State for War had to admit to the House of Commons, the flow of men henceforth

CAPT. SIR HERBERT RAPHAEL, M.P.

Who joined the Sportsman Battalion as a private. He was engaged in raising the 18th Battalion of the King's Royal Rifles.

* The separation allowance granted by the regulations at this period of the war was 7s. 7d. a week to the wife and 1s. 2d. a week for each girl under 16 and each boy under 14 years of age. Towards this a minimum of 3s. 6d. a week was contributed by the soldier from his pay.

OUTSIDE THE TOWN HALL, JOHANNESBURG.
South Africa's call for recruits for German East Africa, and France.

for a time increased. On September 10 Mr. Asquith, in asking the House to sanction an increase of the Army by another 500,000 men, stated that, up to the evening of the previous day, " the number of recruits who have enlisted in the Army since the declaration of war— that is, exclusive of those who have joined the Territorial Force, is 438,000, practically 439,000." These figures, as also that of 33,204, which was given as the total enlisted in the United Kingdom in one day (September 3), were accepted with complacency. But Mr. Asquith hastened to add :

> We do not think the time has come when we ought in any way to relax our recruiting efforts, and when people tell me, as they do every day, " These recruits are coming in by tens of thousands ; you are being blocked by them, and you cannot provide adequately either for their equipment or for their training," my answer is, " We shall want more rather than less ; let us get the men. That is the first necessity of the State—let us get the men." Knowing, as we all do, the patriotic spirit which always—now, of course. in increased emphasis and enthusiasm—animates every class of the community, I am perfectly certain they will be ready to endure hardships and discomforts for the moment, if they are satisfied that their services are really required by the State, and that in due course of time they will be supplied with adequate provision for training and equipment and for rendering themselves fit for service in the field.

The Prime Minister further announced that men who had been attested, and for whom there was no accommodation, were henceforth to be allowed to return home until needed, at 3s. a day. The question of separation allowances was " receiving our daily and constant attention."

Lord Derby had proposed the same day that the separation allowances given in the footnote on page 293 should be raised to 10s. 6d. and 4s. 8d. respectively. Meanwhile, *The Times* urged that payments should be made weekly instead of monthly, as being more compatible with the regular habits and customs of the people. This very desirable reform was put into force on October 1.

So " blocked " with recruits were the military authorities becoming, that on September 11 the height standard for all men other than ex-soldiers enlisting in the infantry of the line was raised to 5 feet 6 inches. This step, however necessary it may have appeared to the over-burdened War Office, had an unfortunate moral effect, for it produced the impression that more men were not really needed after all.

At this moment was announced the composition of the various armies into which the original first new Army had been expanded. It was as follows:

	New Army.
9th to 14th Divisions and Army Troops ...	1st
15th to 20th Divisions and Army Troops ...	2nd
21st to 26th Divisions and Army Troops ...	3rd
27th to 32nd Divisions, of which the infantry were to be selected from the duplicated Reserve Battalions	4th

The formation of a 5th and 6th new army was announced on January 2, 1915.

All this looked beautiful on paper, but, as the Military Correspondent of *The Times* pointed out, we did not possess armies simply because we possessed men:

Good officers, good N.C.O.'s, guns, rifles and ammunition wagons take time to provide, and without a good nucleus of trained professional officers and N.C.O.'s the creation of efficient troops is extremely arduous. . . . There can be little doubt that, so long as the country is in its present mood, we shall be able to raise a million men a year, and gradually to fashion them into a formidable fighting force. But we must not minimize the time needed for creating such a force. An officer, a N.C.O., a gun, a rifle, and a thousand rounds of ammunition all take a certain time to turn out, and nothing but disappointment can ensue if we think that we can do in six months what has taken Germany half a century of effort.

By September 15 the number of recruits raised since August 4 was reported to be 501,580, England having produced 396,751, or 2·41 per cent. of the male population; Scotland, 64,444, or 2·79 per cent.; Ireland, 20,419, or 0·93 per cent.; and Wales, 19,966, or 1·94 per cent.

A SOLDIER ARTIST
Who was wounded at the battle of Ypres busily engaged designing posters for the recruiting campaign.

Mr. Asquith was enthusiastically received in Ireland and Wales on his visiting those parts of the kingdom for the purpose of stimulating the formation in each of a special Army Corps.

TRAINING.
Troops returning from a route march.

RECRUITS AT WHITEHALL.
Marching from the Recruiting Office to the railway station.

Inset : Waiting to be attested.

Nevertheless, by the end of October, 1914, the position with regard to recruiting had begun to cause anxiety to the authorities. The Recruiting Department issued an appeal in which young men were "reminded" that adequate arrangements for accommodation had been made, that steps had been taken to ensure the prompt payment of separation allowance, that the minimum height for recruits had been reduced to the normal standard of 5 ft. 4 in., except for those units for which special standards had been authorized, and that the age limit had been raised to 38, and, in the case of ex-soldiers, to 45. A fortnight later the height standard was again reduced—to 5 ft. 3 in. At this period London was producing an average of only 1,000 recruits a day, Glasgow about 100, Leeds fewer than 40. Recruiting was undoubtedly hanging fire. Men were, it is true, still joining the Territorial Force and various specialized and unofficial corps in fair numbers, but uncertainty as to the Government's intentions with regard to separation allowances and pensions, combined with local prosperity,

the lack of arms and uniforms, and a general failure to "realize the war," had brought recruiting for "Kitchener's Army" to a low ebb.

Mr. Asquith had announced on September 17 that the following new scale of separation allowances would be adopted :—

	NEW SCALE		OLD SCALE	
	s.	d.	s.	d.
Wife *	12	6	11	1
Wife and 1 child	15	0	12	10
Wife and 2 children	17	6	14	7
Wife and 3 children	20	0	16	4
Wife and 4 children	22	0	17	6

* New Scale. whether " on the strength " or not ; Old Scale, " on the strength " only.

These allowances, as already mentioned, were to be payable weekly through the Post office as from October 1.

As for pensions, it was not until November 10 that a new scale was issued. It showed the following increases in respect of the lowest grade of the Service :—

	NEW SCALE		OLD SCALE	
	s.	d.	s.	d.
Widow without children ...	7	6	5	0
Widow with 1 child	12	6	6	6
Widow with 2 children ...	15	0	8	0
Widow with 3 children ...	17	6	9	6
Widow with 4 children ...	20	0	11	0
Motherless children	5	0	3	0
	(each child up to 3, and 4s. each additional child)		(each child)	

TOTAL DISABLEMENT   14s. to 23s.   10s. 6d. to 17s. 6d.
PARTIAL DISABLEMENT 3s. 6d. to 17s. 6d. 3s. 6d. to 10s. 6d.

Writing on November 7, The Times, in discussing the remedies needed to improve recruiting, insisted upon the absolute necessity of a fuller and more adequate supply of news from the front, so far as was consistent with military requirements:

Our Allies in the west do not need this incentive, for the meaning of the war and its horrors is visible to the eyes of their people. The French and Belgians do not require to be told, but our people do. The Press does not urge this view in its own interest, but in the interest of the Allied cause. If France needs more help, as she does, she must let us raise that help in our own way, by showing our people the character of a war which France can see and our people cannot. . . . The Allies must make their choice. They can give the news and get the men, or they can suppress the news and do without the men. . . .

The next remedy lies in the adoption of clearer, more systematic, and more far-seeing methods at the War Office in obtaining recruits and in handling them when enlisted. We are not in the least attacking the War Office, for we consider that it has accomplished marvels, and done far more than the country had any right to expect. The machinery, however, is still inadequate for the enormous demands likely to be made upon it in the next few months, and it should summon to its aid all the best available lay help for this gigantic task of getting more and still more new armies. . . . Above all the Government have got to make up their minds instantly on the subject of pay, separation allowances, pensions and widows' pensions.

Nearly a year was to elapse before, as will be seen (pp. 306–310), the wisdom of this advice to put the business of recruiting in civilian hands was recognized by the Government. *The Times* once more urged the importance of merely attesting recruits and then allowing them to continue their ordinary

RECRUITING FOR THE ROYAL NAVAL DIVISION.

vocations, at Army rates of pay, until they were required. This also was to prove one of the most popular features of Lord Derby's scheme a twelve-month later. Meanwhile the Press of the whole country teemed with discussions

RECRUITING MARCH IN LONDON.
The 24th Middlesex, outside St. Paul's. appeal for 500 new recruits.

CAPTURED WAR TROPHIES WHICH ATTRACTED RECRUITS.

German guns from Loos on view at the Horse Guards Parade, St. James's Park.
Centre picture: New recruits marching across the Parade.

THE RECRUITING CAMPAIGN.

An anti-aircraft gun in the Lord Mayor's Procession in London, November, 1915.

of the desirability or otherwise of compulsory service. The whole of the London district on October 6 yielded only 500 recruits as compared with the high-water mark of over 5,000 in one day in September. Three days later a remarkable illustration of the soundness of the view that the sluggish English mind needs the stimulant of pageantry and music to lift it out of its peaceful groove was to be seen in the effect upon recruiting of the Lord Mayor's show, a naval and military spectacle which aroused the greatest enthusiasm. More men joined the colours in London on that day than on any one day since the rush which followed the outbreak of war. Throughout the country, too, a considerable improvement was perceptible. The issue on November 10 of the new scale of pensions and allowances (see p. 296) no doubt contributed largely to this satisfactory result.

It is needless to repeat the description already given in Vol. V., page 295, of the expedients which were tried during the following months, and which soon tended to resemble compulsion while avoiding either the justice or the effectiveness of that method of recruiting. On November 9, at the Guildhall Banquet, Lord Kitchener had said that he had no complaints whatever to make about the response to his appeal for men, and a week later Mr.

NEW RECRUITS AT THE HORSE GUARDS PARADE.

Asquith, in asking the House of Commons to sanction the increase of the army by another 1,000,000 men, announced that not less than 700,000 recruits had joined the colours since the beginning of the war, not including those in the Territorial Force. But for a time at least the most successful recruiter was the enemy. Such incidents, for example, as the bombardment of Scarborough never failed to produce an instantaneous rush of recruits. But, as *The Times* pointed out, there was a danger lest the presence of more recruits than could conveniently be dealt with at the moment should blind the Government to the necessity of looking forward to the time when the last half-million men should be needed to turn the scale. The Government suppressed recruiting returns and was adamantine in its refusal to discuss the matter, but Lord Haldane, while declaring that the Government saw no reason to anticipate the breakdown of the voluntary system, reminded the House of Lords (on January 8) of the truism that compulsory service was not foreign to the constitution of the

AFTER THE LUSITANIA OUTRAGE.

country, and that in a great national emergency it might become necessary to resort to it. His utterances raised a great outcry in that part of the Press which was opposed on principle to compulsion, but a little reflection might have suggested that the establishment of compulsory service was not in any case conceivable without the consent of Parliament.

On March 1 Mr. Asquith declared that the Government had no reason to be otherwise than satisfied with the progress of recruiting. But before the month was out it became abundantly evident that the whole matter was in an unhealthy state of muddle.

The official attitude appeared to betray a lack of courage and frankness and a nervous unwillingness to face the situation boldly. All that the Government could produce was a

series of vague and humiliating appeals, tempered by speech-making "campaigns" in London and elsewhere, the success of which was largely due to some timely Zeppelin raids and the news of hard fighting round Ypres. Meanwhile the disproportionate enlistment of married as compared with unmarried men continued to be a reproach upon the justice of the voluntary system.

A remarkable speech by Lord Derby at Manchester on April 27 aroused the public, by this time growing weary of the recruiting clamour, to the realization of the over-optimism of the Government. Mr. Lloyd George had said that Lord Kitchener was satisfied with the rate of recruiting. In Lord Derby's opinion, he was perfectly justified in saying that he was satisfied for the moment, but that did not mean that recruiting could not and ought not to be increased. Lord Derby announced that he had Lord Kitchener's authority for saying that he asked that the recruiting efforts should be maintained and that "the time would come —sooner, perhaps, than most people expected— when he would ask for additional and redoubled efforts." That seemed to Lord Derby to mean that "in a very short time they would have made to them an appeal to which none of them would be able to say nay. He thought that there would be a compulsory demand on the services of this country."

On May 18, Lord Kitchener appealed in the

SERGEANT O'LEARY, V.C.,
Who took part in a recruiting campaign organised by the United Irish League of Great Britain, appealing for recruits in Hyde Park.   Inset : Sergeant O'Leary with Mr. T. P. O'Connor, M.P., on the way to the meeting.

A LONDON V.C. AS RECRUITER.

Lance-Corporal E. Dwyer of the East Surrey Regiment, in London on a few days' leave, addressing a meeting in Trafalgar Square.

Inset: Lance-Corporal Dwyer (centre).

House of Lords for 300,000 more recruits, and next day the age limit was raised to 40 and the height standard reduced to 5 ft. 2 in A month later *The Times* published a prophetic letter from Lord Milner :

The State [he wrote] ought not to be obliged to tout for fighting men. It ought to be in a position to call out the number it wants as and when it wants them, and to call them out in the right order—the younger before the older, the unmarried before the married, the men whose greatest value is as soldiers in preference to those who can contribute more to the successful conduct of the war in a civilian capacity, as makers of munitions, transport workers, tillers of the soil or what not. . . .

The present call for another 300,000—any men, just those who choose to listen to it—may succeed or it may fail. If it succeeds, it will still be, like previous levies of the same kind, needlessly disorganizing and wasteful. Many men will go who would be far more use at home than others who will not go. The unfairness of leaving it to individual intelligence or good will to decide who is to bear the burden will become increasingly evident and disturbing to the public mind. And how about the next 300,000 and the next after that ? . . .

The way we are at present going on is unfair to everybody. It is unfair to our splendid men at the front and our gallant Allies. But it is unfair, also, to thousands of men at home, who are unjustly denounced as " slackers," or " cowards," when they are simply ignorant, or bewildered—and who might not be bewildered between the alternating screams for help and pæans of victory ?—or sorely puzzled to choose between conflicting duties. . .

Amid the controversies involved in the formation of the Coalition Government, Mr. Lloyd George, now Minister of Munitions, was alone among members of the Cabinet in speaking out courageously on the subject of compulsory service. At Manchester, on June 3, he informed a meeting of engineers that he had come to tell them the truth. " Unless you know it," he said, as *The Times* had been saying for months past, " you cannot be expected to make sacrifices." Arguing that " conscription " was a question not of principle, but of necessity, he declared, amid cheers, that if the necessity arose he was certain that no man of any party would protest :

" But," he added, " pray don't talk about it as if it were anti-democratic. We won and saved our liberties in this land on more than one occasion by compulsory service. France saved the liberty she had won in the great Revolution from the fangs of tyrannical military empires purely by compulsory service ; the great Republic of the West won its independence and saved its national existence by compulsory service ; and two of the countries of Europe to-day—France and Italy—are defending their national existence and liberties by means of compulsory service. It has been the greatest weapon in the hands of Democracy many a time for the winning and preservation of freedom."

But henceforth, until mid-September, the country was too much occupied with the urgent need for munitions to remember that, as Lord Milner reminded it, " if there was one thing which the war ought to have taught, it was that you have to look ahead, and that you cannot afford to think only of one thing at a time." Six or nine months hence, he added—and his prophecy was to be fulfilled even sooner than he thought—the deficiency of material might have been made good and the great cry once more be for men.

Before the end of June the Government was to recognize the truth which, although pressed upon it from divers quarters, it had hitherto persistently ignored—namely, that the first step towards making the best use of the national resources in men was to discover what men were available. The National Registration Bill, introduced on June 29, and described in Vol. V., page 317, although it abstained from asking for a good deal of the information which the authorities in Continental countries require as a matter of course from every citizen, enabled the Government to take stock of the adult population from the point of view of occupation, warlike or otherwise. " When this registration is completed," said Lord Kitchener

PACKING UNIFORMS FOR THE NEW ARMIES.

at the Guildhall on July 9, " we shall, anyhow, be able to note the men between the ages of 19 and 40 not required for munition or other necessary industrial work, and therefore available, if physically fit, for the fighting line. Steps will be taken to approach, with a view to enlistment, all possible candidates for the Army —unmarried men to be preferred before married men, as far as may be."

With this object returns of men between the ages of 19 and 41 were copied upon so-called " pink " forms for the use of the military authorities, while men engaged on Government work or in essential war industries were " starred " as exempt from the attentions of the recruiting officers. The use of these " pink" forms, and the haphazard principles on which " starring " was carried out, were immediately and, as was clear to detached observers, inevitably to lead to extreme dissatisfaction with War Office methods. This dissatisfaction culminated on the publication (October 5) of a War Office circular of September 30 instructing recruiting officers to " take whatever steps considered most effectual " to induce unstarred men to join the Army. Officers were further enjoined to see " that no unstarred man is able to complain any longer that he is not wanted in the Army as ' he has not been fetched,' " and to report the number of unstarred men who " refuse to give their services to the country by enlisting in the Army, where they are so much needed." So great was the feeling caused by the commencement of this military canvass that it was immediately abandoned.

The number of " starred " occupations, which were at first confined to munition work, Admiralty work, coal mining, railway work, and certain branches of agriculture, tended as time went on to show a very remarkable increase, and undoubtedly led to much " shirking " disguised under the form of engagement in essential industries. It seems quite certain that an enormous number of unmarried men entered " starred " trades with the object of escaping enlistment. There can be no doubt that a far more satisfactory plan would have been to have " starred " individuals without regard to their occupation, but it was probably felt that this task, which in other countries is deliberately performed in peace time, was too extensive to be attempted amid the improvisations of war. Trades, therefore, were " starred " as a whole, and it was not until the abuses of the system became flagrant

THE DERBY RECRUITS.

A great army of British recruits who had enlisted under the group scheme which came to a close on Sunday evening, Dec. 12, 1915. Everywhere the rush of recruits taxed the capacities of the various officers to the utmost. Armlets of khaki cloth bearing a crown cut out of scarlet cloth were served out to all those who had attested.

that the restoration to the " unstarred " list of men who, by the fact of their belonging to " starred " trades, had been " starred " themselves, but who could be shown, nevertheless, not to be essential to those trades, was undertaken by a subsequent and painful process of extraction. By the end of December the list of so-called " reserved occupations " numbered several hundreds, divided into innumerable sub-occupations. With regard to most of these it was clear that they were of vital importance to the proper carrying on of the essential industries of the country. What remained to be made clear was the importance to any of them of any individual man—at all events, so far as the unskilled ranks of labour were concerned.

CAPT. WILLIAM SHORT,
The King's Trumpeter, sounding the "Fall In."

Meanwhile, abundant expressions of support were forthcoming for a National Service movement, summed up in the comprehensive sentence : " Every fit man, whatever his position in life, must be made available, as and when his country calls him, for the fighting line, or, if specially qualified, for national service at home."

It was announced on September 6 that a Committee had been appointed, under the chairmanship of Lord Lansdowne, to advise the Government on the best method of utilizing the National Register " for the successful prosecution of the war." A Cabinet Committee, under the presidency of Lord Crewe, had been sitting during the Parliamentary recess for the purpose of eliciting information as to our military requirements in men. It was understood that the majority had reported that the only decision possible was the introduction of a comprehensive system of national service. Mr. Asquith, adroitly postponing the matter until the last half-minute of a speech in the House of Commons on September 14, permitted himself to raise a laugh by observing that National Service was " a matter which has not escaped

the attention of his Majesty's Government." He added that when the Government, without undue delay, with as much deliberation as the gravity of the subject demanded, arrived at their conclusions, they would present them to the House, and they would become the subject of Parliamentary discussion. During this period, those who urged the Government to make up their minds were commonly represented as desiring to impair " the unity of the country." Such are the trivial catchwords with which English politicians faced the greatest war in history.

On the following day, however, Mr. Asquith made an important statement in which he declared the total numbers in the Navy and Army (including those already serving when the war began, the reservists summoned back to duty in both services, the Territorial Force, and the various special services formed for military and naval purposes) to be " not far short of three millions of men." As for the recruiting, it had kept up for 13 months at " a fairly steady figure," though he regretted that the last few weeks had shown signs of falling off. Lord Kitchener, in the House of Lords, considerably amplified this statement. While, as he said, the response of the country to calls

RECRUITING FOR THE ROYAL NAVAL
AIR SERVICE.

r recruits had been "little short of marvel-
us," he pointed out that the provision of men
maintain the forces in the field depended in
reat degree on a large and continuous supply
recruits, and added : "The provision to
ep up their strength during 1916 has caused
s anxious thought, which has been accentuated
nd rendered more pressing by the recent
lling off in the numbers coming forward to
nlist, although every effort has been made to
btain our requirements under the present
ystems." He very properly closed with the
emark that, though recruiting had declined,
e did not "draw from this fact any conclusion
nfavourable to the resolution and spirit of the
ountry."

The world had yet to learn the full truth
egarding the response to Lord Kitchener's
ppeals. In the absence of figures, which,
vith the idea of misleading the enemy, were
ept strictly concealed, it was impossible to
ay exactly what was the strength of the
ew Armies in the autumn of 1915. But it
vas known in many quarters that the men
eeded to maintain existing and authorised

formations were not being secured, and as the
year went on the situation went from bad to
worse. Sir Edward Carson was subsequently
to show in the House of Commons (December
21) that three of our divisions in the East
which should have numbered 36,000 infantry
were reduced to 11,000 men, or in other words
that we had failed to make good by drafts the
wastage of war in the field. And on the following day Colonel Yate showed that a certain
Second Line Territorial division in England,
due for the front in March, 1916, had only
4,800 infantry in place of its proper 12,000
men.

The total difference between the establishments and the strengths of the Army was
undoubtedly exceedingly serious, and whatever
the actual numbers may have been, it was clear
that affairs were approaching a climax. In spite
of the Prime Minister's appeals for silence, the
House of Commons continued to discuss the
matter with great energy. On September 30 a
statement was issued by a conference of the
Parliamentary Committee of the Trades Union
Congress, the Management Committee of the
General Federation of Trade Unions, the Execu-

RECRUITING IN EDINBURGH.
New Recruits for the 9th Royal Scots in their uniforms.

tive of the Labour Party and members of the Parliamentary Labour Party, in which the conference pledged itself " to assist the Government in every possible way to secure men for service in the Navy, Army, and in munitions works," and for this purpose decided to organize a special Labour recruiting campaign throughout the country. Great " recruiting rallies " were held in London and elsewhere on October 2, and the following days, but the results were meagre in the extreme. The time had come to try new methods and a new man.

The next phase opened with the announcement, on October 6, of the appointment of Lord Derby as Director of Recruiting. Although himself an advocate of national service, Lord Derby had for ten years past done perhaps more than anyone to make the voluntary system a success. A typical Englishman in his straightforwardness and sincerity, Lord Derby had shown himself to possess a remarkable combination of qualities which might well have been utilized long before. His own position and ardent patriotism stood above question. He had an intimate knowledge of the great industrial centres in the North. He was businesslike and immensely industrious. His appointment was hailed with general satis-

faction, not only on account of his personal popularity, but because it was felt to be an advantage that the preliminary work of securing recruits should be in civilian hands, leaving the War Office free to concentrate upon the work of training them after they had been secured.

Forthwith the Labour Recruiting Committee issued an appeal stating that " the responsibility for victory or defeat rests with those who have not yet responded to the call," and declaring that " if the voluntary system is to be vindicated at least 30,000 recruits per week must be raised to maintain the efficiency of our armies." So far as can be seen, this figure only represented *infantry* needs. About 35,000 men per week were really required to keep up existing formations.

On October 15 Lord Derby outlined his scheme* in considerable detail. Starting with the general principle that recruiting should in future be done entirely by civilians, instead of, as in the past, by the military authorities with civilian assistance, Lord Derby explained that the chief responsibility would rest with the

* Lord Derby subsequently explained that the scheme was the work of three Lancashire men—the Secretary to the Territorial Association, and two candidates for Parliament, Unionist and Liberal respectively.

A CAPTURED GERMAN AEROPLANE BEING SET UP ON THE HORSE GUARDS PARADE.

AT THE HORSE GUARDS PARADE.
Recruits answering to their Names.
Inset: Leaving the Horse Guards Parade.

Parliamentary Recruiting Committee and the
Joint Labour Recruiting Committee.   In every
area a local committee, whether already existing
or to be formed, would undertake the work of
canvassing, availing itself of the services of
the political agents of all parties.   A letter
would be sent to every " unstarred " man in
order that he might have a direct appeal and
be unable to say in future that he was not called
upon to join.   The canvass would continue
until November 30.

In a letter to *The Times Recruiting Supple-
ment*, published on November 3, Lord Derby
wrote :

"My conception of an ideal recruiting campaign is to get as many men to enlist under the
voluntary system as would have to come under
a compulsory one.   I have always urged that
it is the duty of every man in this crisis to offer
his services to the State, and for the State
definitely to allot him his position, whether it
be in some branch of his Majesty's forces or in
the munition works, or in one of the indispensable
industries of this country, or even as an indispensable person in a private business.   But it
must be the State and not the individual which
decides a man's proper place in the machinery

of the country.   I hope by the present scheme
not only to ascertain what is each man's right
position, but to induce him voluntarily to take
it.   But before this can be done a man must
actually enlist, not merely promise to do so.
By enlisting men in groups, only to come up
when called upon, and allowing them before
actually joining to appeal to local tribunals to
be put in later groups for reasons which can be
specially urged, we shall be able to allot proper
places to all men in the ' unstarred ' list.   Then
we must carefully examine the whole of the
' starred ' list, and where we find a man
wrongly placed in that list, or a man who,
though rightly placed in it, can be spared

AN INDIAN OFFICER
Addressing a meeting in the Strand, London.

from his industry, that man must be placed in the 'unstarred' list and dealt with accordingly. . . .

"There is no necessity under this scheme for a man when he enlists to join his regiment immediately. He can do so if he wishes ; but if he prefers to be placed in such a group as his age and condition—*i.e.*, married or single—entitles him to enter and only come to the colours when his group is called up for service, he can request the recruiting officer to do this. He has this assurance : groups will be called up strictly in their order, the younger unmarried men before the older men, and all unmarried men, except those who may be proved to be indispensable to their businesses, before any of the married men. The recruiting officer will inform the recruit of the number of his group, which is determined, as stated above, by age and whether married or single. Be it understood, however, that any man who has married since the date of registration will be placed in a group as if unmarried.

"Whether the scheme will be a success or not is in the lap of the gods. No mere numbers will make it a success. The older married man who enlists must not be penalized by being brought forward earlier for active service than he can rightly expect because the younger man has failed in his duty. Each group represents a particular age, and success can only be attained when it can be shown that each group, and therefore each age, has played its part and come forward in something like equal proportions Unless the young unmarried man does come forward this voluntary scheme will not

have succeeded and other methods will have to be adopted. It is essential that faith should be kept with the patriotic men who do enlist. I therefore urge everybody of recruitable age to present themselves to the recruiting officer and let that officer decide if he is physically fit for service. If he is, let him take his proper place in his group. The local tribunals will give fair hearing to the recruit's request that he should be put in a later group owing to his being indispensable to his business."

The groups above referred to were the following :

Unmarried.		Married.	
Age.	Group.	Age.	Group.
18—19†	1	18—19†	24
19—20	2	19—20	25
20—21	3	20—21	26
21—22	4	21—22	27
22—23	5	22—23	28
23—24	6	23—24	29
24—25	7	24—25	30
25—26	8	25—26	31
26—27	9	26—27	32
27—28	10	27—28	33
28—29	11	28—29	34
29—30	12	29—30	35
30—31	13	30—31	36
31—32	14	31—32	37
32—33	15	32—33	38
33—34	16	33—34	39
34—35	17	34—35	40
35—36	18	35—36	41
36—37	19	36—37	42
37—38	20	37—38	43
38—39	21	38—39	44
39—40	22	39—40	45
40—41	23	40—41	46

† No man was to be called up until he had attained the age of 19.

It will be realized from the above that a recruit had the option either of joining the Army at once or of joining the group appropriate to his age and condition, whether married or

DRILLING BY GRAMOPHONE.

HOME FROM THE TRENCHES.

unmarried. In the latter case he was simply attested, received the sum of 2s. 9d. for his one day's "service," and returned to his civilian occupation as a member of Section B of the Army Reserve, to be called up at a fortnight's notice as required in the order of the groups. Local tribunals, to which appeal tribunals were added, were to decide whether a man could rightly claim exemption and whether his claim to be transferred to a later group should be allowed.

In his letter to the "unstarred" men, Lord Derby wrote :

If this effort does not succeed the country knows that everything possible will have been done to make the voluntary system a success and will have to decide by what method sufficient recruits can be obtained to maintain our Armies in the field at their required strength. May I, as Director-General of Recruiting, beg you to consider your own position ? Ask yourself whether in a country fighting as ours is for its very existence you are doing all you can for its safety, and whether the reason you have hitherto held to be valid as one for not enlisting holds good at the present crisis. Lord Kitchener wants every man he can get. Will you not be one of those who respond to your country's call ?

Lord Derby's scheme did not apply to Ireland.

The canvass was carried out for the most part by civilian volunteers of both sexes, chosen by a local sub-committee, the men being above recruitable age or otherwise excused from enlistment. In some cases soldiers were also employed. Under the committee for each Parliamentary constituency branch committees were set up where required in district boroughs, borough wards, and sub-divisions comprising groups of villages. The use of Town Halls, Municipal Offices, Schools, and similar useful buildings was secured as Canvassing Headquarters. Blue cards containing the names of eligible men were supplied to the Chairmen of the Committees, as also duplicate white cards, which were kept as a register of results, and on which the essential particulars entered by the canvassers on the blue card were briefly recorded. The blue and white cards were provided with spaces for the name, address, age, and occupation of the man canvassed, his employer's name and address, and particulars as to whether he was married or single, and the number of his children or other dependents. Attestation sub-committees were appointed to assist the canvassers in getting the men attested, and particularly to collect men willing to join on certain future dates. Travelling inspectors, of position and influence,

were appointed to visit frequently the sub-committees to see that the work was being done efficiently. Railway warrants for those willing to enlist at once were supplied in advance.

The following were the official directions for canvassers issued by the Parliamentary Recruiting Committee :

1. YOU SHOULD CANVASS FOR HIS MAJESTY'S FORCES, WHETHER REGULAR, NEW ARMY, SPECIAL RESERVE OR TERRITORIALS.

2. You will be provided with a card which will give you the authority to call upon recruitable men.

3. The cards that you receive contain names of men who, according to the National Register, can be spared to enlist.

4. Make a point of calling repeatedly until you actually see the man himself. You must not be put off by assurances or statements from other people. Make a special report if ultimately you fail to see him.

5. PUT BEFORE HIM PLAINLY AND POLITELY THE NEED OF THE COUNTRY. DO NOT BULLY OR THREATEN.

6. If he agrees, give him all necessary information as to where and how he may enlist.

7. If he hesitates or refuses, try to find out what are his reasons. Note these carefully. Ascertain whether his difficulties or objections can be removed by furnishing him with information on any specific point (for example, pensions, separation allowances, vacancies in particular regiments), or by some possible action with his employer or relations.

8. Treat your conversations as confidential and do not disclose them except to those authorised to know the circumstances.

9. Note all removals and try to ascertain from neighbours or others the new address.

10. Make careful notes on every card and report daily at the office until your list is completed.

11. Verify all particulars on card (especially age and occupation). Tick if correct.

12. Amend particulars that are incorrect.

13. Ascertain if the man has been discharged from

RECRUITING IN AUSTRALIA.
Outside a Recruiting Office at Melbourne Town Hall.

THE "LION CUBS" ANSWER THE CALL.
A scene outside a Recruiting Office in Ottawa, Canada.

the Navy or Army. If so, extract reason for discharge
and date from his discharge paper. State if reason for
discharge has since been removed.

14. If the man has been refused on account of being
medically unfit or for other reason, insert on the card
the date and place of rejection from his notice paper.
If he is not in possession of a notice paper he should be
told to go to the recruiting office where he was rejected
to get one. Please state carefully cause of rejection—
e.g., under standard, medically unfit, eyesight, etc.

15. If a man has enlisted since the Register was made
up, give regiment and, if possible, date and place of
enlistment.

16. Canvassers must endeavour to get all the men
they possibly can for the Infantry. It is Infantry that
is required to maintain the Armies in the field, and the
issue of the war largely depends on this arm. They
should be told that their services are equally useful
whether they join the Regular, New, Special Reserve, or
Territorial Force.

17. Where a man states that he is employed by a firm
engaged on Government work, reference should be made
to the nearest recruiting officer to ascertain whether
under War Office instructions the man should not be
recruited.

It will be seen that if these instructions were
properly carried out no eligible man would be in
a position to say that he did not know that he
was wanted. No totals were published during
the progress of the canvass. All that could be
gathered was that it was being more successful
in some districts than in others.

The movement thus started was given a
great impetus by the following stirring letter
from the King, published on October 23:

BUCKINGHAM PALACE.
TO MY PEOPLE.

At this grave moment in the struggle between
my people and a highly organized enemy who
has transgressed the Laws of Nations and
changed the ordinance that binds civilized
Europe together, I appeal to you.

I rejoice in my Empire's effort, and I feel
pride in the voluntary response from my
Subjects all over the world who have sacrificed
home, fortune, and life itself, in order that
another may not inherit the free Empire which
their ancestors and mine have built.

I ask you to make good these sacrifices.

The end is not in sight. More men and yet

MEN FROM TRINIDAD IN LONDON.

WAITING THEIR TURN TO ATTEST AT DEPTFORD TOWN HALL.
On the last day of the Recruiting Campaign.

more are wanted to keep my Armies in the Field, and through them to secure Victory and enduring Peace.

In ancient days the darkest moment has ever produced in men of our race the sternest resolve.

I ask you, men of all classes, to come forward voluntarily and take your share in the fight.

In freely responding to my appeal, you will be giving your support to our brothers, who, for long months, have nobly upheld Britain's past traditions, and the glory of her Arms.

GEORGE R.I.

As the result of this and other appeals, a flood of recruits came pouring in even before the formal canvass could be put into operation. There was still, however, as there had been from the first, much difficulty in persuading some employers to allow their employees to enlist, and it was not long before various uncertainties connected with the scheme led to a regrettable, if natural, hesitation on the part of certain classes affected. The married men, in particular, wished to know how they would stand in the event of its being only partially successful. What would happen if, owing to the failure of the unmarried to come forward, the married groups were called up forthwith, and then, after all, compulsory service became necessary? What was really meant by the phrase on the recruiting posters, "Single men first"?

On November 2 Mr. Asquith delivered a speech in the course of which he said:

I am told by Lord Derby and others that there is some doubt among men who are now being asked to enlist whether they may not be called upon to serve having enlisted, or promised to enlist, while younger and unmarried men are holding back and not doing their duty. So far as I am concerned I should certainly say the obligation of the married man to enlist ought not to be enforced or binding upon him unless and until—I hope by voluntary effort, and if not by some other means—the unmarried men are dealt with first.

Now, by Lord Derby's scheme as published, there was no question of attested married men being called up before attested unmarried men. The Prime Minister's characteristically ambiguous statement was, therefore, taken to mean that, before the married men were called up in their groups, compulsion would be applied to the eligible unmarried men in the event of their not enlisting voluntarily.

In point of fact Mr. Asquith explained on November 12 that in his speech he had "pledged not only himself but his Government when he stated that if young men did not, under the stress of national duty, come forward voluntarily, other and compulsory means would be taken before the married men were called upon to fulfil their engagement to serve." But even so, anxieties were not allayed. Many married men enlisted in the belief that they would not be called up until every unmarried man had been compelled to enlist, but Mr. Asquith's fencing replies to questions in the House of Commons soon revealed to them that their position was by no means so clear as they had supposed. As the result of the uncertainty as to what, if anything, the Government meant to do, and the feeling among the married men that they had been enlisted under false pretences, recruiting was thrown back for over a week. Lord Derby, indeed, gave the married men his personal pledge that faith would be kept with them. He added that the day that faith was not kept he would go out of office. In his view, there was no discrepancy between the " other means " of Mr. Asquith's speech of November 2 and the " compulsory means " of Mr. Asquith's explanation of November 12, for the simple reason that there was no alternative to voluntary methods except compulsory methods. But, if Parliament had to be required to consider compulsory service, and refused it, the obligation upon attested married men would not be held binding.

This view was formally expressed by Lord Derby in a letter published on November 20, and was endorsed by Mr. Asquith as correctly expressing the intentions of the Government. Lord Derby wrote :

Married men are not to be called up until young unmarried men have been. If these young men do not come forward voluntarily we will either release the married men from their pledge or introduce a Bill into Parliament which will compel the young men to serve, which, if passed, would mean that the married men would be held to their enlistment. If, on the other hand, Parliament did not pass such a Bill, the married men would be automatically released from their engagement to serve.

By the expression " young men coming forward to serve " I think it should be taken to mean that the vast majority of young men not engaged in munition work or work necessary for the country should offer themselves for service, and men indispensable for civil employment and men who have personal reasons which are considered satisfactory by the local tribunals for relegation to a later class, can have their claims examined for such relegation in the way that has already been laid down.

If, after all these claims have been investigated, and all the exemptions made mentioned above, there remains a considerable number of young men not engaged in these pursuits who could be perfectly spared for military service, they should be compelled to serve. On the other hand, if the number should prove to be, as I hope it will, a really negligible minority, there would be no question of legislation.

Meanwhile strenuous efforts were made to recover the time and men lost by this unfortunate muddle. Lord Derby informed a meeting of the Stock Exchange that " men must come in in very much larger numbers in the next three weeks if they were going to make the position of voluntary service absolutely unassailable. A gradual relaxation of

THE RAW MATERIAL AND THE FINISHED ARTICLE.
Soldiers from the trenches in France welcome their prospective comrades outside a Recruiting Office.

RECRUITING AT THE WHITE CITY: READY TO BE SWORN IN

the formalities prescribed on attestation became visible. The eyesight test for men enlisting on the group system was deferred until they should be called up for service. With the view, doubtless, of swelling the gross total, Civil Servants, who had hitherto considered themselves exempt, were invited by the Government to enlist, the only Departments immune from the attentions of the canvassers being the Admiralty, the War Office, and the Ministry of Munitions. The date for the conclusion of the canvass was extended, first to December 11, and then to December 12. After the latter date enlistment could only be for immediate service without the intervention of the group system. As December 12 drew near the rush of recruits completely overwhelmed the arrangements made for dealing with it. Just as in the early period of the war, men waited for many hours in vain outside the recruiting offices.* In some cases no attempt could be made to carry out a medical examination. The recruiters' instructions appeared to be to attest anyone who presented himself, leaving it to the future to decide whether he had or had not justified his sojourn in Section B of the Army Reserve. The "starring" system, of which so much had been heard, went by the board, "starred" men of all classes and occupations being invited to present themselves with the rest. The local tribunals were, therefore, to be called upon to do over again, on the "starred" man's coming up with his group, the work which had in theory been done at the time of the making of the National Register.

The idea of permitting those who placed their services absolutely at the disposal of the Government to wear an armlet had been suggested as early as September, 1914, by the National Patriotic Association, but nothing came of it, war badges being issued instead, though in a haphazard manner, to some of the men engaged on munitions work. On October 30, 1915, however, it was announced that the Government had decided to issue khaki armlets, bearing the Royal Crown, to the following classes of men :

(1) Those who enlisted and were placed in groups awaiting a call to join the colours.

* It was decided at the last moment to take the names of men still unattested at midnight on December 12 and keep open the group system for them alone for a further three days.

BERMONDSEY'S NEW RECRUITS.
Leaving the Recruiting Office in Jamaica Road for their training camp

(2) Those who offered themselves for enlistment and were found to be medically unfit.

(3) Those who had been invalided out of the Service with good character, or who had been discharged as "not likely to become efficient" on medical grounds.

A good deal of dissatisfaction was aroused in some quarters by this announcement. It was felt that, unless armlets were equally issued to "war workers" who were not supplied with badges, obloquy would fall upon many who in no way deserved it. There was further much dislike of the idea that a man should publicly proclaim himself as medically unfit, and thereby, perhaps, spoil his chance of obtaining employment. On November 15, therefore, the proposed issue to recruits rejected as medically unfit was withdrawn for further consideration. On December 27 it was announced that, after January 15, 1916, armlets would be issued to rejected men, subject to their presenting themselves again for medical examination. Those who had been rejected on account of eyesight or some slight physical defect would now, if they passed the examination, be attested and passed into the Army Reserve. When the rush of recruits came at the finish of the period laid down, the supply of armlets for attested men proved quite inadequate. But even among those who

MIDNIGHT SCENE AT SOUTHWARK TOWN HALL.
Major Jackson swearing-in the new recruits.

duly received their armlets on attestation, a curious reluctance to wear them manifested itself. It is probable that many of those who thus hid their light under a bushel did so from the Englishman's natural inclination to shrink from making himself conspicuous. Others, again, may have been merely prompted by the desire to keep their armlets clean, with a view to preserving them as a memento. But, whatever the cause, it was remarkable to note the almost complete absence of armlets in the streets, and it was not until the King himself expressed the hope that every man entitled to wear an armlet would do so that the practice of wearing them became other than most unusual.

The canvass having been completed, the Government acted, for once, with great promptitude and on December 18 issued a Proclamation, dated December 20, calling up for service the unmarried men belonging to the second, third, fourth, and fifth groups. (See page 308.) The first group, consisting of men between eighteen and nineteen years of age, was left until they should have grown older. The men called up were instructed to present themselves in batches beginning on January 20, 1916. Meanwhile claims for postponement were to be delivered in writing to the clerks of the local tribunals not later than December 30. Men belonging to the following three categories— (1) those " starred " by reason of their occupation on their National Register " pink " forms, (2) those authorized to wear a Government badge denoting that they were engaged upon essential work for the Government, and (3) those actually engaged on a reserved occupation, lists of which had been published in the Press—were not to be called up for actual military service unless it had been decided, after due inquiry by the competent authority, that it was no longer necessary in the national interest to retain them in their civil employment.

Those who had hoped to learn the result of the Derby scheme, and with it the fate of the voluntary system, before the House of Commons adjourned for Christmas were doomed to disappointment. In asking Parliament, on December 21, to sanction the addition to the Army of yet another 1,000,000 men—making the fourth million since August 5, 1914—Mr. Asquith announced that Lord Derby's report had not been received until the previous evening and that, while the figures and the inferences to be drawn from them were receiving from the Government the careful consideration that they deserved, it would be impossible to communicate to the House the results in any detail, or, indeed, at all. " To avoid all possibility of misunderstanding," he repeated the pledge to the married men, which he had given on November 2 (see page 312). Meanwhile, he warned the House of the enormous deductions which would have to be made, under whatever system of recruiting, before it became possible to arrive at the " recruitable maximum." The debate produced nothing except a vague belief that the Derby scheme had failed to bring in the number of young single men which alone, according to Mr. Asquith's pledge, would warrant the calling out of the married groups. One phrase, however, of Mr. Asquith's speech deserves record, if only because it was one more instance of the belated Ministerial acceptance of opinions urged by the Press during the previous year of war. Mr. Asquith laid down the principle that " we should aim at getting potentially every man of military age and capacity, not disqualified by physical or domestic conditions, who is available, consistent with making provision for our other national necessities." Such provisions included the Navy, the business of the production and transport of munitions and the maintenance of those industries on which our subsistence, our social life, and our export trade depend. But this organization is precisely what compulsory service, and compulsory service alone, can achieve in a just and economical manner.

The next few days were spent by a portion of the Press in a form of guessing competition as to the results of the canvass, and deductions according with the preconceived ideas of the newspapers were freely based upon these admittedly conjectural assertions. But even the more violently " anti-conscriptionist " organs revealed an uneasy feeling that, in spite of the final rush of recruits—a rush which only the extensions of the date of closing the list had rendered possible—their confidence that the influx of unmarried men would render the fulfilment of Mr. Asquith's pledge unnecessary was destined to be deceived by events. Gradually there became reason to believe that the gross total of attestations had amounted to nearly 3,000,000 men. But not only owing to the wholesale sweeping into the net of men who were certain to be subsequently rejected on various grounds, but also because a number estimated at between 500,000 and 650,000 of unmarried men had refused to enlist, or had taken refuge in "starred trades" for the purpose of evading the canvasser, the inevitability of some form of compulsion in order to obtain the country's maximum effort had become unmistakably clear.

This would have been a period of considerable anxiety if the public had believed for a moment, as some of Mr. Asquith's most ardent supporters in the Press appeared to invite them to believe, that the Prime Minister would not carry out, in the spirit as well as in the letter, his definite pledge to the married men given on November 2 and confirmed on various subsequent dates.

At a Cabinet meeting held on Boxing Day grave differences of opinion apparently manifested themselves. No decision was arrived at as to the action to be taken on Lord Derby's report. The meeting lasted for two hours and was eventually adjourned until next morning. There is good reason to believe that Mr. Lloyd George intimated that unless Mr. Asquith's pledge were interpreted in the strictest sense he should resign. On December 28, which was to prove an ever-memorable date in English history, the Cabinet sat for two hours and a half and subjected Lord Derby's report to a more thorough analysis than had been possible on the previous day. It was understood that the great majority of the Ministers, all of whom were in attendance, agreed upon the following line of policy :

1. That the Prime Minister's pledge to the married men was binding on the Government as a whole, and not upon Mr. Asquith alone.

2. That the pledge should be redeemed at once.

3. That the principle of Compulsion should be accepted.

4. That the Prime Minister should make an announcement to this effect immediately on the reassembling of the House of Commons on January 4.

It appeared that the Cabinet had decided that the number of single men who had not attested was by no means a "negligible minority." It was, in fact, larger than most Ministers had expected, after the final rush to attest under Lord Derby's scheme. The decision to proceed to compulsion was strongly opposed by a minority of Ministers, among whom were Mr. McKenna, Chancellor of the Exchequer, and Mr. Runciman, President of the Board of Trade. The former was believed to have his own opinion about the military need of more men, but to object mainly on financial grounds and to believe that the financial commitments of the country were already as heavy as it could safely bear. The objection of the President of the Board of Trade was believed to be based on the necessity of maintaining unimpaired the country's export trade. But with regard to the military situation, at all events, it was obvious that Lord Kitchener's opinion was more valuable than Mr. McKenna's, and as for the economic objections it was clear that, if the troops required to win the war were not provided, our financial position would not be worth considering. On the other hand, there was no ground for the assumption that all the men taken for the Army would be withdrawn from productive occupations, thereby necessarily crippling them. The natural remedy would be to replace men of military age by older men, lads and women, and at the same time to make a strenuous effort to reduce expenditure.

The attitude of Mr. Arthur Henderson, representative in the Cabinet of the Labour Party, gave rise, for a moment, to some uncertainty. The Labour members, though suspicious as a whole of changes in our recruiting methods, had never assumed a hostile attitude to compulsion, if the demand for it were backed by the Government of the day. Mr. Henderson decided to consult his colleagues before definitely declaring himself. But, since the working class was as keenly interested in the redemption of the Prime Minister's pledge as any other section of the community, there was no reason to fear serious obstruction from that quarter. The House of Commons contained a small and negligible group of irreconcilable Radicals who were unlikely to be propitiated at any price. Most of them had never had their heart in the war, and had given little help or encouragement to the Government during its progress. The position of the Irish Nationalist members was exceptional. They were determined that compulsion should not be applied to Ireland and at the same time felt that their position might be prejudiced in the eyes of the Empire by the adoption of compulsion for Great Britain alone and the retention of the voluntary system for their own country. It must be remembered that the Derby scheme did not apply to Ireland, which was still recruiting on the old lines.

As for the public at large, the news of the

Cabinet's decision was received without a trace of excitement. The general feeling seemed to be one of quiet satisfaction, tempered by regret that the decision had not been reached long before. It was clear that the idea of "compulsion" had ceased to bear the suggestion of "degradation" attributed to it, incredible as it may seem, by one of the posters of the Parliamentary Recruiting Committee. From the earliest days of the war public opinion had been considerably in advance of the views of its political leaders, and most men had long since made up their minds that they would accept compulsion or anything else from the Government if it were put before them as an indispensable means of victory.

Lord Derby's final report, dated December 20, 1915, was issued on January 4, 1916. Lord Derby wrote :

"The gross figures are as follows :

23RD OCTOBER TO 15TH DECEMBER, 1915
(INCLUSIVE).

	Single.	Married.
Men of military age (a) ...	2,179,231	2,832,210
Number starred	690,138	915,491
Number of men enlisted (b) ...	103,000	112,431
Number of men attested (c) ...	840,000	1,344,979
Number of men rejected (b) ...	207,000	221,853
Total	1,150,000	1,679,263
Men of military age	2,179,231	2,832,210
Presenting themselves ...	1,150,000	1,679,263
Number remaining	1,029,231	1,152,947
Total starred men attested	312,067	449,808
Number unstarred attested	527,933	895,171

(a) Men who joined His Majesty's Army between August 15, 1915, and October 23, 1915, are excluded from these figures.

(b) Whilst total is based on actual records, the distribution as between single and married is only an estimate, but may be taken as substantially accurate.

(c) Actual records.

Grand total of military age ... 5,011,441

Total attested, enlisted, and rejected 2,829,263

Total number remaining ... 2,182,178

"Large as are the figures, I am afraid that on analysis they do not prove as satisfactory as I could have wished. Owing to the great rush of recruits it was impossible in many cases to have more than a most perfunctory medical examination, and the number of men who will be rejected when the various groups are called up and are subject to a proper examination must be very large, the number of men actually unexamined being 925,445. This total includes both 'starred' and 'unstarred' men.

"For the same reason—the great rush of recruits—I fear there may be many instances where men have not been noted as being 'starred,' 'badged,' or belonging to 'reserved' occupations and a deduction must be made on this account.

"Lastly, there are many who will come under the heading of being indispensable, men who are the only sons of widows, sole support of a family, &c.

"My calculations for these necessary deductions have been submitted to Dr. T. H. C. Stevenson, Superintendent of Statistics at the General Register Office, and the following tables are now presented in accordance with his recommendations. The percentages of deductions are my own. They must of necessity be only estimates, but they have been arrived at upon the best information available.

SINGLE MEN ATTESTED.

Total number of single men attested	840,000
Of these the number starred was ...	312,067
The number of unstarred single men attested was therefore	527,933
For final rejection as medically unfit a number of unstarred men have not been examined, say	*260,000
Balance	267,933
Deduct 10 per cent. "badged" and "reserved"	*26,793
Balance	241,140
Deduct 10 per cent. "indispensable"	*24,114
	217,026
As shown above, it is estimated that of the unstarred single men attested those not examined as to medical fitness numbered	*260,000
Deduct 10 per cent. "badged" and "reserved"	*26,000
Balance	234,000
Deduct 10 per cent. "indispensable"	*23,400
Balance	210,600
Deduct 40 per cent. unfit	*84,240
	126,360
Estimated net number available of single men attested	343,386

MARRIED MEN ATTESTED.

Total number of married men attested	1,344,979
Of these the number starred was ...	449,808
The number of unstarred married men attested was therefore	895,171
For final rejection as medically unfit a number of unstarred men have not been examined, say	*445,000
Balance	450,171
Deduct 15 per cent. "badged" and "reserved"	*67,526
Balance	382,645
Deduct 20 per cent. "indispensable"	*76,529
	306,116

As shown above, it is estimated that of the unstarred married men attested those not examined as to medical fitness numbered *445,000

Deduct 15 per cent. " badged " and " reserved " *66,750

Balance 378,250
Deduct 20 per cent. " indispensable " *75,650

Balance 302,600
Deduct 40 per cent. unfit *121,040
————— 181,560

Estimated net number available of married men attested 487,676

(There are probably more married men than single men who are in reserved occupations, and certainly amongst the indispensable class. I have increased considerably the percentage of deductions in both these cases.)

The figures marked * are estimates only.

" I must again draw attention to the fact that the men in the married groups can only be assumed to be available if the Prime Minister's pledge to them has been redeemed by the single men attesting in such numbers as to leave only a negligible quantity unaccounted for.

" On comparing the above figures it will be seen that of the 2,179,231 single men available, only 1,150,000 have been accounted for, leaving a residue unaccounted for of 1,029,231.

" Deducting the number of starred single men who have attested, 312,067, from total number of starred single men, 690,138, leaves 378,071 starred men.

" If we deduct this figure from 1,029,231 (the remainder of single men left who have not offered themselves), it shows a total of 651,160 unstarred single men unaccounted for.

" This is far from being a negligible quantity, and, under the circumstances, I am very distinctly of opinion that in order to redeem the pledge mentioned above it will not be possible to hold married men to their attestation unless and until the services of single men have been obtained by other means, the present system having failed to bring them to the colours.

" I have been at some pains to ascertain the feeling of the country, and I am convinced that not only must faith be kept with the married men in accordance with the Prime Minister's pledge, but more than that ; in my opinion some steps must be taken to replace as far as possible the single men now starred, or engaged in reserved occupations, by older and married men, even if these men have to a certain extent to be drawn from the ranks of

those already serving. Especially does this apply to those who have joined these occupations since the date of the Royal Assent to the National Registration Act. This applies, though naturally in a minor degree, to munition workers.

" There is another point to which I would most earnestly ask the Government to give consideration. I have already drawn attention in my previous Report to the detrimental effect that the issue from time to time of lists of ' reserved ' occupations has had on recruiting. Even since that Report was written further and lengthy lists have been issued. I do not presume to state what are or are not industries indispensable to this country, but if there is to be any further reservation of occupations it is quite clear that the figures I have given above must be subject to a reduction, and I cannot help hoping that there should be some finality to the issue of these lists.

" Before concluding, it might be interesting to give one or two features of the campaign. The figures given above refer only to recruits received between October 23 and December 15, but as I have been in my present office since October 11, I include recruits for immediate enlistment from that date to Sunday, December 19 inclusive, and I also include belated returns of men (61,651) taken in the group system. It has not, however, been possible to allot these latter accurately as between single or married : the majority appear to be men in starred occupations. During that time there have been taken for the Army as follows :—

Immediate enlistment	...	...	275,031
Attestation in Groups	...	...	2,246,630
A gross total of	...	...	2,521,661

" Some of the figures of the take of recruits under the group system for particular days may also be of interest :—

On Friday, December 10, we took	193,527
On Saturday, December 11, we took	336,075
On Sunday, December 12, we took	325,258
On Monday, December 13, we took	215,618
Or a total in the 4 days of ...	1,070,478

" In order, however, to get at the number of men who have offered themselves, it is necessary to add to the above figures those who have been definitely rejected on medical grounds, viz., 428,853. This shows that a total of 2,950,514 men have shown their willingness to serve their country, provided they were able to be spared from their employment and could be accepted as medically suitable.

" There will be additions to make to these numbers, slight, but very significant. In foreign towns where there are English communities, men have banded themselves together to come under the group system. Men have written from Hong Kong, Rhodesia, Cadiz, California, offering to come home to be attested for Army Reserve (Section B)."

In the course of his first Report, which had been dated December 12, and was also issued on January 4, Lord Derby said :

" Many difficulties have been met with, but the chief difficulty has been the unreliability of the starring as distinguishing between those who should and those who should not be taken for the Army. Instead of starring being of assistance, it has been a distinct hindrance to the canvass. More especially is this so in rural and semi-rural areas, owing to the fact that it was known before Registration Day what branches of the agricultural industry would be starred, with the result that many men who had no right to do so claimed to come under these particular headings. The sense of unfairness thus created and the inequality of treatment of farmers has been most detrimental in these areas. The farmer himself is not a starred man, but there are numberless cases of his sons and labourers being starred as cowmen and horsemen, &c., though in many instances it is known that they are not really so engaged.

" It is essential that the starred list should be carefully investigated, and in cases of misdescription the star removed and the man made available for military service. This applies to the starred men in all industries.

" The issue, during the process of canvass, of lists of trades which were to be considered 'reserved occupations' has also proved an obstacle. I recognise that it was essential that such lists should be issued, but the fact remains that trades other than those mentioned in these lists have been applying to be so included, and the men engaged in those trades are expecting to be treated in the same way as 'starred'

men, and have been deterred from coming forward.

" Many men also who would willingly serve find themselves barred from doing so by domestic, financial and business obligations. This especially applies to professional and commercial men, who find difficulties in meeting such obligations as payment of rent, insurance premium, interest on loans connected with their business, and provision for their family, due to the fact that their income is entirely dependent on their individual efforts, and ceases when they join the Colours—separation and dependants' allowances being quite inadequate in such cases to meet these obligations. This applies not only to married men, but also to single men in many cases.

" Another obstacle to recruiting has been the unequal treatment of individuals. Parents and relations especially cannot understand why their sons, husbands or brothers should join while other young men hold back and secure lucrative employment at home.

" Apart from the number of men who have actually enlisted and attested there are many who have promised to enlist when ' So and so ' has also promised to go. There may, of course, be a number of men who make this answer as an excuse. But that it is genuine in a very large number of cases, and is accentuated by bad starring, there is no reason to doubt.

" Further, the system of submitting cases to Tribunals to decide is a novel one and is viewed with some distrust, partly from the publicity which may be given to private affairs, and partly to a fear, which personally I do not share, that cases will not be fairly and impartially dealt with.

" The canvass shows very distinctly that it is not want of courage that is keeping men back, nor is there the slightest sign but that the country as a whole is as determined to support the Prime Minister in his pledge made at Guildhall on November 9, 1914, as it was when that pledge was made. There is abundant evidence of a determination to see the war through to a successful conclusion."

CHAPTER CIV.

THE FRENCH OFFENSIVE IN CHAMPAGNE.

THE key to the military history of the operations in the first part of 1915 is to be found in the munitions question. The shell problem was not confined to Great Britain. In France, although in another form, it became just as acute as in Great Britain, and it was in the course of the operations conducted simultaneously with the British in the spring that the French realized that matters were seriously wrong. When, after the Battle of the Marne, the vital importance of shell supply was forced upon the attention of the French authorities they immediately took steps similar to those taken in Great Britain to provide requisite supplies. They mobilized all their available resources and managed in a very brief space of time very greatly to increase their daily output of shell.

But in the haste to procure shells inferior methods and materials were employed, the drilled shell was provided instead of the forged shell, and the results were not long in revealing themselves in the rapidly growing number of gun bursts along the Western front. It was deficiencies of this nature that brought to a standstill the offensive begun in the early months of the year in the north of France. When those operations ceased, comparative

quiet descended upon the line, while behind it in France the method of shell manufacture was rapidly altered and in Great Britain the output was increased. Throughout the summer, from June to the end of September, action along the French front was confined to fighting for positions, chiefly in the Vosges. As regards the number of men engaged and the extent of front involved, these operations were of a local character. They none the less served a very useful purpose. The enemy was worn out and exhausted by fruitless and costly counter-attacks. He was constantly threatened by a French offensive in Alsace, and this menace acted in some degree as a screen to the preparation of the Allies' plans for a general offensive along an extended front.

By many it had been supposed that after the check of the Artois offensive (described in Chapter CI.) the Western Allies would confine their energies to local operations and to accumulating vast stores of munitions and of men for a gigantic sledge-hammer blow upon the enemy's lines in the spring of 1916.

There were, however, a hundred reasons of an international, of a military, and of a psychological nature which weighed in determining

GERMAN SHELL CASES AS FRENCH TRENCH GUNS.

Lighting the fuse of a battery of four "Crapouillots": French Infantry about to fire their home-made trench-mortars.

General Joffre and Sir John French to make a great effort before the advent of a winter campaign with all its hardships.

The military and political situation in Russia was not the least of these determining factors. The great enemy drive seemed, in spite of the valour of the Russian soldier, to be approaching a triumphant end, and it was the duty of the Western Allies to do their utmost to relieve the pressure upon the Eastern partner. Upon the West these same Russian operations had obliged the enemy to remain entirely upon the defensive and to leave the initiative to the French and the British. The British Army had been solidly reinforced, and had thus been enabled to take over a further stretch of the front in France. Moreover, thanks to this fact and to changes and reorganizations in the French Army, the regrouping of certain regiments and the formation of new forces had become possible. Also, the industrial output of France had been increased to a very large extent, and a vast reserve of several million shells of all calibres had been accumulated.

All these reasons applied with equal strength both to the French and the British Armies in the West, and in a conference between the military and political leaders of both countries simultaneous and co-ordinated action was agreed

upon by the British and the French working together in the north, and by the armies under the direct command of General Castelnau in the centre of the great rampart of civilization.

What that rampart was could be realized only by those who had seen it, who had spent days in the trenches, which were its ultimate expression, who had studied the intricate and vast mechanism which kept it fed and supplied with its multifarious requirements, who had been able to visit the vast caverns in which men sheltered, who had explored the cunningly concealed machine-gun emplacements, who had wandered through acre upon acre of seemingly endless communication trench, tramped over miles of corduroy road, stumbled upon vast sandbag cities, wandered in the new worlds created underneath the ruins of the old in the cellars, drains and graveyards. Nothing so stupendous, so infinitely painstaking, so amazingly ingenious, so solidly resisting, had been seen in the history of war.

The will of man against such a barrier would have been impotent, the great onrush of the Revolutionary Wars suicidal. Science and patience alone could prevail; they alone could render useful the display of the human qualities of bravery and fearlessness, of patriotism and self-sacrifice.

Both science and patience found their expression in the tremendous bombardment which preceded the Allied advance. For weeks the enemy was pounded with high explosive and shrapnel along the whole front. Shell poured from British guns of every calibre, and from the French mountain 65mm. to the great 370mm. howitzers there fell a constant rain of destruction upon the German lines. The trench artillery, from the converted cartridge-case to the big mine-throwers, joined in. High above, favoured by the fine weather, great fleets of aircraft controlled and "spotted" for the artillery, while the heavy guns of the bombardment flotillas threw their loads of explosives and carried destruction far beyond the range of the heaviest field guns on to railway and supply centres or troop concentration points.

This bombardment was carried out for weeks practically along the whole line with the double object of preventing the enemy from seeing at which point the infantry was preparing to follow and of rendering it impossible for the enemy to prepare any serious counter-attacks or to forestall the offensive anywhere along the front.

The great offensive in France, broadly speaking, consisted of three parts. The first arm to begin the attack was the airplane, which, since the beginning of the war, had been very considerably developed and was at last building up, if slowly, a system of aerial tactics and strategy. By the summer of 1915 the existing possibilities of the airplane had become recognized and classified; industry was furnishing the different types of machines required and squadron formations had taken definite shape. The work of the airplane at this stage of the war was split up under three general headings: 1. Reconnaissance. 2. Fight. 3. Bombardment. For each class of work special types of plane had been provided, and each one of them played a vitally important part in the Champagne operations. The aerial activity of the French which had an immediate bearing upon the Champagne offensive began in July, when, as part of the fighting in the Argonne, the railway junctions and supply centres of the Crown Prince's army were vigorously bombarded with explosive shells of high calibre by squadrons of between thirty and forty machines. With these bombplane squadrons went the chaser planes, or Hawks, as they were known to the French Army, powerful machines armed for fighting, which, flying above, ahead and on the flanks of squadrons, acted as escort and engaged any enemy planes which might attempt attack.

GERMAN SHELL CASES AS FRENCH TRENCH GUNS.
Two of the battery of four "guns" fired: two about to be fired.

TWENTY YARDS BETWEEN OPPOSING TRENCHES.
View taken from the top of a French trench, showing a German trench in background.

While all this raiding work was going on behind the enemy's lines, swarms of reconnaissance planes were engaged in the less spectacular but equally dangerous and useful work of photography over the enemy's lines, spotting for the guns, locating artillery positions, and preventing any German planes from discovering the great movements and preparations in progress for the offensive.

All this activity was, however, but an infinitely small part of the really gigantic business of the offensive. Some idea of the nature of the work performed by the various Staffs can be gained from a description of the mapping operations carried out before the Champagne offensive. The cartography of peace even on its largest scale proved quite inadequate and misleading in a siege war where every bend of a stream, every ruined house, every clump of trees, every fold in the ground had to be explored for artillery or machine-gun emplacements, where indeed at some portions of the line the appearance of a new sandbag, a new path worn into the ground might possess significance. The armies had, it is true, been facing each other on practically unchanged lines since the French advance in March, 1915. In trench warfare, however, a map may be out of date in some all-important particular in less than a week, and map correcting and amplification proceeds without a break day after day. The base of them all was, of course, the General Staff map, upon which were fixed the results of aerial

photography, of panoramic photography from the first line trenches, the discoveries of the observation officers, the work of the artists who from points of vantage have turned their talents to military account and hidden in a tree or a ruin have created a new school of realistic landscape painting for the special benefit of the artillery. Some idea of the detail required can be gained from the map of the Champagne front published on pp. 340–1. That is a small-scale production compared with the maps used by company commanders. It is, moreover, a map prepared entirely by the indirect means described. A map of the French position before the offensive would have been crowded with infinitely more minute detail. For in the maze of trenches leading to the front line there was a multitude of opportunities of error—error which might well have been disastrous and thrown the whole supply of men to the front line into terrible confusion. Every yard of the ground had to be studied, labelled, numbered or named. The rough and ready methods of indicating the entrance to a communication trench, signposts of bottles or of sticks, would have been enough for troops used to the position, but arrangements had to be made for the advance of large bodies of supports and reserves who were comparative strangers to the positions, and those arrangements had to be effective, for the whole attack was planned out very much in the methodical manner of a railway time-table, and delay at one point would have meant delay along the line and the adding of fresh difficulties to the problem of keeping regiments in touch with each other in advancing over trench positions.

The problems of the map maker were but a small part in the huge complications of the offensive, the final Staff preparations for which were made while the most intense bombardment in history was in progress.

That bombardment began in the middle of August, and while it was general along the front, there were certain districts which came in for more than their proportionate share of attention from the masses of artillery assembled behind the French front. These special zones going from north to south were (1) Belgian front, (2) Souchez district, (3) Arras, (4) Roye, (5) Aisne, (6) in Champagne between Moronvillers and Souain, (7) Argonne, (8) Woevre. (9) Lorraine. The bombardment remained general (growing in intensity, however, in the Champagne) until three days before the actual infantry operations began, when, without ceasing day after day, night after night, the Champagne front was deluged in shell.

Whatever doubts the Germans may have had about the intentions of the French as to the spot at which they intended to strike hardest were then set at rest. It was in the Champagne Pouilleuse.

The front upon which the French attacked was broad. The previous successes on both sides in the West had ended in check because the front attacked had not been broad enough. In Artois, at Soissons, and in the Argonne each local success scored remained purely tactical.

It was one of the commonplaces current in France throughout the summer of 1915 that Joffre could break through where he wanted to do so. This may have been quite true. If you bring enough artillery—enough of the right kind of shell—to bear long enough upon any given section of the front, the line will break at that point as it did at Festubert, at Souchez, as it did at Soissons, as it nearly did in the Argonne. But the wedge driven into the line had up till then failed to yield any strategical results. On to the narrow fronts threatened both sides were able to concentrate their troops and their material, with the result that troops breaking through the lines had only found themselves confronted with another barrier a little distance farther back. They were unable at any time to get back to the war of manœuvre, to surface fighting, as the Germans managed

AFTER THE FRENCH VICTORY.
German guns captured in the Battle of Champagne. Inset: A German trench gun was devised for throwing bombs.

THREE-STOREYED FRENCH FIELD FORTIFICATIONS.

to do in their great drive in Galicia. As Mr. John Buchan pointed out in *The Times*: " If you can tear a great rent in the enemy's lines—20 or 30 miles wide—then you prevent him repairing the damage in time and with luck you may roll up the ragged edges, force the whole front to retire. That is what von Mackensen did on the Dunajec in the first days of May. He broke Radko Dmitrieff on a 40-mile front and there was no halting till Galicia was lost." That is what Joffre set himself to do in September of 1915 along the Western front, where, it is true, the conditions of the French differed very largely from those of the Germans in their great offensive in the East, both as regards the munition supplies of the enemy and as to their means of communication.

When the tactics and strategy of the operations on the Western front during 1915 are studied, it will be seen that in the fierce spring fighting in Artois, where that remarkable soldier of France, General Petain, gained a widespread reputation outside the ranks of the Army, principles which governed all subsequent fighting were most clearly expressed. Few of those civilians who glibly used and gaily accepted the expression " siege warfare " in describing the war at this period can have had any idea of the terrible accuracy of that description. It was not only siege warfare, but siege warfare, as it were, under a microscope. Any yard of the front might become a bastion and delay advance at the cost of hundreds of lives to the assailants and a minimum of loss to the defenders. The minute localization of this war is shown quite clearly on reference to the *communiqués*. Day after day Europe, the greater part of which was in the war area, waited eagerly for news of events at the sugar refinery or the cemetery of Souchez, at the ferryman's house on the Yser, the crest of Hartmannsweilerkopf in Alsace, the Four de Paris in the Argonne. It was not until 1915 that the French seem definitely to have realized this intense localism of the war, and to have conducted all their operations on that knowledge.

All flanking movements having become impossible since the war settled down into the trench, the task of attacking generals really was to create flanks and effect enveloping movements upon small sections of the front, by thrusting infantry into the enemy's line at different points, much as the dentist's pincers are thrust down into the base of a tooth, and then to eat a way round the village or work to be carried. This operation was repeated time after time in the detailed fighting in Artois in the early summer. It was this principle that Joffre applied on a huge scale to the strategy of the great summer offensive. Powerful and gigantic thrusts were to be made on two sectors of the front, which were, if all went well, to be taken up along the whole line, and all these thrusts, composed of detailed actions much like those in Artois, were to contribute to the execution of that strategy upon a vast scale. The offensive began simultaneously in the north and in the centre. The attack upon the latter section was, by reason of the number of men engaged and the results achieved, by far the more important. The centre of the French line was held by three armies, from left to right, by the 6th, the 5th and the 4th, under General Langle de Cary. It was upon the front held by the latter that the offensive was launched.

If any clear idea of the fighting is desired a very close study of the country is necessary, for, although chosen by history as the stage for some of the most tremendous events in the military history of Europe, the country is by no means simple and straightforward.

The field of battle was that of Attila, and it lies a little to the north of the region through which historians have looked in vain for the exact spot of the great Hun's last stand. Even in time of peace it is a desolate region. Man has had to fight for his living on this ungrateful, tumbling soil of chalk. Fields of saffron, woods of pine and spruce are the chief evidence of agriculture. Roads are few and villages very scarce. Nearly all of them lie on the banks of the small streams which have cut their beds into the chalk hills—the Suippe, the Ain and the Tourbe. The line held by the Germans in this region covered the Bazancourt-Challerange railway at a distance varying from six to nine miles. These were practically the positions which the German General Staff had organized during the advance, and to which they fell back after the defeat of the Battle of the Marne. Naturally very strong, the position had been strengthened by every device of the military engineer until the Germans were justified in calling it the " steel barrier."

Although from the point of view of a general description the country does not vary much from west to east, from a military standpoint it was by no means uniform, and was divided by the French General Staff into six zones.

Going from Auberive, the western end of the line, to Ville-sur-Tourbe in the east, the first zone was constituted by a ridge of about five miles, cut through almost at its centre by the road from St. Hilaire to St. Souplet and the Baraque de l'Epine de Vedegrange. The slopes of this ridge were covered by many small clumps of spruce thinned out very considerably by shell fire and by the timber requirements of trench repairs.

The second zone comprised the hollow of Souain with the village of that name in the bottom, the road from Souain to Somme-Py and the Navarin Farm, about two miles to the north of Souain on the crest of the hills.

The third zone lay to the north of Perthes, and was formed by the slow-moving, monotonous valley, about two miles broad, between the wooded hills of Bricot Hollow and the Mesnil Ridge. This valley was defended by several lines of trenches and closed by several very highly organized heights—the Souain Ridge, Heights 195 and 201, and the Tahure Ridge.

To the north of Mesnil lay the fourth zone, which, from the point of view of the defence, was very strong. The hills in the west, Mamelle Nord and Trapèze, and the Mesnil

Ridge on the east, formed the bastion of the German positions, and were linked up by a powerful trench organization, behind which, as far as Tahure, stretched a broken, wooded country.

In the fifth zone, to the north of Beauséjour, the country was fairly easy. The soil, bare of vegetation, rose gently in the direction of Ripon as far as the Maisons de Champagne Farm.

The strongest point of the line lay to the north of Massiges, where Heights 191 and 199, stretching like an open hand, formed the eastern support of the entire front.

The whole of this front had been connected by the German engineers by a complicated and elaborate system of defence works. By the disposition of the trenches the whole ground had been split up into a series of more or less regular rectangles, each one of which, armed with an abundance of machine guns, was capable of standing a siege in the proper sense of the word, of delaying the advance of the enemy, of becoming a centre of resistance and a rallying point for any counter-attacks.

A study of the map which appears on pp. 340-1 reveals the formidable nature of the German defences. The portion of the line attacked by the French consisted of two main positions separated by two or two and a-half miles. The

ON THE LOOK-OUT FOR AEROPLANES.
Ready to fire a German Anti-aircraft gun.

READY FOR ENEMY AIRCRAFT.
Ingenious French gunners mounted their gun on an improvised platform made from an old disused gun carriage.

first-line defences were extremely dense, and consisted of a complicated network of defence and communication trenches formed by at least three, and in some places by five, parallel trench lines facing the French, and cut up into compartments by lateral defence lines, and thus studded with trench squares of formidable strength. This first line was some 400 yards in depth, and between each trench in it had been placed large fields of barbed-wire entanglement, some of them 60 or 70 yards in depth. The second position consisted on the whole of but one single trench. Here and there was a support trench. Along the whole line this second trench had been constructed on the unseen side of the hill crest, the upper slopes of the hills under the observation of the French being only held by machine-gun sections and artillery spotters, whose advanced posts were linked up by tunnels with the trench behind them. The whole of the couple of miles separating these two positions had been fortified and netted with transversal, diagonal and lateral trench works and communication trenches, which, protected with barbed wire and armed with mitrailleuses, became a by-system of fortifications, capable of putting up a long fight even after the hostile infantry had swept over the positions.

Thanks to forward trench and airplane observation, there was not much about the position which had not been noted by the cartographical survey of the army. Each trench, each bristling clump of shell-stripped tree trunks, had been baptized or numbered on the maps. Artillery positions, supply centres, headquarters behind the line were also known to the French.

It has been said that the airplanes were the first to begin the offensive ; the artillery took it up, and the middle of August saw the beginning of the sustained bombardment upon this section of the front. In the five weeks which preceded the action of the infantry, on no fewer than twenty-five days the front described above was reported in the official *communiqués* as having been violently bombarded. The objects of this bombardment on the first position were fivefold :

1st. Destruction of barbed-wire entanglements.

2nd. Burial of defenders in dug-outs.

3rd. Levelling of trenches and blocking of fire holes.

4th. Closing up of communication trenches and tunnels.

5th. Demoralization of the enemy.

Meanwhile the long-range naval and military

AN ARMOURED TRENCH.

French soldiers holding an armoured trench during a violent German bombardment.

guns were busily employed bombarding head-quarters, camps, railway stations and the Challerange-Bazancourt railway, impeding or interrupting the shell and food supply of the firing line.

On September 22 and 23 remarkably fine weather favoured the airplanes in their spotting work for the artillery, and on the 22nd the bombardment burst into a tremendous roar along the Champagne front, which was sustained at frenzy point until the hour for the infantry advance had struck.

On September 22 all private communications between the zone of the armies and the interior of France ceased. The long suspense of weeks of tremendously significant bombardment was at an end.

On the night of September 24 an extra ration of wine was issued and the men were acquainted with their task by the following General Army Order :

Grand Quartier General, Sept. 23.
General Order 43.

SOLDIERS OF THE REPUBLIC !

After months of waiting which have enabled us to increase our strength and our resources while the enemy was using his, the hour has come to attack and to conquer, to add fresh pages of glory to those of the Marne, of Flanders, the Vosges and Arras.

Behind the storm of iron and fire unloosed, thanks to the labour of the factories of France, where your comrades have worked day and night for you, you will go to the assault together upon the whole front in close union with the Armies of our Allies.

Your dash will be irresistible.

It will carry you with your first effort up to the enemy's batteries beyond the fortified line opposing you.

You will leave him neither truce nor rest until victory has been achieved. On, then, with your whole heart for the liberation of our country, and for the triumph of right and liberty. J. JOFFRE.

Already during September 24 the clouds had been gathering, and although they had remained high enough not to impede the work of air reconnaissance, there seemed no possibility of the rain not being brought down by the tremendous artillery fire on the next day.

When réveille sounded at 5.30 on the morning of the great day, September 25, those who had slept through the din of gunfire awoke to a world of gloom. Clouds heavy with rain swept low across the grey chalky landscape, reflecting on the heavens the monotony of the tumbled, dirty grey landscape. Between 6 and 6.30 the morning coffee was drunk with many a jest merry and lugubrious, and then, conversation being impossible, the men squatted down by the trench wall and smoked and thought of what the day might bring forth. Then, as the time of the attack drew near, the company commanders threw their last glance over their men's equipment, assembled their men where possible, addressed to them their last orders and explained all that was required of them.

The Frenchman, of whatever class he comes, is a man of intelligence. He only gives of his best when he knows what he is fighting for and what he is fighting against. Under a pouring rainstorm which broke at 9 o'clock, in a few brief phrases the general situation and the general scheme of operations of the day were set before the men. Then by the time given by wireless to the Army from the Eiffel Tower the fuses of the artillery behind were lengthened, the officers scrambled out of the advanced parallels with a last shout of " En Avant, mes Enfants " to the men and the wave of " invisible blue " tipped the parapets with foam. The great offensive of 1915 had begun, and all those who took part in it are agreed that no moment of the battle was so thrilling, so soul-stirring and impressive as that which saw the first wave of Frenchmen in blue uniforms, blue steel Adrian casques, with drums of grenades hanging at their waists, burst from the trench in which they had lain hidden for so many months and strike across the intervening No Man's Land for the enemy's lines.

General Castelnau, who was in direct command of the operations, had declared to an officer on his staff : " I want the artillery so to bend the trench parapets, so to plough up the dug-outs and subterranean defences of the enemy's line as to make it almost possible for my men to march to the assault with their rifles at the shoulder."

This desire was at points almost realized, and there is nothing so remarkable in the Champagne Battle of 1915 as the rapidity with which the first line of the enemy was carried by assault and the tremendous obstacles which met the attacking infantry once it had swept over the first-line trenches.

The front was extremely varied. In some points all semblance of resistance had been obliterated by the preliminary bombardment ; in others a little nest of machine guns had remained untouched by the artillery fire and delayed the advance by hours. At one point an entire French Army Corps occupied its section of the first German line with a loss in killed and wounded which did not exceed 150 men ; at another spot men fell in their

FRENCH HEAVY GUNS IN POSITION.

In a well-protected position. French gunners wearing their shrapnel-proof helmets. Inset: After bombarding the German defences.

at several points along the line resistance was maintained. Machine guns were unmasked, the German artillery, which had been too late with its attempt to stop the first advance with a *tir de barrage*, got to work, and along the entire front the fighting settled down into a series of more or less isolated sieges, some of which were successful, while others failed.

It is therefore necessary to describe the fighting in each section of the front in some detail.

In the first section, going from west to east—the section of the Epine de Vedegrange—the German line was situated at the foot of the large wooded ridge. The salients of the line gave to it all the strength of the flanking fire of a fortress, so that the attacking troops were under fire at practically every point along the line from three sides at once. Taking the St. Souplet and St. Hilaire road as marking the centre of this section on the western side, there were no fewer than three of these salients, forming as many entrenched bays swept by machine-gun storms. Here the difficulties of the position were increased by the very considerable support given to the enemy by their artillery, which had been massed in great

hundreds before a position which had either been overlooked by or had resisted the artillery.

The fighting may be divided roughly into two distinct parts. The first waves which went dashing out of the trenches had about 250 yards to cover before they reached the first German line, and such was the dash of the French troops, such were the effects of the artillery fire, that practically along the whole front the first line was taken before noon. Up to this point success had been complete. But

numbers on the Moronvillers plateau to the west of the front attacked.

The first assault, however, carried the sevenfold wave of the French blue line through the first trenches of the Germans up to a supporting trench, where concealed fields of barbed wire which had not been destroyed by the bombardment stayed further progress. The Germans farther to the left, profiting from the fact that that section of the line had not been stormed, organized a counter-attack which, sweeping from west to east, and firmly supported by the guns from Moronvillers, forced the French left back a little. The French right in this small portion of the front held all the ground gained, and on the following days, indeed, pushed farther and farther forward into the labyrinth of trenches, keeping pace with their comrades in the neighbouring section of the line, where the difficulties confronting the assailants were only equalled by the courageous tenacity with which they were overcome.

Upon their positions here the Germans had lavished a vast amount of tackle, and the work of their pioneers in the woods and trenches had made of it one of the most elaborately defended positions of the German centre. A glance at the map will show the tremendous strength of those defences, which consisted of triple, and in places of quadruple, lines of fire trenches, and almost innumerable machine-gun blockhouses, and was reinforced by a very large number of batteries of artillery in positions hidden in the woods of the sloping ground behind. Along this portion, too, the advance met with varying fortune. Again it was the local left—that is to say, the troops operating with their left on the east side of the St. Souplet-St. Hilaire road—that got stopped, this time after they had carried the first trench line, by hidden mitrailleuses which executed great damage on the French. There, where the difficulties seemed greatest, however, the advance was most successful, and the right of the attacking troops carried all four lines of trench—some of them hidden in woods—difficult targets for the French artillery, and rushed about a mile and a half of country, making 900 prisoners, of whom 17 were officers, and capturing two German 77 mm. field guns and five 105 guns.

Farther east, under cover of a fold in the ground, the French got a footing in the German trench line for a distance of about 500 yards, but here again check was called, for the enemy hastily concentrated his artillery fire into the breach, while from the left and the right of it unconquerable machine guns sputtered check, check, check.

FOR THE COMFORT OF FRENCH TROOPS.
Bedsteads used in dug-outs and trenches in Champagne.

Such, briefly described, were the results of the first day's offensive. The results show the general rhythm of the battle right along the line and the principles which inspired both attack and defence. The defence had formed a number of resistance centres separated each from the other by a weaker trench fortification system which was under the protection of the bastions formed by the resistance centres. The French struck boldly for the weaker line, meanwhile getting their teeth into the strong positions, bombing and firing while their comrades got round to the flanks of the bastions and forced surrender or retreat. The position at Auberive-sur-Suippes was one of these resistance points, the district on each side of the St. Souplet-St. Hilaire road, one of the weaker lines ; while the salient to the east of the road once more became formidable.

To the east again, in the semi-circular entrant around Souain, the enemy's defences were more slender, and in this section the French advance was more remarkable.

Here the French lines almost touched the German trenches at the western point, the Moulin, and at the east point of the curve, the Bois Sabot. The French line between those two points was elliptical, and left about 1,000 yards of No Man's Land between the opposing trenches north of the village of Souain. It was in this section of the front that some of the most delicate and dangerous preparatory work of the offensive was carried out. It had been learned by costly experience that against a line well fitted with machine guns it was necessary (unless great loss of life was to be incurred) to bring the attacking troops to within about 200 or 250 yards of their immediate objective. Here to the north of Souain they had to push forward about 800 yards before the offensive began. This was done by sapping out and linking up with parallel trenches, and at times by rushes at night under the glare of searchlights and the cold, scrutinizing eye of the star shells and pistol flares of the enemy. Under fire the men dug themselves in where they dropped, and then dug backwards to the main trenches. In this manner the average distance separating the two lines of trench was reduced to its proper minimum of between 200 and 250 yards.

Here, again, so intricate and detailed were the operations, it was necessary to subdivide the section attacked into three parts corresponding with the direction of the assault, which radiated out from Souain to the west upon the woods of Hills 174 and 167, to the centre along the Souain-Somme-Py road, and to the east along the Souain-Tahure road. In the first two subdivisions up the hill slopes on the west of the curve and in the centre due north the advance was extremely rapid. Here, as along the rest of the battlefield, the assault was unchained at 9.15 a.m. ; in less than an hour the Palatinate and Magdeburg fortifications had been carried, the Von Kluck Trench overrun, and the Harem communication trench, a mile and a quarter behind the first German trench, had been reached. Progress to the north was even more startlingly rapid, for there by ten o'clock, three-quarters of an hour after the first shout of " En Avant," the French had stormed up the hill, swept over Eckmühl Trench and the Gretchen Trench on towards the Navarin Farm, a little south of the Ste. Marie and Somme-Py roads.

On the eastern side of the semicircle things were by no means so easy, a number of machine guns having escaped destruction in the Bois Sabot, at the southern extremity of the curve, and no great progress was realized here on the first day of the offensive.

The wooded region between Souain and Perthes was in many ways the most interesting bit of the battlefield. It had been fiercely fought for in February and in March, when the French, in spite of almost superhuman efforts, only succeeded in getting a footing in the Bois Sabot and in making slight progress to the west of Perthes on Hill 200. The German defences between these two points had then offered an unshakable resistance. This " Pocket," as the French termed the system of defences, constituted one of the most solidly organized resistance centres of the German line, with its Coblentz work and the Hungarian, Rhine, Prague and Elbe Trenches running from north to south, linked up on the north by the horizontal trenches of Dantzig and Hamburg. To the north of the Pocket lay the core of the defence in the fairly thick woods of the Bricot Hollow, which stretched along a front of about a mile and extend northwards for two and a half miles.

East of the Bricot Hollow the country was bare and easy. Its defences were comparatively slender. The first line was formed by a triple row of trenches with about 100 yards between each. Then, after a distance of about three-quarters of a mile, came a solitary support

IN CHAMPAGNE.
French Colonial troops resting after the battle.

trench—the York Trench—beyond which there was nothing until the second German position was reached at Tahure Ridge.

The main blow was struck at this chink in the armour. The left, playing a secondary part, had been ordered to carry the Pocket and subsequently to cooperate in the envelopment of Bricot Hollow, in which work the troops attacking the eastern slopes of the Souain semicircle were to assist.

The attack was carried through without a hitch. The first assaulting line of Frenchmen and the lines of support had already swept over and beyond the first German trenches before the German artillery awoke to what was happening, and began its barrage fire, which,

hindered at every moment by the French gunners, did but little damage to the waiting French troops in the Place d'Armes, the huge caverns scooped out for the cover of large bodies of men.

At 9.45 a.m. the converging column which attacked the salient of the Pocket joined up. The whole position was surrounded and those of its defenders who were left were made prisoners.

Meanwhile the attack upon the main position had made good progress. Almost at the same time that the Pocket was surrounded the first French battalion had got a footing in the southern edge of the Bricot Hollow woods. While they held on, succeeding battalions which

had been working up northwards to the east
of the woods swung round to the left, seized
the support trenches and installed themselves
in the communication trenches, while other
battalions which had advanced north from
Perthes got into the eastern edge of the wood,
where so rapid and surprising had been their
rush that they surprised some of the officers
calmly lying in bed, so great was their confidence
in the resisting power of the " Steel Barrier " of
the first lines.

The York Trench was occupied almost without a shot being fired, but farther to the east
progress was stayed for a while along the
Perthes-Tahure road, where small blockhouses

IN A FRENCH TRENCH.
A Telephone Operator at work.

and pivot-points put up a desperate fight.
One machine gun, tucked away beneath an
armoured shield, did a great deal of damage, and
was only silenced by the drastic step of bringing
up artillery to bear upon it. An infantry
officer, with the help of an artillery non-commissioned officer, got up a gun to within 300
yards of the obstinate machine and destroyed
it at that range. The dam had burst, however,
and through the breach poured in the French
troops. The later waves had hard fighting with
grenade and bayonet before they cleared out
the wooded clumps. But here again their

arrival was a surprise, batteries of artillery were
rushed from the flank and the rear, and the
gunners bayoneted in the act of firing. Thus
in the advance straight to the north of Perthes
10 heavy guns of 105 mm. and five of
150 mm. were captured. The same process was
going on in the woods to the east of Perthes-
Souain-Tahure roads, where one regiment
travelled two and a-half miles in two hours,
capturing 12 guns, five of 105 mm. and seven of
77 mm.

By the end of the afternoon the Souain-
Tahure road had been reached by the first
French regiment. The advance was great, but
already the difficulties of the attackers were
beginning. The incessant downpour rendered
the work of the artillery very difficult, for they
were now firing on new targets, and observation
spotting was impossible. The advance had
taken place over ground terribly broken by
trench and mine, and liaison between the
different units had broken down. In a few
graphic words a French officer thus described
the scene at this period of the attack :

The Germans were busy pouring a converging fire
upon our men from the Souain and the Tahure Ridges.
The bare stretch of country, veiled in driving rain, was
dotted with scattered groups of men, and officers who had
got separated from their men were hurrying about trying
to find them again. I was trying to restore my regimental liaison, and every now and again a junior officer
of another regiment was reporting to me and asking for
instructions. Disorder was apparent, but everywhere
order was working. It took some time to get things
straightened out again, and the work was rendered easy
by the inner laugh we all got out of a young St. Cyrien—
one of those lucky youths who, had it not been for the
war, would still have been studying the Napoleonic
campaigns at the Military Schools. He came up to me
caked in the chalk mud which covered us all. He was
proud of his chalk and flushed with the elation of sensation. He was even prouder of his sword, for with the
utmost gravity and delightful " panache," instead
of giving the hurried hand salute which, on a battlefield
with shells bursting around us, would have been ample,
he must needs draw his sword and with a fine, if completely incongruous, flourish gave me a magnificent
parade-ground salute, as he reported.

Company was linked to company, regiment
to regiment, and in spite of growing fire from
the Germans the line advanced as far as the
slopes of Hill 193 and the Tahure Ridge.
There the men dug themselves in and waited
for dawn and their artillery.

It was in the Mesnil section that the first day
attack met with the most serious opposition.
Here all that was accomplished was done with
great difficulty. In the course of the previous
winter the French had succeeded in getting
a foothold on Height 196. The Germans
remained in Kitchen Gully ; to the east of this

FRENCH WOUNDED IN A VILLAGE CHURCH.
A church close to the fighting lines used by the French Red Cross to shelter wounded soldiers who were moved out of the danger zone. The wounded were arranged in rows down both sides of the church, and rested on small piles of straw which covered the flagstones.

gully was the only portion of the line which the first day's offensive captured.

North of Beauséjour better fortune attended the French. Almost in one dash they broke through the Fer de Lance and Demi-Lune Woods and the Bastion. Some of their troops were carried right through the hill crest of the Maisons de Champagne, bayoneting gunners at their guns as they swept victoriously on. The mine-torn region of Beauséjour, which

MUNITIONS UNDERGROUND.
The entrance to a French ammunition store.

with its deep craters resembled a lunar landscape, was crossed as far as the Bois Allongé in the Maisons de Champagne road. There the enemy gunners knew what was happening, and they had their horses harnessed and were saving the guns when the French infantry wave burst upon them. The line was pierced here with a vengeance. The gap was growing hour by hour. Everywhere war was once more coming to the surface. The armies of France were moving over ground which had not known the tread of Frenchmen for over a year. Guns were coming out of their lairs, harnessing up, and galloping into action over the trench line they had been bombarding for months. Even the cavalry, as they had shared the winter misery with their infantry comrades in the trenches, had been buoyed up with the hope that their day might come, began to move forward. Their hopes of a dart were disappointed, but at one or two points they did useful work. Thus, in this section two squadrons of hussars, dashing across the enemy's *tir de barrage*, were making for the batteries north of the Maisons de Champagne, when they found themselves under the machinegun fire of a section of the German line which was still holding out. Several horses were killed, and the hussars thereupon dismounted, and sabre in hand advanced to the assistance of the infantry. Thanks to this timely, if unorthodox, assistance, the 600 Germans who were still resisting surrendered.

The extreme east of the line hung upon the tremendously strong positions of the plateau of Massiges. Here the Colonial troops, advancing at the double, got right up to the top of the plateau in a quarter of an hour. There

AFTER THE BATTLE.
Excavation made by a German shell.

their progress was stopped for the day by the tremendous machine-gun concentration of the enemy. But enough had been done at this point, whence the enemy had dominated the entire line, to make secure the gains along the rest of the front.

The day's operations were thus summarised in the official *communiqué* of September 26 :

" In Champagne obstinate engagements have occurred along the whole front.

" Our troops have penetrated the German lines on a front of 25 kilometres (15½ miles) to a depth varying between one and four kilometres (five-eighths to two and a-half miles), and they have maintained during the night all the positions gained.

" The number of prisoners actually counted exceeds 12,000 men."

Thus the results of the first day's fighting may be summed up as being entirely successful. The assault at the two ends of the line around Auberive and Servon failed to carry the position, but with heroic tenacity, under converging artillery fire and counter-attacks, the men fought on, and they retained very large forces of the enemy upon their front, pinned the enemy's two wings down, and thus facilitated the work upon the centre. There the " poilu" had done his work well, but already the obstacles which in the days to come finally brought the movement to a check were hanging the advance up at certain points. The night was passed in quiet activity. The Germans appeared to be stunned by the blow given them, and no counter-attack or bombardment came to worry the preparations for the next day's operations. Throughout the night the roads in the rear were filled with the

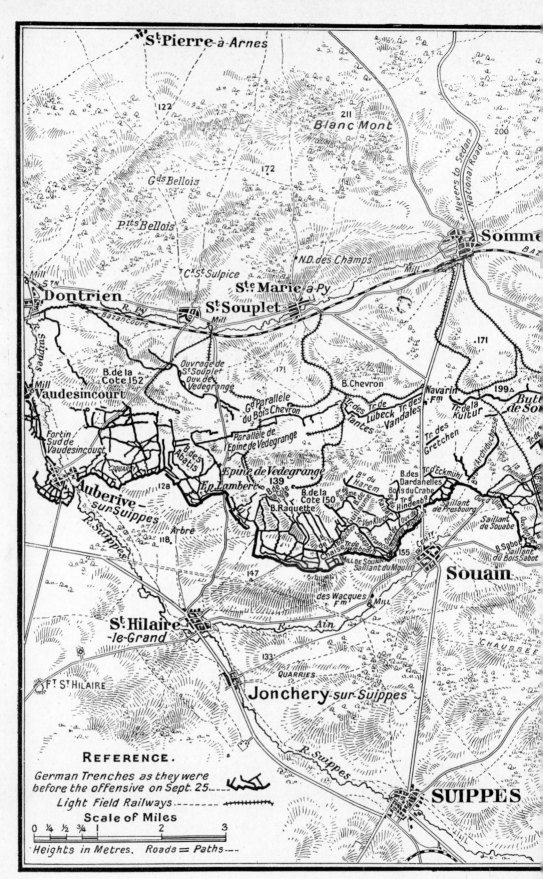

REFERENCE.

German Trenches as they were
before the offensive on Sept. 25.......

Light Field Railways ....

Scale of Miles

0 ¼ ½ ¾ 1   2   3

Heights in Metres.   Roads═══ Paths----

THE GERMAN DEF

(Showing Germ

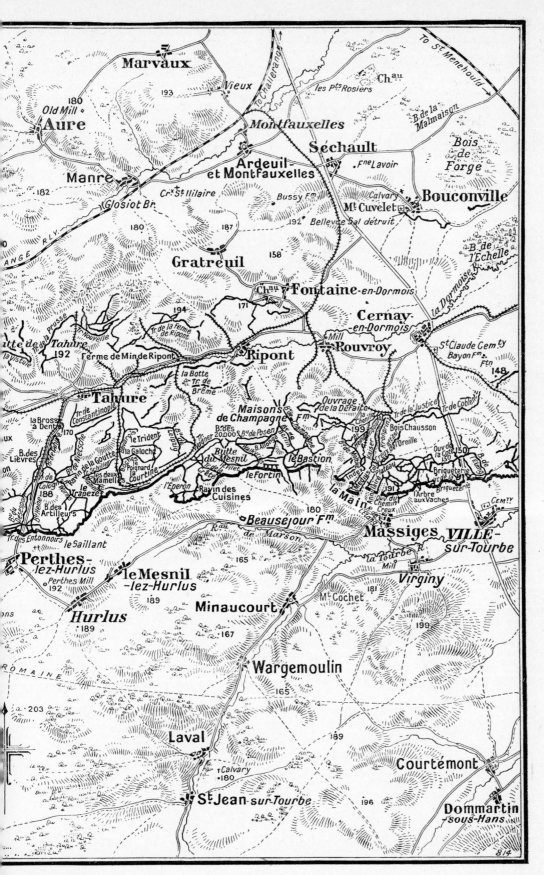

Marvaux
Vieux
193
les P^{ts} Rosiers
Ch^{au}
To St Menehould
To Challerange
180
Old Mill
Aure
Montfauxelles
B de la Malmaison
Séchault
Bois de Forge
Manre
182
Ardeuil-
et Montfauxelles
F^{ne} Lavoir
Glosiot Br.
Cr. St Hilaire
Bussy F^m
Calvary
Mt Cuvelet
Bouconville
180
187
192
Bellevue Sal détruit
158
Gratreuil
B de l'Echelle
ANGE RLY
Ch^{au} Fontaine -en-Dormois
194
171
Cernay-
en-Dormois
la Dormoise R.
Tr. de la Ferme
de Ripont
Tr Nouvelle
Mill
Rouvroy
St Claude Cem ty
tte de Tahure
192
Ferme de Min de Ripont
Ripont
Bayon F^m
F^{tn}
148
la Botte
Tr. de
Brème
Ouvrage
de la Defaite
Tr. de la Justice
Tr. de Coblentz
Tahure
Tr. de Constantinople
Maisons
de Champagne F^m
la Chenil
199
Bois Chausson
la Brosse
à Dents
170
le Trident
la Galoche
B des
20,000
B de Posen
B^e de l'Oreille
Ouv. de
la Côte
150
Ravin de la Goutte
les deux
Mamelles
Butte
du Mesnil
Tr. de Filet
le Bastion
191
l'Arbre
aux Vaches
Briqueterie
B. des
Lièvres
Poignard
la Courtine
Tr. de Crête
le Fortin
la Main
Creux
Cem ty
le Trapèze
l'Eperon
Ravin des
Cuisines
l'Epine de Vedegrange
B. des
Artilleurs
180
Beausejour F^m
Massiges
VILLE-
sur-Tourbe
Tr. des Entonnoirs
le Saillant
R^{au} de Marson
la Tourbe R.
Mill
Perthes-
lez-Hurlus
165
Virginy
Perthes Mill
192
le Mesnil
-lez-Hurlus
181
Mt Cochet
Hurlus
189
189
Minaucourt
199
167
Wargemoulin
165
ROMAINE
203
Laval
189
Courtémont
Calvary
180
St Jean sur Tourbe
196
Dommartin
-sous-Hans
814

AMPAGNE

341

EFFECT OF THE FRENCH SHELL FIRE.
In the distance is seen the remains of a wood, and in the foreground the crater of a mine explosion.

tremendous traffic of supply, of reliefs and reinforcements. Advantage was taken to move up even the heavy artillery, so as to afford support for the continuance of the operation so happily begun.

Going again on the map from west to east, the French had been stayed at the wood bordering the St. Hilaire-St. Souplet road. This they seized on September 27, and on the same day they carried the long Epine de Vedegrange trench, thus getting their teeth into the German second position, where their further progress was stopped by the intact wire entanglements defending the Parallel du Bois Chevron.

In this Vedegrange section the fighting died away after September 28, upon which date the yield of the offensive here was thus stated by the French General Staff : " Capture of nearly 10 square miles of closely fortified country, 44 guns (seven of 105 and six of 150 mm.) and over 5,000 prisoners."

In the Souain section it was not until September 28 that along the whole line the French got into contact with the second German positions. The German defence of the Bois Sabot, composed mainly of machine guns, which had come through the preliminary

bombardment unscathed, had to be enveloped. The circle was completed on the 27th, when the troops coming from the Souain-Tahure road made their junction with the columns attacking to the north of Perthes. A small investing force was left behind, and *parlementaires* were sent to the Germans to point out the hopelessness of further resistance. They were greeted with shots, and in the night the desperate and famished defenders (they had been without food for days) made a forlorn effort to break through.

The greater number of them were killed, and the others, then convinced of the uselessness of further refusal to accept defeat, surrendered.

In front of Perthes, where halt had been called towards noon by the severity of the converging enemy artillery fire, the night was busy, and artillery was brought up right beyond the York Trench to support the next day's movement. The situation of the men was such that they either had to retreat or advance, so at dawn the re-formed regiments pushed forward and got into immediate contact with the second German line from the Souain Ridge to the Tahure Ridge. They even carried one or two advanced parts of that line, but here again they were held up by un-destroyed wire, which lay in great fields on the reverse slope of the hills. Here they lay, digging themselves in, and building up under the guns of the enemy a whole system of defence until October 6.

The *leitmotiv*, as it were, of the succeeding days of the battle was heard strongest in the Mesnil sector. Here even the first day's offensive had spent itself in vain against intact wire, and it was not until six days later that the northern tip of the Mesnil Ridge was captured and the Trapèze on the top of the southern crest encircled.

The most stubborn resistance on September 25 had been encountered on the Main de Massiges. The Germans had some ground for their boast that this position could be held by "two washerwomen and two machine guns," for it was indeed of extraordinary strength. The three hills which run in a south-westerly direction and the valleys between them have the appearance of the back of the first three fingers of a hand. On the Staff maps this similarity is heightened by the network of trenches which cover the heights, which are as close and as complicated as the lines upon a finger. The French had declined the invitation to advance up the open valleys

between these fingers, where certain destruction awaited them, and had struck over the back of the hand, and had got on to the plateau. Here the fighting became one long personal struggle in tunnel and in trench with the bayonet and the grenade. An endless human chain was formed from Massiges, along which grenades were passed from hand to hand to the grenadier parties. The fighting followed a regular course after a fierce bombardment, regulated by flag signals. From the attacking line came a swift avalanche of grenades—the bomb-throwers advancing with bayoneting parties and fighting their way up the narrow trenches foot by foot. A semi-official account of this great feat said :

Having announced in its *communiqué* of September 29 that the French had been unable to take the heights to the north of Massiges, the German General Staff announced, in its *communiqué* of September 30 that Hill 191 had been evacuated because it was taken in the flank by artillery fire. In point of fact, we reached the summit of these heights on September 25, and during the following days completed their conquest. The number of prisoners we made there, together with the still greater number of German corpses which filled the trenches and the communication trenches on Hill 191, bear witness to the bitterness of the struggle. There was no question here of a voluntary evacuation or a retreat in good order, but of a broken resistance and a costly defeat. Our adversaries were holding a for-

AFTER THE FRENCH VICTORY.
A shattered German trench in the Champagne.

THE FRENCH OFFENSIVE IN CHAMPAGNE.

One of the brilliant successes achieved by the French in Champagne was the capture of the village of Tahure and the summit of Butte de Tahure and the famous "Height No. 199."

midable bastion which assured, by flanking works, the security of a great stretch of their front in Champagne. They thought this bastion impregnable. We knew that the saying was current among them, " Hill 191 can be held with two washerwomen and two machine guns."

The possession of this fortress was indispensable to the success of our attack, and the honour of the assault fell to the Colonial Infantry, who wrote a new page of heroism in their history at Massiges. By our first assault on September 25 we reached the summit of the plateau. Our artillery had completely wrecked the slopes and ravines and torn gaps in the barbed-wire entanglements which the enemy had stretched below. The German regiments which occupied Hill 191 at the moment of attack, confident in the solidarity of their fortress, were disorganized and demoralized by the rapidity of our first rush. Their machine guns enabled them to prolong their resistance, but under the weight of our artillery and grenade fire they gave way little by little. Reinforcements selected from the best troops of the Crown Prince's Army were sent to their assistance. These newcomers did justice to their reputation. Overwhelmed by our shells and grenades, they clung to their trenches. "Surrender!" shouted in German the colonel of one of our colonial regiments, who was advancing with his grenadiers and had reached a distance of 30 yards from the enemy. A German lieutenant fired at him and missed. Not one of his men escaped. There are so many corpses in the trenches of Hill 191 that at certain points of the plateau they literally fill up the trenches, and one has to walk over them exposed to the enemy's fire.

Our methodical advance was continued from September 25 to September 30. As the trenches were conquered the Germans, surrounded in the intermediary communication trenches, raised their hands in surrender. We took them prisoners in groups of about a thousand, amongst whom were several officers. One active officer swore at his men. " I can only make them advance with the stick or the revolver," he said. When it felt that the possession of the heights was being wrenched from its grasp, the German General Staff attempted a counter-attack, which debouched from the north-east, but the assaulting troops, as they deployed, came under the fire of our machine guns and artillery, and were swept away in a few moments. The survivors fled in disorder. Our troops, seeing the enemy give ground, continued the fight with joyous ardour. " I can't find men to take the prisoners back," said an officer. They all want to remain up there."

This version of the struggle does but scanty justice to the exploit of the Colonial Corps. The number of German dead which " fill up the trenches " alone testifies to the stubborn resistance which the French had to overcome, and an officer who took part in the fighting was more gallant, and perhaps more accurate, when he declared that " the enemy fought with amazing courage against a still more amazing attack. Time and again the enemy machine guns were only put out of action when the gunners had been bayoneted at their posts. Grenadiers fought with desperation, and so close was the fighting that many of them were killed or wounded by the explosion of their own grenades." The possession of these heights enabled the French to carry by flanking attack the trenches east of the position, which resisted all frontal storming.

The official story of the fighting was contained in the following passages of the *communiqué* issued day by day from the French War Office :

September 26, evening.

In Champagne our troops have continued to gain ground. After crossing on almost the whole front comprised between Auberive and Ville-sur-Tourbe the powerful network of trenches, communication trenches, and forts established and perfected by the enemy during many months, they advanced northwards, compelling the German troops to fall back on the second position trenches, three or four kilometres in the rear.

The fighting continues on the whole front. We have reached the Epine de Vedegrange, passed the cabin on the road from Souain to Somme-Py and the hut on the road from Souain to Tahure. Farther east we hold the farm of Maisons de Champagne.

The enemy has suffered very considerable losses from our fire and in the hand-to-hand fighting. He has left

INFORMATION FROM THE ENEMY.
A German deserter explaining in detail a German position in Champagne to a French officer.

in the works which he has abandoned a large quantity of material, which we have not yet been able to tabulate.

At present the capture of 24 field guns has been reported.

The number of prisoners is increasing progressively, and at present exceeds 16,000 unwounded men, including at least 200 officers.

Altogether, and on the whole front, the Allied troops have taken in two days over 20,000 able-bodied prisoners.

September 28.

In Champagne the struggle continues without intermission.

Our troops are now on a wide front before the second line of the German defences—between Hill 185 (east of the Somme-Py-Tahure road) to the west of the farm of Navarin (on the Souain-Somme-Py road, half way between the two places), the ridge of Souain-Tahure road, and the village and ridge of Tahure.

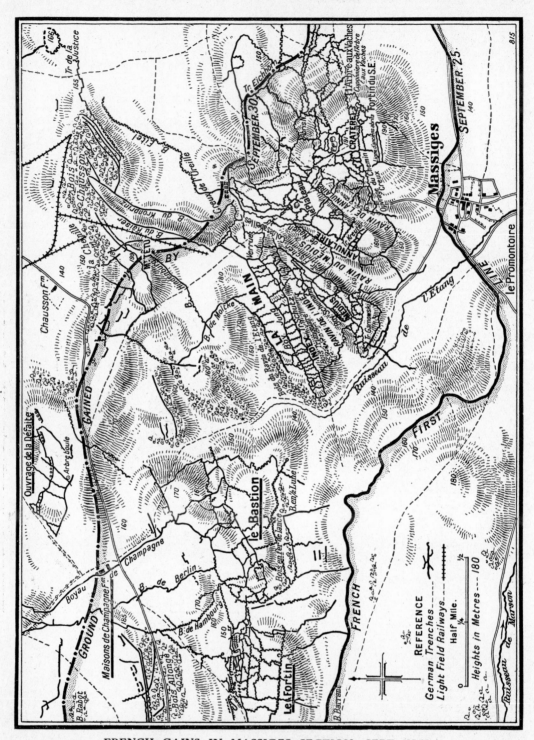

FRENCH GAINS IN MASSIGES SECTION, SEPT. 25-30.

The number of guns captured from the enemy cannot be estimated at the present moment, but it exceeds 70 field pieces and heavy weapons, 23 of which were captured by the British.

The Germans to-day took the offensive in the Argonne, but were stopped.

Four times they attempted an infantry attack on our positions at La Fille Morte, after having bombarded them with projectiles of every calibre and with asphyxiating shells. The enemy was only able to reach at some points our first line trenches, he was stopped there by the fire from our support trenches, and was repulsed everywhere else with heavy losses.

September 28.

In Champagne fighting went on tenaciously along the entire front.

We occupied at several points, notably at the Trou Bricot (about three miles north-east of Souain), north of the Macques Farm, some positions, which we had already passed, in which the enemy still maintained himself.

We made 300 officers prisoners in Champagne, and not 200, as originally reported.

September 29.

In Champagne the Germans are resisting in their reserve positions, protected by extensive and concealed wire entanglements.

We made some further progress towards Hill 185 (west of the Navarin Farm) and towards La Justice, north of Massiges.

In the Argonne, the obstinate attacks delivered yesterday by the enemy, with six to eight battalions, against our first line trenches at La Fille Morte and Bolante resulted in a serious defeat.

The counter-attacks carried out by us in the course of the night permitted us to expel the German infantry from almost all the points where they had been able to penetrate. The ground in front of our trenches is covered with the enemy's dead.

September 30.

The reports which are coming in permit us to measure more completely each day the importance of the success obtained by our offensive in Champagne, combined with that of the Allied troops in Artois.

The Germans have not only been forced to abandon on an extensive front positions which were strongly entrenched, upon which they had orders to resist to the end ; they have sustained losses the total of which in killed, wounded, and prisoners exceeds the strength of three Army Corps.

The total number of prisoners is now over 23,000; the number of guns brought to the rear is 79. Seventeen thousand and fifty-five prisoners and 316 officers have passed through Chalons on their way to their internment destinations.

The clearing of the battlefield and the counting of the arms of every kind, and of the field and trench material which the enemy was obliged to abandon to us, is being proceeded with.

In Artois the progress reported yesterday east of Souchez continued.

October 1.

In Champagne we gained a footing at several points in the German second defensive position west of the Butte de Tahure and west of the Navarin Farm.

At the latter point certain of our troops crossed the German line and advanced determinedly beyond it, but their progress could not be maintained owing to a barrage of artillery fire and very violent flanking bombardments.

Our men are holding firmly the captured positions in the enemy's second line.

South of Ripont (east of Tahure, on the Souain-Tahure-Cernay road) we extended and completed the conquest of the first German position by carrying a part of the important support works known as the "Works of the defeat."

October 2.

In Champagne we stopped dead with our fire a counter-attack in the region of Maisons de Champagne.

The number of prisoners made yesterday evening, in the course of our progress north of Massiges, was 280, including six officers.

In Champagne a *coup de main* between Auberive and l'Epine de Vedegrange enabled us to capture from the enemy more machine guns and about 30 prisoners.

October 4.

In Champagne the Germans bombarded, in the course of the night, our new lines at the Epine de Vedegrange and east of the Navarin Farm. Our troops won a considerable portion of the enemy's positions which formed a salient on the present line north of Mesnil.

In Lorraine German reconnoitring parties attacked two of our posts near Moncel and Sorneville. They were repulsed and pursued until they returned to their lines.

The night was quiet on the rest of the front.

Our air squadrons threw a very large number of projectiles upon the railway stations and lines behind the enemy's front.

To this official record must be added the text of the telegrams exchanged between the Allied Chiefs of State :

PARIS, SEPT. 28.

The Tsar has sent the following telegram to President Poincaré :

"Having received the news of the great success achieved by the glorious French Army, it is with pleasure I seize this happy occasion to express to you and to the valiant Army my warmest congratulations and my sincerest wishes for the future and the unchangeable prosperity of France.

"NICHOLAS."

PARIS, OCT. 1.

King George yesterday sent the following telegram to the President of the French Republic :

"I have followed with admiration the magnificent exploits of the French Army, and seize this opportunity of congratulating you, M. le Président, as well as General Joffre and the whole French nation, on the great success achieved by the valiant French troops since the beginning of our joint offensive.

"GEORGE, R.I."

The congratulations of the President of the Republic to the Army were expressed in the following letter to M. Millerand, Minister of War :

"MY DEAR MINISTER,—The magnificent results produced by our operations in Artois and Champagne enable us to estimate the extent of the victory which the Allied Armies have just won. Our admirable troops have given in this tough fighting new proofs of their incomparable ardour, of their spirit of sacrifice, and of their sublime devotion to the Fatherland. They have definitely asserted their superiority over the enemy.

"I beg you to transmit to the General-in-Chief, to the Generals commanding Army groups and Armies, and to all the Generals, officers, non-commissioned officers, and soldiers, my warmest and most heartfelt congratulations.

"Believe, my dear Minister, in my most devoted sentiments.

"(Signed) R. POINCARÉ."

In this bald official phraseology a thousand epics lay hidden. Concealed in the restrained language of the *communiqué* writer were a thousand feats of arms, each of which was worthy to inspire another Homer. In singing the praises of the French troops the lyric mood

FRENCH CAVALRY CHARGING THE GERMAN GUN POSITIONS IN CHAMPAGNE.

Outstripping their infantry comrades who were dealing with the first-line trenches, the cavalry pushed on to the German gun positions, and were among

is alone permissible. They performed prodigies of valour, and countless are the instances of direct sacrifice for the welfare of the country. In no way is the merit of the French troops' behaviour lessened by a more detailed description of the effects of the French bombardment upon the German trenches. The strength of that line had to be seen to be believed. Shells such as were employed at that moment in the war were about the size of a pillar-box, and did not contain enough high explosive to shatter the shelters and caverns in which the enemy infantry lay waiting with their machine-guns.

General Castelnau had said before the beginning of the offensive that he wanted the bombardment to be so terrific that his men might go to the attack of the opposing trench lines with their rifles at the shoulder. It was the business of M. Albert Thomas, Under Secretary of State for Munitions, to see to it that the realization of this wish was possible. M. Albert Thomas is one of the very few instances in the war up to this period of a man being developed who really was worthy of the circumstances. Known before the outbreak of the war to his political friends and opponents as L'Homme-Chien, on account of his tremendous growth of beard and hair, M. Albert Thomas was recognized rather as one of the coming forces of International Socialism, as an economical writer of the French business man's journal *L'Information*, than as the great " organizer of victory," as his friends did not hesitate to name him in 1915. For a long time he worked behind the scenes, and it was not until long after the Battle of the Marne had flung the invader back from Paris that France as a whole learned that in all matters of artillery and shell supply M. Millerand, who was the Minister of War, had had the benefit of M. Albert Thomas's advice. His position was given official recognition by his appointment to the newly created post of Under-Secretary of State for Munitions, not long after the great shell upheaval in Great Britain and the consequent appointment of Mr. Lloyd George to the new portfolio of the Ministry of Munitions. M. Thomas was inevitably dubbed the French Lloyd George. The service he rendered to France was, to say the least of it, equal to that so splendidly given to Britain by his British colleague, and the title reflected honour upon each. Like Mr. Lloyd George, M. Albert Thomas had to fight against the dead weight of settled convictions, of settled procedure in the minds and methods of bureaucracy. Like Mr. Lloyd George, and perhaps before him, he conquered all those difficulties, and although it may be said that the offensive in Champagne came to an end through a miscalculation, a misunderstanding, a non-realization as to the tremendous quantity of high explosive to blast a way through the main German line, both first and second, in the Champagne, the blame—if blame of any sort there be—cannot be laid at the door of M. Albert Thomas. As he frankly stated to the Paris correspondent of *The Times* while the offensive was still in progress on September 29, there were three lessons to be gained from the success of the Champagne offensive. The first was perhaps the most satisfying. It was that all agitation for shells and for the mobilization of industry (of which the agitation in Parliamentary Committees was by no means the least important) had been " a real and solid work." The writer, who in March had visited the State arsenal of Bourges, who had stayed at the works of Messrs. Schneider & Co. at Le Creusot, was among the first privileged to see the tremendous purpose of French industrial mobilization. The men, who, bare to the waist, and sweating with the work, let loose the flood of molten steel from the furnace, who watched over its safe progress to the moulds, who toiled and troubled at the presses, who pushed backwards and forwards through rollers the long trunk of red-hot steel, the men who measured calibres with a precision such that the thousandth part of a tenth of an inch made all the difference between acceptance and rejection, the old peaceful ladies from Brittany in white lace caps who, with pots of spring flowers before them, stamped out the parts of the shell first, poured the deadly mixture of chemical into the hollow steel cavern of the shells, they all had before them but one aim—- the beating of the Boches. Only this unity of national purpose rendered possible the tremendous shell expenditure of the trench in the Champagne.

The second lesson of the offensive, according to M. Thomas's remarks to the Paris correspondent of *The Times*, was " that the work accomplished had been carried out upon the right lines, and had given the troops the shells they wanted in the qualities and quantities required for the needs of the attack." In other words, all the old Colonial experience— whether it be South African or Moroccan—as

ON THE CHAMPAGNE BATTLEFIELD.
The French Red Cross at work.

to the benefits of shrapnel, had been laid on one side; the special requirements of siege warfare had been met by provision of vast quantities of high-explosive shell which, poured in sufficient quantities upon the opposing front, destroys all semblance of trench, levels the deep-dug line with the rest of the country in a multitude of volcanic explosions.

Never before had such a whirlwind of shell and chemicals been unloosed upon the earth. The unfinished letters found upon the prisoners made in the fighting bear eloquent testimony to the horror of the bombardment. Thus one German soldier, writing on September 24, said: "For two days the French have been fighting like madmen. To-day, for example, one of our shelters was demolished. There were sixteen men in it. Not one remained alive. There are also a great many isolated dead and a great mass of wounded. The artillery fire as quickly as the infantry. A cloud of smoke hangs so thick upon the front of battle that nothing is to be seen. The men are falling like flies. The trenches are nothing but a heap of ruins." In other letters and note-books there is talk of the "rain of shells." A man in the 100th Regiment of Field Artillery, writing on September 25, said: "We have been through bitter hours; it seemed as though the world were crumbling to pieces. We have had many losses; a company of 250 men had 60 men killed last night and a neighbouring battery

lost 16. The following incidents will show you the terrible power of French shells. A shelter, 15 ft. deep, with 12 ft. of earth above it and two layers of timber, was broken like a match." In a report made out on the morning of September 24 by a company commander it is stated, "The French are firing upon us with heavy shells and mitrailleuses; we must have reinforcements quickly; many of the men are no longer good for anything. It is not that they are wounded, but they belong to the Landsturm and the wastage is bigger than our reported losses. Send supplies of food at once; no rations have reached us to-day. We are in urgent need of flares and hand-grenades. Is the sanitary column never going to come?"

On the morning of September 25 the cry of despair was acute. The same officer wrote: "I insist upon having reinforcements. My men are dying of fatigue and lack of sleep. I am without any news of the battalion."

Perhaps one of the most graphic accounts of the bombardment was furnished from German sources. It is that of Professor Wegener, correspondent of the *Cologne Gazette*:

It is Friday morning. During the night we have been hearing the sound of distant gun-fire which in volume and duration has exceeded anything we have experienced since we have been here.

Yesterday evening already the bombardment was exceptionally lively; it then died down towards midnight. But at about 4 o'clock this morning it started afresh, with unprecedented intensity—a typical big-scale bombardment, with shot following shot in one unbroken growl of thunder, like the roll of drums. One hour—two hours—four hours—and still no end to it !

There is excitement in the town. The like of it has not been heard ever since the days when the first German advance passed like a storm over this region. Where is it ? What does it mean ?

The thunder of distant guns can be heard better up on the hills than down in the valley. So I went up to the top of the hill which rises outside the town. And I have just returned. It is now 11 a.m., and the guns are still thundering. It is extraordinary. The roll of the bombardment in the Argonne which preluded the recent French attack on the Marie Thérèse fieldworks lasted from 8 to 11—three hours. This bombardment has already been going on for more than twice as long. And the sound of it, up on the top of the hill . . . ! The whole atmosphere was in a state of dull vibration ; it seemed as if one perceived the sound not only with the ear, but as if one had the physical sensation of being shaken by the air-waves. It was as if the sound came up from the unknown depths of the earth. Indeed, more than anything it was like the uncanny underground growling of a distant volcano in eruption, shaking—as I have repeatedly experienced it in Java and in Martinique—the earth's crust for miles around and making it tremble like a man in a fit of ague.

It was the most remarkable and exciting sensation imaginable. All around, as far as the eye could reach, the countryside lay bathed in a gracious peace, and through the clear, sunlit air, from beyond the sky-line, came these awe-inspiring sounds. It seemed to come straight from the south, or perhaps from south-south-west, and therefore from Champagne. A peculiarly sultry, oppressively hot south wind, a sort of sirocco, unusual in these parts was blowing from that quarter ; and it may be that this wind carried the sound with unwonted clearness.

In any case something tremendous and awful is going on. What it is, whether it is we, or the French, or both, I cannot, as I write these lines, yet tell. But I think that it is likely to be the rolling thunder of French guns, probably between Reims and the Argonne. Nor am I altogether surprised by it. On the contrary, I had, almost with certainty, expected it.

The reader will remember that I recently went out to join General Fleck's Rhenish Corps in Champagne in the expectation that something might happen there during my stay. It is an open secret that we are reckoning with the possibility of an attempt by the enemy to start a new great offensive somewhere on the West front. We are ready for it ; the whole front is in a state of electric tension ; and I am not going too far when I say that there is hope, too, in the hearts of our troops, who are eager for the fray. I cannot state at which point our supreme command primarily expects the attack. At

JAPANESE MILITARY OFFICERS VISIT THE BATTLEFIELD.
The officers, wearing steel helmets, common to the French forces, inspecting a ruined village.

several points perhaps; at many points at once, it may be.

In Champagne itself there was a very strong expectation that this region would be one of the points of attack. For a long time past we have observed the considerable movements, by road and by rail, which have been proceeding along and behind the French front over against us. Prisoners have told us that on the other side, too, there is this peculiar atmosphere of tension. The Chief of Staff of the . . . Army, who received us before we left to join Fleck's Corps, told us the same thing. We have so far not witnessed an attack of the expected kind; but in manifold ways we have learned how an attack of this kind will be parried. There was, thank God, no tendency to minimize the seriousness of a new great lunge forward by the French; but always when we asked, " Do you think they can break through ? " we met with the uniform reply, " Out of the question."

Towards noon the voice of the guns at last was still. Everyone who has heard it on the spot knows how awful and terrible a thing, even for the victor who holds

IN THE FRENCH TRENCHES.
A grenade-thrower.

the ground at the last, is the sound of them, as I heard it to-day, like the rolling of drums.

This bombardment was both moral and material in its effect. While trenches went up in a floating veil of smoke and dust along the front shelters, and batteries were pounded to pieces, and the whole steel barrier was crumbling away, the moral and fighting spirit of the enemy was being undermined through the physical deprivation of sleep and food, and by the sense of isolation brought about by the complete rupture of communications not only with the rear and the source of authority but even with the neighbouring trench defenders. There is no more striking contrast than that to be drawn between the victorious French and the defeated Germans in this battle. For the collapse of their moral, and, indeed, of the whole of their elaborate staff machinery, the Germans cannot claim the mitigating circumstances of complete surprise. Operations which demand an incessant bombardment of many weeks, which demand a close preparation during many months, cannot be held entirely secret, especially with the aeroplane and photography. For many weeks before the storm burst the waiting and eager Frenchmen in the trenches had been taunted by their foe. Day after day placards had been hoisted in the German trenches telling the French in more or less provocative language that the Germans knew they were going to attack, and asking them to screw their courage up to do it at an early moment. Aeroplanes had dropped leaflets among French troops

IN THE FRENCH TRENCHES.
Setting off a flare rocket.

in the Argonne bearing similar taunts and questions.

Already on August 15 General von Ditfurth in an Army order warned his men "to expect the possibility of a great French offensive." On September 22 General von Fleck, who commanded a portion of the German army in Champagne, issued the following order to his troops :

Armeegruppe Fleck, 1 A NR 21845,
Armeegruppenbefehl.

Comrades : Let us swear in this solemn hour that each one of us. no matter where he may be, whether in the trenches, or in the batteries, or in positions of command, no matter where, will do his duty there right to the bitter end. Wherever the enemy may hurl himself to the assault we will receive him with a well-directed fire, and if he reaches our positions we will throw him back at the point of the bayonet, and pelt him with hand grenades.

A BOMB WHICH DID NOT EXPLODE.
The projectile was dropped from a German aeroplane outside a French trench.

If we have the determination to act in this manner, and if we are determined to face death, every enemy attack will be broken by us, and the country may confidently look on this wall of steel constituted by her sons.

Complete surprise was, perhaps, impossible to achieve, but in the limits of possibility the French succeeded in misleading the enemy, who, aware of the general line which was about to be attacked, had not for a moment foreseen the tremendous force which had been gathered behind the French lines for the assault, and had completely miscalculated the means of victory which the French had fashioned for themselves in their war factories, and which they had always possessed in the incomparable valour of the French soldier. The ignorance of the German General Staff as to the magnitude of the blow about to be dealt to the

FRENCH HELIOGRAPHER AT WORK.
Reading distant signals.

Western line is clearly shown by the inadequacy of the steps they took to meet it, for during the artillery preparation they only reinforced their Champagne front with the 183rd Brigade, the 5th Division of the 3rd Corps, and half the 43rd Reserve Division, or, in other words, twenty-nine battalions. This somewhat arrogant contempt of the German General Staff for the offensive capacities of their enemy was reflected right away through the military hierarchy, and received clear illustration in the capture of a number of German officers in the second line, both in Bricot Hollow and at the Epine de Vedegrange. These officers, although they had been informed that a

ON THE BATTLEFIELD.
Collecting trophies.

ON THE BATTLEFIELD.
German prisoners carrying in a blanket one of
their seriously wounded comrades.

Inset : Captured Prussian Guards in their trenches.

front round Soissons, in the Argonne, in the
Woevre, and in Alsace. In the handling of
these reserves, in the manner in which they
were brought into the firing line, there was a
complete absence of that spirit of method
which was the strength of German staff work.
The men were sent off from their billets battalion by battalion, as soon as they were ready
to move, and so pressing was the need that they
were even moved in detachments of a couple
of companies. They reached the front anyhow
and anywhere, as was shown by another
"letter which did not reach him," found on a
soldier belonging to the 18th Regiment, in
which he says :

We started on a mad race in motor-cars through
Vouziers as far as Tahure. There we had two hours of
rest in the rain, and then we started off on a six-hours'
march for our positions. On our way we were wel-
comed so heartily by the enemy's shell fire that only
224 of the 280 men of the second company got to the
trenches safe and sound. These trenches had been
newly dug, were scarcely deeper than four or five inches.
Mines and shells constantly burst around us, and
we had to keep these trenches and look after them for
118 hours without having anything hot to eat. It
cannot be worse in hell. To-day 600 fresh men arrived
for the regiment. In five days we have lost as many
and more.

Units arrived in confusion, and the disorder was shown by the fact that of the regiments of the 5th Division of the 3rd Corps
the 81st was located near Massiges, while one
battalion of the 12th was at Tahure and a
battalion of the 32nd at Bricot Hollow. The
regiments of the 56th Division were strung
along the front in a similarly haphazard

French general offensive could be expected,
were so confident in the resisting strength of
their first line that even after communications
of every sort had been interrupted between
the first and second line they gave not a
thought to the matter, and, as we have seen,
were captured by the victorious French infantry while in their beds.

Everything tends to show that the completeness and the rapidity with which the first
line was rushed constituted that element of
surprise which in war is one of the essentials
of success.

That surprise threw the whole staff work
of the German army into confusion. The
local reserves they had formed to meet the
expected offensive were entirely inadequate,
and they had to throw hurriedly into battle
not only the 10th Corps brought back from
Russia, but even the local reserves of the

manner, the 88th and 35th Regiments at Massiges, the 91st at Souain, and a battalion of the 79th west of Tahure Ridge. So great was the muddle made by the German General Staff in bringing up their reinforcements that on the small stretch of front between Maisons de Champagne and Hill 189 there were on October 2 no less than 32 battalions belonging to no less than twenty-one different regiments. These men were flung into the inferno of battle badly rationed, badly equipped, and lacking proper supplies of ammunition; they were rushed to a front of which their officers had no personal knowledge, without any definite plan save that of stemming the French advance wherever the two lines came into contact, and with no means of establishing their liaison with neighbouring battalions. The haste with which these men were brought into action on positions already completely swept by the French fire, and which had already been mastered by the French infantry, explains a portion of the very heavy losses suffered by the Germans.

The reinforcements the Germans sent did no more than replace their losses, and on the first day of the offensive the enemy was completely incapable of serious resistance, even through his artillery.

It was, indeed, one of the most noticeable features of the first day's fighting that the German artillery was not only badly served and badly equipped with shell, but also it was always late. The tirs de barrage, which are always the first real line of protection against assault, came in on nearly every section of the front after successive waves of French infantry had swept over the barrage zone.

The utmost the enemy could do was to launch a counter-attack upon specially threatened positions, and even then those attacks were only carried out upon very restricted fronts. They were hastily organized and badly conceived, and resulted, as was shown by the fate of the attack launched upon the French on the Massiges heights, in heavy losses. Here it was that the enemy sent forward isolated battalions of the 123rd, 124th, and 30th Active Regiments, and of the 2nd Ersatz Regiment of the 16th Corps. The losses of these battalions as they broke one after the other upon the counter-shock of the French advance were extraordinarily heavy.

The experience of this and similar counter-attacks along the front proved the accuracy of General von Ditfurth's impressions, which had been conveyed to his troops in an army order in which he said, " I have the impression that our infantry at some points confines its action solely to the defensive. . . . I cannot energetically enough protest against such proceedings, which of necessity result in killing the spirit of the offensive among our own men, in wakening and in strengthening the feeling of superiority among our enemies. The enemy is given his full freedom of action, and our own action is subordinated to the enemy's will."

Another sure sign of the decay in the enemy's moral is seen in the numbers of German prisoners, in the manner in which they surrendered as well as in the statements they made to their captors. The Paris Correspondent of *The Times*, in a telegram about

GERMAN PRISONERS
Being conducted to the rear by way of their own communication trenches.

the battle of September 30, thus described the general impression conveyed by the prisoners, and noted the contrast between the attitude of those captured, particularly the officers, and that of the prisoners after the Battle of the Marne :

Everywhere large bodies of Germans left behind in the retreat are surrendering. In this work of clearing up behind the first impetuous dash African cavalry performed excellent service. . . . For the most part the captured prisoners made a good impression. Here and there men who had been cut off for days from their supplies were exhausted and famished, but the majority of the men, although dazed by the violence of the bombardment, were well-nourished, and once they had been captured were delighted to be out of it. Their good humour may be judged from the following little picture, outlined to me by a wounded officer, of some twenty prisoners who had been marshalled under an escort of cavalry. Noticeable among them was a tall, fat, blonde, spectacled German, of the type rendered familiar by the caricaturist. The convoy was rather slow in starting ; when the officer gave the command "En avant, marche," adding the German "Schnell, schnell," this particular man started off with such good-will that he fell, and as he was at the head of the section rolled several feet down the hillside. His comrades in captivity immediately burst into a roar of laughter.

The officers were pained and surprised by their predicament. They accused the French artillery, as they have done before, of "inhumanity," but on the whole they were noticeably less arrogant and more polite than after the Battle of the Marne.

In the creation of this chastened mood the losses inflicted by artillery fire, the nervous tension of living in an inferno of bursting shell, mine, and torpedo, played an enormous part. A lieutenant who was not captured until five days after the offensive was begun, after the terrific rainstorm had ceased, had in his note-book : "Again fine weather. If it would only begin to rain again, or if only the fog would come. But now the airmen will come, and we shall have again torpedo fire and flanking fire upon the trenches. This beastly good weather ! Fog, fog, come to our aid ! "

It is very difficult to state with any accuracy the extent of the German losses in the battle, but from the declarations of prisoners the French were enabled to form a general estimate of the enemy casualties. It was known that at the beginning of September the enemy had some seventy battalions on the Champagne front. Anticipating the French offensive they brought up twenty-nine battalions, so that when the storm broke loose they had, taking into account the normal quota of artillery and engineers, 115,000 men directly engaged in the battle. Between September 25 and October 15 so heavy were the losses of the Germans, either through the preliminary bombardment or in the actual assault or the futile and costly

counter-attacks, that whole battalions had ceased to exist, and the German General Staff was forced to replace almost completely the 115,000 men who had met the first few days of onslaught, and they brought up no less than ninety-three fresh battalions. A man of the 3rd Battalion of the 153rd Regiment, which was engaged on September 26, stated, indeed, that so tremendous were the losses of that regiment that after it had been engaged only for two days—that is to say, after it had suffered one day of sustained bombardment and one day of actual infantry fighting—it had to be withdrawn from action, as it had ceased to present the characteristics of a regiment. The same fate overtook other units, such as the 27th Reserve Regiment and the 52nd Active Regiment after one day of battle ; for on the evening of September 25 the French had captured of the one 13 officers and 933 men, and of the other 21 officers and 927 men.

The losses were undoubtedly heaviest on the German side during the first two days of the actual battle, and it may reasonably be estimated that of the 115,000 men the French had against them about 50 or 60 per cent. were killed, wounded, or captured. The support furnished by the fresh battalions brought up and thrust hurriedly forward under heavy fire lost about 50 per cent.

There was another cause which increased the German net loss. In every country improvements in the medical service have reduced the number of permanently incapacitated wounded men, and had the battle been a normal operation the Germans would undoubtedly have been able to save a great number of their wounded, and return them to the front after a few weeks in hospital. In this Champagne struggle the evacuation of the wounded to the rear was impossible, and it is no exaggeration to state that nearly the entire force defending the first German line became a dead loss to Germany, for in addition to the 20,000 unwounded prisoners were all the wounded, who, in normal circumstances, would have been evacuated. After careful collation of evidence the French General Staff estimated that this dead loss in killed, wounded, and captured amounted to no less than 140,000 men.

The French soldier was his own Homer in the battle, and no poet could improve the splendid virility of the phrases in which the

"GOOD-BYE, COMRADE."

An incident in the battle of Champagne: a commander of a French battalion stops to shake hands with a wounded captain.

thin impetuous aristocrats and the tubby but wiry little bourgeois voiced the glory of the day or uttered their own epitaphs. There in those glorious fields of Champagne the words of Wolfe became a commonplace. An officer in charge of a reconnaissance was wounded mortally. He turned to his sub-lieutenant, saying: "Obey me once more. Carry on the reconnaissance, and leave me to die. We have won. I am happy." A lieutenant who had been wounded for the first time at the Battle of the Marne, and who had been sent back to the front at his own request, had passed through a very violent *tir de barrage* with his men, and was killed on the parapet of the trench he conquered, shouting encouragement to his men: "Bravo, my children; the Boches are clearing out. *En avant! Vive la France!*" A lieutenant-colonel, who had carried his battalion over a mile and a half of country without stopping, was mortally wounded, and as he lay upon the ground, he shouted out: "*En avant!* I can only die once." Countless were the cases in which wounded officers and men lying in the trenches and the communication tunnels begged their comrades to throw them out of the trench on to the fields swept by machine-gun fire, so that they might not impede the traffic up the trench. "Go on," cried one man, who was lying wounded on the road, to an officer, who was stepping aside to avoid him, "I'm wounded. The whole people are the only ones that matter to-day." A captain,

HONOUR TO THE BRAVE: THE SALUTE TO A WOUNDED GENERAL.

General Marchand, who was grievously wounded in the Battle of Champagne, being carried to the rear on a stretcher borne by an officer and three stretcher bearers.

who had been badly wounded by a grenade splinter in the face, refused to go to the rear to have his wound attended to, saying, " I can't stop for a small wound to-day ; death is the only thing that will stop me!" He remained in his trench and fought for five days before he was killed.

This holy fire of heroism descended upon the whole army, and at no time has the democracy of France been more splendidly manifest. Officers' servants accompanied their masters into battle, where their duties did not call them, and when the battlefield was cleared up many of these servants were found lying dead in front of their masters, killed by the same bullet or the same shell. Perhaps the most extraordinary instance of this devotion of the men to their officers is to be found in the official record of the death of a captain in the Colonial Artillery. When he reached the second German trench he fell, shot full in the chest by a German who had raised himself above the parapet. The men around the officer immediately stormed the trench and bayoneted the little group of men of the 30th Prussian Infantry Regiment who defended it. Among the dead they recognized the man who had killed their captain. They took out his body, and while under very hot rifle and machine-gun fire, propped it up against the parapet, near their dying officer, who said, " I'm glad to fight with men like you, and to shed my blood with you for such a cause." When the German body had been placed in position one of the soldiers drew a camera from his haversack, and, still under terrible fire, took a snapshot, of the man who had killed his captain, saying as he turned the film, " We'll send that to the Captain's mother. It will show her that he was avenged."

As an example of the French soldier's complete ignorance of his own bravery the following letter from Sergeant Quittot to the captain commanding a Colonial company should be quoted : " I am in charge of the small post on the left of the hollow road. This morning I noticed that the shots fired upon us came from our left. I went out there and found three Boches in a machine-gun shelter. I killed two of them, who tried to run away, I have the third at your disposal, for I think he may have some useful information. In this shelter there are the machine-gun carriage and some range-finding instruments, twenty-five full boxes of ammunition,

and three reservoirs with rubber tubes, the use of which I don't know. What should I do ? I think there are still more Boches in the other trench. I am at your disposal if you want them put in the soup. I am keeping the prisoner with me."

Here, indeed, was the much-advertised New France. But Old France also had its page of glory. A lieutenant, a man of sixty-two years of age, who had rejoined the army on the outbreak of the war, took part in the first assault and was killed as he cried to his men, " Now then, parade step ; hold your heads high. To-day we're off to the ball." A corporal who had been wounded turned to his sergeant, who lay wounded beside him, saying : " I know I'm going to die ; but what does that matter since it's for France ? " A colonel in command of a Colonial infantry brigade, spent the five minutes before the first offensive was timed to start in fixing his cap and brushing the chalk off his uniform, and at a quarter past nine ordered the regimental flag to be unfurled. Then, as, first along the line, he clambered up the trench ladder to the open field, he turned to those behind him saying : " Gentlemen, my time has come," and fell back, killed by a shell splinter.

The initiative of the French soldier was in a very great degree responsible for the rapidity with which the confusion between the first and second German lines was restored. Men who had lost all their officers seemed to have an instinctive grasp of what was required of them, and pressed forward under the leadership of any private who assumed command. Thus 300 men who had lost all their officers on the eve of September 25 captured a German trench. Finding themselves far in advance of the rest of the line and without support or liaison they evacuated the trench in the night, and the next morning, still without officers and without orders, they set off again, recaptured the trench, and continued to advance.

It is impossible to say whether the officers inspired their men by the countless acts of collective and individual bravery of those September days, whether the men inspired the officers, or whether, faced with a tremendous crisis in the country's history, the whole nation was found equal to the demands made upon it. Among the men there is the case of Sergeant Quittot. At the other end of the military hierarchy is the case of General Marchand. Early in the morning of September 25 the General was in the advanced sap which had been pushed out during the night right up to the German lines, far in advance of the normal trench line. Of the first wave of assault two currents to right and to left advanced without difficulty towards the Navarin Farm. The centre was held up by four machine-guns which had escaped destruction by artillery; officers and men were falling one after the other; there was the inevitable moment of wavering hesitation. Then General Marchand, his pipe in his mouth, and armed with a walking-stick, dashed out, and as he took his place at the head of the hesitating centre, he fell with a bullet through his abdomen. His orderly officer ran to him, and ignoring the order of the General, who said: " I'm hit; my spinal column is broken; leave me alone," had him carried to the rear. Meanwhile his men, fired by his example and the desire to make the Germans pay dearly for their General, swept forward and pierced the German centre.

The results of all this heroism, of all the straining and toiling in the factories of France, of all the vast work of staff preparation which had gone on without a break for five months, were extremely important; for the French victory in the Champagne, although it remained from the military point of view tactical, was almost the first definite notification to the world that initiative along the Western front had passed from the hands of the Germans into those of the Allies.

An attack upon a first line is a very different matter from a simultaneous assault upon a first and second line. In the Champagne months of stationary warfare had enabled the French to get the exact range of every position upon the first line, but when their artillery moved up new range-finding became a necessity, geography became more doubtful, reconnaissance work, having been of necessity entirely aerial, became less reliable. When the French reached the German second line they became aware practically for the first time of the formidable nature of its defence, and, perhaps,

the greatest obstacle to the strategic completion of the French offensive was found in the system the Germans had adopted for defending their second line along the crest of the hill running parallel to the Challerange-Bazancourt Railway. Upon the south-western slopes exposed to land observation there was practically no sign of defensive preparation. Here and there, upon the face of a hill could be seen a few sandbags, an occasional mound of white upturned chalk denoting the emplacement of a machine-gun section or an observation post. These positions, as the French found out after the offensive had been launched, were but the outworks of the main defence. Upon the " other side of the hill," to quote Napoleon's expression, lay the German surprise. It consisted of dense sunken fields of barbed wire, huge pits dug in the chalk soil to a depth of six or seven feet, and, on an area of about seventy yards, filled up to the level of the earth with solid barbed-wire entanglements. Behind these entanglements, which were practically invisible from the air and completely screened by the crest of the hill from the French observers in the forward trenches, lay a whole system of fortification, in which each hill became a bastion, and swept with an enfilading fire of machine-guns and field-guns the zone separating it from the similar bastions to its right and to its left. The post on the exposed side of the hill communicated with the hidden trenches through galleries driven right underneath the hill peak.

This line of defence had remained comparatively untouched by the artillery bombardment, and although the French in subsequent fighting got a footing in it, the exploit of the Germans on the Dunajec in breaking through the Russian front and rolling up its edges was not repeated.

In short, the Champagne offensive was a trial of strength which was in some ways comparable with the victories of Austerlitz and Jena, although it did not achieve so victorious a result. It nevertheless turned very definitely in favour of the Allies, and constitutes one of the finest pages in the military history of France.

CHAPTER CV.

THE BATTLE OF LOOS.

THE great offensive of the French in the Champagne Pouilleuse, described in the last chapter, coincided with the Battles of Loos and Vimy. These were in effect a renewal on a still more gigantic scale of the Battles of Artois, the Aubers Ridge, and Festubert delivered by Generals Foch, d'Urbal, and Sir John French in the preceding May. The same leaders were now to renew their efforts to win their way into the Plain of the Scheldt between the La Bassée salient and the Scarpe, while General de Castelnau between Reims and the Argonne endeavoured to drive back the Germans before him to the banks of the Aisne.

By the third week of September, 1915, thanks to a stream of reinforcements from England, the British Army had extended its right wing to Grenay opposite Loos and Lens, taking over from the French, and consolidating and enlarging most of the trenches which ran southwards from the Béthune-La Bassée Canal to the ridge and plateau of Notre Dame de Lorette. The numbers of the British were sufficient for the coming battle.

It was not with numbers alone, however, that the British Army had been strengthened. The additional troops sent by us to France had all arrived properly equipped with a due proportion of artillery, in addition to which a large number of guns and howitzers had reached the army and furnished it with a material which more than fulfilled expectations, and which indeed produced far greater moral and physical effects on the Germans than the latter had ever believed possible. The British and French attacks were necessarily frontal because the German line was continuous to the sea. Under these circumstances no attack can be successful unless it has been properly prepared by artillery fire. It is necessary to create a point where the infantry can break in. To do this not only must the hostile defences be thoroughly disposed of, but the obstacles in front of them must be swept away before an assault can be successful. To destroy fortifications of the semi-permanent character which the Germans had erected, to blow away parapets, ruin trenches, and the bomb-proof shelters of concrete and iron constructed in them, requires shells of vast weight containing

361

IN NORTHERN FRANCE.
British troops on their way to the trenches.

very large high-explosive bursting charges. By the time the advance was determined on sufficient howitzers and heavy guns were available. The guns which the divisions possessed, 18-pounders, 60-pounders, and 4·5 in. howitzers were ready to play their part in totally destroying the broad belts of barbed wire obstacles which covered the front of the German line. Through these no troops, however gallant, could possibly hope to penetrate so long as the troops in the trenches behind them could bring a concentrated fire from numerous machine guns and rifles to bear on the assailants.

For decisive victories in Artois and Champagne it was not sufficient merely to collect there men, artillery, and munitions. If they knew in advance where Joffre's and French's great blows were to be struck, the German leaders by means of their railroads and motor-traction might accumulate in the Champagne Pouilleuse and in Artois artillery and numbers capable of rendering the Allied efforts nugatory. The German reserves had to be diverted to other points on the four hundred mile long line of battle. To effect this purpose feigned attacks were organized. It was decided that while General de Castelnau delivered the main French attack through the Champagne Pouilleuse, as already described in Chapter CIV., General Dubail, who had mastered some of the gateways into Alsace, should demonstrate, as if he were about to descend from the Vosges to the banks of the Upper Rhine.

At the extreme end of the Allied left wing similar demonstrations were made. On the evening of September 24 Vice-Admiral Bacon sent two monitors and certain auxiliary craft to bombard the next day Knocke, Heyst, Zeebrugge, and Blankenberghe, while with other vessels an attack was made on the fortified positions west of Ostend. In both cases considerable damage was done to the enemy's works. On September 26, 27, and 30 further attacks were made on the various batteries and strong positions at Middelkirke and Westende. From August 22, indeed, the British Admiral with the seventy-nine vessels at his disposal had at frequent intervals bombarded the Belgian coast-line from the mouth of the Yser at Nieuport to the Dutch frontiers. This bombardment, which was especially severe on September 19 and 25, might signify in the German eyes an intention to disembark a large force at Zeebrugge or another point. For some time before the Battles of Loos and Vimy telegraphic and postal communications between Great Britain and the rest of the world were suspended, and the German leaders, after the extraordinary daring of the British landings in the Gallipoli Peninsula, could not safely rule out the possibility of a British disembarkation in the neighbourhood of Ostend behind the end of their right wing.

As a landing on the Belgian coast would be almost certainly accompanied by an attempt of the Allies in the Ypres salient to break through the enemy's lines and advance down the north bank of the Lys on Ghent against the communications of the Duke of Wurtemberg's Army, west of Ghent, orders appear to have been given to General Hely d'Oissel, commanding the French troops wedged between the Belgian Army on the Yser and Bixschoote, and also to General Sir Herbert Plumer to menace the Duke of Wurtemberg with an offensive. This menace was accompanied on September 25 by four holding attacks.

On the 25th the German positions in the Ypres salient and south-westwards to La Bassée were subjected to a tremendous artillery fire, and four attacks were launched by the British. The first was directed at the German trenches east of the Ypres-Comines Canal, the second at those south of Armentières in the region of Bois Grenier, the third from Neuve Chapelle against the Moulin du Piétre, and the fourth just north of the Béthune-La Bassée Canal near Givenchy. The object of the attacks was to draw the German reserves away from the Battles of Loos and Vimy. It was successful.

In the first of these engagements an attack by the 3rd and 14th Divisions of the V. Corps, forming part of the Second Army under Sir Herbert Plumer, was made along a front of about 500 yards between the Ypres-Menin road and the Ypres-Roulers railway. After a severe cannonade, which lasted from 3.50 to 4.20 a.m., a mine was exploded by us north of the Bellewaarde Farm, and the columns of smoke caused by the explosion were still drifting away from the crater, 30 yards across by 30 feet deep, as our men left the trenches. A battalion of the Rifle Brigade was on the left, one of the Oxford and Bucks in the centre, and one of the Shropshires on the right. In reserve behind Sanctuary Wood was a battalion of the King's Royal Rifles, and a battalion of the Somerset L.I. was also held in readiness. The Shropshires had to attack a very strong point south of the Bellewaarde Farm which was powerfully defended with machine guns, but they succeeded, nevertheless, in forcing their way into the German lines, the Grenadiers particularly distinguishing themselves. The right column of the Oxford and Bucks put a machine gun out of action, and then swept through the enemy's positions, clearing the Germans out of their dug-outs and destroying another machine gun. The left column, however, could not make good its footing in the German trenches. As soon as they left their own lines the men came under

ON THE WESTERN FRONT.
Men of the Royal Field Artillery shelling German trenches.

a very heavy fire from the German mitrailleuses, and their failure impeded the general advance. The result was that it was found impossible properly to consolidate the ground gained, and by about 8 a.m. our men with 15 prisoners were withdrawn to their original lines. During the remainder of the day the Germans organized several ineffectual counter-attacks from the Bellewaarde Wood, and heavily shelled our trenches, 300 six-inch shells falling on one small length of line alone.*

The Bois Grenier action was on our side fought by other details of the Rifle Brigade, by the Lincolns and by the Royal Berkshires. The attacks on the left and right were successful, but that in the centre was held up. The British line here curved away from the enemy and formed a re-entrant. The advance was timed for 4.30 a.m. The Lincolns, posted on the left, had the difficult task of storming a strong fort at Le Bridoux, and in successfully accomplishing that feat they not only killed many Germans, but captured 80 of the 106 prisoners taken in the sector. Lieut. Leslie and Cor-

* Second-Lieut. R. P. Hallowes, of the 4th Middlesex Regiment, for his gallantry on this occasion and in the fighting near Hooge up to October 1, gained the V.C.

KEY MAP.

poral Carey crawled forward before the fort had fallen and surprised five Germans in a dug-out. They returned later and captured 18 more. In the centre the Berkshires, revealed by a German searchlight, had to attack a redoubt known as the " Lozenge," where the trenches and dug-outs were exceedingly strong. One private named Jenkins did splendid work by standing behind a traverse and bayoneting seven Germans as they came up round it. Another man was seen squatting on the parapet and sniping coolly from this position. Notwithstanding the gallantry of our men, the Germans substantially maintained their position, with the result that the men of the Rifle Brigade on the right, who had made their attack so swiftly that they caught many of the Germans without their rifles and equipment, and had gained by 6 a.m. the second line trenches, could not maintain contact with the Berkshires on their left. Before 10 a.m. they had fallen back to the German first line trenches. Meanwhile the Germans skilfully massed their reserves under the lee of the Bois Grenier, and, as the main aim of our attack had succeeded, a general retirement was ordered soon after 3 p.m. It was carried out in good order, and a ditch which ran straight in front of the old curved line was retained.

In the Neuve Chapelle sector also a determined effort was made by a battalion of the Black Watch, with the Second Leicesters on one flank and battalions of the Meerut Division of the Indian Expeditionary Corps on the other, to break the German line at the Moulin du Piétre. The Leicesters and Indians were hung up by barbed-wire entanglements which, as at the Battle of the Aubers Ridge, the British artillery had been unable to destroy. The Black Watch, however, rushed the first line German trench, and, with the regimental pipers (one of whom was killed, the other wounded) playing " Hieland Laddie," bombed four more lines of trenches, and, advancing 600 yards or so across an open field, reached the enemy's reserve line near the Moulin du Piétre. But, as both their left and right were exposed to counter-attacks and enfilading fire, the Scotchmen had to be withdrawn. Captain M. E. Park, of the 2/Black Watch, had shown conspicuous courage. From 6 a.m. to 10 a.m. he directed a company of bombers in close and continuous fighting. Captain J. I. Buchan, of the same regiment, who with his men had been gassed by the Germans,

ON THE WESTERN FRONT.
British troops surprise a party of Germans who were busily engaged sapping.

reached the enemy's reserve line trench near the Moulin du Piétre and was wounded in the counter-attack. Major Frederick Lewis, of the 2/ Leicesters, at an early stage of the combat had been hit in the neck by shrapnel, but for three hours he remained at his post directing the attack. After his wound had been dressed he subsequently took command of the battalion; his senior officer having been incapacitated by wounds. Another officer of the Leicesters, Captain W. Carandini Wilson, although badly wounded in the stomach, refused to leave the field until his men were over the parapet of the German trench, while Rifleman Kublir Thapa, of the 3rd Queen Alexandra's Own Gurkha Rifles, who had been severely wounded,

[Russell.

VICE-ADMIRAL BACON

Commanded a squadron of seventy-nine ships, bombarded the Belgian coast line from the mouth of the Yser to the Dutch frontier.

saved, under peculiarly difficult circumstances, two of his countrymen and a badly injured soldier of the Leicesters. For his bravery and devotion Thapa was awarded the V.C.

The attacks near Bois Grenier and Neuve Chapelle suggested that the real offensive might be about to be delivered against the northern, not the southern side of the La Bassée salient. At the Battles of Neuve Chapelle, the Aubers Ridge, and Festubert the aim of the British had been to sever the Germans round La Bassée from Lille by an advance over the ridges north of the La Bassée-Lille Canal.

Further, to mystify the enemy as to our designs on the 25th, Sir Douglas Haig, with portions of the I. Corps, assaulted the German trenches near Festubert and Givenchy, as if a direct attack on the point of the salient was contemplated. In this feint Second Lieut. S. S. John, of the 9th Cheshire Regiment, at the conclusion of the attack, when the British had retired to their trenches, crawled out and saved a wounded officer and about twenty men. The Military Cross was his reward, as it was for Second Lieut. J. K. W. Trueman, of the 6th Wilts, who had taken command of a company and handled it with remarkable skill.

The many efforts from Nieuport to Belfort, accompanied by the bombardment of the whole of the enemy's line, made it difficult for the Germans to decide where the main blow was to be struck, though in a stationary

combat such as here obtained, to keep plans entirely hidden was impossible. Aeroplanes can observe a good deal, and report any large accumulations of men or guns. Spies cannot be entirely eliminated, although it is possible sometimes to deceive them by false orders issued for their benefit. But from their aerial observers the Germans learned little, for the superiority of our men had given them completely the upper hand. Throughout the summer the work of the Royal Flying Corps had gone on continuously, even during the unfavourable weather. The enemy's positions had been photographed, so that plans of his trenches had been constructed and the dispositions of his guns furnished to our gunners. Such work is most tiring and hazardous, for the airmen must remain for long periods within range of the enemy's artillery. The danger from this can be best exemplified by the statement that on one occasion a machine was hit no fewer than three hundred times soon after crossing the German lines, and yet the observer successfully carried out his task. Deeds of this kind show the highest courage, and when it is mentioned that they were almost of daily occurrence the efficiency of the corps can be easily imagined. Nor was it without opposition from the German aircraft. Thus a British airman drove off four hostile machines and then completed his reconnaissance. Another time two officers engaged no fewer than

[Gale & Polden.

MAJOR-GEN. F. V. D. WING,

Who commanded the 12th Division. Killed.

six of the enemy's Taubes and disabled at least one of them.

The notes or photographs taken by the airmen were supplemented as much as possible by observations made on the surface of the ground. Before and during the Battle of Loos many arduous and venturesome feats were performed by British officers and men seeking to learn the height and depth of the obstacles, the positions of which had been detected by the airmen or had been revealed in the negatives of the latter's photographs. The choice of observation stations from which the effect of fire could be telephoned back was a difficult and dangerous duty, which had necessarily to be done on the ground itself. It involved walking many miles with not even the caps of the surveyors visible over the crests of the trenches. Often only periscopes could be used for observation, which was therefore a lengthy business. But this instrument gave in many places insufficient information, and then personal reconnaissance had to be resorted to. For instance, on the nights of September 12–13 and 23–24, Second Lt. M. H. Gilkes, of the First Surrey Rifles, crawled up to the German wire entanglements near Maroc. In the course of his second reconnaissance he was wounded in two places. Second Lt. C. H. H. Roberts, of the same regiment, emulated Gilkes's example.

[*Russell.*

MAJOR-GEN. G. H. THESIGER,
Who commanded the 9th Division.   Killed near the
Hohenzollern Redoubt.

Again, Second Lt. N. R. Colville, of 10/Argyll and Sutherland Highlanders, on August 7 and September 8 and 9, at great personal risk, investigated the formation and wiring of the Hohenzollern Redoubt.

In addition to their reconnoitring work and their personal encounters, our airmen did excellent service by bombing the German communications. During the operations towards the end of September nearly six tons of explosives were dropped on various objectives. The Flying Corps had become the Fifth Arm.

Of the feats of individual airmen some may be here recorded. On September 21, four days before the battle of Loos, Captain L. W. B. Rees, R.F.C., accompanied by Flight Sergeant Hargreaves, sighted a large German biplane armed with two machine guns, some 2,000 feet below them. Though he himself had only one machine gun, Captain Rees spiralled down and dived at the enemy. The latter, whose machine was faster, manœuvred to get Captain Rees broadside on, and then opened a heavy fire. But Captain Rees pressed his attack, and apparently succeeded in hitting the engine of the German biplane, which fell just inside the German lines. Captain Rees had previously engaged in two successful duels in the air. He was awarded the Military Cross.

[*Histed.*

MAJOR-GEN. SIR T. CAPPER,
Who commanded the 7th Division.   Severely
wounded at Loos on September 26th, 1915, died
on the 27th.

BY 'BUS TO THE FIRING-LINE: BRITISH TROOPS ABOUT TO BOARD MOTOR 'BUSES FOR THE TRENCHES.

Another officer who received the same distinction was Second Lieut. S. H. Long, of the Durham Light Infantry and Royal Flying Corps. On September 10 he had, with bombs, put out of action an anti-aircraft battery and had narrowly missed destroying an observation balloon. On September 23 he twice attacked German trains from the low height of 500 feet. While the Battle of Loos was in progress he bombed at a train under heavy rifle fire and damaged the line. Later in the day, in spite of darkness and bad weather, he endeavoured to destroy other trains. The heavy rain prevented his reaching them. Instead, he attacked the railway station of Péronne, which, however, was saved by the anti-aircraft battery in the neighbourhood. Prevented from reaching the station, Long climbed up to 1,500 feet and silenced the gun of a " Rocket " battery.

As mentioned, trains did not escape unscathed from the British airmen. On September 26 Second Lieut. D. A. C. Symington, of the Royal Flying Corps, wrecked a large portion of one moving towards St. Amand. Another airman given the D.S.O. was Lieut. G. A. K. Lawrence. On September 21 he reconnoitred 60 miles within the German lines, being repeatedly attacked by a hostile machine. During the first day of the Battle of Loos he descended to 600 feet from the ground and hit a moving train near Lille. The next day he drove off a German aeroplane which was interfering with our bombing machines. Finally, on September 30, he reconnoitred for three hours in very bad weather. His aeroplane was hit in seventy places by anti-aircraft guns as he was crossing the German lines on his way out.

A last example of the daring displayed by individual airmen. Lieut. C. E. C. Rabagliati, of the Yorks Light Infantry and Royal Flying Corps, and Second Lieut. A. M. Vaucour, of the Royal Field Artillery and Flying Corps, on September 28 reconnoitred over Valenciennes and Douai. They had to fly in thick cloud nearly the whole distance, and their aeroplane frequently got into a " spin." Each time it did so the machine was righted, and the two gallant officers from a height of 2,800 feet, under heavy fire, performed their dangerous task.

Nor should the good work of our anti-aircraft gunners be overlooked. The feat of a Canadian about this date, who had " brought

A TRENCH KITCHEN.
Preparing food on a charcoal fire in the first line trenches.

down eight Hun aeroplanes in three months " is worthy of record.

The feints to deceive the German Higher Command have been mentioned. The services rendered by our airmen and anti-aircraft gunners in preventing German aerial observers from perceiving that the main Allied forces of men and material north of Compiègne were being concentrated between Arras and Béthune, their expeditions to obtain information or to interfere with the German communications have been sufficiently acknowledged. It remains to describe the German positions which French, Foch and d'Urbal had decided to assault on September 25 and the subsequent days.

It will be remembered that in May and June, at the Battle of Artois, General d'Urbal, with the 10th French Army, had, under the eyes of Generals Joffre and Foch, driven the Germans from the plateau of Notre Dame de Lorette, captured the villages of Ablain St. Nazaire and Carency, the White Works connecting Carency with the hamlet of La Targette, the village of Neuville St. Vaast, and the formidable sub-terranean fortress called "The Labyrinth," constructed across the Arras-Lens road. Down the ravine-like valley leading from Ablain St. Nazaire to Souchez on the Arras-Béthune road they had in June gradually forced their way, capturing the sugar refinery and the group of three houses known as the "Mill Malon." On June 17 the cemetery of Souchez was taken, but the Germans, assisted by clouds of poisonous gas, recovered it some three weeks later.

A glance at the map will show the importance of what had been achieved by the French ; but north of Souchez the Germans still clung to the eastern slopes of the plateau of Notre Dame de Lorette and the Bois-en-Hache, and their line extended north of Angres and Liévin in front of the low Loos-Hulloch-Haisnes heights to the Béthune-La Bassée-Lille Canal in the vicinity of La Bassée. South of Souchez it curved eastward of the high road which runs from Béthune through Souchez and La Tar-gette to Arras, and crossed the Scarpe in the outskirts of that battered city.

Between the French and the plain stretching from the Scarpe below Arras to the La Bassée-Lille Canal lay the heights of Vimy. The mining city of Lens is in the low ground to the east of Liévin and south-east of Loos. The capture of either the Loos-Hulluch-Haisnes ridges or of the Vimy heights would oblige the Germans to evacuate Lens.

The loftiest point on the plateau of Notre Dame de Lorette is 540 feet high, but the plateau itself is not sufficiently elevated completely to command the heights of Vimy. The culminating point on the Vimy heights is 460 feet above sea level, and behind Souchez they reach an altitude of 390 feet.

North-east of Neuville St. Vaast the crest of the heights was crowned by the thick wood of La Folie, which the Germans held. They also were entrenched in Thelus, Farbus, Petit Vimy and Vimy. From La Targette the Arras-Béthune highroad winds downwards to the wood-fringed village of Souchez, which lies in a hollow. Before Souchez was reached an isolated building, the "Cabaret Rouge" was encountered. Beyond, on the left of the road, was the cemetery, and a hundred yards farther on the first houses of the village. To the east of the road the ground, intersected by hedges and with here and there a tree, rose gently

upwards towards the dark mass of the La Folie wood, and, north of it, Hill 140. On the heights behind and east of Souchez is Hill 119 and the village and wood of Givenchy-en-Gohelles.

Along the ridge from Hill 119 to Hill 140 were lines of German trenches connected by tunnels with the reserves and the heavy artillery behind the crest. The Vimy heights fall rapidly to the plain, so that troops and guns below the crest were comparatively safe from the French artillery, while the barbed wire entanglements here could not be cut by shrapnel. Nearer the French and halfway down the slope was a sunken road running parallel with the crest. Its lower bank, some 15 feet high, had been prepared for defence by a parapet ; moreover, the Germans had tunnelled down from the road and constructed on the French side great caves, each capable of containing half a company of men. Access to the caves was obtained by flights of steps, securely covered from the view of the French so that when their troops advanced over the roofs of the caves and descended into the road they could be attacked by the enemy issuing from his subterranean refuges.

In the valley below the heights Souchez, its cemetery, the "Cabaret Rouge" and the Château de Carleul, in its immediate vicinity, had been fortified with every device known to the German engineer. The village could be approached from the south and north along the Arras-Béthune highroad, from the south-west and west by the valleys of the streamlets Carency and Nazaire, which join to form the stream of the Souchez. At the head of these valleys were the ruins of Carency and Ablain St. Nazaire. By damming up the Carency and Nazaire streams the Germans had created an impassable swamp, which perforce split in two the French assaulting columns.

Against the north side of Souchez an assault was impossible so long as the Germans retained their trenches on the eastern slopes of the plateau of Notre Dame de Lorette, and in the Bois-en-Hache. To dislodge them from the wood and trenches was difficult, because the advancing infantry would be enfiladed by the German artillery in Liévin, Angres and Givenchy-en-Gohelles. As Sir John French observed, the French 10th Army under General d'Urbal had to attack "fortified positions of immense strength, upon which months of skill and labour had been expended, and which extended many miles."

BOMBERS COVERING A BAYONET CHARGE NEAR LA BASSÉE.

The bombers went before, the assaulting infantry came after them. Most of the bombs were of the rocket kind, and were carried in canvas bags. A piece of webbing which payed out as the bomb was thrown caused the missile to land head downwards so as to ensure explosion.

The task of Sir Douglas Haig, commanding the British First Army, of which the right wing had in September been extended to the region of Grenay, three miles or so north of the plateau of Notre Dame de Lorette and some four miles west of Lens seemed, on the map, easier, because the Loos-Hulluch-Haisnes ridges were on an average only half the altitude of the Vimy heights. But even the largest scale map gives no indication of the difficult problems confronting the British leaders. The plain crossed by the Loos-Hulluch-Haisnes ridges was dotted with villages, factories, mine-works and slag-heaps intersected with trenches. For

BRITISH OFFICERS
With a machine gun.

years before the outbreak of the war industries
had sunk shafts and tunnelled beneath it ; and
for nearly twelve months the plodding Germans
and their enslaved captives had burrowed in
the hollows and thrown up trenches on the
ridges, so that the ground where it was not
covered by buildings or mining refuse resembled the preliminary excavations for a
mighty city.

The lattice work of German trenches—8 or
9 feet deep, mostly cemented or floored and
furnished with wooden platforms for musketry
and machine guns—between Lens and Loos,
Loos and Hulluch, Hulluch and Haisnes, and
Haisnes and La Bassée, was supplemented by
redoubts and observation posts.

Opposite Grenay and west of Loos were two
large slag heaps, known as the Double Crassier,
bristling with mitrailleuses. Nearer Loos the
cemetery and numerous fortified chalk pits
formed a powerful barrier. Behind the dwarf
walls of the graveyard numerous machine guns
were ensconced. On a track leading from
Vermelles to Loos along the crest of the downs
was a German redoubt, 500 yards in diameter,
whence a view could be obtained of Loos,
beyond it "Hill 70," and the outskirts of Lens,
while to the north Hulluch and its quarries,
the hamlet of St. Elie and the village of Haisnes,
in front of which were Pit 8 and the Hohenzollern Redoubt, were visible.

Loos itself, a town which before the war
contained 12,000 inhabitants, of whom none
but the heroine Emilienne Moreau and a
handful of half-starved women and children
remained, was an agglomeration of two-

storeyed miners' cottages clustered about an
ancient village. The principal street ran west
and east, and was lined by roofless shops and
cafés. The parish church, though reduced to
ruins, still served to remind the spectators
of the antiquity of the place. Conspicuous
for forty miles round rose out of Loos the
tracery of the "Tower Bridge," 300 feet high.
It was the name given by our soldiers to two
square towers of steel girders, joined two-thirds
of the way up by others. It was used as a platform for German artillery observers, snipers and
mitrailleuses. The possession of the "Tower
Bridge" midway between La Bassée and the
Vimy heights gave the Germans for observation purposes a considerable advantage over
their foes.

Behind, and south-east of Loos on the
direct road to Lens, was the shaft of Pit 12.
Due east the ground sloped gently up to the
Lens-St. Elie-La Bassée highway and an
eminence dignified by the title of Hill 70.
On the north-east side of Hill 70 was a strong
redoubt. A little to the north of the redoubt
was the coal-mine "14 bis," powerfully fortified,
as also was a chalk pit to the north of it.
East of Hill 70 the ground dipped, and on the
next rise was the village of Cité St. Auguste.

Three thousand yards north of Loos were
the houses of Hulluch strung out along a small
stream. North-west of Hulluch were the stone
quarries converted into a fortress, similar to
that which west of Carency had up to May 11
blocked the French advance on that village.
Behind the Quarries was the mining village
of Cité St. Elie on the Lens-La Bassée road.
Half a mile or so north-west of the Quarries
and five hundred yards in front of the German
trenches was the Hohenzollern Redoubt. It
was connected with their front line by three
communication trenches attached to the defences of "Pit 8," a coal mine with a high and
strongly defended slag-heap a thousand yards
south of Auchy, a village nearly a mile distant
from the banks of the Béthune-La Bassée-Lille
Canal. The villages of Haisnes and of Douvrin east of the railway, Cuinchy - Pont à
Vendin-Lens, which passes between them,
afforded rallying points for the enemy should
he be driven from Pit 8, the Hohenzollern Redoubt and the Hulluch Quarries.

From west to east the German position was
crossed by the Béthune-Beuvry-Annequin-
Auchy-La Bassée road, off which branched a
road through Haisnes and Douvrin cutting the

La Bassée-Lens highway; next by a road from Vermelles by Hulluch to Pont à Vendin; then diagonally by the Béthune-Lens high-road, and lastly by the Béthune-Grenay-Lens railway. Behind the British trenches went south of Auchy the La Bassée-Vermelles-Grenay road and, in the background, was part of the Béthune-Nœux-les-Mines-Aix Noulette-Souchez-Arras causeway. A railway half a mile west of Grenay connected the Béthune-Lens line with La Bassée. Just to its west a smudge of red and white ruins amid the green fields and black slag-heaps indicated Vermelles, the scene of such bloody fighting in the winter months.

The distance between the British and German trenches varied from 100 to 500 yards. They ran parallel south of the Canal up an almost imperceptible rise to the south-west. Between the Vermelles-Hulluch-Pont à Vendin and Béthune-Lens roads the ground rose towards the Germans. South of the Béthune-Lens road, where the trenches crossed a spur, it was the reverse. Long grass, self-grown crops, and cabbages in patches grew on the chalky soil. Dull grey sandbag parapets marked the presence of the German trenches, before which were three separate barbed wire entanglements.

The first line of trenches was well west of Loos, the second running in a slight depression covered part of the town and then turned abruptly east and ran through the middle of Loos. Behind Loos there was a third line. A power-station furnished trenches and dug-

outs with electric light, and an elaborate tele-phone system enabled the German commanders to support any point with infantry and gun fire. Observation posts constructed of rein-forced concrete topped by steel cupolas, machine-gun emplacements encased in concrete and iron rails and "dug-outs" from 15 feet to 30 feet deep, abounded. A typical "dug-out" may be described. To a depth of 20 feet a shaft, boarded in, had been sunk. By means of a pulley a machine gun could be lifted and lowered up or down this shaft as occasion required, and by a ladder the occupants de-scended to a room 6 feet or so high, also boarded. It was furnished with a table and chairs and four sleeping bunks. Out of it a steep staircase led into another trench. Some of these sub-terranean bedrooms had whitewashed walls and were lit by lamps and decorated with pictures. The reader who loves comparisons is recommended to turn or return to the "Com-mentaries" of one of the first great entrenching generals, Cæsar, and study his account of the circumvallation of Alesia. He will then appre-ciate the immense progress which had been made in the engineering branch of the Art of War since the days of the man whose name has been degraded into Kaiser.

By Friday, September 24, the preparations for the great offensive in Artois as for that in the Champagne had been completed. To win the rim of the Plain of the Scheldt and to sur-prise the Germans in their formidable strong-

BY THE ROADSIDE IN LOOS.
A German trench captured by the British.

ON THE NIGHT BEFORE THE ATTACK AT LOOS, SEPTEMBER 24, 1915.

Scouting to ascertain what parts of the German trenches had suffered most from British shells: A party telephoning back to the artillery where to direct its fire.

BEFORE THE BRITISH ATTACK AT LOOS.

The great iron structure—a part of the mining machinery—known to the British soldier as the "Tower Bridge."

holds from La Bassée through Loos and Lens to Vimy, it was necessary not merely to make feints at the enemy's line between Ypres and La Bassée but to station the French and British reserves in such places that their employment at the front would not be plainly evident. Generals Foch and d'Urbal concentrated their reserves in the region of Arras. The Indian Cavalry Corps, under General Rimington, was moved to Doullens, half-way between Arras and Amiens, and 17 miles north-west of Albert. Here, it will be recollected, Foch and French, on October 8, 1914, had settled their plans for the British advance on La Bassée, Lille and Ypres. The presence of these troops at Doullens would, if it came to the knowledge of the Crown Prince of Bavaria, be calculated to make him believe that the offensive would be delivered south of Arras in the neighbourhood of Hébuterne and Albert. Twenty miles north-west of Arras, in the districts of St. Pol and Bailleul-les-Pernes, was the British Cavalry Corps, now under General Fanshawe. The 3rd Cavalry Division, which before and during the First Battle of Ypres had been attached to the IV. Corps, was (less one brigade), on September 21–22, brought into the area behind the latter body, which formed the right of the British in the coming battle. That a portion of the 3rd Cavalry Division should be again under Sir Henry Rawlinson, the leader of the

IV. Corps, if known, would arouse no suspicion at the German Headquarters. Nor, generally speaking, was the fact that the bulk of the British Cavalry was south of the line Béthune-La Bassée any sure indication of the Allied Generals' intention. Yet it had to be near at hand so that if the German line were broken masses of British with French

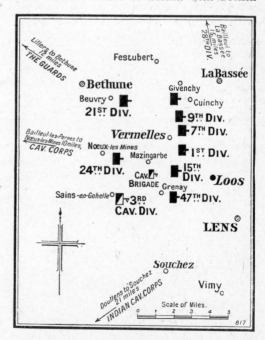

POSITION OF TROOPS BEFORE THE BATTLE.

horsemen could be rushed through the gap into the plain beyond the Hulluch-Loos-Vimy heights, to complete the discomfiture of the enemy.

The XI. Corps formed the main infantry reserve. It comprised the Guards Division under Lord Cavan, composed of the Grenadier, Coldstream, Scots, Irish, and the newly-enrolled Welsh Guards, the 21st and 24th Divisions of the New Army. The 28th Division was also temporarily withdrawn from Sir Herbert Plumer's Second Army at Ypres. The Guards bivouacked in the region of Lillers, ten miles northwest of Béthune. The 21st and 24th Divisions were between Beuvry and Nœux-les-Mines. The 28th Division was brought back from the Ypres salient to Bailleul, north-west of Armentières on the Lys. From a central position like Bailleul it could be directed to any point north or south of the La Bassée Canal. Assuming that these dispositions were by design or accident brought to the notice of the Crown Prince of Bavaria, he would be little the wiser.

The British troops which Sir Douglas Haig was about to launch to the assault were the I. and II. Corps. The I. Corps, with the exception of the details detached for feints at Givenchy and Festubert, was concealed in the trenches from the Béthune-La Bassée Canal to the Vermelles-Hulluch road. It was under the orders of Lt.-Gen. Hubert Gough. Its left wing working eastwards along the Canal was to storm Auchy where the German heavy guns were posted, to seize Haisnes and to take in reverse Pit 8 and the Hohenzollern Redoubt. The 9th Division in the centre was to capture the Hohenzollern Redoubt and then push

on to Pit 8. To its right Lt.-Gen. Gough directed the glorious 7th Division on the Hulluch Quarries and village of St. Elie. South of the Vermelles-Hulluch road was Sir Henry Rawlinson with the IV. Corps. The 1st Division, the 15th Highland Division—part of the New Armies—and the 47th London Territorial Division were to reach the heights between Hulluch and Lens, taking en route the redoubt on the Vermelles-Loos track, the town of Loos, the Double Crassier slag-heaps and east of the La Bassée-Lens highway, the Chalk Pit, Pit "14 bis," the redoubt on the north-east corner of Hill 70, the summit of that hill and the village of Cité St. Auguste.

If Gough succeeded, the La Bassée salient would be turned from the south; if Rawlinson were successful, the city of Lens, the German troops and guns in Liévin and Angres and the northern end of the Vimy heights might be taken. The Allies, whether the French did or did not secure those heights, would have at last obtained access to the Plain of the Scheldt, and a manœuvring battle, in which the superiority of the Allied forces in moral would assert itself, would promptly ensue.

Such was the plan of the Allied leaders. To carry it through they had at their disposal, besides a gigantic artillery, two new weapons—retorts for discharging a gas which stupified, but did not poison, and devices for creating volumes of smoke. If the wind blew from the west, and was strong enough to carry the gas and smoke and was not so strong as to dissipate the clouds of vapour, the tables would be turned on the Germans. Seeing that the enemy relied on his entrenchments to counter-balance the superior fighting qualities of the British

ON THE WESTERN FRONT.
British troops making a road in Northern France.

ON THE WESTERN FRONT.
British troops in the first-line trenches.

and French, it had been a bad mistake for him to employ poisonous gas. The Allies, being civilized, could not pay the Kaiser out in his own coin; their reply was equally effective but lacked the element of diabolical cruelty which commended itself to the enemy. No German suffered the pangs of suffocation or expired in lingering agony after days of hideous suffering as a result of breathing the gas used by the British.

During the early days of the week preceding the battle the weather was fine but the wind was in the east and the gas and smoke would, therefore, be blown across and behind our men. On Friday, September 24, a westerly breeze sprang up. Coming from the British Channel and the season being the late autumn, it brought with it fine rain and mist. The landscape was blurred and the roads, fields and trenches, as each hour passed, became soppy, slippery and muddy. If the wind held, the conditions for the use of gas and smoke the next day would be propitious, but the going would be bad both for the charging infantry and for the reserves who had long distances to march.

All Friday the British and French artillery pounded away at the enemy's wire entanglements, the sand-bagged parapets of the trenches, the quarries, slag-heaps, chalk-pits, red-brick cottages, steel cupolas, patches of wood, and the factories, mining works, villages and towns which formed the position of the enemy. The German batteries replied, but their fire was less effective. As evening fell British and

French aeroplanes ascended and, amidst puffs of bursting shrapnel, passed over the German line. At one point a couple of Aviatiks mounted to meet them, but, declining the combat, were seen to disappear beyond the dim, misty horizon.

To prevent the enemy repairing the breaches in his entanglements and parapets under cover of darkness, shrapnel and machine guns played ceaselessly on the German first line. Behind our front the roads and the communication trenches—great numbers of which had been recently made to facilitate the arrival of reinforcements—were filled with men, guns, and stores. Here were the lorries bringing up ammunition, Red Cross vehicles, cars carrying staff officers, motor cyclists, all pursuing their eastward way. "I was back at the waggon line," writes an officer of artillery, "looking after the storing of our ammunition for the next day. With what quiet and holy satisfaction we brought up load after load of lyddite shell to the gun-pits!" At 8 p.m. Lieut. M. W. M. Windle, of the 8th Devon Regiment, began a letter which he was destined never to finish:

We moved up here last night, and all day long have been listening to the biggest cannonade I've yet heard. I wish I could give you some idea of it. The sound that preponderates is like the regular thump of a steamship's engines. But across this from time to time comes the thunder-clap of a gun being fired, or a shell exploding, while the shells as they pass moan like the wind in the trees.

It's slackened a bit now, but to-morrow it will be twice as loud, excepting during the last few minutes before we go over the parapet. Then, I suppose, machine guns and rifles and bombs will swell the chorus. We have about 200 yards to go before we reach their first system of trenches on the rising ground to our front. I hope that won't present much difficulty, and if the guns have any luck we should top the hill all right. After that there are at least two more systems of defence, each about 1,000 yards apart which it will be up to us to tackle. I wonder whether we shall do it ? . . . Thucydides is a gentleman whose truth I never appreciated so thoroughly before. In his description of the last great effort of the Athenians to break into Syracuse he tells how the officers lectured and encouraged their men right up to the last moment, always remembering another last word of counsel, and wishing to say more, yet feeling all the time that however much they said it would still be inadequate. Just the same with us now. We've all lectured our platoons, but something still keeps turning up, and after all we can only play an infinitesimal part in Armageddon !

Well, we're parading in a minute. Good-night and heaps of love.

To be continued to-morrow !

Strange is the contrast between, on the one hand, this letter, with its reference to the battle which decided that the Athenians of the Age of Pericles, Socrates, and Pheidias should not mould the Greeks into an imperial race, and, on the other, a note found among the effects of a dead German near Loos : " How nice," wrote " Mitzi " in Münster to Adolph, " if Russia makes peace as we expect. Then we can give those damned Tommies a good hammering. They deserve it, the swine ! "

About midnight the artillery officer from whose letter we have quoted turned in for three hours' sleep. At 4 a.m. on Saturday, September 25, the watches of the officers taking part in the preliminary cannonading and the advance were synchronised so that complete unison in the movements and gun-fire might be ensured.

The wind had shifted to a south-westerly direction and so was not coming from exactly the right quarter for the purposes of our gas-and-smoke engineers. As on Friday afternoon, rain fell and mist enveloped the surface of the slopes up which the British and the French to their right were to push their way.

At 4.25 a.m. the intense bombardment opened. The roar produced by the immense assemblage of guns was so terrific that sleepers thirty or forty miles away were awakened. Farther off, damped by the south-westerly wind, the deafening noise diminished to a low-pitched rumble, punctuated by the louder reports of the heavier weapons. This bombardment, unique in British history, had scarce been equalled but not surpassed by those of the Germans in the Eastern theatre in the advance through Galicia and Poland. Equally severe was the overwhelming fire rained that day on the heights of Vimy and the German positions in

Champagne. British and French science had combined to place at the disposal of the Allied armies weapons superior to those forged in German arsenals. The following extract from the same artillery officer's letter, previously quoted, gives the impression made on those who took part in the Battle of Loos :

The air was suddenly torn into a thousand pieces ; screeched and screamed ; and then groaned and shivered as it was lashed again and again and again. Along our section, say, five miles, there must have been 3,000 shells fired in five minutes. If the action was a wide one, the bombardment was the biggest thing as yet in this war.

I wish I could give you some idea of the awful majesty of those few moments, when, as an avenging Angel with a flaming sword the forces of the Allies gave to the Hun the first lash of the scourge prepared for him. The morning, it seemed, was dull (as a matter of fact, I found out afterwards, through discovering myself wet through, it was raining heavily) ; but the flashes of the guns were so continuous as to give a light which was almost unbroken. It flickered, but it never failed. The earth itself quivered and shook with the repeated shocks of the guns. The air was a tattered, hunted thing, torn wisps of it blown hither and thither by the monstrous explosions. We had guns everywhere, and all were firing their hardest at carefully registered points of the German trenches. On every yard of trench at least four shells must have fallen within five minutes, and each shell would have a radius of destruction of at least 20 yards.

Yes, I wish I could give in words some impression of that gunfire. But all I can say is that it was a hundred times greater than any I had experienced before ; and you know I have seen some bombardments. You would think that some metaphor of terror and sublimity would have suggested itself. It didn't. Instead I had the fantastic image in my mind of all the peacemongers of England assembled in a great Temple of Calico, and this temple being split into a million ribands with a horrid screeching and thundering, while the poor devils writhed prone on the ground, faces upturned to the clamour, their necks all awry.

In the faint light which precedes the dawn— at 5.30 a.m.—clouds of gas and smoke issued from the British trenches. Unfortunately, the wind appears to have carried gas and smoke past Pit 8, the Hohenzollern Redoubt, the Quarries and Hulluch. Nevertheless, the pyschological effect of the gas and smoke on the Germans must have been considerable. They could not be sure that the gas was not poisonous and the smoke, through which tore the shells and the sleet of bullets from machine guns and rifles, would, they knew, be soon alive with enemies eager to close with their own special weapon, the bayonet, which the Germans had previously experienced and feared.

While the visible and invisible vapours drifted in the direction of Loos and Liévin, our men, full of suppressed energy, yet bearing an outward calm, waited impatiently in their trenches, ready with their gas helmets.

At last the wished-for moment came. It was 6.30 a.m. In an instant the roar of the

KEEPING OFF A NIGHT ATTACK.

A ruse in the British trenches: Firing star pistols and rifles at once. During a retirement a few men were left behind to personate a company while the British were withdrawing. The men in the trenches fired rifles and star pistols, which successfully bluffed the enemy into imagining that the British were there in force.

guns behind them ceased, but that of the French artillery still went on in rolling thunder as d'Urbal's infantry would not be ready to attack till some minutes after noon. From our trenches sprang lines of soldiers who, with their heads covered in smoke helmets, resembled in appearance divers. They moved forward silently but determinedly through the mist and smoke, and swept like an angry wave against the

trenches of the enemy. A German observer, writing in the *Berliner Tageblatt*, describes from the enemy's standpoint those charges and what preceded and followed them :

Waves of gas and walls of smoke rolled up like a thick mist. The Germans were waiting. They fired madly into the wall of fog.

An officer appeared, sword in hand, out of it, and fell immediately. Then the Germans retreated, for these trenches could not be held at all. A bursting shell

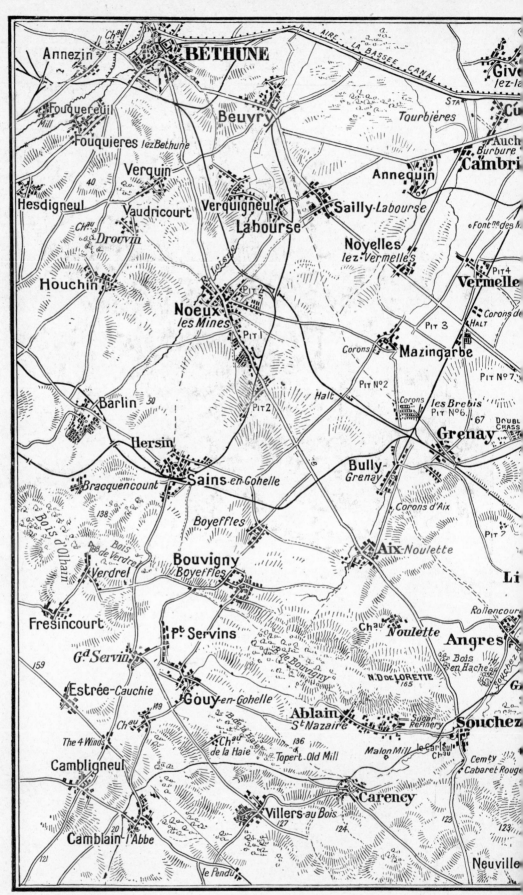

MAP TO ILLU

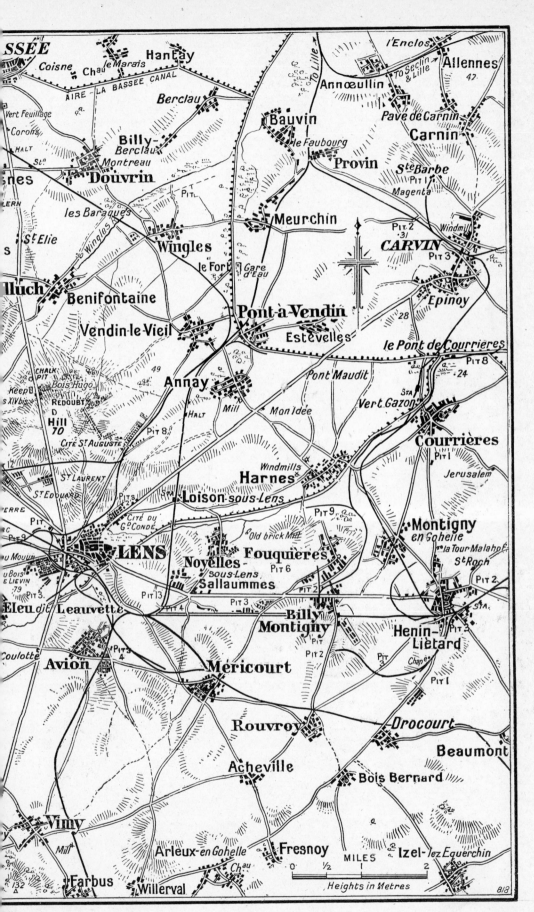

ATTLE OF LOOS.

hurled a machine gun back into a trench. Some of our brave fellows seized it and began to fire. English on the right ! Where ? They are our men ! No ; by Heaven ! they are Englishmen, quite near, not ten yards off, before their uniforms can be recognised in the dark haze. . . .

Suddenly an English company appears unexpectedly. A machine gun sweeps the street. Some fall. An officer rallies them, and forward they come over bodies and blood ! And the machine gun is silent. . . .

Often it was hard to say who was opposite, who was on the flanks or in the rear, friend or foe. And shrapnel burst wherever one turned one's steps.*

A wounded British officer declared later that "hell itself could not be worse. Nothing," he continued, "could be an exaggeration of

---

* *Translated by The Manchester Guardian.*

the horrors of that battlefield ; it was, it is, a veritable shambles, a living death of unspeakable horror even to those who, like myself, were destined to come through it unscathed, bodily at all events. Most of the survivors went through it as through a ghastly nightmare without the relief and joy of awakening." One soldier relates how as he neared the enemy's trench, the butt of his rifle was blown clean away, leaving barrel and bayonet in his hands, how on reaching the trench a Prussian officer covered him with his revolver, and how he ducked and bayoneted the man with his broken weapon.

At 6.35 the British artillery reopened at longer ranges, searching for the enemy's reserves and rear trenches. This second bombardment lasted fully 30 minutes, and was "fierce enough to shake the earth and the heaven."

From the wider we turn to particular features of the Battles of Loos and Vimy. The left wing of Lt.-Gen. H. Gough's Corps (the I.) operating in between the banks of the Béthune-La Bassée Canal and Pit 8 made no progress, though the dead between the Canal and Pit 8 were to be counted in thousands. At this point the British, who were deluged with shells from the La Bassée salient, met with a bloody repulse. Of the deeds of gallantry in that corner of the battlefield we may mention two.

THE HEROINE OF LOOS.

Emilienne Moreau, who, when the British retook the town, carefully dressed the wounds of the British troops. She killed five Germans by throwing grenades and using a revolver. In the above picture she is being decorated by General de Sailly with the Military Cross, as shown in the circle portrait.

AFTER THE BOMBARDMENT.

A Scottish Regiment entered the village of Loos. In spite of the intense bombardment which played around the village, some of the inhabitants were still living in their shattered houses. Those who were rescued were carried to a place of comparative safety.

At Cuinchy, on the border of the canal, Capt. F. R. Kerr, M.B., R.A.M.C., after an unsuccessful attack, crawled over the British parapet and under the fire of the enemy at close range brought in two wounded men. Near Cambrin, a village south-west of Cuinchy, Major H. C. Stuart, of the Reserve of Officers, Highland Light Infantry, gallantly led forward his company, and, though gassed, reorganized what remained of his battalion. Both officers were awarded the D.S.O.

While the combat round Cuinchy, Cambrin

and Auchy was proceeding, Lt.-Gen. Gough threw Major-General G. H. Thesiger, with the 26th and 28th Brigades of the 9th Division, against the Hohenzollern Redoubt and Pit 8. For the gas and smoke to envelop the Redoubt and Pit 8 the wind would have had to be in a due west or north-easterly direction, and, as we have seen, that was not the case. The Hohenzollern Redoubt was a second Labyrinth, and Pit 8, with which, as mentioned, it was connected by three trenches, had been converted into a miniature fortress.

AIMING A RIFLE BY THE PERISCOPE.
In the British first-line trenches.

The 28th Brigade marched east of the Vermelles-La Bassée railway on the Hohenzollern Redoubt, the 26th Brigade penetrated between the Redoubt and the Hulluch Quarries and captured Pit 8. The fighting at these spots beggars description. Here is the picture of a German officer as he appeared to one of his countrymen coming from the redoubt :—

"His legs were covered with clay, his body with filth and dust. His shoulders were half wrenched off ; his hair was grey, and deep furrows stood in his brow. He was hoarse and could not speak coherently. . . . The slaughter was terrible, especially the work of the howitzers and machine guns—all horrible to see."

On that day near Vermelles, Second Lieut W. L. Dibden, of the 2nd Battalion Royal Warwick Regiment, though so exhausted that he could hardly stand, led a party of bombers down a German communication trench.* Wounded three times, Major David McLeod, of the Reserve of Officers, Gordon Highlanders, commanded a company in the attack of the Redoubt till he collapsed on the ground. Captain G. Burrard, of the 52nd Brigade of the R.F.A., under continuous shell and rifle fire,

guided his guns to the close support of the infantry. Major C. W. W. McClean, of the 52nd Brigade, R.F.A., who was wounded, brought up a battery in support and observed the fire from a very exposed position. Lieut. J. B. Hollwey, an artilleryman of the same brigade, laid a telephone wire under very heavy fire. He had scarcely gone 10 yards when he was wounded in the leg. He went on, laid 300 yards more wire, was again wounded, this time his leg being fractured. He lay in the open unable to move for 16 hours, refusing all aid to avoid taking men away from their duties.*

As the result of our efforts part of the Hohenzollern Redoubt was stormed, yet without completely dislodging the Germans from it.

The fighting round the slag heap, the manager's house and the buildings of Pit 8, to the north-west of the Hohenzollern Redoubt, was equally violent, but at first more successful. The 26th Infantry Brigade secured the Pit, Lieut. D. C. Alexander, R.A.M.C., and Lieut. G. H. W. Green, of the 7th Battalion Seaforth Highlanders, here particularly distinguishing themselves. But, owing to the failure of Gough's left, the capture of Pit 8 did not entail the capture of the Hohenzollern Redoubt.

Meanwhile, on the right of the 9th Division the 7th Division, under Major-General Sir Thompson Capper, was living and dying up to its traditions. Swiftly they reached and captured the Hulluch Quarries and then the left of the division pressed forward on Haisnes, the centre to the heights north of St. Elie, while the right attacked that mining village. Capt. A. W. Sutcliffe, of the 3rd, but attached to the 2nd Battalion of the Border Regiment, was commanding the left company of the first line in the attack. On finding that its advance was checked by machine-gun fire from an emplacement called " Pope's Nose," he coolly headed a charge which ended in the capture of the German mitrailleuse. He then reorganised his company and marched it past the Quarries up to the left of the line. He and his men had taken 150 prisoners.

Another remarkable feat was that of Capt. J. E. Adamson, of the 8th Battalion of the Gordon Highlanders. At the head of his company, which was in advance of other detachments, he made across the open for Haisnes. Shells burst around them, rifle fire thinned

---

* He gained the Military Cross.

* Hollwey gained the Military Cross, McLean, Burrard and McLeod the D.S.O.

the little band ; three lines of wire were encountered and, while they cut or hacked their
way through them, mitrailleuses took toll of
the company. Nevertheless, at 8 a.m. the
survivors were in Haisnes and there till 5 p.m.
they remained, causing and suffering heavy
losses. Finally, when almost entirely surrounded, attacked by the enemy's artillery,
bombers, and riflemen from three sides, Captain
Adamson mustered his handful of heroes and
brought them back in good order.*

Thus Lt.-Gen. Hubert Gough with the I. Corps
had in the forenoon driven his right—the 7th
Division and the 26th Brigade—well into the
German position. Pit 8 and the Quarries were
gained and his troops were in or before Haisnes
and St. Elie. But, as the hours rolled by, the
hold on the points gained became more and
more precarious. Haisnes we have seen was
abandoned, and the enemy appears to have
recovered the Quarries. That the British left
wing was in immediate need of reinforcements
was only too apparent.

At 9.30 a.m., an hour after Adamson reached
Haisnes, Sir John French placed the 21st and
24th Divisions of the New Army at Sir Douglas
Haig's disposal, and Haig ordered the commander of the XI. Corps to send them up.
Between 11 a.m. and noon, the central brigades
of these divisions filed past Sir John French
at Beuvry and Nœux-les-Mines respectively.
At 11.30 a.m. the heads of both divisions were
within three miles of our original first line

* Adamson received the D.S.O.. Sutcliffe the Military
Cross.

trenches. Sir John French also directed the
Guards on Nœux-les-Mines which they did
not, however, reach till 6 p.m., and he brought
south of the Lys the 28th Division from Bailleul.

It was unfortunate that the reserves were
not closer to the battlefield, as by noon two
of Sir Henry Rawlinson's divisions of the IV.
Corps by a series of magnificent charges, the
pace of which seems to have deranged the plans
of our staff, had almost torn their way through
the whole of the German line and taken Lens.

Sir Henry Rawlinson, who was assisted to a
greater extent than the I. Corps by the gas and
smoke, had at 6.30 a.m. advanced against the
German positions from Hulluch through Loos
to the Double Crassier. Two brigades of the
1st Division with a third brigade in reserve
marched on Hulluch and the heights south of it.
The 1st Brigade on the left, capturing gun
positions on the way, penetrated into the outskirts of the village, but the brigade on the
right, south of Lone Tree, was hung up by
some barbed wire entanglements which had
escaped the attention of our artillery. Though
the delay occasioned by this misfortune enabled
local reserves of the enemy to concentrate
behind the second line trenches, a detachment
of the 1st Brigade succeeded between 2 and 3
p.m. in getting behind the entanglements and
capturing some five hundred Germans. The
fighting between Vermelles, Le Rutoire and
Hulluch, and in Hulluch itself, was of the most
desperate nature. Near Le Rutoire Sergeant
Harry Wells, of the 2/Royal Sussex Regiment,
when his platoon officer had been killed took

AFTER THE BRITISH ATTACK.
A wrecked church in Loos.

command and led the men to within fifteen yards of the German wire. Nearly half of them were killed or wounded and the remainder wavered. Wells rallied them, and they again advanced, but were compelled to take cover. Again Wells went forward and was shouting to them to come on when he fell dead. The V.C. was awarded to him. Major F. S. Evans, of the 1st/9 Battalion Liverpool Regiment, leading his men with great gallantry to the attack over open ground, fell wounded.†

The 2/Royal Warwicks were stopped by wire before the German first line trenches in front of Hulluch. It was broad daylight, but Private Vickers standing up under a very heavy fire from guns, rifles and machine guns, cut the wires and gained the V.C. Captain Joseph Pringle, of the 1/Battalion Cameron Highlanders, by force of example, induced his men to take and consolidate a position. Captain Douglas Tosetti, of the 8/Battalion Royal Berks, badly wounded in the leg, led his men to the outskirts of Hulluch. Second Lieut. T. B. Lawrence, of the same battalion, when the machine gun officer had fallen, rallied the gun crews, brought two maxims into action, and captured a couple of German field guns. Captain E. R. Kearsley, of the 1/Battalion Royal Welsh Fusiliers, kept cheering on his men to the capture of trenches near the village, and he did not desist until he received his seventh wound. During the night of the 25th, Sergeant-Major Thomas Bluck, of the same regiment, rallied the men retiring before counter-attacks, and was wounded. Private George Peachment, of the 2/King's Royal Rifle Corps, one of the youngest men in his battalion, trying to save the life of an officer, lost his own, but gained the V.C. Second Lieut. T. R. Reid and Captain P. J. R. Currie, both of the same battalion as Peachment, were gassed. Reid, with a machine gun, entered a gap in the enemy's wire and rendered invaluable aid to his comrades; Currie, his senior officers having been gassed and wounded, assumed command of the battalion, and led it forward to the farthest point reached. Under heavy fire, Second Lieut. R. W. Carrigan, R.F.A., took forward two trench mortars to destroy some buildings near Hulluch in which enemy machine guns were working. Captain A. M. Read, of the 1/Northampton Regiment, partially gassed during the morning, moved freely about,

rallying his men. He gained the V.C., but died of his wounds. He was a celebrated Service boxer, and had previously exhibited conspicuous gallantry. He was only 31 when he fell. These all too brief records of heroic deeds will enable the reader faintly to realize the hard fighting round and in Hulluch on the 25th. "I shall never forget," writes an officer who rejoined his regiment that evening, "what those one-and-a-quarter miles which we had gained looked like as I passed through them in the dimness and mist that shrouded that battlefield. The place was an absolute shambles . . . ultimately I found the regiment—all that was left of it. It was hurriedly scratching itself in on either side of the Hulluch road, in front of everything."

The right brigade of the 1st Division had been early held by the barbed-wire entanglements; this did not check the 15th Division (recruited in the Highlands), to the south of the 1st Division. Though their left wing was exposed, yet with extraordinary impetuosity and courage two of the three brigades composing it which had left their trenches at 6.30 a.m., followed a few minutes later by the Reserve Brigade, stormed in the midst of clouds of gas and smoke the redoubt on the Vermelles-Loos track. Before 8 a.m. the right brigade was assaulting Loos from the north, while the left pushed on and seized the Chalk Pit, Pit 14 bis, and Hill 70 with its redoubt, and even reached the village of St. Auguste. The Camerons, meanwhile, had detached a body of grenadiers to help the right brigade of the 1st Division, still struggling with the barbed-wire entanglements south of Hulluch.

Two episodes at the beginning of this amazing charge of the Highlanders may be narrated. Piper Daniel Laidlaw, of the 7th King's Own Scottish Borderers, perceiving that his company was shaken from the effects of the gas, coolly mounted the parapet, marched up and down it, and played the men out of the trench to the assault. He continued playing his pipes till he was wounded. For this splendid action he was awarded the V.C. Captain M. F. B. Dennis, of the same regiment, was wounded immediately before the attack. After being bandaged, he dashed forward, cheering on his men. Wounded a second time, he was carried to the dressing station. From it he staggered after his company, and cheered them on till he received a third wound.

The Chalk Pit, Pit 14 bis, Hill 70 and the

† He received the D.S.O.

THE BRITISH REACH THE GERMAN TRENCHES.

Between bomb and bayonet: German troops who took refuge in their dug-outs—some of which held as many as twenty men—compelled to surrender to the British.

redoubt on its north-east edge, had been occupied by the Highlanders of the New Army, From the houses, cellars and "dug-outs" in Loos, from Cité St. Auguste, and the environs of Lens, the German machine-guns played on the front and rear of our brave troops. In the course of the fighting, Second-Lieut. F. H.

Johnson, of the 73rd Field Company of the Royal Engineers, wounded in the leg, had headed several charges and won the V.C Every German gun in the vicinity was being trained on our men, the enemy was being rapidly reinforced from the north, east and south. But by 9.30 some British artillery had

STORMING OF THE TRENCHES ROUND LOOS. SEPTEMBER 25-27.

British Infantry storming an enemy trench near Loos during the Allied advance in Artois.

been sent up towards Loos, and a brigade of the 21st Division of the New Army appears to have been dispatched later to the assistance of the Highlanders. These were, however, only able immediately to procure effective help from the 47th London Territorial Division on the extreme right of the British 1st Army.

Two brigades of the London Territorials had left their trenches near Grenay at 6.30 a.m. Gas and smoke had preceded them. They had speedily driven the enemy from the greater part of the slag-heaps known as the Double Crassier, and crossing the Béthune-Lens road, advanced on the cemetery and the town of Loos. For long the German machine-gunners in the cemetery maintained their position among the tombs. Finally, the cemetery was stormed, and the main attack on Loos from the south and west with the Highlanders forcing their way in from north and east began. From house to house, from cellar to cellar the Germans were bombed or bayonetted. Numbers surrendered, but many died bravely at their posts. Under the church tower the enemy had laid mines, of which, in the midst of bursting shells, Major E. B. Blogg, of the 4th London Field Co., R.E. (T.F.), cut the fuze, thereby saving the heavy casualties which their explosion would have caused.* Lieut. F. L. Pusch, of the 19th Battalion of the London Regiment (St. Pancras), led a party of bombers, and, going alone into a house, captured seven Germans, one of whom wounded him badly in the face.

After a bloody struggle, Loos was at last in our hands. Among the rescued French inhabitants was Mlle. Émilienne Moreau, a girl of 18, who had lived through the German occupation and now assisted to bandage the British wounded. She killed with her own hand several Germans who attacked wounded Highlanders and Territorials. On November 27 this young heroine was publicly decorated at Versailles with the Croix de Guerre. In pinning the cross on her breast, General de Sailly observed : " I congratulate and admire you, young lady. You do honour to the women of France. You are a fine and inspiring example."

From 6.30 a.m. to noon the British had been assaulting the enemy's position from the Béthune-La Bassée Canal to the environs of Lens, but, all this time, for reasons which have not been explained, the French 10th Army between Grenay and the Labyrinth had not

advanced. A terrific bombardment which had been proceeding for five days had prepared the way for the French infantry, but Generals Foch and d'Urbal postponed their attack till after noon of the 25th, and then, instead of throwing troops towards Lens, confined themselves to assaulting Souchez and the Vimy Heights. That they had excellent reasons for the course pursued may be taken for granted, but one result was that the 47th London Territorial Division, which it had been found necessary to deploy from Grenay to south of Loos as a defensive flank was not able to give much assistance to the Highlanders on Hill 70.

The movements of the French troops must now be described. At 12.25 p.m. Generals Foch and d'Urbal, sent forward their infantry on Souchez. German deserters who had been finding their way to the French lines had acknowledged that the defenders were at their last gasp. On the left our gallant Allies descended the eastern slopes of the Notre Dame de Lorette plateau and made for the Hache Wood, the fringe of which was reached in twenty minutes. With asphyxiating shells and shrapnel and machine-gun fire, the Germans sought to stop the advance, while their batteries from Angres, Liévin and Givenchy-en-Gohelles kept up a ceaseless rain of projectiles. The French attack slackened its pace, but the Souchez stream was reached. In the meantime, down the valleys of the Nazaire and Carency and along the Béthune-Arras highway from La Targette, other bodies of French troops advanced on the Château of Carleul, the " Cabaret Rouge," and the cemetery of Souchez. Simultaneously masses of infantry forced their way to the lower slopes of Hill 119. The cemetery was taken but soon after lost, and the right wing was held up by machine-gun fire. The desperate nature of the opposition belied the statements of the deserters and the strength of the subterranean and other defences on the Vimy heights forced Foch and d'Urbal to put off to the next day their final attack on Souchez.

The unexpected rapidity of the advance of the Highland Division of the New Army, the small measure of success gained by the 1st Division on its left, the precarious position of the 7th Division in the triangle St. Elie-Haisnes - the Hulluch Quarries, and of the 26th Brigade of the 9th Division engaged round Pit 8, the little headway made by the 28th Brigade in its assault on the Hohenzollern

* He subsequently received the D.S.O.

THE BRITISH ADVANCE.
A street in Loos, showing the effect of the bombardment.

Redoubt, the failure of Gough's left wing in its endeavour to advance between the redoubt and the Béthune-La Bassée Canal, coupled with the unexpected strength of the German strong-holds in and round Souchez and on the Vimy heights, deranged the plans of the Allied leaders and gave the Crown Prince of Bavaria an opportunity of delivering, about 1 p.m., a violent and successful counter-attack against the Highlanders who, with some support from the London Territorials, had captured Hill 70, the redoubt on its north-east corner, Pit 14 bis, and some houses on the western edge of the village of Cité St. Auguste. Being new troops who, up to then, like their comrades at Suvla Bay, had had but little training and still less experience of fighting in the open, our troops were at some disadvantage. The hordes of fanatical Germans, too, who were driven by their officers out of Lens and its environs to attack them were far superior to them in num-bers. Nor did the ground afford our men any protection against heavy artillery. Unless there has been time to create deep trenches, dug-outs which cannot be reached by high explosive shells, and broad barriers of wire entanglements to deny access to them, the bravest infantry may

be swiftly dislodged from the Hougoumonts and Plancenoits of to-day. It is true that the British could take refuge in the elaborate subterranean constructions of the Germans, but the very effectiveness of the crushing bombardment which had preceded the offensive had destroyed most of these and had ripped up the barriers of barbed wire.

Under the pitiless rain of bursting shells, the Highlanders and Territorials were slowly driven back. The houses in Cité St. Auguste had to be abandoned, and the redoubt and most of the summit of Hill 70 were by nightfall again in the possession of the enemy. The portion of the 21st Division of the New Army which had mounted the heights to support the Highlanders does not appear to have rendered much effective assistance to them. When night fell, the line of the British First Army was roughly as follows. From the Double Crassier slag-heaps it ran round the south of Loos to the western part of Hill 70, thence close to the western exit of Hulluch, round the west of Hulluch Quarries to Cité St. Elie and Pit 8, where it turned back east of the Hohenzollern Redoubt to our original line—in the region of Vermelles. The line was, however, not continuous, and there were numerous fortified points in it still held by the Germans. The real gains of the day had been the expulsion, capture, or destruction of the Germans in Loos and the taking of the "Tower Bridge" from which the snipers, machine-gunners and artillery observers of the enemy had been shot down in the early hours of the morning. For some unaccountable reason the Germans do not appear to have mined the Tower Bridge as they had mined the ruins of the Church of Loos. To destroy this valuable post for their artillery observers may have seemed to them to be a step which ought not to be taken so long as they retained any foothold on the ridges at the edge of the Plain of the Scheldt.

During the night, which was lit up by the moon and the German star-shells and rockets, the fighting continued. Cité St. Auguste was on fire and the flames gave some light to Hill 70. The scenes in Loos were ghastly. Amidst bursting shells, operations were being performed on the wounded in cellars and dug-outs by the dim illumination of scanty candles. Officers of the Signal Service were crawling about laying wires. Beyond, on Hill 70 and to the south round the Loos chalk pit, Highlanders and Territorials were resisting the frantic attacks of the enemy. The 28th Division,

which had been placed at the disposal of Sir Douglas Haig in the early hours of Sunday the 26, came over the bridges on the Béthune-La Bassée Canal into the trenches previously lined by the troops of the I. Corps, who had been used up in the battle of the previous day and were now snatching a few hours' rest in the muddy, chalky holes and trenches between Pit 8 and Hulluch.

The rain had ceased and the morning broke fine but cold, the sun shone brilliantly, and there was a cloudless blue sky. The Highlanders on Hill 70, who had been vigorously but unsuccessfully attacked half an hour after midnight and again at 5.30 a.m., reinforced by the leading troops of the 21st and 24th Divisions of the New Army at 9 a.m., again advanced. The attack was preceded by a heavy bombardment lasting an hour. In face of the German machine-gun fire, no progress was made. The Germans were now firmly established in the redoubt to the north-east of Hill 70, and at noon they finally dislodged us from Pit 14 bis. During the afternoon the 6th Cavalry Brigade was ordered up to Loos as a garrison, and later the 3rd Cavalry Division was thrown into the town. On the left of the Highlanders the 1st Division renewed its attacks on Hulluch, but the net result of the efforts of the IV. Corps

AFTER THE BRITISH BOMBARDMENT.
A street in Loos, showing the "Tower Bridge" in the background.

THE BATTLE OF LOOS.
Wounded British troops on the way to the dressing station after the attack.

on the 26th was, except for a small gain of ground south of Loos, insignificant from the British standpoint. By nightfall the line bent sharply back from Hill 70 to the north-west as far as the Loos-La Bassée road, which it followed for 1,000 yards, bearing thence north-eastward to near the west end of Hulluch. Northward of that it was the same as it had been on the previous night. As for the I. Corps : its sole success on the 26th had consisted in the recapture of the Hulluch Quarries by the 7th Division. But this gain had been counterbalanced by the fall of its leader, Major-General Sir Thompson Capper, who was severely wounded and died the next morning. The Allied victory at the First Battle of Ypres had been largely due to the courage, energy, and resourcefulness of this most distinguished and capable leader.

The number of German prisoners by now amounted to 2,600 ; nine guns had been taken and numerous machine guns. Our aeroplanes had bombed and derailed a train near Loffres, east of Douai, and another which was full of troops near St. Amand. Valenciennes Station, through which German troops were passing to the battlefield, had also been bombed. Among the officers and men who won distinction that day in the combats round Hill 70 were Captain A. P. Sayer of the 91st Field Company, Royal Engineers, who by his devoted gallantry had restored the action at a critical moment; Private Robert Dunsire of the 13th Royal Scots (Lothian Regiment), who rescued wounded men under peculiarly dangerous circumstances ; and Captain W. W. Macgregor of the Gordon Highlanders, who had the sense to doubt the authenticity of an order sent to him to retire,

THE BATTLE OF LOOS.
After the British attack : A line of wounded.

and by his prompt action in leading his men forward prevented the Germans from turning our flank. Dunsire received the V.C.

Other officers whose names may be mentioned in connection with the same fighting were Lieutenant-Colonel A. F. Douglas-Hamilton, who also gained the V.C. but was killed at the head of his men—the 6th Cameron Highlanders—after he had led them four times back into the fighting line, when the battalions on his right and left had retired. So desperate had been the struggle that at the moment when he was killed he was at the head of no more than fifty men.

In the meantime, south of the British Army Foch and d'Urbal, though they had been unable to lend a hand to the London Territorials and Highlanders, had seized the Hache Wood and the Germans had evacuated Souchez,

whose garrison regained by their communication trenches their second line on the slopes of Hill 119. On Saturday and Sunday, 1,378 prisoners, including a considerable number of officers and a boy aged fourteen years had been taken. Like Carency and Ablain St. Nazaire, Souchez, according to the Kaiser's orders, was to have been held at all costs. When the Germans left it, it was almost level with the ground and resembled the excavations of a buried city of the distant past. The Vimy heights, however, remained to be taken, and how formidable these were the reader will have not forgotten. On the 27th the French confined themselves to making preparations for their attack on Hills 119 and 140.

Monday, September 27, was another wet day, rain falling in torrents during the afternoon. Two divisions of the Prussian Guard

FRENCH TROOPS FIGHTING IN SOUCHEZ CEMETERY.
When the Germans left Souchez it resembled a buried city of the past.

which had been brought back from the Eastern theatre of war had been directed by the Crown Prince of Bavaria to the entrenchments on the Vimy heights. The British Guards division had been moved by Sir John French and Sir Douglas Haig to the neighbourhood of Loos. They were to retake the summit of Hill 70, with the redoubt on the north-east corner of the hill, Pit 14 bis and the adjacent woods and chalk pit, while the London Territorials, the 47th Division, on their right attacked the enemy towards Lens.

For their part the Germans made desperate efforts to dislodge the troops of the 9th Division from the buildings of Pit 8 behind the Hohenzollern Redoubt, and round this point and the redoubt itself furious fighting raged throughout the day. In spite of the most heroic efforts the British holding the Pit were unable to maintain their position. As the day wore on they were slowly forced back to the eastern portion of the Hohenzollern Redoubt. The commander of the 9th Division, Major-General G. H. Thesiger, who had himself proceded to the scene of action, was killed in the course of the fighting. At noon, when the enemy's bombers were successfully working up the "Little Willie" trench towards the redoubt,

Corporal J. D. Pollock of the 5th Cameron Highlanders got out of the trench, walked along the top edge and, under heavy machine gun fire, flung many grenades at the enemy's bombers, and stopped the German progress for nearly an hour till he was wounded and compelled to desist. He was awarded the V.C.

Second Lieut. John Bessell of the 3/Battalion, Dorset Regiment, who was attached to the Royal Fusiliers, made daring reconnaissances to ascertain the position of the bombers in the redoubt. Second Lieut. B. A. Bates of the 3/Battalion York and Lancaster Regiment also did good service recovering a trench. His company had used up their bombs, but taking six men with him he drove out the Germans by rifle and revolver fire. Second Lieut. J. E. French of the 3/Battalion Royal Fusiliers (City of London Regiment), near Vermelles also distinguished himself by his coolness and courage.

In the afternoon, the Guards and the London Territorials, supported by what remained of the Highlanders and by some of the dismounted cavalry from Loos, made on the right of the British line a desperate attempt to counterbalance the enemy's success in the neighbourhood of the Hohenzollern Redoubt. If this gallant attempt of our heroic troops had been successful, the German line between Hulluch and Lens would have been pierced. These charges will be long remembered by the British Army. " Can you imagine," writes a non-commissioned officer, in the machine-gun section of a London Regiment, " the ordinary battle pictures of troops advancing under hell's own shell fire ? I thought such a thing was impossible, now I not only know it's true, but saw it all."

On the morning of September 27 the 1st and 2nd Brigades of the Guards held the recently-captured first line German trenches from a point 500 yards south of Hulluch to the northern houses of Loos. The 3rd Brigade was in reserve behind the town. Lord Cavan's plan was to throw the 2nd Brigade against the chalk pit and the spinney at its north-eastern end, and the mining works of Pit 14 bis, while the 3rd Brigade, so soon as the 2nd Brigade had secured these points, was to

march through Loos and attack Hill 70. The attack of the 2nd Brigade was heralded by a terrific bombardment by the British guns and howitzers. From the trenches occupied by the Guards it was possible to see the objectives across the shallow valley. There before them were the chalk pit with two ruined brick cottages and the spinney round these, the ugly mining works of Pit 14 bis with a lofty chimney, near it a small red house and a collection of entrenchments and sand-bag parapets known as the " Keep." Away to the right was Hill 70, and the redoubt on its farther side hidden by the crest of the hill.

At 4 p.m. the Irish Guards advanced down the valley and at an inconsiderable loss reached the edge of the spinney. Two companies filed off south of it to help the Scots Guards, who, under a very heavy fire of shrapnel, rushed down the slopes, crossed the Hulluch-Loos road, mounted the rise and made for Pit 14 and the " Keep." Their Colonel was wounded

HEROES OF THE BATTLE OF LOOS.
Wounded British troops on the way to the rear.

A VICTORIA CROSS HERO AT LOOS: PIPER DANIEL LAIDLAW, OF THE KING'S OWN SCOTTISH BORDERERS,

Heartens his comrades by playing outside the British trenches under enemy fire.

PIPER DANIEL LAIDLAW.

During the worst of the bombardment of the German trenches near Loos and Hill 70, when the attack was about to begin, seeing his company was suffering from the effect of gas, Piper Laidlaw, with absolute coolness and disregard of danger, mounted the parapet and played his company out of the trench.

and 11 other officers killed or wounded. Notwithstanding a tremendous machine-gun fire, the men pressed on and reached the buildings, while the Irish Guards, at first driven back, rallied and occupied the spinney. On their left, the Coldstream Guards advanced and secured the north-east outskirts of the chalk pit. Two companies of the Grenadiers raced down the hill to support the Scots Guards, struggling round Pit 14 bis, where Captain Cuthbert, D.S.O., at the head of a party, had obtained an entry into the "Keep." He and Lieutenant Ayres-Ritchie and the party with them hung on to the "Keep" until they were almost the only survivors. At nightfall, though the Germans had recovered Pit 14 bis and the "Keep," the Coldstream Guards held the chalk pit, the Irish Guards the spinney, while the Scots and Grenadier Guards dug themselves in from the spinney towards Loos. The retirement of two companies of the Scots and one of the Grenadier Guards was a remarkable sight. They marched back up the hill which they had descended as if they were on parade, and suffered comparatively speaking but little loss.

Meanwhile, the 3rd Guards Brigade, leaving a battalion of the Grenadier Guards in the trenches, crossed in open formation the shell-torn ridge which divided them from Loos. A battalion of the Grenadier Guards entered

Loos on the north-west, with a battalion of the Welsh Guards, who were under fire for the first time, on their right. Some of the Scots Guards followed the Grenadiers. The mass of dauntless men disappeared into the ruins of the town and entered the communication trenches which led towards the summit of Hill 70. As they left the communication trenches they were met by a deluge of gas shells. The Colonel of the Grenadiers, badly gassed, relinquished his command to Major the Hon. Miles Ponsonby. The men were halted and ordered to don their smoke helmets, then the advance was resumed, some companies of the Grenadiers being sent to establish contact with the Scots Guards who had not succeeded in taking Pit 14 bis.

The remainder of the Grenadiers and the Welsh Guards delivered the attack. So long as the advance was across dead ground the losses were few, but when the men reached the crest of Hill 70, and their forms were outlined against the sky, they were greeted with a murderous fire at short range. As the evening drew in the Scots Guards from the reserve joined the combat, but it was impossible to carry the redoubt, and the men were withdrawn behind the crests of Hill 70, where they entrenched, having on their right the dismounted cavalrymen. There they all remained till the evening of the 29th, when the position was taken over by the London

[*Lafayette.*

LIEUT. G. H. WYNDHAM-GREEN,

Seaforth Highlanders. Awarded the Military Cross. He set a splendid example of coolness and bravery under fire when in command. Exposed himself most fearlessly while organising and leading attacks near "Pit 8."

LIEUT.-COL. ANGUS DOUGLAS-
HAMILTON.

Commanded 6th Batt. Cameron Highlanders,
killed on Hill 70. When the battalions on his
right and left had retired, he rallied his own
battalion and led his men forward four times.

PRIVATE A. VICKERS,

2nd Batt. Royal Warwickshire Regt. Went in
front of his Company at Hulluch under heavy
fire, and cut the wires holding up the
battalion.

Territorials. The Highlanders were already
being withdrawn from the Loos trenches. During
the advance of the Guards the London Territorials on their right had captured a wood and
repulsed a severe counter-attack.

On Tuesday, September 28, the Coldstream

Guards, at 3.45 p.m., attacked Pit 14 bis from
the south face of the chalk pit. The British
machine-guns concentrated on the wood east
of it, and the Irish Guards poured in a heavy
rifle fire. Pit 14 bis was reached by the Cold-
streams, but was found to be untenable.

SEC.-LIEUT. A. BULLER TURNER,

3rd Batt. Royal Berkshire Regt. At "Pit 8"
volunteered to lead bombing attack. Practically
alone, he threw bombs incessantly and drove
back the Germans. He has since died of
wounds.

ACTING-SERGT. J. C. RAYNES.

A Batt. 71st Brig., R.F.A. At Fosse 7 de Bethune
went out under intense fire from gas-shells, carried
Sergeant Ayres to safety, gave him his own gas-
helmet, and returned, though badly gassed, to his
gun.

FOR MOST CONSPICUOUS BRAVERY AND DEVOTION TO DUTY:

SEC.-LIEUT. A. J. FLEMING-SANDES,

2nd Batt. East Surrey Regt. Seeing his men retiring at Hohenzollern Redoubt, he jumped on to the parapet in full view of the enemy, who were only twenty yards away, threw bombs, and saved the situation.

SEC.-LIEUT. F. H. JOHNSON,

73rd Field Company, R.E. In the attack on Hill 70, although wounded, led several charges on the German Redoubt. He remained at his post until relieved in the evening.

Away on the left of the battle-field, in drenching rain, the fighting went on round Pit 8. In "Slag Alley" Second Lieutenant A. B. Turner, of the 3rd Berkshire Regiment, gained the V.C. Practically alone he pressed down the communication trench and threw bombs with such accuracy that he drove back the Germans 150 yards. Unfortunately, this gallant officer died of the wounds he received. Second-Lieut. W. T. Williams, of the East Kent Regiment, took charge of a small party of bombers, and during 17½ hours he and they

CAPT. A. MONTRAY READ,

1st Batt. Northamptonshire Regt. During first attack near Hulluch he went out to rally units which were disorganised and retiring. Captain Read was mortally wounded while carrying out this gallant work.

SEC.-LIEUT. R. PRICE HALLOWES,

4th Batt. Middlesex Regt. At Hooge set a magnificent example, threw bombs, and made daring reconnaissances of the German positions. When mortally wounded, continued to cheer his men.

VICTORIA CROSS HEROES IN THE BRITISH ADVANCE.

threw close on 2,000 bombs. The damp fuses had to be lit with cigarettes. Lieut. Williams, though wounded, refused to leave his post, and it was mainly due to his bravery that the trench in which he was posted did not pass into the hands of the enemy.

We have seen that General d'Urbal on the 27th was consolidating his position at Souchez. On the 28th the French troops attacked the Prussian Guards on the Vimy heights. Few French details are available, but, after days of desperate encounters, the western slopes of the heights and a large part of the Wood of Givenchy passed into the hands of our Allies. The losses which had been sustained by the British at the Battle of Loos and by the French in the taking of Souchez, the enormous expenditure of shells, grenades and cartridges used in the attacks, were among the causes which induced Sir John French to break off for the present his offensive. On the morning of September 28 he discussed the situation with General Foch, who, on September 30, sent the 9th French Corps to take over the ground occupied by the British, extending

from the French left up to and including the village of Loos and a portion of Hill 70, which was still being held by the British. This movement was not completed until October 2.

September 28 may be considered to mark the end of the Battle of Loos, as originally designed by the Allied commanders. No great results were obtained by the fighting, which had cost the British Army very heavy casualties. The reasons for the comparative unsuccess were many. In the first place, there were not sufficient reserves immediately available to back up the early successes of the British and consolidate the positions won. This gave time to the Germans to rally and counter-attack. Perhaps the unexpectedly rapid advance of the British had something to do with this. Secondly, the French advance took place six hours after the British. This left the right of the latter exposed to a flank attack. These unfortunate events may have been, and probably were, unavoidable, but the result was that a battle, which if fought under more favourable conditions, might have changed the aspect of the war, was to all intents and purposes a failure.

LOOS.
A Street after bombardment.

CHAPTER CVI.

THE FIGHTING ROUND LOOS, SEPTEMBER 28–OCTOBER 13, 1915.

A S we have seen, the Allied offensive at the Battles of Loos and Vimy had not produced the results which the Allies had expected. The very moderate measure of success achieved by the British and French was, perhaps, symptomatic of the changed conditions of modern warfare. In the history of the Art of War there have been periods when, owing to the weapons, instruments or methods employed by their opponents, military geniuses of the first order have failed to achieve their objects. Hannibal, a century after Alexander the Great had moved from the Danube to the Indus, led an army from Spain across the Alps, routed the Romans at the Trebia, Trasimene and Cannae, but, in face of the trench tactics of Fabius and the permanent fortifications of the Roman and Latin Colonies, was unable to conquer Italy. In the first years of the eighteenth century the great Duke of Marlborough, whose march in 1704 from the Netherlands to the Danube and whose conduct of the Battle of Blenheim showed him to be an original and audacious strategist and tactician, was foiled for a time by the Fabian tactics of Marshal Villars. In both cases the explanation was simple. Neither Hannibal nor Marlborough possessed machinery powerful enough to destroy the entrenchments of their enemies or a preponderance of numbers so great

that the artificial obstacles placed in their paths could be ignored or, at a frightful sacrifice of life, overcome. The disappointment felt in the Allied and some neutral countries because Castelnau, Foch and French had not pierced the German lines was to a large extent irrational. The hostile critics of the Allied Generals—critics hypnotised by the memories of Austerlitz, Jena, Sadowa and Sedan—had forgotten that the Japanese had won no crushing victory over the Russians in Manchuria and that the early successes of the Germans in the West had been due to their immense superiority in point of numbers and armament, and that the success of Mackensen in 1915 was mainly caused by the Russian shortage in ammunition. At the Battle of the Marne when, thanks to Joffre's strategy, the Germans between Paris and Verdun appear to have had no numerical advantage, the Kaiser's soldiers had been worsted. The Battle of the Marne had not, however, been, nor had it led to, " a crowning mercy," while in the First Battle of Ypres it had been demonstrated that masses, theoretically overwhelming, and directed by officers callously indifferent to losses of life or to human suffering were, even when supported by a gigantic artillery, incapable of carrying entrenchments manned by a comparatively small force of trained and brave troops. " The development of arma-

IN THE LINE OF FIRE.
French Women running to shelter during a violent bombardment.

ments," Lord Kitchener observed on November 9, 1914, "has modified the application of the old principles of strategy and tactics and reduced the present warfare to something approximating to siege operations." So far as the Western Theatre of War was concerned, that statement had not been gainsaid by subsequent events. At the Battles of Neuve Chapelle and Artois the British and French had —on the map—made only trifling advances. The Germans with poisonous gas had in April, 1915, struck a felon blow at the defenders of the Ypres salient, but the ruins of Ypres still remained in the possession of the Allies. In the last week of the following September, assisted by soporific gas and clouds of smoke, the British and French had tried to blast, bomb and bayonet their way through the German lines in Artois and Champagne, but the results described in Chapters CIV. and CV. were regarded by many as incommensurate with the expenditure of life and munitions.

Nevertheless in both areas the Allies had secured substantial gains. General de Castelnau had drawn nearer to the Bazancourt-Grand Pré railway and, if the Germans could be deprived of that important lateral line of communication, the position of the enemy south of the Aisne and in the northern glades of the Ardennes would become precarious. Generals Foch and d'Urbal, too, had forced the Germans out of Souchez, as in May and June they had dislodged

them from Carency, La Targette, Neuville St. Vaast and the Labyrinth. The French 10th Army was, moreover, slowly worming its way up the Vimy heights. Lastly, Sir Douglas Haig had taken the Double Crassier slag-heaps, the ruins of the town of Loos, the western slopes of Hill 70, the chalk pit to its north, and part of the Hulluch Quarries and the Hohenzollern Redoubt, albeit the losses of the British in the Battle of Loos had been so great that on September 28 the French 9th Corps at the urgent request of the British generalissimo had been detached by Foch to take over the Double Crassier, Loos, and the trenches leading out of Loos towards Hill 70.

The progress of d'Urbal and Haig might appear to be small, but it brought them close to the rim of the Plain of the Scheldt. The importance which the German Higher Command attached to holding that rim was evidenced by the honeycomb of subterranean defences which the Germans had constructed in the chalky ridges from La Bassée southwards to the banks of the Scarpe, and by the desperate efforts which during the days following the Battle of Loos they made to retain their grip on the rim and to recover the approaches to it lost by them in the fighting from September 25 to 28.

Apart from the tactical disadvantages they would be under if they were driven into the Plain of the Scheldt, and if the southern face of the La Bassée salient were enfiladed, there was this to be taken into account by the Germans. With infinite pains a vast burrow of fortifications had been created between La Bassée and the Scarpe. The German troops believed those fortifications to be impregnable. If that belief were discovered to be erroneous, the moral effect on the Germans might be enormous. It would be tantamount to a confession that the Western Allies were their superiors in scientific warfare. The Germans had nowhere in the Western theatre of war carried entrenchments so formidable as those between La Bassée and Vimy. The Labyrinth and the Hohenzollern Redoubt were, as it were, test cases. If the Hohenzollern Redoubt, like the Labyrinth, had to be abandoned, a sense of discouragement might sink into the minds of the Germans in Artois, and thence permeate to the rest of the huge horde defending the four hundred miles of trenches on the Western front. As a panic in one considerable sector would entail the collapse of his whole line, and the best specifics against panics were counter-attacks, the Crown Prince of Bavaria made numerous attempts to drive back the Allies to their original positions.

From the tactical standpoint the main effects of the Battles of Loos and Vimy had been to accentuate on the south the German salient at La Bassée, and to create a second German salient running from the environs of Lens through the outskirts of Liévin and Angres, and by Givenchy en Gohelle, and the Vimy heights to the Scarpe below Arras. On the side of the Allies the corresponding salient created by their victory commenced near Cuinchy on the Béthune-La Bassée-Lille Canal. It went south-eastwards by the Hohenzollern Redoubt, the Hulluch Quarries, the western exit of Hulluch, and the Chalk Pit taken by the Coldstream Guards to the edge of Hill 70; thence it turned westwards round the south of Loos and the Double Crassier to the Allied trenches at Grenay.

The Cuinchy-Hulluch-Grenay salient measured at its base only some five miles, and, taking into consideration the range of modern artillery, it was obvious that the British and French troops holding it were in a peculiarly perilous position. The French 10th Army had, indeed, cleared the enemy out of his trenches on the eastern slopes of the plateau of Notre Dame de Lorette

WRECKAGE IN NORTHERN FRANCE.
British Transport Column passing through a shell-shattered village.

opposite Angres, and had taken the Bois en Hache and Souchez, but on September 28, when the British Generalissimo was requesting that the 9th French Corps should be sent to occupy the southern face of the Cuinchy-Hulluch-Grenay salient, General d'Urbal's attempts to seize Givenchy en Gohelle, the neighbouring woods and the Vimy heights, met with a stout resistance from the two divisions of the Prussian Guards detailed by the Crown Prince of Bavaria to prevent d'Urbal turning from the south the German positions between Grenay and Angres.

On Wednesday, September 29—a day of biting winds and torrential rain—the Germans made several attacks on the British position north-west of Hulluch. The fighting was very severe and continued throughout the day, but except on the extreme left, where the enemy gained about 150 yards of trench, the assaults were beaten off. In the course of them Second Lieutenant Alfred Fleming-Sandes, of the 2nd Battalion East Surrey Regiment, gained the V.C. for conspicuous gallantry at the Hohenzollern Redoubt. He had been sent to command

MINING OPERATIONS.
Destruction of a German trench by a mine.

a company shaken by continual bombing and machine-gun fire. The men had only a few bombs left; the troops to their right were retiring, and isolated soldiers were beginning to file off to the rear. Fleming-Sandes grasped the situation at a glance. He collected a few bombs, jumped on to the parapet, and threw them at the advancing Germans, who were not 20 yards away. Almost immediately he was very severely wounded by the explosion of a grenade. Struggling to his feet, instead of seeking medical assistance, he rushed forward and threw his remaining bombs, being soon afterwards again badly wounded. But for the action of Fleming-Sandes it is probable that his company would not have rallied, and that the position at this most important point of the battlefield might have become very critical.

Close by, in the "Big Willie" trench which ran eastward from the Hohenzollern Redoubt, Private Samuel Harvey, of the 1st York and Lancaster Regiment, was also that day winning the V.C. A heavy bombing attack had been made by the enemy, and, as in the previous case, our men's bombs had dwindled to a small number. Harvey volunteered to fetch some, but, owing to the communication trench being blocked with wounded and with reinforcements, he was obliged to cross the open ground under intense fire. He was eventually wounded in the head, but ere he fell he had brought up no less than thirty boxes of bombs. Had he failed to do so, the enemy might, perhaps, have taken the whole of the trench.

Among the other heroic deeds on September 29 performed by Britons, two others may be mentioned. Near Vermelles Captain C. H. Sykes, of the 6th Battalion Royal Fusiliers, City of London Regiment, when some troops on his left were bombed out of their trench, charged at the head of a dozen men and recovered it. Not content with that, he continued to advance, and only fell back because he was not supported. Later in the day, under heavy shell fire, he supported a company which was retreating before superior numbers. The next morning this brave officer was wounded. Not far off Second Lieutenant R. J. H. Gatrell led a squad of bombers against a German bombing party which had succeeded in capturing a trench 350 yards long. Gatrell and his men retook it.

Meanwhile, d'Urbal's 10th Army in the small hours of the night of the 28-29th, and during the 29th, had succeeded in reaching Hill 140,

A GERMAN REDOUBT BLOWN UP BY A BRITISH MINE.

which was the culminating point on the Vimy heights and the orchards south of it. They had taken 300 prisoners, mostly belonging to the Prussian Guard. The German *communiqué* of September 29, after truthfully stating that a portion of the ground evacuated north of Loos had been recovered by the Germans, admitted that the French had been partly successful " in the district of Souchez and Neuville."

The 29th was noteworthy, too, for an action near Ypres, in the Hooge region. The enemy fired a mine close to our trenches south of the Ypres-Menin road, and gained a temporary footing in the British first-line trenches. Nearly the whole of the lost position was regained on the 30th by counter-attacks.

During Thursday, September 30, when the troops of the 9th French Corps began to file

AIRMEN AS INFANTRY.
Men of the Royal Naval Air Service in the trenches.

into the trenches and dug-outs on the Double Crassier, the combats along the northern face of the Cuinchy-Hulluch-Grenay salient continued. The struggle between the contending forces was especially severe in the vicinity of the Hohenzollern Redoubt. Second-Lieutenant R. J. H. Gatrell again distinguished himself. He led a counter-attack of bombers to recover the trenches of a battalion to his left, and obliged the Germans to retire behind their barricades. For his services on this and the preceding day he was awarded the Military Cross, as was Second-Lieutenant S. C. Godfrey, of the 2nd Battalion Royal Scots Fusiliers, who from 6.30 p.m. till 5 a.m. on October 1, by his initiative and personal bravery, stopped the advance of the enemy who had entered " Gun Trench." At this point we insert a graphic description by Mr. John Buchan, who visited the battlefield on September 30.

I have to-day had the privilege of visiting the battlefield of Loos. Let me describe its elements. A low ridge runs northward from the Béthune-Lens railway to the high ground south of La Bassée. It sends off a spur to the north-east, which is the Hill 70 of the *communiqués*. In the angle between the two lies the village of Loos. The German first position was along the crest of the western ridge ; their second was in the hollow just west of Loos ; their third runs to-day through Cité St. Auguste and along the slopes to the north.

To reach their old front trenches one leaves the Béthune-Lens high road near the houses called Philosophe. In front is a long easy slope so scarred with trench lines that I can only compare it to the Karroo, where tussocks of grass are sparsely scattered over the baked earth. Only in this case the earth is white The coarse herbage springs from a light chalk, and the sandbagged parapets are further patches of dull grey. Looking from the high road, the sky-line is about a thousand yards distant, and beyond it rise the strange twin towers of Loos, like the rigging of a ship seen far

off at sea. The place is not very " healthy "—no hinterland is—but, though the shelling was continuous, the trenches were fairly safe.

Beyond the old British front trench you pass through the *débris* of our wire defences and cross the hundred yards of No Man's Land, over which, for so many months, our men looked at the enemy. Then you reach the German entanglements, wonderfully cut to pieces by our shell-fire. There our own dead are lying very thick. Presently you are in the German front trenches. Here, in some parts, there are masses of German dead, and some of our own. This is the famous Loos-road redoubt, a work about five hundred yards in diameter, built around a tract from Loos to Vermelles which follows the crest of the downs. It is an amazing network, ramified beyond belief, but now a monument to the power of our artillery. It is all ploughed up and mangled like a sand castle which a child has demolished in a fit of temper. Fragments of shell, old machine-gun belts, rifle cartridges, biscuit tins, dirty pads of cotton wool are everywhere, and a horrible number of unburied bodies.

But the chief interest of the Redoubt is the view. The whole battlefield of our recent advance is plain to the eye. Below, in the hollow, lie the ruins of Loos around the gaunt tower. Beyond is the slope of Hill 70, with the houses of Lens showing to the south-east of it. North, one can see Hulluch and the German quarries, and farther on St. Elie and Haisnes, hidden in a cloud of high explosives, and west of them the site of the Hohenzollern Redoubt and the ill-omened slag-heap, Fosse 8. It is that sight rare in this present war, at least in the northern section—an old-fashioned battlefield. It is all quite open and bare and baked. The tactical elements can be grasped in a minute or two.

And, to complete the picture, the dead are everywhere around one, high explosives and shrapnel boom overhead, the thresh of an airplane's propeller comes faint from the high heavens, and up towards Fosse 8 there is a never-ending mutter of machine-guns. Only living soldiers seem to be absent, for, though battle is joined two miles off, scarcely a human being is visible in the landscape.

I came home late this evening through a wonderful scene. A clear blowing autumn sky was ending in a stormy twilight. Far off in the sky a squadron of airplanes glimmered like white moths against the sullen blue. Battalions were marching down from the trenches, khaki and tartan alike white with chalk mud from the rain of yesterday. They had none of the haggard, weary look of most troops in such circumstances, but laughed and joked and had a swagger even in their fatigue. Other battalions, very spruce and workman-like, were marching off. They are stout fellows to look at, these soldiers of the New Army. Interminable transport trains choked all the road, so that one had leisure to study the progress of the thick rain clouds from the west through the skeleton webs which once were cottages.

At a certain Corps Headquarters where I had tea there were many old relics. I saw the alarm bell which had once hung in the Loos-road Redoubt. I saw, too, a strange fragment of steel which fell a long way back from the front, and which could belong to no German type of shell. It looked like a piece of a burst gun, but where it came from heaven alone knows. Among the captured German field guns outside the chateau was a Russian machine-gun, which must have been taken on the Eastern front. That little gun had seen life since it first left its factory in Odessa.

Everywhere in our troops there seems to be the quickening of a new hope. You can see it, too, in the civil population. The inhabitants of the towns behind the front have seen too much of war, and have grown apathetic. But the other day they lined the streets and cheered the tattered remnants of a battalion return-ing from action. And you can see it most of all among the French. The great news from Champagne—of the charge of Marchand's Colonials, of the brigades that have gone clean through all the German lines and are now facing open country—is reflected in a brighter eye and a stiffer bearing even among those clear-eyed and upstanding men.

To-night, I passed a knot of French soldiers in their new horizon blue, and they were singing some marching song, from which I caught the word "Prussians." Perhaps it was the old song of the men of Dumouriez :

> *Savez-vous la belle histoire*
> *De ces fameux Prussiens ?*
> *Ils marchaient à la victoire*
> *Avec les Autrichiens. . . .*

A famous general is reported to have said, with a pardonable mixture of metaphors, that, if the French once got their tails up, they would carry the battlement of heaven. Let us hope that, for our incomparable Allies and for ourselves, "the day of glory has arrived."

Though the French did not, in the words of the general quoted by Mr. Buchan, "carry the battlement of heaven," they made (on Friday,

BUILDING A TRAVERSE IN A
FRONT-LINE TRENCH.

BRITISH DISPATCH RIDERS.

Motor cyclists break their journey at a French shanty in order to replenish their stock of petrol.

October 1) further progress up the heights of Vimy, pushing forward in the Wood of Givenchy and capturing 61 prisoners belonging to the Prussian Guard. Two German counter-attacks, one on a small fort taken the day before in the Givenchy Wood, the other on the trenches south of Hill 119, were completely repulsed. In addition there were numerous combats—in which the grenade played the chief part—to the east and south-east of Neuville - St. Vaast. Nothing of importance appears to have occurred on the British front.

The next day, Saturday, October 2, was memorable for the death, which occurred in the afternoon, of Major-General F. D. V. Wing, C.B., commanding the 12th Division. Born in 1860, he was the only son of the late Major Vincent Wing. He was gazetted lieutenant in the Royal Artillery in 1880 and held a variety of Staff appointments, including that of A.D.C. to Lord Roberts in 1903, and the command of the Royal Artillery 3rd Division Southern Command in 1913–14. Like so many other of our officers, he had seen active service in South Africa, having been present at the actions of Talana, Lombard's Kop, and Laing's Nek. In the Great War he had been wounded and mentioned in dispatches.

Wing was the third General of Division who had been killed since the opening of the Battle of Loos. The deaths of the other two, Major-

BRITISH INFANTRY CAPTURE THE WOOD COVERING THE CHALK PIT NEAR HILL 70.

General G. H. Thesiger, C.B., and Major-General Sir Thompson Capper, have been already referred to. As their biographies illustrate the world-wide activities of the Old Army which was now fast vanishing, it may not be inappropriate to furnish some brief particulars of the careers of these two officers.

Thesiger, the elder son of the late Lieutenant-General the Hon. Charles Wemyss Thesiger and a grandson of the first Lord Chelmsford, was born in 1868, and educated at Eton. He received his commission in the Rifle Brigade in 1890. He was a graduate of the Staff College and held a number of Staff appointments. In the Nile Expedition of 1898 he was present at the Battle of Omdurman and was mentioned in dispatches. During the South African War he fought at Lombard's Kop and helped in the defence of Ladysmith, where he was severely wounded. Subsequently, while on the staff, he took part in several of the operations—including the action at Belfast—which led up to the reduction of the Transvaal.

More varied had been the services of Sir Thompson Capper. The third son of the late William Copeland Capper, of the Indian Civil Service, who was one of the besieged residents in Lucknow, Capper joined the Army in 1882, serving in the East Lancashire Regiment. He obtained his company in 1891, and went through many campaigns with distinction in India and Africa, gaining the medal with clasp for the Chitral Relief Force in 1895, a brevet majority and other rewards for services in the Sudan in 1898, and the D.S.O., the Queen's Medal (with six clasps), the King's Medal (with two clasps), and the brevet rank of Lieutenant-Colonel during the South African War. His military work, however, was not confined to the field, for he was for some time a professor at the Staff College, and later the first commandant of the new Staff College created in India. In 1911 he became Brigadier-General in command of the 13th Infantry Brigade. Capper, as Commander of the 7th Division, had before, at and after the first Battle of Ypres, made for himself a name which will never be forgotten. Early in the summer of 1915 an unfortunate accident in the course of some experiments with hand grenades caused him serious injury, and he was obliged to relinquish his command for a time. When sufficiently recovered to return to the front, he was reappointed to his old division.

The extract from a letter written on October 2 shows the almost-light-hearted spirit in which the men of the New Armies approached their duties :—

I have massaged the bacon into a proper semblance of martyrdom and eaten breakfast. I feel refreshed. The Germans, those curious freaks who live quite close to us, have been hurling high explosives into a wood behind us all the morning, for some reason best known to themselves—there is certainly nothing *in* the wood worth a bullet, let alone a shell. Now I sit on the fire step wrapped in my great coat—a place in the sun—feeling very home-sick and Coliseumy and cold, and

HIGHLANDERS IN THE TRENCHES.
An Officer inspecting a respirator.

listen to the weird noises La Bassée way, like the rumblings of the belly of Silenos.

I have nothing to offer for your birthday—not even a nose cap has lately come my way—so my benediction must suffice and the wish that you may one day add your graceful presence to this happy family circle—shall we say in the spring ; for it would be an ill wish indeed to hasten any friend's footsteps out here in mid-winter —and it is as cold as the devil, and a wind that 'ud melt the marrow on yer and make you shake with the ague. Glory be to God !

.   .   .   .   .   .

We had rather a tragedy the other night. On the right of the X—— Regiment's line and included in it is a place called the "Tambour." The Tambour might be described as a long bow, in which there is a distance of about 30 yards between the bow itself and the string, and about 60 yards between the bow and the Germans. The Tambour is still heavily mined from end to end by the Germans. Well, J. B., commanding D company, granted one of his subalterns (an awfully nice fellow— M. T——, second lieutenant) leave to go out with a patrol to inspect the German barbed wire in front of the Tambour. T—— went with a corporal, and, picking their way gingerly round the mine craters, they went out to the wire. Half an hour later the corporal returned alone, and said that he had got separated from T——, and had looked for him but couldn't find him. He had heard a shot, seen the flash near to, and thought T—— was hit. He was sent out again to find him, failed, and came back. This, of course, was at night. B—— telephoned for the elder T——, who came up at once. Corny T—— is a great hefty fellow, strong as an ox, and he went out to look for his brother. He went out three

ASSAULT BY BRITISH BOMBERS.

Hurling the deadly missiles into the German trenches. The Infantry were behind, each with two bombs,
and after handing these to the throwers, rushed in themselves with the bayonet.

separate times, and at length found him dead by the
German barbed wire. He carried him back slung on
his shoulders. He is getting the D.C.M. or V.C. for that.
I don't suppose he particularly wants it.*

On the day when that letter was written such
scenes as the following were being enacted,
probably within gun-shot of the writer. Captain

* Published by the *Manchester Guardian*.

W. H. Tapp, of the 2nd Dragoon Guards, who
had taken a plane table into the front line of
trenches near Loos, under continuous fire was
fixing observation points and correcting con-
tours on a map of Hill 70. Captain B. J.
Hackett, of the Royal Army Medical Corps,
whose battalion had run out of dressings for

the wounded, was walking a thousand yards in the open exposed to shells and bullets to obtain a fresh supply. Captain N. Freeman, of the 2nd Battalion Cheshire Regiment, holding the right of a trench near Vermelles, was after sunset during the night of the 2nd-3rd exchanging bombs with the enemy. He did not leave his post until he was almost surrounded. That same night Lieutenant B. S. Browne, of the R.A.M.C., was—also near Vermelles—searching for and carrying back wounded lying between our own and the enemy's line. The enemy kept firing at him and the ground was lit up by flares.

Sunday, October 3, was no day of rest for either the British or their Allies. The French 9th Corps had by now relieved entirely the British troops defending the southern face of the Cuinchy-Hulluch-Grenay salient. In the afternoon the Germans opened a violent bombardment on the northern face. It was followed by several attacks over the open against the British trenches between the Hulluch Quarries and the Vermelles-Hulluch road. These attacks were repulsed with severe loss to the enemy, but north-west of the Quarries the Germans succeeded in recapturing the greater portion of the Hohenzollern Redoubt. All the while the struggle for the Vimy heights went on, and the Germans claim to have repulsed French attacks south of Hill 119 and to have recaptured a portion of a trench north-east of Neuville-St. Vaast. Whether the German claims were justified or not is uncertain. What is, however, established is that the next day, October 4, General d'Urbal's troops were desperately fighting in the Givenchy Wood and on Hill 119. They carried the Cinq Chemins cross-road but subsequently lost it.

There was now a short lull in the struggle raging between the Béthune-La Bassée Canal and the Scarpe. The British and French were consolidating their positions, the Germans preparing for the counter-attack by which they hoped to recover the whole of the ground relinquished by them at the Battle of Loos. The counter-attack was not long in coming. The advance of the British between Hill 70 and Hulluch, where they had gained ground varying from over 500 to 1,000 yards in breadth, had alarmed the Crown Prince of Bavaria, and he was determined, if possible, to dislodge the Allies from the salient.

At 10.30 a.m. on the morning of Friday,

IN NORTHERN FRANCE.
British troops getting a dummy gun into position.

ON THE WESTERN FRONT.
The Duke of Cornwall's Light Infantry in the first-line trenches.

October 8, high explosive and other shells began to rain on the British front line and support trenches. An enemy aeroplane for a time circled above them registering the fire. It was driven off; but the intensity of the bombardment continued to increase. At 3.20 p.m. rifle and machine-gun fire from all points of the crescent-like German position opened. Bombardment and fusillade ceased half an hour later. Meanwhile eight or ten German battalions prepared to attack the French between Grenay and Hill 70. Twelve more battalions mustered in or near the woods opposite the Chalk Pit, north of Hill 70. Six to eight battalions were deployed in the trenches and slag-heaps near the Hohenzollern Redoubt, to which sector of the battle-field the bulk of the British Guards Division had been recently moved from the direction of Loos. The 1st Division, with apparently some details of the Coldstream Guards, was disposed from Hulluch to the Chalk Pit. It was against the 1st Division and the Guards that the main German attack was to be made.

About 4 p.m. four lines of Germans shoulder to shoulder appeared, line succeeding line, above the parapets of the trenches, which in the neighbourhood of the Chalk Pit were in places only 120 yards from our own. Behind them columns of the enemy issued out of the woods, buildings and villages to support the attack. Instantly the British Artillery and the French Soixante Quinze guns showered shrapnel on the advancing foe. Our machine-guns were turned on and the men emptied their magazine rifles at the surging waves of Germans and the masses in rear of the latter.

It was the story of Mons and Ypres over again.

An officer present who observed the carnage declared that the affair resembled "bowling over nine-pins." In a few seconds the ranks of ambling Germans had been reduced to a number of little groups, divided from each other by dead or wounded men. The less severely wounded were crawling on their hands and knees towards their own trenches. Some of the enemy lay down and tried to return the fire. Such of them as were not hit by bullets were killed or wounded by the shrapnel.

Only at a very few points did the enemy reach our positions. For example, near Loos a strong party of Germans captured two hundred yards of trench, but Lance-Sergeant Oliver Brooks, of the 3rd Battalion Coldstream Guards, on his own initiative led a party of bombers to drive them out. He succeeded in regaining possession of the lost ground, and for his fearlessness, presence of mind and promptitude was awarded the V.C. As a rule, however, the enemy gained nothing by his reckless attacks and heavy bombardment. The shells had destroyed the sapheads and a large section of the front trench occupied by a company of the 2nd Battalion Coldstream Guards commanded by Captain H. C. Loyd; nevertheless he and his men repulsed two determined bomb attacks. The assaults in the centre near the Chalk Pit failed entirely, not a German getting to within forty yards of our men. Between Hulluch and the Quarries the enemy was similarly beaten off, and the British, pursuing the flying foe, secured a German trench west of the hamlet of St. Elie. Only at one point in the " Big Willie " trench of the Hohenzollern Redoubt did the Germans effect an entry. Here Lieutenant G. G. Gunnis, of the 3rd Battalion Grenadier Guards, leading his men with great dash, attacked the Germans in flank and rear, drove them helter-skelter into the open, and, killing or wounding large numbers, effected the recapture of "Big Willie." The French 9th Corps lost a small portion of the Double Crassier slag-heaps, but by midnight the German counter-attack had ended in complete failure. After the charges a tremendous artillery duel had followed, which had resulted in the British guns gaining the ascendancy about 5 p.m. Violent and repeated attacks on the French positions south-east of Neuville-St. Vaast had also been utterly repulsed. The Allies lost very few men in the battle of October 8, and the number of dead Germans in front of their lines in the Cuinchy-Hulluch-Grenay salient alone was estimated at from 7,000 to 8,000.

The bloody repulse inflicted by Sir John French and General d'Urbal on the Germans who had attacked the positions in the Cuinchy-Hulluch-Grenay salient and on the Vimy heights was followed by a number of minor engagements. On the 9th the enemy delivered some futile attacks against the redoubt captured from him in the wood of Givenchy-en-Gohelle.

On the night of the next day, October 10, the 4th Regiment of the Prussian Grenadier Guards charged the French trenches in the Bois-en-Hache, but were beaten off with heavy loss, 100 prisoners being taken ; 174 more prisoners were secured a few hours later by our Allies. Among them were six officers, some of them belonging to the 1st Grenadier Regiment. The French *communiqué* of October 11 states "that very marked progress had been made in the valley of Souchez, west of the Souchez-Angres road, and to the east of the redoubt in the Givenchy wood, and that ground had been gained on the Vimy heights towards the wood of La Folie." During the evening of October 12 the Germans assaulted the French lines north-east of Souchez, but were everywhere completely foiled.

From October 9 to 13 neither side was inactive in the Loos salient. Numerous aerial duels took place, in most of which our airmen were successful, though one of our machines appears from the German report to have been brought down east of Poperinghe. This was perhaps the aeroplane which Sir John French stated at the time to have been lost. According to the German *communiqué*

BARBED WIRE IN FRONT OF A GERMAN TRENCH WRECKED BY SHRAPNEL FIRE.

Lieutenant Immelmann, on October 10, compelled, too, a British battle-biplane to descend north-west of Lille. Of the incidents which occurred in the four days' fighting, one deserves to be recorded because it shows under what nerve-racking conditions the British gunners had to work. On October 11, at Fosse 7 de Béthune, A Battery, of the 71st Brigade Royal Field Artillery, was being heavily bombarded by armour-piercing and gas shells. Sergeant Ayres was wounded, and the battery was ordered to cease fire. Amidst bursting shells and choking from gas fumes, Sergeant J. C. Raynes rushed across to assist his comrade. He bandaged him and returned to the battery, which again

A CORNER OF A CAPTURED GERMAN TRENCH.

German notice-boards in background.

opened fire. A few minutes later "Cease Fire" was a second time ordered, and Sergeant Raynes, calling on two gunners to help him—both of whom were shortly afterwards killed—went out and carried Sergeant Ayres into a dug-out, at the mouth of which a gas shell promptly burst. With splendid courage Raynes dashed out, fetched his own smoke helmet, put it on Ayres, and, himself badly gassed, staggered back to serve his gun. Not many hours elapsed before Raynes also was wounded. He and seven other soldiers were in a house called after Mr. J. M. Barrie's play, "Quality Street." A "Jack Johnson" blew

in the building. Four of the men were buried by the falling bricks and timbers. The remaining four found themselves imprisoned in the cellar. The first to be dug out was Raynes. He was wounded in the head and, leg, but insisted on remaining under heavy shell fire in order that he might help in the rescue of the others. Then, the moment his wounds were dressed, he rejoined his battery, which was again being violently shelled. The V.C. was an almost inadequate recompense for such magnificent conduct.

On October 13 the Germans made a fierce attack on the French round Souchez and on the Vimy heights, while Sir Douglas Haig once more assaulted the Hohenzollern Redoubt and the German position from that point to half a mile or so south-west of Hulluch.

The Crown Prince of Bavaria's attack on d'Urbal was preceded by a terrific bombardment, followed by repeated charges into the Bois-en-Hache and against the French trenches east of the Souchez-Angres road. In addition, attacks were made against the redoubt in the Givenchy wood and the adjacent trenches, and at several other points on the Vimy ridges. Despite the enormous losses incurred by them, the Germans succeeded only in capturing a few sections of trench in the Givenchy wood. Everywhere else they were flung back just as they had been on October 8.

The Germans near Vimy had attacked down hill, but Sir Douglas Haig, in the literal sense of the word, had an up-hill task. The battle of Wednesday, October 13, and the succeeding days was another attempt by the British to extend upwards the northern face of the Cuinchy-Hulluch-Grenay salient. It was accompanied by a holding attack made by the Indian Corps to the north of the La Bassée Canal, in which Second Lieutenant R. J. J. Bahadur, of the Indian Native Land Forces, who was attached to the 39th Garhwal Rifles, gained the Military Cross. He had shown great gallantry in one of the holding attacks on September 25, the first day of the Battle of Loos. In the evening of October 12 he had been wounded in the arm by a rifle bullet, but during the fighting on October 13 he refused to leave the firing line, and commanded a double company with great ability, being severely wounded in the neck. The holding attack by the Indian Corps was magnified by the German Higher Command into an imaginary general attack by the British from Ypres to La Bassée,

PAYING THE GERMAN IN HIS OWN COIN.
The British charge under cover of smoke and gas.

AFTER THE BRITISH ATTACK.
A crossroads in Loos.

which, according to the enemy, was repulsed by the Germans. As a matter of fact, the only other fighting by the British on October 13 was that about to be described.

On the morning of October 13 the wind blew steadily from the west. The air was raw and chilly. A thick Scotch mist covered the ground, and the drizzling rain seemed the harbinger of another of those torrential down-pours which had interfered with the move-ments of the British, French and German troops at the Battle of Loos and afterwards. As the hours, however, passed, the rain ceased, the mist cleared off, and the battlefield was bathed in a warm, autumnal sunlight. The wind was more propitious for a British gas and smoke attack than on September 25. Since the Battle of Loos our stores of shells had been replenished, and the night before the North Midland Division of Territorials had replaced the Guards in the trenches from Vermelles to the region of the Hulluch Quarries.

Far off to the right a column of bright and smokeless flames leapt out of Liévin. For two days a fire had been raging in that village. To the north-west on the horizon were dimly visible the outlines of the battered town of La Bassée. Along the British front blotches of red marked the presence of what remained of the villages of Vermelles and Le Routoire. Between them and La Bassée rose the lofty chimneys of the factories and the black, ugly

slag-heaps of Pit 8 and Haisnes. The open spaces—stubble-field, cabbage patches and the like—were strewn with unburied corpses and broken weapons. Huge holes recorded the activities of the gunners who for a year had been ploughing up with their shells this area, once the home and playground of so many miners and their families. Behind the hostile lines groups of miners and peasants were even now phlegmatically toiling at their daily tasks.

Suddenly, at noon, a bombardment com-parable with that which had preluded the Battle of Loos began. Tongues of fire leaping from the ground flashed as it were a warning to the Germans of the storm of shells descend-ing on them. In the rear British observa-tion balloons hung motionless. Aeroplanes buzzed backwards and forwards.

From hundreds of spots in the German line pillars of black smoke ascended. Fleecy white puffs marked where the shrapnel was bursting, a green or pinkish blob—which swiftly vanished—that an asphyxiating shell from the answering German guns had exploded. In the distance buildings crumbled away and clouds of chalky smoke told that trenches and dug-outs which a few minutes before had been the refuges of soldiers chatting to each other had been upturned.

An hour passed by. Then from the British lines near Vermelles a dense cloud of white smoke, fringed below with red and green, drifted towards the Hohenzollern Redoubt. By the time it had left our trenches it was half a mile broad. Slowly it settled on the Redoubt, the slag-heap behind it, and the buildings of Pit 8.

Meantime our men in the trenches were getting ready. Most of them had discarded their overcoats; all had a few bombs of different varieties. That chiefly used was somewhat larger than a duck's egg, which it resembled in shape. A small ration of rum had been served out to warm the blood and steady the nerves. Except in a few cases this was a superfluous precaution, for few of the soldiers showed, at all events outwardly, any signs of uneasiness. "Fifteen minutes before the charge," relates one of them, " a gallant lad was telling me anecdotes of his school days in the most matter-of-fact fashion." Towards 2 o'clock an order was passed along the lines that the smoke helmets should be put on. They were not, however, to be drawn over the nose and mouth. Five minutes later another order reached the waiting men— to pull the helmets completely over their faces. The charges were timed for 2 p.m.

Sir Douglas Haig had decided that the Midland Division of Territorials was to storm the Hohenzollern Redoubt, while the troops on their right were to attack the Hulluch Quarries and the trenches between them and the village of that name. South of Hulluch an effort was to be made in the direction of Pont à Vendin.

Seen from our lines opposite it, the Hohenzollern Redoubt, shaped like a bean, hid everything from view except the top of a slag-heap and the roof of the house formerly occupied by the manager of Pit 8. The Redoubt had a frontage of some 500 yards. On the gentle rise leading to Pit 8, it stood well out from the main line trench of the Germans in front of the pit. The side farther from the British was connected with that line by two trenches—the northerly one had been christened by the British "Little Willie," the other was known to them as "Big Willie." Between Little Willie and Big Willie two other trenches ran back to the German entrenchments, behind which, west of Pit 8, was the slag-heap above referred to, called "The Dump." To the left of the Dump were four rows of one-storeyed miners' cottages At the back of them ran the Pit railway, which connected the coal-mine with the railroad from La Bassée to Grenay. Beyond the railway were other rows of cottages, known as the Corons de Pekin. East of the Dump and the Pit railway stood three buildings—Les Trois Cabarets. Well in the background were the considerable villages of Auchy and Haisnes.

Though our artillery had pulped most of the

AFTER A BATTLE.
A scene in a village street in Flanders.

ON THE WESTERN FRONT.

buildings and had blown in large parts of the trenches and many of the dug-outs, the problem set the Midland Territorials was perhaps as, or even more, formidable than that which the London Territorials or the Highlanders of the New Army had been asked to solve on the morning of September 25. In the preceding days the enemy, reinforced by companies of the Prussian Guards, had been gradually recovering their hold on the Redoubt. Only a portion of the Big Willie trench was now in our possession. A sap had, however, been run out by us towards the Little Willie trench. Beneath or through the Dump the enemy's engineers had constructed timbered galleries leading to casemates, from the loopholes of which machine guns pointed in all directions. From the cellars of the ruined cottages and mine buildings other machine guns protruded. In dug-outs 30 feet or so deep lurked bombers ready, the moment the British attack was launched, to emerge into the open. Their wooden-handled grenades on explosion by the mere concussion caused blindness. Doubtless the nerves of the defenders had been shaken by our terrible bombardment, doubtless they were confused, if not overcome, by the fumes of the British gas, and owing to the smoke cloud they could only see dimly their assailants. But the gas and smoke affected the British no less than themselves and, when the cloud had passed or been dissipated, the chance of the Germans would come.

A few minutes before 2 p.m. the British guns lifted from the Redoubt and began to search the trenches and buildings behind it, and at 2 p.m. the charge was delivered by the Territorials. It has been described with a wealth of detail by one of them :

I have a very indistinct recollection of anything until I had covered the 200 yards which separated the British lines from the first trench of the Redoubt. The din of the firing and the excitement of the moment once I was over the parapet left me in such a whirl that it was some time before I knew really what I was doing and grew sufficiently cool to experience the thrill and joy of battle.

Already the battalions were becoming mixed, and I found myself with Leicesters and 5th Lincolns. I rather think the 4th Lincolns, in their eagerness to get at the enemy, had started a little before their time, as I caught up with some of the Leicesters before they had passed the German first line. The bullets dropped ceaselessly by, and the German artillery had got the range beautifully. The shells, high explosive and shrapnel, were coming over in showers. The sight of the shrapnel exploding is not particularly encouraging. The projectile bursts fairly low in the air with a terrific bang. A huge cloud of black smoke is given off which curls and whirls so violently that it reminds one of the surface of a whirlpool. It is strangely different from the British shell

which bursts with a soft "pop" and gives off white smoke.

I found the barbed wire in front of the trench had been blown to bits by our guns. Without staying to look at the trench I crossed it by a plank and went forward. I jumped into the German second trench. At one place a Leicester sergeant, shot through the stomach, was lying across the floor of the trench. None of us knew how to deal with a man wounded as he was, and I suggested he should lie with his knees up, and he did. I believe I was right, but I only mention the fact as an illustration of how useful to the soldier a little knowledge of first-aid would be on the field.

German equipment, bags of bombs, and dead bodies lay half buried everywhere ; their taste for smart colours seems strongly developed ; a bag of bombs I unearthed was all the colours of the rainbow. These bombs were of the type most commonly used by the Huns. They were pestle shape. The "head" is a

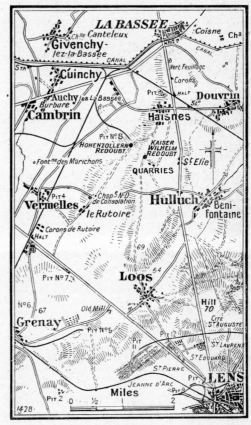

tin containing the explosive, with a wooden handle attached. A loop of thin string projects from the end of the handle. The thrower grasps the handle, pulls out the string (by which act he lights the fuse), and throws. The fuse is a $7\frac{1}{2}$ sec. one, I believe.

Urgent messages were passed from man to man, and presently a Stafford officer came down the line and told us to "stand fast" for a time. He was a jolly little chap ; his face was streaming with perspiration, but he was all smiles, and seemed as happy as if he was at a picnic. On the right of us was a trench— whether a communication trench, or a part of the trench we occupied curving sharply back to the German third line, I knew not, but it apparently met our trench almost at right angles. Corporal Davies detected a party of German bombers working their way towards us. At first only their bluish-grey helmets could be seen, and as our fellows were wearing similarly coloured smoke helmets, some doubt existed as to whether they might not be British—in fact a message was sent down

ENEMY AIRCRAFT IN SIGHT.

that the men were 4th Lincolns and Monmouths. All doubt was removed when the party went past a spot where the trench side had caved in, for then their bluish-grey uniforms could be plainly seen. We opened fire and they returned the compliment.

I got on my feet with the purpose of regaining the trench, when a voice cried, " Can you do anything for me, chum ? Looking round I saw a poor fellow lying about 10 yards from the communication trench. His face was ashy pale. Two of us ran to him and found he had been hit high up in the right thigh by a piece of shell. We tried to carry him to the trench, but before we had got a couple of yards the other fellow left me. The poor chap was in such pain, and could hardly bear to be touched. I dare not drag him in by myself for fear of getting a lot of dirt into the wound. I bandaged him as best I could, and he was very grateful, poor chap ; his only fear seemed to be that I should get hit while attending to him. On getting back to the trench I sat down for a momentary rest. Near by was another man sitting down. His hand was at his head. It was evident all would soon be over. Just then I was conscious of the sensation akin to receiving a tremendous " clout " on the back of the head, and my interest in the war suddenly ceased.

The bullet did not penetrate my pate, but glanced off. Everything seemed very confused for a few

seconds, and then I was aware that something warm was running down my neck. A kindly Leicester bound up the wound with a " first field dressing," and told me to get back to the dressing station. I climbed over the parapet and presently caught up with a 4th Lincoln who had been shot through the back and was crawling along as best he could. I asked him if he could walk across if I put my arm round him, but he said very sensibly he preferred to crawl, it was safer. Fearing he might suddenly lose his strength or some mishap might occur, I decided to stay with him instead of running on, and we crawled along together. He was very cheerful, in spite of the pain he was enduring. He had a magnificent helmet fastened to his belt. It was of shiny black leather, ornamented in brass, and had probably been worn by some stalwart Prussian Guard.

We soon found ourselves in a procession of halt and lame, all wending their way to the same spot. It was wonderful how some of them managed to walk at all. I left the Stamford man at the first dressing station. It was filled with patients, and the medical officer asked me if I could walk to the village. I said " Yes," and proceeded down the long trench.

At Vermelles I boarded an ambulance car, which reached Béthune Hospital about 7.30 p.m.

I waited several hours in the corridor, and during all the time never heard a word of complaint. The wounded were too grateful that their lives had been spared, and were thinking too much of their pals in the Redoubt to complain of the pain they were enduring themselves. The chaplain came in and took all hearts by storm by his first two questions :—" Have we lost many boys ? " " Yes, sir, a great lot." " Did you kill any Germans ? " ' Heaps, sir : they went through the mill, I can tell you, far worse than us." " That's good," he said, fervently. You see, he was an Englishman before he was a chaplain. He bared his head and every one stood up. " Oh God, we thank Thee for having spared these men's lives," he prayed, and a deep and earnest " Amen " came from every throat. His short prayer concluded, the Lord's Prayer was repeated. I never heard the familiar sentences so sincerely and gratefully uttered as they were that night by the tall chaplain and the weary, blood-stained men in the gloomy corridor.

Eventually the ambulance arrived, and I spent the night at a clearing house near Béthune.

At first the attack seemed as if it would be completely successful. The Leicestershires and Lincolnshires in the centre swept clean over the Redoubt itself, and reached that portion of the German main line called the Fosse trench. Enfiladed by machine-gun fire, only a small number, however, of our men were able to get

BARBED-WIRE DEFENCES IN FRONT OF A GERMAN TRENCH.

BRITISH SIGNAL SERVICE IN FRANCE.
A linesman repairing a wire broken by shell-fire.

into the trench. A party of the Lincolnshires managed to bring some machine guns up to within sixty yards of it. Behind their fire the mass of the Leicestershires and Lincolnshires, supported shortly afterwards by the Monmouths, dug themselves in ; after the Monmouths came the Sherwood Foresters. Meanwhile a party of bombers, who were reinforced by some of the Leicestershires, had made their way into Little Willie trench, where for hours a desperate struggle went on. Lieutenant C. H. F. Wollaston, of the 1/5th Leicester Regt., though wounded in the back and arm, organized a bombing party up Little Willie and held up

A COMMUNICATION TRENCH.

Scene in German trench after a bombardment : the dead and wounded half buried under the falling roof and sides.

the enemy for hours till his bombs were exhausted. Captain J. C. Warren, of the 1/7th (Robin Hood) Battalion Sherwood Foresters, with a party of four men, performed a similar feat, finally withdrawing across the open into the western face of the Redoubt, where he built a barrier and held it for fourteen hours.

To the right of the Redoubt the South Stafford-shires led the advance, but they were unable, in face of the German machine-gunners, grenadiers and riflemen, to reach at a bound the portion of the Big Willie trench retained by the enemy. Nevertheless, individuals and small parties pressed on, and the North Stafford-shires advanced to their assistance. A bombing party of the South Staffordshires from our portion of the Big Willie trench executed a flank attack. They gained 30 yards and constructed a new barricade, but were soon driven back to the old one. Second Lieutenant Hubert Hawkes, of the 1/5th South Stafford-shire Regiment, particularly distinguished him-self in this fighting. Among other deeds of daring performed that day in or near the Redoubt two more may be mentioned. Corporal J. L. Dawson, of the 187th Company, Royal Engineers, when the trenches were crammed with men half stupefied by German poisonous gas, walked backwards and forwards along the parados fully exposed to a very heavy fire. Finding three leaking gas cylinders, he rolled them some sixteen yards away from the trench, and then fired rifle bullets into them to let the gas escape. Captain M. H. Barton, of the Royal Army Medical Corps, tended and brought in wounded under fire, and also rallied and sent forward men who had become scattered.

The assault on the Hohenzollern Redoubt had thus met with a certain amount of success. To the east we had captured a trench on the north-western face of the Hulluch Quarries, and, south-west of St. Elie, trenches behind the Vermelles-Hulluch road and the south-western edge of the Quarries. South and west of Hul-luch we had gained 1,000 yards of trench, but had been shelled out of it. It was near Hulluch that a most gallant action by one of our artillerymen was performed. Captain H. N. Fairbank, of the 117th Battery R.F.A., gal-loped up his guns, and from a spot where he could not hide them kept up an effective fire at short range. Hard by Second Lieutenant N. Martin, of the 3rd Battalion Queen's Own Cameron Highlanders, showed dauntless courage. In a German communication trench, when one officer of his company had been killed, another wounded, and three parties of bombers killed or disabled, he threw bombs himself until there were no more to hand, and then with his revolver and afterwards with a rifle held the barricade until he was relieved by some other bombers.

The next day, October 14, in the morning, another effort was made to gain entirely the Big Willie trench. One battalion of the Sherwood Foresters attacked it from the Redoubt; another battalion of the same regiment advanced along it from the portion already in our hands. But, so strong were the German defences, it was found impossible to bring the attack to a successful issue. It was on this day that Captain

AFTER THE BATTLE OF LOOS.
British wounded entraining for the base.

ANTI-AIRCRAFT GUN IN ACTION.

Charles Vickers, of the Sherwood Foresters, secured the V.C. When nearly all his men had been killed or wounded, and only two were left to hand him bombs, Captain Vickers, fired at and bombed by the Germans from front and flank, held a barrier for several hours. His retreat was cut off, but instead of endeavouring to make his way back, he stayed where he was until he was severely wounded. By his orders a barrier had been built behind him to ensure the safety of the trench. The fighting continued in the Redoubt until the 15th, when the 2nd Guards Brigade relieved the North Midland Territorials.

The Battle of Loos and the subsequent fighting had cost the British over 50,000 men. Judged by the standards of the Great War, this was perhaps not an inadequate expenditure for the results obtained. As in the case of the Battle of Artois, delivered by Foch and d'Urbal in May and June, the Germans had been driven from a number of positions which they had fondly believed to be impregnable. On October 19 Sir John French was able to describe the topographical gains in the following words :

"The new front now leaves our old line at a point about 1,200 yards south-west of the southern edge of Auchy-lez-La Bassée and runs thence, through the main trench of the Hohenzollern Redoubt, in an easterly direction, 400 yards south of the southern buildings of Fosse No. 8 to the south-western corner of the Quarries.

"We also hold the south-eastern corner of the Quarries, our trenches running thence south-east parallel to, and 400 yards from, the south-western edge of Cité St. Elie to a point 500 yards west of the north edge of Hulluch.

"The line then runs along the Lens-La Bassée road to the chalk pit, 1,500 yards north of the highest point of Hill 70, and then turns south-west to a point 1,000 yards east of Loos Church, where it bends south-east to the north-west slope of Hill 70 and runs along the western slopes of that hill, bending south-west to a point 1,200 yards south of Loos Church whence it runs due west back to our old line.

"The chord of the salient we have created in the enemy's line measured along our old front is 7,000 yards in length ; the depth of the salient at the chalk pit is 3,200 yards."

The men, or some of them, of the New Armies had shown courage worthy of the heroes of Mons, Le Cateau, the Marne, and Ypres. The Territorials engaged had more than justified the expectations of the officers who had trained them. The whole army was convinced of its superiority to the enemy on a fair field of battle.

We may well conclude our review of the great offensive delivered by the Allies in the autumn of 1915 with some extracts from an article in which the Military Correspondent of *The Times* (January 20, 1916) considered the lessons of the whole series of offensives in the West. Starting from the fundamental doctrine that, the centre of gravity of the German military power being in the West, "it is here that we should amass a superior force in order to seek victory which will be decisive, the writer said :

The main point is that it does not matter so very much where we fight Germans, so long as we fight Germans, and not their allies and dupes to whose fate Germany is indifferent, and it is easier for us to kill Germans in their present positions in the West than it is anywhere else. Even if these present positions were approximately maintained by the enemy we could make him suffer such losses in them that we could maintain the

A SKIRMISH WITH THE ENEMY.
A party of French Infantrymen on the edge of a wood.

A FRENCH PATROL.
Scouting in the outskirts of a village.

A FRENCH GUN IN ACTION.

rate of wastage, which must, in the end, bring him down. In this respect we have done better in each successive fight in the West, and as the number of our heavy guns and howitzers continues to grow, and the supply of shells mounts up, we can make each fresh attack upon him with greater profit, and impose more sacrifices upon him when he attacks us.

But, it is urged, we cannot break the German lines, and what is the use of attacking them if, in such attacks, we lose more men than he does ? These visions of breaking the German lines ; these dreams of swallowing the whole German Army at a gulp ; these half a dozen objectives given to our infantry in an attack and carrying them far beyond the support of their artillery ; these massed Corps of Cavalry ready to stream through the famous G in Gap, have never appealed to the writer very much, since they have appeared to him to be based upon a fallacy—namely, the expected resurrection of the manœuvre battle, which, like good Queen Anne and Roland's mare, is unfortunately dead.

How can we expect to break the German lines in one battle ? There are lines upon lines, and when we have taken the Aubers Ridge and the Vimy Heights there will be Lille, the Dendre, the Scheldt, the Meuse, the Rhine, and many more lines, as there will be for us if the Germans attack us, so that this basic idea of breaking the line, good for Trafalgar, is really quite out of place. It is even harmful, for when we win a serious victory like that of September last, when we dispose of 150,000 Germans and capture 150 German guns, we are not content because we have not attained the unattainable and our cavalry have not streamed through the famous Gap. It is lucky that they have not, because the country is unrideable, covered with obstacles, and confines cavalry to roads where a division can be held up by a few machine guns. But if, leaving these really puerile plans aside, and abandoning the idea of breaking the line, we had said before September 25 that we were going to cause the Germans 150,000 casualties and to bring home 150 of their guns, we should have considered the accomplishment of this purpose a great feat, and we should have been satisfied instead of dissatisfied with the result.

Moreover, this misconception of the real problem leads to heavy and unnecessary losses. The writer showed, after Neuve Chapelle, that there were two ways of attacking the enemy's lines, one of which was to grip

and hold, and the other to go on after capturing the enemy's first lines with the idea of breaking through and winning a decisive battle. We took Neuve Chapelle and its immediately surrounding defences with little more than 2,000 casualties, but, going on into the blue, we did no good ; we ran into the German reserves, and we came back to the lines first captured with nothing more gained and with 10,000 more of our men on the floor. The same underlying idea of finishing off the Germans at a blow recurs in our May and September offensives, which equally cost us heavy losses, because we were not content to occupy and consolidate our first gains, and to postpone a further advance until our guns had moved forward and were ready once more to support with their admirable fire our incomparable infantry. We and the French have exhausted the possibilities of the theories upon which our tactics were based in the battles of 1915, and our next business is to set out to find better, with experience as our searchlight.

After some detailed examination of the need for greater cooperation by the Allies, the Military Correspondent of *The Times* stated the following conclusions :

What is true for the whole great strategic theatre is also true for each front. If the operation which we propose is likely to extend beyond forty-eight hours, it is quite obvious that, unless the whole German front is attacked, or at all events menaced and harried, our enemy has a simple game to play, for using his railways again, as well as motor transport, he rushes up the reserves of all neighbouring sectors to the front which we are attacking, and meets us at length in equal force. What Werder did on the Lisaine in 1871, and Foch did at Ypres, German generals are doing now. Most, if not all, of our attacks have been condemned to sterility in advance because we have attacked on narrow fronts, have spun out our operations, sometimes over weeks, and by maintaining a passive attitude on other parts of the front have placed all the trumps in German hands. The 100 German battalions which met the French in Champagne rapidly grew to 200 because the neighbouring sectors remained quiescent, and so it has been with us, on a smaller scale.

A general offensive by all the Allies at once, and a general offensive on each front, are the tactics which will hurt Germany the most, and they are therefore to be commended. They are being rendered more possible every day by the rapid increase of our heavy howitzers and munitions generally, enabling us to devote an increasingly large number of heavy guns to all our sectors, and to maintain a good rate of fire for a longer time. It is not the case that we have yet delivered a serious attack without any concern for our supply of shells. Neither we nor the French have been wholly so fortunate as that, but as time goes on each one of our attacks will be more deadly from the artillery point of view, and we may often enjoy the luxury of driving the enemy out of his trenches by shell fire alone.

The long periods of quiescence, which are unacceptable in principle and yet elapse between one of our attacks and another, are largely due to want of shells, and when we have a practically unlimited supply we can do much better. If we carry on in the future as we have in the past, we do not get forward with our war of attrition, but rather get back, and with the experience now behind us we must change our tactics to the changed conditions. Hitherto the old conception of the infantry as the queen of battles has ruled. Our actions have, on the whole, been fought with this dominating idea in our minds. The guns have provided the overture, but when the curtain has been rung up we have always discovered the infantry as chief actors. The infantry remains the principal arm, and we can never make too much of it nor use it with too violent energy when the opportunity arises. But the predominance of modern artillery in present-day fighting has become most marked, and it is a question whether, in this trench warfare, we should not use the infantry as a complementary arm, and see what happens when we subordinate its action to that of the guns. If we knock to pieces the first line system of hostile trenches and

obstacles with our shells, form our *barrage* of fire beyond, counterbatter the German artillery more effectively, and then use our infantry to occupy and consolidate the ground gained, and await the advance of our guns to fresh positions before we continue our attack, we may hope to gain solid successes and to cause the enemy much greater loss than we suffer ourselves.

SPOILS OF WAR AFTER A BATTLE.
French soldier collecting rifles and other articles left behind by the Germans.
Inset: A collection of shells, bombs, hand grenades, and boxes of ammunition gathered in the German trenches in Champagne.

THE EDITH CAVELL MEMORIAL SERVICE IN ST. PAUL'S CATHEDRAL, OCTOBER 29, 1915.

"We give Thee hearty thanks, for that it hath pleased Thee to deliver Thy servant, Edith, out of the miseries of this sinful world."

CHAPTER CVII.

THE EXECUTION OF MISS CAVELL.

Miss Cavell's Life-work—Her Labours in Brussels during the War—Her arrest—First efforts of the American Legation—The trial—German and British ideas of justice—How the German officials planned the execution—Mr. Brand Whitlock's final appeal —Miss Cavell's death—German excuses—Baron von Bissing—Feeling in England and France—American opinion of the crime.

WHILE the great movements described in the last chapter were developing an event occurred in Brussels which sent a wave of horror and resentment throughout the world, equalled only by the universal indignation aroused by the sinking of the Lusitania. Miss Edith Cavell, an Englishwoman, head of a Nursing Institution in Brussels, was secretly tried by a German court-martial on the charge of aiding English, French and Belgian soldiers to escape from Belgium, and on October 12 was hastily executed. There was much in the circumstances attending this event and in the surroundings of the trial and execution to stir the wrath and pity of the world—wrath against the men who had by a military technicality done a brave woman to death, and pity for the nurse who had paid the penalty of her life for her work of mercy.

Miss Edith Cavell was a daughter of the Rev. Frederick Cavell, for forty years vicar of Swardeston, Norfolk. She received her training as a nurse at the London Hospital, entering there in 1896 and later being appointed staff nurse. After some experience in Poor Law nursing she went to Belgium, in 1900, on the invitation of Dr. Depage, a distinguished medical man who had established a training institute for Belgian nurses in a suburb of Brussels. Dr. Depage was anxious to modernize the system of sick nursing in Belgium. Up to this time the nursing had mainly been done by the nuns of religious establishments or by women drawn mainly from the domestic servant class. Catholic families when sick were nursed by the nuns; the numerous non-Catholic sections of the public had to rely upon the other class.

Miss Cavell threw herself with enthusiasm into her new mission. The Institute, whose influence was felt throughout Belgium, grew until it became the centre of a large nursing organization. When, at the outbreak of the War, Dr. Depage was called to military service and made the head of a military hospital with the Belgian Army, Miss Cavell continued the work in Brussels. Everyone who came in contact with her was agreed that she was a capable leader and a woman of fine character, worthy to take a place in the noble list of great nurses, the list with the name of Florence Nightingale at the head.

After the advance of the German armies upon Brussels in 1914 Miss Cavell was allowed to remain there. When the tide of war brought many German wounded to the Belgian capital she and her assistants nursed them equally with the Belgian wounded. The fighting around Namur and Mons, and the retirement of the French and British armies in the late summer and autumn of 1914, left one legacy for Belgium. A number of English and French soldiers, cut off from their companies during the retreat, hid themselves in trenches, in woods, or in deserted houses, attempting to avoid capture. Many were caught and in some instances, at least, were executed immediately they were caught. Others were sheltered by kindly farmers, who gave them civilian clothing, employed them on their land and allowed them to remain until opportunity arose for them to cross the frontier into Holland. Belgian soldiers whose regiments had been broken during the early fighting there also hid about the country, waiting for chances to escape. They too, in some cases, were shot when captured, and the common belief in Brussels was that this was their usual fate. When Miss Cavell was asked in Court during her trial why she had helped English soldiers to escape, she replied that she thought that if she had not done so they would have been shot by the Germans and that, therefore, she thought she only did her duty to her country in saving their lives.

The fugitives, hiding in the country, looked around to see who could help them. Miss Cavell was a prominent worker. Her care of the sick and the wounded brought her in touch with all classes. As was only natural, the men approached her. That she did help some of

MISS EDITH CAVELL.

The British nurse who was condemned to death and shot by order of the German Military authorities at Brussels, October, 1915.

these men to escape from the death that would probably have been their fate had they been caught is not denied. The German authorities claimed that she enabled 130 men to leave Belgium. How far this figure was correct there is no evidence to show.

The German administration, then steadily tightening its hold upon all sides of Belgian life, became suspicious of her. The system of espionage in Belgium had by now been developed to a very fine point. Spies were put upon the track of Miss Cavell. It is said that one spy went to her as a fugitive, begged her to help him, and then betrayed her.

Miss Cavell was arrested on August 5, 1915, and sent to the military prison of St. Gilles, where she was placed in close, solitary confinement. The Germans declare that she made no effort from the first to conceal the fact that she had taken pity on some of the fugitives and had given them assistance. She knew that in doing this she was committing a military offence. Those who met her immediately before her arrest say that she anticipated a short term of imprisonment. She evidently

MISS CAVELL WITH HER
FAVOURITE DOGS.

did not dream—at that time no one dreamed—that the German authorities would shoot a woman with premeditation for taking pity on and showing mercy to the helpless.

Mr. Brand Whitlock, the American Minister in Brussels, who represented British interests there during the War, acted promptly when news was brought to him of Miss Cavell's arrest. Mr. Whitlock, who had been American Minister to Belgium for nearly two years, was well known as an author and reformer before he entered the diplomatic service. The grandson of an Abolitionist and the son of a Methodist minister, he started life as a newspaper reporter in Toledo, Ohio, and later on became a lawyer. He attracted wide attention in 1905 by his campaign as a political reformer. He was elected Mayor of Toledo in that year and was subsequently re-elected for three further terms. As a lawyer, as an author, and as Mayor of Toledo, his great characteristics were a profound human sympathy and a passion for justice. The case of Miss Cavell aroused—if acts may speak for a man's thoughts—his most intense sympathy. He at once took the matter up with the German

authorities, and used every possible means to ensure that she should have a fair trial. He wrote to the Civil Governor of Belgium, Baron Von der Lancken, asking that M. de Leval, a representative of the Legation, might see Miss Cavell, and also informing him that he had been requested by telegraph to take charge of Miss Cavell's defence without delay. The German authorities did not reply to this letter. Mr. Whitlock wrote again. The German Civil Governor then wrote back refusing to allow anyone to see Miss Cavell, declaring that she had confessed her guilt and informing Mr. Whitlock that she would be defended by a Mr. Braun. The essential parts of the reply were :

She has herself admitted that she concealed in her house French and English soldiers, as well as Belgians of military age, all desirous of proceeding to the front. She has also admitted having furnished these soldiers with the money necessary for their journey to France, and having facilitated their departure from Belgium by providing them with guides, who enabled them to cross the Dutch frontier secretly.

Miss Cavell's defence is in the hands of the advocate Braun, who, I may add, is already in touch with the competent German authorities.

In view of the fact that the Department of the

MISS CAVELL WITH SOME MEMBERS OF THE NURSING STAFF.

Miss Cavell (X) was the head of a nursing school at Brussels. In the above group she is seen in dark uniform, seated on the right of Dr. Depage, the Belgian doctor.

MR. BRAND WHITLOCK.
The American Minister to Belgium.

Governor-General as a matter of principle does not allow accused persons to have any interviews whatever, I much regret my inability to procure for M. de Leval permission to visit Miss Cavell as long as she is in solitary confinement.

Mr. Braun, it turned out, had been prevented by some unforeseen circumstance from undertaking the defence and had handed it over to Mr. Kirschen, a Roumanian, practising in Brussels. M. de Leval, the Councillor of the American Embassy, at once communicated with Mr. Kirschen. M. de Leval stated in his subsequent narrative of events :—

I at once put myself in communication with Mr. Kirschen, who told me that Miss Cavell was prosecuted for having helped soldiers to cross the frontier. I asked him whether he had seen Miss Cavell and whether she had made any statement to him, and to my surprise found that the lawyers defending prisoners before the German Military Court were not allowed to see their clients before the trial, and were not shown any document of the prosecution. This, Mr. Kirschen said, was in accordance with the German military rules. He added that the hearing of the trial of such cases was carried out very carefully, and that in his opinion, although it was not possible to see the client before the trial, in fact the trial itself developed so carefully and so slowly, that it was generally possible to have a fair knowledge of all the facts and to present a good defence for the prisoner. This would especially be the case for Miss Cavell, because the trial would be rather long, as she was prosecuted with thirty-four other prisoners.

I informed Mr. Kirschen of my intention to be present at the trial so as to watch the case. He immediately dissuaded me from taking such attitude. which he said

would cause a great prejudice to the prisoner, because the German judges would resent it and felt it almost as an affront if I was appearing to exercise a kind of supervision on the trial. He thought that if the Germans would admit my presence, which was very doubtful, it would in any case cause prejudice to Miss Cavell.

Mr. Kirschen assured me over and over again that the Military Court of Brussels was always perfectly fair, and that there was not the slightest danger of any miscarriage of justice. He promised that he would keep me posted on all the developments which the case would take and would report to me the exact charges that were brought against Miss Cavell and the facts concerning her that would be disclosed at the trial, so as to allow me to judge by myself about the merits of the case. He insisted that, of course, he would do all that was humanly possible to defend Miss Cavell to the best of his ability.

The trial opened on Thursday, October 7. Miss Cavell was one of thirty-five prisoners brought before the Court at the same time. The German authorities believed that they had discovered a widespread conspiracy for espionage and for the escape of fugitives. Among the prisoners were several women : the Princess Maria de Croy, the Comtesse de Belleville, Mlle. Louise Thulier, a teacher in Lille, and Mme. Ada Bodart, of Brussels. Among the men were M. Philip Baucq, an architect of Brussels ; M. Louis Severin, a chemist of Brussels ; M. Herman Capian, an engineer of Wasmes ; M. Albert Libier, of Wasmes, and another chemist. M. Georges Derbeau.

THE MARQUIS DE VILLALOBAR.
Spanish Minister at Brussels.

It is interesting to contrast at this stage, the difference between the British and German methods in the trial of persons charged with military offences in war time. In England a woman, of whatever nationality, is tried, not by court martial, but by a civil court. She is brought before a tribunal which holds a preliminary enquiry, taking a summary of the evidence. She is always assisted by a lawyer, a complete record of the evidence, oral and documentary, is given to her through her lawyer, and she is allowed an interval to prepare for defence. At the trial, the lawyers for the defence have the same opportunities as are given to the accused in an ordinary case in peace time. In the last case that occurred in the United Kingdom, before the Cavell case in Brussels, a woman of German birth was charged with espionage. She had been acting in association with a male spy, and was detected travelling to various points in order to collect information about our naval defences. She was tried before three civil judges of the High Court and a jury, and was convicted, in the words of Sir John Simon, then Home Secretary, "of deliberate and

GENERAL BARON VON BISSING.

The German Governor of the occupied portion of Belgium.

persistent spying for the purpose of providing the enemy with important information." She was found guilty. For this offence, infinitely more serious from every point of view than the charge brought against Miss Cavell, she was sentenced to ten years' imprisonment. She had the right of appealing against this sentence.

Contrast this method, with its ample precautions to ensure justice for the accused, with the methods employed in the trial of Miss Cavell. She was kept in solitary confinement for over nine weeks, without an opportunity of consulting even her legal advisers. During this time she was subjected to cross examination. Statements said to have been made by her, admitting her guilt, were transmitted by the German authorities to the lawyers who subsequently would have to undertake her defence. Her trial before a court martial was held in a language she did not understand— German; the questions in her cross-examination being put in German and then translated into French. It was obviously impossible to plan any adequate scheme of defence with the lawyer, whom she saw for the first time when the trial began, a lawyer who had no opportunity of studying the documents of the prosecution. After her sentence, the fact of the conviction was kept as secret as possible

BARON VON DER LANKEN AND DR. VON SANDT.

The Baron (on left) was the head of the political department of the Governor-General of Belgium, through whose action a reprieve for Miss Cavell was refused. Dr. von Sandt was the German Chief Civil Administrator of Belgium.

COLONEL BARON VON STRACHNITZ.
Ex-Commandant of Brussels.

and her accusers were evidently so fearful that even at the eleventh hour a plea of mercy might prevail, that they had her shot within nine hours. Had there been any outward tumult, or had the military trial taken place on the field of war, this haste might have been excused. But there was no tumult or disturbance, and the trial, so far from taking place in a military camp, occurred in a city where the Germans had for months established and maintained a civil administration.

The fullest account of the trial itself was given in the report of M. de Leval to Mr. Whitlock :

Miss Cavell was prosecuted for having helped English and French soldiers, as well as Belgian young men, to cross the frontier and to go over to England. She had admitted by signing a statement before the day of the trial, and by public acknowledgment in Court, in the presence of all the other prisoners and the lawyers, that she was guilty of the charges brought against her, and she had acknowledged not only that she had helped these soldiers to cross the frontier, but also that some of them had thanked her in writing when arriving in England. This last admission made her case so much the more serious, because if it only had been proved against her that she had helped the soldiers to traverse the Dutch frontier, and no proof was produced that these soldiers had reached a country at war with Germany, she could only have been sentenced for an attempt to commit the " crime " and not for the " crime " being duly accomplished. As the case stood the sentence fixed by the German military law was a sentence of death.

Paragraph 58 of the German Military Code says,

" Will be sentenced to death for treason any person who, with the intention of helping the hostile Power, or of causing harm to the German or allied troops, is guilty of one of the crimes of paragraph 90 of the German Penal Code."

The case referred to in above said paragraph 90 consists in—

". . . conducting soldiers to the enemy . . . (viz., " dem Feinde Mannschaften zuführt ").

The penalties above set forth apply, according to paragraph 160 of the German Code, in case of war, to foreigners as well as to Germans.

In her oral statement before the Court Miss Cavell disclosed almost all the facts of the whole prosecution. She was questioned in German, an interpreter translating all the questions in French, with which language Miss Cavell was well acquainted. She spoke without trembling and showed a clear mind. Often she added some greater precision to her previous depositions.

When she was asked why she helped these soldiers to go to England, she replied that she thought that if she had not done so they would have been shot by the Germans, and that therefore she thought she only did her duty to her country in saving their lives.

The Military Public Prosecutor said that argument might be good for English soldiers, but did not apply to Belgian young men whom she induced to cross the frontier, and who would have been perfectly free to remain in the country without danger to their lives.

Mr. Kirschen made a very good plea for Miss Cavell, using all arguments that could be brought in her favour before the Court.

The Military Public Prosecutor, however, asked the Court to pass a death sentence on Miss Cavell and eight other prisoners among the thirty-five. The Court did not seem to agree, and the judgment was postponed.

M. Kirschen now apparently thought that he had done all that was required of him. The trial lasted two days, ending on Friday, October 8. On Saturday M. de Leval, receiving no report from M. Kirschen, tried to find him, but failed. Then on Sunday he sent him a note, asking him to send his report to the Legation, or to call there on Monday morning at 8.30. M. Kirschen did not come even then, so M. de Leval called at his house, but was informed that he would not be there until the end of the afternoon. The American Councillor at once went to another lawyer interested in the case of a fellow prisoner, and was then told—the information having apparently been given out in order to prevent outside attempts to interfere with the execution of the sentence— that judgment would be passed only the next morning; that is Tuesday morning. Mr. Kirschen subsequently declared that he had not promised to communicate with the American Legation after the trial. His action, or rather his lack of action, drew very severe censure on him.

The political department of the Governor-General of Belgium had given the American Legation positive assurance that it would be fully informed of developments in the case. At 6.30 p.m. on Monday night Mr. Conrad, of the Political Department, had positively informed the Legation in answer to its other inquiries that sentence had not been pronounced, and he again renewed his previous assurances that he would not fail to inform the American officials as soon as there was any news. At this time the sentence of death had already been pronounced.

On Monday evening at eight o'clock M. de Leval was privately and reliably informed that the judgment of the court-martial had been passed at five o'clock that afternoon, that Miss Cavell had been sentenced to death, and that she would be shot at two o'clock the next morning. There were only six hours left in which to attempt to save her. He hurried to his chief with the news. Mr. Brand Whitlock was ill, unable to leave the house. He wrote, however, a moving letter to Baron von der Lancken, the Civil Governor, with his own hand.

My dear Baron,—I am too ill to present my request to you in person, but I appeal to the generosity of your heart to support it and save this unfortunate woman from death. Have pity on her !
Yours sincerely,
Brand Whitlock.

Armed with this, and with a plea for clemency (requête en grace) addressed to the Governor-General, Mr. Hugh Gibson, the First Secretary of the Legation, and M. de Leval, hurried to the Spanish Minister, to beg his cooperation. They found him at dinner. He at once joined them, and they went together to the house of the Civil Governor to appeal for clemency. What followed is best told in the official report of Mr. Gibson :

Baron von der Lancken and all the members of his staff were absent for the evening. We sent a messenger to ask that he return at once to see us in regard to a matter of utmost urgency. A little after 10 o'clock he arrived, followed shortly after by Count Harrach and Herr von Falkenhausen, members of his staff. The circumstances of the case were explained to him and your note presented, and he read it aloud in our presence. He expressed disbelief in the report that sentence had actually been passed, and manifested some surprise

that we should give credence to any report not emanating from official sources. He was quite insistent on knowing the exact source of our information, but this I did not feel at liberty to communicate to him. Baron von der Lancken stated that it was quite improbable that sentence had been pronounced, that even if so, it would not be executed within so short a time, and that in any event it would be quite impossible to take any action before morning. It was, of course, pointed out to him that if the facts were as we believed them to be, action would be useless unless taken at once. We urged him to ascertain the facts immediately, and this, after some hesitancy, he agreed to do. He telephoned to the presiding judge of the court-martial and returned in a short time to say that the facts were as we had represented them, and that it was intended to carry out the sentence before morning. We then presented, as earnestly as possible, your plea for delay. So far as I am able to judge, we neglected to present no phase of the matter which might have had any effect, emphasising the horror of executing a woman, no matter what her offence, pointing out that the death sentence had heretofore been imposed only for actual cases of espionage, and that Miss Cavell was not even accused by the German authorities of anything so serious. I further called attention to the failure to comply with Mr. Conrad's promise to inform the Legation of the sentence. I urged that inasmuch as the offences charged against Miss Cavell were long since accomplished, and that as she had been for some weeks in prison, a delay in carrying out the sentence could entail no danger to the German cause. I even went so far as to point out the fearful effect of a summary execution of this sort upon public opinion, both here and abroad, and, although I had no authority for doing so, called attention to the possibility that it might bring about reprisals.

The Spanish Minister forcibly supported all our representations and made an earnest plea for clemency.

Baron von der Lancken stated that the Military Governor was the supreme authority (" Gerichtsherr ")

REV. H. STERLING GAHAN.

The British Chaplain at Brussels, who visited Miss Cavell at the prison of St. Gilles on October 11, 1915, the day before she was executed by the Germans.

MR. AND MRS. CAVELL.
The mother and father of the late Miss Cavell.

in matters of this sort; that appeal from his decision could be carried only to the Emperor, the Governor-General having no authority to intervene in such cases. He added that under the provisions of German martial law the Military Governor had discretionary power to accept or to refuse acceptance of an appeal for clemency. After some discussion he agreed to call the Military Governor on to the telephone and learn whether he had already ratified the sentence, and whether there was any chance for clemency. He returned in about half an hour, and stated that he had been to confer personally with the Military Governor, who said that he had acted in the case of Miss Cavell only after mature deliberation; that the circumstances in her case were of such a character that he considered the infliction of the death penalty imperative; and that in view of the circumstances of this case he must decline to accept your plea for clemency or any representation in regard to the matter.

Baron von der Lancken then asked me to take back the note which I had presented to him. To this I demurred, pointing out that it was not a "requête en grâce," but merely a note to him transmitting a communication to the Governor, which was itself to be considered as the "requête en grâce." I pointed out that this was expressly stated in your note to him, and tried to prevail upon him to keep it; he was very insistent, however, and I finally reached the conclusion that inasmuch as he had read it aloud to us, and we knew that he was aware of its contents, there was nothing to be gained by refusing to accept the note, and accordingly took it back.

Even after Baron von der Lancken's very positive and definite statement that there was no hope, and that under the circumstances "even the Emperor himself could not intervene," we continued to appeal to every sentiment to secure delay, and the Spanish Minister even led Baron von der Lancken aside in order to say very forcibly a number of things which he would have felt hesitancy in saying in the presence of the younger officers and of Mr. de Leval, a Belgian subject.

His Excellency talked very earnestly with Baron von der Lancken for about a quarter of an hour. During this time Mr. de Leval and I presented to the younger officers every argument we could think of. I reminded them of our untiring efforts on behalf of German subjects at the outbreak of war and during the siege of Antwerp. I pointed out that, while our services had been rendered gladly and without any thought of future favours, they should certainly entitle you to some consideration for the only request of this sort you had made since the

beginning of the war. Unfortunately, our efforts were unavailing. We persevered until it was only too clear that there was no hope of securing any consideration for the case.

"Our failure has been felt by us as a very severe blow," Mr. Whitlock wrote later. None could have done more than he and his assistants did.

How was Miss Cavell standing the strain? Fortunately there is full evidence of her bearing at this time. M. de Leval, who showed throughout the greatest energy and devotion in working for Miss Cavell, had made application on the Sunday evening that he and the British chaplain, the Rev. H. Sterling Gahan, might be permitted to see Miss Cavell in gaol. This was at first refused, but on Monday evening, after the sentence of death had been passed, Mr. Gahan was allowed to visit her. Mr. Gahan subsequently wrote a simple and moving statement of what took place:

To my astonishment and relief I found my friend perfectly calm and resigned. But this could not lessen the tenderness and intensity of feeling on either part during that last interview of almost an hour.

Her first words to me were upon a matter concerning herself personally, but the solemn asseveration which accompanied them was made expressly in the light of God and eternity. She then added that she wished all her friends to know that she willingly gave her life for her country, and said: "I have no fear nor shrinking; I have seen death so often that it is not strange or fearful to me." She further said: "I thank God for this ten weeks' quiet before the end." "Life has always been hurried and full of difficulty." "This time of rest has been a great mercy." "They have all been very kind to me here. But this I would say, standing as I do in view of God and eternity, I realise that patriotism is not enough. I must have no hatred or bitterness towards anyone."

We partook of the Holy Communion together, and she received the Gospel message of consolation with all her heart. At the close of the little service I began to repeat the words "Abide with me," and she joined softly in the end.

We sat quietly talking until it was time for me to go. She gave me parting messages for relations and friends, She spoke of her soul's needs at the moment and she received the assurance of God's Word as only the Christian can do.

Then I said "Good-bye," and she smiled and said. "We shall meet again."

The German military chaplain was with her at the end and afterwards gave her Christian burial.

He told me : "She was brave and bright to the last. She professed her Christian faith and that she was glad to die for her country." "She died like a heroine."

Few details were allowed to be known of the final scene. It was reported at the time that Miss Cavell fainted on the way to her death and was shot by the officer in command of the party while lying unconscious, but it seems to be certain that the execution was carried out in the usual military manner. The place of burial was kept secret, and the people of Brussels tried in vain to learn it, that they might, in some way or other, show their appreciation of Miss Cavell's great courage. The opportunity was denied them.

The story of the execution aroused the world—except Germany! Various Germans in official positions expressed the greatest surprise that people should make so much to-do about the death of one woman. This was the view of Baron von Bissing, the Military Governor of Brussels. Shortly after the execution of Miss Cavell Mr. Karl Kitchin, a staff correspondent of the New York World, visited Brussels to learn the German defence in this case. He was received with open arms and given every facility. He saw all most closely concerned in it, from Baron von Bissing to Mr. Gahan. Baron von Bissing openly expressed his astonishment that an American thought it worth while paying a visit to Brussels over such an affair. "I cannot understand why the world is interested in the case," he said, "when thousands of innocent people have died in the war, why should anyone become hysterical over the death of one guilty woman ?" In the course of conversation he clearly revealed that the German authorities had hurried on the execution not merely because Miss Cavell had helped fugitives to escape, but because they wanted to make her an example to awe the Belgians. He said :

A few years in prison is not sufficient punishment for an offence of this kind. For punishment in a case of this nature is meted out to deter others from committing the same offence. If the Cavell woman had been sent to prison she would have been released in two or three years—at the end of the war. Amnesty is usually granted to all prisoners convicted of offences of this nature, espionage, and so forth, when peace is made.

We have only recently uncovered a big spy system here in Belgium. Important military matters have been communicated to the enemy for some time. I will not go into details, but I will say that this Cavell woman was aware of their activities—had guilty knowledge of much of their work. Such a system of spying assails our very safety and we proceeded to stamp it out.

The Cavell woman was not charged with espionage. The charge of aiding the enemy's soldiers to escape which was made against her was sufficiently serious. Her death was deplorable—but I do not see why it should occasion such hysteria in America.

"I cannot understand why so much has been made of this unfortunate affair in your country," remarked the representative of the official Press Bureau to the visitor. Baron

THE VICARAGE AT SWARDESTON, NEAR NORWICH,
where Miss Cavell was born.

von der Lancken, the Civil Governor, declared that as the execution was purely a military affair, he did not interfere. It would have been a breach of etiquette if he had done so. Baron von Bissing himself, it was declared, could not have pardoned Miss Cavell after her conviction by a court martial without exceeding his military function. The only appeal was to the Kaiser, who had no cognizance of the affair until after the execution. The man responsible for that execution was Major-General von Haesler, Military Commander of the district. In short it was a trivial affair. One woman more or less—what difference did it make ?

But this was not the view that the world took. "Sir Edward Grey is confident that the news of the execution of this noble English-

> The last letter from my mother was dated 27th Jan. If this reaches you will you send her a line to say all is well here – she is naturally very anxious and I do not know whether she gets my letters. There are not many opportunities of sending –
>
> What do you do these days, are you still farming, or is that given up? I like to look back on the days when we were young and life was fresh & beautiful and the country so adorable & sweet.
>
> Many thanks for your kind letter my dear cousin from
>
> Yours affectionately
>
> Edith
>
> 11 March 1915

FACSIMILE OF LETTER SENT BY MISS CAVELL TO HER COUSIN IN ENGLAND, MARCH, 1915.

woman will be received with horror and disgust not only by the Allied States, but throughout the civilized world," wrote our Foreign Minister to the United States Ambassador in London, when the account of the execution was forwarded to him. "Miss Cavell was not even charged with espionage, and the fact that she had nursed numbers of wounded German soldiers might have been regarded as a reason in itself for treating her with leniency. The attitude of the German authorities is, if possible, rendered worse by the discreditable efforts successfully made by the officials of the German civil administration at Brussels to conceal the fact that sentence had been passed and would be carried out immediately."

The tale of Miss Cavell's death came like a trumpet call to the British nation. It showed once again the real character of the enemy this country was fighting. To the soldiers in Flanders it gave a fresh battle-cry, and to civilians at home it served to re-emphasize the need of greater effort and greater sacrifice.

The King and Queen and Queen Alexandra wrote to Miss Cavell's mother expressing their sympathy and their horror at the appalling deed. "Men and women throughout the civilized world, while sympathizing with you, are moved with admiration and awe at (your daughter's) faith and courage in death," wrote Lord Stamfordham, for the King and Queen. Queen Alexandra sent this message: "The women of England are bearing the greatest burden of this terrible war, but by all the name of Miss Cavell will be held in the highest honour and respect. We shall always remember that she never once failed England in her hour of need."

A memorial service was held at St. Paul's Cathedral, and long before the hour of commencement the church itself was full, and a great, silent, orderly crowd thronged in St. Paul's Churchyard without. Every class was there, from Queen Alexandra to six hundred nurses, from soldiers in khaki to the representatives of the City Corporation. The beating drums and the band of the 1st Life Guards, rolling and crashing as the "Dead March in Saul" was played at the end, closed an almost overwhelmingly impressive display of national grief. Various memorials were planned and carried out, but perhaps the greatest proof of how the execution had touched the heart of our nation was the quickening of recruiting, the increase in individual service and the evidence on all sides that this example by one woman of duty well done had helped all England to realize its obligations still more fully.

The French people showed how deeply they had been touched. The Minister of Public Instruction gave orders that the teachers of the Paris schools should relate the story of the martyrdom of the heroic victim and comment on it. "The great and sublime figure of Edith Cavell stands forth among the black horrors of this war as a living image of outraged humanity," he declared. The nation found a niche for Miss Cavell in the gallery of great women who have helped France, the women who, from Jean d'Arc to Madame Roland, have given their life for *la patrie.* Municipalities named streets after her, and artists chose her final sacrifice for their theme on canvas and in stone.

Mr. Frederick Palmer, the well-known war correspondent, returning to America in November, 1915, told his countrymen that when he left the trenches at the front the British soldiers, before a charge, would shout all along the line, "For Miss Cavell"! "Miss Cavell's execution did more for recruiting than all the Zeppelin raids," he said. "I happened to be with the French when the news of her death was received. Its effect on the troops was instant, electric. The woman's sacrifice had a Joan of Arc character that struck home to the French heart. Officers spoke of it as an event that had done more to cement the alliance of France and England to fight to the last man than all the speeches of statesmen and conferences of generals. Miss Cavell's picture, taken from the newspapers, is pinned on cottage walls all over France. Deep as the impression was on the civil population of both England and France, it was slight beside that made on the soldiers."

From Allies and from neutrals alike came messages of sympathy and of indignation. Nowhere, perhaps, was the emotion deeper than in the United States. The American people were aroused in many ways. Their national dignity was offended, because their representatives had been slighted when attempting to save the Englishwoman. But this resentment counted for little as compared with the genuine wrath at an act of barbarous inhumanity to a woman. Even German-Americans, who had stoutly defended the doings of their armies in the early days of the invasion of Belgium, now could do little save make excuses and express regrets.

It would be difficult to extract from the multitude of American newspaper denunciations of the crime isolated passages that would give any adequate idea of the depths and intensity of the feeling. Happily the American view was summed up in a statement by Mr. James M. Beck, formerly Assistant Attorney-General of the United States, and one of the leaders of the New York Bar. Three brief extracts will show its tenour:

Those who have regarded the Supreme Court of Civilization—meaning thereby the moral sentiment of the world—as a mere rhetorical phrase or an idle illusion should take note how swiftly that court—sitting now as one of criminal assize—has pronounced sentence upon the murderers of Edith Cavell. The swift vengeance of the world's opinion has called to the bar General Baron von Bissing, and in executing him with the lightning of universal execration has for ever degraded him.

The laboured apology of Dr. Zimmermann, and the

swift action of the Kaiser in pardoning those who were condemned with Miss Cavell, indicate that the Prussian officials have heard the beating of the wings of those avenging angels of history who, like the Eumenides of classic mythology, are the avengers of the innocent and the oppressed.

"*Greatness*," wrote Æschylus, "*is no defence from utter destruction when a man insolently spurns the mighty altar of justice.*"

This is as true to-day as when it was written, more than two thousand years ago. It is but a classic echo of the old Hebraic moral axiom that "the Lord God of recompenses shall surely requite."

You, women of America. Will you not honour the memory of this martyr of your sex, who for all time will be mourned as was the noblest Greek maiden, Antigone, who also gave her life that her brother might have the rites of sepulture ? Will you not carry out in her name, and for her memory, those sacred ministrations of mercy which were her lifework ?

Make her cause—the cause of mercy—your own !

BARBED WIRE ERECTED BY THE GERMANS ALONG THE DUTCH-BELGIAN FRONTIER.
In the wire compound is the body of a man who was killed by the frontier guard whilst trying to escape from Belgium.
Inset : Two of the Guards.

INDEX TO VOLUME VI.

ILLUSTRATIONS IN VOLUME VI.

PORTRAITS.

PLACES.

MAPS AND PLANS.

WAR ATLAS
(PAGED SEPARATELY).

The Times
HISTORY AND ENCYCLOPAEDIA OF THE WAR

WAR·ATLAS

CONTENTS

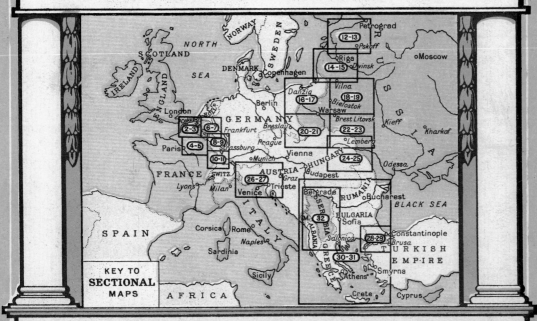

KEY TO SECTIONAL MAPS

Published by the Times Publishing Company, Printing-house-square, London, E.C.

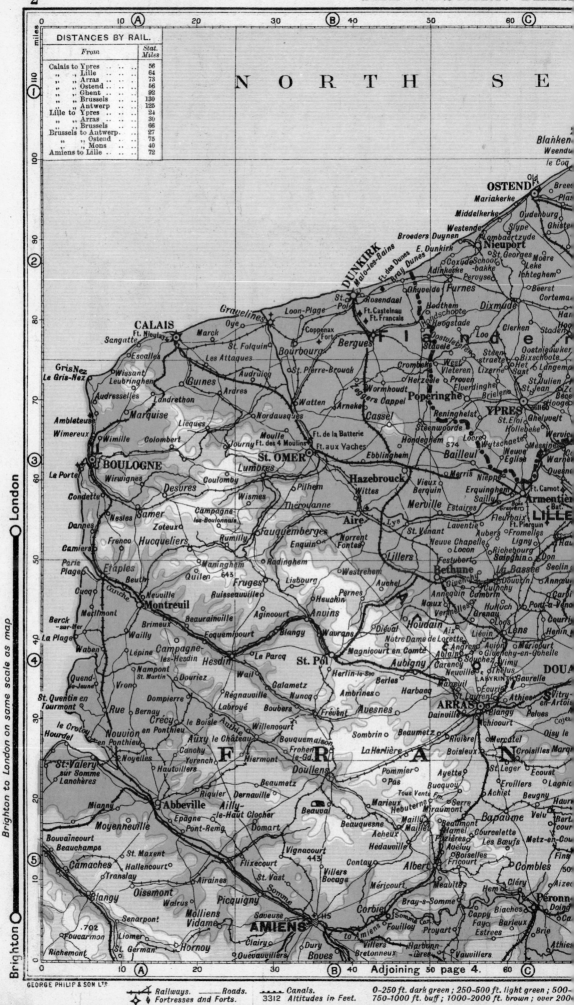

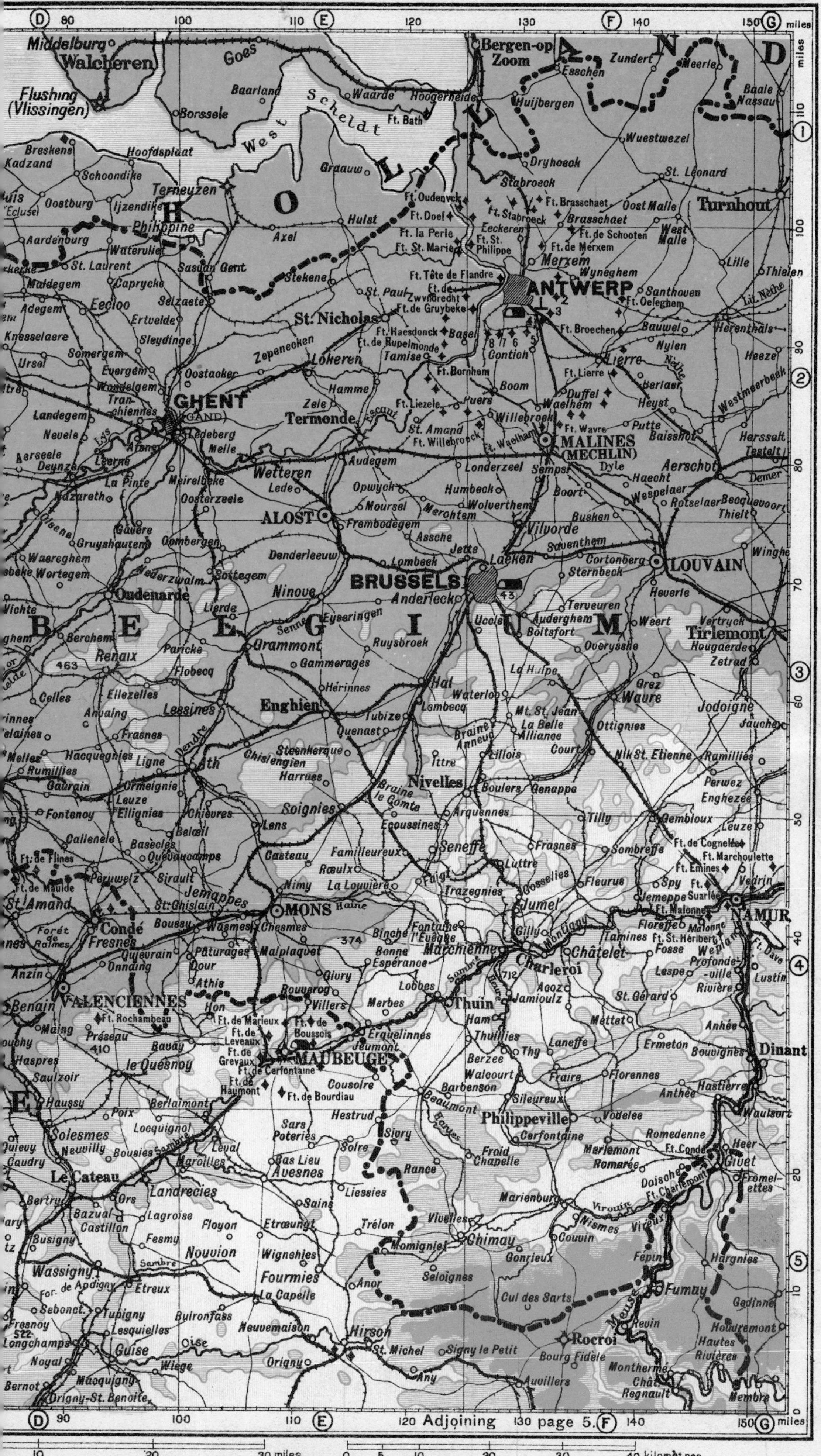

Middelburg Walcheren
Flushing (Vlissingen)
Goes
Bergen-op-Zoom
Zundert Meerle
Esschen
HOLLAND
Baale Nassau

Breskens Kadzand
Schoondike
Terneuzen
IJzendike
Oostburg
Philippine
Aardenburg
St. Laurent
Maldegem
Adegem
Eecloo
Knesselaere
Somergem
Ursel
Evergem
Wandelgem
Landegem
Nevele
Aerseele
Deynze

Borssele
Hoofdsplaat
Baarland
Graauw
Waarde Hoogerheide
Ft. Bath
Huijbergen
Dryhoeck
Stabroeck
St. Leonard
Turnhout
West Malle
Oost Malle
Lille Thielen
Lit. Nethe
Heeze
Herenthals

Ft. Oudenvek
Ft. Doel
Ft. la Perle
Ft. St. Marie
Ft. Tête de Flandre
St. Paul
Ft. de Zwijndrecht
Ft. de Gruybeke
Eeckeren
Ft. St. Philippe
Ft. Stabroeck
Ft. Brasschaet
Brasschaet
Ft. de Schooten
Ft. de Merxem
Merxem
ANTWERP
Wyneghem
Santhoven
Ft. Oeleghem
Nylen
Berlaer
Westmeerbeek

Axel Hulst
Stekene
Zepenecken
Lokeren
St. Nicholas
Ft. Haesdonck
Basel
Ft. de Rupelmonde
Tamise
Contich
Ft. Bornhem
Ft. Lierre Lierre
Heyst

GHENT (GAND)
Ledeberg Melle
Wetteren
Hamme
Termonde
Zele
St. Amand
Ft. Willebroeck
Willebroeck
Boom
Waelhem
Duffel Waelhem
Ft. Wavre
MALINES (MECHLIN)
Sempst
Dyle
Aerschot
Demer

ALOST
Audegem
Opwyck
Moursel
Frembodegem
Assche
Londerzeel
Humbeek
Woluerthem
Boort
Busken
Wespelaer
Rotselaer Becquevoort
Thielt

BELGIUM
Oudenarde
Ninove
Denderleeuw
Lombeek
Jette Laeken
Sternbeck
Cortenberg
LOUVAIN
Heverle
Winghe

Renaix
Grammont
Gammerages
Hérinnes
BRUSSELS
Anderlecht
Ucole
Auderghem
Boitsfort
Overysshe
Weert
Vertryck
TIRLEMONT
Hougaerde
Zetrad

Lessines
Enghien
Tubize
Quenast
Hal
Lembecq
Waterloo
Braine l'Alleud
Mt. St. Jean
La Hulpe
Grez Waure
Jodoigne
Jauche

Soignies
Nivelles
Boulers Genappe
Tilly
Gembloux
Leuze
Perwez
Enghezée

Lens
Casteau
Seneffe
Frasnes
Sombreffe
Ft. de Cognelée
Ft. Marchoulette
Ft. Emines

MONS
Chesmes
Binche
Marchienne
Charleroi
Châtelet
Jemeppe
Spy Ft.
Vedrin
NAMUR
Ft. Dave

Condé
Fresnes
Malplaquet
Bonne Espérance
Froid Chapelle
Fontaine l'Evêque
Gilly
Fosse
Profondeville
Lustin

VALENCIENNES
Ft. Rochambeau
Bavay
le Quesnoy
MAUBEUGE
Erquelinnes
Thuin
Beaumont
Philippeville
Dinant

Solesmes
Le Cateau
Landrecies
Avesnes
Sars Poteries
Sivry
Marienbourg
Chimay
Rocroi
Fumay
Givet

The map is divided into 25 mile squares

Adjoining page 6.

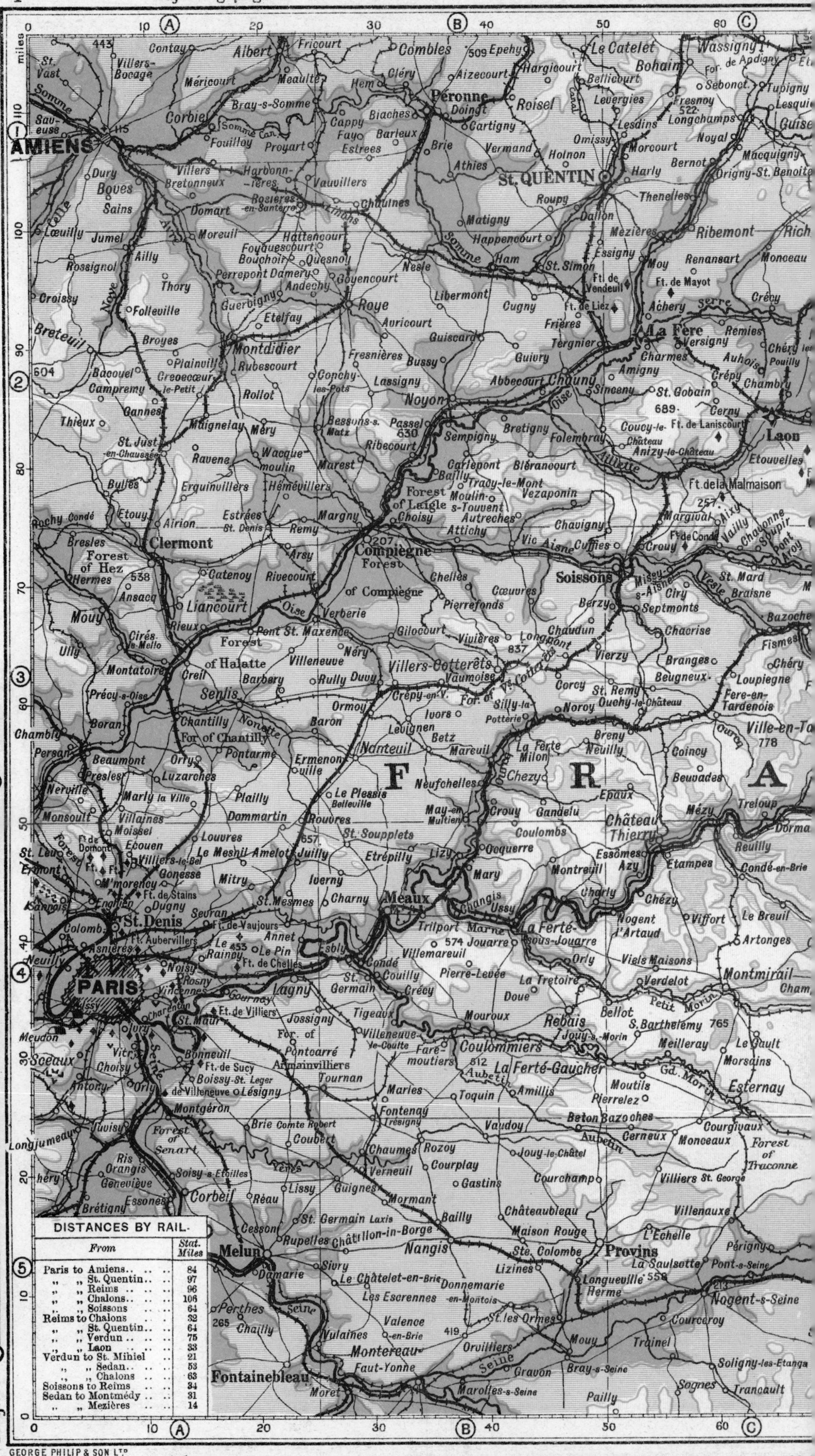

Grid reference letters: (A) (B) (C) across top and bottom; 1, 2, 3, 4, 5 down left side.

Scale markings: miles 0 10 20 30 40 50 60

Left margin (vertical): London   Brighton   Brighton to London on same scale as map

Principal place names (selection, north to south, west to east):

St. Vast, Sau-euse, Somme, Contay, Villers-Bocage, Méricourt, Albert, Fricourt, Combles, 509 Epehy, Le Catelet, Bohain, Wassigny, For. de Andigny, Tupigny, Lesqui, Guise, Méaulte, Hem, Cléry, Aizecourt, Hargicourt, Bellicourt, Levergies, Sebonct, Fresnoy 522, Longchamps, Macquigny, Noyal, Bray-s-Somme, Cappy, Fayo, Biaches, Péronne, Doingt, Roisel, Lesdins, Omissy, Morcourt, Bernot, Drigny-St. Benoite

Amiens, 115, Corbie, Somme Can., Fouilloy, Proyart, Estrées, Brie, Vermand, Holnon, St. Quentin, Harly, Thenelles, Ribemont, Monceau, Rich

Dury, Boves, Sains, Villers-Bretonneux, Harbonn-ières, Vauvillers, Chaulnes, Athies, Matigny, Roupy, Dallon, Mézières, Essigny, Renansart

Lœuilly, Jumel, Moreuil, Rosières-en-Santerre, Hattencourt, Foyquescourt, Quesnoy, Nesle, Libermont, Ham, St. Simon, Moy, Ft. de Mayot, Crécy, Achery

Rossignol, Ailly, Thory, Folleville, Guerbigny, Andechy, Roye, Auricourt, Guiscard, Cugny, Frières, Tergnier, Ft. de Liez, Ft. de Vendeuil, La Fère, Versigny, Remies, Chéry, Pouilly

Breteuil, 604, Bacouel, Campremy, Gannes, Broyes, Plainville, Crevecœur-le-Petit, Rubescourt, Montdidier, Fresnières, Bussy, Conchy-les-Pots, Lassigny, Noyon, Guivry, Abbecourt, Chauny, Amigny, Sinceny, St. Gobain 689, Cerny, Chambry, Laon

Thieux, Maignelay, Méry, Rollot, Bessons-s-Matz, Passel, 630, Ribecourt, Sempigny, Bretigny, Folembray, Couy-le-Château, Anizy-le-Château, Etouvelles, Ft. de Laniscourt

St. Just-en-Chaussée, Ravena, Wacque-moulin, Marest, Bailly, Carlepont, Bléraucourt, Tracy-le-Mont, Vezaponin, Ft. de la Malmaison, 257

Erquinvillers, Hémévillers, Estrées, St. Denis, Margny, Forest of Laigle, Moulin-s-Touvent, Choisy, Autreches, Attichy, Chavigny, Margival, Aixy, Vailly, Chaudun

Clermont, Arsy, Remy, 207, Compiègne Forest, Chelles, Cœuvres, Vic Aisne, Cuffies, Crouy, Ft. de Condé, Soupir, Pont Arcy

Bresles, Forest of Hez, Hermes, 538, Ansacq, Liancourt, Rivecourt, Oise, Verberie, of Compiègne, Pierrefonds, Soissons, Missy-s-Aisne, Ciry, Septmonts, Chaorise, Braisne, St. Mard, Bazoche

Mouy, Cirès-le-Mello, Rieux, Pont St. Maxence, Néry, Gilocourt, Vivières, Longpont 837, Berzy, Vierzy, Branges, Fismes, Chéry

Ully, Montataire, Creil, of Halatte, Villeneuve, Rully, Duvy, Villers-Cotterêts, Vaumoise, Corcy, St. Remy, Beugneux, Loupeigne, Fère-en-Tardenois

Précy-s-Oise, Senlis, Barbery, Ormoy, Crépy-en-V., For. de Villers-Cotterêts, Silly-la-Potterie, Noroy, Ouchy-le-Château

Chambly, Boran, Chantilly, For. of Chantilly, Pontarmé, Nonette, Baron, Levignen, Ivors, Betz, Breny, Neuilly, Coincy, Ville-en-To, 778

Persan, Beaumont, Presles, Orry, Luzarches, Ermenon-ville, Nanteuil, Mareuil, La Ferté Milon, Chézy, Epaux, Beuvades, Treloup

Nerville, Monsoult, Villaines, Marly la Ville, Plailly, Le Plessis-Belleville, Neufchelles, Crouy, Gandelu, Mézy, Dorma

Moissel, Ebouen, Villiers-le-Bel, Gonesse, Dammartin, Rouvres, May-en-Multien, Coulombs, Château Thierry, Reuilly

Ft. de Domont, Ermont, Enghien, Ft. de Stains, Mitry, St. Soupplets, Lizy, Cocquerre, Essômes, Azy, Etampes, Condé-en-Brie

St. Leu, Sannois, Montmorency, Le Mesnil-Amelot, Juilly, Etrépilly, Mary, Montreuil, Charly, Chézy, Viffort, Le Breuil, Artonges

Colomb, St. Denis, St. Aubervilliers, Le Pin, Ft. de Chelles, Iverny, Charny, St. Mesmes, Meaux, Trilport, Marne, La Ferté-sous-Jouarre, Jouarre 574, Orly, Viels Maisons, Montmirail

Neuilly, Asnières, Noisy, Rainey, Sebly, Changis, Ussy, Nogent d'Artaud, Verdelot

Paris, Rosny, Vincennes, St. Maur, Lagny, St. Germain, Condé, Couilly, Crécy, Pierre-Levée, Doue, La Tretoire, Rebais, Petit Morin, Bellot, S. Barthélemy 765, Montmirail

Sceaux, Choisy, Orly, Ft. de Vaujours, Annet, Le Pin, Gournay, Jossigny, Tigeaux, Mouroux, Jouy-s-Morin, Meilleray, Le Gault, Esternay

Antony, Montgéron, For. of Pontcarré, Villeneuve-le-Comte, Faremoutiers, Coulommiers, La Ferté-Gaucher, Moutils, Morsains

Meudon, Vitry, Juvisy, Bonneuil, Ft. de Sucy, Armainvilliers, Tournan, Marles, Toquin, Amillis, Pierrelez, Gd. Morin, Courgivaux

Longjumeau, Ris Orangis, Boissy-St. Léger, de Villeneuve, Lésigny, Fontenay-Trésigny, Vaudoy, Beton Bazoches, Cerneux, Monceaux, Forest of Traconne

Geneviève, Essonnes, Brie Comte Robert, Coubert, Chaumes, Rozoy, Courplay, Courchamp, Aubetin, Villiers St. George

Brétigny, Corbeil, Réau, Lissy, Guignes, Mormant, Gastins, Courchamp, Châteaubleau, Villenauxe, Périgny, L'Echelle

St. Germain Laxis, Rupelles, Châtillon-in-Borge, Nangis, Bailly, Maison Rouge, Ste. Colombe, Provins, Pont-s-Seine

Melun, Cesson, Sivry, Le Châtelet-en-Brie, Lizines, Longueville 555, La Saulsotte

Damarie, Perthes, 265, Chailly, Les Escrennes-en-Montois, Donnemarie, St. les Ormes, Nogent-s-Seine

Fontainebleau, Moret, Seine, Valence-en-Brie, 419, Oruillers, Mouy, Courceroy

Vulaines, Montereau-Faut-Yonne, Gravon, Bray-s-Seine, Soligny-les-Etanga

Marolles-s-Seine, Pailly, Sagnes, Trancault

Legend (bottom):

Railways.   Roads.   Canals.
Fortresses and Forts.   3312 Altitudes in Feet.

0-250 ft. dark green; 250-500 ft. light green; 500-
750-1000 ft. buff; 1000-2000 ft. brown; over 2000

GEORGE PHILIP & SON LTD

DISTANCES BY RAIL.

From		Stat. Miles
Paris to	Amiens..	84
" "	St. Quentin..	97
" "	Reims..	96
" "	Chalons..	106
" "	Soissons..	64
Reims to	Chalons..	32
" "	St. Quentin..	64
" "	Verdun..	75
" "	Laon..	33
Verdun to	St. Mihiel..	21
" "	Sedan..	53
" "	Chalons..	63
Soissons to	Reims..	34
Sedan to	Montmédy..	31
" "	Mézières..	14

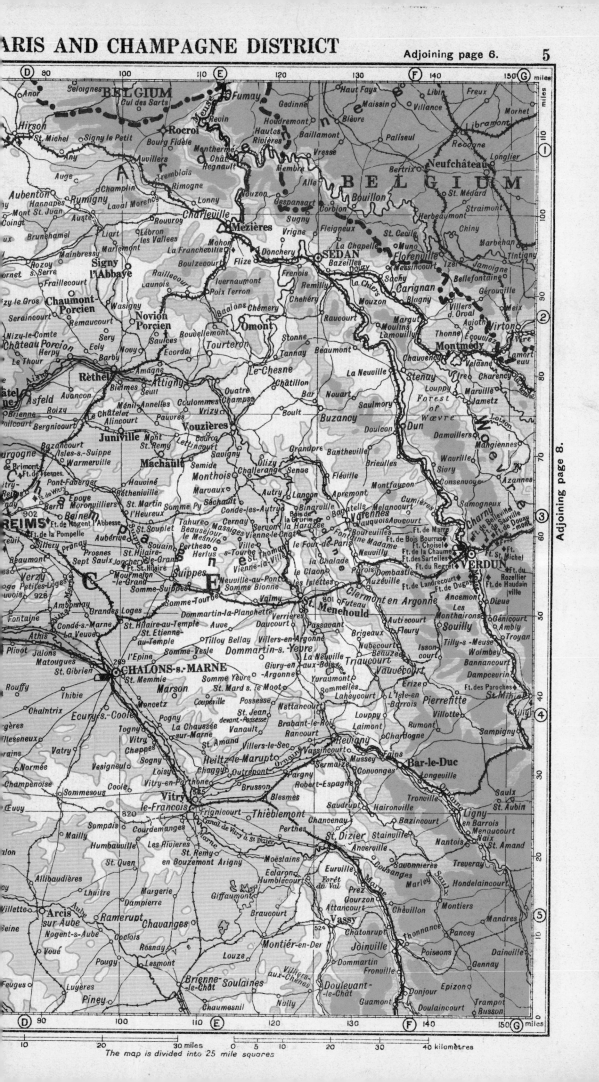

Adjoining page 8.

The map is divided into 25 mile squares

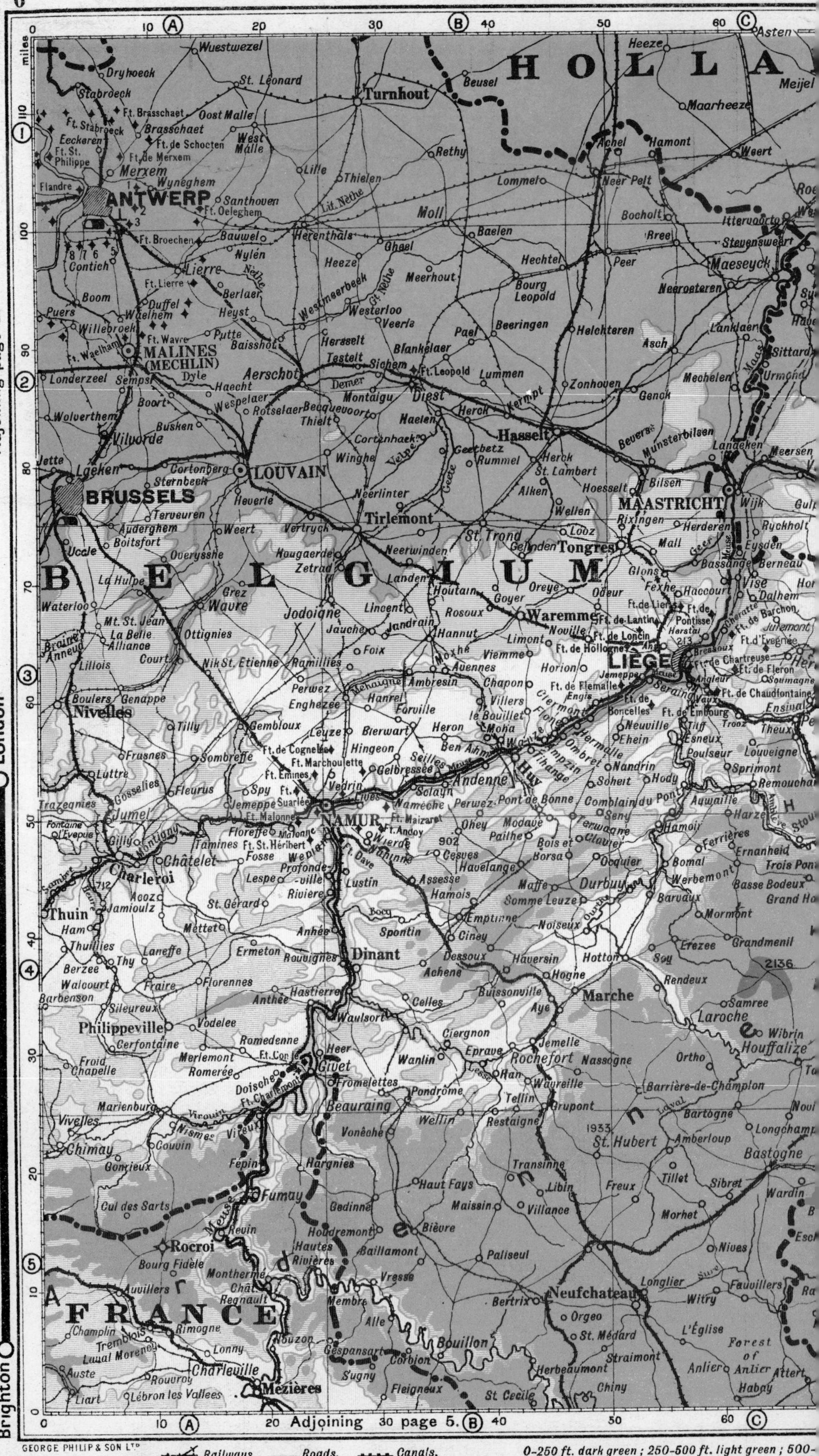

6

HOLLA[ND]

BELGIUM

FRANCE

Major places: ANTWERP, MALINES (MECHLIN), BRUSSELS, LOUVAIN, MAASTRICHT, LIÉGE, NAMUR, CHARLEROI, DINANT, Marche, St. Hubert, Bastogne, Neufchateau, Bouillon, Mezières, Charleville, Rocroi, Philippeville, Nivelles, Waterloo, Wavre, Tirlemont, Hasselt, Tongres, Waremme, Huy, Andenne, Thuin, Châtelet.

Other places (selection): Wuestwezel, Dryhoeck, Stabroeck, St. Léonard, Turnhout, Beusel, Heeze, Maarheeze, Meijel, Asten, Oost Malle, West Malle, Rethy, Achel, Hamont, Weert, Merxem, Wynéghem, Lille, Thielen, Lommel, Neer Pelt, Santhoven, Moll, Bocholt, Itervuort, Herenthals, Ghael, Baelen, Bree, Maeseyck, Neeroeteren, Hechtel, Bourg Leopold, Peer, Asch, L'anklaer, Sittard, Beeringen, Helchteren, Mechelen, Genck, Diest, Herck, Kermpt, Zonhoven, Landeken, Meersen, Aerschot, Sichem, Lummen, Münsterbilsen, Bilsen, St. Lambert, Hoesselt, Beverst, Wijk, Ryckholt, Eysden, Berneau, Vise, Dalhem, Glons, Fexhe, Haccourt, Bassange, Oreye, Odeur, Ste. Trond, Looz, Rixingen, Mall, Herderen, Houtain, Rosoux, Goyer, Hannut, Moxhe, Viemme, Horion, Jemeppe, Seraing, Boncelles, Esneux, Poulseur, Louveigne, Sprimont, Remouchamps, Aywaille, Hamoir, Durbuy, Barvaux, Bomal, Werbemont, Marche, Hotton, Rendeux, Samree, Laroche, Houffalize, Ortho, Longchamps, Amberloup, Tillet, Sibret, Wardin, Rochefort, Nassogne, Grupont, Tellin, Wellin, Restaigne, Libin, Transinne, Villance, Freux, Morhet, Nives, Longlier, Witry, Fauvillers, Bertrix, Orgeo, St. Médard, L'Église, Chiny, Habay, Straimont, Herbeaumont, St. Cecile, Corbion, Sugny, Fleigneux, Vresse, Alle, Membre, Bouillon, Paliseul, Bièvre, Maissin, Haut Fays, Gedinne, Houdremont, Baillamont, Hautes Rivières, Revin, Monthermé, Chât. Regnault, Nouzon, Gespansart, Mézières.

GEORGE PHILIP & SON LTD

Legend:
✈ Railways. ── Roads. ···· Canals.
✦ Fortresses and Forts. 3312 Altitudes in Feet.

0–250 ft. dark green; 250–500 ft. light green; 500–750–1000 ft. buff; 1000–2000 ft. brown; over 200[0]

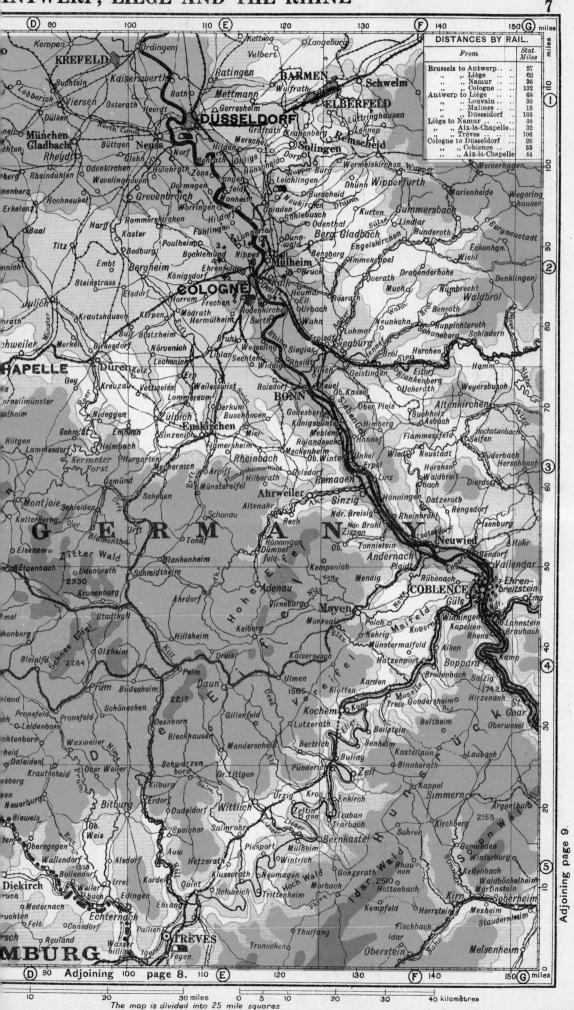

DISTANCES BY RAIL.	
From	Stat. Miles
Brussels to Antwerp ..	27
,, ,, Liège ..	62
,, ,, Namur ..	36
,, ,, Cologne ..	132
Antwerp to Liège ..	68
,, ,, Louvain ..	30
,, ,, Malines ..	15
,, ,, Düsseldorf ..	105
Liège to Namur ..	38
,, ,, Aix-la-Chapelle ..	32
,, ,, Trèves ..	106
Cologne to Düsseldorf ..	26
,, ,, Coblence ..	55
,, ,, Aix-la-Chapelle ..	44

Adjoining page 9.

Adjoining page 8.

10   20   30 miles   10   20   30   40 kilometres
The map is divided in 25 mile squares

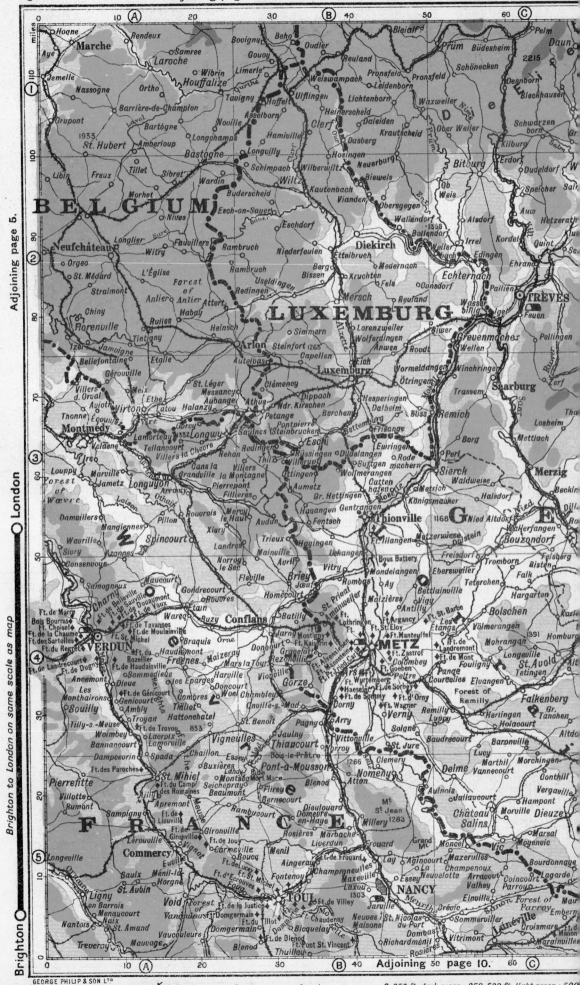

Adjoining page 5.

Brighton to London on same scale as map

London ○ Brighton

GEORGE PHILIP & SON Ltd

Railways. ———— Roads. ‒‒‒‒ Canals.
Fortresses and Forts. 3312 Altitudes in Feet.

0–250 ft. dark green; 250–500 ft. light green; 500
750–1000 ft. buff; 1000–2000 ft. brown; over 20

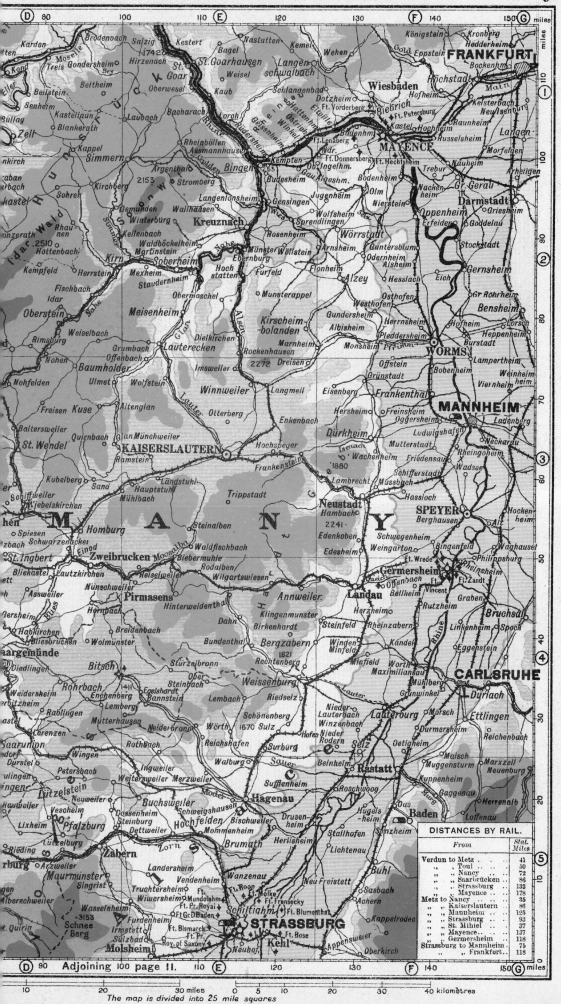

The map is divided into 25 mile squares

DISTANCES BY RAIL.	
From	**Stat. Miles**
Verdun to Metz	41
" " Toul	50
" " Nancy	72
" " Saarbrücken	86
" " Strassburg	133
" " Mayence	178
Metz to Nancy	35
" " Kaiserslautern	86
" " Mannheim	125
" " Strassburg	93
" " St. Mihiel	37
" " Mayence	137
" " Germersheim	118
Strassburg to Mannheim	75
" " Frankfurt	118

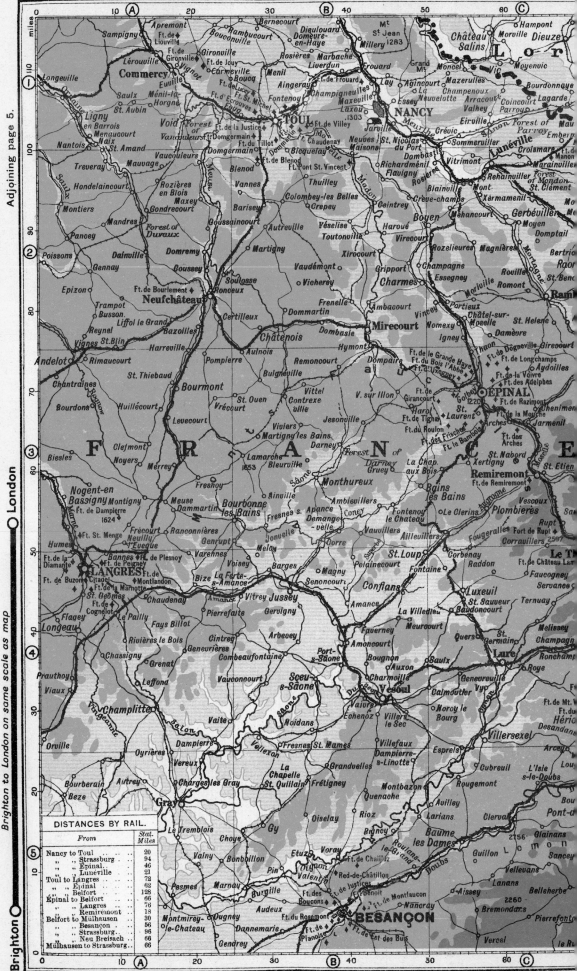

THE WESTERN THEA

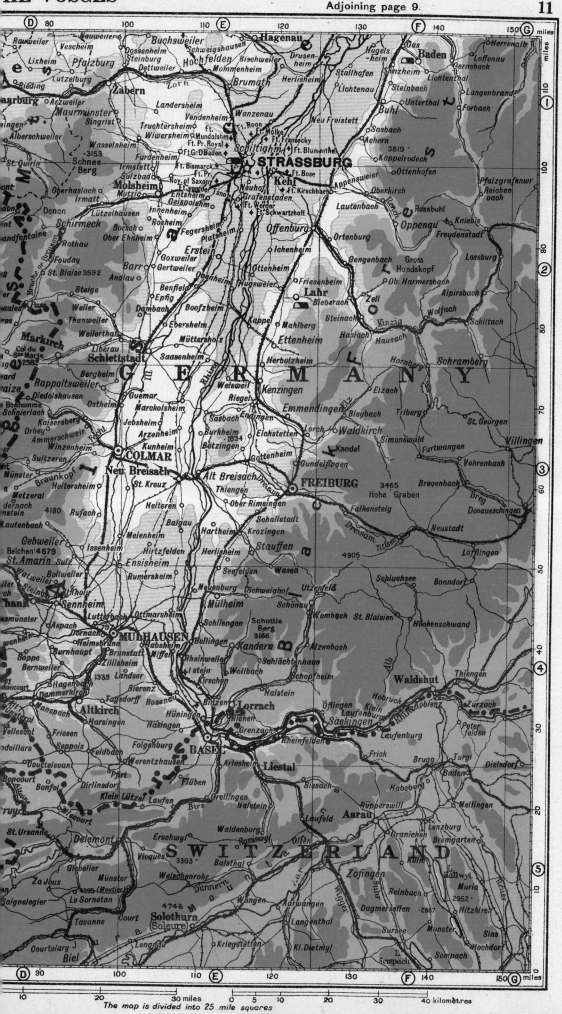

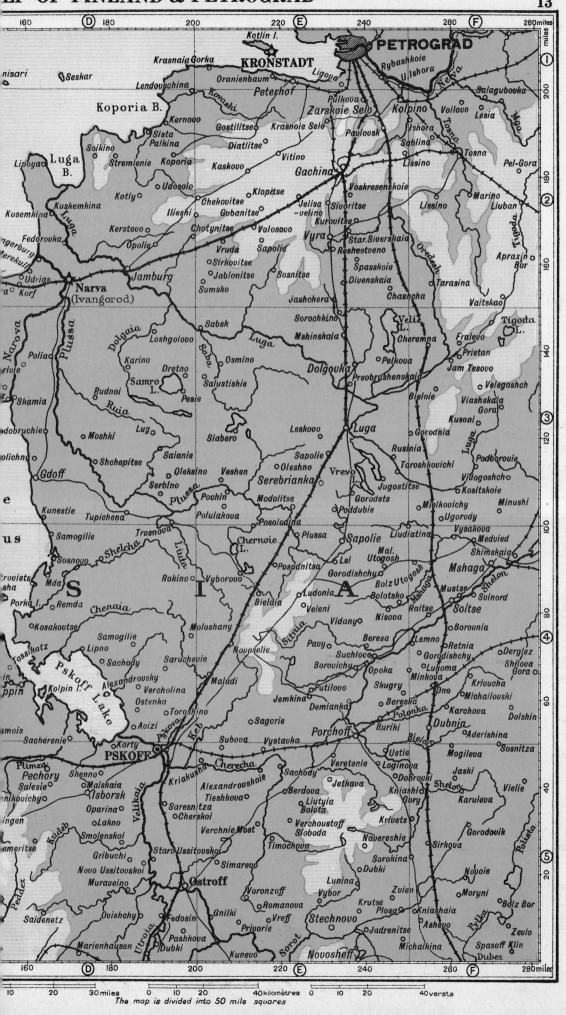

Kotlin I.

Krasnaia Gorka

KRONSTADT

PETROGRAD

Rybashkoie

Ulshora

Neva

Salagubovka

nisari | Seskar

Lendovschina

Oranienbaum

Ligova

Peterhof

Pulkova

Voilovo

Lesia

Mga

Koporia B.

Kernovo

Kovashi

Gostilitse

Zarskoie Selo

Kolpino

Ishora

Tosna

(I)

200

Sista Palkina

Diatlitse

Krasnoie Selo

Pavlousk

Sablina

Tosna

Pel-Gora

180 (2)

Soikino

Stremlenie

Koporia

Kaskovo

Vitino

Gachina

Voskresenskoie

Lissino

Marino

Liuban

Luga B.

Lipoya

Udosolo

Klopitse

Chekovitse

Jelisa -velino

Sivoritse

Lissino

Tigoda

Kotly

Ilieshi

Gubanitse

Kurovitse

Apraxin Bor

Kuskemkina

Kerstovo

Chotynitse

Volosovo

Vyra

Star. Siverskaia

Tarasina

160

Fedorouka

Opolie

Vruda

Sapolie

Reshestveno

Spasskoie

Vaitskao

Udrias

Jamburg

Jablonitse

Sosnitse

Divenskaia

Chashcha

Tigoda L.

Korf

Sumsko

Jashchera

Sorochkino

Velia L.

Fralevo

140

Dolgaia

Sabsk

Luga

Mshinskaia

Cheremna

Pristan

Polia

Karino

Loshgolovo

Saba

Osmino

Pelkova

Jam Tesovo

Skamia

Rudnoi

Dretno

Salustishie

Dolgouka

Preobrashenskaia

Velegoshch

Samro L.

Pesie

Bieloie

Viashskaia Gora

(3)

Moshki

Lug

Siabero

Leskovo

Luga

Gorodnia

Kusoni

120

Shohepitse

Saianie

Sapolie

Rusinia

Podborovie

Gdoff

Oleksino

Veshen

Oleshno

Vrevo L.

Taroshkovichi

Vidogoshch

Serbino

Serebrianka

Gorodets

Jugostitse

Mielkovichy

Kositskoie

Kunestie

Pochin

Modolitse

Poddubie

Ugorody

Minushi

Tupichena

Poluiakova

Posolodina

Liudiatina

Vysakova

100

Samogilie

Trosnova

Chernoie L.

Plussa

Sapolie

Medvied

Sosnovo

Shelcha

Liuta

Posadnitsa

Mal. Utogosh

Shimskaia

Porka I.

Remda

Rokino

Vyborovo

Lsi

Gorodishchu

Bolz Utogosh

Mshaga

Mustse

Svinord

Chenaia

Bieldia

Ludonia

Belotsko

Raitse

Soltse

Kosakoutse

Moloshany

Veleni

Vidany

Nisova

Borounia

80 (4)

Samogilie

Lipno

Sachody

Saruchevie

Novoselie

Pavy

Beresa

Lemno

Retnia

Derglez

Alexandrousky

Vercholina

Maladi

Borovichy

Suchlovo

Opoka

Gorodishchy

Lukoma

Minkova

Dno

Shilova Gora

Ostenka

Putilovo

Skugry

Krivucha

Michailouski

Toroshino

Jemkina

Demianka

Bereska

Karchova

Dolshin

Avizi

Sagorie

Polonka

Buriki

Dubnia

Aderishina

60

Sacherenie

Subova

Vystavka

Porchoff

Bielao

PSKOFF

Ustie

Mogileva

Sosnitza

Plinza

Korty

Cherecha

Veretenie

Loginova

Jaski

Pechory

Shenno

Kriakusha

Sachody

Dobrouki

Shelon

Vielie

40

Salesie

Malskaia

Alexandrovskoie

Berdova

Jetkava

Kniashia Gory

Karuieva

nkovichy

Isborsk

Tieshkova

Liutyia Bolota

Krivets

Oparina

Saresnitza

Cherskoi

Verchoustoff Sloboda

Navereshie

Gorodovik

Lakno

Verchnie Most

Timochova

Sorokina

Sirkova

Novoie

20

Smolenskoi

Staro Ussitovskoi

Simarevo

Dubki

Polista

Gribuchi

Novo Ussitouskoi

Lunina

Zvien

Moryni

Muraveino

Ostroff

Voronzoff

Vybor

Krutse

Plosa

Kniashaia

Bolz Bor

emeritse

Romanova

Stechnovo

Ashevo

Pyka

Zevlo

Saidenetz

Ovishchy

Gnilki

Vreff

Privorie

Jadrenitse

Michalkina

Spasoff Klin

Marienhausen

Pashkova Dubki

Kunevo

Sorot

Novosheff

Dubez

The map is divided into 50 mile squares

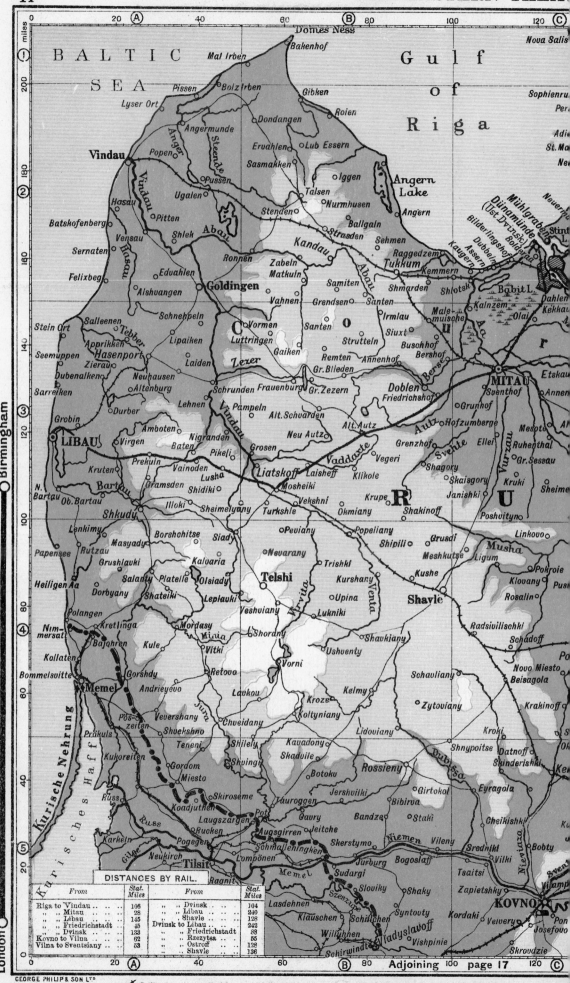

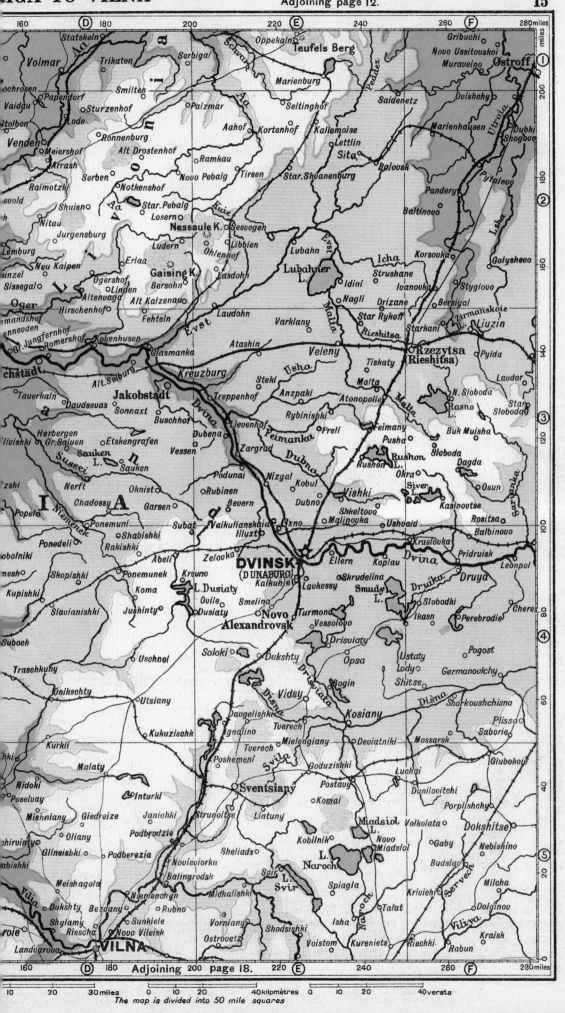

The map is divided into 50 mile squares

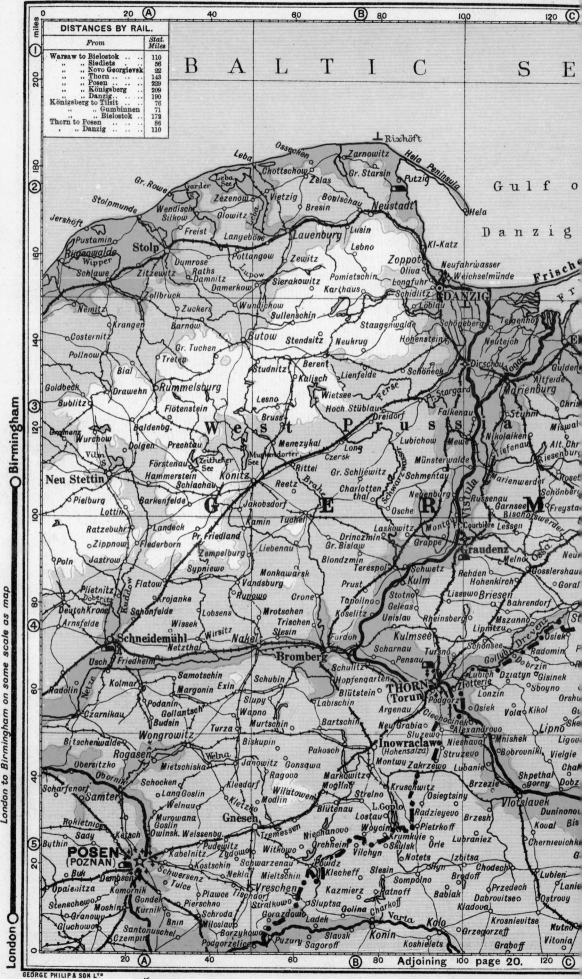

DISTANCES BY RAIL.	
From	Stat. Miles
Warsaw to Bielostok	110
" " Siedlets	56
" " Novo Georgievsk	22
" " Thorn	143
" " Posen	229
" " Königsberg ..	209
" " Danzig	190
Königsberg to Tilsit	76
" " Gumbinnen ..	71
" " Bielostok ..	172
Thorn to Posen	86
" " Danzig	110

BALTIC SE

Gulf o

Danzig

London to Birmingham on same scale as map

Birmingham

London

GEORGE PHILIP & SON Lᵗᵈ.

✦ Railways.   ___ Roads.   .... Canals.
✦ Fortresses and Forts.   3312 Altitudes in Feet.

0-250 ft. dark green ; 250-500 ft. light green ; 500-75
750-1000 ft. buff ; 1000-2000 ft. brown ; over 2000 f

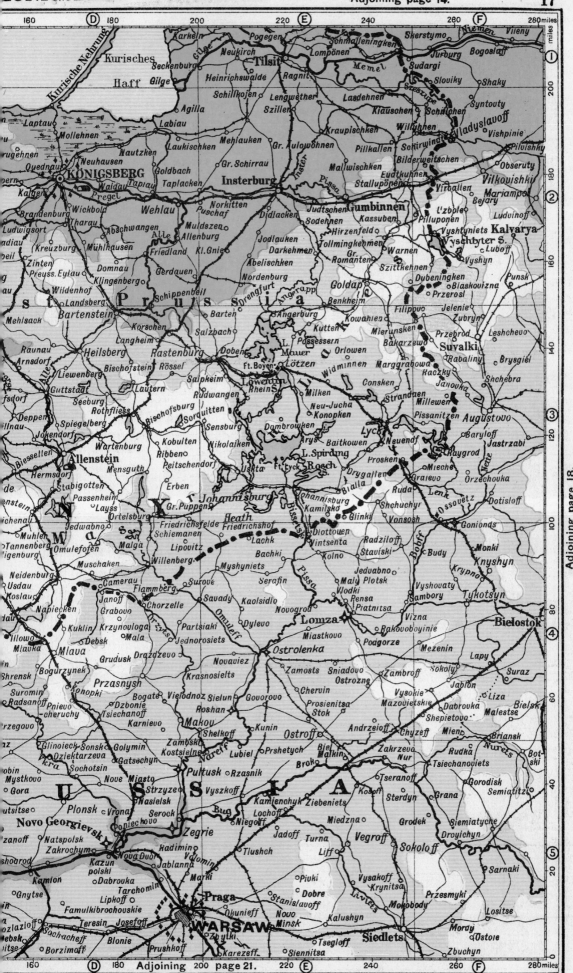

The map is divided into 50 mile squares

miles 0   20 (A)   40   60 (B) 80   100   120 (C)

Adjoining page 17.

London to Birmingham on same scale as map

Birmingham

London

Shaky
Tsaitsi
Zapietshky
Svenz.
Vilampolsha
Kornialoff
Rumshyshki
Chabishki
Meishagola
Balingrodsk
Michalis.
KOVNO
Koshedary
Dukshty
Bezdany
Niemenchyn
Rubno
Vorniani
Syntouty
Kordaki
Veivery
Ponemon
Zyzmory
Shylamy
Riescha
Sunkiele
Novo Vileisk
Ostrovetz
Vladyslavoff
Josefovo
Jeroie
Landvarovo
VILNA
Sloba
Vishpinie
Skroudzie
Darsunishki
Troki
Rukbiny
Shuprany
Oshr
Piloishky
Preny
Uzagose
Soroktalary
Miedniki
Pavlovo
Obseruty
Plotyski
Virshtany
Stoklishki
Rudzishki
Rudniki
Jashany
Zodoff
Grauzyshky
Vilkouishki
Balvierzyski
Puni
Olsh
Betary
Mariampol
Dusmiany
Olkieniki
Solechniki
Smol
Traby
Ludvinoff
Rumbovitse
Daugi
Orany
Biniakony
Eishyshki
Veronoff
Subotniki
Kalvarya
Olita
Niemonoitsie
Kolesniky
Radun
Zyrmuny
Lipnishki
Iuie
Novina
Simno
Przelaie
Zervina
Dubiche
Ditva
Morino
Nik
Luboff
Miroslaw
Merech
Martsinkantse
Zablotie
Myto
Lida
Dielatychy
Vyshyn
Urdomin
Sereie
Dubiche
Sobatenzy
Dytew
Pieski
Vsielub
Punsk
Lozdzieje
Vielsieia
Druskieniki
Koba
Novy Duor
Vasitishki
Lebeda
Ruda
Novogrud
Zubryn
Zegary
Koptsioff
Przevalek
Porzeche
Radzivoninshki
Bielitsa
Leshcheuo
Seiny
Kadus
Horo.
Oseryo
Jeziory
Ostryna
Zoludek
Orla
Suvalki
Brysgiel
Shchebra
Augustovo Canal
Sdookinie
Goshaio
Grandzieze
Dombrovo
Shchuchyn
Viazoviets
Ochunova
Augustovo
Holynka
Lipsk
GRODNO
Skidel
Lamionk
Dzienciol
Novoielaya
Baryloff
Jastrzabi
Dombrovo
Nobol Duor
Niemen
Lunno
Dubno
Mosty
Vk Vola
Koloushchina
Dvorzets
Potse
Orzechouka
Suchovol
Sidra
Indura
Volpa
Malkov
Piaski
Malkoviche
Shchara
Moltschad
Gonionds
Dotisloff
Janoff
Kuznitsa
Odelsk
Holno
Ros
Derechyn
Holinka
Dereunoye
Nou.M
Krypno
Monki
Korytsyn
Josienovka
Sokolka
Krynki
Mala Brzoslowitsa
Volkouysk
Zelva
Slonim
Polonka
Knyshyn
Tykotsyn
Vasilkoff
Vela Brzoslovitsa
Holynka
Mstsiboff
Izabelin
Jeziernitsa
Shirovichy
Shilovichy
Zlatorya
Tsaoroschch
Bielostok
Grudek
Rozany (Ruschana
Bitten
Lapy
Zabludoff
Jalovka
Suisloch
Porozoff
Lyskoff
Bulla
Domonovo
Suraz
Rybele
Nareff
Nareff
Strzel
Novy Duor
Manchyki
Kosoff
Chemiely
Shur
Liza
Kleniki
Nareuka
Smolenitsa
Malestse
Chishi
Forest of
Bielovies
Kozly
Jasiolda
Sieletz
Briansk
Orla
Bielovies
St. Vola
Nurets
Botski
Omialenez
Prushany
Berezakartuzka
Bobrevich
Gorodisk
Cheremeza
Kletzchely
Dmitroviche
Malech
Signiviichi
Telech
Semiatitzi
Verchouichi
Linouka
Corsk
Sdsitovo
Siemiatyche
Zamasty
Sasnovka
Plosk
Chamsk
L.Sporoti
Oza
Vysoko-Litousky
Kamieniets Litousky
Besdesh
Melnik
Sarnaki
Strygoff
Horodets
Antopol
Drogit
Janoff
Niemieroff
Voltchin
Cherrauchytse
Kobryn
Snitovo
Broduit
Lositse
Bug
Shabinka
Blota
Glinna
Miedzurzech
Janoff
Neple
BREST LITOVSK
Rokitnitsa
Horodets Canal
Mokre
Ostoje
Krzevitsa
Biala
Krzna
Brzyluki
Ruda
Novosiolki
Dyoim
Radzistoff
Harki Lyubas

GEORGE PHILIP & SON Ltd.

Railways.   Roads.   Canals.
Fortresses and Forts.   3312 Altitudes in Feet.

0-250 ft. dark green ; 250-500 ft. light green ; 500-750
750-1000 ft. buff ; 1000-2000 ft. brown ; over 2000 ft.

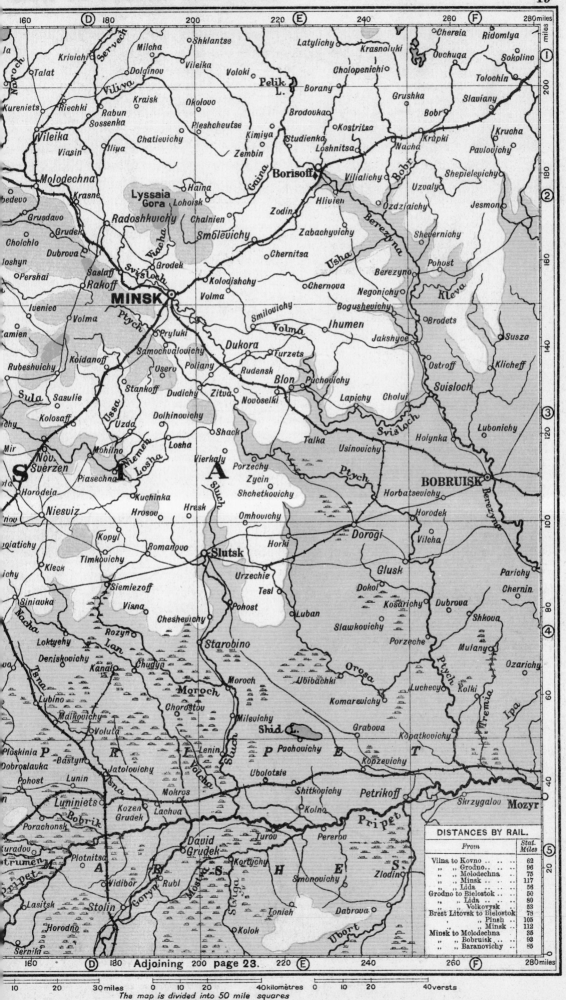

DISTANCES BY RAIL.

From	Stat. Miles
Vilna to Kovno ..	62
" " Grodno ..	96
" " Molodechna ..	75
" " Minsk ..	117
" " Lida ..	56
Grodno to Bielostok ..	50
" " Lida ..	80
" " Volkovysk ..	53
Brest Litovsk to Bielostok ..	78
" " Pinsk ..	105
" " Minsk ..	112
Minsk to Molodechna ..	35
" " Bobruisk ..	93
" " Baranovichy ..	85

10 20 30 miles   0 10 20 40 kilomètres   0 10 20 40 versts

The map is divided into 50 mile squares

London to Birmingham on same scale as map

Birmingham ○

London ○

DISTANCES BY RAIL.

From	Stat. Miles
Warsaw to Lublin	112
" Ivangorod	67
" Siedlets	56
" Cracow	218
" Lodz	80
" Breslau	245
" Chenstochova	139
Przemysl to Jaroslau	20
" Cracow	147
Lodz to Breslau	140
" Cracow	172
" Kalish	65
Cracow to Breslau	155
" Tarnoff	47
" Ivangorod	205

GEORGE PHILIP & SON Lᵀᴰ

✈ Railways. —— Roads. ---- Canals.
✦ Fortresses and Forts.   3312 Altitudes in Feet.

0-250 ft. dark green; 250-500 ft. light green; 500-750
750-1000 ft. buff; 1000-2000 ft. brown; over 2000 ft

GERMANY

AUSTRIA

P

BRESLAU (WRACLAW)

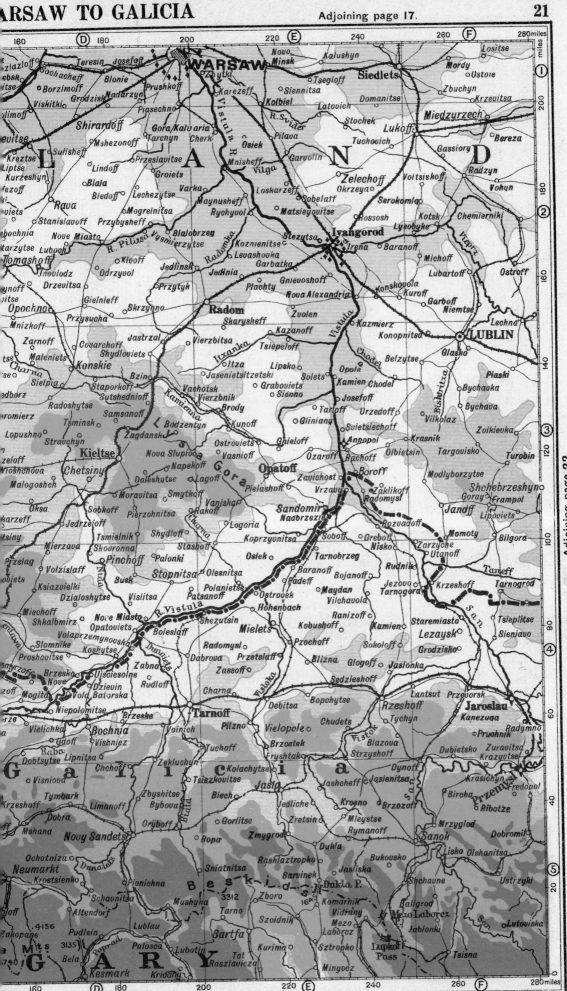

Adjoining page 22.

The map is divided into 50 mile squares

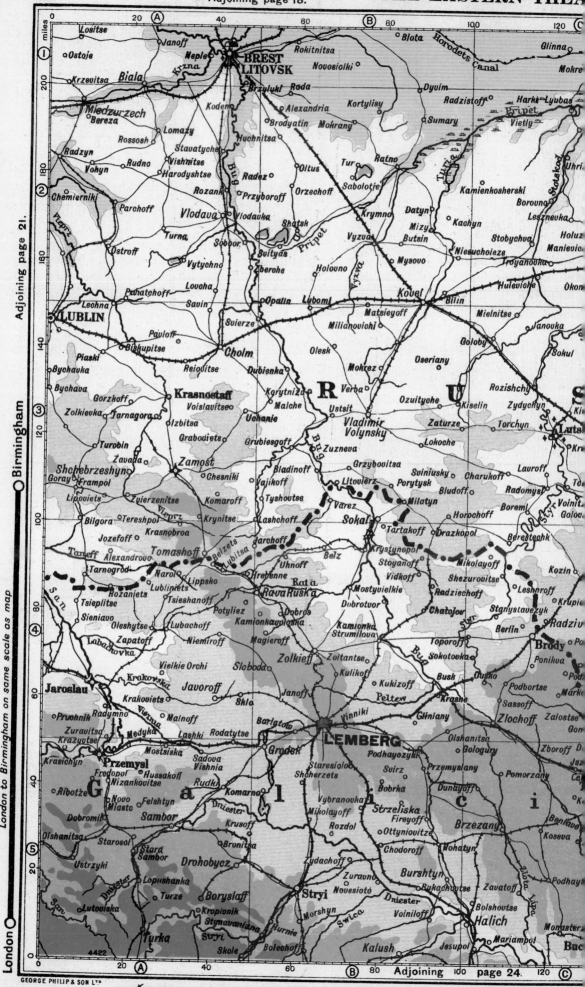

GEORGE PHILIP & SON Lᵀᴰ

Railways. —— Roads. ╍╍ Canals.
✦ Fortresses and Forts.   3312 Altitudes in Feet.

0–250 ft. dark green; 250–500 ft. light green; 500–750
750–1000 ft. buff; 1000–2000 ft. brown; over 2000 ft.

London to Birmingham on same scale as map   Birmingham   London

Adjoining page 21.

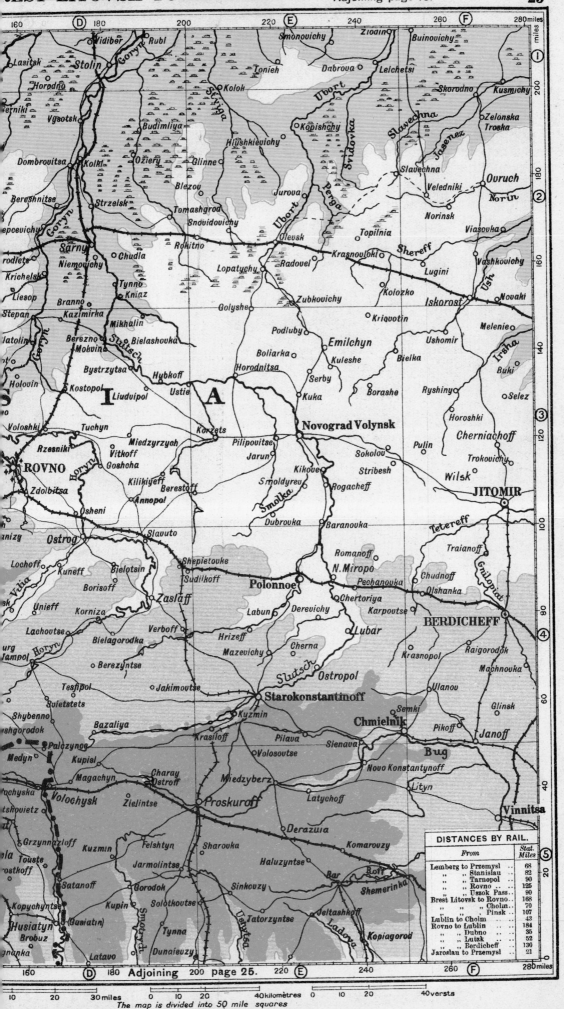

Widiber
Rubl
Smonovichy
Zioain
Buinovichy
Lasitsk
Stolin
Goryn
Tonieh
Dabrova
Lelchetsi
①
Horodno
Skorodno
Kusmichy
Verniki
Vgsotsk
Budimliya
Styriga
Kopishchy
Slavechna
Zelonska
Troska
②
Dombrovitsa
Kolki
Oziery
Glinne
Hlushkievichy
Jasenez
Bereshnitse
Blezov
Jurova
Perga
Slavechna
Veledniki
Ovruch
Norin
Strzelsk
Tomashgrod
Snovidovichy
Ubort
Norinsk
Viasovka
repoevichy
Goryn
Olevsk
Topilnia
Ⓐ
Sarny
Rokitno
Radovel
Krasnovloki
Shereff
Lugini
Vashkovichy
rodiete
Niemovichy
Chudla
Lopatychy
Ush
Novaki
Krichelsk
Tynno
Kniaz
Zubkovichy
Kolozko
Iskorost
③
Liesop
Branno
Kazimirka
Mikhalin
Golyshe
Kriovotin
Ushomir
Melenie
Stepan
Berezno
Bielashovka
Podluby
Emilchyn
Bielka
Ryshiny
Irsha
Buki
Matolin
Mokvin
Slutsch
Kuleshe
Selez
Holovin
Bystrzytsa
Hybkoff
Horodnitsa
Serby
Borashe
Horoshki
Kostopol
Ustie
Ⓐ
Kuka
Cherniachoff
Voloshki
Liudvipol
Korzets
Novograd Volynsk
Pulin
Wilsk
ROVNO
Tuchyn
Miedzyrzych
Pilipovitse
Sokolov
Trokovichy
Zdolbitsa
Vitkoff
Goshcha
Jarun
Kikove
Stribesh
JITOMIR
Osheni
Kilikiyeff
Berestoff
Smoldyrev
Rogacheff
Ⓣ
Ostrog
Annopol
Smolka
Baranovka
Tetereff
Traianoff
Lochoff
Slavuto
Dubrovka
Romanoff
Kuneff
Bielotsin
Shepietouke
N. Miropo
Chudnoff
Gnilopiat
Borisoff
Sudilkoff
Pechanovka
Ojshanka
Unieff
Zaslaff
Polonnoe
Chertoriya
Karpoutse
BERDICHEFF
④
Korniza
Labun
Derevichy
Raigorodok
Lachoutse
Verboff
Hrizeff
Lubar
Krasnopol
Machnovka
Bielagorodka
Mazevichy
Cherna
Ulanov
Horyn
Berezyntse
Slutsch
Ostropol
Glinsk
Tesfipol
Jakimoutse
Starokonstantinoff
Semki
Svietstets
Kuzmin
Chmielnik
Pikoff
Janoff
Shybenno
Bazaliya
Krasiloff
Pilava
Sienava
Bug
shgorodok
Palczynog
Volosoutse
Novo Konstantynoff
Medyn
Kupiel
Magachyn
Lityn
Charay
Ostroff
Miedzyberz
Latychoff
Vinnitsa
⑤
achyska
Volochysk
Zielintse
Proskuroff
Grzynnazloff
Kuzmin
Felshtyn
Derazuia
Komarouzy
la Touste
Sharovka
Haluzyntse
Roff
rosthoff
Jarmolintse
Bar
Shemerinka
Satanoff
Gorodok
Sinkovzy
Kopychyntse
Kupin
Solotkoutse
Jeltashkoff
Husiatyn (Gusiatin)
Tatorzyntse
Ladova
Kopiagorod
Brobuz
Tynna
Dunaieuzy
Ⓔ
nanka
Latavo

10 20 30 miles	0 10 20 40 kilomètres

The map is divided into 50 mile squares

DISTANCES BY RAIL.	
From	Stat. Miles
Lemberg to Przemysl ..	68
" " Stanislau ..	82
" " Tarnopol ..	90
" " Rovno ..	125
" " Uszok Pass..	90
Brest Litovsk to Rovno..	168
" " Cholm..	70
" " Pinsk..	107
Lublin to Cholm ..	43
Rovno to Lublin ..	184
" Dubno ..	35
" Lutzk ..	52
" Berdicheff ..	130
Jaroslau to Przemysl ..	21

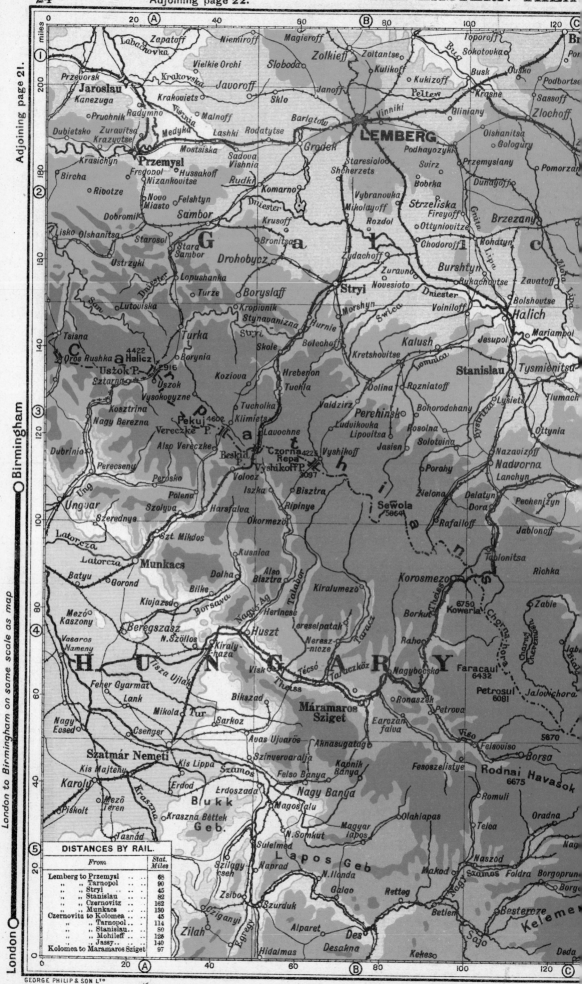

London to Birmingham on same scale as map

○ Birmingham

London ○

DISTANCES BY RAIL.

From		Stat. Miles
Lemberg to Przemysl	..	66
,, ,, Tarnopol	..	90
,, ,, Stryi	..	45
,, ,, Stanislau	..	82
,, ,, Czernovitz	..	162
,, ,, Munkacs	..	130
Czernovitz to Kolomea	..	45
,, ,, Tarnopol	..	114
,, ,, Stanislau	..	80
,, ,, Mohileff	..	125
,, ,, Jassy	..	140
Kolomea to Maramaros Siget		97

GEORGE PHILIP & SON Lᵀᴰ

✳✳ **Railways.**   —— **Roads.**   ---- **Canals.**
✦✦ **Fortresses and Forts.**   3312 **Altitudes in Feet.**

0-250 ft. dark green ; 250-500 ft. light green ; 500-75
750-1000 ft. buff ; 1000-2000 ft. brown ; over 2000 f

Adjoining page 23.

The map is divided into 50 mile squares

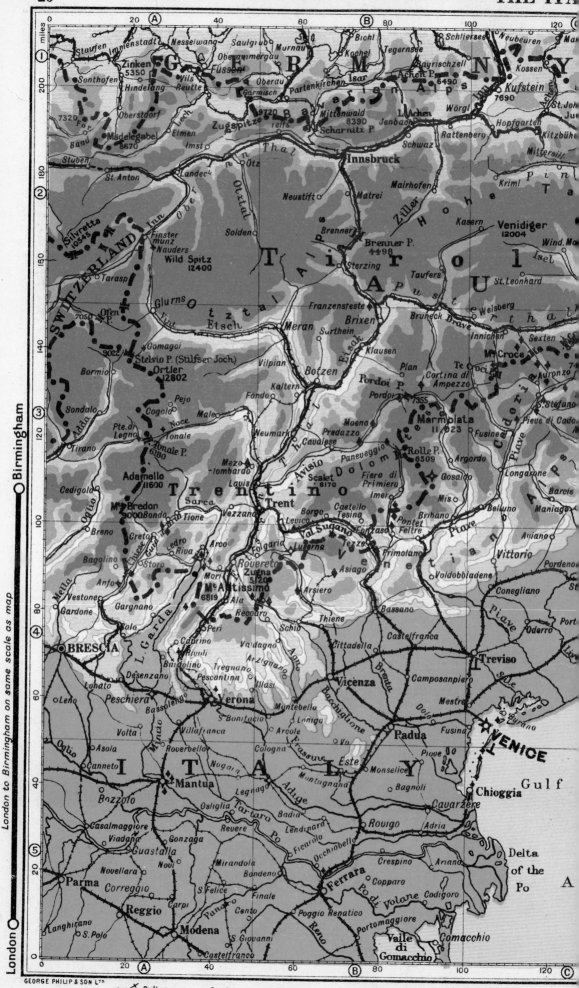

Railways. —— Roads. ···· Canals.
Fortresses and Forts. 3312 Altitudes in Feet.

0-500 ft. dark green; 500-1000 ft. light green; 1000-20
2000-4000 ft. buff; 4000-6000 ft. brown; over 6000 ft.

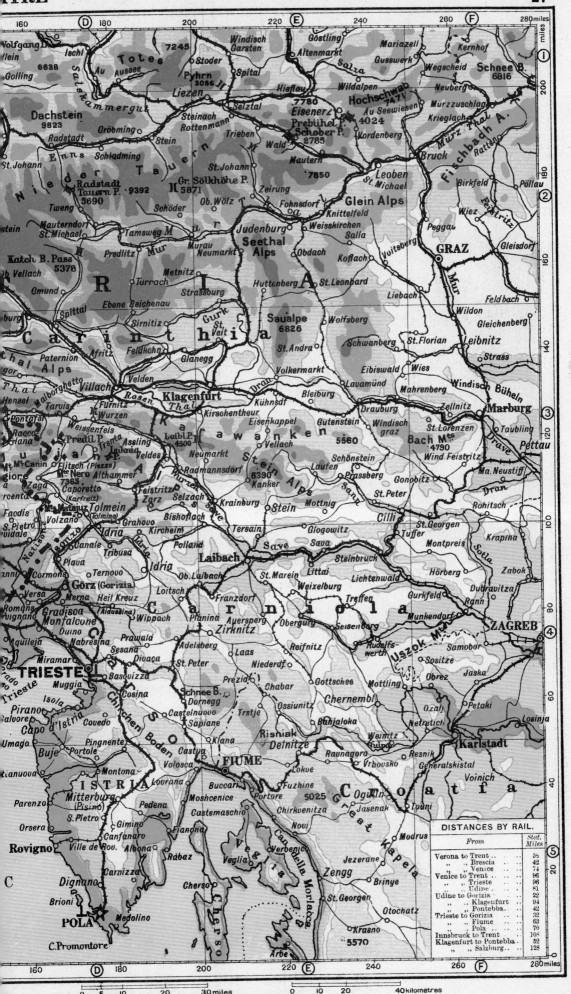

40 miles

(A) 26°   20   (B) 40   60 27°   80

Brighton to London on same scale as map

London

Brighton

BULGARIA

Adachli

Yatajik

Akche Alan

Ortakeui

Kuchuk Derbend

Biyuk Derbend

Pishmankeui

Dogan Hissar

Adarmishli

Budoma

Rumjik

Dedeagatch

Maritza

Pt Dragutina

C.Gremea

Kastron

Imbros

C.Kepháli

Chermen

Mustafa Pasha

Hadikeui

Marash

Arda

Karagach

Sarihadir

Kilkikeui

Geukje Bunar

Kara Kilissa

Karajali

Kizil Deli

Demotika

Mandra

Saltikeui

Sufli

Yan Veran

Kadikeui

Vakuf

Keupli

Bidigli

Sarkhanli

Germekkeui

Ipsala

Ferejik

Koskur

J. Gala

Chatal Tepe

Enos

Chelebi

Yazeuren

Ayazma

Erikli

Karachali

Gulf of Xeros (Saros)

Yeni Keui

Bergaz

Gallipoli

Kartunus

Galata

Suvla Pt & Bay

Ungerdere

Anafarta

Yalova

Sari Bair

Anzac

Gaba Tepe

Maidos

Kilid Bahr

Achi Baba

Krithia

C.Tekeh

Sedd-ul Bahr

Kum Kale

Yeni Shehr

Yeni Keui

Beshik B.

Tenedos

Pt Kum

Tenedos

Burgus

Ezine

Havaras

Karayusuf

ADRIANOPLE

Akhorkeui

Havsa

Urlu

Kuleli Burgas

Uzun Keupri

Chepkeui

Kara Bunar

Kozkeui

Taila Dagh

Beyendik

Bulgarkeui

Keshan

Yabuldak

Mauria

Grabunar

Kizkaban

Maharis

Ibrije

Xeros Is.

Pt Bakla

Bulair

Karayusuf

Kukiler

Yenije

Kavakli

Osmanjik

Baba Eski

Pavlo

Lahana

Ergene

Hairobolu

Chene

Khaskeui

Meriap

Yurgach

Tash Umuj

Himetkeui

Karajageul

Malgara

Ereke

Gasutova

Mahmudkeui

Kuru Dagh

Khoja-cheshme

Bairamich

Ursha

Kavak

Hexamili

C.Inje

Arapli

Heraklitsa

Merefte

Sharkeui

Kamaraes

Aksaz

C.Kara

Deirmenjik

C.Boz

Gureje

Chardak

Lapsaki

Tokatkyr

Doghanji Keui

Kirjalar

Bergaz Chai

Bergaz

Ahmedlar

Bigha

Shab Dagh 3009

Nagara

Chanak

Dardanus

Erenkeui

Terziler

Karajalar

Kumkeui

Ruins of Troy

Ishiklar

Biyuk Tepekeui

Bairamich

Mendere

Bunarbashi

Kazdagh Karakeui

Karabei

Kirk ◆ **Kilissa**

Kukiler

Yenije

TURK

Havsa D.

Maritza

Ergene

Ana Su

Ortajakeui

Ferada

Ainarjik

Tekfur Dagh

Naibkeui

Kastambul

Emerli

Yurtuk

Hora

C.Kara

Karabr Pt E

Dimetok

ABDAL DAGH

223↑

Inova

Chan Bazarkeui

Karakeui

(A)

(A) 26°   20   (B) 40   60 27°   80

✈ Railways.
✦ Fortresses and Forts.

—— Roads.
3312 Altitudes in Feet.

0-250 ft. dark green; 250-500 ft. light green; 500-750
750-1000 ft. buff; 1000-2000 ft. brown; over 2000 ft.

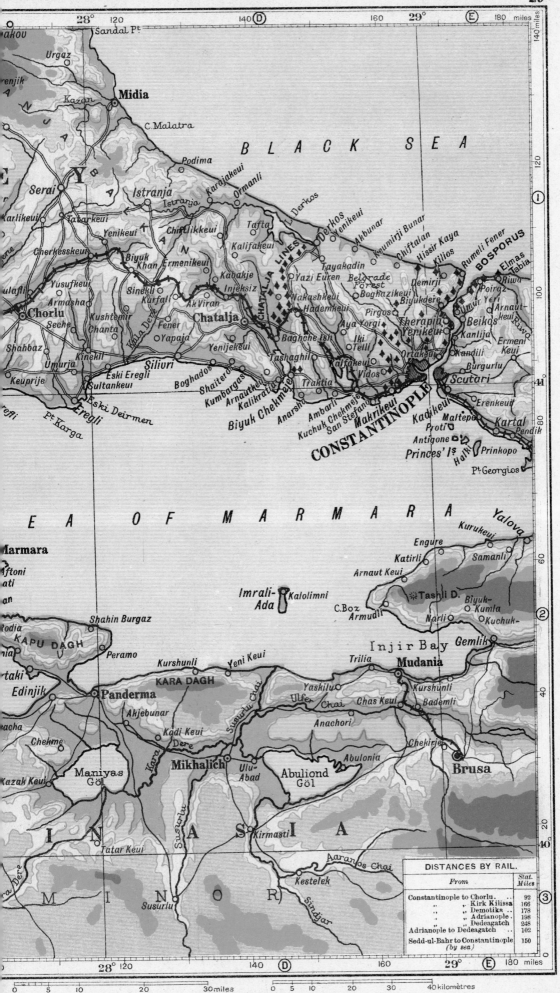

DISTANCES BY RAIL.	
From	Stat. Miles
Constantinople to Chorlu	92
,, ,, Kirk Kilissa	166
,, ,, Demotika	178
,, ,, Adrianople	198
,, ,, Dedeagatch	248
Adrianople to Dedeagatch	102
Sedd-ul-Bahr to Constantinople (by sea)	150

THE BALKAN PENINSULA SHOWING THE INTERNATIONAL BOUNDARIES.

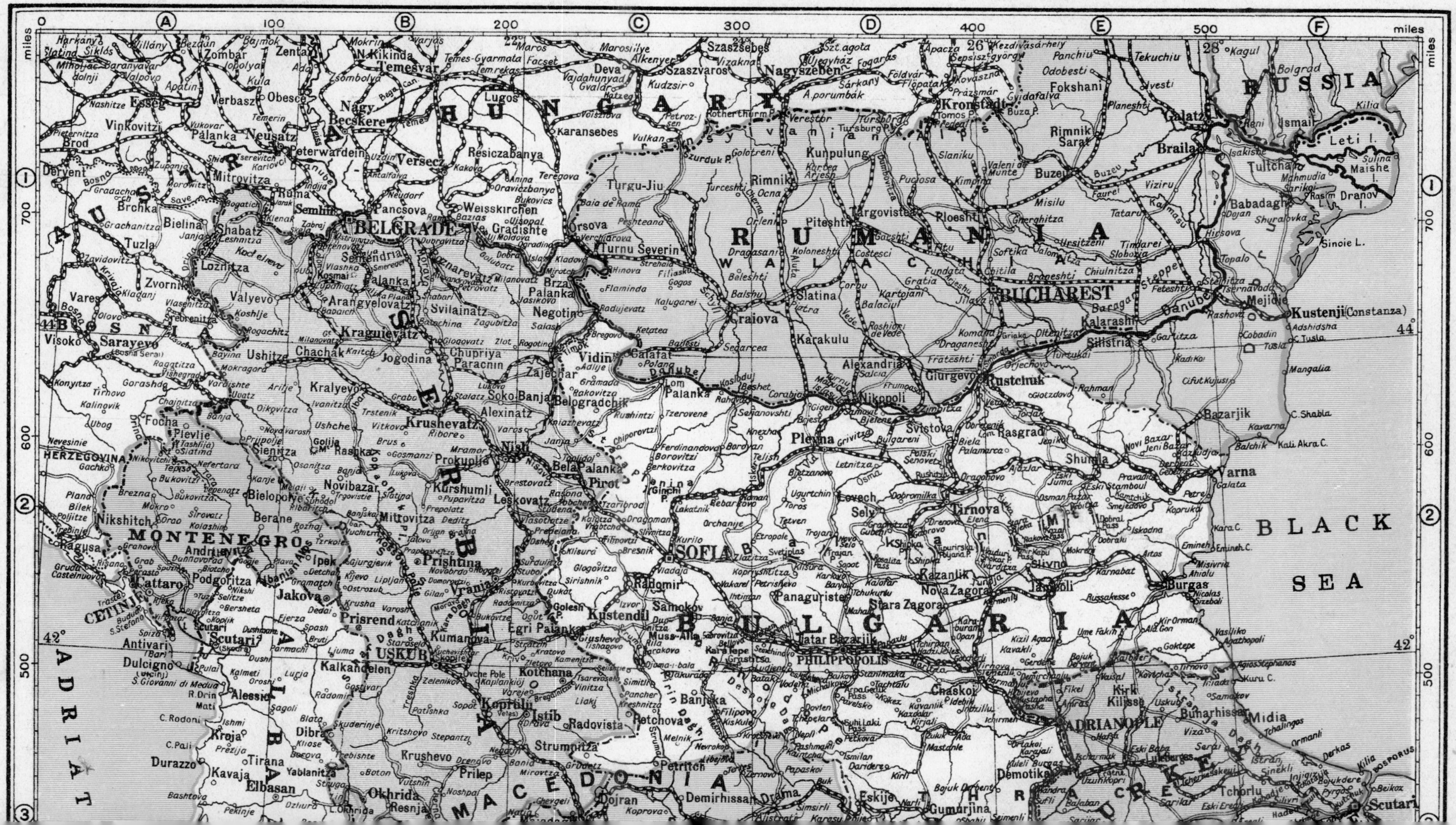

RUSSIA

RUMANIA

WALLACHIA

TRANSYLVANIA

HUNGARY

BULGARIA

SERVIA

BOSNIA

HERZEGOVINA

MONTENEGRO

ALBANIA

MACEDONIA

THRACE

BLACK SEA

ADRIAT

BUCHAREST

BELGRADE

SOFIA

USKUB

PRISHTINA

PHILIPPOPOLIS

ADRIANOPLE

BURGAS

CETINJE

Scutari

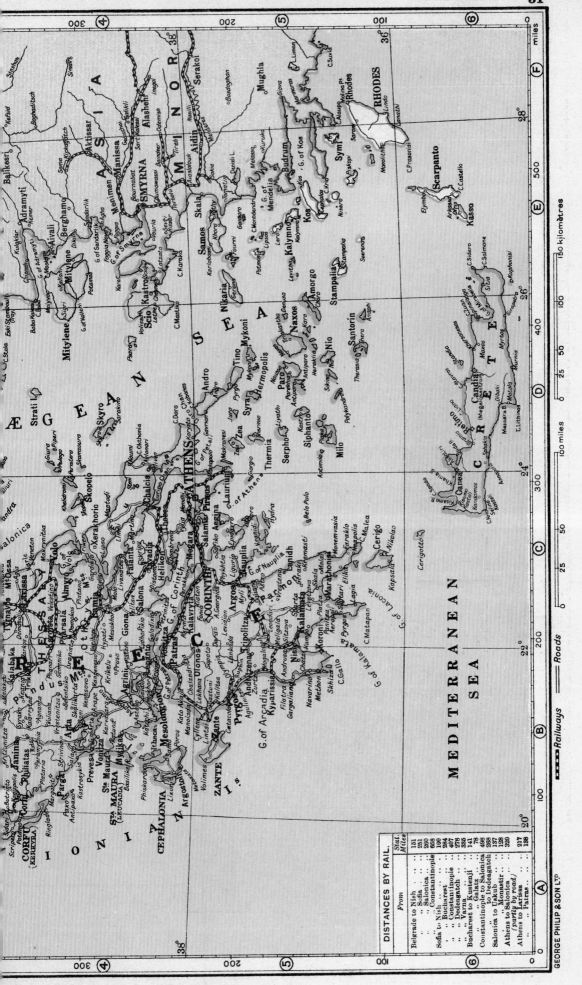

31

Railways ▪▪▪▪ Roads ═══

Railways. —— Roads.
Fortresses and Forts.

0-500 ft. dark green; 500-1000 ft. light green; 1000-2000 ft. yellow; 2000-4000 ft. buff; 4000-6000 ft. brown; over 6000 ft. olive.
The map is divided into 50 mile squares

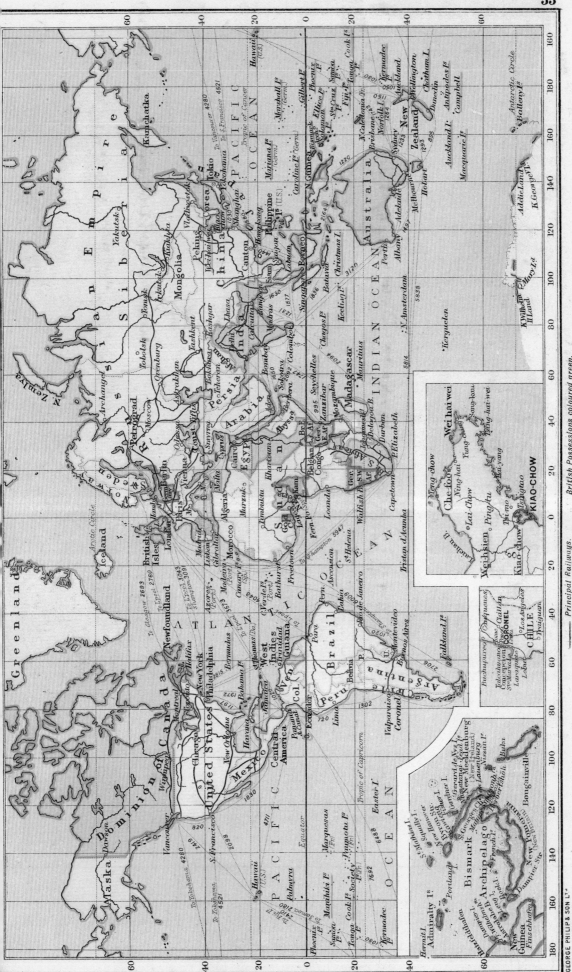

Principal Railways.
Steamer Routes
(Distances in Nautical Miles).

British Possessions coloured green.
German Possessions coloured brown.

THE NORTH SEA AND BALTIC

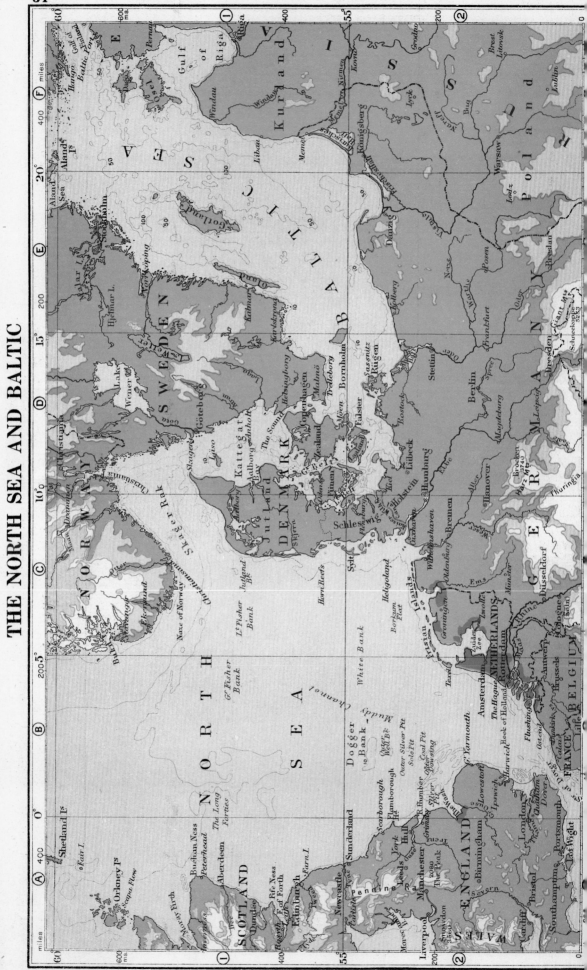

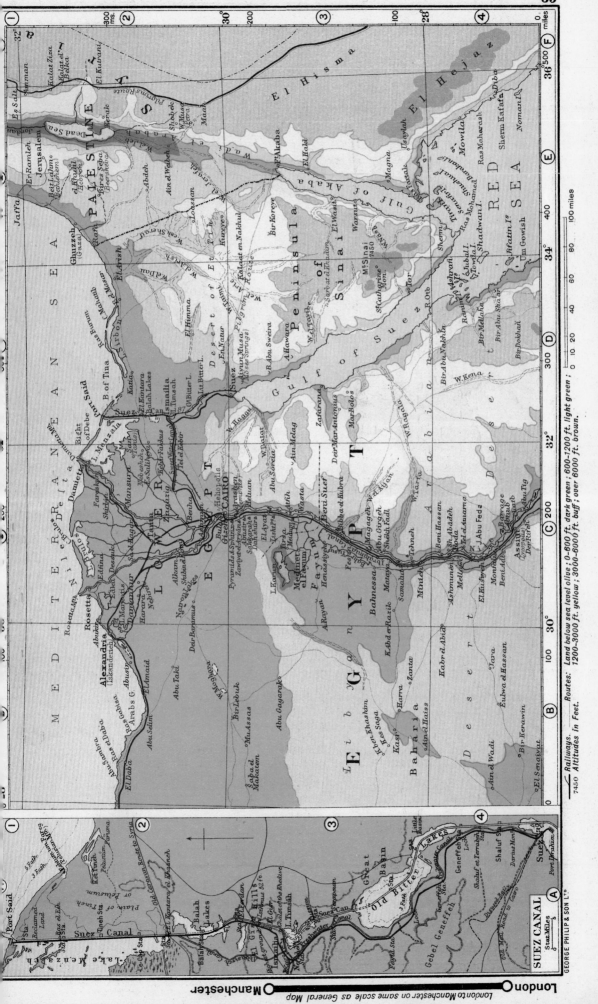

SUEZ CANAL.

Stat. Miles.

GEORGE PHILIP & SON Lᵗᵈ

London to Manchester on same scale as General Map.

○London   ○Manchester

Railways.   Routes: Land below sea level olive; 0–600 ft. dark green; 600–1200 ft. light green;
7450 Altitudes in Feet.   1200–3000 ft. yellow; 3000–6000 ft. buff; over 6000 ft. brown.

0   10   20   40   60   80   100 miles

MEDITERRANEAN SEA

LOWER   EGYPT

L i b y a n   Desert

U p p e r   G Y P T

PALESTINE

Jerusalem

Dead Sea

Peninsula of Sinai

Gulf of Akaba

A r a b i a n   Desert

RED SEA

Gulf of Suez

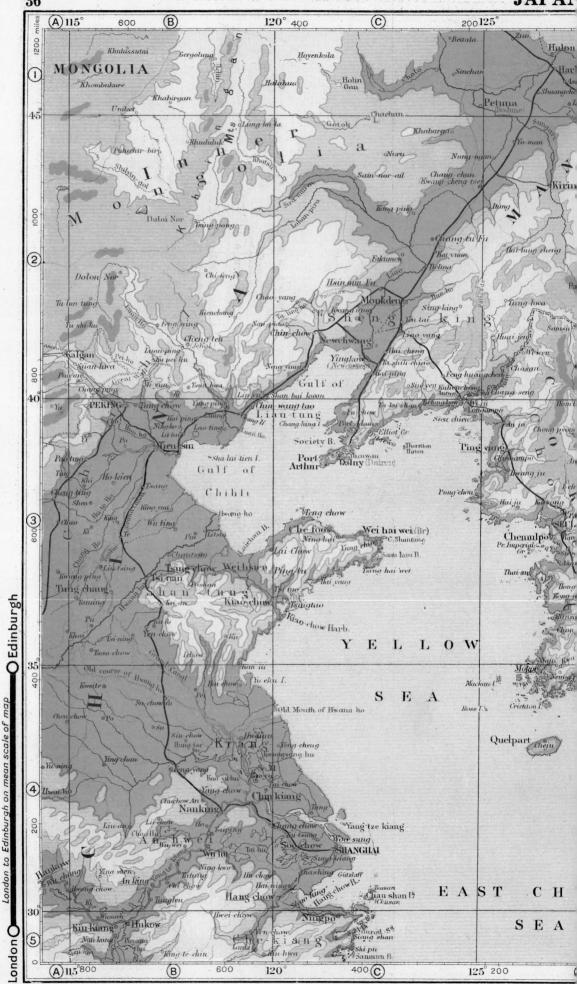

Railways.

0-600 ft. dark green; 600-1200 ft. light green; 1200-3000 ft. yellow;
3000-6000 ft. buff; 6000-9000 ft. brown; over 9000 ft. olive.

London to Edinburgh on mean scale of map

London ○ ○ Edinburgh

Totomosiri I.

Sakhalin

C. Notoro

La Perouse Strait

C. Nosshup

C. Soya

Rebunshiri I.

Wakanai

Rishiri I.

Teshiwo

**HOKKAIDO
(YEZO)**

Yagashi

Shibetsu

Kunidoe

Mashike

Asahigawa

Hitsushumbetsu

Ishikari R.

C. Novoshzov
(Kamoi Saki)

Otaru

Sapporo

Porohoi

Yubari

Sutsu

Iwanai

Tomakomai

Z

Okushiri

Volcano
Bay

Muroran

Endermoshor

Urakawa

Esashi

Mori

Hakodate

Yesan S.

Siwokubi
Str.

Shiriyo
Saki

Tanabu

Fukuyama

Tsugaru

Bikuni

Kogen

C. Shirakami

Taura

Ominato

Abmori

Shirinebi

Same

Hirosaki

Hachinohe

Fukaura

Odate

Shimoda

Noda

Yoshiro
Nuido Saki

Hanawa

Funakawa
Tsuchizaki

Uhita

Miraishi

Miyako

Namaita

Obonai

Yokote

Ishi

Sakata

Kisawa

Tsuruhoka

Tsuchiyo
Ishinomaki

Murokawa

Sendai

Ognohama
Kadzu

Sado

Mito

Shiogama

Aikawa

Yamagata

Niigata

Shibata

Yonezawa

Nakamura

Wajima

Sudzu Saki

Fukushima

Kashiwazaki

Nagaoka

Shirakawa

Nanao

Iwaeki

Takata

Niida

Nara

Fushiki
Takaoka

Nagano

Ashio

Otsunomi

Mito

Kanazawa

Toyama

Maebashi

Tochigi

Ishioka

Matsumoto

Takasaki

Kawagoye

Rawagoye

Inohoga

Takayama

Fukui

Gifu

TOKIO

Chiba

Kyoga Misaki

Wakasa
B.

Kurina

YOKOHAMA

Tsu

Yokoska

Matsue

Tottori

Miyadzu

Ohma

Byoa

Nagoya

Naako

Tateyama

Saigo

Kyoga Misaki

KIOTO

Shimidzu

Shizuoka

Oshima

Oki I.

Dogo I.

Dozen

OSAKA

Okato

Hamamatsu

Mishima

Matsue

Sakai

Atsugi

Shimoda

Hiroshima

Itozuki

Nozuki

Wakayama

Hino Misaki

Shingu

Nii Sh.

Kochi

Miyake Sh.

Matsuyama

Seven Isles
of Izu

Muroto Saki

Oshima
Suwo Misaki

Hachijo Sh.

Kiushiu

Kumamoto

Isa Saki

Awoga Shima

P A C I F I C

Miyazaki

Oki

Tori Saki

Volcano I.

San Francisco I.

Tanega Shima

O C E A N

St Peters
Fort Sh.

Shichi-to I.
(Linschoten I.)

Lots Wife

S E A   O F

J A P A N

Matsu Shima

Liancourt I.

STRAIT

PACIFIC OCEAN

Treaty Ports are underlined.

Mean Scale

0   50   100   200   300 miles

TURKEY IN ASIA, PERSIA & THE CAUCASUS

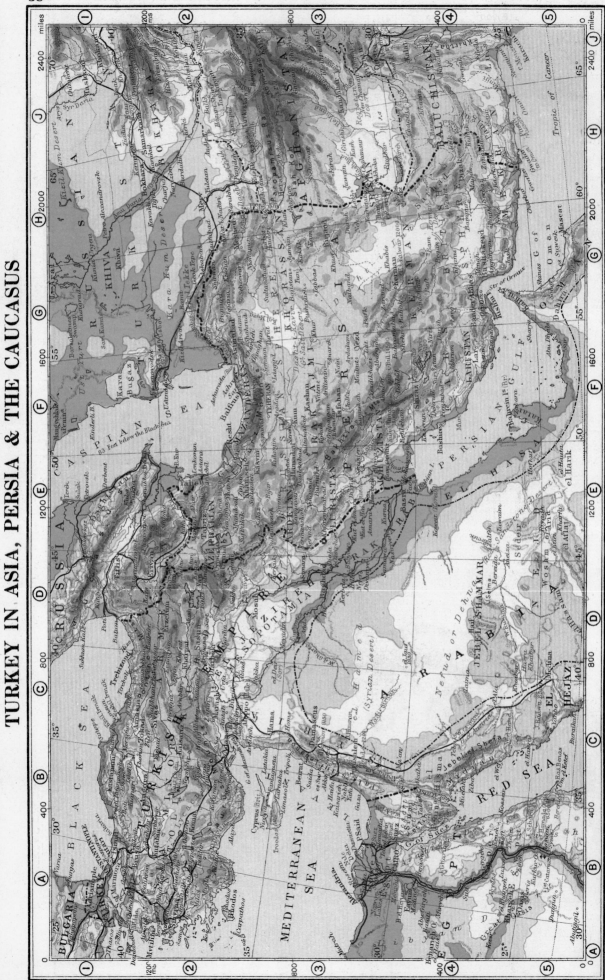

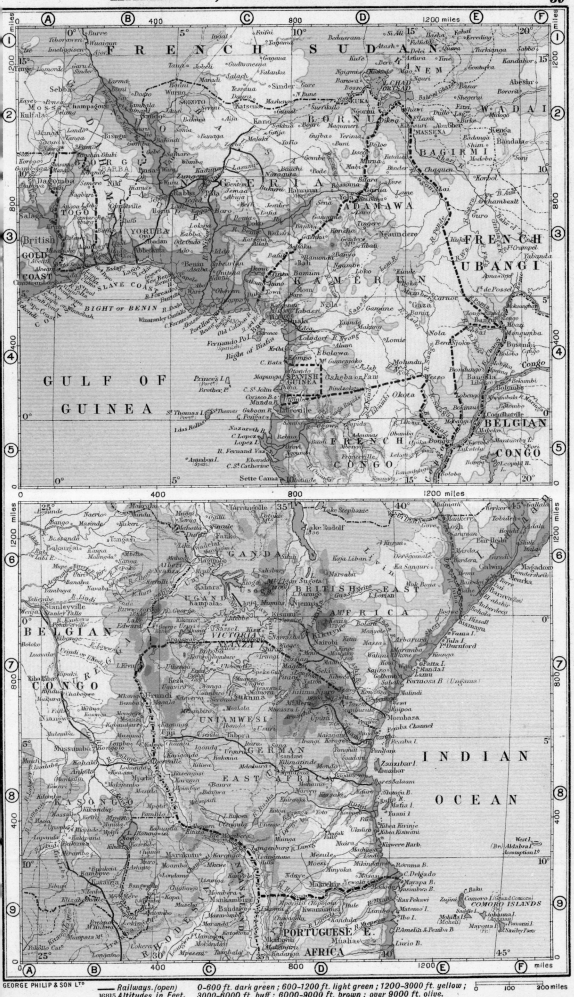

—— Railways. (open)   0-600 ft. dark green ; 600-1200 ft. light green ; 1200-3000 ft. yellow ;
16815 Altitudes in Feet.   3000-6000 ft. buff ; 6000-9000 ft. brown ; over 9000 ft. olive.

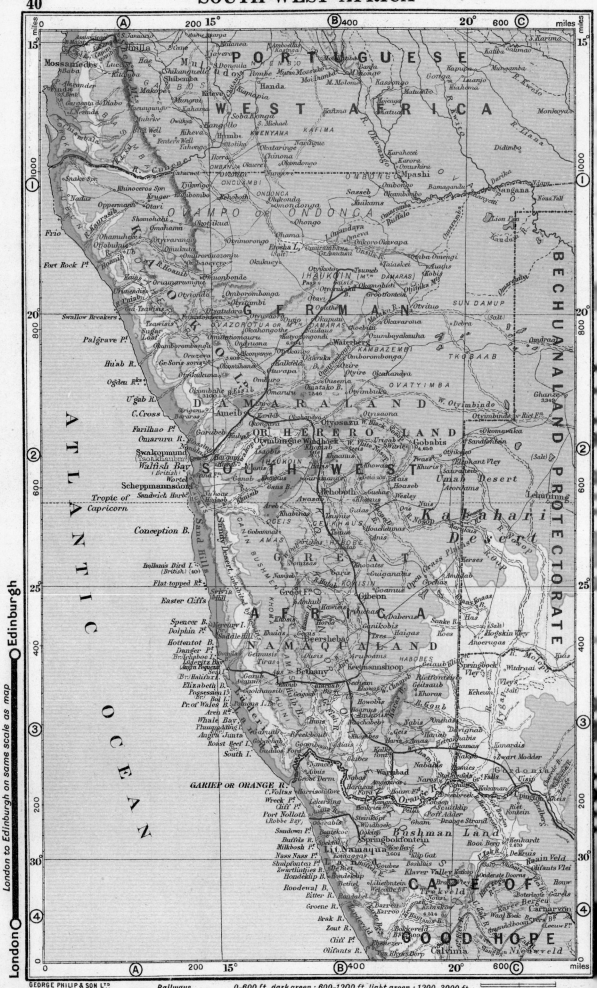

—— Railways.
3312 Altitudes in Feet.

0-600 ft. dark green; 600-1200 ft. light green; 1200-3000 ft.
yellow; 3000-6000 ft. buff; over 6000 ft. brown.

London to Edinburgh on same scale as map

○ Edinburgh

London ○

STATISTICS RELATING TO BELLIGERENT COUNTRIES

LIST OF PLACE NAMES

STATISTICS RELATING TO BELLIGERENT COUNTRIES.

THE BRITISH EMPIRE.

AREA AND POPULATION, DECEMBER 13, 1913 (ESTIMATED).

	Area. Square miles.	Population. Males.	Population. Females.	Population. Total.	Population per square mile.
United Kingdom (including Isle of Man and Channel Islands)	121,432	22,016,661	23,353,869	45,370,530	373·5
India	1,802,112	161,294,820	153,791,552	315,086,372	174·8
Self-governing Dominions—					
Australia (Commonwealth)	2,974,581	2,313,035	2,141,970	4,455,005	1·5
New Zealand (Dominion)..	104,751	531,910	476,558	1,008,468	9·6
Canada (Dominion)	3,729,665	3,821,067	3,383,771	7,204,838	1·9
Newfoundland	42,734	122,578	116,092	238,670	5·6
South Africa (Union)	473,184	3,069,392	2,904,002	5,973,394	12·6
Colonies, Protectorates, etc.—					
Basutoland..	11,716	184,102	220,405	404,507	34·6
Bechuanaland (Protectorate) ..	275,000	62,712	62,638	125,350	0·5
Rhodesia (S. and N.)	439,575	—	—	1,593,559	3·6
Uganda (Protectorate)	121,437	—	—	2,843,325	23·4
East Africa (Protectorate) ..	247,600	—	—	2,402,863	9·7
Ceylon	25,481	2,175,030	1,931,320	4,106,350	161·2
Northern Nigeria (Protectorate).. ..	256,200	3,435,743	5,833,257	9,269,000	36·2
Southern Nigeria (Protectorate).. ..	79,880	—	—	7,857,983	98·4
Gold Coast	80,235	755,446	746,347	1,501,793	18·7
Sierra Leone	24,908	363,197	472,374	1,403,132	56·3
West India Islands	12,227	789,253	890,356	1,688,609	138·1
Other Colonies, etc. ..	450,282	—	—	4,734,252	
Total British Empire	11,273,000	—	—	417,268,000	37·0

NOTE.—The figures of population are based on those obtained by the Census of 1911 (April 1), and as estimated for December 31, 1913. After the declaration of war on Turkey, November 5, 1914, Egypt and the Sudan were annexed to the British Empire. Their areas are estimated at 363,181 square miles and about 985,000 square miles respectively, with populations of 11,300,000 and 3,000,000, but these figures are only approximate. At the middle of 1914 the population of the United Kingdom was estimated at 46,089,249.

THE UNITED KINGDOM.

REVENUE.

The revenue for 1913–14, the last year undisturbed by the War, was £198,242,897 ; that for 1914–15, which included the produce of fresh taxation necessitated by the War and not in the original Budget for the financial year, was £226,694,080. The expenditure for 1913-14 was £197,492,969 ; that for 1914-15 was £560,473,533. By far the greater part of the war expenditure in these years was met by the issue of loans. On March 31, 1914, the nominal amount of the Funded Debt was £586,717,872. It was £583,290,097 on March 31, 1915, but the unfunded debt on that date amounted to £497,486,258.

COMMERCE.

	1915.	1914.	1913.
	£	£	£
Imports (total) ..	853,756,279	696,635,113	768,734,739
Exports (British) ..	384,647,336	430,721,357	525,245,289
Re-exports	98,797,123	95,474,166	109,575,037

Imports.—The United Kingdom's imports consist mainly of food and raw materials ; in normal years from 20 to 25 per cent. of the total is made up of articles wholly or mainly manufactured. Wheat and other cereals, meat, butter, sugar, fruit, and tea are usually the largest items among foods ; and cotton, wool and other textiles, timber, rubber, metallic ores and hides are the principal raw materials landed. In 1913 the imports were thus composed :

	£
Food, drink, and tobacco	290,202,323
Raw materials and articles mainly un-manufactured	281,822,444
Articles wholly or mainly manufactured..	193,602,375
Miscellaneous	3,107,597
	£768,734,739

Exports.—The exports (British) of the United Kingdom consist principally of articles wholly or mainly manufactured, of which the biggest items are cotton yarns and fabrics, iron and steel goods, woollens and worsteds, machinery and chemicals, drugs, etc. Of the raw materials shipped the greater part is coal, coke and manufactured fuel. In 1913 the exports of the four classes were as follows :

	£
Food, drink and tobacco	32,587,942
Raw materials and articles mainly un-manufactured	69,904,992
Articles wholly or mainly manufactured..	411,368,358
Miscellaneous	11,383,997
Total	£525,245,289

There is always a large excess of imports over exports which represents (a) sums due to the United Kingdom for freights earned by shipowners, and (b) interest on British investments abroad.

MERCANTILE MARINE OF THE EMPIRE.

The net tonnage of the sailing and steam vessels on the Register in the United Kingdom and the principal parts of the Empire at the end of 1913 was as follows :

	Net Tons.
United Kingdom..	12,119,891
India	107,774
Australia	436,054
New Zealand	159,310
Canada	897,062
Newfoundland	152,715
Straits Settlements	86,416
Hong Kong	62,017
West India Islands	71,282

Including the tonnages of the other parts of the Empire the total for the whole was 14,168,274 tons. Of this total 12,403,231 tons consisted of steamers.

FRANCE.
AREA AND POPULATION.

—	Area. Sq. miles.	Population Number.	Per sq. mile.
France	207,075	39,601,509	191·2
Algeria	222,067	5,563,828	25·0
Other Colonies in Africa	3,962,234	20,918,915	5·3
Colonies in Asia ..	310,176	14,773,000	47·6
„ „ America	35,222	450,900	12·8
„ „ Oceana	8,744	81,100	9·3
Total Colonies ..	4,538,443	41,787,743	9·2
Total France and Colonies	4,745,518	81,389,252	17·1

The largest cities in France were, according to the census of 1911, Paris (2,888,000), Marseilles (551,000), and Lyons (524,000).

The principal rivers of France are the Seine, Loire, Saone and Rhone.

COMMERCE.

	1913. £	1912. £
Imports (special) ..	335,744,000	329,232,000
Exports (special) ..	275,172,000	268,504,000
Debt	1,255,938,000	1,246,480,000

The articles most largely imported into France before the war were wool, cereals, coal and coke, cotton, machinery, raw silk, hides, wine, coffee, copper and rubber. The principal exports were silk and cotton textiles, skins and furs, raw wool, automobiles, woollen textiles, wine.

France exports most largely to the United Kingdom, and she imports from it to a fair extent. Arrivals from Germany and the United States formed the next largest proportions of the total value of her imports before the War, and from Belgium and Russia she also received a considerable volume of goods. In the export list Belgium stood second to the United Kingdom before the War, Germany coming third; the United States, Switzerland and Italy were fairly good customers.

MEANS OF COMMUNICATION.

In 1913 the mercantile marine of France amounted to 2,201,164 tons, of which 1,793,310 tons were steamers.

The length of railway open in 1913 was 31,391 miles.

RUSSIA.
AREA AND POPULATION.

—	Area. Sq. miles.	Population Number.	Per sq. mile.
Russia in Europe ..	1,867,737	125,683,800	64·6
Poland .. .	43,804	11,960,500	254·5
Finland	125,689	3,196,700	24·6
Caucasus	181,173	12,512,800	66·4
Siberia	4,831,882	9,788,400	1·8
Central Asia ..	1,366,832	10,957,400	7·5
	8,417,117	174,099,600	20·7

The above figures are estimates for 1913. They do not include an area of about 317,468 square miles consisting of inland lakes.

The largest cities in Russia are Petrograd (2,018,596 inhabitants), known as St. Petersburg until September 1, 1914, and Moscow (1,173,427 inhabitants). Other large towns are Warsaw (756,426), Riga (500,000) and Odessa (449,673).

The revenue of Russia for 1913 was £362,704,500, and her expenditure, £357,601,800. The debt amounted on January 1/14, 1914, to £931,600,000.

Russian money is expressed in roubles; before the War the sterling exchange rate was usually expressed as 9.458r.—£1, making the rouble worth about 2s. 1d.

COMMERCE.

	1913. £	1912. £
Imports	129,014,000	123,687,000
Exports	150,196,000	160,318,000

Russia is a very large producer of food and raw materials, especially wheat, rye, barley, butter and eggs, and raw flax and timber. Germany is the largest customer for Russian produce, and from Germany more than half Russia's imports came in most years before the War. The United Kingdom's share of business with Russia has been much less than that of Germany, but was much larger than that of any other country.

MEANS OF COMMUNICATION.

Russia is still poorly supplied with means of communication considering its enormous size. The railway mileage open at the end of 1912 was 48,902 miles. Various new lines were under construction when the War broke out. There is a considerable internal lake, river and canal traffic. The ocean-going mercantile fleet consisted in 1913 of 1,216 vessels, of 974,178 tons, of which 716 vessels, of 790,075 tons, were steamers.

ITALY.

Area, 110,632 square miles. Population (1911), 35,597,784, or 321·8 per square mile.

Principal cities, with their populations: Rome, 579,285; Naples, 723,208; Milan, 599,200; Turin, 427,733; Palermo, 341,656; Genoa, 272,077; Florence, 232,860.

ITALIAN OVERSEA POSSESSIONS.

—	Area. Sq. miles.	Population Number.	Per sq. mile
Eritrea	45,800	450,000	9·8
Tripoli & Cyrenaica	400 000	528,000	1·3
Italian Somaliland..	139,000	400,000	2·8
Tientsin Concession	18	17,000	944·4
Total ..	584,818	1,395,000	2·3

Revenue (year ending June 30) 1913–14, £113,741,000; expenditure, £114,528,000.

COMMERCE, 1913.

	1913. £	1912. £
Imports (special)	145,511,000	148,077,000
Exports (special)	100,157,000	95,877,000

Italy's largest imports are wheat, coal and coke, cotton, timber, hides and machinery. She exports chiefly raw and thrown silk (undyed), cotton manufactures, dried fruits, silk manufactures and wine. Before the War her imports came chiefly from Germany, the United Kingdom, the United States, France, Austria-Hungary and Russia. She exports most largely to Germany, the United Kingdom and the United States, but to a much smaller extent than she receives goods from those countries. Exports to Switzerland, from which she takes little, are fairly large. She sends to Austria-Hungary rather less than she buys from the Dual Monarchy, as a rule. There is a considerable trade with Argentina in both directions.

MERCANTILE MARINE.

The merchant vessels on the register amounted in 1913 to 1,521,942 tons, of which 1,274,127 tons were steamers.

The length of railway open in 1913 was 11,165 miles.

BELGIUM.

AREA AND POPULATION.

Area, 11,373 square miles; population (1910), 7,423,784, or 652 per square mile.

The Belgian Congo has an area estimated at about 900,000 square miles, with a population of about 15,000,000. The largest town is Antwerp, with 320,650 inhabitants.

COMMERCE.

	1913. £	1912. £
Imports (special)	183,345,000	198,320,000
Exports (special)	143,073,000	158,029,000

The principal imports are wool, wheat, cotton, raw hides, coal and rubber. The biggest exports are iron and steel, flax and flax yarns. Rubber obtained from the Congo is also an article of importance, as are also to a less extent rolling stock and machinery.

Belgium imports, as a rule, most largely from France; Germany coming second in the list of countries of origin, and the United Kingdom third, in 1913. A fair amount comes from Holland, which is also a good customer for Belgian goods. The arrivals from Argentina were fairly large before the War.

The Belgian mercantile marine was 181,637 tons in 1912.

There were about 2,917 miles of railway open in 1912.

SERBIA.

Area, 18,650 square miles. Population, 2,911,701, or 144 per square mile. Capital, Belgrade (90,000 inhabitants).

The revenue in 1913 was £5,230,600, which equalled the expenditure for the year.

The imports were £4,244,000, and the exports £4,676,000 in 1912. The chief articles of importation are cotton yarns and goods, iron and steel, machinery, hides (raw) and leather. The chief exports are wheat, meat and maize. Formerly there was a large export of swine, but this had shrunk to small dimensions some years before the War, owing to the difficulties put in the way of the Serbian merchants by the Austro-Hungarian Government.

Serbia's largest trade was with Austria-Hungary and Germany. Imports from the United Kingdom were on a moderate scale.

JAPAN.

AREA AND POPULATION, 1914.

	Area. Sq. miles.	Population Number.	Population Per sq. mile.
Japan	147,650	53,596,894	366·0
Korea	84,103	16,499,806	196·2
Formosa	13,840	3,612,184	260·9
Pescadores	47	—*	—
Japanese Saghalien	13,154	55,476	4·2
Total	258,794	73,764,360	285·0

* No official figures; estimated at about 55,000.

The principal cities are Tokyo (the capital), with a population of 2,033,320; Osaka, 1,424,596; and Kioto, 442,462.

The revenue (ordinary) for the financial year ended March 31, 1914, was £57,542,805, and the expenditure (ordinary), £41,563,580. The extraordinary revenue amounted to £14,654,744, and extraordinary expenditure to £15,799,812.

COMMERCE.

		1914. £	1913. £
Imports		59,573,572	72,943,164
Exports		59,110,146	63,246,021

The principal articles imported into Japan are raw cotton, oil cake, rice, brown sugar, sulphate of ammonia, wool, and soya beans. The chief exports are raw silk, cotton yarn, silk tissues, copper, coal, grey shirtings and sheetings, refined sugar, tea, matches, and twilled tissues.

A large proportion, in some years nearly 50 per cent., of the total imports comes from Asiatic countries, and of this about one-half comes from British India; the next largest amounts are sent from Great Britain, the United States, China, Germany, the Dutch Indies, French Indo-China and Australia.

MEANS OF COMMUNICATION.

At the end of 1914 the tonnage of Japanese merchant shipping was 2,202,517 gross tons, of which 1,593,357 gross tons were steamers.

In 1913–14 the aggregate mileage worked was 7,291 miles, of which 5,473 miles were represented by the State, 1,121 by private lines, and 697 miles by the South Manchuria Railway.

GERMANY.

AREA AND POPULATION.

	Area. Sq. miles.	Population Number.	Population Per sq. mile.
Prussia	134,619	40,165,219	224·0
Bavaria	29,292	6,887,291	234·4
Saxony	5,789	4,806,661	829·5
Würtemberg	7,534	2,437,574	323·2
21 Other States	25,942	8,755,234	337·5
Alsace-Lorraine	5,605	1,874,014	333·5
Total	208,781	64,925,993	310·4

Colonial Possessions :—

	Area. Sq. miles.	Population Estim. 1913.
Togo	33,700	1,032,346
Cameroon	291,950	3,600,591
German S.W. Africa	322,450	94,386
German E. Africa	384,180	7,651,106
Kiauchau	200	168,900
Kaiser Wilhelm's Land	70,000 ⎫	
Bismarck Archipelago	20,000 ⎬	463,300
Soloman Isles	4,200 ⎭	
Caroline, Pelew, Marianne and Marschall Isles	960 ⎱	122,000
Samoan Isles	1,000	35,000
	1,128,640	13,167,629

The chief city of Germany is Berlin, the capital of Prussia, the population of which in 1910 was 2,071,000. Among other large cities and towns are Hamburg (931,000), Munich, capital of Bavaria (596,000), Leipzig, in Saxony (590,000), Dresden, capital of Saxony (548,000), Cologne, in Prussia (517,000), Breslau, Prussia (512,000).

There are three great rivers in Germany, the Rhine, the Elbe, the Oder, and many others of minor importance.

FINANCE OF THE EMPIRE.

		1913–14 £	1912–13 £
Revenue, Ordinary and Extraordinary		184,801,660	141,902,000
Expenditure		184,801,660	141,902,000
Debt		236,037,000	242,743,000

COMMERCE.

		1913. £	1912. £
Imports (general)		560,335,000	568,962,000
Exports (general)		509,965,000	476,140,000

Germany's principal imports before the War were cotton, hides and skins, wool, chemicals, wheat, barley, timber, copper, coffee, iron ore, grease, palm kernels, etc., coal, eggs and bran. The chief exports were iron and steel and manufactures thereof, chemicals, drugs, dyes, etc., machinery, coal, cotton manufactures, grain, flour and meal, hides and skins, leather and silk manufactures.

Germany bought largely from the United States, Russia, the United Kingdom and Austria-Hungary, and exported most to the United Kingdom, Austria-Hungary, Russia, France, the United States and Holland.

MEANS OF TRANSPORTATION.

The mercantile marine consisted in 1913 of 5,082,061 tons, of which 4,743,046 tons were steamers.

There were 1,600 miles of ship canal open. The Kiel Canal is 61 miles in length. The railway mileage was 37,823 miles.

AUSTRIA-HUNGARY.
AREA AND POPULATION.

	Area.	Population	
	Sq. miles.	Number.	Per sq. mile.
Austria	115,802	28,567,898	247·0
Hungary ..	125,609	20,886,487	165·0
Bosnia-Herzegovina	19,768	1,898,379	96·0
Total ..	261,179	51,352,764	196·6

The principal cities of the Dual Monarchy are Vienna (2,031,000), Budapest (880,000).

The most important river is the Danube.

FINANCE.

	1913. £	1912. £
Revenue :		
Austria	144,207,000	132,221,000
Hungary ..	94,339,000	81,453,000
Expenditure :		
Austria	144,196,000	132,682,000
Hungary ..	94,337,000	83,886,000
Debt :		
Austria (1912)		519,631,000
Hungary (1912)		274,702,000

COMMERCE (AUSTRIA-HUNGARY).

	1913. £	1912. £
Imports	141,433,000	148,200,000
Exports	115,129,000	113,911,000

The articles most largely imported before the war by Austria-Hungary were raw cotton, coal and coke, machinery, raw wool, maize, hides and skins and coffee. The chief exports were eggs, coal (chiefly lignite), hides and skins, glasswares, cotton manufactures, malt, and leather manufactures.

Before the War Austria-Hungary usually obtained more than one-third of her imports from Germany, and sent to that country about one half of her exports. Other countries' figures were much smaller. The United States sent a fair amount, but took little ; the arrivals from and shipments to the United Kingdom have been nearly equal of late years. Russia and British India sent fair amounts and bought little. Italy bought more than she sent.

MEANS OF COMMUNICATION.

Austria-Hungary had, in 1913, 1,011,414 tons of merchant shipping, of which 1,010,347 tons were steamers.

The railway mileage of Austria was 14,512 miles, and that of Hungary 13,333 miles.

TURKEY.
AREA AND POPULATION.

	Area.	Population	
	Sq. miles.	Number.	Per sq. mile.
Turkey in Europe ..	10,882	1,891,000	187
Asia Minor ..	199,272	10,186,900	52
Armenia and Kurdistan	71,990	2,470,900	34
Mesopotamia ..	143,250	2,000,000	9
Syria	114,530	3,675,000	33
Arabia	170,300	1,050,000	6
Total ..	710,224	21,273,800	30

The principal cities in European Turkey are Constantinople (1,200,000 inhabitants) and Adrianople (100,000) ; those in Asiatic Turkey are Smyrna (260,000), Bagdad (150,000), Damascus (150,000).

FINANCE.

	1913. £	1912. £
Revenue	28,248,000	28,665,992
Expenditure ..	30,095,000	34,420,000
Debt	151,656,000	—

COMMERCE.

	£
Imports (1912)	39,591,852
Exports (1912)	21,746,662

Turkey imports largely textiles and on a small scale cereals, sugar and metals. Her chief exports are textiles, fruit, tobacco and cereals.

MEANS OF COMMUNICATION.

Turkey's mercantile marine amounted in 1913 to 157,298 tons, of which 111,848 tons were steamers.

The length of railway open was 3,882 miles.

BULGARIA.

Area, 43,305 square miles ; population, 5,500,000 (estimate 1914) ; per square mile, 110.

The capital is Sofia, population (in 1910) 102,812.

FINANCE.

	1913. £
Revenue	5,765,344
Expenditure	4,732,832
Debt	35,145,572

COMMERCE.

	1913. £
Imports	6,850,042
Exports	3,728,185

Bulgaria's chief imports are textiles, machinery, metals, hides, cattle and cereals ; and she exports wheat, attar of roses, maize and hides, skins, etc.

More than half her imports came from Austria-Hungary and Germany in 1913, and her chief customers were Germany, Belgium and Austria-Hungary.

The length of railway open in 1913 was 1,384 miles.

Name	Page	Square
Capo d'Istria	27	D 4
Caporetto (Karfreit)	27	D 3
Cappy	4	B 1
Caprino	26	A 4
Caprycke	3	D 2
Cardiff	34	A 2
Carency	2	C 4
Carignan	5	F 2
Carinthia	27	D 3
Carlepont	4	B 2
Carlisle	34	A 2
Carlsruhe	9	F 4
Carmeville	10	A 1
Carnic Alps	26	C 3
Carnières	3	D 5
Carniola	27	E 4
Carnizza	27	D 5
Carnot	39	E 4
Carnotville	39	B 3
Carpathian Mts.	24	A 3
Cartigny	4	B 1
Carvin	2	C 4
Caska	32	C 6
Caspian Sea	38	E 1
Cassandra	31	C 3
Cassandra, G. of	31	C 3
Cassandra Pen.	31	C 4
Cassel	2	B 3
Casteau	3	E 4
Castelfranca	26	B 4
Castelnuovo	27	D 4
Castelnuovo	30	A 2
Castello C.	31	E 6
Castello Tesina	26	B 3
Castemaschio	27	E 5
Castillon	3	D 5
Castua	27	D 5
Catacolo	31	B 5
Catenoy	4	A 3
Cattaro	30	A 2
Cattenhafen	8	B 3
Caucasus	38	D 1
Cavalese	26	B 3
Cawdry	3	D 5
Cebroff	24	C 2
Cedigolo	26	A 3
Ceintrey	10	B 2
Celle R.	4	A 1
Celles	3	D 3
Celles	6	B 4
Celles	11	D 2
Cepcevichy	23	D 2
Cephalonia I.	31	A 4
Cepha os	31	E 5
Certontaine	3	F 5
Cerigo I.	31	C 5
Cerigotto I.	31	C 6
Cerra R.	32	D 2
Cernay	5	D 3
Cernay	5	E 3
Cerneci	32	D 2
Cerny	4	C 2
Cerovitza	32	C 4
Cervignano	27	D 4
Cesves	6	B 4
Cetatea	32	D 3
Cetinje	30	A 2
Chabar	27	E 4
Chaber	32	B 5
Chabishki	15	D 5
Chachaj	32	A 7
Chachak	32	B 3
Chacrise	4	C 3
Chad (or Tsad), L.	39	D 2
Chaalsey		
Chaillon	8	A 4
Chalandritza	31	B 4
Chalcidice	30	C 3
Chalcis	31	C 4
Chaldshilar	32	C 8
Chalet of the Khedive	35	A 3
Chalin	16	C 5
Challerange	5	E 3
Chalons	5	D 4
Chalons-sur-Marne	5	D 4
Cham R., West	40	B 3
Chambezi R.	39	C 9
Chambi	39	C 8
Chambley	8	B 4
Chambry	4	C 2
Chamob R., West	40	B 3
Champagne	10	C 2
Champagney	10	C 4
Champenoux	10	C 1
Champigneulles	10	B 1
Champillon	5	D 3
Champlin	5	D 1
Chamsk	18	C 5
Chan Bazarkeui	28	C 2
Chan Chai R.	28	C 2

Name	Page	Square
Chanak	28	B 2
Changis	4	B 4
Chanishte	32	C 7
Chapon	6	B 3
Char	32	B 5
Charay Ostroff	25	D 2
Charbar	38	H 4
Chardak	28	B 2
Chardeh	38	F 2
Charevo	32	D 6
Charency	5	F 2
Charkoff	16	B 5
Charlerois	3	F 4
Charleville	5	E 2
Charlotten	12	B 3
Charny	4	B 4
Charmes	4	C 2
Charmes	10	B 2
Charna	21	E 4
Charna R.	21	D 3
Charna R.	21	E 3
Charny	5	F 3
Charny Cheremosh R.	24	C 4
Charnydunayets	20	C 5
Chartouysk	23	C 2
Charukoff	22	C 3
Chas Keui	29	D 2
Chashcha	13	E 2
Chaskoi	30	D 3
Chatai Kepe	28	B 2
Chatalia	29	D 2
Château Porcion	5	D 2
Château Regnault	5	E 1
Château Salins	10	C 1
Château Thierry	4	C 4
Châtelet	3	F 4
Châtel-sur-Moselle	10	C 2
Châtenois	10	B 2
Chatham	34	B 2
Chatievichy	19	D 2
Châtillon	5	D 2
Chatillon-sur-Marne	4	C 3
Chatojov	22	B 4
Chatynichy	19	D 4
Chaudun	4	B 3
Chaulnes	4	B 1
Chaumont-Porcien	5	D 2
Chamny	4	B 2
Chaushkoi	32	C 6
Chautsun	36	B 3
Chauvency	5	F 2
Chaux	11	D 4
Chavigny	4	B 2
Chavonne	4	C 3
Chazin	27	F 5
Chchoff	21	D 5
Chechina	32	C 4
Che-foo	36	C 3
Chehatina R.	32	A 4
Chehéry	5	E 2
Cheikishki	14	C 5
Chekovitse	13	E 2
Chelebi	28	B 2
Chelles	4	B 3
Chémery	5	E 2
Cheniely	18	C 4
Chenierniki	22	A 2
Chemulpo	36	D 3
Chenaia R.	13	D 4
Chene	28	C 1
Chenichmit		
Chenstochova	20	C 3
Chepkeui	28	B 1
Cheratte	6	C 3
Cherecha R.	13	E 5
Cheremna	13	F 3
Cheres	15	F 4
Cherkesskeni	29	C 1
Chermen	28	B 1
Cheremeza	18	A 5
Chernembl	27	E 4
Cherna R.	30	D 1
Cherna R.	32	C 7
Cherniacfoff	23	F 3
Chernievichki	16	C 5
Chernik	32	D 6
Chernin	19	F 4
Chernitsa	19	E 2
Chernoie I.	13	E 4
Cherovene	32	E 4
Cheiravchytse	18	B 5
Cherskoi	13	D 5
Cherso	27	E 5
Cherso I.	27	E 5
Chertoriya	23	C 3
Chervin	17	E 4
Chéry	4	C 3
Chéry les Pouilly	4	C 2
Cheshevichy	19	E 4
Chesmeh	31	E 4

Name	Page	Square
Chesmes	3	E 4
Chesniki	22	A 3
Chestin	32	B 3
Chestobroditza	32	A 3
Chetsiny	21	D 3
Chézy	4	C 4
Chézy en-Orxois	4	B 3
Chiese R.	26	A 3
Chievres	3	E 3
Chifta an.	29	D 2
Chiftlikeui	28	B 2
Ch.ftikkeui	29	D 2
Chilindrin	32	D 7
Chimay	3	F 5
China	36	B 4
Chin-Kiang	36	A 4
Chinkovtze	25	D 3
Chinoff	20	C 2
Chin wang-tao	36	B 3
Chiny	5	F 2
Chioggia	26	C 5
Chioppo	39	C 4
Chipneh	31	E 4
Chiporovtzi	32	D 4
Chirchen Boden	27	D 4
Chirkvenitza	27	E 5
Chishi	18	A 4
Chislengien	3	E 3
Chitila	30	E 1
Chiulnitza	30	E 1
Chiusaforte	27	D 3
Chivres	4	C 2
Chmielnik	23	E 4
Chmielnik	25	F 2
Choch	20	B 2
Chocholoff	20	C 5
Chodech	16	C 5
Chodel	21	E 3
Chodel R.	21	E 3
Chodoroff	24	B 2
Choisy	4	B 2
Cholchlo	19	D 2
Cholm	22	A 3
Choma	23	C 1
Chongara	29	C 1
Chorlu	29	C 1
Chorlu R.	29	C 1
Chorna-Lora Mts.	24	C 4
Choro	31	D 5
Chorostkoff	25	D 2
Chorzelle	17	D 4
Chouilly	5	D 4
Chotin	25	D 3
Chotynitse	13	D 2
Christiania	34	D 1
Christiania Fiord	34	D 1
Christiansand	34	C 1
Chrosczütz	20	B 3
Chrupishta	32	C 8
Chrzanoff	20	C 4
Chudets	21	E 4
Chudla	23	D 2
Chudyn	19	D 4
Chugali Falls	39	D 8
Chukas	32	A 7
Chumowassi	31	E 4
Chumsk	23	D 4
Chuprenja	32	D 4
Chupril	32	B 5
Chupriva	32	C 3
Churkli	32	C 8
Chvridany	14	A 1
Chyzeff	17	E 4
Ciechocinek	16	B 4
Ciergnon	6	B 4
Cilicia	38	B 2
Cilli	27	F 3
Ciney	6	B 4
Cirés-le-Mello	4	A 3
Cirey	11	D 2
Ciry	4	C 3
Cittadella	26	B 4
Cittanuova	27	D 5
Ciuperceni	32	D 3
Cividale	27	D 4
Clary	3	D 5
Clavier	6	B 4
Clert	8	B 2
Clerf R.	8	B 2
Clémency	8	B 3
Clemery	8	B 5
Clermont	4	A 3
Clermont	5	D 2
Clermont	6	B 3
Clermont en-Argonne	5	F 3
Clerken	2	C 2
Cléry	4	B 1
Clinnaia	25	E 4
Clocher	2	B 5
Cobadin	30	F 1
Coblence	7	F 4
Coboop	40	B 3
Codroipo	26	C 4
Coeuvres	4	B 3

Name	Page	Square
Cogolo	26	A 3
Coincourt	10	C 1
Coincy	4	C 3
Creil	4	A 3
Coingt	5	D 2
Cojeul R.	2	C 4
Col du Bonhomme	11	D 3
Col du Ste. Marie	11	D 2
Colmar	11	E 3
Cologne	7	E 2
Colombert	2	A 3
Colombey	8	B 4
Comacchio	26	C 5
Comblain du Pont	6	C 3
Combles	4	B 1
Comines	2	C 3
Commercey	10	A 1
Compagne-les-Boulonnais	2	A 3
Compiègne	4	B 2
Conception B.	40	A 2
Concevreux	4	C 3
Conchy-les-Pots	4	B 2
Condé	3	D 4
Condé	4	A 2
Condé-en-Brie	4	C 4
Condé-les-Autry	5	E 3
Condé-sur-Marne	5	D 4
Condette	2	A 3
Conegliano	26	C 4
Conflans	8	B 4
Congo R.	39	E 5
Consdorf	8	B 2
Consenvoye	5	F 3
Consken	17	E 3
Constantinople	29	D 3
Conray	4	A 1
Conthill	8	C 5
Contich	3	F 2
Coosenberg	7	D 3
Copenhagen	34	D 1
Coppenax Fort	2	B 2
Coquilhatville	39	E 4
Corabia	30	D 2
Corbény	5	D 2
Corbie	4	A 1
Corbion	5	F 1
Corbu	30	D 1
Corby	32	D 2
Corcieux	11	D 3
Corcy	4	B 3
Corea	36	D 2
Corea Strait	36	D 4
Corfu	31	B 4
Corfu (Kerkyra) I.	31	A 4
Corinth	31	C 5
Corinth, G. of	31	C 4
Corisco B.	39	C 4
Corlatelu	32	D 2
Cormicy	5	D 3
Cormons	27	D 4
Cormontreuil	5	D 3
Cormor R.	27	D 3
Corninon	11	D 3
Corno Mt.	26	C 3
Corny	8	B 4
Coronel	33	Insel.
Corravillers	10	C 3
Corsk	18	B 5
Cortemarck	2	C 2
Cortenhaeken	6	B 2
Cortina d'Ampezzo	26	B 3
Cortonberg	3	F 3
Cosina	27	D 4
Costanza (Kustenji)	30	F 1
Costesci	30	D 1
Coucy-le-Château	4	C 2
Coulombs	4	B 2
Coulommes	5	E 2
Couommiers	4	B 4
Counfanaro	27	D 5
Coulomby	2	A 3
Courcelette	2	C 5
Courcelles	8	C 4
Courland	14	B 3
Courmont	4	C 3
Courrières	2	C 4
Court	3	F 3
Courtelevant	11	D 4
Courrai	3	D 3
Cousolre	3	E 4
Couvin	5	F 5
Covarchoff	21	D 4
Covedo	27	D 4
Coxyde	2	C 2
Cracacani	25	D 5
Cracow	21	C 4
Craonne	4	C 2
Crecy	4	C 2

Name	Page	Square
Crécy en Ponthieu	2	A 4
Creil	4	A 3
Crépy	4	C 2
Crépy-en-V.	4	B 3
Creta Verde Mt.	26	C 3
Crete I.	31	D 6
Creto	26	A 4
Crévic	10	C 1
Crève-champs	10	B 2
Crevecœur	3	D 5
Crevecœur-le-Petit	4	A 2
Crkvena	32	D 5
Croatia	27	F 5
Croce Carnico, Mte.	26	C 3
Croce Mt.	26	C 3
Croisill s.	2	C 4
Croismare	10	C 2
Croissy	4	A 2
Crombeke	2	C 2
Crouy	4	B 3
Crouy	4	C 3
Crveni	32	D 4
Csacza	20	C 5
Ctesiphon	38	D 3
Cucq	2	A 4
Cuffies	4	C 3
Cugny	4	B 2
Cuinchy	2	C 4
Cul des Sarts	5	E 1
Cumières	5	F 3
Cunene R.	40	A 1
Cuxhaven	34	C 2
Cyllene	31	B 5
Cyprus	38	B 2
Cysoing	3	D 3
Czempin	16	A 5
Czernovitz	25	D 4
Cziasnau	20	B 3
Czorna Repa Mts.	24	B 3
Czortkoff	25	D 3

D

Name	Page	Square
Dabek	20	C 3
Dabie	20	C 1
Dabrova	20	C 4
Dabrova	21	D 4
Dabrovitse	16	C 5
Dabrovka	17	F 4
Dabrovody	25	C 2
Dabuvka	17	D 5
Daltzeele	2	C 3
Dagda	15	F 3
Daghiani	32	B 8
Daghstan	38	E 1
Dagö I.	34	F 1
Dahlen	14	C 2
Dahn	9	E 4
Dainville	2	C 4
Dairen (Dainy)	36	C 3
Dajti	32	A 7
Daleiden	8	B 2
Daleshytse	21	D 3
Dalheim	8	B 3
Dalhem	6	C 3
Dailon	4	B 1
Dalny (Dairen)	36	C 3
Dalstein	8	C 3
Damanhur	35	C 2
Damaraland or Herero Land	40	A 2
Damasuli	31	C 4
Dambach	11	E 2
Damery	4	A 2
Damèvre	10	C 2
Damietta	35	C 2
Damietta Mouth	35	C 2
Damme	3	D 2
Dammer	20	B 3
Dammerkirch	11	D 4
Dampcevrin	5	F 4
Damvillers	5	F 3
Danduschany	25	E 4
Danischin	20	B 2
Daniushevo	19	C 2
Danjoulin	11	D 4
Dankowzy	25	D 3
Dannes	2	A 3
Danube, R.	32	B 2
Danzig	16	B 2
Danzig, G. of	16	C 2
Darabani	25	D 4
Darachofl	25	C 2
Darah	38	F 4
Darda	32	B 7
Darda	32	B 8
Dardanelles	28	B 2
Dardanus	28	B 2
Dar-es-Salaam	39	D 8
Daridere	30	D 3